# MYSTICISM

# MYSTICISM

## Experience, Response, and Empowerment

Jess Byron Hollenback

The Pennsylvania State University Press
University Park, Pennsylvania

To *my beloved parents,*

*Byron C. Hollenback*
*and*
*Mildred Ann Konik-Hollenback*

*and to*
*Kees Bolle, mentor and friend*

Library of Congress Cataloging-in-Publication Data

Hollenback, Jess Byron, 1948–
Mysticism : experience, response, and empowerment / Jess Byron Hollenback.

    p.      cm. — (Hermeneutics, studies in the history of religions)
    Revision of author's thesis (Ph.D.)—UCLA, 1989.
    Includes bibliographical references and index.
    ISBN 0-271-01551-9 (cloth : alk. paper)
    ISBN 0-271-01552-7 (pbk. : alk. paper)
    1. Mysticism—Comparative studies.   2. Parapsychology—Religious aspects.
  I. Title. II. Series: Hermeneutics, studies in the history of religions (University
Park, Pa.)
  BL625.H644   1996
  291.4'22—dc20                                    95-47064
                                                   CIP

It is the policy of The Pennsylvania State University Press to use acid-free paper for
the first printing of all clothbound books. Publications on uncoated stock satisfy
the minimum requirements of American National Standard for Information Sciences—
Permanence of Paper for Printed Library Materials, ANSI Z39.48-1992.

# Contents

# PART II
## How Tradition Shapes Both the Mystical Experience and the Mystic's Responses to It

### Book Three: Mysticism Among the Oglala Lakota: The Visions of Black Elk

### Book Four: The Mysticism of Saint Teresa of Avila

# Preface and Acknowledgments

This study differs from other published works on comparative mysticism in five important ways.

First, this book places greater emphasis on the cross-cultural significance of recollective practices (methods of one-pointedly focusing attention) within the totality of the lives of mystics. It shows that not only do recollective practices generate mystical states of awareness, but they also play a critical role in generating the extraordinary phenomena that often accompany those states of consciousness. It demonstrates that many of the ascetic disciplines of mystics, their requirements for solitude, and their ways of praying derive their rationale from the need either to preserve or facilitate recollective concentration of the mind.

Second, this book contains a lengthy analysis of a common but largely ignored accompaniment of recollective practice and mystical experience, a phenomenon that I have called the "empowerment" of a mystic's imagination, thoughts, emotions, and volitions. This empowerment is a peculiar and radical enhancement of these four faculties that often emerges when the mystic tightly focuses his or her attention by the practice of recollection. Under conditions of recollective empowerment, these faculties not only objectify themselves so that they form the visionary landscape that the mystic perceives, but they also exhibit noetic possibilities, that is, they can sometimes function as supernormal channels of perception, locomotion, and communication. The cross-cultural persistence of empowerment is demonstrated here and shown to play a significant role in constructing the perceptual and existential environments within which mystics dwell during their visions, ecstasies, and journeys to the spiritual world.

Third, this book explains why a significant class of mystical experiences exhibits a strong sensitivity to influences from the mystics' religiohistorical

viii Preface and Acknowledgments

context. While some contemporary scholars have demonstrated that the influences mystics receive from their environments decisively shape the character of what they perceive, feel, and know in their encounters with the spiritual world, they have paid less attention to the psychological mechanisms that cause this close fit between the content of a mystic's experience and his or her underlying theological and mythological matrix. I argue that the fundamental contextuality that many mystical experiences exhibit originates from a concurrent empowerment of the individual's mind, will, and imagination. Those same methods of trance induction (or recollection) that bring about the initial mystical state of consciousness are likely to lead to conditions of mental and imaginational empowerment. The unconscious ideas, desires, and expectations of individual mystics then "materialize" into a visionary landscape that is structured according to the particular system of mythology that the individual mystic takes for granted as providing a true description of reality and humankind's destiny within that reality. When empowerment is concurrently present, it practically guarantees that there will be a close fit between a mystic's experience and perceptions and the system of mythology that he or she takes for granted. By making explicit this important link between empowerment and the fundamental contextuality of mystical experience, this book is unique among comparative studies of mysticism.

Fourth, this book draws attention in an unusual way to limitations inherent in the contextualist paradigm that dominates current scholarship on the interaction between mystics and their religious and cultural environments. Although I confirm the contextualist thesis, I also show that contextualist scholars who assert or imply that mystical experiences are merely psychosomatic enhancements of the mystic's religious beliefs are making exaggerated claims. I suggest that various sorts of supernormal experiences, such as clairvoyance, telepathy, and precognition that sometimes accompany mystical states of consciousness, do not appear to be explicable in terms of the contextualist paradigm. What Henri Corbin terms the "noetic possibilities" of the empowered imagination—that is, its ability to function as a supersensory organ of perception, communication, and knowledge—provide a powerful, though unusual, argument against the view that the empowered imagination does nothing more than "project" or exteriorize the contents of the mystic's unconscious mind and will.

Fifth, this book makes use of a large body of literature that the majority of scholars of mysticism have almost completely ignored, namely, the autobiographies and other writings of nineteenth- and twentieth-century European and American mediums, clairvoyants, and out-of-body travelers.

This literature provides a gold mine of information about recollective practices, mystical experiences, and the supernormal manifestations that sometimes accompany them.

This study rejects the idea that visionary experiences are an inferior type
of mystical consciousness. A significant number of scholars, both past and
present, display a bias against visionary forms of mystical experiences
where vivid sensory images and illuminations dominate the field of consciousness.[1] They assume that genuine mysticism, or its most highly developed forms, ought to be both aniconic and acosmic, that is, both devoid of
sensory imagery and radically world-negating. This presupposition has had
the unfortunate consequence of leading some investigators to banish visionary experiences from the domain of mysticism altogether,[2] creating an
unduly restrictive definition of mysticism that suffers from the defect of
being somewhat ethnocentric. It takes as normative for all of mysticism a
type of aniconic mystical experience that appears only within the cultural
milieu of the universal religions. I am unaware of any examples from preliterate tribal religious traditions where individuals cultivated and valued
aniconic states of consciousness. Does this mean, then, that we are to regard oral cultures as devoid of mysticism? Acceptance of this constricted
definition of mysticism actually marginalizes many of the better-known
mystics who developed their visionary spirituality within the cultural matrix of the great universal religions. Should we no longer regard Ibn al-
'Arabi and Hildegard of Bingen as mystics simply because visions and
voices played an important role in their encounters with God and the spiritual world?

I object to exiling visions, locutions, and illuminations from the domain
of mysticism because, if we do so, we lose sight of a number of fascinating
questions that pertain to the psychology of trance: How and why does
recollective concentration sometimes transform the imagination into an ex-
transensory organ of perception and knowledge? How is it that the habitual
cultivation of trance can sometimes make it possible for an otherwise unre-
markable eagerness to apprehend something to become transformed into
clairvoyant and telepathic "alertness"? How and why does it happen that,
under conditions of recollective trance, light acquires peculiar properties

1. See, for example, Rudolf Otto, *Mysticism East and West* (New York: Macmillan,
1976 [1929]), p. 89; Walter Stace, *Mysticism and Philosophy* (Philadelphia: J. B. Lippincott,
1960), pp. 47 and 49; Robert K. C. Forman, "Mysticism, Constructivism, and Forgetting," in
Forman, ed., *The Problem of Pure Consciousness* (New York: Oxford University Press,
1990), p. 7.
2. Forman, "Mysticism," p. 7, and Stace, *Mysticism and Philosophy*, pp. 47 and 49.

and powers that it never manifests in ordinary waking consciousness? In each of these cases, there is a close link between the cultivation of trance and a peculiar form of transcendence. In each of them, the condition of trance activates a remarkable power within a human being that causes mental faculties, mental states, and mental objects to exceed their usual limitations, functions, and capacities in a dramatic fashion. The point I wish to make is simply this: Transcendence, along with trance, is one of the central elements of mysticism. We seriously impoverish our understanding of mystical transcendence if we restrict ourselves to those examples of it that come from the most highly abstracted states of divine union or yogic absorption where all images, forms, and earthly passions fall away. Visionary forms of mysticism with their apparitions, supernormal enhancements of the senses, and experiences of supersensible illumination broaden our comprehension of mystical transcendence by displaying more "concrete" types of transcendence that bear at least some resemblance to processes or phenomena with which we are familiar through the course of everyday sense-experience.

This book would never have been possible without the unstinting efforts of Professor Kees Bolle on my behalf throughout the years. As my mentor at UCLA he enkindled and nurtured my interest in the history of religions. His passionate devotion to the highest standards of scholarship and the extraordinary range and depth of his knowledge within the history of religions have been an inspiration to me. For all his generous efforts, for the breadth and depth of his scholarship, for his constant encouragement of my scholarly endeavors, and for the gift of awakening my interest in a field that has given me great intellectual and professional satisfaction, I want to express my warmest appreciation and deepest respect.

Those scholars who reviewed the manuscript for Penn State Press deserve special thanks. I deeply appreciate the considerable time they devoted to this task and the helpful suggestions and criticisms they made.

I also want to thank the staff of Penn State Press for their role in bringing this book to completion. I especially thank senior editor Philip Winsor for his encouragement and assistance. I deeply appreciate the constructive suggestions and enormous amount of labor that my manuscript editor, Patricia Mitchell, made during the course of copyediting. The efforts of the Press marketing manager, Lisa Bayer, and her staff are also very much appreciated.

Finally, I want to thank my parents for their encouragement and interest in my work and simply for just being there.

# Introduction

## What Mysticism Is

From the moment we awake until the moment we fall asleep, the vast majority of us spend our time silently talking or thinking to ourselves. A few individuals whom we call mystics have mastered the difficult art of shutting off this habitual interior dialogue. This inner silence that mystics cultivate cannot develop unless the individual first learns how to tightly focus his or her attention so that the mind and imagination no longer wander aimlessly from one object, thought, or feeling state to another. When this mental background noise ceases as a consequence of the mystic's successful endeavors to focus his or her attention, a dramatic change in the mystic's mode of consciousness takes place, a metamorphosis that is just as radical (sometimes even more so) as that transformation that occurs during the shift from the waking state of awareness to the dream state. This dramatic metamorphosis of the waking consciousness caused by simultaneously focusing the attention and quieting the mind, together with the responses in both deed and thought that it generates, is what I call "mysticism."

It is clear from this description that mysticism incorporates two important elements: a distinctive mode of experience or consciousness and the individual's responses to that unusual modality of experience. It is evident, then, that the term "mysticism" is not synonymous with "mystical experience," for the latter refers only to the first of these two elements. "Mysticism" is instead a comprehensive term incorporating both the mystical experience and the individual's response to it. Because of this dual reference inherent in the term "mysticism," a study of this phenomenon must accomplish two basic tasks. First, it must shed light on those particular attributes that distinguish the mystical mode of consciousness from other modes of consciousness. Second, it must delineate the manifold ways that men and women have responded in both thought and deed to those extraordinary types of experience. In order to accomplish these two tasks, I have divided this study into two parts. Part I, "Mystical Experience: Its Principal Features and Accompaniments," analyzes the peculiarities of the mystical state of consciousness. Part II, "How Tradition Shapes the Mystical Experience and the Mystic's Response To It," focuses more heavily on the nature of the mystics' particular responses to their unusual experiences.

# Why a New General Study Is Needed

There is an urgent need today for a new general study of mysticism that is not only broadly comparative in its treatment of the subject but also sensitive to its fundamental contextuality or historicity.[1] There are two main reasons why a new general study of mysticism with these features is long overdue.

First, most general studies of mysticism are grossly out of date. For example, the general studies of mysticism that are most widely read today, namely, William James's *The Varieties of Religious Experience* and Evelyn Underhill's *Mysticism,* were first published in 1902 and 1911, respectively. As a result, these two books do not convey the extraordinary advances in our knowledge of mysticism that have taken place since they were published. For instance, the last eighty years have produced many highly specialized studies of mysticism from non-Christian religious traditions,

---

1. When I speak of a "general" study of mysticism, I am opposing it to those highly specialized analyses of mysticism that focus on examples of the phenomenon drawn from one particular religious tradition or that are tightly restricted in their temporal focus. In contrast to these highly specialized studies of mysticism, a general study of mysticism possesses both cross-cultural and temporal breadth in its choice of examples.

To speak of the intrinsic "contextuality" or "historicity" of mysticism is just another way of saying that the contingencies inherent in every mystic's historical, religious, and cultural environment decisively determine the perceptual and affective content of the mystical state of consciousness itself, the meditational techniques that the mystic employs to induce it, the nature of his responses in thought and deed to the experience, and the way that he describes this experience to others. In other words, references to the "contextuality" or "historicity" of mysticism are just other ways of reiterating that almost every aspect of this complex phenomenon is historically and culturally conditioned.

studies that are frequently of very high quality.[2] In addition, the scholars of the last eighty years have also translated into European languages an abundance of mystical texts and autobiographical accounts of mystical experiences thereby making these writings easily available to European and American scholars.[3] Furthermore, thanks to the painstaking fieldwork of ethnographers and cultural anthropologists during the last eighty years, present-day scholars have a far deeper and more sophisticated understanding of the cultures and religious experiences of preliterate peoples than James, Underhill, and their contemporaries possessed.[4] These significant advances in our knowledge of the major non-Christian religious traditions and the religious traditions of preliterate cultures make it possible to do comparative studies of mysticism on a more solid foundation than was imaginable at the time that James and Underhill were writing.

In short, when viewed from today's perspective, both Underhill's and James's studies of mysticism suffer from ethnocentricity and a lack of comparative breadth. For example, neither of the two authors deals with mysticism in tribal religions. Underhill's classic makes generalizations about

2. See, for example, Gershom Scholem, *Major Trends in Jewish Mysticism* (New York: Schocken Books, 1961); Moshe Idel, *Kabbalah: New Perspectives* (New Haven: Yale University Press, 1988); A. P. Elkin, *Aboriginal Men of High Degree,* 2d ed. (New York: St. Martin's Press, 1978); Annmarie Schimmel, *Mystical Dimensions of Islam* (Chapel Hill: University of North Carolina Press, 1975); Henry Corbin, *Creative Imagination in the Sufism of Ibn 'Arabi* (Princeton: Princeton University Press, 1969); John Blofield, *The Tantric Mysticism of Tibet* (New York: Dutton, 1970).

3. See, for example, Pantañjali, *The Yoga-System of Pantañjali,* trans. James Haughton Woods (Delhi: Motilal Banarsidass, 1977); Gopi Krishna, *Kundalini: The Evolutionary Energy in Man* (Berkeley: Shambala, 1971); *The Tibetan Book of the Dead,* trans. Lama Kazi Dawa Samdup, and ed. W. Y. Evans-Wentz (New York: Oxford University Press, 1960); David Snellgrove, ed. and trans., *Four Lamas of Dolpo* (Cambridge, Mass.: Harvard University Press, 1967); Tson-kha-pa, *Calming the Mind and Discerning the Real,* trans. Alex Wayman (Delhi: Motilal Banarsidass, 1979); Bhadantacarya Buddhaghosa, *The Path of Purity,* trans. Bhikku Nyanamoli (London: Pali Text Society, 1923); Henry Corbin, *Spiritual Body and Celestial Earth: From Mazdean Iran to Shi'ite Iran* (Princeton: Princeton University Press, 1977); William C. Chittick, *The Sufi Path of Knowledge: Ibn al-Arabi's Metaphysics of Imagination* (Albany: SUNY Press, 189); W. Montgomery Watt, *The Faith and Practice of Al-Ghazali* (London: George Allen & Unwin, 1953); Jalal al-Din Rūmī, *Discourses of Rūmī,* trans. A. J. Arberry (New York: Samuel Weiser, 1972); *The Secret of the Golden Flower,* trans. Thomas Cleary (New York: HarperCollins, 1991); Raymond J. DeMallie, *The Sixth Grandfather: Black Elk's Teachings Given to John G. Neihardt* (Lincoln: University of Nebraska Press, 1984).

4. See, for example, Report of the Fifth Thule Expedition, 1921–24: The Danish Expedition to Arctic North America in Charge of Knud Rasmussen; Knud Rasmussen, *Intellectual Culture of the Iglulik Eskimo* (Copenhagen: Gyldendanske Boghandel, Nordisk Forlag, 1929); Elkin, *Aboriginal Men;* S. Shirokogoroff, *The Psychomental Complex of the Tungus* (London: Kegan Paul, Trench, and Trubner, 1935).

the essential nature of mysticism that are based on an excessive reliance on Christian examples. It claims to be a comparative treatment of mysticism yet lacks any in-depth discussion of Buddhist or Hindu mysticism.

Even later prominent works that seemed to promise broadly comparative treatments of mysticism, such as Rudolf Otto's *Mysticism East and West* and Daisetz Suzuki's *Mysticism Christian and Buddhist,* fail to deliver on those implied promises.[5] Both studies narrowly focus on just two religious traditions and one type of mystic, those mystics who exemplify the *via negativa,* that is, that type of mysticism that stresses the utter transcendence of the divine or sacred from all that is creaturely.[6] (Because these mystics of the via negativa emphasize how neither God nor the sacred can be described by analogies drawn from created things, they tend to describe or postulate mystical encounters with God (or the sacred) that are devoid of forms, vivid imagery, or supernormal accompaniments.) As a result of this restricted focus, these two studies by Otto and Suzuki also lack breadth.

The second major reason why a new general study of mysticism is urgently needed today is that, during the last twenty years or so, a major paradigm shift has occurred in the way that scholars study mysticism, a shift away from an "essentialist" view of mysticism toward one that is explicitly "contextualist."[7] At the time that James and Underhill wrote, most scholars downplayed the significance of the institutional, social, and historical settings within which mystics had their experiences. Those context-sensitive elements of mysticism and mystical experience were usually dismissed as being of secondary importance compared to those aspects of the phenomenon that were cross-culturally invariant. To use a hypothetical example, that earlier generation of scholars would not have shown much interest in either the specifically Buddhist elements in a Japanese monk's experience of *satori* or in the specifically Christian elements in one of Saint Teresa of Avila's "intellectual" visions. Instead, they would have focused most of their attention on delineating the transculturally invariant characteristics that both experiences shared. Recent scholarship on mysti-

5. Rudolf Otto, *Mysticism East and West* (New York: Macmillan, 1976 [1929]). Daisetz Teitaro Suzuki, *Mysticism Christian and Buddhist* (London: George Allen & Unwin, 1957).
6. Otto's *Mysticism East and West* compares Hindu and Christian mystics.
7. The most prominent advocate of this new paradigm is Steven T. Katz. Katz states his preference for the label "contextualist" over the label "constructivist" that some of his intellectual opponents, such as Robert Forman, have applied to him in his "Mystical Speech and Mystical Meaning," in Steven T. Katz, ed., *Mysticism and Language* (New York: Oxford University Press, 1992), p. 34, n. 9.

cism displays a much greater respect for the role that context plays in shaping every facet of both the content of the mystical experience itself and the ways that mystics and their religious communities respond to their experiences.

# The Essentialist (or Perennialist) View

The "essentialist" view of mysticism (also known as the perennial philosophy or "perennialist" view)[8] assumes that behind the multiform descriptions and interpretations of visions, locutions, and revelations of mystics from various cultures there is an invariant common core of experiences essentially unaffected by the individual mystic's particular historical situation, social status, cultural environment, and religious commitments. In other words, the essentialists assume that the dissimilarities that loom so prominently when one compares mystics' reports of their experiences are only apparent—superficial features that disguise the fact that, deep down, all mystical experiences arise from a common core experience that is, for all intents and purposes, the same everywhere and at all times.[9] The investigator's primary goal is to isolate this supposedly unchanging "essence" of mysticism from the obscuring veil of culturally conditioned interpretations that mystics unavoidably spread over it in the course of their attempts to render this seemingly ineffable core experience into language understandable to their contemporaries. Basically, the essentialists take it for granted that content and context, experience and interpretation, dwell in sovereign

8. The term "essentialist" was coined by Philip Almond to describe the approach that the contextualists were opposing. See Almond, "Mysticism and Its Contexts," in Robert K. C. Forman, ed., *The Problem of Pure Consciousness* (New York: Oxford University Press, 1990), p. 212. The terms "perennial philosophy" or "perennialism" are the more frequently used synonyms for essentialism. See Forman's article, "Mysticism, Constructivism, and Forgetting," in his *Problem of Pure Consciousness*, pp. 3–4, where he uses these two terms instead of "essentialism."

9. For example, Evelyn Underhill claims that the historical study of mysticism is not very useful "since mysticism avowedly deals with the individual not as he stands in relation to the civilization of his time, but as he stands in relation to truths that are timeless. All mystics, said Saint-Martin, speak the same language and come from the same country." Evelyn Underhill, *Mysticism: A Study in the Nature and Development of Man's Spiritual Consciousness* (New York: E. P. Dutton, 1961), p. xiii, also p. 96. One can find similar statements about the transhistorical nature of the mystical experience in William James, *The Varieties of Religious Experience: A Study in Human Nature* (New York: Collier Books, 1961), p. 329; and Friedrich Heiler, *Die Bedeutung der Mystik für die Weltreligionen* (Munich: Ernst Reinhardt, 1919), p. 6.

independence of each other. Interpretations are either "added on" to experiences after the experiences occur or else they are generated by the experience. Essentialists take it for granted that the relationship between experience and interpretation, content and context, is a one-way street with all
the traffic moving from experience to interpretation rather than the reverse. In a similar fashion, the essentialists also claim that insofar as religious doctrines relate to mystical experiences at all, they are derived postexperientially from mystical states of consciousness instead of the other
way around.

These assumptions cause the essentialists to underestimate the role that
context plays in shaping the perceptual and existential content of a mystic's experience. For example, Evelyn Underhill wrote that

> attempts . . . to limit mystical truth—the direct apprehension of the
> Divine Substance—by the formulae of any one religion, are as futile
> as the attempt to identify a precious metal with the die which con-
> verts it into current coin. The dies which the mystics have used are
> many. Their peculiarities and *excrescences* are always interesting
> and *sometimes* significant . . . But the gold from which this diverse
> coinage is struck is always the same precious metal.[10]

For the essentialists, conceptual systems such as theologies, mythologies,
and philosophies may play a role in determining how mystics retroactively
interpret their experiences, but they do not shape the perceptual and existential content of the experience itself. Consequently, they are mere "excrescences" of secondary importance in the study of mysticism. They are
like the die that stamps a piece of gold into a coin—the essence of the gold
is in no way affected by the operations of the die upon it.[11]

---

10. Underhill, *Mysticism: A Study in the Nature and Development of Man's Spiritual Consciousness,* 12th ed. (New York: World Publishing, 1955), p. 96 (emphasis mine). The well-known scholar of Islamic mysticism, A. J. Arberry, also took for granted that "mysticism is essentially one and the same, whatever may be the religion professed by the individual mystic: a constant and unvarying phenomenon of the universal yearning of the human spirit for personal communion with God." A. J. Arberry, *Sufism: An Account of the Mystics of Islam* (London: George Allen & Unwin, 1950), p. 11.

11. William James expressed a similar view about the purely "secondary" role that reli-
gious doctrines and beliefs play in the experiential dimension of religious life when he wrote that "when we survey the whole field of religion, we find a great variety in the thoughts that have prevailed there, but the feelings . . . and the conduct . . . are almost always the same, for Stoic, Christian, and Buddhist saints are practically indistinguishable in their lives. *The theo-ries which Religion generates, being thus variable, are secondary;* and if you wish to grasp its

Henri Delacroix's *Études d'histoire et de psychologie du mysticisme* (Studies of the history and psychology of mysticism) shows how even vigorous partisans of the historical approach to the study of mysticism were sometimes blinded to the full extent of its contextuality. For instance, even though Delacroix opens with statements about the importance of studying mysticism in its historical context,[12] many of his subsequent assertions indicate that he failed to consider the possibility that the innermost core of the mystical state of consciousness—that simultaneous experience of divine union coupled with the obliteration of the ego—might itself be a historically conditioned artifact.[13] He asserts, for example, that during the experience of mystical contemplation, the Christian mystic begins to sense that he not only intimately knows the Object he is contemplating, but he also *is* the Object that he contemplates. In this simultaneity of being and knowing "the notions and acts proper to Christianity disappear. . . . It seems to me that there is in mysticism an aversion for all that is formalized, an ambition to the infinite or the indefinite that goes beyond all dogmas and ritual acts. Christian mysticism does not escape this rule."[14] These remarks suggest that Delacroix has exempted the Christian mystic's experience of divine union from the historical process. These assumptions about the transhistorical nature of the mystical experience relegate the historian's analytical activities to the "shallower" phenomena of mysticism. Delacroix implies that historians must remain content with leaving the analysis of the "deep" structures of the mystical experience to the psychologists and satisfy themselves with a humbler role, that of analyzing how each mystic's particular historical milieu determines both the specific types of meditational techniques that he or she uses to bring about contemplative states of awareness and the specific ways that he or she responds to experiences of divine union.[15]

Even as late as the 1960s and 1970s prominent scholars continued to assume that there were no serious problems with the essentialist approach

---

essence, you must look to the feelings and conduct as being the more constant elements" (emphasis mine). Quoted from James, *Varieties of Religious Experience* (New York: Collier, 1970), pp. 390–91.

12. Henri Delacroix, *Études d'histoire et de psychologie du mysticisme: les grandes mystiques chrétiens* (Paris: Felix Alcan, 1908), pp. i–iv.

13. I reject Delacroix's view that all mystical experiences involve some form of union with the divine or that they always involve a dissolution of the feeling that one exists as a separate ego.

14. Delacroix, *Études d'histoire*, p. 370; see also pp. vii–viii for similar remarks.

15. Ibid., pp. 370–75.

to the study of mysticism. In 1975, Frits Staal expressed the opinion that "we can only make progress in the study of mysticism if we direct our attention away from the superstructures and back to the experiences themselves."[16] What Staal meant by the term "superstructures" were those philosophical, doctrinal, and mythological frameworks that form the basis for the way that the mystic interprets and responds to his own experience. Like James, Underhill, Stace, and other essentialists,[17] Staal took it for granted that for a scholarly investigation of mysticism to be truly interesting and worthwhile, it must place its main emphasis on the task of disentangling the "pure" transhistorical, transcontextual mystical experience from those historically conditioned ideological matrices or superstructures that simultaneously veil the pure experience from our sight and determine the way that an individual mystic responds to and interprets it.

## The Contextualist View

The contextualists assert that the essentialists' fundamental assumption about the relationship between experience and interpretation, content and context, suffers from a serious flaw. The essentialists took it for granted that a mystic's religious presuppositions and commitments do not shape the content of his or her experience while it is occurring but, instead, they shape the way that he or she interprets or otherwise responds to it after it has taken place. In short, the essentialists assumed that context-dependent elements in mysticism only played a role postexperientially. The contextualists, on the other hand, pointed out that the relationship between context and content, interpretation and experience, and religious doctrine and religious experience was one of reciprocity. In other words, the contextualists argued that religious doctrines do more than just shape the way that mystics interpret their visions after they have occurred. It also frequently happens that religious doctrines shape the perceptual and existential land-

16. Frits Staal, *Exploring Mysticism: A Methodological Essay* (Berkeley and Los Angeles: University of California Press, 1975), p. 189.

17. Walter Stace implies the underlying sameness of mystical experiences when he asserts that there is an amazing similarity between the descriptive language of the Upanishads and certain Christian mystics of the via negativa such as Ruysbroeck "so long as these latter confine themselves to uninterpreted description. But as far as interpretation enters into and permeates their descriptions, the phraseologies . . . tend to diverge radically." Walter T. Stace, *Mysticism and Philosophy* (Philadelphia: J. B. Lippincott, 1960), p. 94; see also pp. 34–36, 131–32.

scape of a mystic's vision while it is taking place. The contextualists argued that the relationship between experience and interpretation, content and context, was a two-way, not a one-way, street. Those cultural factors that determine how a mystic interprets his or her visions and revelations after they have taken place can just as often shape those experiences while they are in the process of occurring. "Interpretations" are not just items "added on" to mystical experiences retroactively. The assumptions that generate those interpretations also play a role in creating the experiences while they are being formed. Steven Katz, whose own writings have been most responsible for generating the recent paradigm shift toward contextualism,[18] emphasized the reciprocal rather than one-way interaction between context and experience when he observed that "the experience itself as well as the form in which it is reported is shaped by concepts which the mystic brings to, and which shape, his experience."[19]

The contextualist thesis affirms not only that context-dependent elements such as mythologies, religious doctrines, soteriological and eschatological expectations, religious symbols, and philosophies determine the specific ways that a mystic interprets and responds to his or her experiences after they have taken place but it also affirms that these same context-dependent elements shape and color the actual perceptual and existen-

18. See Steven T. Katz, ed., *Mysticism and Philosophical Analysis* (New York: Oxford University Press, 1978); idem, *Mysticism and Religious Traditions* (New York: Oxford University Press, 1983). Other recent works on mysticism and religious experience that adopt a contextualist approach include Wayne Proudfoot, *Religious Experience* (Berkeley and Los Angeles: University of California Press, 1985), esp. pp. 107–8, 123–24; Moshe Idel, ed., *Mystical Union and Monotheistic Faith: An Ecumenical Dialogue* (New York: Macmillan, 1989), esp. pp. 3–4, 7–8; and Philip Almond, *Mystical Experience and Religious Doctrine* (New York: Mouton Publishers, 1982), pp. 164–66. It should be noted, however, that although Almond generally has high praise for the contextualist approach to the study of mysticism, he finds Katz's assertion that context completely determines the nature of a mystical state of consciousness to be an overstatement. If Katz is right, Almond asks, then how do we account for mystical experiences where the mystic incorporates new elements that were alien to his religious upbringing? Furthermore, Almond points out that Katz assumed that there were no transcontextual, contentless mystical states of consciousness. Almond feels that Katz's assumption should not be accepted uncritically. See Almond, *Mystical Experience*, pp. 166–69, 174–76.

19. This quotation is taken from Katz's own essay, "Language, Epistemology, and Mysticism," in Katz, *Mysticism and Philosophical Analysis*, p. 26. Another passage from this same essay further reinforces the formative role that the mystic's religious and cultural context plays in shaping the content of his experiences: "Mystical experience is 'over-determined' by its socio-cultural milieu . . . the mystic brings to his experience a world of concepts, images, symbols, and values which shape as well as colour the experience he eventually and actually has" (p. 46).

tial content of those experiences while they are in the process of forming. This insight has some important implications and advantages.

First, the contextualist thesis implies that mystical experience in its "pure" state (free from all context-dependent influences) simply does not exist.[20] To imagine that we can disclose mystical experience in its "pure" state once we have peeled away all the retrospective interpretations that have overlaid it is methodologically naive because, from the very moment that a mystical experience begins to form, the assumptions, concepts, and expectations that the mystics have carried with them into the experience from their respective cultures and religious traditions are already at work shaping what they will see, hear, and feel. The contextualist maintains that there is never a moment, from the time that a mystical experience begins to form until the time that it is over, when it is not being shaped by those context-dependent elements. Indeed, some of the more radical exponents of the contextualist position have gone so far as to argue that mystical experience is nothing but a spiritual landscape and existential situation that the mystic's mind and imagination fashion out of the expectations, moods, and presuppositions that his or her culture and religion have implanted. Robert Gimello claimed that "mystical experience is simply the psychosomatic enhancement of religious beliefs and values or of beliefs and values of other kinds which are held religiously."[21] Given such extreme contextualism, it makes no sense at all to imagine a "pure" or "immediate" mystical experience prior to or independent of context-dependent influences. It is not just mystical experiences that share this extreme sensitivity to context. Wayne Proudfoot argues that all emotional states share this dependence on context. Emotions presuppose particular concepts and beliefs. "An individual's beliefs about the causes of his bodily and mental states enter into the determination of the emotions he will experience. The attribution of causes of one's experience will also prove to be crucial for the identification of an experience as religious."[22]

---

20. Thus Katz asserted emphatically that there was one crucial assumption that led him to publish the first of his two books, namely, the notion that "*there are no pure (unmediated) experiences.*" Quoted in Katz, *Mysticism and Philosophical Analysis*, p. 26.

21. Robert M. Gimello, "Mysticism in Its Contexts," in Katz, *Mysticism and Religious Traditions*, p. 85. In his often-ignored classic study of religious trance, Ernst Arbman expressed a similar view that mystical experiences simply convert preexisting beliefs and ideas into objects of actual experience. See Ernst Arbman, *Ecstasy or Religious Trance: In the Experience of the Ecstatics and from the Psychological Point of View*, 3 vols. (Stockholm: Svenska Bokforlaget, 1963–70), 1:347.

22. Proudfoot, *Religious Experience*, p. 108.

A second implication of the contextualist thesis is that the context-dependent elements of the mystical experience acquire an intellectual dignity that they did not possess within the essentialist framework. For the contextualists, it is not just the invariant universal elements within mystical experiences that constitute its vital and "essential" features (we assume here for the sake of argument that such invariant universals exist). The historically conditioned and culturally specific elements within the mystical experience are just as essential in determining its nature as the zygote is to the mature organism. These context-dependent elements shape the structure, perceptual landscape (in the case of visions), and mood of the mystical experience from the instant that it begins to develop in much that same way that the chromosomes in the zygote determine the developmental sequence, physical features, and probable lifespan of an organism. For this reason, the contextualists cannot accept Underhill's characterization of religious doctrines, mythologies, and philosophies as merely "peculiarities and excrescences" of inferior and incidental significance for understanding the nature of mystical experience.[23]

Third, the contextualist thesis gives the scholar a far more plausible explanation for the striking heterogeneity exhibited in mystics' descriptions of their experiences. The essentialists assume that all mystics' experiences are fundamentally the same after one has peeled away all the postexperiential interpretations that have become encrusted over them.[24] But how is it really possible for an experience that is supposedly identical for all mystics to generate such heterogeneous descriptions of what it is? The contextualists argue far more plausibly that the reason why mystics describe their experiences so differently from each other is that the experiences that they describe really are different. There is no identity of content at all. Moreover, the contextualists have no difficulty explaining why the mystics' experiences differ so radically from each other: Each particular mystic's experience derives its structure and emotional mood from a unique configuration of historically specific and culturally specific concepts, assumptions, and expectations that, during the mystical state of consciousness, become transformed from mere objects of belief into objects of actual experience.

It was not until the late 1970s that Steven Katz and the other contributors to *Mysticism and Philosophical Analysis* inaugurated the paradigm shift that made contextualism the dominant model governing the scholarly

23. Underhill, *Mysticism* (1955), p. 96.
24. Stace, *Mysticism and Philosophy*, p. 94.

investigation of mysticism. Although the contextualist approach originated long before Katz and his collaborators wrote their essays, those earlier contextualists did not succeed in overthrowing the then dominant essentialist consensus.[25] The contextualist view triumphed in the 1970s because the intellectual climate in almost all fields of the humanities and social sciences had become thoroughly imbued with the notion that a culture's worldviews, its systems of social relations, and its linguistic conventions actively structure how an individual perceives the world.[26] These paradigm shifts in other disciplines stressed the active rather than passive role that culture and the imagination played in the process of perception. When measured against these dynamic models of how the human psyche and culture shape an individual's perception and experience, the passive role that the essentialists assigned to both these agents in the perceptual process began to appear naive and obsolete. It would not be long before these more dynamic models of the psyche and culture would influence the way scholars studied mysticism.

# Recent Critics of Contextualism

Today the contextualist paradigm appears to have scored a resounding triumph over its essentialist predecessor. Nevertheless, critics have recently

25. It is important to realize that contextualism did not originate with Steven Katz and his collaborators. While it is certainly true that his *Mysticism and Philosophical Analysis* did a great deal to inaugurate the paradigm shift toward contextualism, a few earlier scholars had articulated the key contextualist idea that the mystic's environment shapes not only his interpretations and responses to his experience but also its content. For example, Philip Almond has pointed out that as early as 1909, Rufus Jones had asserted in *Studies in Mystical Religion* (London: Macmillan, 1909) that "there are no experiences of any sort which are independent of preformed expectations or unaffected by the prevailing beliefs of the time. . . . Mystical experiences will be, perforce, saturated with the dominant ideas of the group to which the mystic belongs, and they will reflect the expectations of that group and that period" (quoted in Almond, "Mysticism in Its Contexts," in Forman, *Problem of Pure Consciousness,* p. 212). Similarly, in 1938, John Morrison Moore insisted in a typically contextualist fashion that the relationship between experience and its interpretation was one of reciprocal interdependence. "It is misleading to think of an interpretation as simply 'growing out of' an experience. The relation of experience and interpretation is reciprocal and complex rather than being a simple one-way relation of dependence" (John Morrison Moore, *Theories of Religious Experience* [New York: Round Table Press, 1938], p. 187).
26. See Forman, *Problem of Pure Consciousness,* pp. 4–5, and also Almond's essay in that same book, p. 212.

begun to challenge some of its assumptions and implications.[27] The gist of their objections is that while they concede that the contextualist paradigm is epistemologically more subtle than its essentialist predecessor, the more radical advocates of contextualism carry contextual determinism to unacceptable extremes. For example, Philip Almond has pointed out that some of Steven Katz's statements suggest that "the mystic *cannot but* experience in contextually determined ways."[28] Almond suggests that Katz is implying that all elements and facets of the mystical experience are context-dependent and cannot emerge unless the mystic's environment has prepared the way for their appearance.

Critics have raised several valid objections to this radical expression of contextual determinism. First, as Forman explains, extreme contextualism has difficulty accounting for elements of novelty in mystical experience.[29] However, critics do concede to the contextualists that in innumerable cases of mystical consciousness objects of belief that the mystic acquired before the mystical state of awareness occurred become transformed during the moments of mystical revelation into actual objects of perception. The stigmatization of Saint Francis of Assisi provides one with an excellent example of this transformation of prior beliefs and expectations into objects of actual experience. Saint Francis's cultural environment was pervaded with an intense devotion to the sacred humanity of Jesus and His sufferings on the cross. Moreover, Saint Francis displayed an exceptional sensitivity to this popular devotion to Christ. He was consumed with an intense desire to live his life exactly as Christ had lived it while He was on earth, even to the point of imitating His sufferings. It is therefore not at all surprising that Saint Francis later received a mystical vision where Christ spoke to him and then imprinted the wounds of His Passion on Saint Francis's flesh. This stigmatization of Saint Francis, therefore, is a perfect illustration of how thoroughly context can shape the content of a mystic's experiences.

There are also many other cases in the literature of mysticism where

27. Philip Almond was one of the first scholars to point out flaws in the contextualist paradigm (see his *Mystical Experience and Religious Doctrine*, pp. 166–80). However, the most detailed critique of the contextualist position can be found in Forman, *The Problem of Pure Consciousness*, which focuses on delineating the weaknesses of contextualism. Forman and his collaborators use the term "constructivism" instead of "contextualism" to refer to the viewpoint they are criticizing. However, as I pointed out in note 4 above, Katz prefers to use the term "contextualist" to refer to his own methodological orientation, which is why I adopted the term "contextualism" rather than use Forman's term.

28. Almond, "Mysticism and Its Contexts," in Forman, *Problem of Pure Consciousness*, p. 213.

29. Forman, *Problem of Pure Consciousness*, pp. 19–20.

something alien to the received tradition intrudes into the mystic's experience.[30] In those cases, the scholar faces difficulties if he or she tries to
explain these alien intrusions as by-products of the mystic's previously
held beliefs and expectations. Let us consider several examples of preternatural experiences that seem to be inexplicable in terms of the contextualist paradigm.

The first example is a case of spontaneous, involuntary clairvoyance that
the prominent twentieth-century Irish medium Eileen Garrett described in
her autobiography, *Adventures in the Supernormal*. She relates that one
evening while she was touring Germany, she spent the night at an inn. As
she was getting ready to go down to dinner, she experienced a peculiar
pricking feeling in the nerves and a sensation of goose-flesh in her back.
She then "saw" a man hanging by the neck from a beam in the cellar
twitching spasmodically. This clairvoyant image of the dying hanged man
continued to haunt her during her stay at the inn. Garrett claimed that she
had no prior knowledge of how the man had met his death and yet, as she
was able to verify later, she had correctly "seen" the circumstances of his
tragic end. Here we have an example of a visionary experience that was
not shaped by the mystic's prior beliefs and expectations. Garrett suggested that, in this particular case, the only explanation that seems to
make sense is that her clairvoyant vision resulted from an invasion of her
consciousness by the discarnate spirit of the hanged man.[31] Such types of
possession and invasive clairvoyance constitute an important class of preternatural visionary experiences that elude full explanation in terms of the
contextualist paradigm.[32]

30. In *Problem of Pure Consciousness*, Forman notes that, in contrast to what one would
expect if the contextualist thesis that mystical experiences are the psychosomatic enhancements of religious beliefs and expectations were universally valid, mystics often find that
completely unexpected elements intrude into their experiences. Thus he cites the example of a
practitioner of transcendental meditation who was totally surprised by novel "fingerlike sensations" on the top of her head during her deeper meditative states as well as the sensation
that "her cranium seemed to open up like flower petals" (p. 21). (This is probably not a very
good example of an utterly novel element intruding into a mystic's field of awareness because
it would seem to me that a devoted practitioner of Maharishi Mahesh Yogi's transcendental
meditation would probably have heard about the topmost chakra, the thousand-petaled lotus
at the top of the skull, which certain schools of Yoga claim can be activated during the
highest states of mental concentration.)

31. See Eileen Garrett, *Adventures in the Supernormal* (New York: Creative Age Press,
1949), pp. 210–13; for her explanation, see pp. 213–14.

32. I would also draw the reader's attention to cases of "traveling clairvoyance" and telepathy that sometimes occur during out-of-body experiences or trance states (see Chapters 8–9,
11–12).

An overly rigid contextual determinism would also seem inadequate as
an explanation for some cases of spontaneous mystical experience such as
Richard Maurice Bucke's episode of what he called "cosmic consciousness."[33] It is difficult to imagine how the preternatural illumination that
surrounded Bucke and surprised him during this moment of supreme joy
could have been fully explicable as a by-product of his cultural milieu since
it was experienced as something completely new and unexpected. (However, Bucke's subsequent interpretations of this experience were another
matter, for they were clearly influenced by a blend of Darwinism, Christianity, and philosophical materialism.)

Cases of mediumistic clairvoyance and telepathy, possession by what
appear to be the discarnate souls of deceased individuals, the perception of
auras, and spontaneous mystical experiences that shatter the recipient's
previous expectations and assumptions about the nature of the world suggest that even though contextualism is an explanatory and hermeneutic
paradigm of great intellectual power, it has its limits. As useful as this
model is, according to Almond, "we must be wary of too crude an application of it."[34]

I suggest that certain types of preternatural experiences associated with
supernormal perception, mediumship, and spirit possession offer the best
examples of aspects of mystical experience that elude full explanation in
terms of the contextualist paradigm. However, my focus on those particular phenomena as counterexamples to the contextualist thesis is unusual.
Most of the critics of contextualism claim that the "pure consciousness
event" or "contentless [mystical] experience" serves as the best example of
a transcontextual mystical experience. Robert Forman has defined this
"pure consciousness event" as "a wakeful though contentless (nonintentional) consciousness."[35] During this particular mystical state of awareness,
the mystic is no longer aware of either his or her own mental processes or
any object of consciousness (hence, it is a nonintentional form of awareness). Furthermore, it is a state of mystical consciousness devoid of forms,
images, and symbols. As Almond described it, "it is a state in which the
distinctions between the knower, the act of knowing, and what is known
are obliterated."[36] Since these pure consciousness events or contentless

33. Richard Maurice Bucke, *Cosmic Consciousness* (New York: E. P. Dutton, 1969), pp.
9–10.
34. Almond, *Mystical Experience,* p. 168.
35. Forman, *Problem of Pure Consciousness,* p. 8.
36. Almond, *Mystical Experience,* p. 174.

mystical experiences appear to be states of wakefulness where there is no longer awareness of any object, the critics claim that they contain nothing at all that is historically or culturally conditioned. They are supposedly completely transcontextual events, unmediated or "pure" mystical states that are experientially indistinguishable from one another.[37] Examples of such pure consciousness events would include the highest trance-state in Sāṃkhya-Yoga, known as *samādhi* without support (*asamprajñāta samādhi*), which immediately precedes the attainment of "isolation" or *kaivalyam;* the highest trance state that the Theravada Buddhists call the trance of "the cessation of sensation and conceptualization"; and the elevated state of consciousness that Meister Eckhart called "rapture."

There are two problems with using pure consciousness events as examples of transcontextual mystical experiences. First, if Forman suggests (in contrast to Katz), that "a formless trance in Buddhism may be experientially indistinguishable from one in Hinduism or Christianity,"[38] he has no way of verifying this assertion because, so far as I know, there are no *firsthand* autobiographical descriptions of what it is like to experience the Buddhist "trance of cessation" or the condition of *asamprajñāta samādhi* (samādhi without the support of any meditation object) mentioned in the Yoga-Sūtras of Patañjali.[39] Second, one should also bear in mind that neither the Buddhist trance of cessation nor the condition of asamprajñāta samādhi constitute the ultimate goal of their respective recipients' meditational practices. They are only religiously useful if they lead respectively to Buddhist nirvana or to the state of kaivalyam described in Patañjali's system of Yoga. As I argue in Chapter 31, it is a mistake to consider nirvana and kaivalyam as equivalent states of consciousness because, despite their ideational, perceptual, and affective abstractness, they preserve a distinctive soteriological particularity that forbids one from taking them out of

37. For example, in *Problem of Pure Consciousness,* Forman asserts that "a formless trance in Buddhism may be experientially indistinguishable from one in Hinduism or Christianity" (p. 39).

38. Ibid., p. 39.

39. I am alluding here to the distinction that Peter Moore made between first-order (autobiographical), second-order (impersonal, stereotyped, and conventional accounts of mystical experience often encountered in sacred scriptures or Yoga treatises), and third-order (theological or liturgical texts that do not refer directly to the mystical experience itself or do so only in a very oblique fashion) accounts of mystical experience. I do not know of any *first-order* descriptions of either the Buddhist trance of the cessation of sensation and conceptualization or of asamprajñāta samādhi. See Peter Moore's "Mystical Experience, Mystical Doctrine, Mystical Technique," in Steven Katz, ed., *Mysticism and Philosophical Analysis* (New York: Oxford University Press, 1987), p. 103.

their religious context. They are also conditions of penetrating insight into truths that are definitely not equivalent. After all, nirvana presupposes the insight that all things are devoid of an eternally existent self or soul whereas kaivalyam presupposes the existence of such an eternally existing entity (*puruṣa*) that Buddhism categorically rejects.

## Mysticism and the Supernormal

Thus far, I have drawn the reader's attention to three major defects that have marred the principal general studies of mysticism: (1) they are seriously out of date, (2) they suffer from an ethnocentric and Eurocentric bias that causes them to base most of their generalizations about the nature of mysticism on Western European Christian examples of the phenomenon, and (3) they have paid insufficient attention to the role that context plays in shaping the existential and perceptual content of mystical experiences. Those earlier general studies of mysticism also suffer from a fourth weakness—they do not pay sufficient attention to the supernormal or "miraculous" phenomena that so frequently accompany mystical states of consciousness.[40]

The average person commonly associates the words "mysticism," "mystical," and "mystic" with both the possession of and exhibition of "miraculous" or supernormal powers. This popular assumption that the adjectives "mystical" and "miraculous" are synonymous does have some factual basis. After all, the various genres of mystical literature—the biographies and hagiographies of saints and mystics, the legends and mythical narratives about them, the descriptions of celestial (or otherwise quintes-

---

40. I use the adjectives "supernormal" and "paranormal" to designate those phenomena of nature (such as poltergeists) or the human mind (telepathy and clairvoyance) that, by the mere fact of their occurrence, imply—if accounts of them be true—that natural forces or potentialities exist that are capable of either producing effects that transcend the normal limitations and operations of matter or conveying information to an individual that he could not have otherwise acquired by means of his five physical senses, his scientific instruments, or by means of inferences based on data from those two sources. The words "supernormal" and "paranormal" do not necessarily imply divine agency and they are not synonymous with the term "supernatural" since there is no reason to suspect that the supernormal phenomena of mysticism lie outside the domain of nature. The existence of such phenomena, if it is to be admitted, simply implies that our knowledge of nature is incomplete. It is also important to realize that many mystical experiences do not contain any admixture of the supernormal. Consequently, it is a serious mistake for scholars to act as though the adjectives "supernormal" and "mystical" are synonymous.

sentially "spiritual") modes of existence,[41] and even quite a few of the mystics' autobiographies—repeatedly interweave descriptions of mystical states of consciousness with accounts of miraculous powers and events. Those documents not only portray the mystic as the perfectly "spiritual" individual who, by virtue of exceptional spiritual purity and refinement enjoys the singular privilege of directly communing with God, but they also depict the mystic as the miracle-worker,[42] an individual who is capable of, among other things, levitating,[43] reading the thoughts of others,[44] seeing auras,[45] journeying to the spirit-world,[46] clairvoyantly witnessing distant events,[47] moving physical objects by purely mental or spiritual operations,[48] and spiritually healing the sick.[49]

Unfortunately, many scholars dismiss these supernormal accompaniments as only marginally significant for deepening our understanding of

41. For example, in *City of God,* Augustine not only describes heaven as a place and mode of existence where human beings enjoy an unending, blissful, and direct communion with God but he also portrays it as a realm and mode of being where the inhabitants possess the miraculous powers of discerning other people's thoughts (book 22, chap. 29) and effortlessly move their bodies from one place to another by merely wishing themselves there ("Wherever the spirit wills, there, in a flash, will the body be" [book 22, chap. 30]). Augustine of Hippo, *The City of God,* abridged ed., trans. Gerald G. Walsh, S.J., et al. (Garden City, N.Y.: Image Books, 1958), pp. 540, 541.

42. The portrayal of Moses in the Book of Exodus serves as an excellent illustration of the way that sacred literature so often depicts the mystic as both a miracle-worker and an intimate companion of God. Thus Moses not only spoke with God in solitude on top of Mount Sinai (Exodus 34) and during his encounter with Him in the burning bush (Exodus 3:2–6) but, as God's agent, Moses also possessed such miraculous powers as the ability to turn the waters of the Nile into blood and populate the desert with frogs (Exodus 7:17–21 and 8:1–6).

43. In his autobiography, D. D. Home, the famous nineteenth-century American medium and mystic, claimed that numerous people had seen him levitate during his trances. See D. D. Home, *Incidents in My Life* (Secaucus, N.J.: University Books, 1972 [1862]), pp. 38–39.

44. Jalal al-din Rūmī, *Discourses of Rūmī,* trans. A. J. Arberry (New York: Samuel Weiser, 1972), pp. 52–53. The phenomenologist of mysticism and clairvoyant Gerda Walther describes one of her own telepathic experiences in *Phänomenologie der Mystik* (Olten und Freiburg im Breisgau: Walter Verlag, 1955), pp. 64–65.

45. Walther, *Phänomenologie der Mystik,* pp. 68–69.

46. Knud Rasmussen, *Intellectual Culture of the Iglulik Eskimo,* vol. 7, no. 1 of the Report of the Fifth Thule Expedition, 1921–1924: The Danish Expedition to Arctic North America in Charge of Knud Rasmussen, 10 vols. in 11 (Copenhagen: Gyldendanske Boghandel, Nordisk Forlag, 1929), pp. 76, 95, 124–27.

47. See Martin Lings, *A Sufi Saint of the Twentieth Century: Shaikh Aḥmad al-'Alawī* (Berkeley and Los Angeles: University of California Press, 1973), pp. 69–70; Home, *Incidents in My Life,* p. 11.

48. Home, *Incidents in My Life,* pp. 33–35; Sylvan Muldoon and Hereward Carrington, *The Projection of the Astral Body* (New York: Samuel Weiser, 1974), pp. 273–75.

49. Home, *Incidents in My Life,* pp. 14–15; 2 Kings 5:1–15 (the incident where the prophet Elisha cures Naaman of his leprosy).

mysticism and the mystical life.[50] It is easy to see why they have this attitude. After all, most mystics from the "universal" religious traditions[51] do
warn their followers that a fascination with supernormal phenomena or a
desire to exhibit "miraculous" powers is a serious hindrance to spiritual
perfection.[52] Second, many scholars also come to the study of mysticism
with the assumption that mystical experiences filled with visions, powerful
emotions, and paranormal manifestations are relatively inferior to those
mystical states of consciousness devoid of such phenomena. Thus, they
take it for granted that those ineffable, imageless sensations of divine presence exemplified by Saint Teresa's "intellectual visions," the Buddhist
"trance of cessation" (*asamprajñāta samādhi*), constitute the "highest"
forms of mystical experience.[53] Third, many scholars tend to disregard the

50. Rudolf Otto stands out as a typical example of this scholarly attitude that takes a
rather dim view of visions and the paranormal accompaniments of mysticism. See his *Mysticism East and West*, pp. 89–91. Gerda Walther and Henri Corbin are two exceptions to this
common scholarly view. Walther minutely examines the various supernormal phenomena
and states of consciousness (for example, how one "sees" auras, the subtle differences that
distinguish phenomena generated by the human psyche [*seelische*] from those that appear to
come into his consciousness from some spiritual [*geistige*] source, the distinctive characteristics of telepathic and clairvoyant awareness) in order to show how they differ significantly
from hallucinations, phantasms of the imagination, and objects fashioned reflectively by the
memory. See Walther, *Phänomenologie der Mystik*, esp. pp. 24–45, 56–75, 110–21. Corbin
draws attention to the extraordinary transformation of the imagination that occurs during
mystical experience. See his discussions of the "creative imagination" and "active imagination," *himmah* and enthymesis in Henry Corbin, *Creative Imagination in the Sufism of Ibn
'Arabī* (Princeton: Princeton University Press, 1969), esp. pp. 3–4, 179–81, 222–24. There
are strong parallels between Corbin's descriptions of both the "creative imagination" and
enthymesis and the phenomenon I have termed the "empowerment of the imagination (see
Book 2, Chapters 8–9).
51. "Universal" religious traditions, in contrast to tribal or primal religions, are those that
actively seek converts and concern themselves with the salvation or well-being of all of humankind not just a particular ethnic group. Buddhism, Islam, and Christianity are examples
of universal religious traditions.
52. For example, in the Christian mystical tradition, see Saint John of the Cross, *The
Ascent of Mount Carmel*, 3d rev. ed., trans. E. Allison Peers (Garden City, N.Y.: Doubleday,
1958), pp. 105, 242–43, 370; Walter Hilton, *The Stairway of Perfection*, trans. M. L. de
Mastro (Garden City, N.Y.: Image Books, 1979), book 1, chap. 11. In the Islamic tradition,
see Sharafuddin Maneri, *The Hundred Letters*, trans. Paul Jackson, S.J. (New York: Paulist
Press, 1980), pp. 40–41. For Hinduism, see Patañjali, *Yoga-Sūtra of Patañjali*, trans. J. R.
Ballantyne and Govind Sastri Deva (Delhi: Indological Book House, 1971), book 3, v. 38,
and Bhojarāja's commentary on the same. For Buddhism, see the comments of Burmese master Sunlun Sayadaw regarding those practitioners of meditation who become fascinated by
supernormal powers in Jack Kornfeld, *Living Buddhist Masters* (Santa Cruz, Calif.: Unity
Press, 1977), p. 96.
53. See Rudolf Otto's disparaging remarks about what he calls "illuminist" mysticism in
his *Mysticism East and West*, pp. 89–91. It is also interesting to note that some recent
scholarship on mysticism continues to exhibit discomfort in the presence of types of mystical

paranormal dimension of mystical experience because they come to the study of mysticism with a positivistic or psychologistic bias, that is, they take it for granted that episodes of clairvoyance, telepathy, out-of-body travel, and veridical dreams or visions are nothing more than hallucinations that are generated from inside the mystic's own subconscious.[54]

Even among those scholars who acknowledge that visions and supernormal phenomena are an important part of the mystical life, there is very often a tendency for them to focus most of their attention on either enumerating the ways that these experiences affect the mystic's behavior or describing the various kinds of visions, auditions, and extraordinary phenomena that occur in the mystical life.[55] This functional and phenomenological (or descriptive) emphasis is certainly a legitimate and important focus of inquiry. However, it seems to me that these two foci of inquiry, together with the three assumptions mentioned in the preceding paragraph, bypass important and interesting questions about the relationship between mystical states of consciousness and paranormal phenomena. For example, why is it that supernormal phenomena so often accompany mystical experiences? Is there any relationship between the hallucinatory and imaginational processes of the human mind that create dreams, visions, and fantasies and the processes that generate supernormal manifestations? Is it possible that the closer study of these supernormal accompaniments of mystical experience might bring forth data that challenges the validity of psychologism, the view that everything in a mystical state of consciousness originates from within the mystic's own mind?

I contend that a closer look at the supernormal phenomena that some-

---

experience where such supernormal phenomena are present. Thus Robert Forman—borrowing Ninian Smart's working definition of mysticism (Smart, "Interpretation and Mystical Experience," *Religious Studies* 1 [1965]: 75)—sweeps the supernormal element in it under the rug by "restricting the term 'mysticism' to experiences not described with sensory language" (Forman, *Problem of Pure Consciousness*, p. 7). As a result, those forms of transcendental consciousness where images, visions, locutions, symbols, and powerful affective states occur are set aside in a separate category labeled "visionary phenomena" to distinguish them from the formless and affectless "mystical" states of consciousness. Such an excessively restricted definition of mysticism eliminates such classic examples of mystical experience as Saint Paul's vision on the road to Damascus and Saint Teresa's experience of the transverberation.

54. James Leuba was a classic example of this positivistic view of mystical and paranormal experience. Thus he wrote that "Hallucinations . . . may convince the mystic that he sees and hears, unhampered by opaque obstacles and distances, or that he travels bodily through space at his good pleasure" (James Leuba, *The Psychology of Religious Mysticism* (New York: Harcourt, Brace & Co., 1925), p. 27.

55. See, for example, Underhill, *Mysticism*, pp. 266–97.

times accompany mystical experience deepens our understanding of mysticism in several ways. First, this closer analysis of the paranormal dimension of mysticism reemphasizes the central importance of recollective concentration as an element of the mystical life. Mystical states of consciousness, many forms of supernormal perception such as telepathic sensitivity, clairvoyance, and the ability to see auras, and certain supernormal powers of action such as out-of-body travel and psychokinesis usually do not become manifest until an individual has first one-pointedly focused his or her mind, will, and emotions. In short, both mystical and paranormal phenomena share a common genesis in the recollective act. That is why mystical states of awareness and supernormal powers of both perception and action so often occur in tandem with each other—they are the by-products of a recollected mind.

Second, exploring this linkage among paranormal experiences, mystical states of consciousness, and the practice of recollection reveals some very interesting features of the imagination that most scholars have previously ignored.[56] For one thing, some paranormal phenomena that accompany mystical experiences are the result of the imagination becoming both an organ of veridical (accurate) perception and a means of supernormal locomotion.[57] This metamorphosis of the imagination (which I have called the "empowerment" of the imagination) normally occurs only when the mystic's mind has become recollected. The experience of quite a few mystics suggests that the imagination is not just a weaver of fantasies, dreams, and illusions but that, under conditions of recollective concentration, it can sometimes transport the mystic to distant locations and sometimes give the mystic accurate knowledge of what is occurring there.

This notion that the imagination can function noetically, that is, as an organ of perception and knowledge, is really not all that strange. As I demonstrate in Chapters 9 through 11, the imagination also displays noetic functions in other quite ordinary contexts. For example, it appears that the imagination helps us to "hallucinate" correct optical perception. Scientists have shown that even though the human eye is an imperfect camera,

56. Henry Corbin is an exception to this generalization for he is especially sensitive to the phenomenon of the imagination acting as an organ of perception. He continually cautions his readers against the danger of confusing the active imagination, referred to by some Shi'ite Sufis, with mere fantasy. "The notion that the Imagination has a noetic value, that it is an organ of knowledge, is not readily compatible with our habits" (Corbin, *Creative Imagination in the Sufism of Ibn 'Arabī*, p. 180).

57. For a more detailed analysis of how the imagination can sometimes function as an organ of supernormal perception and action, see Chapter 9.

we see objects accurately in spite of this defect because the imagination actively intervenes in visual perception to compensate somehow for the inaccuracy of the image on the retina. It would seem, therefore, that the hallucinatory mechanisms that normally are at work in dream construction and in the normal fantasy-creating activities of the imagination also appear capable of playing a vital role in guaranteeing the accuracy of optical perception.

This realization that the illusion-producing elements of the human psyche can sometimes have noetic functions by serving as an organ of supernormal perception and by playing an active role in guaranteeing the accuracy of visual perception challenges the validity of psychologism and positivism.[58] Showing that the imagination actively participates in shaping visual perception challenges the assumption of positivism and psychologism that perception is a purely passive reception of sense-data. It also challenges the assumption that the imagination and the creations of the human imagination (for example, religions) only operate to hinder an accurate perception of reality by creating a tissue of pleasing illusions that substitutes for accurate knowledge of how things really are. When one realizes that the imagination, under conditions of recollective concentration, can sometimes serve as an organ of supernormal perception, it is clear that the imagination and other hallucinatory processes of the human mind play a far more complex role in the apprehension and appropriation of reality than most scholars have heretofore realized. The lesson to be learned from this is that mystical experiences and the supernormal phenomena that often accompany them are not just bizarre marginalia of human cultural and psychic life but rather windows into a realm where we can see the imagination and other illusion-producing processes of the human mind operating in their most fully developed manner.

Focusing on the supernormal accompaniments of mystical states of consciousness also brings another benefit—it sheds light on why mystical experiences are so context-dependent. As I demonstrate in Chapters 9 and 15 that metamorphosis of the imagination that I call its "empowerment" not only transforms it into an organ of supernormal perception and locomotion but also causes it to objectify the contents of the mystic's conscious and subconscious thoughts and desires. This process of objectification ensures that there will almost always be a close fit between what a mys-

---

58. For example, see Chapter 15 for my refutation of psychologism.

tic sees and hears during visions and revelations and the cultural expectations that he or she brings to those experiences. By examining the supernormal dimensions of mystical experiences, one comes to know not just that mystical experience exhibits an intrinsic contextuality but one also learns about one of the reasons why it exhibits that dependence on context.

Detailed attention to supernormal phenomena not only sheds light on why so many aspects of the mystical state of consciousness exhibit context-dependence but it also sheds light on the limits of contextuality in mystical experience. While it is true that a significant number of supernormal phenomena associated with mystical states of awareness derive from the recollective metamorphosis of the individual's imagination, transforming it into an organ of paranormal perception and locomotion, and that this transformed or "empowered" imagination is exceptionally sensitive to influences from the mystic's environment, there are other extraordinary phenomena that occasionally take place that do not appear either to originate from within the mystic's psyche or to exhibit context-dependence. Earlier in this introduction, I referred to a case where the medium Eileen Garrett felt her field of awareness suddenly invaded by an accurate clairvoyant impression of a man who had committed suicide by hanging. This particular clairvoyant impression neither originated from within her own unconscious or conscious mind (since she knew nothing of the gruesome event that had invaded her awareness) nor did it result from any prior process of cultural conditioning or religious indoctrination (since it was simply a picture of the unfortunate man's last moments in the basement). I discuss in Chapter 13 other similar examples where material of an apparently extrapsychic origin (coming from a source outside the mystic's conscious or subconscious mind) overwhelms the medium's or mystic's field of awareness. In summary, data of this sort deserves closer scholarly investigation despite its very unusual nature because (1) it presents concrete examples of material that eludes explanation in terms of the contextualist model of mysticism, (2) the apparently extrapsychic origin of the material is one more challenge to the psychologistic and positivistic models of the human mind, and (3) it reveals that, as important as the recollectively empowered imagination is in the creation of some types of supernormal experiences that accompany mystical states of awareness, there are still other sources that can generate paranormal material that enters into the mystic's or medium's field of consciousness.

# Principal Objectives of This Study

My first objective in this work is to present a broad comparative historical treatment of mysticism that will not only interest the scholar but also remain easily accessible to the layperson. I especially stress that this comparative study of mysticism is historical and contextual because most earlier treatments of this phenomenon, as well as quite a few recent ones,[59] have either underestimated or altogether ignored the crucial role that historically and culturally contingent factors play in shaping the emotional and perceptual content of the mystic's ecstasies, visions, and locutions. I demonstrate, in opposition to Staal, Underhill, James, Arberry, Stace, and Heiler, that their more or less implicit notion of a "pure" noumenal mystical experience is an empty theoretical construct.[60] I maintain that—aside from the few types of paranormal phenomena that appear to originate from outside the psyche of the mystic—it is impossible to isolate the content of a mystical experience from its religious and cultural matrix. Consequently, I repeatedly show that not only are the "external" aspects of mysticism (that is, the mystic's interpretations of his or her experiences, responses in deed to visions and revelations, and techniques of inducing such experiences) historically and culturally conditioned but that the mystic's historical and cultural environments decisively determine the perceptual and affective content of the innermost core of even the most "elevated" visionary revelations or spiritual insights.

My second objective is to draw attention to the ubiquity of recollection (one-pointed concentration of mental and emotional attention) in the genesis of both mystical states of consciousness and the numerous types of paranormal phenomena that sometimes occur in tandem with them. I also show how the need to preserve recollectedness plays a decisive role in the way that the mystic interacts with the world.

59. For example, James, *Varieties of Religious Experience* (1902) and Underhill, *Mysticism* (1911); Staal, *Exploring Mysticism* (1975), esp. pp. 173, 189; Stace, *Mysticism and Philosophy* (1960).

60. Immanuel Kant used the term "noumenon" to refer to the thing-in-itself, that is, the object as it really is independently of the way that our sense organs or laboratory instruments distort it when they present it to our consciousness. Kant explained what he meant by noumenon in his *Critique of Pure Reason* when he wrote that "if we call certain objects 'appearances,' 'sensed entities,' or 'phenomena,' we distinguish our awareness of them from what they are in their own nature. In so doing, the objects-themselves are placed in opposition to the sensed entities. . . . All those objects which are not sensed we may call 'intelligible entities' (noumena)." Quoted in Immanuel Kant, *An Immanuel Kant Reader,* trans. and ed. Raymond Blakney (New York: Harper and Brothers, 1960), pp. 77–78.

My third objective—and this is one of the most unusual aspects of this study—is to draw attention to the importance of *enthymesis,* or what I have termed the "empowerment" of thought, will, and imagination as a significant process that shapes visionary landscapes, ensures that a mystic's experiences will seem to confirm empirically the truths that his religious tradition proclaims in its myths or scriptures, and transforms the imagination and will into "organs" of supernormal perception. ("Empowerment," or "enthymesis," as used in this work, refers to that peculiar simultaneity between thinking and being that often operates during mystical experiences. Under conditions of enthymesis, visionary landscapes and spiritual environments behave as though they are constructed out of the mystic's thoughts or desires.)

My fourth objective is to try to do justice to the paranormal dimension of mysticism. I try to explain why supernormal manifestations such as telepathy, clairvoyance, and out-of-body experiences so often accompany mystical states of consciousness. I also go one step further and show why out-of-body travel, clairvoyance, telepathy, and the perception of auras are not just sideshows peripheral to our understanding of mysticism but rather phenomena that can actually deepen our understanding of it in unexpected ways.

My fifth major objective is to make this study a broad cross-cultural treatment of mysticism. I do not restrict this analysis solely to those mystics who claim allegiance to one of the principal world religions—Christianity, Islam, Buddhism, and Hinduism. I go further and also discuss mysticism as it appears among such preliterate peoples as the Lakota, the Australian Aborigines, and the Eskimo.

# Organization of This Study

A word is in order about the organization of the chapters. I have organized the material into two parts and four books, with thirty-one chapters. Part I deals with the nature of mystical experience. Book One is simply designed to give the reader an immediate grasp of the salient features that distinguish the classic mystical experience. For this purpose I focus on four mystical experiences that exhibit its principal characteristics in an especially pronounced manner. I warn the reader, however—and buttress this warning with numerous examples—that the seven characteristics that I distill from these classic experiences are subject to a wide range of variation in the degree that they become manifest in any one mystic's experience. Book One also draws the reader's attention to the essential contextuality of the mystical experience (Chapter 4). In addition, I devote a considerable amount of space in Book One (Chapter 5) to the very important phenomenon of recollection, that mental discipline that is responsible for producing most mystical states of consciousness as well as many of the supernormal manifestations referred to in religious and mystical literature. Book Two primarily centers around the problem of clarifying the relationship between mystical experiences and the supernormal phenomena that sometimes accompany them.

Part I focuses mainly upon the mystical experience and I say relatively little about the mystic's response to his or her experience there. I attempt to rectify this initial imbalance in Part II by shifting the focus toward mysti*cism*, that is, the totality comprising both the mystic's experience and his or her responses to that experience. Part II, comprising Books Three and Four, demonstrates how the mystics' religiohistorical environments and social situations determine not only the particular content of their extraordinary states of consciousness but also how they determine the specific character of the numerous ways that they respond to those experiences. Books Three and Four delineate how (1) the mystics' deeds and desires that arise in response to their visions and ecstasies, (2) their particular interpretations of those experiences, (3) the distinctive criteria they use to separate religiously significant experiences from those that they regard as insignificant or even harmful, (4) the onset and cessation of those states of consciousness as well as their intensification and diminution, and (5) their ultimately constructive or destructive mental and emotional effects, all display a remarkable sensitivity to inputs that mystics receive from both "tradition" and those people whom they acknowledge as religious and social authorities.

I devote Book Three to the study of a turn-of-the-century Lakota mystic, Black Elk. Book Four deals with the sixteenth-century Spanish Carmelite mystic, Saint Teresa of Avila. Books Three and Four are not intended to be biographies of the two mystics but they do employ enough biographical material to situate the experiences of Black Elk and Teresa in their respective historical and cultural contexts. This choice of mystics from two radically different religious traditions was deliberate. I did it not only to set up a contrast that would exhibit the contextuality of both mystics' experiences and responses to their experiences in the sharpest possible manner but I also hope to draw attention to some important differences that separate mysticism in tribal religions from those forms that originate in the universal religions. For far too long scholars have ignored the forms of mysticism found in tribal religions. Consequently, they have taken as normative those expressions of mystical spirituality that have originated in the universal religions. This neglect of tribal mysticism allows an ethnocentric bias to creep into their descriptions of the phenomenon. Hopefully, attention to the spirituality of Black Elk will help scholars become more aware of how their explicit and tacit commitments to the ultimate ethical, existential, and philosophical concerns of the universal religions have shaped their approaches to the subject of mysticism.

# PART

# I

# MYSTICAL EXPERIENCE: ITS PRINCIPAL FEATURES AND ACCOMPANIMENTS

# Book One

# The Nature of Mystical Experience

# 1

# The Mystical Experience:
# A Preliminary Reconnaissance

From time to time in history, one encounters singularly gifted men and women called mystics, individuals who have often played pivotal roles as innovators, revitalizers, and reactionary conservators of their respective religious traditions. A quick glance at the more prominent names from among their ranks provides convincing proof of their historical and religious significance. Muhammad, Paul, Jesus of Nazareth, Gautama Buddha, Moses, Augustine of Hippo, Plotinus, the prophet Ezekiel, Ibn al-'Arabī, al-Ghazzālī, Black Elk, and Milarepa make up the list of famous mystics who have made their mark in the history of their respective religious traditions. What particular gift distinguishes mystics from ordinary men and women? The answer is their susceptibility to certain unusual states of consciousness by means of which they come into direct contact with a domain of experience that almost always remains inaccessible to the human mind in its ordinary waking state. While conscious or in a trance-state, mystics enter into another world, a realm of "spiritual" things, beings, and powers. Although these spiritual phenomena usually remain imperceptible to the five physical senses in their normal mode of operation, this mystical state of consciousness often brings these spiritual entities into the mystic's field of awareness with a compelling vividness and concreteness equaling or even surpassing that of ordinary sense objects.

The religious, cultural, and social importance of mystics does not, of course, derive solely from their unusual experiences. Their importance also derives from their remarkable ability to endow any kind of symbolism, mythology, or metaphysic (including even nineteenth-century European materialism)[1] with a hitherto unsuspected dimension of significance and

1. The Spiritualist mediums of nineteenth-century Europe and America, with their exhibitions of poltergeist phenomena and ectoplasmic manifestations, show that some nineteenth-

meaning, as well as their peculiar penchant for having spiritual experiences that seem to empirically confirm for them and their co-religionists that the nature of reality is actually congruent with the description provided by their respective scriptures and myths. With respect to the first point, Paul's and Muhammad's reinterpretations of events and personages in the Old Testament serve as examples of how mystics can play a major role in endowing the myths and symbols of their particular religious traditions with a new meaning. With respect to the second point, as important as mystics' contributions have been to the development of new hermeneutic frameworks and symbolisms within religious traditions, it is equally important that a mystic's religious community also exerts a powerful influence on both the content of his peculiar experiences and the distinctive manner in which he responds to them. In short, the relationship between the mystic and his community is one of reciprocal interdependence, a fact that no study of mysticism can afford to ignore. It is a serious error to regard the mystical experience as though it were simply the consequence of some purely intrapsychic process that exists in total isolation from the mystic's historical and cultural milieu.

What features distinguish "mystical" experience from other types of experience? In an attempt to answer this question, I display four classic examples of this phenomenon, one after another, so as to bring the distinctive features of mystical experience into the sharpest possible relief. However, the reader should bear in mind that because the existential coloration of each mystic's particular experience, as well as that experience's distinctive imagery and symbolism, remain indissolubly determined by the mystic's cultural and religious environment, mystical experiences necessarily exhibit a remarkable degree of diversity. For this reason, no matter which four examples one chooses to illustrate the essential features of this mode of experience, one must recognize that these choices can only give the reader a partial insight into the range of variation that occurs within the phenomenon. This means that some of the characteristics I isolate as common to each of these classic episodes will manifest themselves weakly, if at all, in other mystics' experiences.

---

century mystics attempted a novel reconciliation of materialistic science and the Christian dogma of the reality and immortality of the human soul. Their experiences of those phenomena seemed to prove to them that religion could be saved from the criticisms of scientific materialists because they claimed that their capacity to produce ectoplasms and poltergeists indicated that the soul had a material aspect and was, therefore, like the matter of Newtonian physics, eternally subsistent.

# Four Examples of Mystical Experience

## An Eskimo Shaman's Enlightenment

In the following narrative, Aua, an Iglulik Eskimo from the northwestern coast of Hudson Bay, describes the unusual experience that came to him the moment he first realized that he had become a shaman. He had sought instruction from many famous shamans, but their teaching had apparently not yet given him any significant results. Aua withdrew into solitude (a traditional shamanic practice among the Eskimo) where, for a time, he seems to have undergone a period of great mental distress and instability. After he had withdrawn, he related to Rasmussen:

> I soon became very melancholy. I would sometimes fall to weeping, and feel unhappy without knowing why. Then, for no reason, all would suddenly be changed and I felt a great, inexplicable joy, a joy so powerful that I could not restrain it, but had to break into a song, a mighty song, with room only for the one word: joy, joy! . . . And then in the midst of such a fit of mysterious and overwhelming delight I became a shaman, not knowing myself how it came about. But I was a shaman. I could see and hear in a totally different way. I had gained my *quamanEq,* my enlightenment, the shaman-light of brain and body, and this in such a manner that it was not only I who could see through the darkness of life, but the same light also shone out from me, imperceptible to human beings, but visible to all the spirits of the earth and sky and sea, and these now came to me and became my helping spirits.
>
> My first helping spirit was my namesake, a little aua [a female shore-spirit somewhat akin to a small elf]. When it came to me, it was as if the passage and the roof of the house were lifted up, and I felt such a power of vision, that I could see right through the earth and up into the sky; it was the little aua that brought me all this inward light, hovering over me as long as I was singing. Then it placed itself in a corner of the passage, invisible to others, but always ready if I should call it.[2]

2. This narrative is quoted in Rasmussen, *Intellectual Culture of the Iglulik Eskimo*, pp. 118–19.

## A Modern Hindu Awakens Kundalini

My second example of a mystical experience recounts the story of how Gopi Krishna, a contemporary practitioner of yoga, first aroused that peculiar vital energy that hatha yoga treatises call *kuṇḍalinī*. This strange, subtle, spirit-like energy resides in a latent unmanifest state within the lowest of those subtle energy centers or *chakras* that supposedly line the backbone but that are invisible to ordinary visual or anatomical inspection. The practitioners of hatha yoga maintain that when an individual becomes adept at certain techniques of mental concentration, he begins to excite this normally dormant energy into a state of activity. Once this happens, kundalini begins to move like a luminous fluid up the spinal cord, its movements upward being accompanied by a dramatic transformation in the yogin's mode of consciousness.

Gopi Krishna's dramatic arousal of kundalini culminated seventeen years of meditational practice in which he had finally learned how to sit undistractedly in yoga postures for hours, breathing slowly and rhythmically while he simultaneously centered his entire attention on a luminous lotus that he imagined as glowing at the very top of his head. Gopi Krishna had therefore already attained considerable success in *prāṇāyāma*, the technique of mental concentration through "visualization" and breath control that constitutes one of the cornerstones of yoga.

One day, while Gopi Krishna was totally absorbed in contemplating the imaginary lotus, he suddenly felt a peculiar sensation at the base of his spine. However, as soon as he began to pay attention to this strange sensation (and thus divert his previously focused attention from its exclusive concentration on the glowing lotus), he noted that the feeling began to dissipate. On the other hand, if he kept his attention tightly centered on the lotus despite this strange feeling at the base of his spine, the sensation reappeared. He repeated this procedure several times, holding his attention fixedly on the glowing lotus despite the steadily intensifying strength of the spinal sensation. Then something snapped.

> Suddenly, with a roar like that of a waterfall, I felt a stream of liquid light entering my brain through the spinal cord.
>
> Entirely unprepared for such a development, I was completely taken by surprise; but regaining self-control instantaneously, I remained sitting in the same posture, keeping my mind on the point of concentration. The illumination grew brighter and brighter, the

roaring louder. I experienced a rocking sensation and then felt myself slipping outside of my body, entirely enveloped in a halo of light. It is impossible to describe the experience accurately. I felt the point of consciousness that was myself growing wider, spreading outward while the body, normally the immediate object of its perception, appeared to have receded into the distance until I became entirely unconscious of it. I was now all consciousness, without any outline, without any idea of a corporeal appendage, without any feeling or sensation coming from the senses, immersed in a sea of light simultaneously conscious and aware of every point, spread out, as it were, without any barrier or material obstruction. I was no longer myself, or to be more accurate, no longer as I knew myself to be, a small point of awareness confined in a body, but instead was a vast circle of consciousness in which the body was but a point, bathed in light and in a state of exaltation and happiness impossible to describe.[3]

## Saint Paul's Conversion to Christianity

The biblical story of Saint Paul's dramatic conversion to Christianity stands out as the most well-known instance of a mystical experience in all of religious literature. One can find three accounts of this momentous event in the Acts of the Apostles, specifically, Acts 9:3–8, 22:6–13, and 26:12–19, each of which varies in certain details from the others.[4] For example, in the accounts given in Acts 9 and 22, Paul is described as being blinded by his illumination, whereas that given in Acts 26 makes no mention of this fact. Similarly, in Acts 9, Paul's companions heard a voice but could not see Christ speaking to Paul. This text also remains silent on whether or not they saw the light that illumined him. Acts 22, on the other hand, relates that Paul's companions saw light but heard no voice. The description in Acts 26 remains silent on whether his companions heard the

3. Gopi Krishna, *Kundalini: The Evolutionary Energy in Man* (Berkeley: Shambala, 1971), pp. 12–13.

4. One must bear in mind that Luke was the author of Acts, not Paul. As was traditional in Greco-Roman historiography, Paul's speeches in Acts were actually Luke's free compositions. (See Norman Perrin and Dennis C. Duling, *The New Testament: An Introduction*, 2d ed. [San Diego: Harcourt Brace Jovanovich, 1982], p. 132.) We will therefore never know how closely Luke's version of events corresponded to what actually took place. Nevertheless, Luke's account of Paul's conversion displays all the classic features of an experience of mystical illumination.

voice, but it implies that they all witnessed the light since they all fell to the ground along with Paul.[5]

The following description of Paul's conversion from Acts 26:13–19 forms a part of Paul's speech to King Agrippa countering the charges that the Jewish Sanhedrin had lodged against him. He relates that he was on his way to Damascus to persecute the Christian community there when

> at midday as I was on my way. . . . I saw a light brighter than the sun come down from heaven. It shone brilliantly around me and my fellow travelers. We all fell to the ground and I heard a voice saying to me in Hebrew, "Saul, Saul, why are you persecuting me? It is hard for you, kicking like this against the goad." Then I said, "Who are you, Lord?" and the Lord answered, "I am Jesus, and you are persecuting me. But get up and stand on your feet, for I have appeared to you for this reason: to appoint you as my servant and as a witness of this vision in which you have seen me, and of others in which I shall appear to you. I shall deliver you from the people and from the pagans, to whom I am sending you to open their eyes so that they may turn from darkness to light, from the dominion of Satan to God, and receive, through faith in me, forgiveness of their sins and a share in the inheritance of the sanctified."
>
> After that, king Agrippa, I could not disobey the heavenly vision.[6]

## Saint Augustine's Vision of the Infinite Light

The next account of a classic mystical experience comes from Saint Augustine's famous autobiography, *The Confessions*. It describes an illumination experience that came to Augustine during a time when he had immersed himself in the study of Neoplatonism shortly before his final conversion to Christianity. In this passage Augustine writes as though he were talking to God. He related that, one day, with the help of God,

> I entered into my inmost being. This I could do, for you became my helper. I entered there, and by my soul's eye, such as it was, I saw above that same eye of my soul, above my mind, an unchangeable

---

5. The reader should note that even though Paul seems to be the one talking, this is Luke's secondhand version of the event.

6. Acts 26:13–19 (Jerusalem Bible).

light. It was not this common light plain to all flesh, nor a greater light, as it were, of the same kind, as though that light would shine many, many times more bright, and by its greater power fill the whole universe. Not such was that light, but different, far different from all other lights. Nor was it above my mind, as oil is above water, or sky above earth. It was above my mind because it made me, and I was beneath it, because I was made by it. He who knows the truth, knows that light, and he who knows it, knows eternity.[7]

From these four examples, it is easy to see that the mystical experience is a mode of awareness that differs sharply from both the dream-state and ordinary waking consciousness.

7. Augustine of Hippo, *The Confessions of St. Augustine,* trans. John K. Ryan (Garden City, N.Y.: Image Books, 1960), book 7, chap. 10, pp. 170–71.

# 2

# Distinctive Features of the Mystical Experience

## Seven Common Characteristics

Most mystical experiences exhibit seven distinctive attributes that, when taken together, distinguish them from other modes of human experience.

1. The mystical experience is a radical, trans-sensory metamorphosis of the subject's mode of consciousness that takes place while he or she is awake.
2. It is a mode of consciousness that gives the subject both privileged access to and knowledge of those things that his or her particular culture and religious tradition regards as ultimately real. In other words, it is no mere "perception" of another domain of experience—it is a revelation that concerns those things that are of supreme ontological significance for that individual's particular cultural and religious community.[1]
3. It is an experience that gives the subject privileged knowledge about those matters that his or her religious tradition considers to have the utmost importance for human salvation. In other words, it gives mystics knowledge about matters that are of ultimate soteriological concern to their communities.[2] This is yet another sense in which the mystical experience is not mere "perception" but rather something that compels a response to it with all of one's being.

1. Ontology is that branch of philosophy that deals with the ultimate nature of being, of that which exists. Hence, the term "ontological" means simply that which pertains to what is ultimately real.
2. The word "soteriological" means of or pertaining to the process which leads to salvation. Soteriological knowledge is therefore something quite distinct from ontological knowledge.

4. It is heavily laden with affect.
5. It is an illumination that is both literal and metaphorical.
6. It is fundamentally amorphous and its content historically conditioned. The mystical experience is amorphous insofar as it has no predetermined form. The particular images, insights, emotional states, and volitions that it generates derive most of their specific character and intensity from religious and philosophical assumptions that the mystics bring with them into the experience prior to its onset. Moreover, the content of each mystic's experience validates the mythology or metaphysic that he or she takes for granted as being self-evidently true. In other words, there is not only an *essential* contextuality to the mystical experience but also a *reciprocal* interdependency between the presuppositions that underlie a mystic's interpretation of his or her experience and the content of that experience. For this reason, it is inappropriate to speak of either the experience or its interpretation as though one were epistemologically prior to the other.
7. It is a mode of experience that usually has its genesis in the recollective act.

It is important to remember that these seven characteristics display a wide variation in the degree to which they become manifest in any individual mystic's particular set of experiences. In other words, some mystical experiences will not exhibit all of these attributes; for instance, even such seemingly fundamental characteristics of the phenomenon as the preternatural illumination and intense affectivity may be weak or even lacking altogether in a particular mystic's experiences while most of the other elements are present.[3] I have chosen mystical experiences of an ideal type in order to bring out the characteristics of the phenomenon as sharply as possible. The variability of the phenomenon will become clearer as I proceed.

I will now discuss the first four characteristics of mystical experience. The more detailed discussions of illumination, the amorphousness and historicity of mystical experience, and the linkage between the practice of recollection and the genesis of mystical states of consciousness require that they each receive a separate chapter.

3. Many of Robert Monroe's out-of-body experiences lack the intense affectivity and luminous manifestations so commonly a part of other mystics' experiences. For example, see Robert A. Monroe, *Journeys Out of the Body* (Garden City, N.Y.: Doubleday, 1971), pp. 46–47.

# Characteristic 1: Mystical Experience is a Radical, Trans-sensory Metamorphosis of the Subject's Waking Consciousness

The first thing that strikes the observer when he examines each of the four narratives quoted in Chapter 1 is that, in each case, the mystic's mode of awareness underwent a dramatic change while he was in the midst of a waking state of consciousness. Nothing in Aua's, Gopi Krishna's, Paul's, or Augustine's descriptions suggests that any one of them had been dreaming when their particular visions or experiences of a divine voice had overwhelmed them. In each case, the mystic remained conscious not only immediately prior to its onset but also during the event. Each of them remembered what took place while it was in progress even though the actual moments of the experience brought about a condition of isolation from the ordinary waking mode of awareness.

The co-presence of this condition of conscious awareness appears to differentiate the four mystical experiences from those states of hypnotic hyperesthesia that take place in deep trance-states. In deep trance-states, although the subject may become, while he is hypnotized, acutely sensitive to phenomena that ordinarily lie beneath the threshold of his ordinary waking awareness, he finds that he cannot afterward recall what he had perceived during that time.

One must not exaggerate the differences between deep hypnotic trances and mystical experiences even though most mystical experiences do, indeed, take place when the subject is alert. After all, some mystical states bring about such a degree of abstractedness from the world of ordinary waking awareness that the mystic forgets what took place while they were happening. For instance, Teresa of Avila mentioned that that blissful ecstasy, which she called the "union of all the faculties," paralyzed her memory, imagination, and understanding so that she could never remember what had taken place while it had been in progress. Because it crippled her memory, she could no longer remember the subject on which she had been meditating immediately prior to its onset. Because it paralyzed her imagination, she found out that she could no longer imagine anything while it was taking place. Moreover, this condition of delightful swoon took away her power of understanding so that she could comprehend neither what she read nor the words spoken to her. She could have a minimal awareness that printed words were in front of her or that spoken words were impinging on her ears but the meaning or significance of these events could not register. This cognitive, imaginational, and intellectual paralysis made her completely unable to describe what took place during this condition of divine union.[4] Although Teresa's amnesia was a condition of blissful forgetfulness whereas the amnesias of most hypnotized subjects fail to stir up such intense and beneficial aftereffects, one must not forget that quite a few mystical experiences are rather humdrum affairs that carry little in the way of affective impact.[5] Consequently, the absence or presence of blissful emotions does not serve as an adequate criterion for differentiating mystical trance from hypnotic trance. Furthermore, one must realize that the hypnotic condition and the mystical trance-state share one very important feature: each comes about when individuals put themselves (or allow themselves to be put) in a state where their minds have become totally focused upon one thing—that is, either on some meditational object (such as Christ's appearance at His Passion) or else on some object that is presented by a hypnotist.[6]

When I refer to the "trans-sensory" character of the mystical mode of consciousness, I am observing that the mystic seems to perceive the objects of his or her visions and locutions by means of some faculty other than the five physical senses. I employ the term "trans-sensory" rather than "extra-sensory" in order to emphasize that mystical experiences do not necessarily involve any supernormal faculty of perception. While trans-sensory does not exclude those extrasensory modes of perception that appear to operate in experiences of clairvoyance, telepathy, and precognition,[7] most mystical experiences seem more akin to hallucinatory phenomena than

4. Teresa of Avila, *The Life of St. Teresa of Jesus: The Autobiography of St. Teresa of Avila*, trans. and ed. and with an introduction by E. Allison Peers (Garden City, N.Y.: Image Books, 1960), pp. 174–79.

5. For example, Monroe frequently experienced mystical states where he found himself outside of his body looking at a realm of being that seemed to him as real as the physical world. For the most part, he gives one the impression that his out-of-body episodes were just jaunts that happened to be occurring in an unusual manner but that, aside from the novelty of their manner of occurrence, were otherwise experienced as though they were completely ordinary events. See Monroe, *Journeys Out of the Body*, pp. 46–48.

6. For further discussion of the all-important function of mental concentration in the genesis of mystical experiences and supernormal phenomena, see Chapters 5, 8, and 11.

7. Although there is no reason to consider most mystics' visions to be anything other than hallucinations, some visions (and auditions) do appear to mix supernormally received information into the hallucinatory material. Other visions and locutions that convey supernormally received information have almost no hallucinatory ornamentation at all. I deal with this relationship between the hallucinatory fabrications of the imagination and the supernormal accompaniments of mysticism in more detail in Chapters 9, 11–12.

they do to supernormal manifestations.[8] In short, I use "trans-sensory" because it allows me to include both hallucinatory and supernormal phenomena within the domain of mystical experience with the added advantage of pointing one toward the quasi-sensory nature of those types of perceptions that take place during mystical states. Mystics do not just see and hear strange things in their visions and locutions but they "see" and "hear" them in a peculiar way that has analogies with optical and auditory sensation yet preserves a distinctive character of its own.

If one examines the four examples of the mystical experience that I have selected, one can see that each of those mystics either explicitly or implicitly presupposed that his unusual experience involved some sort of perceptual faculty other than the five physical sense organs. For instance, Aua stressed that his shamanic enlightenment allowed him to "see and hear in a totally different way" for he could now perceive things that were otherwise invisible to ordinary people such as the spirits and the shaman-light that radiated from his body. It is clear from his description that both of those objects were completely invisible to people who could only see by using their physical eyes. Moreover, Aua also mentioned that his new power of vision allowed him to see right through the earth and up into the sky. This implies that Aua not only had the capacity to see visions but that, like many other Eskimo shamans, he probably also possessed a supernormal faculty of clairvoyance. Even though Aua did not explicitly associate his particular illumination with the advent of supernormal powers, the Iglulik generally maintain that the illuminated shaman possesses the power to perceive telepathically the thoughts that are in peoples' minds as well as the power to leave his or her physical body in order to go on ecstatic journeys to visit the realms of the spirits and the dead.[9] The story of how the shamaness Uvavnuk acquired her inner light explicitly relates that telepathy and the power to undertake ecstatic journeys to the spirit-world went hand-in-hand with the illuminated state. Thus Uvavnuk informed Rasmussen that on one especially dark night, while she had stepped outside to urinate, there suddenly appeared before her a glowing ball of fire in the sky that came rushing toward her. She tried unsuccessfully to escape from it as its appearance frightened her. As it entered her everything be-

8. The continuity of hallucinatory and supernormal phenomena is discussed at some length in Chapter 9.

9. The Iglulik disagree with respect to how they would explain these ecstatic journeys to the spirit-world. Rasmussen noted that some of his informants claimed that it was only the spirit or soul of the shaman that did the traveling whereas others claimed that it was the physical body of the shaman that made the journey. See Rasmussen, *Intellectual Culture of the Iglulik Eskimo*, p. 124.

came luminous and then she lost consciousness. Immediately after she regained consciousness, she found out that she had become a shamaness for "there was nothing that was hidden from her now." Soon she began to use this telepathic sensitivity to reveal all the taboo violations that had been committed by those in her house. Not only did this illumination confer upon her this supposed telepathic sensitivity to the thoughts and hidden actions of others but it also gave her the capacity to visit the interior of the earth so that she could journey there in spirit to procure game from the mistress of animals, Takānakapsâluk.[10] The remarkable thing about Uvavnuk was that "as soon as she came out of her trance she no longer felt like a shaman; the light left her body and she was once more quite like an ordinary person. Only when the spirit of the meteor lit up the spirit light within her could she see and hear and know everything, and become at once a mighty magician."[11] This intimate juxtaposition of transsensory (both hallucinatory and supernormal, in this case) perceptual manifestations with the onset of illumination recurs constantly in the literature of mysticism. It is apparent that among the Eskimo the onset of mystical experience involved a radical alteration of the shaman's mode of consciousness. This transformation of awareness gave the shaman perceptual insights that transcended those that he or she could have known or inferred on the basis of information acquired from the five physical sense organs.

The dissimilarity of Gopi Krishna's mystical mode of perception from that which operates during ordinary sense-experience also comes out clearly in his description of how he awakened kundalini. One will recall that he stressed that when he "saw" this interior illumination, he apparently perceived it while his physical senses were inoperative. Thus he saw this liquid light "without any idea of a corporeal appendage, without any feeling or sensation coming from the senses."[12] Since his ordinary faculties of sight and touch seemed to be anesthetized, it is more appropriate to describe his perception of this inner luminosity as quasi-visual rather than visual because it was more akin to the kind of "seeing" that occurs in dreams and hallucinations than it was to ordinary physical sight.

Augustine also suggests that his perception of the infinite light took place by means of some trans-sensory perceptual faculty that he referred to as "my soul's eye." Moreover, he took care to explicitly note that this interior illumination was not "this common light plain to all flesh" but a

10. Ibid., pp. 122–23.
11. Ibid., p. 123.
12. Gopi Krishna, *Kundalini*, pp. 12–13.

type of luminosity completely different from it.[13] Furthermore, this difference in types of light was not a difference of mere magnitudes of intensity but rather a difference in nature for it somehow conveyed to him that it was an emanation of the divine essence.

The description of Paul's conversion in Acts implies that he perceived the divine illumination in a nonsensory way. Nevertheless, if one assumes that the light he "saw" was mere physical light, then how can one explain how it could shine much brighter than the midday sun and also radiate outward from both his companions and himself? This certainly suggests that Paul perceived his illumination in a transsensory manner. In Paul's own writings he sometimes alludes to a faculty of spiritual discernment that appears to be something quite different from ordinary sense perception. For example, in 1 Corinthians 2:14 he declares that the things of the Spirit seem nonsensical to the ordinary man. They seem foolish and "beyond his understanding because [they] can only be understood by means of the Spirit." To be sure, one must not infer that every time Paul used the word "Spirit" he necessarily intended that it refer to some subtle, nonphysical perceptual faculty. Nevertheless, his famous ecstatic ascent to the third heaven that he mentioned in 2 Corinthians 12:1–7 suggests that he had experienced out-of-body states similar to those that Rasmussen's Eskimo informants described when they spoke of their souls journeying to the land of the dead and to the realm of the mistress of animals.[14]

This association of mystical experience with one or more transsensory, and even supernormal, faculties of perception and cognition recurs as a constant theme in mystical literature. Throughout the world, in the most diverse religious traditions, people frequently assume that mystics are also men and women who have been gifted with extraordinary powers of discernment. Indeed, they often assume that such extraordinary powers constitute an essential prerequisite for the deeper forms of spiritual insight and wisdom. Thus Aua mentioned that no man could claim to be a shaman unless he also possessed the power to see spirits and talk to them, something that no ordinary man immersed solely in the experiential horizons of his physical senses could ever hope to do. Similarly, there is a passage in the Bhagavadgītā where, in order to reveal the awesome grandeur of his divine nature, Krishna unveils his true form to Arjuna and strips away the veil of appearances that made people think that he was merely Arjuna's

13. Augustine, *Confessions,* book 7, chap. 10, pp. 170–71.
14. Rasmussen, *Intellectual Culture of the Iglulik Eskimo,* pp. 122–24.

charioteer. Krishna prefaced this revelation of his divinity by stating that true knowledge of his divine being required that one first possess a special supernormal faculty of perception.

> Of course, with the ordinary eye
> You cannot see me.
> I give you divine vision.
> Behold my absolute power!
>
> With these words, Viṣṇu
> The great Lord of mystic power
> Gave Arjuna the vision
> Of his highest, absolute form.[15]

The foregoing observations demonstrate that mystical experience does not come about unless the subject has first activated one or more trans-sensory modes of perception and cognition. The kind of sense-experience available to people in their ordinary waking state of consciousness is incapable of giving them any direct, tangible encounter with the "spiritual" world and its denizens. We do not see spirits with our eyes. If we see them at all, we do so by means of some trans-sensory mode of perception. Consequently, there is a genuine sense in which the things of the spirit remain truly hidden from the ordinary run of men and women.

## Characteristic 2: Mystical Experiences Give the Subject Both Privileged Access to and Knowledge of What Religious Traditions Regard as Ultimately Real

Three out of the four experiences I have chosen exemplify privileged access to what is regarded as the ultimately real with exceptional clarity. For example, Gopi Krishna stated that his awakening of kundalini gave him the impression he had somehow come in contact with something that was endowed with a higher degree of reality than the phenomena of the physical world. Thus he wrote that his encounter with this strange luminous energy had given him the sensation that he was now perceiving "a reality before which all that I treat as real appears as unsubstantial and shadowy,

15. *The Bhagavadgītā*, trans. Kees W. Bolle (Berkeley and Los Angeles: University of California Press, 1979), 11:8–9.

a reality more solid than the material world reflected by the other senses, more solid than myself, surrounded by the mind and ego, more solid than all I can conceive of including solidity itself."[16] This impression that the experiential domain revealed through mystical experience possesses a higher degree of reality than the physical world occurs repeatedly in mystics' accounts of their experiences. Augustine's language in describing his vision of the Infinite Light also points to its ontological superiority to the physical world. Thus he characterized the peculiar illumination he "saw" with his soul's eye as not only the very source of his own being ("it was above my mind because it made me") but also that which was eternal and supremely true.[17] Paul leaves one no doubt that he, too, regarded his vision on the road to Damascus as an encounter with supreme reality. For example, in Philippians 3:21, Paul speaks about Christ, the Son of God, as equal to the Father in His power over all of creation for he proclaims that at the end of the world Christ will be able to transform the physical bodies of men into replicas of His glorious Body "by the same power by which He can subdue the whole universe." In other words, the Christ whom Paul encountered in his vision was none other than the Supreme Reality Itself.

That experience of so-called cosmic consciousness that overwhelmed Richard Bucke one evening furnishes us with one of the most perfect examples of how mystical experiences often give their recipients a compelling sensation that they have not only contacted ultimate reality itself but also comprehended its nature. Bucke relates that as he was driving home from a poetry-reading session in a warm mood of "quiet, almost passive enjoyment," he suddenly discovered that he was

> wrapped around as it were by a flame-colored cloud. For an instant he thought of fire, some sudden conflagration in the great city; next, he knew that the light was within himself. Directly afterwards came upon him a sense of exultation, of immense joyousness accompanied or immediately followed by an intellectual illumination quite impossible to describe. Into his brain streamed one momentary lightning-flash of the Brahmic Splendor which has ever since lightened his life; upon his heart fell one drop of Brahmic Bliss, leaving thenceforward for always an aftertaste of heaven. Among other things he did not come to believe, he saw and knew that the Cosmos is not dead matter but a living Presence, that the soul of man is immortal, that the universe is so built and ordered that with-

16. Gopi Krishna, *Kundalini,* p. 233.
17. Augustine, *Confessions,* book 7, chap. 10, p. 171.

out any peradventure all things work together for the good of each and all, that the foundation principle of the world is what we call love.[18]

This description clearly demonstrates that Bucke did far more than just perceive something unusual. His vision was more than just a perception of something, it was also, as he put it, a blissful "intellectual illumination," a type of experience that conveyed to him what he regarded as an unshakeable insight about the foundational principles of the cosmos.

Not surprisingly, Bucke's ontological and metaphysical concerns were those that preoccupied many of his philosophically inclined contemporaries. Like them, he, too, was concerned with the following questions: What is the nature of the relationship between "matter" and "spirit"? Which of these two entities has greater ontological dignity; that is, which of the two is more "real" than the other? Is spirit autonomous from matter? If so, what evidence supports this conclusion? Bucke thought that his experience of cosmic consciousness helped him to resolve these metaphysical questions by giving him empirical evidence for the ontological priority of spirit over matter. After all, this vision showed him that "the cosmos is not dead matter but a living Presence." Bucke also thought that he had saved Christianity from vulgar philosophical materialism because his vision had proved to his own satisfaction, at least, that "the soul of man is immortal" and that the universe is not cold and indifferent to human beings but, in some peculiarly sensed and empirically demonstrable way, loving and concerned about their welfare. He and his secularized contemporaries could now once again live confidently in a reenchanted universe that was alive, loving, and endowed with personality. His vision had directly demonstrated that the dreary, impersonal, and inanimate cosmos of the philosophical materialists and positivists was a fallacy. Furthermore, this vision had convinced Bucke that the Christ of the New Testament was none other than the experience of cosmic consciousness itself.[19] When one acknowledged this admittedly unusual interpretation of Christ as an experience rather than as a man, there was no problem bringing the Bible into harmony with science since one could now accept an interpretation of Christ that was free of all the mythological baggage that had made Christianity and science so incompatible in the past.

18. Richard Maurice Bucke, *Cosmic Consciousness: A Study in the Evolution of the Human Mind* (New York: E. P. Dutton, 1969), pp. 9–10.
19. Bucke explicitly identified Jesus Christ with the phenomenon of cosmic consciousness. "The saviour of man is Cosmic Consciousness—in Paul's language—the Christ." Ibid., p. 6.

The absence of these ontological concerns among the Eskimos helps to explain why Aua's mystical experience had nothing at all to say to him about such matters. Such abstract philosophical questions were utterly irrelevant to their pressing existential needs: to stay in contact with the world of the spirits and to avoid those forms of pollution that would turn the spirits against them causing thereby famine, sickness, and death in the community.[20] For this reason, the preeminent theme in Aua's experience is not "intellectual" illumination but rather that mode of illumination that brings him into contact with the spirits, those all-important beings whose help humanity needs and whose whims the community must placate in order to survive in the world.

The kinds of mystical consciousness (states of samādhi) that one finds described in Buddhist literature also fail to come across as any sort of revelation of ultimate reality. The reason for this absence of ontological concern is rooted in the fundamental Buddhist assumption that all forms of eternally existing ultimate reality or substance are illusions. Buddhists have always contended that the attainment of nirvana is impossible as long as one mistakenly imagines that any kind of phenomenon, be it an object, a state of consciousness, or some product of a state of consciousness, possesses a self; that is, exists eternally. According to this view, any person who craves a mystical state of consciousness in the deluded hope that cultivating it and immersing himself in it will give him an insight into the ultimate nature of reality by that very fact attributes to it a self. This delusion would be one of the most serious obstacles to nirvana.[21]

The aforementioned Buddhist and Eskimo examples show that the general tendency of mystical experiences to give both access to and convey knowledge of something that seems like ultimate reality does admit of significant exceptions. Religious traditions that either criticize the quest for knowledge of ultimate reality as a waste of time (such as Buddhism) or that have existential concerns that remain completely indifferent to such a quest (such as Iglulik Eskimo shamanism) do not create the conditions that generate ontological revelations of the type that Bucke, Augustine, and Gopi Krishna experienced. The reverse is also true. Those cultural environ-

20. Rasmussen describes the central religious concerns of the Iglulik Eskimos in Rasmussen, *The Intellectual Culture of the Iglulik Eskimo*, pp. 54–58, 62–63.

21. One can find examples of this Buddhist refusal to ontologize, that is, attribute an ultimate reality to any kind of experience whatsoever, in Tson-kha-pa, *Calming the Mind and Discerning the Real . . . from the Lam rim chen mo of Tson-kha-pa*, trans. Alex Wayman (Delhi: Motilal Banarsidass, 1979), pp. 92 and 442n.; as well as in Alexandra David-Neel, *Magic and Mystery in Tibet* (Baltimore: Penguin Books, 1971), pp. 283–87.

ments that value the quest for knowledge about either God, the ultimate nature of reality, or the nature of matter tend to generate mystical experiences where the illuminated individual seems to feel that he or she is in contact with that which is supremely real and abiding. It is clear that this particular feature of the mystical state of consciousness exhibits a large degree of context-dependence.

## Characteristic 3: Mystical Experiences Give the Subject Privileged Access to and Knowledge About What Religious Traditions Claim Have Soteriological Importance

Moses' encounter with God in the burning bush (Exodus 3:2–17) and Paul's vision on the road to Damascus (Acts 26:13–19) stand out as the classic stereotypes of the mystical experience in the religious literature of the West. Especially prominent in both is an encounter with God that bestows upon the mystic a message or commandment that becomes crucial for the salvation of both himself and his religious community. Moses must now set his people free from their bondage in Egypt and lead them to the Promised Land and Paul must now accept Christ as his Savior and Lord and preach the Gospel to the gentiles. The decision that each of these men made to obey the visionary commandments became a decisive turning point in both the sacred and profane histories of their respective religious communities. These two examples suggest that one of the significant features of the mystical experience is that it possesses soteriological relevance; that is, it contains material that is important to the salvation of the individual and his community.

The visions of Gopi Krishna and Aua would certainly validate this last suggestion. Like the experiences of Moses and Paul, those of Gopi Krishna and Aua also took form as conversion experiences. In Aua's case the experience suddenly converted him from an ordinary man into a shaman, and in Gopi Krishna's case it brought about both a radical transformation in the way he lived and a serious disturbance of his mental and physical equilibrium.[22] Moreover, Gopi Krishna maintained that the awakening of kundalini was not just a private matter bereft of any significant impact on the world around him. Instead, his own illumination convinced him that

---

22. It caused him to quit his job as a civil servant so that he could devote himself full time to meditation.

the happiness and welfare of mankind depend upon its adherence to the yet unknown laws of this evolutionary mechanism, known in India as *kundalini* which is carrying all men towards a glorious sense of consciousness with all their capacities to act, love, and enjoy intact, enhanced rather than diminished but functioning in subjection to a cultivated will.[23]

The activation of kundalini is an event fraught with potential for humankind's salvation for this kundalini energy is none other than that evolutionary mechanism that is supposedly responsible for the highest cultural achievements of humanity. When people learn how to activate and direct this energy constructively, they will eventually achieve a transcendent state of consciousness and fulfillment that the present state foreshadows only dimly. This conception of the salvational process is, to be sure, vastly different from the traditional soteriologies of the various schools of Yoga that have developed throughout history in India. Specifically, insofar as human beings must now try to live in harmony with the "laws" of this evolutionary "mechanism," Gopi Krishna's soteriology incorporated a response to the modern theory of evolution and the modern ideologies of progress through the advancement of science and the scientific method, notions to which he had been exposed as a result of his exposure to a European style of education. It is a soteriology redolent with the language and the method of science but, for that reason, is no less a scheme of salvation. However, now it is not gods who speak out of the luminous cloud to Gopi Krishna in order to teach him how he must be saved. His salvation now depends on his willingness to act like the present-day savior-figure, the scientist, for he must learn to probe this "energy" the way every scientist studies any phenomenon that comes to his attention, that is, in such a way that he can discern the "laws" that govern its manifestation.

Aua's enlightenment had a significant soteriological value for his community because it gave him the coveted power to make the spirits his helpers and companions as well as the vitally important power to travel to the spirit-world so that he could placate the spirits after the polluting actions of men and women had angered them and caused them to send bad weather or withhold the game animals on which everyone depended for subsistence. According to the Eskimo, the tragedy of humankind resides in the fact that almost all the food we eat has a soul that does not perish with the death of the creature we have killed and eaten. Consequently, the souls

23. Gopi Krishna, *Kundalini*, p. 241.

of these killed animals must be treated with respect and never subjected to insult (such as when someone violates a taboo).[24] Unfortunately, men and, especially, women can never completely avoid occasions when they unintentionally violate one or more of the elaborate and onerous taboos. When these inevitable pollutions accumulate, the shamans are the only ones who can journey to where the spirits dwell and convince them to restore health, good weather, or game animals to humans.[25]

To regard all mystical experiences as soteriologically important to the one who has them, however, is a mistake. Some mystics' visions are surprisingly mundane affairs. For example, Robert Monroe had numerous out-of-body experiences where all he did was visit friends to see what they were doing at a distant location.[26] On the other hand, there were also other occasions when Monroe's journeys to the spiritual world brought him into an exquisitely beautiful, ineffably meaningful, condition of total peace and harmony he called the "Perfect Environment." He described it as a "place or condition of pure peace, yet exquisite emotion." One feels that one is floating in a cloud "swept by rays of light in shapes and hues that are constantly changing, and each is good as you bathe in them as they pass over you. Ruby-red rays of light, or something beyond what we know as light, because no light is ever felt this meaningful."[27] There is also an ineffable sense of music and musical harmony that pervades this celestial environment. Monroe went on to describe this Perfect Environment as "the purity of a truth of which you have had only the glimpse." Most important, one had many companions there. "They do not have names, nor are you aware of them as shapes, but you know them and you are bonded to them with a great single knowledge."[28] This example shows that, even for the same individual, mystical visions can vary markedly in significance and emotional impact. One must therefore not regard the conversion experiences of Paul and Moses as typical. Many mystical experiences have no soteriological significance whatsoever either to the individual who has them or to his or her religious community.

It is also worth noting that Augustine's vision of the Infinite Light stands out from the rest of the four examples of mystical experience by its relative absence of soteriological force. In other words, the vision resolved on-

24. Rasmussen, *The Intellectual Culture of the Iglulik Eskimo*, p. 56.
25. Ibid., pp. 109–11.
26. For instance, see Monroe, *Journeys Out of the Body*, pp. 46–47, 48–49.
27. Ibid., pp. 123–24.
28. Ibid., pp. 124–25.

tological problems rather than soteriological ones. It was certainly not a proximate cause of his conversion to Christianity for that event occurred some time after this particular vision. This vision of the Infinite Light occurred during Augustine's Neoplatonist phase and, as one would expect, its content embodied Plotinus's intellectualism. Although this particular vision aroused his feelings of love and awe, its principal import was that it helped him to resolve an intellectual problem, the problem of whether or not God existed and how He existed in a manner that was beyond any possibility of representing Him in an image. In any case, it does not appear to have had any immediate impact on his will in any way comparable to the voice that he later heard speak to him in the garden.[29]

One would not expect Buddhists to have mystical experiences laden with soteriological import for reasons that I have already mentioned above and, indeed, one does not find such saving visions described in their literature. Visions of great splendor do appear in Buddhist literature but the idea that the experience of any particular mystical state of consciousness could have any significance for an individual's salvation—that is, it could serve as a proximate cause of him or her entering nirvana—would have seemed ridiculous to them because such an attitude would have been tantamount to committing one of the greatest spiritual errors—attributing to a transient state of consciousness an eternally subsistent self that was not subject to the defilements of karma and the sufferings that go with subjection to the laws of karma. One does not enter nirvana merely by entering into trances. One enters into nirvana only when one comprehends in a penetrating manner that all phenomena whatsoever—even the most elevated trance-states—are impermanent and ultimately productive of suffering when one acquires a craving for them.

## Characteristic 4: Mystical Experiences Are Laden with Affect

The popular stereotype of the mystical experience invariably portrays it as a phenomenon with an overwhelming emotional intensity. Like Moses standing before the burning bush or Muhammad before the blazing throne

---

29. Compare Augustine, *Confessions,* book 7, chap. 10 (the vision of the Infinite Light), with book 8, chaps. 8–12 (the voice in the garden).

of Allah,[30] the typical mystic is always depicted as standing in awestruck astonishment before the divine presence or else he or she is portrayed as overwhelmed by blissful transports of ecstasy. This popular image of the mystical experience is not all that misleading. The four examples I have quoted suggest that the mystical experience is, indeed, anything but emotionally neutral. After all, Aua described his enlightenment as an unrestrainable joy that somehow projected him into another world.[31] Gopi Krishna spoke of his awakening of kundalini as an event that filled him with feelings of "exaltation and happiness impossible to describe."[32] Paul fell down to the ground in awe of the light and voice that came to him, and Augustine wrote that his experience of the Infinite Light made him tremble "with love and awe."[33] One could cite innumerable other instances of this sort where intense emotional states accompany mystical experience. In these instances the mystic does not confront the object of his experience as though it were a mere percept, a mere thing, an "it." As Bucke so aptly put it in describing his own experience, the object of the experience seems to become a "living" presence, simultaneously alive and intelligent.[34] Mystical experience might be more accurately described as an encounter rather than a mere perception for "perception" erroneously suggests an emotionally flat "I-It" relationship between subject and object, whereas the term "encounter" conveys more accurately the sense of anticipatory excitement that grips mystics as they confront the spiritual world and the beings or persons they may find there.

Even though it is very common for mystical experiences to manifest themselves in an emotionally overpowering way, this is by no means always the case. As I have already pointed out above, many (though not all) of Robert Monroe's out-of-body experiences had no emotional impact at all. He simply found himself looking at something going on that he otherwise would not have seen if he had been in his ordinary waking state but, other than that, there was no difference between the "spiritual" mode of perception and ordinary sight.

30. This mythical narrative of Muhammad's ascension to heaven and his appearance before the throne of Allah can be found in Mircea Eliade, *From Primitives to Zen: A Thematic Sourcebook of the History of Religions* (New York: Harper & Row, 1977), pp. 517–20.
31. Rasmussen, *Intellectual Culture of the Iglulik Eskimo*, p. 118.
32. Gopi Krishna, *Kundalini*, p. 13.
33. Augustine, *Confessions*, book 7, chap. 10, p. 171.
34. Bucke, *Cosmic Consciousness*, pp. 9–10.

# 3

# The Nature of
# Mystical Illumination

One of the most common phenomena associated with mystical states of consciousness is a preternatural illumination that can take several different forms. Sometimes it becomes manifest as a brilliant aura that seems to emanate from either the mystic or the particular beings that the mystic encounters in the spiritual world.[1] At other times it seems as though it is the whole environment that is suffused with radiance rather than individual beings within it.[2] On other occasions, the preternatural illumination seems to be localized within a system of subtle physiology (for example, kundalini energy seems to be a peculiar liquid light that is localized within the spinal canal).[3]

## Characteristic 5: Mystical Experience Brings About an Illumination That Is Both Literal and Metaphorical

### Preliminary Observations

Each of the four mystical experiences I chose as examples of the phenomenon as well as Moses' vision of the burning bush and Bucke's experience of "cosmic" consciousness were experiences that involved the subject in a peculiar sort of illumination or photism. This illumination takes place in both a literal and figurative sense.

One speaks here of illumination in the literal sense insofar as each of the mystical experiences referred to by Moses and Bucke caused the subject to

1. Aua's illumination provides us with an excellent example of this. See Rasmussen, *Intellectual Culture of the Iglulik Eskimo*, pp. 118–19.
2. See Bucke, *Cosmic Consciousness*, pp. 9–10.
3. See Gopi Krishna, *Kundalini*, p. 12.

perceive a peculiar kind of preternatural light. It is a most peculiar sort of light because, on the one hand, it bears many similarities to the kind of light that one normally perceives through one's physical organs of sight while, on the other hand, it also possesses qualities that radically set it apart from that sort of illumination we see with our corporeal eyes. Saint Augustine brought out this distinctive quality of mystical light when he emphasized that what he had perceived in his vision was "not this light plain to all flesh, nor a greater light, as it were, of the same kind . . . but [something] different, far different from all other lights."[4]

One speaks of the mystical experience as involving an illumination in a metaphorical or figurative sense as well because it usually happens that the moment of literal illumination coincides with a moment of spiritual insight or awakening. The mystic has, to use the slang expression, "seen the light," that is, he has gained an insight or received some sort of revelation that would never have come to him in his ordinary waking state of consciousness. One observes that the moment when the mystic first perceives a preternatural luminosity almost always coincides with that instant when he claimed that he had, for the first time, acquired genuine insight into those matters that his particular culture or religious tradition presupposes are matters of ultimate soteriological and ontological concern.[5] For example, that first moment when Aua perceived the "shaman-light of brain and body,"[6] that is, was illuminated in the literal sense, was also the first moment when he recognized that he had the power to see spirits (this was illumination in the metaphorical sense for he now had knowledge of spiritual things). Similarly, Saint Paul was not only literally illumined by the light from heaven but he was also illuminated metaphorically when Christ revealed to him that He was the Lord and that Paul's purpose in this life was to spread the Gospel to the gentiles (Acts 26:13–19).

Several other peculiar qualities of this mystical light deserve a more extended comment.

First, the mystic light is not identical to the ordinary light that illumines the physical world. It is analogous to physical light but not identical to it.

4. Augustine, *Confessions*, book 7, chap. 10, p. 170.

5. Mircea Eliade has noted this persistent connection between the onset of mystical illumination and the transformation of the mystic's profane mode of being into one that is spiritual rather than profane. He wrote that "a meeting with the Light produces a break in the subject's existence, revealing to him—or making clearer than before—the world of the Spirit, of holiness, and of freedom; in brief, existence as a divine creation." Mircea Eliade, *The Two and the One* (New York: Harper & Row, 1965), p. 77.

6. Rasmussen, *Intellectual Culture of the Iglulik Eskimo*, p. 118.

All of the four experiences cited in Chapter 1 show that although the photism shines in a manner that bears many similarities to the way that physical light shines, there is always something else about the phenomenon that
renders a facile analogy with physical light completely misleading. For instance, Aua's description indicated that it possessed several strange properties that ordinary light never has. First, he mentioned that it was an "in-
ward" light, that is to say, it seemed as though it were a luminosity of the
brain rather than a physical light generated from a source outside himself.
Second, Aua described this light as being invisible to the five physical
senses and to ordinary human beings but visible to spirits. It was therefore
a phenomenon that required for its perception some sort of spiritual "organ" of vision. Third, Aua's own body appeared—at least to the spirits—
as though it were luminous, a contradiction to ordinary experience.
Fourth, although Aua did not explicitly mention supernormal powers coming to him with his illumination, other Eskimos link the onset of mystical
illumination with the onset of supernormal capabilities.[7]

The peculiarities of the mystical light come out even more prominently
in Gopi Krishna's account. His descriptions of kundalini as a stream of
"liquid light" that quite literally roars up from the base of the spine to the
top of the skull where it overflows in a shower of light depict a sort of
luminosity that, aside from the fact that it shines, bears no other analogy
to any luminous manifestation one encounters in the waking state. Moreover, Gopi Krishna made it clear that while he was perceiving this strange
luminescence, he was unconscious of any feeling or sensation coming from
his physical senses. Unlike ordinary light, he could only perceive this mystical light by means of a trans-sensory "organ" of perception since his
physical senses were deadened at the time that he "saw" it. Finally, one
notes there seems to have been a direct proportionality between the intensity of Gopi Krishna's illumination and the degree to which he had abstracted himself from sense experience—for example, if he allowed the
physical sensation at the base of his spine to distract him from focusing

7. For example, one will recall that Uvavnuk claimed that she possessed the ability to
read others' thoughts and to see their secret transgressions only when she had preternatural
light within her body (see Rasmussen, *Intellectual Culture of the Iglulik Eskimo*, pp. 122–
24). Franz Boas also noted the widespread belief among the Eskimos of Hudson Bay and
Baffin Island that when shamans possess that interior light they also possess various supernormal powers such as clairvoyance, telepathy, and the ability to travel out of their bodies.
See Franz Boas, *The Eskimo of Baffin Land and Hudson Bay,* from the notes collected by
George Comor, James S. Mutch, and E. J. Peck, in *Bulletin of the American Museum of
Natural History,* vol. 15, pts. 1–2 (New York: Published by Order of the Trustees, 1901–7),
pp. 133–34.

exclusively upon the imaginary lotus in his head, he noticed that the sensation quickly dissipated and with it any possibility of perceiving the photism.[8]

The biblical description of Paul's vision (Acts 26:13–19) further confirms the alien nature of this mystical light. Although this account does not go into much detail, it does indicate that the luminosity of his vision differed from physical light because it shone "brighter than the sun" and radiated outward from both Paul and his companions.

As I have noted in Chapter 1, Augustine's description of the Infinite Light accentuated its difference from physical light. Three details especially merit comment in this context. First, Augustine mentioned that he did not perceive this interior light with his physical eye but rather with something that he called "my soul's eye." Second, he also described this light as somehow being the well-spring of creation. In a most peculiar manner, this luminosity conveyed the impression to him that it was that creative potency that gave rise to all that exists. Third, it was not a light that Augustine perceived in an emotionally neutral manner as usually happens when ordinary physical objects are illuminated by the sun or a streetlight.[9] Like all of the other mystical photisms cited in Chapter 1, it was a peculiar radiance that elicited a profound existential response from the subject.

Even though photisms very frequently accompany mystical experiences, it also happens rather often that they are absent. For example, when Black Elk received a clairaudient premonition about the presence of game animals from a coyote, this event took place without any accompanying experience of illumination.[10] Similarly, many of what Saint Teresa called her "intellectual visions" came to her without any concomitant sensation of exterior or internal illumination and yet she regarded these particular contacts with God as the most spiritual of her visions notwithstanding their lack of luminous accompaniments.[11] Many of Monroe's ecstatic dissociations also exhibited a great degree of variation with respect to the extent to

8. Gopi Krishna, *Kundalini*, pp. 12, 16.

9. Augustine, *Confessions*, book 7, chap. 10, p. 170.

10. Raymond J. DeMallie, ed., *The Sixth Grandfather: Black Elk's Teachings Given to John G. Neihardt* (Lincoln: University of Nebraska Press, 1984), p. 208.

11. Saint Teresa explicitly distinguished the intellectual vision from any sort of visionary manifestation that involved an interior illumination. During her intellectual visions, she had an indubitable consciousness that God was present beside or in the interior of her soul and yet this certainty did not derive from seeing Him there with either the eyes of the body or the eye of the soul. In this ineffable imageless vision, God "presents Himself to the soul by a knowledge brighter than the sun. I do not mean that any sun is seen, or any brightness is perceived, but that there is a light which, though not seen, illumines the understanding so that the soul may have fruition of such a blessing." Teresa of Avila, *Life of St. Teresa of Jesus*, p. 250; for references to its assumed superiority to visions with images, see ibid., pp. 249, 259.

which they manifested the phenomenon of photism. For example, he related that he repeatedly experienced a series of strange illumination experiences that preceded the actual onset of his first out-of-body episode.[12] Nevertheless, most of the time no unusual luminous manifestations intruded into what he "saw" during those times he was actually dissociated from his body.[13]

## The Diversity of Luminous Manifestations in Mystical and Religious Literature

Although some form of preternatural luminosity very frequently accompanies mystical experiences regardless of the religious tradition one examines, one must never lose sight of the extraordinary variability of these luminous manifestations. For example, the phenomenon of kundalini as described by Gopi Krishna displays features that have no counterpart in the other accounts.[14] The other mystics' descriptions of their experiences neither associate any unusual spinal sensations with the onset of their illuminations nor do any sensations of light rushing up the spine occur while their illuminations are in progress. In a similar vein, one notes that Augustine's description of the Infinite Light says nothing about this radiance that would suggest that it emanated from his own body or surrounded other beings or men.[15] Aua, on the other hand, specifically mentioned that his shaman-light radiated outward from within himself so that his body had a luminous appearance to the spirits.[16] Such manifestations of luminous beings and spiritual human beings are extraordinarily abundant in mystical literature. Moreover, these luminous personages and spirits exhibit this preternatural radiance in very diverse ways. For this reason, an analysis of these variations can be helpful in displaying with special clarity the fundamental diversity of illumination phenomena.

For example, when Moses came down from Mount Sinai with the Tablets of the Covenant, "the skin on his face was radiant. . . . And when Aaron and all the sons of Israel saw Moses, the skin on his face shone so much that they would not venture near him" (Exodus 34:29–30). Religious texts quite often portray the person who enjoys an extraordinary

12. Monroe, *Journeys Out of the Body*, pp. 22–25.
13. For example, note how the visionary experiences described lack any sort of photism. Ibid., pp. 46–47, 51–54, 55–57.
14. Gopi Krishna, *Kundalini*, pp. 12–13.
15. Augustine, *Confessions*, book 7, chap. 10, pp. 170–71.
16. Rasmussen, *Intellectual Culture of the Iglulik Eskimo*, pp. 118–19.

proximity to the divine or who possesses an exceptional degree of spiritual wisdom as someone who radiates light from his or her body.[17] One notices that such supremely spiritual persons tend to become luminous in this manner when they are either in the process of transmitting exceptionally significant sacred revelations to their religious communities or conveying spiritual power to someone. For example, Moses' luminescence did not become manifest on just any occasion but only on those occasions when either he had to communicate the most important messages of God to His chosen people or else when he was enjoying his most intimate moments of communion with Yahweh. What is true about the quintessentially spiritual individual also applies to the divine being from whom the mystic receives his revelation. Thus not only is Moses radiant when he has come down from the mountain after talking to Yahweh but Yahweh Himself is depicted in that same text as even more refulgent with light than Moses. Indeed, He shines so brightly that Moses cannot look at His face directly for that would certainly kill him. Consequently, Moses has to content himself with looking at Yahweh's back. One of the traditions about Muhammad's Night Journey (mi'raj), his ecstatic ascension to Heaven where he met Allah face to face, relates that when Muhammad stood before Him on His throne Muhammad's sight was so dazzled by the brilliance that radiated from Allah that he had to close his eyes in order to avoid blindness.[18]

Nicholas Motovilov's famous conversation with the great Russian holy man Seraphim of Sarov refers to an incident in which Motovilov witnessed the saint's body grow luminous at that moment when both men believed that the Holy Spirit had actually become intimately present in their midst. Just as the Bible relates that Moses' proximity to God on Mount Sinai had caused Moses to radiate a brilliant light, Seraphim, through his prayers, had brought down the Holy Spirit so that It dwelt both within himself and Motovilov. In both incidents, intimate contact with the supremely sacred resulted in bodily luminescence. According to Motovilov, both he and Seraphim were engaged in a profound conversation about what it really meant to be in the grace of the Holy Spirit. Motovilov asked the saint, "How could one recognize the presence of this sanctifying Spirit?" While this discussion was taking place, Seraphim was simultaneously engaging in silent mental prayer asking God to bestow His most Holy Spirit on his

17. The Chāndogya Upanishad 4:14.2 refers to the wise man who knows Brahma as someone whose face is radiant. Thus: "Your face, . . . shines like a Brahma-knower's. Who pray, has instructed you?"

18. This scene is narrated in Eliade, *From Primitives to Zen*, p. 518.

questioner. Seraphim later explained that he knew that his mental prayer had actually reached God for subsequent events showed him that the Holy Spirit had indeed come down among them both in the form of a brilliant effulgence that Motovilov saw emanating from Seraphim's body. Motovilov described this episode:

> Then Father Seraphim took me firmly by the shoulders and said:
> "We are together, son, in the Holy Spirit of God! Why lookest thou not on me?"
> I replied:
> "I cannot look, father, because lightning flashes from your eyes. Your face is brighter than the sun and my eyes ache in pain!"
> Father Seraphim said:
> "Fear not, my son, you too have become as bright as I. You too are now in the fullness of God's Spirit, otherwise you would not be able to look on me as I am."

He then went on to relate that

> after these words I looked on his face and there came over me an even greater reverential awe. Imagine the center of the sun, in the dazzling brilliance of his midday rays, the face of the man who talks with you. You see the movement of his lips and the changing expression of his eyes, you hear his voice, you feel someone grasp your shoulders; yet you do not see the hands, you do not even see yourself or his figure, but only a blinding light spreading several yards around and throwing a radiance across the snow blanket on the glade and into the snowflakes which besprinkled the elder and me. Can you imagine the state in which I then found myself?[19]

The notion that the most profoundly sacred things and beings exhibit a luminosity that possesses an intensity directly proportional to their degree of participation in a spiritual mode of existence is a universal feature of light symbolisms in religions throughout history and throughout the world. In no tradition where there is a sacred literature that alludes to or describes luminous manifestations can one find any exception to this rule: When something exhibits a brilliant luminosity, the intensity of its lumi-

19. G. P. Fedotov, ed., *A Treasury of Russian Spirituality* (New York: Sheed & Ward, 1948), pp. 274–75.

nescence signifies that it is something supremely sacred or supremely spiritual.[20]

Luminous epiphanies are not the exclusive privilege of mystics who come from within the Jewish, Christian, or Islamic religious environments. For instance, Gerda Walther cited a report of a similar sort of illumination experience that came from India in 1936. In that year Hans-Hasso von Veltheim-Ostrau visited the ashram of the famous Hindu mystic Sri Ramana Maharshi. The German doctor noted that it often happened that when (and only at that time) the great yogin went into *samādhi* (deep trance) his body would begin to radiate light. "The blackness of his body transformed itself gradually into white. This white body became brighter and brighter as though he were illuminated from within and began to shine! . . . During my further sojourns in the ashram, I experienced this same phenomenon each time when I looked at the Maharshi in samādhi, but only then."[21]

I have already emphasized that Moses and Seraphim only became self-luminous when they enjoyed the most intimate kinds of communion with God. Maharshi's luminescence did not appear to have derived from any intimacy with a personal God but instead appears to have stemmed from his ability to put himself into an especially deep trance. Entrance into this trance-state allowed him to comprehend by direct experience a truth that all followers of *advaita* (nondualistic) Vedānta hold quintessentially sacred, namely, that the individual soul (*ātman*) is none other than the eternally subsistent Reality (*brahman*) that gives rise to all that is created. It is clear from this last observation that the luminous manifestations one encounters in mystical literature do not arise from only one particular type of sacred contact. Exceptionally intimate contact with the sacred as it is expressed in any religious metaphysic or mythology gives rise to photism. Theistic religions have no monopoly on this phenomenon.

One important detail about the descriptions of self-luminous beings and individuals merits further attention since it points to the fundamental diversity of illumination phenomena so well. One notices that the brightness that surrounded Moses, Seraphim of Sarov, and Sri Ramana Maharshi did not exhibit any internal structure. The narrators simply depict the light as a structureless brightness that surrounds the holy man. However, there is a

20. In this particular instance, I am using the term "spiritual" to refer to that which has the modality of soul or spirit, that is, that which is completely unfettered by the physical, temporal, and perceptual constraints of matter.

21. Quoted from Walther, *Phänomenologie der Mystik*, p. 196.

64          THE NATURE OF MYSTICAL EXPERIENCE

genre of Western European literature about paranormal manifestations
dating from the nineteenth and twentieth centuries that refers to the phenomenon of the human aura, a luminosity that spiritually and clairvoyantly gifted people sometimes "see" surrounding *all* human beings, not
just saints. Three things differentiated these auras from those luminous
surrounds that enveloped the holy men mentioned above: First, the aura is
always described as a luminous structure that varies in intensity and surrounds all individuals whether they be saints, sinners, or "average." Second, the aura is not just a structureless radiance—it has a complex inner
structure and texture. Third, its presence, intensity, and texture is supposedly correlated to the mood, health, and personality traits of its owner.
Thus the absence of an aura or a dramatic diminution in its intensity supposedly portends either the death or serious illness of the individual.[22]
However, although the aura primarily indicates the mood, health, and
overall personality traits of the individual, its magnitude of brightness and
clarity is often described as directly proportional to the degree to which its
possessor is clairvoyantly gifted or intimate with sacred things.

Walther gives an excellent description of what she "sees" whenever she
examines someone's aura.[23] First of all, she notes that the aura is not seen
with the physical eyes but with some other extra-ocular faculty of perception. To be sure, it often seems as though one is simply seeing an aura with
one's eyes but in such cases what is actually happening is that one is simply superimposing the extra-ocular image over the visual image so that the
two seem to coincide.[24] Second, she perceives that the aura is the most
intimately "personal" thing about an individual that he possesses. It is
even more distinctive and individual than a person's face or portrait. Each
person's aura has a distinctive pattern of colors, a distinctive structure
(granularity, degrees of clarity, or opacity), and a distinctive emotional
impact on the one who perceives it that makes it, like that individual's face
or fingerprint, an infallible means of identifying him or her.[25] Even though
the structure of the aura varies with an individual's swings in mood and
health, the overall pattern still remains uniquely stamped with his or her

22. For an example of this, see Edgar Cayce, *Auras* (Virginia Beach, Va.: A.R.E. Press,
1973), p. 8.
23. Gerda Walther, the author of a phenomenological study of mysticism, *Phänomenologie der Mystik* (1955), was a student of the famous philosopher Edmund Husserl
and the continental reporter for the American Society of Psychical Research during the 1930s.
24. Gerda Walther, "Some Experiences Concerning the Human Aura," *Journal: American
Society for Psychical Research* 26 (September 1932), p. 342.
25. Walther, "Some Experiences," p. 343.

identity just as a person's face or handwriting style are always identifiable as his or her own even though they go through substantial changes with age. Third, the aura possesses an inner structure of which the colors, degree of transparency or opacity, and brightness or dullness convey the most intimate information about that individual's level of spiritual development, mood, and health.

> It is of the greatest difference imaginable whether the "same" color is more or less luminous and transparent or material and dull. One may say the color is about the same; and yet it makes an enormous difference whether it is the "yellow" of a painted wall or a sunbeam. It is just the same with the "colors" of the aura. The aura will be brighter, luminous, and transparent—so to say—the more spiritual its owner is, and it will be dull or opaque if its owner is a more or less materialistic undeveloped person.

Fourth, Walther stressed that the aura was not a creation of the imagination. It appears to be as objectively real as any other physical object to one who is gifted with auric sight. For example, she noted that when she compared her own perceptions of a particular individual's aura with the descriptions which other similarly gifted friends of hers made (without being told beforehand about what Walther had seen) of that same individual's aura, the two descriptions coincided.[26]

Other sources confirm Walther's descriptions of the aura as a luminous halo that, far from being a formless brightness, is instead a type of light that possesses a complex inner structure. For instance, one of Shafica Karagulla's informants told her that she perceives the aura as an

> "energy body or field" which sub-stands [sic] the dense physical body, interpenetrating it like a sparkling web of light beams. This web of light frequencies is in constant movement. . . . This energy body extends in and through the dense physical body and is a replica of the physical body. She insists that any disturbance in the physical structure itself is preceded and later accompanied by disturbances in this energy body or field. Within this energy body . . . she observes eight major vortices of force and many smaller vortices. As she describes it, energy moves in and out of these vortices, which look like spiral cones. . . . Breaks or disturbances in the spiral

26. Ibid., p. 344.

cone have to do with some function of the physical body in that area. If any of these major vortices shows a dullness or irregularity or "leak" in this central point or core, she looks for some serious pathology in the physical body in the area.[27]

This account of the aura's structure shows that the aura seems to be connected to a system of subtle physiology not even hinted at in the descriptions of the luminous epiphanies of Seraphim and Sri Ramana Maharshi. Even though Karagulla's informant did not describe the aura in exactly the same way as Walther did, both accounts emphasize that the human aura is a highly structured type of luminous phenomenon that surrounds an individual and gives a clairvoyantly sensitive person a great deal of information about his health, basic personality traits, and emotional state. Moreover, in both accounts, the ability to "see" the aura does not signify that the percipient is in any way particularly favored by God or in any particularly privileged contact with the sacred.

Nevertheless, there are significant points of contact between experiences of mystical illumination and experiences of auric vision. First, neither the aura nor the mystic light are ordinarily perceptible to corporeal vision. One usually sees the aura or the mystic light only if one has disengaged oneself from the process of physical sense perception and awakened a latent transsensory faculty of perception that normally remains unmanifest as long as the mind is preoccupied with processing information that comes into it from the imagination and the five senses.[28] Second, in both cases, exceptional brightness of the light not only indicates a high degree of spiritual development but also that the one who radiates it has "psychic" gifts, that is to say, is gifted with a supernormal faculty or faculties of perception or action. With regard to the correlation between the brightness of the aura and the degree of spiritual development of its possessor, the "psy-

27. Shafica Karagulla, *Breakthrough to Creativity* (Santa Monica, Calif.: De Vorss, 1967), pp. 124–25. The mention of "vortices" suggests parallels with that system of subtle physiology described by hatha yoga, specifically, the chakras or "wheels" that supposedly line the spine and that are successively activated when the yogin awakens kundalini from its latent state. It is quite possible that Karagulla's informant had learned about the hatha yoga system of subtle physiology through Theosophical circles and that this contact shaped the way that she experienced the aura. This might help to account for the differences between her account of the inner structure of the aura and that given by Walther in "Some Experiences."

28. In other words, most of the time, the ability to "see" the mystical illumination and the capacity to "see" auras both presuppose that the subject has become recollected, that his mind and will have become totally focused and quieted. I deal with this phenomenon of recollection in some depth in Chapter 5.

chic" Caroline Larsen has written that "in the Spirit World, the color of the aura defines the quality of the spirit. All darker colors denote a low state of development. As the spirit progresses upward the colors of the aura become continually brighter."[29] Just as Moses and Seraphim became most brilliantly luminous when their contact with God became most intimate, something quite similar appears to hold true about that "spirit world" accessible to twentieth-century Western European and American psychics, mediums, and out-of-body travelers. The degree of luminosity in their auras is directly proportional to their degree of intimacy with the spiritual world. Matthew Manning, contemporary poltergeist medium, has noted that

> certain colors in an aura appeared to denote particular traits in a person's character. By finding out what colors surrounded people I knew well, I found that each color was representative of a particular facet of their character. . . . If someone had a predominantly fiery or temperamental character, then the predominant color in their aura was red. If they were also kind and generous, they might have this red bordered by blue or purple. . . . For some reason unknown to myself, the clarity and intensity of the colors varies a great deal from one person to another. An interesting observation I have made is that the aura is particularly evident and clear when it surrounds those who have any degree of psychic gifts, especially if they are in the habit of using them.[30]

Manning's description is especially interesting for it suggests that establishing intimate proximity to the sacred, regardless of the way that each religious tradition defines its specific nature, has the same effect on the human aura as developing and utilizing supernormal faculties of perception. In other words, both activities intensify the brightness of the aura. This fact should not be surprising for the folklore of mysticism has often depicted those who enjoyed a privileged intimacy with the sacred as persons who also had a concomitant ability to manifest supernormal powers of perception or action.

It is worth noting that Walther drew a distinction, based upon self-observation, between spiritual (*geistige*) experiences of illumination and

29. Larsen quoted in Muldoon and Carrington, *Projection of the Astral Body*, p. 286.
30. Matthew Manning, *The Link* (New York: Ballantine, 1974), p. 78.

mental or psychical (*seelische*) experiences of illumination.[31] According to Walther, the multicolored aura that most clairvoyants have described that supposedly gives them information about the mood, health, and spiritual development of the person whom it surrounds acquires its particular color-ation and distinctive pattern from the ego-center of its possessor. (She maintains that the ego-center or psyche is not to be confused with a per-son's spirit.) The individual's deepest motivations and aspirations, hates and loves, all of which originate in his or her ego-center, imprint a unique, "individual" pattern on the aura. The multicolored pattern of that aura generated from within the core of each individual's psyche paints a picture of that person's distinctive personality traits and emotional quirks in much the same way that the spectrum of each star gives an indication of its chemical composition, temperature, and magnetic field strength. In con-trast to this aura that appears to originate from a person's ego-center, Walther also noted that there was a spiritual aura that was not "colored" in the ordinary sense of the word. This spiritual aura is not colored in the sense that it does not appear to be either blue, green, red, yellow, or any mixture of these colors of the spectrum. Instead, the spiritual aura appears as a "more or less intense *white* light"[32]—white in the sense that it is the color that represents the blending together of all the primary colors of the spectrum. Just as white exceeds all the other primary colors the spiritual aura transcends the more superficial egocentric individuality of the mental aura because it originates from that supra-individual spiritual primary es-sence (*geistiges Grundwesen*) that supposedly lies at the very core of a human being's deepest self and that must not be confused with the individ-ual's ego-center. Walther maintained that it was not the ego-center but rather the spiritual primary essence that makes contact with God during a mystical experience.

According to Walther, spiritual illuminations, whether they come from the spiritual primary essence of man or from God, have one feature in common—they are not colored with the primary colors of the spectrum. The reason for this is that these illuminations come from beyond the ego-center so it makes sense that their "spectrum" would not display the par-ticular markings of an individual's ego in much the same way that the spectrum of a cold red star could not possibly be expected to display the

31. In this particular instance I am using the term "psychic" simply to refer to that which pertains to the psyche or soul (*Seele*). As such, it does *not* mean "psychic" in the sense of that which pertains to the supernormal.

32. Walther, *Phänomenologie der Mystik*, p. 151.

spectral peculiarities of a supernova. The aura only possesses primary colors or their composites when the ego-center influences its structure. Since illuminations from the spiritual primary essence transcend the ego-center, they are not subject to its influences. This peculiar way that spiritual colors transcend the particularistic individuality of the colors that characterize the mental aura comes across in a statement Walther made when she tried to describe the peculiar way that the spiritual aura was white. That white light that comes from one's spiritual primary essence (as distinguished from God's spiritual primary essence) is indeed

> similar to the divine light of the Spirit except that the divine [light] has a "golden" tinge and is infinitely richer than either the "white" light of the human spirit or the limited "color" of his individual psychical [*seelische*] aura for the divine light is not partially tinged with the "color" of a particular, individual primary essence. . . . Yet neither is it devoid of color but rather it is infinitely rich as if it subsumed all those "colors" in itself—displayed, however, as a unity, not as juxtaposed, so that even in that abundance of colors it never becomes "colorless" or "garishly colored."[33]

Walther also noted that this description of how the "color" of divine illuminations possesses a supra-individual fullness that goes beyond the "limited" individualized coloration patterns characteristic of those auras that originate from an individual's ego-center has its analogue in the different quality of feeling-experiences that originate from the ego-center and the spiritual primary essence. In other words, the affective timbre of those feelings of love that originate from deep within one's ego-center differ profoundly from the much more subtle and complex feelings of love that stream into one's field of awareness from a divine source.[34] Like the spiritual "colors" in an aura, the spiritual emotions have an extra dimension, an extra depth, richness, and impact that their psychically originated counterparts do not possess.

These descriptions of auras and how they differ from the radiance ascribed to certain exceptionally favored saints and holy men has the merit of exhibiting to a small degree some of the essential multiformity inherent in the illumination experiences that one encounters in mystical literature. They also point to a rule that applies to most of the luminous manifesta-

33. Ibid.
34. Ibid., p. 117.

tions that one encounters in mystical and parapsychological literature—the greater the clarity and intensity of a preternatural light, the closer is its proximity to that which possesses ultimate ontological or soteriological significance. Conversely, the more this preternatural luminosity exhibits dullness or opacity, the more distant it is from the sacred and spiritual.

This rule gains confirmation from many varied sources. For example, in Plutarch's work *On the Instances of Delay in Divine Punishment,* he described a vision that came to Thespesius of Soli while he lay unconscious after having suffered a nearly fatal fall. During this spell of unconsciousness, Thespesius claimed that he had journeyed in his spirit to the other world and seen the souls of the dead and learned about the fate that awaited them. He saw that the souls of the deceased were luminous. Some souls, he recounted to Plutarch, "were like the full moon at her purest, and emitted one smooth, continuous, uniform color; over others there were scales, so to call them, or slender weals; others were quite dappled and strange to look upon, branded with black spots like those of serpents."[35] Thespesius then went on to explain what these colors and blotches meant:

> those motley colors upon the souls . . . come from every source.
> There is the dusky, dirty red, which is the smear made by meanness
> and greed; the fiery blood-red of cruelty and harshness. . . . For
> down on earth vice brings out the colors, while the soul is turned
> about by the passions and turns the body, but here, when these
> have been smoothed away, the final result of purgation and chas-
> tisement is this, that the soul become radiant all over and of one
> hue.[36]

Plutarch's account shows remarkable parallels to the descriptions of aura colorations that the previously cited authors have given us. However, the most important thing about his tale is its assertion that souls become more luminous and clearer in color the more they become spiritually purified. Spiritual degradation is here equated with a darkening and mottling of the soul's luminosity.

An apocryphal book of the Bible, *The First Book of Adam and Eve,* claims that the fall of humanity from Paradise coincided with the loss of its "bright nature," an inner light that Adam and Eve possessed when they

---

35. Plutarch, *Selected Essays of Plutarch,* trans. A. O. Prickard, 2 vols. (New York: Oxford University Press, 1913–18), pp. 207–8.
36. Ibid.

were still in the Garden of Eden. Thus one reads that when God expelled Adam and Eve, Adam wept and said to God,

> "O God, when we dwelt in the garden, and our hearts were lifted up, we saw the angels that sang praises in heaven, but now we do not see as we were used to do; nay, when we entered the cave, all creation became hidden from us." Then God the Lord said unto Adam, "When thou wast under subjection to Me, thou hadst a bright nature within thee, and for that reason couldst thou see things afar off. But after thy transgression thy bright nature was withdrawn from thee; and it was not left to thee to see things afar off, but only near at hand; after the ability of the flesh, for it is brutish."[37]

Once again, the text describes sacred existence, spiritual existence, as a mode of being where one has an interior light. Consequently, the Fall not only involved humanity's expulsion from Paradise but it also deprived him of that inner radiance that spiritual beings possess. The text also associates possession of this spiritual radiance with the supernormal gift of clairvoyant sight for when Adam is expelled and loses this inner light, he also loses the ability to "see things afar off." As I already noted in Chapter 2 when I discussed the experience of Eskimo shamans, one repeatedly encounters this intimate connection between interior illumination and supernormal abilities in mystical literature.

The autobiography of the contemporary Hindu holy man Baba Muktananda contains several incidents that provide further cross-cultural verification of my claim that manifestations of preternatural light always signify that the luminous individual has come into intimate proximity to the sacred or to some "power" that emanates directly from it. Muktananda's spiritual emancipation took place at that moment when his guru transferred some of his spiritual power (shakti) to him. Muktananda depicted this spiritual power that flowed from his guru into himself as a peculiar kind of luminosity that radiated from his guru's eyes. This transmission of luminescent spiritual power occurred in the following way: "He stood facing me directly. He looked into my eyes again. Watching carefully, I saw a ray of light entering me from his pupils. It felt hot like a burning fever. Its light was dazzling. . . . As that ray emanating from Bhagawan Nitya-

---

37. *The Lost Books of the Bible and the Forgotten Books of Eden* (Cleveland: World Publishing Co., 1963), chap. 8: "The First Book of Adam and Eve."

nanda's pupils penetrated mine, I was thrilled with amazement, joy, and fear."[38]

Not only did Muktananda learn by experience that the possession of spiritual power went hand in hand with the possession of an interior light, but he also learned that if the things or persons that embody spiritual perfection exhibit this preternatural radiance, the converse also held true, namely, that states of being that incarnate the ultimate in spiritual degradation exhibit a corresponding diminution of this light. Muktananda related that when he once had the misfortune of finding himself spiritually present in hell, he found that he "could see light but no sun. In that region I lost all my radiance."[39]

*The Tibetan Book of the Dead* also exemplifies this principle that the brilliance and clarity of a preternatural light reflects the soteriological dignity of that person or environment that radiates it. The author(s) of this text taught that when a man dies his disembodied consciousness journeys through various postmortem realms of existence (*bardo* realms) seeking rebirth in a new body. The possibility of the individual's eventual salvation depends on his or her ability to either avoid rebirth altogether or, failing that, to at least choose rebirth in a bardo realm that will be conducive to his or her eventual liberation. How does the dead person make the right choice? As each possible realm of rebirth presents itself and offers the dead person a place of refuge, these presentations take the form of luminous epiphanies and hallucinatory landscapes that differ from each other in the intensity of their brightness and clarity of color. The quality of light that shines forth from each of these manifestations is usually the crucial indicator on which the deceased must base his or her decision as to whether or not he or she should seek refuge there and be reborn in that realm. Thus one reads that on the second day of postmortem existence two kinds of illuminations present themselves to the deceased. At the beginning

> the aggregate of thy principle of consciousness, being in its pure form . . . will shine as a bright, radiant white light . . . with such dazzling brilliancy and transparency that thou wilt hardly be able to look at it. And a dull, smoke-colored light from Hell will shine alongside. . . . Act then so that thou wilt not fear that bright, daz-

38. Baba Muktananda, *Play of Consciousness* (California: Shree Gurudev Siddha Yoga Ashram, 1974), p. 59.
39. Muktananda, *Play of Consciousness,* p. 114.

zling, transparent white light. . . . Be not fond of the dull, smoke-colored light from Hell.[40]

What one saw applied to the human aura here applies to states of post-mortem existence for it is obvious that the clarity (transparency) and intensity of an illumination is assumed to be directly proportional to its potential for bestowing spiritual benefits to the one who chooses it. As was the case with Plutarch's narrative, the duskiness and dullness of a preternatural radiation signified that that person or environment that emitted it was spiritually debased or spiritually debasing in its effects.

This description of the varieties of luminous phenomena that can occur in association with mystical experience does not exhaustively cover the subject. I have only discussed the brilliant photisms. "Cold," low-intensity luminous manifestations also emerge during trance conditions, such as that described in nineteenth-century Spiritualist literature, which contains frequent references to dim lights or glows that emanated from ghosts, "astral" doubles or Doppelgängers, ectoplasms, and other diaphanous spirit entities that entranced mediums supposedly created during such seances. The Lakota *yuwipi* ritual[41] and the Sisala fetish-priest's ceremony of summoning the spirits to activate his ritual paraphernalia also involve the production of sparklike or globular spirit-lights that can only be seen in darkness and that appear to depend on the induction of trance to become manifest.[42] In each case, whether the luminous apparition be bright or dim, its appearance usually depends on the antecedent production of a trance-state. Moreover, their presence almost invariably signifies that some aspect of the sacred, whether it be beneficial or malignant, has erupted into the profane sphere of existence.

As is the case with almost every other characteristic of the mystical experience, the preponderance of evidence indicates that the particular form that these photisms take depends to a large extent upon environmental factors rather than on intrapsychic ones. In short, mystical illuminations

40. *The Tibetan Book of the Dead,* trans. Lama Kazi Dawa Samdup, and ed. W. Y. Evans-Wentz (New York: Oxford University Press, 1960), p. 109.

41. *Yuwipi* is a Lakota ritual in which those who have had sacred visions or sacred dreams from the stone spirits attempt to locate lost objects clairvoyantly. See John Fire Lame Deer and Richard Erdoes, *Lame Deer: Seeker of Visions* (New York: Simon & Schuster, 1972), pp. 196, 267.

42. During the course of my doctoral oral exam, Professor Eugene Mendonsa related that he had once witnessed these spirit-lights descend from the ceiling to the rattles and other ritual paraphernalia of the Sisala fetish-priest while the priest was in the process of consecrating these implements of his trade.

are historically conditioned. For example, Paul's illumination on the road to Damascus bears an unmistakable resemblance to Moses's encounter with Yahweh in the burning bush. In both instances, each man perceived a strange light, heard a divine voice issue from it, and then received a command that he felt compelled to obey. This juxtaposition of illumination and a commanding divine voice was the prototypical mystical experience in the Jewish prophetic tradition to which Paul, a Pharisee, had been very much committed at the time immediately prior to his conversion. Gopi Krishna's particular type of illumination, on the other hand, reflected his exposure to hatha yoga. Nothing in any hatha yoga text describes visions where divine beings speak to yogins and command them to do things. However, they do describe a liquid light that comes to life at the base of the spine and then rushes up it to the top of the head.[43] In other words, hatha yoga texts describe the very same system of subtle physiology that Gopi Krishna activated. Like Paul's vision on the road to Damascus, the content of Gopi Krishna's experience conformed to a previously existing model that his religious tradition had given him. In a similar fashion, no religious text from ancient Israel describes any phenomenon even remotely analogous to kundalini or the system of subtle physiology associated with it. For that reason, it is hardly surprising that prophets and mystics within that tradition never reported anything similar to what Gopi Krishna experienced—they had no religiously sanctioned model for such experiences.

43. For references to kundalini as a brilliant luminosity associated with a condition of blissful ecstasy, see *Sat-Cakra-Nirūpaṇa*, v. 51: "Thereafter, in Her [referring to Kundalini as the consort of Shiva] subtle state, lustrous like lightning and fine like the lotus fibre, She goes to the gleaming flame-like Shiva, the Supreme Bliss and of a sudden produces the Bliss of Liberation." Quoted in Arthur Avalon (pseud. for Sir John Woodroffe), *The Serpent Power, being the Sat-Cakra-Nirūpaṇa and Paduka-Pañcaka* (New York: Dover, 1974), p. 460. References to kundalini as a flamelike, heat-generating luminosity that rushes up the center of the spine can be found in *Haṭhayogapradīpikā*, 3:66–69, 4:18–20, 4:41, in Svātmārāma, *The Haṭhayogapradīpikā of Svātmārāma with the Commentary Jyotsnā of Brahmānanda* (Adyar, India: Adyar Library and Research Center, 1972), and in the *Yogakuṇḍalī Upanishad* in *Thirty Minor Upanishads*, trans. K. Narayanasvami Aiyar (El Reno, Okla.: Santarasa Publications, 1980; reprint of 1914 ed.), p. 263.

# 4

# The Fundamental Contextuality
# of Mystical Experience

The four visionary experiences described in Chapter 1 exhibit a significant degree of heterogeneity that the careful scholar should not overlook. Indeed, the differences among those four visions point to an important characteristic of the mystical state of consciousness, its intrinsic contextuality or historicity, that is to say, its perceptual and existential content exhibits a high degree of sensitivity to the mystic's cultural context and historical situation.

## Characteristic 6: Mystical Experience Is Fundamentally Amorphous and Its Content Is Historically Conditioned

When I say that the mystical experience is amorphous, I am observing that its content (and its effects) differ from one religious tradition to the next.[1] In other words, Eskimo shamans do not have the same types of mystical experiences as Christian mystics. No Eskimo shaman insulated from contact with Christianity would ever have a vision where he would receive the stigmata in the manner of Saint Francis of Assisi; Saint Francis would not have had a vision where an *aua* (elf-spirit) would have become his spirit-helper. In each case, the appearance of those respective phenomena would have been completely alien to the mystic's religious values and expectations. Saint Francis would never have developed a relationship with an elflike shore spirit, even if he had heard of such a thing, because that sort of commerce with a nonangelic being would have been looked on by both him and his contemporaries as a spiritual intercourse with demons, some-

1. Gershom Scholem has discussed the essential amorphousness of mystical experience in *On the Kabbalah and Its Symbolism* (New York: Schocken Books, 1969), pp. 8–9.

thing certain to merit Hell. In the same vein, Aua would never have been imprinted with the stigmata by his helping spirits because the concept of crucifixion was alien to the Eskimo as was the notion that any such act could have redemptive value.

It should now be clear that when one says that mystical experience is amorphous this is simply another way of stating that, in the vast majority of cases, one can never isolate either its content or its effects from the mystic's historical context.[2] Indeed, the content of almost every mystical experience seems to be structured in such a manner as to empirically validate or otherwise legitimize many elements of that description of reality that are either expressly or implicitly present in the mythologies, dogmas, or rituals that form the core of that religious tradition to which the mystic adheres. Not only do mystics empirically confirm the existence of a domain of experience that remains inaccessible to the five senses but also the structure of what they perceive to be ultimate reality is consistent with the descriptions given or implied of it by the revelation(s) or rituals that found their particular religious traditions. For example, if that specific mythology or conglomerate of ritual practices presupposes the existence of animal helping spirits and places a high religious value on cultivating their friendship—as did the religions of the Iglulik and the Lakota—then mystics from those particular religious traditions will tend to have visions and locutions where they see these helping spirits appear in front of them and speak to them.[3] Not only will the mystics from these theriomorphic religious traditions[4] have experiences where these spirit-animals appear to them but these mystical encounters will present these animal spirits of folklore and myth with extraordinary vividness. They will seem as real to these Lakota and Iglulik mystics as any object that our five senses present to us during the waking state. This was certainly true in Aua's case for, after his illumination, he knew by direct experience rather than by hearsay

---

2. As is usual with generalizations about mysticism and mystical experience, there are always exceptions. Some clairvoyant impressions appear to invade consciousness in ways that indicate that the resulting experience is not a product of the mystic's prior expectations or cultural upbringing. See Garrett, *Adventures in the Supernormal*, pp. 210–13.

3. In addition to the Iglulik examples cited in Chapters 1 and 2, see DeMallie, *Sixth Grandfather*, pp. 114–42, where Black Elk's Great Vision contains a great number of spirits in animal form.

4. The term "theriomorphic" means having the form of an animal. As one would expect, the religious traditions of hunting peoples and hunter-gatherer peoples abound in myths and narratives of mystical experiences where spirits and superhuman beings have the form of animals.

that the spirit beings referred to in Iglulik mythology and folklore really did exist. After his illumination, Aua no longer merely believed that spirits existed—he knew that they did. Mystical experiences thus exhibit the remarkable ability to endow the most diverse types of mythological objects and beings with a compelling sense of concreteness and personality. Even the most unusual or bizarre elements in the mythological complex, for instance, the aua of Iglulik folklore, can become vividly present to a mystic raised in that tradition. This capacity of the mystical experience to exhibit an almost infinite plasticity in reifying and rendering concretely present the beings, objects, and spiritual locales posited by the mythology of any given religious tradition constitutes one of its most significant features.[5]

Gopi Krishna's awakening of kundalini serves as an excellent illustration of how a mystic's experience can empirically verify the mythology or doctrine of his religious community. Gopi Krishna admitted that a long time before his initial illumination, he had read that there was a "certain vital mechanism called *kundalini,* connected with the lower end of the spine which becomes active by means of certain exercises, and when once roused carries the limited human consciousness to transcendental heights."[6] It is evident from this statement that the content of Gopi Krishna's experience did not arise out of a vacuum for he had already been exposed to the idea that there was a peculiar vital energy localized in the spine that was associated with the production of a transcendental state of consciousness. His own experience empirically proved, at least to his own satisfaction, that this kundalini energy did indeed exist in much the same form as this unnamed text had described it. One will recall that at the beginning of his experience of arousing kundalini, he felt a strange sensation at the base of his spine. Shortly thereafter, he heard a roaring noise and then perceived a stream of "liquid light" enter his brain "through the spinal cord." A few days after this initial awakening of kundalini, Gopi Krishna had another experience of this illumination coursing up his spine into the top of his head only this time it was also accompanied by sensations of heat, as though "a scorching blast of hot air had passed through my body."[7] This description corresponds quite closely to that given of kundalini in the classic hatha yoga treatise, the *Haṭhayogapradīpikā.*

5. This amorphousness or plasticity of the mystical experience, and by extension, its extreme sensitivity to historical context, may have its roots in the peculiar empowerment of the imagination and will that takes place when the mind has become recollected.

6. Gopi Krishna, *Kundalini,* p. 14.

7. Ibid., p. 16.

When the Apāna [one of the five vital "breaths"] rises upwards and reaches the sphere of fire, then the flame of the fire becomes lengthened, being fanned by Apāna.

When the Apāna and the fire join Prāṇa [that one of the five "breaths" that one breathes in through the lungs], which is by nature hot, then the heat in the body is greatly intensified.

By reason of that, the Kundalini which is asleep, feeling the extreme heat, is awakened, just as a serpent, struck by a stick hisses and straightens itself.

Then it enters the Suṣumnā [the hollow of the spine], like (a snake) which enters its hole.[8]

It is clear that this passage, despite its highly symbolic language, is implying that the arousal of kundalini up through the center of the spine generates heat. Other passages in that same text also associate the arousal of kundalini with a state of mental steadiness (*manonmani*) and a sensation of bliss. For example, the author of that text declared that "when the Prāṇa flows through the Suṣumnā, the Manonmani state is attained."[9] In addition, he also stated that when the yogin who has aroused kundalini and thereby entered the state where the mind stops fluctuating (manonmani), "an indefinable bliss ensues."[10] The parallels between these allusions to the liberating experience of arousing kundalini and the content of Gopi Krishna's mystical experience are unmistakable. The light going up the spine, the sensation of heat, the mental concentration, and the experience of ecstatic bliss are all alluded to in the text and present in Gopi Krishna's own experience. None of the experiences of mystical illumination that one encounters outside of India and Tibet link together a light coursing up through the hollow of the spine and the generation of heat in the way that Gopi Krishna's did. Eskimo shamans, Augustine, Paul, Moses, and William Bucke never referred to this strange sensation of heat associated with the rushing of light up the center of the spine. For this reason, one must conclude that Gopi Krishna's prior exposure to hatha yoga determined the peculiarities of his illumination experience. His mystical experience was therefore anything but spontaneous—it was historically and culturally conditioned.

8. Svatmarama, *Haṭhayogapradīpikā*, 3.66–69, pp. 49–50.
9. Ibid., 4.20, p. 65.
10. Ibid., 4.30, p. 67.

The amazing sensitivity of the mystical experience to the subject's religious and philosophical assumptions also comes across in another incident in his life. A few days after he had first aroused kundalini, Gopi Krishna began to fall into a terrifying mental state that made him think that he was going insane. This distressing condition continued for a long time. Searching through the yoga treatises for some clue to his mental condition, he found nothing for they all implied that success in arousing the serpent fire (kundalini) could only lead to a condition of bliss rather than one of acute anxiety. One day, as he talked to his brother-in-law about his condition, his brother-in-law told him that his own guru had remarked that if kundalini were awakened through any other subtle nerve (*nāḍī*) than the one going up through the center of the spinal cord, madness could result. Furthermore, if the liquid light coursed through the *pingalā* nerve (that subtle nerve associated with the sun in hatha yoga texts) that lay to the right of the spinal cord, there was a grave danger of the yogi burning to death from the psychic heat that it generated.[11] This suggestion subsequently played a significant role in Gopi Krishna's experience. One will recall that a few days after he had awakened kundalini his body felt a scorching sensation. Shortly after his talk with his brother-in-law, he ate a small piece of food at a festival and then experienced this scorching sensation with much greater intensity than he had ever experienced it before. He suddenly felt a sinking sensation in his stomach and then a "fiery" stream of energy entered his head. He felt as though he were literally burning alive. At that point when it seemed that he would either die or go completely mad, he recalled his brother-in-law's remarks. It then occurred to him that maybe he had awakened kundalini through the wrong subtle nerve. Instead of directing it through the spinal cord, he was making it go through the pingalā nerve. It also occurred to him that he might try to activate the energy that flows through the *Iḍā* (the subtle nerve associated with the moon in hatha yoga) nerve on the left side of the spine. According to hatha yoga, this vital energy of the Iḍā possesses the opposite qualities of the vital energy that courses through the pingalā, for it has a cooling effect whereas the latter generates heat. By an effort of intense mental concentration, Gopi Krishna tried to make the cooling energy of the Iḍā nerve move up through the center of his spine so that it would neutralize the heat of pingalā. The results seemed to empirically confirm what the

11. Gopi Krishna, *Kundalini*, p. 61.

exponents of hatha yoga had said about the nature of the vital energies that course through the body's subtle nerves.[12]

> I distinctly felt the location of the nerve and strained hard mentally to divert its flow into the central channel. Then . . . a miracle happened. There was a sound like a nerve thread snapping and instantaneously a silvery streak passed zigzag through the spinal cord, . . . pouring an effulgent, cascading shower of brilliant vital energy into my brain, filling my head with a blissful lustre in place of the flame that had been tormenting me.[13]

It is highly significant that from this moment on Gopi Krishna never suffered either the tormenting anxiety or the sensation of unbearable heat.

One could hardly ask for a better demonstration of how context determines the content of mystical experience. It is clear that Gopi Krishna's acceptance of hatha yoga as an authoritative system of subtle physiology and religious praxis dominated the content of both his mystical and his schizophrenic episodes. It taught him that proper meditation could cause a luminous vital energy to go up through the center of the spine and bring about a blissful state of consciousness. This was exactly what he experienced during his first illumination. However, this system of yoga also provided him with another possible experiential scenario, his later experience of madness and internal heat. This is a form of madness that one never encounters in Western European psychiatric literature, where mystics, neurotics, and schizophrenics have never been exposed to the hatha yoga system of subtle physiology.[14] The system of hatha yoga provided Gopi Krishna with a model that he could follow to cure the particular form of schizophrenia that it had apparently enabled him to develop. In other words, this example demonstrates that not only does the mystical experience empirically verify the existence and reality of elements within a particular tradition of religious mythology and doctrine but it also suggests that the stability and revelatory value of a mystical state of consciousness

12. I speak of the physiological entities postulated by hatha yoga as subtle because one cannot perceive them by means of any visual or microscopic inspection. One can only discern them if two conditions are satisfied: one must take it for granted that this system of subtle physiology really exists in the manner described and also be in a trance-state.

13. Gopi Krishna, *Kundalini*, p. 66.

14. I am not saying that mysticism is a form of neurosis or schizophrenia. Many mystics are neither neurotic nor schizophrenic. I am simply observing that the specific content of schizophrenic experiences and mystical experiences is determined to a great degree by contextual factors such as the individual's religious and philosophical assumptions and practices.

depends, to an important extent, on the mystic's capacity to locate his own experiences within a framework of interpretation that has become accepted by a significant group within that cultural or religious community.

Within a religious tradition as heterogeneous as Hinduism, one should not be surprised to discover that there exists a corresponding diversity of mystical experiences. Indeed, even among the narrow confines of the relatively small group of Hindus who claim to have successfully awakened kundalini, one observes considerable differences in the content of their experiences of illumination. These experiential variations appear to reflect the different degrees of each yogin's exposure to the full range of the traditional teaching concerning kundalini yoga and the different degrees of their allegiance to those teachings. For example, although Gopi Krishna and Baba Muktananda both claimed that they had awakened kundalini, the content of their respective experiences differed significantly. Muktananda's autobiography makes it clear that his education imbued him with a profound acquaintance with and reverence for the traditional Hindu scriptures and deities. Gopi Krishna, on the other hand, was an agnostic at the time that he had his first mystical experiences, although he did practice a nontheistic form of yoga.[15] Muktananda seems to have accepted far more literally than Gopi Krishna the descriptions of kundalini and the subtle physiology associated with it that one finds in the traditional treatises on hatha yoga. For example, at one point Muktananda referred to a devout couple who had "completely purified the centers of all the mantras and deities situated in the six *chakras*."[16] This statement about the six *chakras* (or subtle vortices of energy that, according to hatha yoga, supposedly line the spine) and the presence of mantric syllables and deities within them indicates that Muktananda's understanding of hatha yoga came from Tantric sources such as the *Sat-Chakra-Nirūpaṇa*.[17] Because Muktananda accepted the theistic Tantric formulations of hatha yoga, his mystical experiences exhibit a theistic content missing in the experiences of the more rationalistic and agnostic Gopi Krishna. Thus, at one point Muktananda began to experience divine beings and heavenly realms as though they really existed. "After my visits to heaven, hell, and Nagaloka, I developed full faith in the truth of the scriptures. So far I had considered self-realization alone valid and rejected heaven, hell, and the world of gods and all

15. See Gopi Krishna, *Kundalini*, pp. 32–38.
16. Muktananda, *Play of Consciousness*, p. 12.
17. A text translated in Avalon, *Serpent Power*, pp. 317–479.

that as unreal. But now I was fully convinced that the scriptures were absolutely true; only our understanding of them is deficient."[18]

When one compares this passage with the mystical experiences of Gopi Krishna, one notes that Gopi Krishna's are utterly devoid of theism and references to the heavens and hells of traditional Hindu mythology. Gopi Krishna awakened kundalini without ever once intimating that any of these experiences had projected him into either Heaven or Hell. He never interpreted even his most terrifying experiences as though he had somehow been given a foretaste of hellish existence. This absence of theism is not at all surprising for, unlike Muktananda, Gopi Krishna had received a Western scientific education that had caused him to become skeptical about traditional theistic Hinduism.[19] Agnostic and rationalist that he was, he never abandoned Yoga or the spiritual yearnings of his youth. Nonetheless, his spirituality, when set against the luxuriant theism of Muktananda's, seems almost skeletal in its theological simplicity. Gopi Krishna thought that the only theologically important element in Hinduism was yoga, with its emphasis on the process of self-realization, because this aspect of Hindu spirituality, provided that one abstracts it from its theistic matrix, contains nothing that is offensive to the canons of scientific rationalism.[20] Consequently, Gopi Krishna was quite willing to jettison the entire theistic, ritual, and mythical accompaniments of traditional Hinduism as mere figments of human imagination that had no solid basis in empirical fact. Gopi Krishna was himself aware of how his rationalism had shaped the content of his experiences and caused them to diverge from the more traditional descriptions given in Tantric literature. He drew attention to the fact that his own experiences made no mention of the numerous chakras and deities that are referred to in Tantric treatises on hatha yoga. He attributed their absence to his skepticism about their existence.

> I never practiced yoga by Tantric methods. . . . If I had done so with a firm belief in the existence of the lotuses [the chakras], I might well have mistaken the luminous formations and glowing discs of light at the various nerve junctions along the spinal cord for lotuses, and in the excited state of my imagination might even have been led to perceive the letters and presiding deities in vivid form.[21]

18. Muktananda, *Play of Consciousness*, pp. 128–29.
19. Gopi Krishna, *Kundalini*, pp. 32–38.
20. Ibid., pp. 34–36.
21. Ibid., pp. 174–75.

For Gopi Krishna, belief in the existence of deities that live within the energy vortices or chakras that line the spinal cord was no more than the result of an overheated imagination that had been exposed to Tantric teachings.

The scientific rationalism and empiricism that Gopi Krishna acquired from his college and secondary school education influenced not only the content of his experiences in the manner shown above but it also influenced the way that he interpreted them. Whereas the Hindu traditionalist Muktananda interpreted his visions and illuminations as concrete proof that the heavens, hells, and deities of Hindu mythology really did exist as they were depicted in the Tantras, epics, and Purāṇas, Gopi Krishna interpreted his experiences like a scientist by focusing, instead, on the way that his illuminations had opened up a whole new domain of phenomena to scientific investigation. Thus he noted that his experience of awakening kundalini had demonstrated the existence of "an extremely subtle and intricate mechanism located in the sexual region" of the human body which scientists had hitherto ignored. He went on to observe that this subtle physiological mechanism, when properly activated, brings about a dramatic metamorphosis of the brain so that "a superior type of consciousness" becomes manifest. Some day, he declared, this superior state of consciousness will become the possession of all of humankind not just the possession of a spiritual elite.[22] Gopi Krishna could accept the subtle physiology described by hatha yoga texts but only under certain conditions that did not conflict too deeply with his scientific education. In a fashion typical of a scientific empiricist, he claimed that his mystical illumination had empirically demonstrated a new biological fact. Since it had always accepted experience as the ultimate arbiter of truth, science now had to concede that the subtle physiology postulated by hatha yoga really did exist. However, it was under no obligation to accept those aspects of yoga that suggested magical hocus-pocus alien to the fundamental premises of the scientific worldview, notions such as deities residing in the subtle energy vortices that line the spinal canal. Gopi Krishna's hatha yoga was a bowdlerized version of the traditional system culled of all mythological debris so that it could be made compatible with scientific rationalism and empiricism. In this way he effected a synthesis of Hinduism and science.[23]

22. Ibid., pp. 175–76.
23. Gopi Krishna's synthesis of science and religion bears comparison with the attempt of some nineteenth- and twentieth-century Western European mystics and mediums to reconcile scientific materialism and Christianity. Nineteenth-century Spiritualism attempted to show,

The structure of Saint Paul's vision displayed a similar dependence on his ancestral religious tradition. As a Pharisaic Jew, Paul's education taught him to revere the prophets and redemptive events of the Old Testament, a fact that his attempts to harmonize the Old Testament with Christ's novel message abundantly proved. For this reason, it is hardly surprising that his vision followed a paradigm that the Old Testament had already established, one best exemplified in the prophetic visions of Moses and Ezekiel. If one juxtaposes Paul's illumination experience with that of Gopi Krishna, the resulting contrast shows how those Old Testament models provided him with the blueprint for his vision on the road to Damascus.

First, Paul's vision followed the prophetic pattern of Moses and Ezekiel insofar as all three mystical experiences appear to have arisen spontaneously rather than as the product of any meditative effort. Paul never questioned the idea implicit throughout the Old Testament that God sends visions and the gift of prophecy to those whom He chooses for reasons that usually remain unfathomable to men. In contrast, the kundalini yoga that Gopi Krishna practiced attributes little or no soteriological role to divine grace. Instead, it proclaims that liberation can only come about as the result of heroic meditative effort directed toward awakening the goddess Kundalini from her slumbers at the base of the spine. Given such assumptions, it stands to reason that records of spontaneous awakenings of kundalini energy unaided by prior meditative endeavors appear very rarely, if at all, in the literature of hatha and kundalini yoga. It would appear, then, that the spontaneity of Paul's vision on the road to Damascus was no accident. Its unexpected and unpremeditated onset was part of a traditional pattern of prophetic mystical experiences.

Second, in marked contrast to both Gopi Krishna and Aua, the visions of Paul, Moses, and Ezekiel always linked the onset of the visionary apparition and its accompanying illumination to the presence of a divine voice that each prophet felt obliged to obey. This persistent juxtaposition of illumination and locution is exactly what one would expect to find, and what one actually does find, in both Old and New Testament mystical

---

among other things, that materialistic science did not have to be incompatible with the existence of an immortal soul. Spiritualist mediums, by focusing on the production of physical phenomena such as telekinesis and poltergeist manifestations, thought that they had found empirical proof for the materiality of soul-substance. Since this purported soul-substance was another form of matter, the soul could be subjected to scientific study and in this way religion could be saved from positivists' claims that it was an irrational and unreal delusion.

experience given the great religious prestige that both religions accord to the prophetic calling. Each of those two religious traditions starts from the common assumption that humanity's fall resulted from a primordial act of disobedience to God's will. Consequently, salvation becomes inseparable from human endeavors to learn to obey His will perfectly. Given the soteriological importance of obedience to the will of a divine being, it stands to reason that the divine voice, that vehicle by which God makes His will known to human beings, acquires a religious significance that it cannot be expected to possess in kundalini yoga for, in kundalini yoga, obedience to God's will contributes little or nothing to human salvation. Instead, what saves humanity from endless rebirth is the cultivation of mental discipline coupled with knowledge of how attachment and aversion forge chains of karmic bondage. For this reason, it is not surprising that Gopi Krishna's arousal of kundalini was unaccompanied by any admonishing voice.

The obvious elements of continuity in Paul's visionary and auditory mystical experiences with earlier Old Testament models must not lead one into the serious error of thinking that mystics never innovate. Quite the contrary, however deeply the mystics' enculturated religious assumptions condition the content of their visions and locutions (as well as the nature of their responses to them), it also happens that their experiences frequently cause them to see new meanings or dimensions of significance in the mythological heritage or religious practices of their communities. It is also possible for their experiences to display a marked sensitivity to recent changes in the existential preoccupations of the age within which they live or recent contacts with some new group or subculture. Paul's vision on the road to Damascus definitely fell into the latter category. Even though his contacts with Christianity prior to the onset of this vision had apparently been those of a hostile observer and persecutor,[24] these antagonistic contacts apparently still made a deep subconscious impression on him because his vision came from the same crucified God whom that despised sect revered. Paul's acceptance of the novel idea that Christ was the Messiah promised in the Old Testament was the central feature of his vision, something so completely at variance with his Pharisaic upbringing that it forced him to develop a new religious hermeneutic to reconcile this revelation with the Old Testament promises to Israel.

The content of mystics' experiences exhibits a great deal of responsive-

24. According to Acts 7:58 and Acts 8:1, Paul had given his consent to those actions that had caused the martyrdom of Stephen and he may actually have been physically present at both Stephen's defense of himself before the Sanhedrin and his subsequent execution.

ness to changes in the existential preoccupations of a culture or group. For example, the Latin Christianity of the fifth and sixth centuries did not show much theological, iconographic, or popular concern for the vulnerability of Christ in His Sacred Humanity. Indeed, when one looks at the accounts of mystical experiences that date from this period, for instance, those that Augustine or Gregory the Great allude to or describe in their works, one notices that visions of Jesus are conspicuously absent. What one finds instead are visions of an ineffable light devoid of all corporeal form.[25] Moreover, this strange effulgence somehow conveys to the mystic absolute certainty that it utterly transcends the taint of materiality (that is, it is something purely spiritual) and that it is immutable. These characteristics of the ineffable light are similar to the characteristics of the most perfect divinity described in Platonic and Neoplatonic literature. It is clear from this that the central theological and existential preoccupations of Neoplatonism, a concern for God's incorporeality, His freedom from any sort of form, and His changelessness had insinuated themselves into the core of these two Christian mystics' experiences. Here one encounters in a Christianized form the notions of Xenophanes and Plotinus that state that the oneness of God necessarily implies His transcendence of any corporeal form and one also encounters the persistent Orphic theme that the body is a tomb, that the things of the flesh prevent human beings from seeing spiritual things as they truly are. Augustine's and Gregory the Great's mystical experiences suggest that the more highly educated Christians of their day were still deeply preoccupied with the problems and categories that they had inherited from the late Greco-Roman philosophers.

Visions of Christ, more specifically, those that accentuated His sufferings and the vulnerability of His Sacred Humanity, did not become a prominent element in Christian mystics' experiences until sometime around the beginning of the twelfth and thirteenth centuries when the rise of the mendicant orders and the various groups associated with devotion to the Passion of Jesus began to express a deep shift in the Christological focus of the Latin Church. Whereas the Carolingian period stressed the Lordship of Jesus at the expense of His Sacred Humanity, these new expressions of monastic and lay piety began to lay greater emphasis on Christ's likeness to the ordinary human. This new emphasis on His Sacred

25. For examples of such visions, see Augustine, *Confessions*, book 7, chap. 10; book 7, chap. 23; and book 9, chaps. 23–25. For references to Gregory the Great's allusions to mystical experience, see Dom Cuthbert Butler, *Western Mysticism* (New York: Harper & Row, 1966), pp. 72–74, 76–78.

Humanity portrayed Jesus not as the distant and stern world ruler or *pantocrator* of Carolingian iconography but rather as a pitiable, vulnerable human being who had to endure horrible suffering because of His love for the ordinary human. It is not surprising that mystics' visionary experiences began to reflect this Christological shift. Henceforth, there is a pronounced tendency for Christ to appear in mystics' visions and He does so either as the mystic's loving companion desirous of human friendship and loyalty or else He is shown suffering for human sinfulness.

One can see this transformation in the content of mystics' experiences if one juxtaposes a vision of the sixteenth-century Franciscan Tertiary Catherine of Genoa, with one of Gregory the Great's descriptions of contemplation. Catherine's contemporary biographer described the following vision that came to her shortly after she had decided to become associated with the Franciscan Tertiaries. "Our Lord, desiring to enkindle still more profoundly His love in this soul, appeared to her in spirit with His Cross upon His shoulder dripping with blood, so that the whole house seemed to be all full of rivulets of that Blood which she saw to have been all shed because of love alone."[26] This vision is completely focused on the person and image of the human Christ, His love for humanity, and the hideous suffering He had to endure because of that love. As such it is worlds apart from that far more "intellectual" and "abstract" spirituality that typified the mystical experience of fifth- and sixth-century Christians. When Gregory alludes to the mystic's experience of God in contemplation, there is no reference at all to the humanity of Jesus, His desire for human companionship, or to His suffering for our sake. "When we raise the gaze of our mind to the ray of the supernal Light, we are clouded over by the obscurity of our weakness. While man is yet weighed down by the corruptible flesh, he is by no means able to see the eternal Light as it is."[27] Majestic as this Light is when one experiences it, there is nothing human about it that elicits our feelings of sympathy or friendship. As such it presupposes a notion of divinity that places God in a situation that is far more removed from the sphere of everyday human life than that notion of divinity that predominated during the later Middle Ages.

The extraordinary prominence of telekinetic phenomena[28] in the super-

26. Quoted in Friedrich von Hügel, *The Mystical Element of Religion as Studied in Saint Catherine of Genoa and Her Friends,* 2 vols. (London: J. M. Dent & Sons, 1961), 1:108.

27. Quoted in Butler, *Western Mysticism,* p. 88.

28. "Telekinesis" means that type of movement or alteration of physical objects that comes about in a nonmechanical manner solely by means of either the activity of the human

normal experiences of those Christian and non-Christian mystics and mediums who associated themselves with the nineteenth-century Spiritualist
movement serves as one more illustration of how changes in the content of
mystics' experiences develop in tandem with shifts in the existential preoccupations of their respective cultures. Prior to the nineteenth century, very
few Christian mystics ever went into trance states that produced what people later called the "physical phenomena" of mysticism—spirit rappings,
poltergeist manifestations, the materialization of physical objects, or the
extrusion of quasi-material ectoplasm. The reason for their absence in the
literature of earlier Christian mysticism is obvious, the people of those
earlier periods took it for granted that those particular "physical phenomena" could only originate from a demonic source.[29] Given this assumption,
no sane Christian mystic would ever deliberately cultivate such manifestations for, if he did so, he would risk the accusation of witchcraft. The only
exceptions to this general abhorrence of physical manifestations in Christian mystical experience were stigmatization and levitation. The former
was acceptable because late medieval Christianity so deeply revered the
ideal of imitating Christ's exemplary life and sufferings. Stigmatization
seemed to offer compelling proof that Christ had set His seal on a mystic's
holiness. For example, when Christ spoke to Saint Francis in a vision just
before He imprinted him with his stigmata, He told him that the stigmata
were a reward for his faithfulness in trying to imitate Him and that they
were to serve as a tangible sign that Christ regarded him as one of his own.[30]
The Church's toleration of levitation also probably stemmed from its
repeated appearance in Scripture. After all, Christ and the Virgin Mary
had ascended visibly into Heaven and the Bible also taught that the souls
and resurrected bodies of the righteous would levitate to Heaven at the
Last Judgment. Even though levitation was a "physical" phenomenon of
mysticism, its persistent association in Scripture with saintliness and holiness would have militated against it being lumped together with such de-

---

mind and will or else by means of the activity of some supposedly discarnate "spiritual"
entity that exists in complete independence of the human psyche.

29. Herbert Thurston's collection of poltergeist accounts contains numerous instances of
such phenomena that occurred prior to the nineteenth century. In almost every one of those
earlier accounts, the narrator contemporary with the event assumed that the Devil or one of
his minions had produced it. See Herbert Thurston, S.J., *Ghosts and Poltergeists* (Chicago:
Henry Regnery Company, 1953), pp. 69–90, and chap. 7: "Poltergeists in Earlier Centuries,"
pp. 329–37.

30. *The Little Flowers of St. Francis,* trans. Raphael Brown (Garden City, N.Y.: Image
Books, 1958), pp. 191–93.

monic manifestations as poltergeists and spirit rappings, especially when these levitations took place, as they often did, during Communion or prayer.

A comparison of the autobiographies of two devout Christian mystics, the nineteenth-century American medium D. D. Home (1833–86) and Saint Teresa of Avila (1515–82), immediately reveals a striking difference in both their ultimate religious goals and the content of their respective mystical experiences. Like most of her late medieval predecessors, Saint Teresa stressed that human beings can only fulfill their highest spiritual vocation when they try to imitate perfectly the exemplary life of Christ, a life of perfect charity, of perfect obedience to God's will, and a perfected willingness and courage to suffer anything for His sake.[31] This longing to live a life in imitation of Christ shaped the content of many of Saint Teresa's visions and locutions. Most of them fell into one of three general categories. A significant group of them took the form of admonitions from Christ that advised her to take courage and show a more perfect willingness to abandon everything worldly for His sake.[32] Another took form as radiant, overwhelmingly beautiful apparitions of Jesus.[33] Still another took the form of tender conversations between her and Christ with exchanges of mutual love and fidelity just as though the two were lovers.[34] In short, Teresa's visions and locutions exhibited a markedly Christocentric focus, a characteristic that arose because the imitation of His life and exemplary deeds had become the central existential preoccupation of the Catholic monks and nuns of Teresa's time.

Home's mystical experiences did not have this Christocentric focus, even though he considered himself a devout Christian. A perusal of his autobiography and the numerous mystical experiences that he described therein shows that apparitions of Jesus or locutions from Him played very little role in his communications with the spiritual world. Instead, what one finds there is a record of seances where spirits, working via the entranced Home,[35] exhibited their power over matter by lifting heavy objects without the assistance of any mechanical agency and gave empirical proof of the

31. Teresa of Avila, *The Complete Works of St. Teresa of Jesus,* 3 vols., trans. E. Allison Peers (London: Sheed & Ward, 1978), 3:24–25 (*Book of Foundations*) and p. 227 (*Interior Castle*).
32. For an example of this, see Teresa of Avila, *Life of St. Teresa,* trans. Peers, pp. 228–32.
33. Ibid., pp. 258–68.
34. Teresa of Avila, "Spiritual Testimonies," pp. 337–38.
35. See Home, *Incidents in My Life,* pp. 49–50.

existence of an afterlife realm to those participating in the seance by revealing private information concerning one of the participants or his relatives about which only the individuals involved could have known.[36] In other words, Home's mystical experiences had become a series of laboratory experiments that produced externally visible alterations of matter that materialistic skeptics could observe in order to verify empirically that such things as "spirit" and the "spiritual world" really did appear to exist as entities open to scientific investigation. Thanks to these experiments it became possible to verify scientifically, or so it seemed, that the central tenets of Christianity were true—that the soul was immortal, that spirit existed, that it could prevail over brute matter, and that, for that reason, the miracles referred to in the Bible really had occurred.[37]

It is clear that this de-emphasis on the person and words of Jesus Christ had a great deal to do with the enhanced prestige that science enjoyed in the eyes of most mid-nineteenth-century men and women, Christians and skeptics alike. Home, like many of his American contemporaries, was haunted by the fear that the triumph of Newtonian science would completely destroy religion by reducing all phenomena to matter in motion. The materialistic ideology spawned in the wake of Newtonian physics seemed to threaten with extinction or irrelevance everything that pertained to religion and the spiritual order, especially miracles and the notion that there were such things as spirit, spiritual beings, and spiritual worlds. More specifically, many thoughtful European and American men and women of the nineteenth century assumed that one's faith in the Bible stood or fell on the question of whether or not biblical miracles and communications from spirits and angels had some sort of explanation congruent with the principles of Newtonian physics.

Home and his Spiritualist contemporaries saw no reason why the biblical miracles should have been exclusively restricted to ages past. After all, such a restriction contradicted one of the cornerstones of science, Galileo's notion that the laws of nature operate identically in every place and in every period of time—there are no special laws of "planetary" motion as

36. Ibid., pp. 52–53, gives a typical example.

37. In this regard it is worth noting a statement that one of Home's anonymous friends made in the preface to the first edition of *Incidents in My Life* (1863). Home's friend applauded Spiritualism and the physical phenomena that Home and other Spiritualist mediums produced because they had been "redeeming multitudes from hardened atheism and materialism, proving to them, *by the positive demonstration which their cast of mind requires,* that there is another world—that there is a nonmaterial form of humanity—and that many miraculous things which they have hitherto scoffed at, are true" (emphasis mine). Ibid., p. xvii.

Kepler had thought but only general laws of motion that apply to all moving bodies whatsoever.[38] It is no exaggeration to say that this problem of establishing the compatibility of materialistic science with biblical miracle became one of the most pressing existential concerns that preoccupied thoughtful religious individuals of the nineteenth century. It is hardly surprising that Christians who shared this new existential concern became less and less preoccupied with the extent to which their deeds and intentions conformed to the will of God. Instead, they began to focus more and more of their efforts on the task of trying to prove that the miracles and promises of eternal life in the Bible were scientifically tenable, that is to say, congruent with the materialistic and mechanistic presuppositions of Newtonian science.

Home gives one abundant evidence that this new focus of existential concerns motivated his life's work. Whereas Saint Teresa saw her spiritual vocation as a quest that centered around the endeavor to bring her own will into perfect conformity with God's will, Home regarded his vocation as a mission to, as he put it, "convince the infidel, cure the sick, and console the weeping."[39] This set of goals sounds mundane enough until one realizes that, for Home, convincing the infidel, curing the sick, and consoling the weeping did not mean engaging in a merely verbal defense of religion, giving the sick the right medicines, or merely reassuring the grief-stricken. Instead, Home saw his spiritual calling as that of a miracle worker in an age of materialistic science. Home would convince the skeptic by manifesting telekinetic phenomena through his mediumistic powers. These demonstrations of mind over matter would give the skeptic that "positive," concrete, experimental proof that the miracles of the Bible have a scientific foundation. He would console the weeping by proving experimentally that spirits who had died really could come back from the grave

---

38. In the conclusion to his autobiography, *Incidents in My Life,* Home quoted W. Beecher approvingly when Beecher declared, in a truly Galilean manner, that

> the physiology, the anthropology of the bible . . . will be found to harmonize with the general principles of human experience in such matters in all ages. If a theory be adopted everywhere else but in the bible, excluding spiritual intervention *in toto,* and accounting for everything physically, then will the covers of the bible prove but pasteboard barriers. Such a theory will sweep through the bible and its authority, and its inspiration will be annihilated. On the other hand, if the theory of spiritual inspiration be accepted in the bible, it cannot be shut up there, but must sweep its way through the wide domain of 'popular superstitions,' as they are called, separating the element of truth on which these superstitions are based. (p. 233)

39. Ibid., p. 8.

and tell people things that they would have no other way of knowing if it were not true that they still continued to exist after the decay of their bodies. And finally, he would cure the sick, not principally by medicines, but by thaumaturgy—further proof that spirit could work miracles even in his day and age. Given these assumptions about his vocation and the pressing religious need to prove that miracles had some scientific basis, it is easy to see why the content of Home's mystical experiences differed so greatly from those of earlier Christian mystics.

The extraordinary display of telekinetic phenomena that supposedly became manifest on many occasions during the course of Home's life as a medium testifies to the remarkable plasticity of the mystical experience. It shows that the mystical state of consciousness exhibits an almost limitless capacity to create a private and, in some cases, even a public domain of experience which becomes perceptually congruent with virtually any system of mythology or set of fundamental assumptions about the nature of reality and humanity's place within it—provided that the mystic embraces that mythic structure with sufficient conviction. The particular visual, auditory, tactile, and affective content of a mystical experience is historically conditioned.

My emphasis on the historically conditioned nature of mystical experience has one very important corollary: It requires that there be a reciprocal rather than a one-way relationship between interpretation and experience. In other words, it implies that interpretation is not merely something that the mystic just "adds on" to his ot her experience after it has already occurred and he or she is beginning to reflect upon it.[40] Instead, the mythological and philosophical structures that form the basis of the mystic's retrospective interpretations are already actively shaping the content of the experience as it is in the process of taking place.[41] For example, it is absurd to content oneself with saying that Gopi Krishna merely interpreted his experience of mystical illumination as the kundalini energy rushing up his spine and that, aside from this interpretation he placed upon it, his experience was otherwise pretty much identical to the illuminations of Saint Paul, Aua, and Saint Augustine. Gopi Krishna did far more than just "in-

40. Robert Gimello has written one of the most penetrating analyses of this reciprocal interrelationship between interpretation and experience in "Mysticism and Meditation," in Katz, *Mysticism and Philosophical Analysis*, p. 176.

41. See Chapter 15, where I point to one of the psychological roots of this reciprocity between experience and interpretation when I discuss the phenomenon of imaginational and emotional "empowerment."

terpret" this energy as the kundalini energy referred to in the treatises of hatha yoga. He actually experienced it in much the same manner that the hatha yoga treatises said that it should be experienced. It is a very serious error to say that Gopi Krishna had an illumination experience that, aside from the way he interpreted it, was in all other respects essentially identical to the illumination experiences of Aua, Augustine, and Paul. Gopi Krishna's sensation of "liquid light" roaring up his spine and flowing over the top of his head had no parallel in the illumination experiences of these other three mystics. The system of hatha yoga by which Gopi Krishna had interpreted this experience gave him far more than just that framework by which he interpreted it. It is also clear that it actually played a crucial role in creating the experience itself for not only had Gopi Krishna admitted that he had been exposed to the teachings of hatha yoga prior to its onset but the characteristics and behavior of the light he actually experienced also conformed very closely to the kundalini energy described in those texts. From these two facts it would appear that those texts played a decisive role in structuring the actual content of his experience. This inference receives further reinforcement when one recognizes that no mystic ignorant of this kundalini energy as it is depicted in the hatha yoga texts has ever had an experience of illumination that conforms so closely to the one that those treatises describe.

# 5

# Recollection and Mystical Experience

The analyses of the distinctive characterstics of mystical experiences in Chapters 2 through 4 focused on matters relating to the *content* of those experiences. I will now direct the reader's attention to the *process* that most commonly triggers these unusual states of consciousness.

## Characteristic 7: Mystical Experiences Have Their Genesis in the Recollective Act

### What Is Recollection?

The practice that Christian contemplatives refer to as "recollection" forms an essential aspect of the mystical life within Christianity and other religious traditions. Indeed, any study of mysticism that ignores the fundamental connection between recollection and mysticism renders itself seriously inadequate. A study of the interconnection between the two phenomena is crucial to any scholarly analysis for three reasons. First, recollection serves as an almost universal technique for inducing mystical experiences. Second, it not only functions as a technique that brings about the mystic's initial encounter with the spiritual world but it can also function as one of the chief means of deepening the intensity of that contact. Third, when one comprehends how recollection functions as an aid to mystical contemplation, one acquires a clearer understanding of how the external aspects of religious life can either reinforce or debilitate the mystic's inner life.

Recollection refers to that procedure wherein the mystic learns to focus one-pointedly his or her mind, will, imagination, and emotions on some object or goal. This focused total mobilization of the mystic's affective and intellectual powers, if successfully carried out, eventually shuts down the incessant mental chattering that is normally present as a kind of background noise behind all our activities in the waking state. Once mystics stop this process of silently talking to themselves, they transform their mode of consciousness and begin to have their first tangible encounters with that spiritual world that otherwise remains imperceptible to the five senses.

I deliberately chose the term "recollection" to denominate this process of one-pointedly centering the mind and "heart"[1] (instead of the perhaps more familiar terms that often function as synonyms, for example, "meditation," "contemplation," "stilling the mind," and "centering the mind one-pointedly" [ekāgratā in Sanskrit]) because Christian mystics have always emphasized that not only does the recollective process bring the purely "mental" functions such as thinking and intellection into a tightly focused state but that the emotions, the will, and the imagination also participate in this act of total concentration. Terms such as "stilling the mind" and "centering the mind one-pointedly" have the disadvantage of accentuating the mental and ratiocinative aspects of the recollective process at the expense of its volitional and affective aspects. I avoided the term "contemplation" because it tends to be used by Christian mystics to refer to the final rather than the preliminary stages of the mystical path and because it also has the inappropriate contemporary meaning of merely thinking deeply about something. "Meditation" is often used with contrary meanings. Whereas translators of Buddhist documents often use "meditation" to refer to a process of concentration that shuts down the activities of the discursive intellect, Christian manuals on how to pray often use the term to refer to a process of preparation for interior prayer that mobilizes this same discursive intellect in order to quicken the subject's feelings of devotion and repentance. In short, the Christian usage of "meditation" refers to a very early stage of the contemplative path where the subject has not yet quieted the activities of his or her discursive intellect whereas the Buddhist usage presumes that the mystic has already done so. The Christian usage renders the word inadequate for my purposes since it presupposes the continued activity of the discursive intellect,[2] something

1. By "heart" I refer, of course, not to the physical organ but rather to the entire panoply of man's affective powers, namely, the will, the imagination, and his emotions and feelings.
2. I use the term "discursive" to refer to that aspect of man's intellect or reason that is always either involved in thinking about things and their interrelationships or else imagining projects that the individual might or ought to be doing and why it should be doing them. The

inconsistent with that one-pointedness of attention that constitutes the essence of the recollected state of consciousness.

## Recollection in Christian Sources

The crucial problem that any mystic has to solve is this: How does one make contact with this "spiritual" realm when it is inaccessible to the five physical senses? Gregory of Nyssa stressed the extrasensory character of mystical encounters with the divine when he declared that "the contemplation of God cannot function in the realm of sight or hearing; it even escapes the ordinary exercise of our intellect. 'For eye hath not seen, nor ear heard.'" He then went on to say that "the man who would approach the knowledge of the mysteries must first purify his conduct of all sensuous and animal behavior, he must wash from his mind any opinion based on sense-perception."[3] In other words, purifying one's conduct of all sensuality and crude animal needs serves as the only way to attain knowledge of these supersensible mysteries because it helps one to purge one's mind from opinions based on sense-perception. However, it is important to note that Gregory stated that good conduct was only the beginning, not the guarantee, of that process that leads one to contemplation of God.[4] In and of themselves, good conduct and right thinking do not lead one into the direct presence of God while one is in this life.

According to Gregory, the decisive step on the path to transcending the limitations of sense-experience and enjoying a direct encounter with the presence of God comes when the aspirant begins to focus his or her mind and "heart" on God to the exclusion of everything else. Gregory described these benefits of recollective practice in his treatise *On Virginity*. He began by comparing the human mind to a stream that flows from a spring, dissipating itself by branching out in many different directions. As long as this continues to take place, its flow is weakened and it becomes almost useless for irrigating the soil.

---

typical subject matter of fifteenth- and sixteenth-century manuals of discursive meditation were reflections about such subjects as the ways that one had sinned against God that day, how much Christ really must have loved us to have endured the humiliations He endured for us in His Passion.

3. Gregory of Nyssa, *From Glory to Glory: Texts from Gregory of Nyssa's Mystical Writings*, trans. Herbert Musurillo (Crestwood, N.Y.: St. Vladimir's Seminary Press, 1979), p. 98.

4. The term "contemplation," when employed by Christian mystics, refers to the direct experience of God's presence.

So, too, . . . is it with the human mind. If it spreads itself out in all directions, constantly flowing out and dispersing to whatever pleases the senses, it will never have any notable force in its progress towards the true Good. But now recall the mind from all sides, and make it collect itself . . . without scattering and wasting itself: then the mind will find no obstacle in its rise to heaven and in its grasp of the true meaning of reality.[5]

This process of focusing the mind is a phenomenon of the utmost importance in mysticism. Throughout the world, in the most diverse religious and cultural circumstances, focusing the mind (and the "heart") serves as the chief method that mystics use in order to bring about their mystical experiences and free themselves from a state of being that is exclusively conditioned by sense-experience.

Like Gregory of Nyssa, many other prominent Christian mystics made explicit references to recollection as an essential element in man's struggle to enjoy the direct presence of God. For example, Pope Gregory the Great stated that the perfect contemplation of God and mystical illumination were impossible without the practice of recollection. He wrote in his *Homilies on Ezekiel* that

he who keeps his heart within, he it is who receives the light of contemplation. For they that think immoderately of external things know not what are the chinks of contemplation from the eternal light. For that infusion of incorporeal light is not received along with images of corporeal things; because while only visible things are thought of, the invisible light is not admitted to the mind.[6]

Thus it followed that allowing the mind to wander in an undisciplined way after images of fleshly things and the desires for them constituted the most serious hindrance to the contemplative life. As long as this mental and emotional wandering took place, it was impossible to receive any inkling of the spiritual things that lie hidden from the corporeal eye and receive the divinely given grace of illumination.

Bernard of Clairvaux wrote of the preparation for the mystical life in a similar vein when he stated that the monk cannot attain the angelic life

5. See Gregory, *From Glory to Glory*, p. 103.
6. Quoted in Butler, *Western Mysticism*, p. 72.

that is his highest earthly ideal, unless he has first learned to subject his mind to the strictest discipline. He asserted that there were two kinds of death, physical death and the "good death" of contemplation that trans-figures the way a monk experiences the world and elevates his soul to an angelic purity, making it indifferent to the temptations and distractions of the world. However, he cautioned that this "good death" was not possible unless the monk was "able by purity of mind to fly over the phantasmata of corporeal images that rush in from all sides. Unless you have attained to this do not promise yourself rest. You are mistaken if you think that short of this you find a place of quiet, secret solitude, serene light, a dwelling of peace." However, once the monk reaches this degree of purity of mind, his soul is able to come into the "august company of the blessed spirits."[7]

One also discovers that recollection was an essential method of bringing about mystical experiences among the Protestant mystics. For example, in the first of Jacob Boehme's *Dialogues on the Supersensual Life,* a disciple asks his spiritual master what he needs to do in order to come to see God and hear Him speak. The master answers that this would only be possible if the disciple were able to focus his mind, will, and imagination to the degree that his concentration succeeded in blocking out the usual cacoph-ony of sensory and mental images that pour into it from all sides.

> When thou standest still from the thinking of Self and the willing of Self, when both thy intellect and will are quiet, and passive to the expressions of the Eternal Word and Spirit; and when thy soul is winged up and above that which is temporal, the outward senses and the imagination being locked up by holy abstraction, then the Eternal Hearing, Seeing, and Speaking will be revealed in thee, and so God heareth and speaketh through thee. . . . Blessed art thou therefore if thou canst stand still from self-thinking and self-willing, and canst stop the wheel of thy imagination and senses; forasmuch as hereby thou mayest arrive at length to see the great Salvation of God, being made capable of all manner of divine sensations and heavenly communications since it is nought indeed but thine own hearing and willing that do hinder thee, so that thou dost not see and hear God.[8]

7. These passages from Sermon 42:4–6 of Bernard's *Sermons on the Canticle* are quoted in Butler, *Western Mysticism,* pp. 115–16.

8. Jacob Boehme, *Dialogues on the Supersensual Life* (London: Methuen, 1901), pp. 13–14.

## The Affective Dimension of Recollection

The various authors cited above emphasized different aspects of the recollective process. On the one hand, Gregory of Nyssa stressed that recollection checked the wanderings of the mind and made no reference to the affective and volitional side of the process while Jacob Boehme, on the other hand, stressed that recollection involved far more than just the mind—as an act of focusing, it also mobilized the will and imagination as well. Is recollection, then, a purely mental act of concentration, a focusing of the intellectual powers or does it equally involve the will, imagination, and the emotions? A careful reading of the texts supports this alternative. Although some texts and authors seem to accentuate the mental and intellectual aspects of the recollective process, it is always understood that, to some degree at least, the imagination, will, and the emotions participate in and reinforce the effort of concentrating the mind.

One notices this affective dimension of recollection in Indian mystical traditions. While the *Yoga-Sūtras* attributed to Patañjali give one the initial impression that the spiritual liberation acquired by mastering Yoga takes place as the result of a purely mental act, a silencing of the thought-production process, a closer reading shows that this view is mistaken. To be sure, at the very beginning of the treatise, the author defines Yoga as "the hindering of the modifications of the thinking principle."[9] However, it is clear that Patañjali took it for granted that the cessation of thought would not occur unless the yogin's practice of the virtues and his asceticism had simultaneously brought his will, imagination, and emotions under his firm control. The yogin's effort of self-control was a total existential mobilization wherein all aspects of his personality and mind coordinated themselves in order to mutually reinforce his efforts to quiet both the internal chattering of his thoughts and the emotional and imaginational turbulence that accompanies that internal dialogue. Consequently, the author declared that "through the practicing of benevolence, tenderness, complacency, and disregard towards objects (that is, persons who are respectively in possession) of happiness, grief, virtue, and vice, the mind becomes purified." Bhojarāja's commentary on this passage amplifies this statement by observing that although these purificatory measures are only external, and therefore not an intimate portion of Yoga itself, they are "valuable (not so much in themselves, but) as aids in effecting the important matter, so by exercising benevolence, etc., which are moods of mind opposed to aversion

9. Patañjali, *Yoga-Sūtra of Patañjali* (Ballantyne ed.), 1.2, p. 9.

and covetousness, the mind, in which composure has (thereby) been produced, becomes fitted for meditation."[10] In a similar vein, the author of the
sūtra asserted that profound devotedness toward the Lord (Īśvara) that
involved a complete dedication and consignment of all one's actions to
him, also functioned as a "preeminent" means of abstract meditation.[11]

One of the ways that Theravada Buddhists focus their attention is by
staring fixedly at colored discs known as *kasiṇas*. The monk stares at the
disc until the afterimage remains as vividly present when the eyes are
closed as it was when the eyes were open. When the afterimage retains that
vividness for a long period after the eyes are closed that is a sign that the
meditation has been successful and that the mind has achieved one-pointedness of attention. It is clear from Buddhaghosa's description of this process in *The Visuddhimagga* (*The Path of Purity*) that fixing the attention in
this manner requires more than just the act of staring at the kasiṇa. The
meditator must also mobilize his emotions during the act of gazing at the
disc. Thus Buddhaghosa tells the monk that when he starts to concentrate
his attention on one of these colored discs, he ought to regard this inanimate object of his meditation as though it were "a precious jewel," adopt
a "reverential attitude" toward it, and bind his heart to it "in a loving
mood."[12] Elsewhere in the same text, Buddhaghosa states that "ecstasy
arises in a short time . . . [to one] who is devoted to the sign [meditation-
object]."[13] Eliciting feelings of devotion makes it easier for the meditator to
concentrate his attention on the object.

Jacob Boehme, Bhojaraja, and Buddhaghosa suggest that whenever mystics talk about silencing the mind or controlling mental functions, their
techniques of mental regimentation simultaneously imply a correlative regimentation of the will, the imagination, and the emotions. In short, one
must always regard the phenomenon of recollection as a manifestation
that involves both the mind and the "heart."

## Recollection in Other Religious Traditions

The use of recollection as a technique for inducing mystical experiences is
not restricted to Christianity or Yoga. For example, one also finds numerous testimonies to the importance of recollection among the Sufis.

10. Ibid., 1.33, pp. 27–28.
11. Ibid., 1.23, p. 22.
12. Bhadantacariya Buddhaghosa, *The Path of Purity*, 3 vols., trans. Pe Maung Tin (London: Pali Text Society, 1929), 2:143.
13. Ibid., 2:149.

Writing at the beginning of the tenth century, al-Junayd declared that he who desires to follow in the footsteps of the prophets must learn to give up everything that would divert him from total devotion to God.

> Know that your devoted attention to anything in this world, whether it be small or great, is a barrier between you and the next world, a means of obscuring your vision when it should be clear. Stop your consciousness from giving its attention to that which when perceived will make you lacking and inadequate. Purify your consciousness, make clean your inward thoughts by exclusive concentration on the main purpose, by complete and exclusive devotion, being of simple purpose.[14]

This passage indicates clearly that al-Junayd considered the recollective act to be not only an act of focusing the mind or consciousness on God but also an act that incorporated an affective aspect insofar as it required that the subject become filled with an "exclusive devotion" to Him. Al-Ghazzālī made similar demands of the worshiper who desired intimate contact with God. Thus, he wrote in The Niche of Lights (Mishkat al-Anwar) that "the first stage of prophets is their translation into the World of Holy Transcendence away from the disturbances of the senses and imagination."[15] True vision demands that the mystic suppress the activities of his senses and his imagination. Failure to do this will make it impossible for him to see the World of the Invisible. However, "with the suppression of sense, some of the lights prophetical may become clarified and prevail, inasmuch as the senses are no longer dragging the soul back to their own world, nor occupying their whole attention."[16]

Perhaps the best-known Sufic method of recollection is the *dhikr,* a type of interior prayer in which the devotee mentions Allah's name repeatedly day after day, until saying the words "O Allah, O Allah, O Allah" becomes a habit that even carries over into sleep. Once this recitation becomes automatic the audible recitation of these words should cease. In its place the prayer becomes an interiorized, totally absorbing inner remembrance and thought of God. Eventually, according to Schimmel, "the *dhikr* should permeate the mystic's whole being so that in constant *dhikr*

14. al-Junayd, The Life, Personality, and Writings of al-Junayd, trans. and ed. Ali Hassan Abdel-Kader (London: Luzac & Co., 1962), p. 145.

15. Abū-Hāmid Muhammad al-Ghazzali, Mishkat al-Anwar, trans. W. H. T. Gairdner (Lahore, Pakistan: Sh. Muhammad Ashraf, 1952), p. 133.

16. Ibid., p. 142.

he forgets the recollection of everything else."[17] This technique ultimately leads the Sufi to an ecstatic contemplation of God.

The fundamental importance of mental control as the royal road to liberation and salvation is also attested to in the Vedic Upanishads. In the *Katha Upanishad* one finds the famous parable of the soul as a chariot rider. The body is here seen as the chariot in which the soul rides, while the intellect (*buddhi*) is the driver, the mind (*manas*) serves as the reins, and the senses are the horses. The man without understanding, the parable declares, allows his senses to be uncontrolled, just as a chariot driver could lose control and be driven by vicious horses.

> He, however, who has understanding,
> Whose mind is constantly held firm—
> His senses are under control,
> Like the good horses of a chariot driver.
>
> He, however, who has not understanding
> Who is unmindful and ever impure
> Reaches not the goal
> But goes on to reincarnation (*samsāra*)
>
> He, however, who has understanding
> Who is mindful and ever pure
> Reaches the goal
> From which he is born no more.
>
> He, however, who has the understanding of a chariot-driver
> A man who reins in his mind—
> He reaches the end of his journey,
> That highest place of Vishnu.[18]

Other Indian traditions of mysticism also stress the importance of recollection. In the *Vivekachūdamani* (*The crest-jewel of discrimination*), Śankara attests to the great soteriological significance of focusing the mind, imagination, and will. He says that first, the aspirant must cease desiring sense-objects and brooding on them. He achieves this cessation of desire

17. Anne-Marie Schimmel, *The Mystical Dimensions of Islam* (Chapel Hill: University of North Carolina Press, 1975), p. 171.
18. Katha Upanishad 3:6–9, in *The Thirteen Principal Upanishads*, trans. Robert E. Hume (New York: Oxford University Press, 1975), p. 375.

by not engaging in selfish actions.[19] For Śaṅkara, liberation involves not only the destruction of desires but also the exclusion of mental and imaginational fluctuations of any kind. The realization that the *ātman* (the Self) and the *brahman* (the foundational principle of the universe) are identical only comes about in the experience of *nirvikalpa samādhi*, a condition in which all imaginational activity ceases (*nir* = "free from," *vikalpa* = "imagination"). Śaṅkara then goes on to say that "when the Ātman, the One without a second, is realized by means of the nirvikalpa samādhi, then the heart's knot of ignorance is totally destroyed."[20] The dissolution of ignorance requires that the renunciant be

> calm, self-controlled, perfectly retiring from the sense-world, forbearing, and devoting himself to the practice of *samādhi*, always reflect[ing] on his own self being the Self of the whole universe. Destroying completely by this means the imaginations which are due to the gloom of ignorance, he lives blissfully as Brahman, free from action and the oscillations of the mind.[21]

One can see, then, that liberation depends upon the aspirant one-pointedly focusing his mind and will on the fact that his individual Self is identical with the Supreme Self (*brahman*) that underlies all cosmic processes. It is as though once he reaches nirvikalpa samādhi, the subject almost literally becomes that upon which he focuses his mind and will. As Śaṅkara later points out

> the man who is attached to the Real becomes Real through his one-pointed devotion just as the cockroach thinking intently on the Brahmara is transformed into a Brahmara. [According to popular belief, when a cockroach is caught by a predatory worm known as the brahmarakita, it turns the same color as the worm because of its fear]. Just as the cockroach, giving up the attachment to all other actions, thinks intently on the Brahmara and becomes transformed into that worm, exactly in the same manner, the Yogi, meditating on the truth of the Parātman, attains to It through his one-pointed devotion to that.[22]

19. Śaṅkara, *Vivekachūḍamani*, trans. Swami Mahavananda (Calcutta: Advaita Ashram, 1966), v. 317, p. 124.
20. Ibid., v. 353, p. 139.
21. Ibid., v. 355, pp. 139–40.
22. Ibid., v. 358, p. 141.

It is worth noting that Śaṅkara affirms the importance of the affective dimension of recollection for, as the last quotation demonstrates so clearly, the yogin can only attain that liberating insight that the ātman and brahman are identical if he is devoted to the Real to the exclusion of everything else. Liberation is not just a matter of the right control of the mind and thoughts but also of the feelings.

Together with the practice of good conduct (sīla) and the cultivation of discernment (vipaśyanā in Sanskrit; vipassanā in Pali), the practice of calming the mind (śamatha in Sanskrit; samatha in Pali) serves as one of the cornerstones of the Buddhist's struggle to realize nirvana. The cultivation of śamatha has a two-fold function. By focusing the mind śamatha intensifies the vigor of one's resolutions that otherwise become weakened in proportion to the degree to which the mind is scattered and it makes one's insight into the true nature of phenomena as devoid of any permanently abiding substrate or self much more penetrating.[23]

One Buddhist text, the Dhammapada, opens with the assertion that "all that we are is the result of what we have thought: it is founded on our thoughts, it is made up of our thoughts. If a man speaks or acts with an evil thought, pain follows, as the wheel follows the foot of the ox that draws the wagon."[24] Because a man is what he thinks, it follows that it is a matter of the utmost importance that he control his thoughts and desires. This is impossible without a tightly disciplined mind.

> As a fletcher makes straight his arrow, a wise man makes straight his trembling and unsteady thought, which is difficult to guard and difficult to hold back. . . . Those who bridle their mind which travels far, moves about alone and is without a body, and hides in the chamber (of the heart), are freed from the bonds of Mara (the tempter). If a man's thoughts are unsteady, if he does not know the true Law, his knowledge will never be perfect.[25]

The implications of this statement in the Dhammapada have been explored in great depth and detail throughout the history of Buddhism. It is perhaps within the Yogacara school and its offshoots that they have been carried to their greatest extremes. One Tibetan treatise, "The Yoga of Knowing the Mind, the Seeing of Reality," traditionally attributed to

23. Tson-kha-pa, Calming the Mind and Discerning the Real, pp. 89–93.
24. The Dhammapada, trans. Irving Babbitt (New York: Oxford University Press, 1936), 1.1, p. 3.
25. Ibid., 1.33 and 1.37, p. 8.

Padma-Sambhava and inspired by Yogacara teachings, claims that the phenomenal world is only a mental construct, a creation of our minds. According to this source, the only reality is mind—all else is an illusory fabrication of mind. For this reason, one can only attain emancipation if one silences the mental activity that gives rise to this phenomenal world and conjointly develops a penetrating insight into its true nature as devoid of a self (devoid of any permanently existing substrate) and productive of suffering (*dukkha*). When one accomplishes this, one's mind becomes like an ocean whose surface is no longer agitated by the wind. The quieted mind is therefore like a mirror that perfectly reflects the objects that come before it. "Mistake not, by not controlling one's thoughts, one errs. By controlling and understanding the thought-process in one's mind, emancipation is attained automatically."[26]

This emphasis on control of the mind is also found in Japanese Buddhism. For instance, a contemporary practitioner of Soto Zen, Rosen Takashina, describes the central teaching of his school as also being predicated on controlling one's thoughts. This school offers the interpretation that the Buddha did not wish to teach the reading of scriptures, asceticism, or austerities. Instead, he wanted to teach man how to set his mind and body in order so that he could experience the true wonder of his own self-nature. According to Soto Zen, one can only achieve this goal if one learns to stop one's thoughts. "Being without thoughts is the object of Zen meditation; the control of body and mind is only a method of reaching it. When a body and mind have been controlled, then from the ensuing absence of thoughts are born naturally and rightly brilliant understanding, perfect Buddha-wisdom, reading of the scriptures and devotion, asceticism and austerities."[27]

There are suggestions that recollection was also a crucial aspect of preparation for the ecstatic experiences of shamans among tribal peoples. Knud Rasmussen related that among the Caribou Eskimo a man became a shaman only after many arduous trials. The first requires that the novice shaman undergo a month-long vigil of absolute solitude, cold, and hunger. The purpose of this ordeal is to make Pinga, the mistress of the caribou, his helping spirit, for it is only by her assistance that he can hope to ac-

26. "The Yoga of Knowing the Mind, the Seeing of Reality," in *The Tibetan Book of the Great Liberation*, ed. W. Y. Evans-Wentz (New York: Oxford University Press, 1975), p. 233.

27. From Rosen Takashina, *Zetto Zemni* (1953), cited in Edward Conze, trans., *Buddhist Scriptures* (Baltimore: Penguin Books, 1960), p. 138.

quire shamanic powers. During this month-long deprivation and isolation, his teacher tells him to think and desire only one thing: Pinga should own him. Describing his own initiation, Rasmussen's Caribou Eskimo informant told him: "As soon as I had become alone, Perqanaq [the informant's instructor] enjoined me to think of one small thing all the time I was to be there, to want only one single thing, and that was to draw Pinga's attention to the fact that there I sat and wished to be a shaman."[28] It is interesting to note here that Rasmussen's informant stresses the simultaneously intellectual and the affective nature of the recollective process for not only did his instructor tell him to focus his thoughts on Pinga but he also told him to concentrate his desires upon her as well.

The Australian Aborigines also appear to have used some form of recollective technique to generate those particularly acute supernormal powers and sensibilities that their "clever men" supposedly possess. For instance, A. P. Elkin observed that the clever man does not seek his supernormal knowledge or power through drugs or dancing "but rather through quietness and receptivity, meditation and recollection, observation and inference, concentration and decision."[29] This emphasis on mental and emotional focusing is also present in certain acts of magic and sorcery. In the ceremony of pointing the bone, a method for killing someone at a distance, the sorcerer performs this ritual by concentrating on his intended victim in ways similar to those used in Tantric Buddhist "visualization" techniques. "The performer must concentrate his thoughts on the victim; he must vi-

28. Knud Rasmussen, *Intellectual Culture of the Caribou Eskimos,* vol. 7, nos. 2 and 3 of the Report of the Fifth Thule Expedition, 1921–24: The Danish Expedition to Arctic North America in Charge of Knud Rasmussen, 10 vols. in 11 (Copenhagen: Gyldendalske Boghandel, Nordisk Forlag, 1930), p. 53.

Sergei Shirokogoroff, the Russian anthropologist who investigated shamanism among the Tungus peoples, also linked the reputed paranormal abilities of their shamans to the mastery of recollection. He writes:

> In the state of great concentration, the shamans and other people may come into communication with other shamans and ordinary people. Among all Tungus groups this is done quite consciously for practical needs, especially in urgent cases. . . . To achieve such a communication, the person must *think* about another person and formulate the desire, e.g., "please, come here" (to a given locality). This must be done until one "sees" the person called or until one "knows" that the person perceives the call.

Shirokogoroff, *The Psychomental Complex of the Tungus* (London: Kegan Paul, Trench, and Trubner, 1935), pp. 117–18. Notice that the Tungus assume that effective recollective praxis not only involves focusing the attention but also mobilizing the desires and the will.

29. A. P. Elkin, *Aboriginal Men of High Degree* (Sydney: Australian Publishing Co., 1945), p. 25.

sualize him, and transmit to him the thought of illness or death, of having a 'bone' in his inside. . . . Using the traditional mechanism in the prescribed way and saying the prescribed words in a quiet undertone, helps in his concentration and direction of the mind."[30]

These examples demonstrate the ubiquity of recollective techniques throughout the world in all cultural and religious strata. They clearly show that focusing the thoughts, will, imagination, and emotions constitutes one of the fundamental methods that men and women universally employ whenever they wish to achieve the supernormal states of consciousness or power that are so often associated with mystical experiences. One must now consider how the process of recollection can further deepen this initial encounter with that realm of phenomena accessible to the mystical state of consciousness but inaccessible to the five physical senses.

## How Recollection Functions After the Onset of the Mystical State

Sustained and effective practice of recollection results in a radical transformation in one's mode of consciousness and state of being. However, establishing this initial contact with the "spiritual" world is rarely the end of the mystic's quest. Frequently the onset of the mystical experience produces a dramatic change in the mystic's ritual or ethical behavior.[31] In such cases, the mystic's response to this novel mode of experience centers around the need to modify what one might call the "external" aspects of religious life, how he or she interacts with others. However, it sometimes happens that the onset of this new mode of experience demands a more "interior" type of response, in which case the mystic does not remain content with simply making contact but wishes to go further and deepen that contact. Another struggle begins that demands the continuation of the recollected state at a higher level of proficiency. This is necessary because the mystics' initial encounters with the "spiritual" world often give them what

30. Ibid., p. 48.

31. Few religious traditions regard the production of mystical experiences as an end in itself. For example, most mystics from the nontribal religious traditions such as Islam, Christianity, and Buddhism do not value mystical experiences because they produce a blissful state of consciousness or because they give them access to occult knowledge. Instead, they usually assume that these experiences are valuable because they make it much easier for the one who has them to conform himself more perfectly to the ethical ideal of his respective religious tradition. After all, if one learns by direct experience rather than mere hearsay that the Holy Trinity or Allah really exists as a concretely experienced presence in the spiritual world, it stands to reason that one will become more scrupulous in obeying His commandments.

they consider to be a whole new host of distractions that they must learn to ignore or suppress in order to gain salvation. One confronts the strangely ironic situation that their success in suppressing the myriad distractions that emanate from the imagination and the five physical senses simply bring them into a new state of consciousness in which a whole new host of more subtle distractions need to be suppressed. These distractions are the result of a newly awakened capacity for triggering hallucinatory processes similar to those that operate during dreaming and a now activated capacity for perceiving super-sensible cognitions and experiences. In short, the mystic has replaced the physical and mental distractions of ordinary psychic and sensory life with a whole new set of distractions that emanate, or seem to emanate, from the "spiritual" world itself. Referring to this newly awakened condition of consciousness that arises when thoughts have ceased, the Tibetan Buddhist text *The Path of Knowledge: The Yoga of the Six Doctrines* asserts that "the state of quiescence thus realized is not a state devoid of all sensuous experiences; for phenomena appearing like smoke, and mirage, and fireflies, and dull light like that of a lamp, or the glimmer of twilight, and a cloudless sky, and other phenomena, too numerous to be enumerated illumine it in a supernormal manner."[32] It is clear from this description that the focusing of thoughts and emotions that takes place during recollection does not necessarily bring about a state of consciousness devoid of all forms and images.

It is important to realize that the extraordinary state of consciousness that the practice of recollection often activates gives mystics a supernormal faculty of perception and knowledge.[33] For example, telepathy and clairvoyance frequently accompany the recollected state.[34] Similarly, recollected

32. *The Path of Knowledge: The Yoga of the Six Doctrines* in *Tibetan Yoga and Secret Doctrines,* 2d ed., ed. W. Y. Evans-Wentz (New York: Oxford University Press, 1971), p. 197.

33. Mystical experiences and supernormal experiences such as telepathy and clairvoyance are not necessarily synonymous. For example, a Christian mystic may have a vision of Christ's Sacred Heart. This vision may resemble or actually be a hallucination but this does not mean that it was a supernormal phenomenon, that is, a phenomenon that conveyed information about something that would otherwise have been impossible to acquire by means of either the five senses or inference. However, *all* supernormal experiences are mystical states of consciousness because they usually become manifest only when the individual's mind is in a recollected state.

34. See Gerda Walther, "On the Psychology of Telepathy," *Journal for Psychic Research* 25, no. 10 (October 1931), p. 442; Eileen Garrett, *Telepathy: In Search of a Lost Faculty* (New York: Creative Age Press, 1945), pp. 173–74; and see Chapter 13.

mystics may for the first time begin to perceive auras or luminous phenomena (photisms) of the sort that Gopi Krishna and Aua experienced. At other times, the recollected mystics may sense that they are standing outside of their own physical bodies and that they are able to transport themselves magically to distant places as quickly as they can think about going there. They may experience indescribable feelings of bliss and with a transfigured "interior" sight they may envision paradisiacal landscapes of compelling vividness and concreteness. Sometimes this recollected state brings supernatural revelations in its wake.

Despite the potentially extraordinary nature of the phenomena that often accompany the recollected state, most of the universal religions[35] consider recollected states accompanied by visual and auditory phenomena as relatively inferior states of spiritual attainment, at least when they are compared to what each tradition considers the spiritually perfect state to be.[36] Thus Islamic, Christian, Hindu, and Buddhist mystics often describe the "highest" states of mystical consciousness in terms that suggest that they are radically free of forms, images, and voices of any kind whether they be of a sensible or supersensible character. Al-Ghazzālī alludes to this freedom from forms and images that occurs when the mind enters into the most elevated states of consciousness. When a novice first learns how to completely sink his mind in the recollection of God to the exclusion of every other thought, he first undergoes that transformation of consciousness just referred to—he begins to see revelations and visions. "The mystics in their waking state now behold angels and the spirits of the prophets. . . . *Later a higher state is reached; instead of beholding forms and figures,* they come to stages in the way which it is hard to describe in language; if a man attempts to express them, his words inevitably contain what is erroneous"[37] (emphasis mine). In other words, the "higher" mystical experi-

35. I use the term "universal religion" to indicate those religions that claim that their message of salvation applies to all of humankind not just a particular tribe or social group. Islam, Christianity, and Buddhism stand as the classic representatives of this type of religious tradition. The opposite type of religious tradition is the tribal religion, a religion that limits its soteriological appeal to only one tribe or social group. As a general rule, universal religions seek converts whereas tribal religions do not.

36. It is essential to avoid the mistake of thinking that there is one universally identical state of spiritual perfection. Each religious tradition creates its own distinctive ideal of spiritual perfection that embodies a unique configuration of ethical, ritual, and experiential conditions. In short, nirvana as a state of spiritual perfection is not at all equivalent to that ideal of Christian spiritual perfection embodied in John of the Cross's notion of divine union.

37. W. Montgomery Watt, *The Faith and Practice of al-Ghazzālī* (London: George Allen & Unwin, 1970), pp. 60–61.

ences possess an ineffability that transcends even supernormal forms and images.

The history of Christian mysticism exhibits numerous instances in which the highest states of mystical experience and spiritual perfection are depicted as though they were states of being where the mystic was free from any craving for supernormal forms, images, and auditory phenomena. Thus Saint John of the Cross declared that in order to obtain the most perfect union with God, the soul

> must never reflect upon the clear and distinct objects which have passed through its mind by supernormal means. . . . For we must bear in mind this principle: the greater heed the soul gives to any clear and distinct apprehensions whether natural or supernatural, the less capacity and preparation it has for entering into the abyss of faith, wherein are absorbed all things else. For, as has been said, no supernatural forms or kinds of knowledge which can be apprehended by the memory are God, and, in order to reach God, the soul must void itself of all that is not God.[38]

From this passage it is evident that even the supernaturally perceived forms and images received in the sublimest states of mystical ecstasy are hindrances to a true union with God.

Buddhism and certain forms of Hinduism exhibit a similar emphasis on the formless and imageless character of the more advanced states of mystical consciousness. As one saw in the case of Śaṅkara, the perfection of mystical wisdom only occurs in the condition of nirvikalpa samādhi where a radical cessation of imagining and conceptualizing takes place. In a similar vein, Patañjali and his commentators stress that the highest mystical state of consciousness, asamprajñāta samādhi (the trance-state that takes place without the support of any kind of meditational object or image whatsoever),[39] is a condition in which the activities of imagining and perceiving both sensible and supersensible objects have completely ceased because consciousness no longer has any object on which to focus its attention.[40]

38. John of the Cross, *Ascent of Mount Carmel*, 3.7.2, p. 370.

39. I return to this important point in much more depth in Chapter 31—the spiritually liberated state in Yoga, *kaivalyam* (isolation), is not synonymous with asamprajñāta samādhi. Although the latter is the immediate precursor to isolation, it is not coterminous with it.

40. Patañjali, *Patañjali's Yoga Sūtras: With the Commentary of Vyāsa and the Gloss of Vācaspati Miśra*, trans. Rama Prasada (New Delhi: Oriental Books Reprint Corporation,

Buddhist writings imply that a similar absence of forms and images characterizes the higher trance-states.[41] For example, in *The Path of Purification* (*Visuddhimagga*), Buddhaghosa described a very elevated and highly prized state of trance which he called "the trance of cessation." The path that led to it involved a progression of trance-states each of which became more and more "abstract" and free of imagery, form, and affectivity than the one that had preceded it. The first trance-state that the monk had to master on his path to the trance of cessation merely required that he isolate himself from sensual pleasure while the reasoning and reflective faculties still functioned. The second trance (*jhāna*) began when the monk suppressed the activities of those reasoning and reflective faculties. However, in this condition of one-pointed attentiveness, the monk still experienced a sensation of bliss. The third degree of trance began when even this feeling of bliss had subsided. There were several more "abstract" trance-states after this emotionless one until the monk arrived at those peculiar states of being (*samāpatti*) known respectively as "the realm of infinity of consciousness," the "realm of nothingness," and then the "realm of neither perception nor yet non-perception." Only after he has mastered this last abstract and formless trance-state does the monk finally enter into the trance of cessation, that condition where all mental activity, even consciousness of the most abstract type of object, utterly ceases.[42] It is taken for granted that these highest types of trance-state cannot become manifest if one turns one's recollected mind to the production of supernormal visionary states and feats of magical power.

These higher mystical states of consciousness free from forms, imagery, and auditions usually only come about if one continues to practice recollectedness after entering into those initial mystical states of consciousness that supervene when one is at the rather early stages of learning how to concentrate the mind and emotions. In other words, there are degrees of recollectedness. It is only by a persistent effort at focusing the mind, imagination, and emotions that the initial mystical experiences laden with forms, imagery, and strong feelings can be stripped of them. In most of the

---

1978), 1.18 (Vyāsa's commentary) and 1.20 (Vācaspati Miśra's gloss), pp. 34 and 38, respectively.

41. In Chapter 31, I show that Buddhists do not identify nirvana with any particular type of trance-state. The higher trance-states simply function as aids to realizing nirvana but must never be confused with the final goal itself.

42. For the relevant passages in Buddhaghosa's famous work, see Henry Clarke Warren's anthology, *Buddhism in Translations* (New York: Atheneum, 1974), pp. 384–90.

universal religions, the practice of recollection does not cease with the attainment of a condition in which one hears voices or sees visions or otherwise acquires supernormal powers. On the contrary, most of the mystics from those traditions look on indulgence in such supernormal capacities as a serious hindrance to the attainment of spiritual perfection because these pleasures and novelties become a new set of distractions that divert the mind from its focus on the supreme religious goal of that particular tradition or else they give rise to feelings of pride and egoism.

Awareness of this led Sharafuddin Maneri to assert that the miraculous experiences which sometimes come to Sufis often end up by becoming another form of idolatry that they must fight to overcome.

> Just as infidels, because of their attachment to some idol, are enemies of God but can become saints by cutting themselves from their idols, . . . Sufis have their idols, namely, miracles. If they become satisfied with miracles, they will be put to shame and be dismissed from the divine Presence, but if they cut themselves off from miracles they move closer to God and become united to Him.[43]

Consequently, if the Sufi wants to deepen or sustain his contact with God, he must redouble his efforts to separate himself from all that interposes itself between him and the divine. This requires not only a continually renewed avoidance of worldly distractions but it also requires a constant recollective vigilance that extends to those distractions that originate from the spiritual world.

The *Yoga Sūtra* of Patañjali contains what is perhaps the clearest explanation of why continued recollectedness is necessary if one is to achieve liberation from the round of rebirths. As already noted, the trance-state immediately antecedent to release from suffering and rebirth, asamprajñāta samādhi, is one where there is a total absence of any kind of form or image whatsoever. Patañjali makes it clear that this elevated state of consciousness cannot occur if the yogin allows himself to become fascinated by his newly acquired capacity to manifest magical powers that derives from his mastery of the lower trance-states. He declared that "these fruits are obstacles in the way of meditation." Bhojarāja's commentary on this passage explains that "the aforesaid fruits become obstacles to the ascetic closely devoted to meditation (because his) meditation becomes relaxed by

43. Sharafuddin Maneri, *The Hundred Letters*, pp. 40–41.

reason of joy, wonder, etc."[44] To reach the perfection of Yoga practice one must preserve one's recollectedness even in the face of these beguiling supernormal phenomena. Giving one's attention to these supernormal distractions is essentially no different than giving in to those distractions caused by the five physical senses. Both types of distractions prevent the development of the formless trance-states and that condition of spiritual detachment essential to liberation.

Diadochus of Photike was a fifth-century Christian and author of a text, "On Spiritual Knowledge and Discrimination." According to Diadochus, the higher mystical stages cannot be achieved unless one learns to maintain a perfect recollectedness even in the presence of those visionary beguilements that emerge when the aspiring monk first awakens his hitherto dormant spiritual faculties. "You should not doubt that the intellect, when it begins to be strongly energized by the divine light, becomes so completely translucent that it sees its own light vividly. This takes place when the power of the soul gains control over the passions."[45] Quoting Paul, he goes on to say that such luminous apparitions can often also be Satan masquerading as an angel of light. For this reason he says that Paul "teaches us that everything which appears to the intellect, whether as light or as fire, if it has a shape, is a product of the evil artifice of the enemy. So we should not embark on the ascetic life in the hope of seeing visions clothed with forms or shape, for if we do, Satan will find it easy to lead our soul astray." Having established that only formless illuminations can be of divine origin, Diadochus concludes with the observation that visions with forms are deleterious because they destroy the monk's one-pointed focus of mind, imagination, and will that leads him to God. "Our one purpose must be to reach the point when we perceive the love of God fully and consciously in our hearts—that is, with all your heart, and with all your soul . . . and with all your mind."[46]

Buddhist writings also attest to the importance of ignoring the supersensory faculties and powers that are experienced when the monk has learned to meditate with some degree of proficiency. Buddhist masters teach that these phenomena become distractions that disturb meditation. One contemporary disciple of the Burmese Theravada master Sunlun Sayadaw declares that once a certain level of meditational attainment has been reached,

44. Patañjali, *Yoga-Sūtra of Patañjali*, 3.38; and Bhojarāja's commentary, p. 85.
45. Diadochus of Photike, "On Spiritual Knowledge and Discrimination," in *The Philokalia*, trans. G. E. H. Palmer et al. (London: Faber & Faber, 1979), vol. 1, p. 265.
46. Diadochus, "On Spiritual Knowledge," 1: 265.

the yogi sometimes becomes more perceptive to extrasensual things.
. . . Because of this power the yogi can see what others cannot see,
he can hear what others cannot hear. People come to consult him
and his predictions come true . . . thus he has degenerated from a
Vipassana yogi to a shaman. But after some time, as the distractions
of the new vocation grow more varied and the practice of meditation grows less intense, the answers turn out to be less and less
accurate. . . . The yogi is left with an interrupted practice.[47]

Sunlun Sayadaw's disciple likened a yogin who indulged in the minor attainments of meditational practice to a man who "keeps lifting up the tail
and patting the behind of the little iguana he has caught."[48]

Thus far I have established that recollection plays an important role in
the mystical life in two ways. First, it serves as the means whereby mystics
acquire their initial experiences of a supersensible realm of being or else
acquire for the first time an experience of living contact with the divine.
Second, even after this initial transcendent experience takes place, the continued practice of recollection is necessary. This enables mystics to avoid
becoming distracted by supernormal phenomena, a diversion that most
mystics in the universal religions would consider a serious hindrance to his
quest for spiritual perfection.

## Recollection and the External Aspects of the Religious Life

But how does the recollective process relate to the life of religious action?
One of the crucial challenges that every mystic confronts is the task of
reconciling the seemingly contradictory requirements of the contemplative
life and those of the life of action. I use the phrase "life of action" in a very
broad sense to refer to the most varied types of religious activity. For example, the life of action may involve not only the kinds of action that
occur in a ritual setting but it may also refer to the quite different kinds of
action and behavior that stem from fulfillment of the obligatory ethical
precepts of a given religious tradition or the kinds of action that are of a
more voluntary nature such as pious acts of asceticism. At first glance, it
may seem as though the need for mental stillness and freedom from outside disturbances stands radically opposed to any commitment to the "external" performative dimension of the religious life that every tradition

47. Jack Kornfield, *Living Buddhist Masters* (Santa Cruz, Calif.: Unity Press, 1977), p. 96.
48. Kornfield, *Living Buddhist Masters,* p. 96.

imposes upon its adherents. This tension between these poles of the mystical life has sometimes led mystics into an antinomian position from which they dismiss all the ritual, sacramental, and ethical paraphernalia of the religious tradition as insignificant. Such antinomian mystics claim that only the inner experience of God's presence is religiously significant and that, as a consequence, fulfilling the ethical and ritual precepts has no value. While one must not underestimate the tension that gives rise to this propensity toward religious antinomianism, one usually finds that most mystics manage to avoid succumbing to it. Indeed, most of them succeed remarkably well in reconciling the two conflicting demands: the need for contemplative stillness on the one hand and the religious duty of following the ethical and ritual precepts on the other. One of the most important ways they achieve this reconciliation between action and contemplation is by ensuring that the entirety of their external religious life functions as an integral part of the recollective process.

The complementary nature of religious action and contemplative recollection emerges most clearly in the writings of the Christian monastics. For example, in Cassian's *Conferences* the author states that perfect contemplation depends upon achieving purity of heart or dispassion (*apatheia*). Basically, his conception of purity of heart incorporates recollectedness for it is a condition of perfect detachment in which there is both single-mindedness in place of a chaos of ideas and an equanimity in the face of bodily discomforts or worldly anxieties. Like almost all other mystics, Cassian insists that the attainment of this condition is the sine qua non for all advancement along the path to contemplation. Cassian declares that all of the monk's ascetic practices are structured to bring about this purity of heart.

> Whatever can guide us towards purity of heart is to be followed with all our power . . . it is for this end—to keep our hearts eternally pure—that we do and endure everything, that we spurn parents and home and position and wealth and comfort and every earthly pleasure. If we do not keep this mark continually before the eyes, all our travail will be futile waste that wins nothing and will stir in us a chaos of ideas instead of single-mindedness.[49]

According to Cassian, the need for ascetic practices does not therefore originate in a morbid religious guilt but rather in the very practical neces-

49. John Cassian, "The Conferences of Cassian," in Owen Chadwick, *Western Asceticism* (London: SCM Press, 1958), pp. 197–98.

sity of laying the foundations for that stillness of both mind and emotions that is so crucial to progress in the mystical life. Ascetic practices guarantee that the heart will be as free as possible from distraction by the bodily passions. Without this freedom, thoughts and imaginational phantasms distract the contemplative, preventing him from enjoying an immediate sensation of His presence.

Not only do ascetic practices and humility reinforce the process of recollection, but success in recollection also reinforces one's humility and desire to pursue the ascetic practices more energetically. Ascetic practice and recollection reciprocally reinforce each other. Cassian affirms this when he states that

> the discipline of the body and spirit on the one side and unceasing prayerfulness on the other, cannot help having a mutual effect upon the other. The keystone to the arch of all virtues is perfect prayer and without this keystone the archway becomes rickety and insecure. And conversely, without the virtues no one can attain the continued serenity of prayerfulness.[50]

Other Christian monastic texts demonstrate that Cassian's idea of the unity of recollection and asceticism is not an isolated one. For instance, William of St. Thierry, a Cistercian monk, wrote in *The Golden Epistle* that the exercise of virtue reinforces contemplation. He makes it very clear that one of the chief functions of the virtue of obedience is that it helps to prevent the mind and imagination from wandering when they should instead be focusing on sacred matters. He notes that in a soul that has not been shaped by obedience, the mind and imagination constantly flutter from one fantasy and desire to the next thereby distracting the mind from holy and spiritual matters. It is always engaged in questioning, seeking novelty, and idle curiosity. "For this reason, devout simplicity . . . needs to be shaped by a discipline of obedience."[51] William later goes on to say that "regulating his food and clothing, his work and his rest, his silence and his solitude and everything to do with the formation or the needs of the outward man, it leaves the brother who is obedient, patient and tranquil, free from trouble and anxiety."[52] Manual labor works in much the same way as obedience because it can also reinforce recollection. Thus William de-

50. Cassian, "Conferences," p. 214.
51. William of St. Thierry, *The Golden Epistle* (Kalamazoo, Mich.: Cistercian Publications, 1976), p. 35.
52. William of St. Thierry, *Golden Epistle*, p. 37.

clares that manual labor performed in the proper spirit can be of great assistance to contemplation. Instead of finding it a hindrance to contemplation,

> the serious and prudent soul is ready to undertake all work and is not distracted by it but rather finds it a means to greater recollection. It keeps in sight not so much what it is doing as the purpose of its activity and so aims at the summit of all perfection. The more faithfully such an effort is made the more fervently and the more faithfully is manual work done and all the energies of the body are brought into play. The discipline imposed by good will forces the senses to concentrate.[53]

One can easily find examples of the close relationship between recollection and external practice in other religious traditions. The literature of Sufism has many examples of this tendency to make the external religious life serve the process of recollection. Sufis repeatedly declare that their practices enable them to realize concretely the central mystery of Islam, the absolute unity of God.[54] This experience is impossible so long as one allows anything to come between oneself and God. This abandonment of all that is not God takes place during those private moments of recollective intimacy as well as in the course of the life of religious action. Sharafuddin Maneri, for example, declares that one of the major purposes of abandoning sins is

> to ensure that evil desires are broken, and that the tendencies of human nature are brought to heel, with the result that a person does not turn aside from God! There is one further purpose—that a person's heart may be governed by the thought of remembering God, and having been freed from the shackling tendencies of human nature, the heart might become purified for the task of remembering God and attaining a true vision of Him.[55]

This theme that living the Islamic precepts functions as a sort of exteriorized recollective process recurs throughout the Sufi tradition. Just as recollection as a psychological operation aims at cutting off "interior" mental

53. Ibid., pp. 40–41.
54. Schimmel, *Mystical Dimensions of Islam*, p. 17.
55. Sharafuddin Maneri, *The Hundred Letters*, p. 70.

and imaginative distractions, the act of fasting attacks egoistic distractions. "The cycle of eating requires preoccupation with the self and anyone who is preoccupied with himself becomes hidden from the Beloved."[56] In a similar fashion, Sharafuddin Maneri also interprets almsgiving as a recollective act. He says that the true lovers of God make sure that "everything that has a form is offered up by them as a gift so that their relationship toward us men might be severed completely."[57] In Sufism, as in Christianity, there is an integral, harmonious connection between the life of action—ethics, asceticism, ritual—and the life earnestly devoted to the contemplative recollection of God. Both exterior religious actions and the interiorized practice of recollection can help to bring the mystic's mind, will, and imagination to a tightly focused and exclusive remembrance of God.

In the *Yoga Sūtra* religious action is also portrayed as a means of facilitating recollectedness. The author of this text explicitly lists religious observances (*niyama*) and forbearance (*yama*) from such things as killing, stealing, and lying as two of the "eight things subservient (to concentration)." The other things accessory to mental fixation listed in that text include physical activities (such as *prāṇāyāma*, regulation of breathing) that also facilitate recollectedness. It seems clear from the commentary that the author intends to emphasize that these recommended practices are not to be regarded as ethical or ritual prescriptions that have a value in and of themselves.[58] Rather, they are intended instead to assist in attaining the central goal of Yoga—stopping all forms of mental modification.

The foregoing discussion concerning the complementary relationship between what I have termed the "life of action" and recollection points to one of the most fascinating aspects of mysticism: mystics do not just passively receive a religious tradition. When they incorporate its ethical (or ritual) practices into the act of recollection itself, they give those acts a deeper, and perhaps altogether novel, meaning and significance. For example, to use William of St. Thierry's phraseology, only the "spiritual" man can begin to fully grasp the deeper significance of the unquestioning obedience and the manual labor that is demanded of all monks. For the beginner, whom William refers to as the "animal" man, the deeper significance of these obligations eludes his understanding. He can never go beyond seeing these requirements as anything more than constraints that restrict his freedom but that he must nevertheless unhesitatingly yet uncomprehend-

56. Ibid., p. 130.
57. Ibid., p. 132.
58. Patañjali, *Yoga-Sūtra of Patañjali*, 2.29, and Bhojarāja's commentary, p. 54.

ingly perform. Such is his condition as long as he remains only a beginner. Thus, the animal man must be content to receive the tradition in a purely passive manner. In contrast, the "spiritual" man, whom William portrays as having attained a high degree of mastery in the practice of recollection, goes beyond seeing these obligations as constraints that restrict his freedom and spontaneity. He begins to realize instead that the performance of them in the proper spirit can serve as the very foundation and precondition of his newly discovered possibilities for spiritual freedom and understanding. The tradition is then no longer something passively and sometimes grudgingly received and obeyed but something actively and joyfully embraced.[59]

Mystical life is to a great extent a struggle against distractions of all kinds, sensible, supersensible, emotional, imaginational, and even physical. Success in this quest largely depends upon how well the mystic is able to ignore or suppress them. This struggle does not just take place solely within the inner sanctum of the mystic's own mind but it also embraces the existential totality of his or her life. Because all elements of the mystic's life blend together as a remarkably coherent and reciprocally interrelated whole, the study of how recollection functions within that totality is important. If one is to truly understand mysticism, one must go beyond seeing recollection merely as a technique. It is far more than that. It is a focal point around which both the mystic's active and interior life revolve and reciprocally intensify each other.

59. William of St. Thierry, *The Golden Epistle*, pp. 97–98.

# 6

# Mystical Experience and Schizophrenic Experience

Mystical experience is a contextually determined state of consciousness and orientation of the will that usually supervenes only when an individual enters into the condition of recollectedness. As the mystic begins to achieve more profound degrees of recollective abstraction from the world, visions, auditions, and photisms frequently impinge on his field of awareness, replacing the sense-impressions from the five physical sense organs that had formerly dominated his field of consciousness. This intimate association between the onset of the recollected state and the onset of varied hallucinatory manifestations suggests that mystical experience and schizophrenia are different sides of the same coin.[1] After all, if one considers that the processes that generate schizophrenia and the processes that generate mystical experiences both produce a hallucinatory excitement of the mind, is it illogical to assume that the two phenomena are intimately related to each other? Is the schizophrenic a failed mystic and the mystic a successful schizophrenic?

The possible connection between mystical experience and mental illness has not escaped the attention of scholars. For example, James Leuba

---

1. I do not mean to imply that all such "hallucinatory" phenomena (visions, voices, tactile sensations of presence) are "unreal," existing only in the imagination of the beholder. As I point out in Chapters 9, 11, and 12, some hallucinatory phenomena occasionally appear to incorporate veridical material into their content; that is, they refer to objectively verifiable events about which the percipient otherwise had no physically explicable means of knowing. Some hallucinatory phenomena can incorporate telepathic, clairvoyant, or precognitive material.

I do not differentiate between the manifold forms of schizophrenia. When I use the term "schizophrenia," I am referring only to those forms of it that give rise to auditory, visual, or tactile hallucinations. Paranoid schizophrenia and delusions of grandeur, though often labeled "schizophrenia," are often devoid of hallucinations. The hallucinatory and non-hallucinatory forms of schizophrenia may actually be very distinct forms of mental pathology.

claimed that Saint Paul's mystical ecstasies did not differ in any essential way from the hallucinatory manifestations that accompany epileptic seizures. Leuba asserted that the apparent difference between epilepsy and mystical ecstasy originated solely from the different ways that one interprets the two otherwise identical phenomena. The religious mystic "interprets" his or her experience as the work of God whereas the epileptic does not.[2] The former interpretation tends to produce a subjective experience that is usually regarded as and felt to be beneficial in its effects whereas the latter interpretation tends to produce subjective experiences that are unsettling and destructive in their effects. William James also asserted that mystical experiences bore a close relationship to the delusional experiences of the insane, noting that in both cases one observes that the mystic and the insane patient accord the same ineffable importance to the smallest and most insignificant events. Both the mystic and the mentally deranged invest texts and utterances with hitherto unsuspected dimensions of meaning, and both individuals experience the same sorts of visions, auditions, and impulses that appear to come from a source outside the subject's psyche. The only thing that differentiates the experience of the genuine mystic from his or her delusional counterpart is that the former generates positive emotions that enhance the subject's sense of well-being; the latter generates negative emotions, feelings of desolation rather than consolation. For these reasons, James concluded that the mystical experiences and the delusional experiences of the insane stemmed from the same psychological mechanism. Both "mysticisms" originated "from that same mental level, from that great subliminal or transmarginal region of which science is beginning to admit the existence, but of which so little is really known. That region contains every kind of matter: 'seraph and snake' abide there side by side."[3] Are the hallucinatory phenomena that accompany mystical experiences and the delusions of the insane really blood brothers, as James would have us believe? The preponderance of evidence suggests that there is no simple "yes" or "no" answer to this question.

One cannot deny that the onset of mystical experiences can sometimes have deleterious psychological effects. For example, three days after Gopi Krishna first awakened kundalini and the mystical state of consciousness that accompanied that event, he noticed that his previous ability to concentrate his attention had begun to fail him completely and that the quality

2. Leuba, *Psychology of Religious Mysticism*, pp. 213–14.
3. James, *Varieties of Religious Experience*, p. 334.

of that radiance that had illuminated him from within underwent a radical and disturbing metamorphosis.[4] The inner illumination that formerly gave him a sensation of exultation and bliss now began to shine with a sinister coppery glow that produced acute feelings of anxiety and depression.[5] The next few months became a waking nightmare. He was continually beset with moods of intense and unrelenting anxiety. Food became utterly repulsive to him so that he sometimes went for weeks on end eating almost nothing. He felt his center of consciousness undergo the most peculiar and startling sensations of expansion and contraction. He intimated that there were times when he experienced hallucinations in which the menacing coppery-colored glow would assume terrifying shapes and forms as if evil faces were leering at him. Finally, he noticed that, with the exceptions of his feelings of terror and anxiety, his emotions seemed to have shriveled up—he no longer felt any traces of affection for his children, his wife, or any of the things that had formerly given him pleasure.

A comparison of Gopi Krishna's symptoms with those that recovered schizophrenics relate in their autobiographies suggests that Gopi Krishna's practice of recollection had apparently precipitated an attack of acute schizophrenia. Except for the sensation of liquid light roaring up and down his spine filling his head with sparks, a peculiar symptom that appears to have derived its specific content from his previous exposure to hatha yoga treatises, Gopi Krishna's experiences during this period of psychic disintegration were anything but unique. His revulsion from food,[6] his inability to concentrate his attention,[7] his moods of unrelenting terror and anxiety,[8] his hallucinations,[9] and the withdrawal of affect from things that

4. Recovered schizophrenics repeatedly mention that the inability to focus attention is one of the hallmarks of the schizophrenic consciousness. This feature of the schizophrenic consciousness stands in sharp contrast to the mystic's proficiency in recollective concentration of the mind.

5. This psychotic episode is described in Gopi Krishna, *Kundalini*, pp. 48–69.

6. Mark Vonnegut noted that the onset of his schizophrenic symptoms coincided with a complete distaste for food. At one point, he went for twelve days without eating anything. Mark Vonnegut, *The Eden Express* (New York: Bantam Books, 1976), p. 152.

7. Vonnegut mentioned that an exceptionally hypertrophied tendency to become distracted constituted one of the essential characteristics of his schizophrenic states of consciousness. Because of this, the simplest tasks became almost impossible to perform. "I was so distractible that even very simple tasks were impossible to complete." Vonnegut, *Eden Express*, p. 268.

8. See *Autobiography of a Schizophrenic Girl*, with analytic interpretation by Marguerite Sechehaye (New York: New American Library, 1970).

9. Vonnegut, *Eden Express*, pp. 96–100; *Autobiography of a Schizophrenic Girl*, p. 77.

had formerly given him pleasure (*anhedonia*)[10] fall into the standard pattern of behavioral and perceptual abnormalities that characterizes the schizophrenic experience. One must therefore conclude from the case of Gopi Krishna that the onset of recollectedness can sometimes bring about genuine schizophrenic psychosis.

Although the example of Gopi Krishna suggests that it is unwise to draw too rigid a boundary between the domains of mystical experience and schizophrenic experience, most of the evidence indicates that there are good reasons for regarding the two phenomena as distinct from each other. The visual and auditory hallucinations and the distortions of affect that occur during schizophrenia cripple the subject's capacity to draw reasonable inferences from the data presented to his perceptions. Mystical visions and locutions do not do this. For example, mystics very frequently hear voices. Nevertheless, these mystical voices usually respect the rules of polite conversation. They almost always answer in response to one of the mystic's specific emotional needs or requests and once they give their answer or declaration, they withdraw and then quiet resumes.[11] They do not continue babbling on and on like some spiritual variant of the town gossip. Furthermore, these mystical auditions do not impair the mystic's capacity for rational inference. The mystic preserves his ability to critically evaluate what he has seen or heard during his visions and locutions.

The voices that become manifest during schizophrenia do not respect the rules of polite conversation; they often chatter incessantly. Indeed, the schizophrenic frequently hears a cacophony of voices simultaneously uttering contradictory commands. For example, John Perceval noted that during his worst periods of psychosis the simple act of eating breakfast became an ordeal because various spirit voices would then assail him, saying, "Eat a piece of bread for my sake." "No, no!" another one would scream

10. *Autobiography of a Schizophrenic Girl,* p. 79. Her descriptions make it clear that catatonic states do not destroy the ability to perceive but rather the ability to affectively respond to that which one perceives.

11. For instance, on one occasion Saint Teresa became deeply concerned about her confessor's suggestion that she give up all her secular friendships so that she could devote herself undistractedly to spiritual matters. Was such a radical degree of renunciation really necessary in order to fulfill her vows or was it excessive scrupulosity? She prayed for guidance on this question. During one of those prayers, God favored her with a rapture in which He spoke to her, telling her, "I will have thee converse now, not with men, but with angels" (*Life of Teresa of Jesus,* trans. Peers, pp. 231–32). Once God had uttered these words, the conversation ended. The question Teresa had asked Him had been answered and there was no further need for continuing the conversation.

at the same time, "eat this instead . . . don't eat that! Eat this instead."[12] Amid such a welter of contradictory commands, the subject's ability to behave and think in a rationally ordered manner becomes progressively weakened.[13]

One can say the same thing about the visual hallucinations that take place during the two different modes of experience. The mystic's visual hallucinations generally last for only a short period of time and occur only within a rather strictly delimited set of circumstances. Consequently, they do not interfere significantly with his or her normal ocular perception or ability to function in social situations. When those particular vision-inducing circumstances change, the hallucinations cease. Perceval's autobiography contains examples that exhibit this fundamental difference between the schizophrenic and mystical type of visual hallucination. For example, he mentioned that some months before the onset of his madness, he experienced what appears to have been a genuine precognitive vision. He related that during one trip to Dover on his way to France, he paused a few moments for an intense prayer. While praying fervently, he saw a vision of three faces, all of which were wearing the same type of peculiar traveling cap. One of these three figures made him shudder with horror. Soon he saw two people get into his coach dressed with traveling caps identical to those that he had seen in his vision. They were nice enough men so he wondered why one of the hatted figures had elicited such disgust and horror. Later on, he came to the port city and saw a third man wearing the same sort of hat. Now he knew the reason for his former feelings of revulsion. This third man swore horribly and continually, a thing that so repelled Perceval's prudish sensibilities that he reprimanded him.[14] It is significant that Perceval alluded explicitly to the brevity of this vision. It quickly came and went without intruding further on his waking consciousness. This was a marked contrast to the behavior of the visual and audi-

12. John Perceval, *Perceval's Narrative: A Patient's Account of His Psychosis, 1830–1832,* ed. Gregory Bateson (New York: William Morrow & Company, 1974), pp. 60–61.

13. Perceval related that eventually the constant babble of contradictory commands, threats, and accusations that he received from the voices caused him to completely lose his capacity for critical judgment. He described this moment when his reason vanished: Suddenly he heard, "the sound of a slight crack, and the sensation of a fibre breaking over the right temple . . . it was succeeded by a loss of control over certain of the muscles of my body, and was immediately followed by two other cracks of the same kind . . . accompanied by an apparently additional surrender of the judgment. In fact, until now I had retained a kind of restraining power over my thoughts and belief; I now had none. . . . My will to choose to think orderly was entirely gone." Perceval, *Perceval's Narrative,* p. 44.

14. Ibid., p. 260.

tory hallucinations that developed after the onset of his madness. These hallucinations did not exhibit the decorous behavior of the precognitive vision for they constantly barged into his waking consciousness without any respect for his own wishes or social propriety. After his insanity developed, Perceval "became like one awake yet dreaming, present to the world in body, in spirit at the bar of heaven's judgment seat; or in hell, enduring terrors unutterable."[15]

Monroe furnishes us with another example of the "limited" character of the hallucinatory states that accompany mystical experiences. He frequently had visual hallucinations during those periods when he experienced the sensation that his "spiritual body" was slipping away from his physical body and journeying to other dimensions of reality.[16] However, it is significant that these hallucinations did not occur at any other time. When the out-of-body trance-state was over, the visual hallucination ceased and did not further interfere with or intrude into his ordinary waking state of consciousness nor did these hallucinations and the emotions they generated ever cripple his capacity for rationally ordered inference and critical judgment. Schizophrenic visual hallucinations, on the other hand, develop in a far more insidious manner and have a much greater intrusive effect on both the perceptions and the emotions. Moreover, they last much longer than their mystical counterparts. For example, Renee, the authoress of *Autobiography of a Schizophrenic Girl,* wrote that she spent two years in analysis trying to combat an assemblage of terrifying visual hallucinations that she referred to as "the Enlightenment" or "Land of Light," an eerie landscape suffused with an "implacable" blinding luminosity that was so pervasive that it completely obliterated all shadows. This land of metallic, smooth surfaces seemed illimitably vast, completely flat, and cold like a landscape on the moon. Worst of all, this seemingly inescapable, unchanging, and interminable hallucination transformed people into robotic figurines whose gestures and actions appeared to her as empty and alien, devoid of all human warmth, spontaneity, personality, and intelligence.[17] In contrast to Monroe's out-of-body visions and the other mystical visions described above, Renee's hallucinatory Land of Light invaded almost every aspect of her waking life paralyzing her with an unbearable tension and anxiety that progressively crippled her ability to function in any socially acceptable manner.

15. Ibid., p. 44.
16. Monroe, *Journeys Out of the Body,* pp. 22–28.
17. *Autobiography of a Schizophrenic Girl,* pp. 32–34.

Schizophrenic experiences differ in a second way from mystical experiences insofar as they create a condition where recollectedness becomes almost impossible. Mystical experiences, on the other hand, usually have their genesis in a recollective act. Consequently, they presuppose the subject's ability to bring his or her mind into a focused state of attention, the exact opposite of that condition that schizophrenics describe.

I have already observed above that during his schizophrenic phase Gopi Krishna had great difficulty focusing his attention,[18] a marked contrast to the ease with which he had been able to do this before this psychotic episode began. In addition, it is significant that his recovery commenced at that very moment when he restored his ability to focus his attention and bring his mind into a state of quiet.[19]

The autobiographies of many other cured schizophrenics also mention that this condition of profound distractedness stands out as one of the principal characteristics of the schizophrenic state. For example, Mark Vonnegut asserted, "I was so distractible that even very simple tasks were impossible to complete."[20] He would start pruning a tree, for instance, and then find it difficult to complete the task because every tiny detail of the tree or the task itself, the feel of the bark, the particles of sawdust floating to the ground, the feel of his muscles moving, completely (yet in very rapid succession) absorbed his attention so that it became impossible for him to concentrate on anything for any significant length of time.[21] Renee also alluded to this state of distractedness for she mentioned that she constantly "sought distraction in games and conversation" because they warded off the intense fears that accompanied her initially intermittent excursions into the Land of Light. Her need for constant distractions to keep the Land of Light at bay became so pronounced that it appeared to others as though she were a hysterical and hyperactive child.[22] I have also noted that Perceval's final descent into madness coincided with a complete loss of his ability to concentrate or direct his thoughts.[23] I conclude from these obser-

---

18. Gopi Krishna, *Kundalini,* pp. 48, 54–55.

19. Ibid., p. 66.

20. Vonnegut, *Eden Express,* p. 268.

21. Ibid., p. 99.

22. *Autobiography of a Schizophrenic Girl,* p. 26. Renee's excessive absorption in the details of people's faces and gestures recalls Vonnegut's successive absorptions in the details of tree pruning; see Vonnegut, *Eden Express,* p. 37.

23. The climax of his madness began at that moment when he heard a noise inside his head that sounded as though something had cracked or snapped within his right temple. "Until now I had retained a kind of restraining power over my thoughts and belief; I now

vations that this distractedness, this pathological inability to concentrate, is one of the most important characteristics that differentiates the hallucinatory experiences of the mystic from those of the mentally ill.

It is worth noting that Ernst Arbman's comprehensive study of the phenomenon that he called "religious trance" or "ecstasy" also placed a similar emphasis on the presence of recollectedness as the principal point of differentiation between religious ecstasies and the hallucinatory manifestations associated with various types of mental pathology such as schizophrenia and hysteria.[24] He argued that although the auditory and visual hallucinations and trances that occur during the course of hysteria exhibit many parallels to their counterparts in the experiences of the mystics, mystical experiences (or what he called "religious trances" or "religious ecstasies") differ from hysterical states insofar as mystical states of consciousness are "nothing but [the] direct continuation, an anormal intensification . . . of the states of religious '*recueillement*' [recollection] that almost without exception precede it," whereas hysterical states of consciousness almost never originate as the result of the subject's deliberate recollective efforts.[25] Arbman maintained that the mystic always tightly controlled the onset of his mystical states, even in those cases where the experience subsequently escaped his or her conscious control as in cases of spirit possession, whereas the onset of hysterical states usually occurred spontaneously.[26] Arbman also noticed that it was not the mystic's subconscious that determined the content of his or her extraordinary states of consciousness but rather the conscious will. In other words, the devotional objects that mystics deliberately choose as the focal points for their recollective endeavors subsequently function as the structural underpinning for their mystical states of consciousness. The reverse holds true in the hysterical states of consciousness. In those conditions, the victim's autonomous subconscious complexes continually rise to the surface against, or at least without the collusion of, his or her conscious will. It is these upwellings of subconscious material that determine the hallucinatory landscape of the hysteric's visual and auditory hallucinations.

The relatively transient character of mystical experiences also distinguishes them from the experiences of the schizophrenic. For the most part,

---

had none; I could not resist the spiritual guilt and contamination of any thought, of any suggestion." See Perceval, *Perceval's Narrative*, p. 44.

24. Arbman devoted most of his discussion to hysteria rather than schizophrenia.

25. Arbman, *Ecstasy or Religious Trance*, 3:42.

26. Ibid., 3:210.

the hallucinatory manifestations, the ecstatic transports, and the other affective upheavals that accompany mystical experience rarely last for more
than a few minutes or hours, occasionally a few days. In addition, once the
mystic's trance, ecstasy, or vision ends, his perceptual faculties rapidly return to normal. For example, none of Monroe's out-of-body experiences
ever seem to have lasted for longer than the period of a dream and it
always happened that within a few minutes of feeling his "spirit body"
reenter his physical body his sight and hearing would return to normal just
as one's own sight and hearing quickly return to normal when one stops
dreaming and begins to wake up.[27] I must also add that I have no evidence
that would suggest that the visions of Aua, Augustine, Paul, or William
Bucke ever lasted for longer than a few minutes or hours. The perceptual
and emotional dislocations that accompany schizophrenic experience, on
the other hand, often endure for many years.[28] Renee, the patient who
wrote *Autobiography of a Schizophrenic Girl,* experienced the dreadful
"Land of Light" almost continually from the time she was about twelve or
thirteen years old until she was into her twenties. Perceval's period of mental and emotional derangement lasted for about fifteen or sixteen months.[29]

In summary, most of the evidence presented above points to an essential
dissimilarity between mystical experience and schizophrenic experience.
Most important, the vast majority of mystical experiences originate from
some sort of recollective effort. They arise as products of the subject's
conscious will. The majority of schizophrenic experiences, on the other
hand, do not originate from any deliberative recollective effort. Instead,
they come to birth more or less spontaneously as the unexpected consequence of severe emotional trauma, drug abuse, or causes unknown. In
contrast to the recollectively generated visions and locutions of the mystic,
the schizophrenic's spontaneously generated hallucinations and affective
states do not respond very well, if at all, to the subject's conscious will.
Furthermore, the schizophrenic's hallucinations and the emotional states
that accompany them cripple the victim's faculties of critical judgment and
orderly thought at the same time that they progressively invade every domain of his or her waking consciousness for longer and longer periods of

27. Monroe, *Journeys Out of the Body,* pp. 224–26. In this particular discussion Monroe
stresses how easy it is to exit from the out-of-body state when one wishes to do so. It is often
impossible, on the other hand, for schizophrenics to willfully terminate their hallucinatory
experiences.
28. Arbman, *Ecstasy or Religious Trance,* 3:376.
29. *Autobiography of a Schizophrenic Girl,* p. 27; *Perceval's Narrative,* p. 3.

time. Mystical experiences generally last for only a brief period of time, however. They do not cripple the individual's capacity for critical and orderly thought or imperiously intrude on the mystic's waking state of consciousness since they usually restrict their occurrence to the time of trance. When the trance is over, the disruptive effects on normal waking consciousness cease.

I have adduced enough evidence to conclude that even though both schizophrenic experience and mystical experience activate the hallucinatory processes of the mind, they usually do so in significantly different ways. It is therefore a mistake to regard the schizophrenic as though he were simply a failed mystic and it is likewise a serious error to regard the mystic as though he or she were just a successful schizophrenic.

# 7

# What Is Mystical Experience?

Mystical experience is that amorphous, well-ordered, historically conditioned, trans-sensory metamorphosis of the waking consciousness that usually supervenes only after the individual has achieved recollectedness.

The most important feature of this definition is the connection it makes between the mystical transformation of consciousness and the process of recollection. If one probes the autobiographical statements of almost any mystic carefully enough, one is almost certain to find allusions to some form of mental and emotional focusing and, more often than not, an acknowledgment of its role in generating the mystical state of consciousness. This is not to deny that there are cases where mystical experiences come about spontaneously (for example, William Bucke's experience of cosmic consciousness, Saint Paul on the road to Damascus, and Moses' revelation of the burning bush). However, many of these examples of spontaneous experience such as those of Paul and Moses are not firsthand descriptions. Consequently, one cannot say that the particular mystics involved may not have consciously or unconsciously practiced some form of recollective act prior to the onset of their supposedly "spontaneous" visions or locutions. One must also bear in mind that it is possible that recollectedness can come about without the subject being consciously aware of how he got himself into that state. In any case, the overwhelming preponderance of evidence indicates that recollective techniques are the germinal source of mystical experiences.

The adjective "amorphous" points to another extremely important aspect of mystical experience, its essential formlessness. As I demonstrated in Chapter 2, the mystical state of consciousness does not manifest itself in the same manner every time. Some mystical experiences have an overwhelming affective impact whereas others may manifest themselves in a rather humdrum manner, merely bringing about an emotionally neutral change in the landscape that the mystic is looking at. Some mystics experience the phenomenon of photism to a marked degree while others do not. Some mystical experiences are accompanied by out-of-body travel while others are not.

This definition also lays a great deal of emphasis on the historically conditioned nature of the mystical experience. As I pointed out in Chapter 4, the content of that amorphous state of consciousness that transpires after the onset of recollectedness is extremely sensitive to the mystic's particular cultural and historical environment. The particular objects, symbols, and images that mystics see, the sensations that they feel, the words that they hear, the particular moods, activities, and orientations of the will that experience evokes—all these things derive from those particular existential preoccupations that mystics consciously and unconsciously receive from their religiohistorical environments.

My definition also draws attention to the trans-sensory character of the mystical state of consciousness. This term "transsensory" simply means that mystical experiences are an ever-shifting blend of hallucinatory phantasms and supernormal perceptions. Sometimes the hallucinatory component dominates entirely, in which case the mystical experience is hard to distinguish from the waking dream. At other times, the supernormal component can dominate the mystical experience completely shutting out the hallucinatory, dreamlike images to replace them with direct, unembellished clairvoyant or telepathic perceptions, perceptions as clear and objectively valid as anything one might see or hear with one's physical eyes. At yet other times, the mystical experience may be a roughly equal mix of hallucination and supernormal perception. In that case, hallucinatory embellishments disguise the veridical information in a manner analogous to the way that the arcane symbolism in a dream often hides its real meaning or message. The prefix "trans" in this term also draws attention to the fact that one cannot perceive the objects that one "sees" or "hears" during a mystical experience by means of the normal operations of the five physical senses. One must suppress the latter in order to bring about the mystical vision and audition.

When I speak of mystical experiences as "well-ordered," I am noting that they differ significantly from the hallucinatory phenomena that take place during certain types of schizophrenia and hysteria. In contrast to their schizophrenic counterparts, the emotional states, perceptions, and phantasmagoria that occur in mystical experience do not cripple the individual's capacity for critical thinking or rational inference or intrude into his or her normal waking state of consciousness for more than a brief period of time.

This definition of mystical experience differs from most other characterizations or definitions of mysticism because it says nothing about the particular object of that experience. Instead, it focuses primarily on its mode of genesis, its essential amorphousness, and its acute sensitivity to cultural and historical conditioning. Mystical experiences may or may not bring the individual face to face with God. Whether or not they do so depends on whether the notion of divinity is a significant element in the mystic's religious or historical environment. They may or may not help the mystic to escape bondage to the reincarnation cycle (saṃsāra). Whether or not they do so once again depends on whether escape from saṃsāra is a soteriologically significant goal in his religious tradition. One can say the same thing about those experiences of "union" or "oneness" with some absolute being or reality that are often brought up as essential attributes that distinguish the mystical states of consciousness from all other analogues. Mystical experiences have no essential connection to states of "union" or "oneness" with the Absolute. They will only manifest themselves as experiences of union if the individual's religious tradition accords soteriological significance to such forms of fusion or identity with the Divine or Absolute reality.

# Book Two

# Psychological and Parapsychological Aspects of Mystical Experience

# 8

# The Phenomenon of Ex-stasis and Its Variations

In the Introduction I observed that the ability of an individual to have mystical experiences frequently, though by no means always, went hand-in-hand with a tendency for him or her either to manifest or to experience a wide range of paranormal phenomena, for example, clairvoyance, telepathy, out-of-body travel, the ability to influence objects at a distance, the ability to go through physical objects without hindrance. The persistent association of mystical experience and the supernormal constantly surfaces in both legendary and autobiographical narratives of mystics' lives. For instance, in his famous tenth-century compendium of Sufi doctrine, *Kitāb al-ta' arruf*, Kalābādhī acknowledged that all Sufis agree "in affirming the miracles of the saints . . . such as walking on water, talking with beasts, traveling from one place to another or producing an object in another place or at another time."[1] One finds a similar juxtaposition of mystical experience and miracle in Christianity, Hinduism, and Buddhism.[2] This intimate connection between mystical experience and the paranormal is as pervasive in the religious literature of tribal societies as it is in the universal religions. For example, Franz Boas noted that the Hudson Bay Eskimo attributed all sorts of miraculous powers to their shamans, maintaining that when one of them receives his illumination his supernormal powers increase in direct proportion to the intensity of this inner luminosity. Its presence confers such reputed powers as the capacity to undertake ecstatic

1. Abū Bakr al-Kalābādhī, *The Doctrine of the Sufis*, trans. A. J. Arberry (Lahore, Pakistan: Sh. Muhammad Ashraf, 1976), p. 62.
2. Gregory the Great, *Dialogues, Book II: Saint Benedict*, trans. Myra L. Uhlfelder, The Library of Liberal Arts (Indianapolis: Bobbs-Merrill Company, 1967), pp. 10–20; Muktananda, *Play of Consciousness*; Gopi Krishna, *Kundalini*, pp. 210–12; Patañjali, *The Yoga-System of Patañjali*, trans. James Houghton Woods (Madras: Motilal Banarsidas, 1977), book 3; Kornfield, *Living Buddhist Masters*, p. 96; Buddhaghosa, *Path of Purity*, 1:432–33.

flights to visit spirits, accomplish work by mere wish, kill by mere wish, know the thoughts of others, locate game clairvoyantly, and locate lost objects supernormally.[3] Black Elk similarly combined a capacity for mystical experience with an ability to travel clairvoyantly outside of his body and to supernormally locate game.[4] Sergei Shirokogoroff has also observed that among the Tungus of Siberia there existed a widespread belief that shamans possessed not only the ability to communicate with spirits but that they also had telepathic and clairvoyant powers.[5] The universality and persistence of this linkage between mystical experience and supernormal phenomena suggests that the relationship between the two is of an essential rather than merely accidental nature. For this reason, a study of how they are connected merits careful attention.

## Ecstasy and Ex-stasis Distinguished

One cannot fully understand the connection between mystical experience and supernormal powers of action and perception unless one comprehends how each is related to that peculiar mode of being that accompanies the phenomenon of ex-stasis. References to either the phenomenon of ex-stasis[6] or to that distinctive mode of being that accompanies it appear repeatedly and with great frequency in descriptions of mystical experiences as well as in the biographies, both factual[7] and mythical,[8] of mystics, seers, mediums, magicians, and shamans. I generally employ the term "ex-stasis" rather than the more familiar word "ecstasy" in order to distinguish the etymological sense of ecstasy from its more common usage as a synonym for bliss. Ecstasy often appears in mystical literature to refer to an intense state of exaltation, bliss, and thrilling excitement that is often of such intensity

3. Boas, *The Eskimo of Baffin Land and Hudson Bay,* pp. 133–34.

4. DeMallie, *Sixth Grandfather,* pp. 252–55 and 208, respectively.

5. S. Shirokogoroff, *The Psychomental Complex of the Tungus* (London: Kegan Paul, Trench & Trubner, 1935), pp. 117–18.

6. See Rasmussen, *The Intellectual Culture of the Iglulik Eskimos,* pp. 110–30; Gopi Krishna, *Kundalini;* DeMallie, *Sixth Grandfather,* pp. 111–42.

7. Catherine of Siena, *The Dialogue,* trans. Suzanne Noffke, O.P., Classics of Western Spirituality Series (New York: Paulist Press, 1980), chap. 79; Teresa of Avila, *Life of St. Teresa of Jesus,* chap. 20.

8. See reference to Muhammad's ascension to the throne of Allah during his famous Night Journey in Eliade's collection of mythical narratives, *From Primitives to Zen,* pp. 517–20.

that the mystic loses awareness of both his or her physical environment and body. Gopi Krishna's awakening of kundalini was a good example of this.

Ecstasy also has a second connotation that implies an even more radical process of abstraction from the body and the physical world. This is what I call its etymological sense, "ecstasy" in the sense of "ex-stasis," that sensation or feeling that mystics, psychics, mediums, and other specialists in the paranormal often have of literally seeming to stand outside of themselves as though they were looking at their bodies from a vantage point exterior to it. In ex-stasis either a part or all of the subject's consciousness-principle, usually conceptualized as the "soul" or "spirit," separates from the physical body and it is this disembodied soul-substance or spirit-substance that is reputed to be the agency that performs deeds or perceives things that are otherwise impossible while one is in the ordinary waking state subject to the normal limitations of the physical body.

Several terms are synonymous with "ex-stasis." For example, Saint Teresa of Avila declared that the terms "rapture," "elevation," "flight of the spirit," "transport," and "ecstasy" all referred to essentially the same phenomenon—that moment when, as she put it, "the Lord gathers up the soul, just (we might say) as the clouds gather up the vapor of the earth, and raises it till it is right out of itself."[9] Nineteenth- and twentieth-century writers who have been exposed to Theosophy or other occultist movements often use the term "astral projection" as a synonym for ex-stasis though there is nothing related to the stars in such a phenomenon. Those contemporary writers who wish to describe the phenomenon of ex-stasis in a more "scientific" fashion have begun to use the terms "bilocation," "out-of-body experience," and "autoscopic hallucination" to refer to it. Henceforth, I use the terms "ex-stasis," "out-of-body experience," and "astral projection" interchangeably.

# Ex-Stasis in Folklore and Legend

The following Taoist tale illustrates that, even at the level of folklore and legend, humans have long recognized that he who masters the technique of ecstasy likewise becomes the master of supernormal powers, a despiser of worldly pleasures and a partaker of a mode of being that is radically

9. Teresa of Avila, *Life of St. Teresa of Jesus*, chap. 20.

"other" than normal waking experience—themes that are common in much of mystical literature in other cultural settings as well. The story relates that there was once a wizard possessing miraculous powers who came to the court of King Mu. Much like the Eskimo shaman to which Boas referred, this magician could go through fire unharmed, fly through the air without falling, pierce metals and stone, change the shape of objects and even the thoughts of people. The king immediately became captivated by this wizard and did everything he could in order to get him to stay at his court, putting the entire palace at his disposal, entertaining him with the finest food, clothing, music, dancing, and even women from his own harem. However, none of these worldly splendors impressed the wizard in the least for he utterly despised them and could only be induced to stay with the greatest difficulty. One day, however, the magician "invited the king to accompany him upon a journey whereupon the magician began to rise from the ground and the king, clutching at his sleeve, was carried up and up, till they reached the sky." In other words, the magician took the king on an ecstatic journey.

Once the ecstatic condition supervened, the king immediately began to notice a dramatic change in the qualitative character of his experience and mode of being. Shortly after he began his ecstatic travels, the king arrived at the magician's house above the clouds. However, he immediately noticed that this was no mere celestial replica of an ordinary house. The narrator relates that "in this house, nothing that his ears and eyes heard and saw, nothing that his nose and mouth smelt or tasted was in the least like what the king was accustomed to in the world of man. This, he thought, must surely be Stainless City, Purple Mystery, Level Sky, Wide Joy—one of the palaces of God." Then the King looked down on his palace from this celestial viewpoint and what once seemed so beautiful and opulent now appeared as though it were a mere bump on the ground, completely unworthy of the time and concern he had put into it during his reign. In short, as a result of his ecstatic condition, the king became acutely aware of the radical inadequacy of purely mundane existence. The wizard then continued to take the king further on their ecstatic journey beyond even the sun and the moon to a region completely alien to normal experience. The narrative described it as a realm of light so dazzling that the king could not see and a roaring noise filled the place with a deafening roar. Terrified, the king pleaded with the wizard to go back. The king then found himself sitting just as he had been when the magician had first summoned him to join him on his journey.

In response to his question "Where have I been?" the servants told King Mu that he had merely been sitting among them in silence the entire time he had been engaged in his journey with the magician. When he had recovered from his shock and puzzlement, the king asked the wizard to explain what had occurred. The wizard told him that his journey was not a physical journey but a journey of the soul. "I took you," the wizard replied, "upon a journey of the soul. Your body never moved. The place where you have been living was none other than your own palace." The wizard continued by telling the king that only his habitual doubts about the possibility of such miraculous events prevented him from acquiring the wizard's own fantastic powers. Once he had been told this the king was so impressed that he gave up his concubines and concerns about the state and "devoted himself henceforth to distant journeys of the soul."[10]

# Ex-static Experiences and Mystical Experiences

If one compares descriptions of mystical experiences with the account of an ecstatic journey given above, one immediately notices several themes common to each. First, both types of experience refer to a drastic change that occurs in the subject's mode of being. Like the mystic, the ecstatic finds himself thrown into an experiential domain that is alien to anything he encounters in his ordinary waking consciousness. Second, both the narratives of mystical experiences and those of ecstatic journeys almost always sooner or later refer to experiences of preternatural illumination. This is certainly true of the story of King Mu narrated above. Third, in the description of King Mu's ecstatic journey and in the description of mystical experiences there seems to be a fundamental incompatibility between spiritual and supernormal attainments and attention to purely mundane concerns. Fourth, one observes that supernormal powers frequently accompany both ecstatic journeys and mystical experiences conferring on both the ecstatic and the mystic a certain freedom from the material constraints that normally condition and limit the scope of human action and experience. And finally, both the mystical experience and the ecstatic journey are more than mere perceptions. They are revelations as well, that is to say, because they are means of insight into matters of ultimate concern,

10. Arthur Waley, trans., *Three Ways of Thought in Ancient China* (London: George Allen & Unwin, 1974), pp. 63–67.

one cannot experience them indifferently but rather must respond to them with one's whole being just as King Mu felt impelled to respond to his ecstatic journey by abandoning worldly pleasures and the affairs of state.

This close linkage of ex-stasis with revelations bearing a profound ontological or soteriological relevance appears again and again in the literature of mysticism and in legend. For instance, Black Elk's Great Vision, that all-important revelation that subsequently guided his whole life and determined his vocation as a medicineman, took the form not only of an encounter between himself and the spirit-beings he called the Six Grandfathers but it also possessed all the characteristics of a typical out-of-body experience such as the one King Mu had. Like King Mu, Black Elk also followed his spiritual guides on an ecstatic journey that took him up through the clouds to a celestial dwelling where many wonders were revealed to him. And finally, Black Elk discovered that, as the visionary experience ended, he began to be aware that his physical body had actually remained in one place the entire time of his vision. He began to observe himself and his surroundings as though he were looking at them from a vantage point outside of his body. As he came out of his ecstatic trance and looked down from the cloud he had been traveling on in his vision, he could see his own tipi, his body lying inside it, and his parents stooping over him as he slowly came out of his swoon.[11]

The idea that the moment of ex-stasis (here understood as levitation, a literal lifting up of the physical body) coincides with revelations of soteriological importance also finds expression in Saint Catherine of Siena's *Dialogue*. Saint Catherine asserts that sometimes when the saintly soul becomes so inebriated with the love of God, God unites with that spirit in such a way as to give it a foretaste of the heavenly bliss that awaits it after death. At such a time, even though the soul is still weighed down with the body, "she receives the lightness of the spirit. Often, therefore, the body is lifted up from the ground because of the perfect union of the soul with me [God] as if the body had become light." In this condition one's mode of being radically changes for "the eye sees without seeing, the ear hears without hearing, the hand touches without touching, the feet walk without walking."[12] For Catherine, the condition of ex-stasis signifies an event of cardinal religious importance—the most perfect union of the individual soul with God that is possible while one is still in the flesh. Catherine considered ex-stasis to be an attenuated replica of that

11. DeMallie, *Sixth Grandfather*, p. 142.
12. Catherine of Siena, *The Dialogue*, chap. 79.

soteriologically ultimate relationship to God that a person will have once he achieves salvation.

Among that collection of theurgic and philosophical writings dating from around the third century that were later attributed to the legendary pagan wise man Hermes Trismegistus one finds suggestions that the cultivation of ecstatic experiences formed an integral part of the philosopher's quest for wisdom. These Hermetic writings repeatedly stress that wisdom is only achievable when one radically casts aside the impediments to true spiritual perception and insight that the body imposes on the soul. At one point the author of one of these texts asserts that if one wishes to be able to perceive the unchangeable unity that is the source of all that has shape and color, it is first necessary to begin to see by means of something other than physical sight. Then the seeker must "go forth from the body to behold the Beautiful, let him fly up and float aloft, not seeking to see shape or color, but rather that by which these things are made, that which is quiet and calm, stable and changeless."[13] Once again a familiar pattern repeats itself—like the mystical experience, ex-stasis brings about a revelation concerning matters of ultimate concern, a revelation unavailable to one who thinks only in terms of the limited categories of experience given to human beings through their five corporeal senses.

One can observe this same threefold coincidence of ex-stasis, revelation, and a transformation of the subject's perceptual modality from one that is corporeal to one that is spiritual and incorporeal yet another time in the famous legendary account of Muhammad's ascension to heaven. The narrative begins when the Angel Gabriel places the Prophet on a magic carpet. The magic carpet then floats him into the awesome and dazzling presence of Allah—a presence that Muhammad (as the supposed narrator) describes as "a thing too stupendous for the tongue to tell of or the imagination to picture." The brilliance of the illumination radiating from the throne was so intense that Muhammad had to cover his eyes for he feared blindness. When he did so, he related that "Allah shifted my sight (from my eyes) to my heart, so with my heart I began to look at what I had been looking at with my eyes. It was a light so bright . . . that I despair of ever describing to you what I saw of His majesty." After having spent a long time enraptured in the visionary contemplation of Allah's splendors, and while still in a condition of ex-stasis, Muhammad then received his commission as a prophet. Allah followed this by promising Muhammad's new

13. *Hermetica,* trans. Walter Scott, 4 vols. (Oxford: Clarendon Press, 1924), 1:543.

religious community the entire earth as a place for purification and worship and added to that His promise to give Muhammad "the Master of all Books, and the guardian of them, a Qu'ran." Having made this covenant, Allah withdrew His presence. This withdrawal of the divine presence corresponded to the moment when Muhammad began to descend from the celestial throne back to where the Angel Gabriel was waiting for him.[14] Here, once again, one notices a very clear and intimate association between the moment of mystical illumination and that of ex-stasis. Indeed, the time frame of revelation was completely coincident with the time that Muhammad was in the ex-static condition for the revelation ended when he began his descent.

The five descriptions of ecstatic experiences or of what takes place within them show several unmistakable parallels to descriptions of mystical experiences. Indeed, it is difficult to distinguish descriptions of the two from each other since both share emphasis on the ineffability and revelatory quality of their experiences, references to a preternatural luminosity, references to the awakening of an incorporeal mode of perception, and frequent allusions to paranormal capacities of action. These parallels suggest that it is probably not very fruitful, at the purely experiential level, to draw a distinction between the ecstatic condition of being and mystical experience. Nonexperiential criteria should furnish a more useful means of elaborating distinctions between mystics and other specialists in the occult or paranormal. However, like most generalizations about mysticism, this one requires a significant qualification—not all cases of ex-stasis lead to experiences of illumination and vice versa. Thus, Sylvan Muldoon records a large number of out-of-body experiences but he never mentions illumination nor does he ever refer to the experience of having encountered a living presence as do so many mystics and other ex-statics. Instead, his out-of-body experiences have a prosaic, matter-of-factness to them that resembles in its unemotional facticity the ordinariness of our own everyday perceptual experiences. This prosaic ordinariness of his ex-static experiences is poles apart from the sublime raptures of Teresa of Avila and from that awe-inspiring bliss that once overwhelmed another out-of-body traveler when he suddenly felt himself to be at the very source of all things.[15] Similarly, one notes that not all mystics mention that they had had out-of-body experiences. For example, although Augustine of Hippo abundantly

14. Eliade, *From Primitives to Zen,* pp. 518–20.
15. Monroe, *Journeys Out of the Body,* pp. 122–25.

refers to mystical illuminations in his *Confessions*, he never refers to experiences of ex-stasis.

## Ex-stasis and "Secular" Mystics

How do descriptions of out-of-body experiences taken from contemporary "secularized" individuals compare with those descriptions of ex-stasis that have come to us from other cultural and religious traditions? One will find that the modern descriptions of these experiences show remarkable similarities to those that emerge from other religious traditions. Moreover, the contemporary accounts possess the additional advantage of giving the reader a much more detailed description of what occurs while one is in this condition. For this reason they constitute exceptionally valuable documents that allow one to unveil the interrelationships that link mystical and ex-static experiences to paranormal phenomena.

There are some excellent contemporary autobiographical accounts of ex-stasis that possess a three-fold merit: (1) they describe the phenomenon of out-of-body experience and its paranormal accompaniments in great detail, (2) they do so in as rational and matter-of-fact a manner as possible, striving to remain objective in their descriptions of what occurred, and (3) they discuss techniques for inducing these ecstatic experiences. Specifically, Robert Monroe's classic *Journeys Out of the Body* (1971) and Sylvan Muldoon's *The Projection of the Astral Body* (1929) qualify with respect to the above-mentioned criteria of merit as the best autobiographical descriptions of ex-static experiences. Although the subsequent discussions in this book will principally focus on these two accounts, there are also many other descriptions of this phenomenon. Some are autobiographical[16] while others come from large collections of short firsthand descriptions that various compilers have culled from magazine and newspaper accounts,[17] fragmentary references in literature, medical and psychological journals, and surveys run under the auspices of the British and American Societies for Psychical Research.

16. See Oliver Fox, *Astral Projection* (Secaucus, N.J.: Citadel Press, 1979). Caroline Larsen's description of her out-of-body experiences are quoted in Muldoon and Carrington, *Projection of the Astral Body*, pp. 283–87.

17. For example, Celia Green, *Out-of-the-Body Experiences* (Oxford: Institute of Psychophysical Research, 1968); F. W. H. Myers, *Human Personality and Its Survival of Bodily Death* (New Hyde Park, N.Y.: University Books, 1961); Robert Crookall, *The Study and Practice of Astral Projection* (Secaucus, N.J.: University Books, 1966).

Robert Monroe's first ex-static experiences did not appear suddenly but were instead the final result of a gradually intensifying series of puzzling psychological events. He first began to notice something unusual about himself one afternoon as he lay down on his sofa. Out of the north at about a thirty-degree angle in the sky a sensation of a beam of warm light touched his body. Monroe noticed that he could not see any visible ray or beam and that, furthermore, a ray of sunlight would not have been able to strike him from such a northerly exposure. He also noticed another striking peculiarity about this beam of light—when it touched him he became temporarily paralyzed while his entire body seemed to be shaking violently or "vibrating."[18] This strange sensation came and went several times without any further incident except that it began to give him some anxiety that perhaps he might be suffering from epilepsy or some other brain disorder.

After he had entered this "vibrational" state several times during the course of the next few days, Monroe began to notice another odd phenomenon that bears some comparison with Gopi Krishna's first awakening of kundalini. When he closed his eyes during one such vibratory episode, he observed that the "shaking" motion seemed to have taken the visual form of a ring of sparks with his body as its central axis. He saw this luminous ring of sparks even with his eyes closed and noticed that it oscillated up and down his body starting at the head and going down to the toes and back up again. A sensation of "roaring" accompanied its passage over his head.[19]

Several months later, as he lay waiting for one of those "vibration" states to pass so that he could get to sleep, he noticed that he had one of his arms over the edge of the bed and that he was just touching the rug with the tips of his fingers. Then, for no particular reason, he suddenly decided to push his fingers on down into the rug. Much to his surprise he felt that his fingers were penetrating the rug and touching the floor underneath. He continued this process of pushing until it felt as though his arm had gone through the floor as well. He then noticed that he was wide awake although he still felt that his arm was through the floor. As the vibrations of his body began to fade he became anxious that he might get his arm stuck in the floor. He then yanked his arm up to his body and then

18. Monroe, *Journeys Out of the Body*, p. 22.
19. Ibid., p. 24. Once again notice how this roaring noise compares to analogous phenomena in Gopi Krishna's mystical illumination. One will also recall that in the Taoist tale, King Mu's entry into the realm of light was also accompanied by a roaring noise.

looked at the floor but could see no hole where his arm had supposedly been.

Monroe's first exteriorization occurred when, some weeks after the last incident (as he was dropping off to sleep), he began to fall into the vibrational state again. At that moment the thought came to him about how enjoyable it would be if he were flying in a glider. Almost immediately he noticed the sensation of his shoulder against a wall that he discovered was none other than the ceiling of his bedroom. Much to his surprise, Monroe discovered that he was floating in the air like a balloon bouncing gently off the ceiling. When he looked down from the ceiling, he saw his wife lying in his bed next to another man. He wondered, "Who on earth is sleeping with my wife?" Imagine his surprise when he found that that person was none other than himself![20]

Monroe's awareness of the exteriorization phenomena just described above went through several stages. At first he became conscious only of the "feeling" that his hands were stretching elastically through the floor. It was only several weeks later that the sensation of exteriorization actually became a visual awareness that his consciousness and perceptual faculties were somehow dissociated from his body lying on the bed. At this stage he had apparently not yet seen his "astral" double. However, shortly after his first exteriorization experience, he was also able to see a semitransparent duplicate of his physical body as it began to dissociate. This event took place when Monroe was lying on a couch experiencing what he called "very smooth vibrations." As he lay there feeling these smooth vibrations course through his body, he unfolded his arms and began to move them. Lo and behold! his physical arms were still folded over his chest but the arms that were actually responding to his wishes for movement were diaphanous, glowing, ghostlike arms that he could see through. When he experienced the sensation of his fingers wiggling, it was his transparent, ghostlike "astral" fingers that responded to his wishes for movement while his physical fingers remained motionless like the rest of his physical body. These ghostlike arms and fingers felt completely normal while it was his physical arms and fingers that seemed devoid of sensation. What was even more bizarre, Monroe found that he could push his ghostlike hands right through the bookshelf that lay next to his couch. His diaphanous appendages were behaving just as though he were a ghost![21] One can see that at this point Monroe had not only managed to exteriorize his consciousness

20. Ibid., pp. 25–28.
21. Ibid., p. 167.

and sensations but that he had also exteriorized a diaphanous, luminous, quasi-material "soul substance" that ordinarily coincides with the physical body but which, during ex-stasis, moves out of coincidence with it.

I shall now summarize some of the principal features of Monroe's out-of-body experience. First, the condition at first had the quality of a waking dream, tending to occur at that interface between sleeping and waking known to psychologists as the hypnagogic state. Like a dream, certain aspects of the environment were subject to what resembled hallucinatory distortion—for example, the sensation of stretching one's arm past its natural length until it went through the floor. However, unlike a dream, the subject was perfectly conscious. Second, a kind of waking catalepsy preceded the actual movement of dissociation. The physical body remained rigid and unable to respond to the will. Third, Monroe noted the presence of a peculiar sensation of vibration that coincided with the onset of a cataleptic state and that also served as a necessary preliminary to the dissociation of consciousness and the duplicate body. The fourth feature of the experience was, of course, the actual dissociation of both the consciousness-principle and the quasi-material duplicate body from the physical body. In some mysterious way, this diaphanous counterpart to the physical body actually possessed the capacity to perceive—see, feel, and hear—without the physical sense organs being present from its vantage point, in this case the ceiling. Fifth, the dissociated counterpart possessed both remarkable elastic properties as evidenced by its capacity to stretch through the floor and the ability to penetrate solid objects without hindrance. In short, it seemed to somehow defy the laws of gravity and materiality just as though it were a ghost.

Muldoon's initial out-of-body experience shared all of the five characteristics I delineated above. That is, it appeared to be some sort of hypnagogic waking dream; it occurred while he was in a paralyzed cataleptic condition; he experienced the same sense of rhythmic vibrations that went, as he put it, in "an up-and-down direction"; he possessed an awareness of a diaphanous replica which witnessed his own physical body on the bed, and this ghostlike double of his physical body was capable of penetrating solid objects without any difficulty. However, it would be a serious mistake to assume that all out-of-body experiences are identical. Despite these significant parallels to Monroe's exteriorizations, Muldoon's own dissociations had several distinctive characteristics. First of all, there is no mention of the ring of sparks or inner illumination that Monroe mentioned in his own narrative. Second, Muldoon noticed that his astral counterpart was connected to his physical body by an infinitely elastic cable that attached to the back of the head of his "double" and to the space between the eyes (the so-called third eye referred to in treatises of hatha yoga) of his material body.[22] This astral cord is a common feature in descriptions of out-of-body experiences but it is conspicuously absent in Monroe's accounts.

# The Diversity of Exteriorization Phenomena

These differences that I have just noticed between the out-of-body experiences of Muldoon and Monroe point toward a more general problem that arises when one talks about ex-stasis, namely, the diversity of exteriorization phenomena which appear both in the literature of mysticism and parapsychology. While it is true that a great many exteriorization phenomena involve the simultaneous dissociation of the consciousness-principle (and the perceptual apparatus) and the quasi-material counterpart to the physical body, it also very commonly happens that only the consciousness-principle dissociates without there being any corresponding awareness of a "second" body. This particular type of "asomatic" exteriorization characterized Gopi Krishna's initial illumination for although he sensed that he was slipping out of his body, he states that he did so "without any outline, without any idea of a corporeal appendage."[23] Many instances of traveling clairvoyance or telepathy seem to fall into this category of exteriorization phenomena.[24] Other dissociative phenomena involve the witnessing of one's double or Doppelgänger but in such a way as to imply that the double is communicating to either the physical body or some other dissociated part of one's self. Thus, according to Crookall, one "projector" claimed that he saw "a perfect double of myself. . . . My image stood smiling at me, and in an instant I was up in a corner of the room and could see *both* myself *and* the image in the doorway."[25] Here one seems to observe two dissociated second bodies. Rabbi Nathan, a Kabbalistic writer from around the thirteenth century refers to another kind of Doppelgänger phenomenon in which there was only one second body present but in which it seemed to speak to a consciousness that was still, to some extent,

22. Muldoon and Carrington, *Projection of the Astral Body*, pp. 50–53.
23. Gopi Krishna, *Kundalini*, p. 13; see also Green, *Out-of-the-Body Experiences*, pp. 34–37.
24. Walther, "On the Psychology of Telepathy."
25. Crookall, *Study and Practice of Astral Projection*, p. 35 (emphasis mine).

localized in the physical body. "Know that, for the prophets, the full secret of prophecy is this—that he suddenly sees the form of his own self stand before himself, forgets his self and it (the self) is carried away from him. And then he sees before himself the form of his own self as it speaks with him and proclaims the future to him."[26]

In yet other Doppelgänger phenomena the consciousness appears not to be exteriorized at all but remains resident in the physical body with only the second body exteriorized. Archbishop Frederick once wrote to the famous psychical researcher and physicist Oliver Lodge that he once saw an "apparition . . . of myself, looking interestedly and delightedly at myself. . . . After I and myself had looked at each other for the space of about five seconds, my ghostly self vanished."[27] There is no evidence at all that the archbishop's consciousness was present in his ghostly double. This unconscious kind of double forms a sharp contrast to the "conscious" doubles that Monroe, Muldoon, and others so often describe.

# The Continuum of Exteriorization Phenomena

This last observation brings one to a rather interesting fact. As one can begin to see, there seems to be a sort of continuum of exteriorization phenomena. At the top of the continuum are those out-of-body experiences typified by the accounts of Monroe and Muldoon in which there is a simultaneous exteriorization of the consciousness-principle (and the perceptual apparatus) and the ethereal counterpart of the physical body. At the bottom of the continuum one would place unconscious projections such as that of the Archbishop in which there was no apparent consciousness transferred to the second body at all. Because they occur without awareness of a diaphanous counterpart, "asomatic" exteriorizations would represent a "less fully developed" form of exteriorization than would the "full" out-of-body experiences (represented by Monroe and Muldoon). However, such exteriorizations would still be more fully developed than the "unconscious" projection of Archbishop Frederick. Even further down the continuum than Archbishop Frederick's Doppelgänger would be such exteriorization phenomena as ghosts, poltergeists, or the appearance of

26. Gershom Scholem, "Eine Kabbalistische Deutung der Prophetik als Selbstbegegnung," *Monatsschrift für Geschichte und Wissenschaft des Judentums* 74 (1930), p. 288.
27. Quoted in G. N. M. Tyrrell, *Apparitions* (New York: Collier, 1953), p. 144.

someone's "double" without the sender having been aware that he or she were projecting it.[28] In most cases, ghosts and poltergeists seem to be produced without the sender being aware of their existence or behavior.[29] These last three phenomena rank at the very bottom of this continuum for not only is the exteriorization devoid of any consciousness or personality of its own but the sender is also not even aware that he or she has projected it. A notch above these exteriorizations are the materialization phenomena or ectoplasms that some mediums claim to be able to produce. Although these ectoplasms are not invested with the subject's consciousness-principle, they are at least subject to some extent to the medium's control.

These observations demonstrate the true complexity of exteriorization phenomena. Nevertheless, despite their diversity, I have suggested that these distinctive exteriorization phenomena lie along a continuum. I use this image of the continuum because I want to suggest that these diverse forms of exteriorization phenomena are generated by focusing a common psychical or spiritual energy in different ways. I want to suggest, in other words, that the poltergeist that is emitted without the medium's knowledge of its existence and that also appears to be a blind force without any apparent consciousness of its own is, at least with respect to its energy source, really not all that different from either an insentient ectoplasm extruded by an entranced medium or a fully conscious astral double that clairvoyantly perceives events that are happening at a distance from the sender's physical body. I base this hypothesis on the fact that some mystics and mediums who develop the capacity for full out-of-body experiences also claim that sooner or later they acquired other paranormal abilities such as telepathic sensitivity, the ability to travel clairvoyantly, a sensitivity to auras, automatic writing, the ability to produce telekinetic manifestations.[30] The reverse is also true—that is, a person who first develops a sensitivity to auras or who is a poltergeist medium may later develop an ability to travel out of his or her body.

28. For an example of a case where an individual projected his astral body without being conscious that he was doing so, see Fox, *Astral Projection,* p. 61.

29. An extreme example of such poltergeist manifestations that seem to have had their source in an individual who, at the time they were taking place, had no awareness that he was their cause, can be found in Manning, *The Link,* pp. 25–36.

30. For some examples, see Chapter 9, the section entitled "Paranormal Accompaniments of the Ex-static Mode of Being."

# 9

# *Enthymesis:* The Ex-static Recollective Empowerment of the Mind, Will, and Imagination

## Proximity to the Sacred and the Peculiar Enhancement of the Potency of Thoughts and Desires

Time after time religious texts confront readers with the notion that those who dwell in intimate proximity to the sacred, whether they be divine or human, gain the ability to substitute either their thought or their will for the laws of nature. In other words, willing and thinking become transfigured in such a way that whatever one thinks or wills immediately comes to pass. Thus, in the *Corpus Hermeticum* one reads that "with God, to will is to accomplish, inasmuch as, when he wills, the doing is completed in the self-same moment as the willing."[1] Al-Hujwiri, writing about the miracles of the Sufi saints, gives an analogous example of how living in close proximity to the sacred results in a dramatic empowerment of thought. His own spiritual teacher once told him that it really was not necessary for a spiritual master to visit his pupils in person. It was sufficient for him to simply think about them and he would be in their presence. "To traverse distance is a child's play; henceforth pay visits by means of thought."[2] In a similar vein, when Augustine describes the purely spiritual existence of the saints in heaven, he too mentions that in that blessed state their wills become omnipotent for "wherever the spirit wills, there in a flash will the body be."[3] Yet not only will the saints possess this supernal potency of their volitional powers in Heaven, but they will also have the

1. *Hermetica,* 1:301.
2. ʿAli B. ʿUthmān al-Jullābī al-Hujwīrī, *The Kashf al-Maḥjūb,* trans. Reynold A. Nicholson (London: Luzac & Company, 1976), p. 235.
3. Augustine, *City of God,* p. 541.

ability to read others' thoughts and see clairvoyantly without the need of bodily eyes.[4] Saint Augustine's descriptions of the supernormal powers that those who dwell in Heaven possess bear some surprising resemblances to what Franz Boas had written concerning the powers that Eskimos attributed to their fully illumined shamans. Illumination not only gives the shaman the ability to visit spirit beings and to influence them but it also gives him an omnipotent will. Thus Boas relates that the shaman can kill people by merely willing them dead and that "he can accomplish work by mere wish." Furthermore, like the blessed saints in Augustine's portrayal of Heaven, the Eskimo shaman also has clairvoyant powers and the capability of reading other people's thoughts.[5]

# The Preternatural Enhancement of Thought and Will During Ex-stasis

This radical empowerment of thought and will (as well as a concomitant predilection for other forms of supernormal action and perception) that these examples illustrate does not exist only at the levels of folklore and myth—it also forms an integral part of the experience of ex-stasis. This fact is of cardinal importance for understanding both the nature of mystical experience and its relationship to the paranormal.

Monroe noticed that from time to time during his out-of-body experiences he would visit people while in that state and witness events that actually took place as he described them even though his physical body was not present there.[6] These instances of traveling clairvoyance convinced him that, despite the perceptual distortions and dreamlike atmosphere that characterized most of his out-of-body experiences, these ex-static journeys were not mere hallucinations or subjective fantasies.[7] Nonetheless, he had to concede that these moments when one could supernormally acquire valid information about events in the physical world occurred infrequently. Why was this so? Monroe concluded that the principal barrier to accurate traveling clairvoyance while in the out-of-body state derived from that radical empowerment of the thinking and willing faculties that invari-

4. Ibid., pp. 540, 534–36.
5. Boas, *The Eskimos of Baffin Land and Hudson Bay*, pp. 133–34.
6. Monroe, *Journeys Out of the Body*, pp. 46–48, 55–57.
7. Ibid., p. 31.

ably accompanies exteriorization. He noticed that when one "travels" in
an out-of-body experience, one simply has to "think" of the person or
place at the end of one's destination and one somehow begins to travel
rapidly toward it.[8] However, the directive power of thought is so great that
one's out-of-body navigational system becomes exceedingly sensitive to
subtle changes in one's thoughts or moods. Consequently, it becomes very
difficult to control one's destination.

> [One's] navigational system is too accurate. It works by what and
> whom you think. Let one small thought emerge dormantly for just
> one micro-second, and your course is deviated. Add to this the fact
> that your conscious mind may be in conflict with the super-
> conscious as to what should be that destination, and you can begin
> to appreciate why so many experiments to produce . . . evidential
> data have ended in failure.[9]

For this reason, gathering accurate clairvoyant information requires that
one exercise tight control over one's thoughts. Recollectedness is essential
not only for attaining mystical experience but also for the achievement of
clairvoyance and controlled travel while in the out-of-body state.

But what happens when one's thoughts are not so tightly controlled
during exteriorization? One then finds oneself projected into an experiential domain structured in accordance with one's "concretized" thoughts,
desires, and emotions—both conscious and unconscious.[10]

As one can easily imagine, the radical empowerment of thought and will
that takes place during the time one is engaged in out-of-body travel has
dramatic consequences. For reasons that should be easy to understand in
light of my previous remarks, during ex-stasis one usually does not travel
to locations or persons in the *physical* world (that domain Monroe refers
to as "Locale I"). To be sure, journeys to places or persons in the physical
world of ordinary waking consciousness do occur occasionally such as
when the subject travels clairvoyantly but these types of visitations are
generally infrequent. Instead, most out-of-body experiences take place in
that peculiar experiential domain that Monroe called "Locale II." In contrast to Locale I, Locale II was an experiential realm created when one's

8. Ibid., p. 62.
9. Ibid., p. 63.
10. This "concretization" or objectification of thoughts, desires, and emotions is the phenomenon known as *enthymesis* or "empowerment."

thoughts (and the thoughts of others alive and dead), innermost desires, and emotions immediately concretize and "objectify" themselves.

> Superseding all appears to be one prime law, Locale II is the state of being where that which we label thought is the well-spring of existence. It is the vital creative force that produces energy, assembles "matter" into form, and provides channels of perception and communication. . . . As you think, so you are. . . . No cars, boats, airplanes, or rockets are needed for transportation. You think movement and it is fact. . . . "Mere" thought is the force that supplies any need or desire, and what you think is the matrix of your action, situation, and position in this greater reality.[11]

Even the objects, landscape, and sense of apparent solidity in this environment are nothing more than constructions of objectified thought. Monroe emphasized that what he meant by "thought" must not be interpreted too abstractly as mere ideation. He clearly intended for the term to incorporate—as did the term "recollection"—a synesthetic fusion of intellectual, volitional, and emotional components. "In Locale II, reality is composed of deepest desires and most frantic fears. Thought is action, and no hiding layers of conditioning or inhibition shield the inner you from others [the beings one encounters there], where honesty is the best policy because there is nothing else."[12]

One immediately notices unmistakable structural parallels between Locale II as an experiential domain constructed out of the concretization of one's thoughts and desires and the dream state as a domain that also is formed out of the concretizations and projections of one's unconscious thoughts and desires. To put it somewhat clumsily: during ex-stasis one is consciously experiencing the contents of one's own unconscious (and perhaps that of others). The experience of being in Locale II bears many analogies to that of dreaming while awake—indeed, as one shall see below, controlling the content of one's dreams actually constitutes a technique for going into ex-stasis. The following parallels between Locale II and the dream-state point to an essential continuity between the two phenomena: (1) both the dream realm and Locale II are nonmaterial environments that coexist with and interpenetrate the physical world; (2) the close relationship of the two is suggested by the fact that most out-of-body experiences

11. Monroe, *Journeys Out of the Body*, p. 74.
12. Ibid., p. 77.

occur during the hypnagogic state intermediate between waking and sleeping; and (3) just as Freud considered the structure of dreams to be shaped around the fulfillment of one's deepest wishes, one finds this also to be the case in Locale II.

Monroe was not the only one who referred to this peculiar empowerment of thought and will that occurs in the ex-static mode of being. For example, Robert Crookall's collection of short firsthand descriptions of out-of-body experiences contains several examples.[13] Similarly, Alexandra David-Neel, the intrepid traveler and student of Buddhism, relates that she once met a woman in a remote village of Tibet who claimed that she had traveled outside of her body. When that happened the woman had

> remained inanimate for a whole week. She said that she had been agreeably astonished by the lightness and agility of her new body and the extraordinary rapidity of its movements. She had only to wish herself in a certain place to be there immediately; she could cross rivers, walking upon the waters, or pass through walls. There was only one thing she found impossible—to cut an almost impalpable cord that attached her ethereal being to the material body which she could see perfectly well sleeping upon her couch. This cord lengthened out indefinitely but nevertheless, it sometimes hampered her movements.[14]

One cannot help but notice the same structural continuities in this woman's description of her out-of-body state and those of Monroe and Muldoon. For example, one observes that thought is all-powerful, that she apparently was in a cataleptic state when it occurred, and that her "double" could go through physical objects. She even refers to that infinitely elastic "cord" tying the physical to the ethereal counterpart that Muldoon so often mentioned as a prominent part of his ex-static experiences.[15]

Not surprisingly, Muldoon also commented on the dramatically transformed quality of thought and will in the out-of-body experience. He wondered, for example, how it could happen that the astral doubles of the physical body always seemed to have clothes when one would expect them

13. Crookall, *Study and Practice of Astral Projection*, pp. 30, 38, 44, 96. See also Anonymous, *The Boy Who Saw True* (London: Neville Spearman, 1974), p. 135. In this account a spirit describes the nature of the astral plane to the twelve-year-old author. This book is a record of his diary of childhood paranormal experiences.

14. David-Neel, *Magic and Mystery in Tibet*, p. 29.

15. Muldoon and Carrington, *Projection of the Astral Body*, pp. 76–82.

to be nude. He discovered that the kind of aura or luminosity that emanated from the second body responded immediately to one's thoughts.

> It is my belief that the clothing is formed from the aura. . . . No one need worry about awakening in the astral and being abashed because he is nude, for his aura surrounds him, and no sooner does he begin to think about his clothing than he will discover that his thoughts have already formed or materialized clothing for him. . . . On one occasion, I noticed the clothing forming itself out of the emanation surrounding my astral body when only a few feet out of coincidence.[16]

Like Monroe, he emphasized that the omnipotence of thought and will was not simply a feature of incidental importance but instead fundamental to the entire structure of the out-of-body experience and its environment.

> Everything in the astral plane seems to be governed by thought—by the mind of the projector. As a man thinks, so is he! When I think of trying to convey what this implies, I almost give up in despair and realize how insignificant is my ability to express myself. So I can only say again—as one is in his mind he becomes in reality, when he is in the astral body. If you ever learn to project consciously, you will be amazed at the response which follows your thoughts. . . . It seems almost unbelievable, but the subconscious will can bring about the result before the conscious thought is completed. You may think of going to a friend's house and before you have completed the thought, you are there![17]

Muldoon is careful to add that it is not just the *conscious* thoughts or ideations that concretize themselves into an out-of-body environment. As was the case with Monroe, the deeper, inmost subconscious motivations seem to be the most powerful in this regard, though, with discipline and practice, one's conscious thoughts can just as effectively control the content of these experiences.[18] This is a significant point on which I elaborate below.

16. Ibid., p. 284.
17. Ibid., pp. 286–87.
18. Ibid., pp. 289–90.

# The Empowered Imagination as a
# Source of Objective Knowledge

Both Muldoon and Monroe make it very clear that, despite obvious analogies to dream experience and imagining, it would be wrong to regard the experiential world of the ex-static as though it were a purely subjective affair. Locale II is not always a merely private hallucination or fantasy of omnipotence as so many psychological reductionists might think for there are fairly numerous occasions when the ex-static's thoughts or desires paranormally transcend the boundaries of the purely subjective. The accounts of Muldoon and Monroe provide some fascinating examples of this type of phenomenon where the ordinarily solid boundaries between the subjective and objective domains of experience begin to blur.

One will recall that Monroe once stated that in Locale II thought "is the force that produces energy, assembles 'matter' into form, and provides channels of perception and communication."[19] It would be a serious error to think that this power of thought to produce energy and assemble "matter" into form extends no further than the confines of the subject's private dream experiences. The following example demonstrates, if it be accepted as factual, that the ex-static's transfigured powers of thought and will are capable not only of producing energy and "creating matter" in the realm of dreams but that they can also do so in the physical world as well. Indeed, evidence such as this which pointed to the transsubjective efficacy of thought and will played a crucial role in Monroe's own conversion away from the smug positivism of a comparatively unreligious man who had also been given training in the "hard" sciences. At first Monroe was convinced that his exteriorization experiences were nothing more than private hallucinations, self-hypnotic fantasies, or even schizophrenic delusions. However, when he recognized that they could from time to time take on a transsubjective significance, he began to challenge the premises of that psychologism which, up until that time, he had accepted uncritically.

One day Monroe decided to try an experiment in which he attempted to visit a close friend of his by the name of "R.W.," who was vacationing at a location on the New Jersey coast unknown to him. He then lay down on his bed, "went into a relaxation pattern, felt the warmth (high order vibrations), then thought heavily of the desire to 'go' to R.W." Monroe then found himself exteriorized in her presence. She was sitting down with two

19. Monroe, *Journeys Out of the Body*, p. 74.

teenage girls talking and drinking something. Since he wanted to ensure that R.W. would remember his visit, he reached over to her while in the second body and pinched her. He noticed that she immediately let out a yell when that happened. Monroe then returned to his physical body and ended the experiment. A few days later, when she had returned from her trip, he queried her about what she had been doing at the time of his exteriorization. She acknowledged that she had been sitting with two teenage girls, thus confirming Monroe's description of them drinking soft drinks and talking. However, R.W. mentioned nothing about the pinch. Monroe then asked her if she were sure that nothing else had happened during her conversation with the two girls. She again said that nothing remarkable had occurred. Exasperated at her failure to remember the astral pinch he had given her, Monroe then asked her, "Don't you remember being pinched?"[20] R.W. then looked at Monroe, astonished. "Was that you?" she asked. She then went to Monroe's office and showed him the two bluish bruise marks that were located at exactly the place on her body where he had pinched her while exteriorized.[21]

This out-of-body experiment presents one with a fascinating example of the phenomenon of traveling clairvoyance simultaneously occurring with telekinesis (the ability to alter the state of matter at a distance without physically touching it). It also serves as an excellent illustration of how thought really does serve as "the force that produces energy, assembles matter into form, and provides channels of perception and communication" while one is exteriorized.[22]

First, this experience shows that the concretization of thoughts that occurs as a result of empowerment is not always merely subjective. In Monroe's example an empowered thought and volition had objective effects in the physical world that could be verified by someone other than Monroe. Consequently, this example indicates that ex-stasis is a condition that is capable of causing thoughts and desires to become objectified and concretized not only subjectively but also objectively.

Second, this experiment with R.W. shows that ex-static empowerment transfigures thoughts and desires in other ways. It makes thought "serve as a channel of perception and communication."[23] What exactly does this

20. This amnesia bears interesting resemblances to the amnesia that frequently occurs during hypnotic trances.
21. Monroe, *Journeys Out of the Body*, pp. 55–57.
22. Ibid., p. 74.
23. Ibid.

mean? It means that an empowered thought or desire acts as a sense organ capable of gaining information. For example, all Monroe had to do when he wanted to find R.W. at a location unknown to him was to get into the mental state preparatory to projection and then "think" about visiting her. This act of thought and desire, apparently all by itself, accomplished two things simultaneously. It projected him into her presence and revealed her location to him even though Monroe claimed that he had no way of knowing where she had been staying. Somehow, merely thinking about where she might be triggered a process of information gathering. This information-gathering activity of Monroe's empowered thoughts and desires accurately determined both her location and the kinds of activities she and her friends were performing for he not only arrived at where she was but once there he was also able to discern accurately what R.W. and her friends were doing at the time of his astral visit.

Third, empowered thought provided "force that produces energy" insofar as it somehow provided the energy that transported Monroe to where R.W. was and allowed him to gather clairvoyant information while he was there. To use the terminology of physics, ex-statically empowered thought has the capacity to do work that "mere" thought never possesses.

Fourth, insofar as thought "assembles matter into form," it is quite obvious that Monroe's empowered thought about pinching R.W. actually became instrumental in altering the condition of her physical body. Mere thought never has the ability to alter the state of matter outside a person's own physical body.

This example shows that it is a serious mistake to imagine that ex-static empowerment only operates on the individual's mind, emotions, and imagination in a purely subjective way. The empowered imagination does indeed construct the "objects" within that visionary landscape Monroe called Locale II, but that is not all. Examples of this sort—and, as one will soon see, this example is by no means a unique instance of the empowered imagination having an objective impact—show that the boundaries between a person's subjective universe and the objective world of physical reality that we ordinarily take for granted as being sharp, rigid, and unbridgeable are really quite fluid. Sense-experience teaches us that this boundary is sharp. However, under certain exceptional conditions (especially apt to occur during ex-stasis or mystical illumination), what an individual concocts in his or her imagination can sometimes become immediately experienced as an objective datum perceptible to others. Under those circumstances, the boundaries between real and imaginary begin to dissolve in a most peculiar way. It is in this sense that one may speak of the empowered imagination as possessing a trans-subjective efficacy.

To summarize, I have noticed that in ex-stasis thought and will become transformed in the following ways:

1. At the level of purely subjective experience, thought and will immediately concretize themselves so that these exteriorizations of thought and will furnish the total context of one's subjective experience during ex-stasis.
2. Occasionally, these thoughts concretize themselves trans-subjectively, that is to say, one's thoughts and desires may objectify themselves so that others experience them as though they were "real" elements of their physical environments.
3. What one thinks and wills can, in a mysterious fashion, serve as a channel of paranormal perception and communication as well as the energizing impulse that is capable of directing the "second" body or consciousness to the object of its desires. In other words, the thought "I want to see X," when one makes it in an ex-static mode of consciousness, is occasionally capable of somehow conveying the subject to X, establishing a paranormal perceptual link between the subject and X, and setting up a paranormal means of communication between the two locales and persons.

# Paranormal Accompaniments of the Ex-static Mode of Being

Like the mystics whom I have discussed in Chapter 8 Monroe reported other supernormal concomitants besides the clairvoyance and telekinesis that accompanied his ability to travel outside of his body. For example, he noticed that he possessed a supernormal enhancement of his perceptual faculties. Ex-static sight was something quite different from physical sight despite superficial similarities. "It isn't physical "seeing" at all. You learn that you can "see" in all directions at once, without turning the head, that you see or don't see according to the thought, and that when examined objectively, it is more an impression of radiation than a reflection of light waves."[24] Much the same is true of ex-static hearing. Touch, however, remains closely analogous to its physical counterpart with the exception, of course, that one's "astral" limbs and body can go through matter without hindrance.

In the course of his out-of-body travels, Monroe also manifested a faculty akin to telepathy. This "new means of sensory input" involved the capacity to recognize people, not by the way they looked but rather

> through an undisguised awareness of their prime personality habits and thoughts. This is most remarkable because it seems infallible, with the innermost self appearing to radiate patterns, much as the composition of a star . . . can be analyzed by its spectrograph. I suspect that such emanations cannot be shut off by the individual, so there can be no covering over of the inner self to hide it from view.[25]

This new telepathy-like faculty seems inseparably linked to the proclivity of the ex-static imagination to objectify one's innermost desires and thoughts. Consequently, when one is exteriorized, one not only creates a subjectively experienced realm of one's own concretized thoughts and desires but also encounters the objectifications created by the thoughts and desires of other people. One can then translate these objectifications back into the particular thoughts and wishes to which each objectification corresponds. This capacity bears comparison with Augustine's description of Heaven when the thoughts of the saints not only carry their bodies instantaneously to where they wish to go but also where the saints also have the concomitant ability to penetrate beneath disguises and read the thoughts of others.[26]

Monroe sometimes manifested another supernormal sensibility, precognition. Unlike traveling clairvoyance or the ability to affect matter at a distance, these precognitive manifestations occurred in a way that was completely independent of his willing and thinking processes. These episodes of precognition only took place in a condition of relaxation when Monroe's mind was stilled. Once his mind had achieved recollectedness, he was primed to receive the precognitive vision though its appearance was

24. Ibid., p. 184. See Chapter 8 for a similar example of extra-ocular vision taken from the famous legend of Muhammad's mi'rāj or Night Journey; see also Eliade, From Primitives to Zen, pp. 518–20, for quote.

25. Monroe, Journeys Out of the Body, p. 184.

26. Augustine of Hippo, The City of God, trans. Gerald G. Walsh et al. (Garden City, N.Y.: Image Books, 1958), book 22, chaps. 29–30, pp. 540–41.

completely beyond his ability to control. When a precognitive vision did appear, Monroe would first experience a hissing sound in the forebrain and then have the sensation of a door opening up behind which was a scene where some event was taking place. He would then find himself looking at an event just as though he were dreaming, only this viewing of the precognitive vision would take place while he was fully awake. The precognitive vision "would be superimposed directly over outside stimuli. I could perceive both quite readily."[27]

It is significant that Monroe drew an analogy between these precognitive visions and dreams. His need to draw such a parallel suggests that there might be essential continuities between dream processes and precognition.[28] Indeed, Monroe admitted that at first he could not recognize that these precognitive visions were any different than dreams. It was only after one of these dreams came true that he recognized their precognitive character. Aside from this, these visionary "openings" were much like any other dream experience, for those same processes of symbolic distortion that operate in ordinary dreaming were also present in the visionary manifestations. When one examines the following supposedly precognitive vision, one observes how what actually happened became distorted just as though it were a dream.

The experience began when Monroe saw the little door swing open along with the hissing noise in the forebrain, exposing a dream scene in which he was in the process of boarding an airplane. He noticed his friend "D.D." boarding the plane, and a woman in front of him was very nervous and agitated. The plane took off but didn't seem to gain altitude properly, flying low over streets with cloverleafs as though it were following a freeway. The stewardess rather nervously told the passengers that the plane was going to follow the "under the wire" route. He noticed the plane flying between numerous high-tension wires toward a clearing in the sky. The plane suddenly dropped, hit the street, threw him out, bounced again, and crashed. A few weeks after this dream, Monroe noticed that as he was getting on a bus to go from New York to the Newark airport for a flight to North Carolina, a man got aboard the bus who bore a striking

27. Monroe, *Journeys Out of the Body*, p. 145.
28. J. W. Dunne, *An Experiment with Time* (London: Faber & Faber, 1973), proposed the interesting theory, based on both his own dream experiences and those of others, that dreams contain not only imagery that symbolically recapitulates the events or desires one had prior to the dream itself but that they also contain symbolically disguised material that pertain to coming events. According to this theory, dreams not only contain retrocognitive elements but also precognitive elements.

resemblance to his friend D.D. Similarly, he noticed an agitated woman in a seat in front of him who was angry over a baggage mix-up. As the bus drove along the freeway toward the airport he noticed that the bus kept going under high-tension wires. In other words, it was not a plane that went under the wires over a freeway but the bus going to the plane that went over the freeway and under the wires. The precognitive vision was thus distorting factuality much like a dream. When he boarded the plane it did indeed fly low through a thunderstorm (the idea of flying the "under the wire" route) and emerged into a clearing but it did not crash. What did happen four days later was that Monroe suffered a heart attack.[29] This apparently was what the "crash" in the precognitive vision referred to in a distorted fashion. Comparing the two accounts one can see how the precognitive vision actually distorted the future events in much the same manner as Freud noticed that the manifest content of a dream represents a distortion of its latent content, the dream's supposedly "true" message. This parallelism between dreams and precognitive vision fortifies my earlier suggestion that there might be profound continuities between this extraordinary paranormal manifestation and the very ordinary processes that are at work during sleep.

With the exception of telepathy, the close connection between ex-stasis and paranormal phenomena also comes forth with remarkable clarity in Muldoon's autobiography. The linkage between ex-stasis and clairvoyance seemed particularly obvious to him. Indeed, in his opinion ex-stasis was an essential prerequisite for clairvoyance. In a letter to his literary collaborator, Hereward Carrington, Muldoon wrote:

> You have asked . . . if I have ever seen anything while in the astral which I did not know existed, and later verified by seeing it in the physical. Certainly! This is nothing unusual to do, while consciously projected. I have often gone into houses, and noted things—later going there in the physical and seeing everything as I saw it in the astral. . . . *But when in coincidence I have never had a clairvoyant vision in my life—not one.*[30]

Not only did ex-stasis awaken Muldoon's otherwise dormant clairvoyant faculties from time to time but, as was the case with Monroe, Muldoon also observed that during his out-of-body journeys the ex-static analogs to

---

29. Monroe, *Journeys Out of the Body*, pp. 146–51.
30. Muldoon and Carrington, *Projection of the Astral Body*, p. 39 (emphasis mine).

the physical senses underwent a subtle but profound transformation. Like Monroe, he too noted that "during astral projection the subject may see out of different parts of his astral body, that is, he may lie on his back in the air and see what is taking place below him—while looking in the opposite direction with his eyes!"[31] At other times—this is not mentioned in Monroe's account—and only when his exteriorized body was nearly in coincidence to his physical body, Muldoon noted that he sometimes had the capacity to simultaneously see his physical body from both the perspective of his astral counterpart and to see his astral body from the perspective of his physical eyes.[32]

One of the more unusual, though infrequent, abilities that Monroe and Muldoon each manifested was that of telekinesis. In Monroe's case, the ability to affect matter was unequivocally linked to his exteriorizations since it was only when his astral body had pinched his friend R.W. that her body was actually affected. Muldoon, however, recorded several instances in which he affected objects by dreaming about them without there being any unmistakable evidence that his second body was present where the object was situated. He once started a metronome ticking merely by dreaming he was standing next to it—not even touching it. He then awoke from the dream immediately. Two seconds later the metronome began to tick. A few nights later this same set of events repeated itself.[33] During another dream incident, what Muldoon acted out in the dream actually came to pass just as he dreamed he was doing it. What is even more surprising is that it continued even after he had awakened. He was in the process of having a dream when he suddenly became conscious that he was doing so. At the time he was dreaming that he was in his backyard by an old oil drum. He took (in his dream) a large monkey wrench and began to bang on the oil drum. The noise of the blows quickly woke him up from his dream. However, he and his neighbors continued to hear the noise even though no one was seen outside.[34] Muldoon did record, however, an instance of telekinesis that definitely seems to have occurred as a result of action committed by his second body.

Once when he was in great pain from a stomach ailment Muldoon awoke in agony and tried to summon his mother from the other room but could not wake her. When he attempted to get up and walk to her he

31. Ibid., p. 203.
32. Ibid., p. 106.
33. Ibid., pp. 40–41.
34. Ibid., p. 275.

fainted from the pain, got up, and then collapsed a second time. As he struggled to get up again he suddenly found himself exteriorized in her room. There he saw both his mother and his little brother sleeping on a bed. He then became unconscious for a moment, awoke from his momentary amnesia and discovered that his mother was standing on the floor and his brother almost off the bed with both of them speaking in astonishment about how the mattress had lifted up and thrown them out of bed. Muldoon then went back into his physical body that was lying on the floor beside his own bed where he had fainted. He was then able to summon his mother successfully. When she arrived, she was too excited to notice that he was on the floor; she began to tell him animatedly about how spirits had lifted both of them out of her bed.[35]

Much like Monroe, Muldoon exhibited frequent tendencies for precognitive experiences. Again in a manner similar to Monroe, Muldoon also observed that precognitive manifestations, unlike telekinetic phenomena or traveling clairvoyance, were not at all subject to direction or control from the subject's thinking or willing faculties.[36] Muldoon's precognitive experiences differed from those of Monroe in two respects, however. First, though the experiences would take place as if he were dreaming, Muldoon noticed that he was out of his body at the time the precognitive dream was occurring. Monroe, on the other hand, specifically mentioned that the precognitive visions he had did not occur while he was in an ex-static condition but instead took place in that state of recollective relaxation and quiet that immediately precedes exteriorization.[37] Second, Muldoon never experienced the hissing noises, perceptions of a door opening, or peculiar sensations in the forehead that enabled Monroe to distinguish his precognitive visions from ordinary dreams. In contrast, Muldoon noted that his precognitive dreams were indistinguishable from other dream experiences he had while exteriorized except that events occurred in them that later actually took place.[38]

Just as Monroe and Muldoon manifested a wide range of paranormal abilities in addition to their penchant for out-of-body travel, one finds that specialists in other kinds of paranormal manifestations likewise tend to exhibit their paranormal capacities in a wide range of areas. In other words, it is generally the case—though by no means always—that if some-

35. Ibid., pp. 273–74.
36. Ibid., p. 301.
37. Monroe, *Journeys Out of the Body*, p. 145.
38. Ibid., pp. 300–301.

one manifests a special gift, an inclination toward clairvoyance, for instance, that person will also have at least an occasional predilection for one or more of the following supernormal phenomena: out-of-body travel, telepathy, precognition, poltergeist mediumship, automatic writing, an ability to see auras, or an ability to see by means other than physical sight.

Eileen Garrett exemplified this tendency of many mystics and mediums to develop paranormal sensitivities in a variety of areas, for she not only exhibited clairvoyant and mediumistic gifts but also claimed that she was able to "see" diaphanous spirit-beings, to perceive auras, to put herself into telepathic rapport with people, and to sense future events precognitively.[39] Like Muhammad seeing through the "heart" rather than through the eyes during his ascension to Allah's throne,[40] and like Muldoon's and Monroe's descriptions of how their senses underwent a peculiar metamorphosis during ex-stasis,[41] Garrett described a rather similar expansion of her sensory faculties. "Difficult as it may be to accept, the fact is that I found myself *seeing* more easily and clearly through my fingertips and the nape of my neck than through my eyes; and *hearing* and *knowing*, for instance, came through my feet and knees."[42] Garrett also mentioned that she was occasionally subject to out-of-body projections.[43] In this regard, it is not surprising to discover that, despite the tangential nature of her references to these exteriorization episodes, she seems to have been aware of something analogous to that process whereby thoughts become concretized and objectified for she noted at one point that she began "to feel and sense the thoughts of people as forms of light that moved to their destinies impacting and dissipating according to their natures and the force with which they had been projected. I came to know that thoughts are dimensional things which become clothed with form and life as they are born."[44]

One can see this same aptitude for different kinds of paranormal manifestations in Justinius Kerner's famous biography of the early-nineteenth-century spirit-seer, Frederika Hauffe, more familiarly known as the Seeress of Prevorst. The Seeress was most renowned for her capacity to see spirits and the clairvoyance that she demonstrated on numerous occasions. In

39. Garrett, *Adventures in the Supernormal*, pp. 9–10, 18–19, 189–91, 194–98.
40. See Eliade, *From Primitives to Zen*, p. 518.
41. See Monroe, *Journeys*, p. 184; and Muldoon, *The Projection of the Astral Body*, p. 203.
42. Garrett, *Adventures in the Supernormal*, pp. 90–91.
43. Ibid., pp. 22, 87.
44. Ibid., pp. 86–87.

addition to these abilities, at certain times she was also able to act as a poltergeist medium, establish telepathic contact with other people, and obtain information about future events.[45] Kerner also documented what I have observed in Muldoon, Monroe, and Garrett concerning the kind of perceptual transformation that takes place during ex-stasis and deep trance-states for he asserted that the Seeress was capable of reading the contents of a sealed envelope by sensing its contents not with her eyes but through the pit of her stomach.[46] At other times, "she frequently had no feeling or consciousness of existence, except at the pit of her stomach; she seemed to herself as if she had neither head, hands, nor feet. At these times she perceived everything with closed eyes; but she could not tell whether she saw objects or felt them."[47] Moreover, during states of perfect clairvoyant vigilance, she maintained that her thoughts came not from her own mind or imagination but instead "wholly from the spirit and the epigastric region."[48]

From these descriptions it is evident that, like numerous mystics and ex-statics, the Seeress possessed a faculty for paranormal perception that was analogous to but not identical to sense perception. And not surprisingly, one finds that she was subject to frequent out-of-body episodes. Kerner mentions that, like other persons who have had the faculty of seeing spirits, "she was frequently in that state in which persons . . . perceive their own spirit out of their body, which enfolds it as a thin gauze. She often saw herself out of her body, and sometimes double."[49] Although the Seeress did not herself refer explicitly to being in possession of this peculiar empowerment of thought that is so often characteristic of the ex-static condition, she did mention that spirit-beings depend upon the objectification of thoughts when they try to communicate with the living. Once she asked a poltergeist if it heard other people speaking. The spirit told her, "I hear them through you. When you hear others, you think what they speak, and I read your thoughts."[50] From this example, it is clear that the objectification of thoughts constitutes a significant feature of the existential landscape of disembodied spirits.

The contemporary poltergeist medium Matthew Manning recorded a

45. See Justinius Kerner, *The Seeress of Prevorst,* trans. Mrs. [Catherine] Crowe (London: J. C. Moore, 1845), pp. 45, 84–86, 97–99, 252–53.
46. Kerner, *The Seeress of Prevorst,* pp. 75–76.
47. Ibid., p. 97.
48. Ibid., p. 108.
49. Ibid., pp. 57–58.
50. Ibid., p. 201.

similar clustering of paranormal aptitudes that accompanied his remarkable gift for serving as an intermediary for a wide range of telekinetic phenomena and luminous manifestations. For example, Manning found it easy to induce an out-of-body experience.[51] He later discovered that he possessed an exceptional talent for automatic writing and that the poltergeist manifestations would decline in severity and frequency the more he focused his energies in the direction of automatic writing.[52] Manning also noticed another interesting phenomenon—if he learned to get himself into that peculiar state just preparatory to automatic writing without actually engaging in it, he would suddenly find that he could see auras around people.[53] As a result of this paranormal perceptual faculty, he claimed that he could tell by the color and texture of a person's aura what kind of a personality they possessed and from what, if any, illness they suffered.

These examples should suffice to demonstrate that just as a propensity toward mystical experiences very frequently (though not invariably) awakens a wide variety of hitherto dormant supernormal faculties, a tendency to manifest ex-static experiences produces the same result. As noted in Chapter 8, the biographies of ex-statics and mystics are replete with descriptions of paranormal powers attributed to them, which suggests that the mystical experience very often (although once again, not invariably) incorporates the ex-static mode of being. Consequently, it is clear that without a full understanding of how an ex-static condition can induce paranormal phenomena, one can never hope to comprehend fully the supernormal dimension of mysticism. These facts also suggest that the different paranormal powers and sensitivities that are ready to rise to the surface during the conditions of ex-stasis and mystical consciousness become manifest in accordance with subtle shifts in the way that the mystic or medium directs the focus of his or her attention.[54]

51. Manning, *The Link,* p. 66.

52. Ibid., p. 77. Manning noticed that although he was the agent responsible for producing poltergeists, he was not aware, at the time that they were actually happening that he was in the process of generating them. They seemed to emanate from him unconsciously. Poltergeist manifestations appear to be an unconscious form of exteriorization in contrast to the conscious exteriorizations of Monroe (*Journeys Out of the Body*) and Muldoon and Carrington (*Projection of the Astral Body*).

53. Ibid., p. 78.

54. Recall that Manning's ability to see auras required only a very subtle shift in the direction of his attention from what would otherwise have been an ability to exhibit automatic writing. He had to get himself into that peculiar state that immediately preceded the onset of automatic writing but not go into that state. The ability to see auras then developed (see Manning, *The Link,* pp. 77–78). Monroe's precognitive sensitivity only became manifest

# Techniques for Empowering Thought, Will, and Imagination

## Recollection Is the Key to the Empowerment of Thought, Will, and Imagination

One of the things so difficult to understand about mystical experience and the ex-static mode of being is that both conditions seem to defy the canons of common sense. For example, we know that in everyday life our thoughts and desires have no capacity to immediately actualize themselves as they do when one is having an out-of-body experience. Thus, even though I may *think* about moving an object from one side of the room to the other, that object will remain completely unaffected by my thoughts or wishes. Similarly, I may wish that I were in the presence of a distant friend but unless I hop on the bus or get in a car and go there that desire will never come to pass. However, as I demonstrated above, many mystics and ex-statics claim that sometimes during ex-stasis or illumination those same thoughts, desires, and imaginings that in everyday life possess absolutely no ability to objectify themselves suddenly begin to exhibit a peculiar kind of power to concretize themselves not only subjectively but, at times, even objectively. What factors seem to be responsible for effecting this sudden transformation?

Recollection serves as the principal means for bringing about that empowerment of thought, will, and imagination that (1) constitutes one of the fundamental characteristics of ex-static experience and (2) also functions as one of the prerequisites for the exercise of many paranormal

---

if he got himself into that state of consciousness that immediately preceded exteriorization but did not actually go to the next step and allow himself to exteriorize (Monroe, *Journeys,* p. 145). The famous medium Eileen Garrett noted that telepathic sensitivity, clairvoyance, and clairaudience "almost undoubtedly are varying manifestations of the same function" (Garrett, *Telepathy,* p. 13). Finally, one will also recall that only the most subtle shifts of attention during the dream state or hypnagogic state are necessary to manifest very different types of consciousness. If one enters either the dream-state or hypnagogic state and then succumbs to the lure of the dream images, one lapses into ordinary dream consciousness. On the other hand, if one enters those conditions and refuses to allow one's attention to be distracted by the lure of dream images, then it is possible to enter modes of consciousness where exteriorization is possible and the empowerment of the imagination takes place. In this state of empowerment, the imagination can sometimes function as an extraphysical organ of perception and knowledge, something impossible during ordinary dreaming (see Chapters 9 and 15).

powers of perception and action. This fact should not occasion any surprise for one will remember that in Chapter 5 I observed that mystics were almost unanimous in claiming that a person can only transcend the experiential and perceptual limitations of corporeal sense-experience if he learns to shut out sensory distractions and anxieties, stops the incessant internal chattering of his mind and imagination, and masters the ability to one-pointedly focus his mind, will, imagination, and emotions on achieving whatever object or goal his particular religious tradition considers to be the consummation of what is spiritually perfect. One will recall that in Chapter 5 I observed that mystics often mentioned that when an individual has finally mastered recollective techniques, he concomitantly awakens otherwise dormant capacities for exercising supernormal powers of perception and action. The accounts of ex-statics, clairvoyants, and mediums make it clear that recollection plays a role in their lives analogous to the one which it plays in the lives of mystics. In other words, (1) recollection is the chief means for both attaining the condition of ex-stasis and the concomitant empowerment of thought, will, and imagination that accompanies it and (2) recollection is the chief means for acquiring and perfecting supernormal powers.

## Monroe's Technique of Progressive Relaxation

If one looks at the progressive relaxation techniques that Monroe used to induce his out-of-body experiences, one will see that the practice of recollection furnished him with his chief method for attaining both dissociation from the physical body and the empowerment of his thought and will. Every step in his dissociative technique emphasizes the cardinal importance of one-pointedly concentrating the mind, keeping a tightly focused control over one's thought processes and emotional states, and studiously avoiding any distraction from petty anxieties and sense-impressions. Consequently, Monroe counsels that when one prepares to project he must be utterly relaxed—both mentally and physically—otherwise the experiment will fail. To ensure this relaxation he continues, "No pending appointments or anticipated calls for your services or attention must clutter up your thoughts."[55] Monroe further elaborates on the techniques necessary to bring about that progressive mental and physical relaxation necessary for projection and repeatedly stresses the importance of a tightly focused con-

55. Monroe, *Journeys Out of the Body*, p. 207.

centration. The first stage of this process, or what Monroe called Condition A, consisted of the effort to maintain consciousness while suspended in the hypnagogic state, that transitional condition between waking and sleeping. This, of course, required a high degree of mental and physical self-control; otherwise, it was extremely easy simply to fall asleep. To get into Condition A, it was necessary to lie down as though one were going to sleep. As the individual begins to sink into sleep, he or she must focus attention on something. The ability to stay indefinitely in this borderline state between sleeping and waking without actually going to sleep, with one's eyes closed and attention tightly focused on some object, person, or event, indicates that the individual has moved beyond Condition A into Condition B. The second stage of the dissociation process, Condition B, supervenes when the individual no longer feels the tension of concentration and lets go of the image on which he or she had fixated attention in Condition A and simply stares at the blackness in front of him. At this stage, hallucinatory phenomena of various sorts may develop but if the would-be projector is not distracted or disturbed by them they eventually fade away and he or she sees nothing except darkness in front of the eyes. Condition C begins when the would-be projector tries to "deepen" consciousness while in Condition B. By deepening consciousness, Monroe meant that the individual gradually moved from the hypnagogic borderland into the sleep-state while still maintaining conscious awareness. In this deepening of consciousness, the individual learns to maintain conscious awareness while deliberately cutting off, first, the sensation of touch, then the sensations of taste, smell, hearing, and sight in that order.[56] It is evident that Monroe is advocating one of the most important recollective methods, abstracting oneself from sensory inputs and distractions. This kind of mentally induced anesthesia of the corporeal senses eventually brings about a transformation in the individual's mode of consciousness just as it does every night when we cut off awareness of sensory inputs as we go to sleep and then shortly afterward begin to go into the mode of consciousness known as dreaming.[57] Condition D takes place when the

56. Ibid., pp. 208–9.
57. In this context, it is very interesting to note that there are numerous reports of out-of-body experiences that have been induced as a result of medical anesthesia (see Crookall, *Study and Practice of Astral Projection,* pp. 118–31, for examples). It seems that by chemically cutting off sensory inputs, anesthesia imitates those processes of sensory deprivation that occur every night as we drop off to sleep and that also are a result of the recollective

aspiring projector achieves Condition C, not while sleeping or tired but instead when fully awake and refreshed. Monroe remarks that this latter qualification is important for "to enter the relaxation state full of energy and wakefulness is greater insurance for maintaining conscious control" over the content of the resulting experience.[58] Without it the dreamlike experiences that follow successful completion of his relaxation and recollection techniques become chaotic and no longer subject to conscious control just as do our ordinary dream experiences.

The achievement of Condition D does not yet bring about dissociation. For that condition to occur Monroe believed that it was necessary to go further and induce the state of "vibration" referred to in earlier descriptions of his out-of-body experiences. Once again, Monroe stresses that maintaining concentration and tight control over one's will and thought processes is all-important. One must constantly endeavor to go as deeply into the sleep-state as possible and yet not fall asleep. This requires an extraordinary power of self-control and concentration. In order for dissociation to take place, it is necessary for the individual to "descend" to Condition D while remaining deeply relaxed yet completely alert. Then he must begin breathing rhythmically through the mouth, concentrating on the blackness in front of his eyes. Monroe continues by telling the would-be projector to stare fixedly at an imaginary spot in the blackness a foot away from his forehead, then progressively shift that imaginary spot away from his forehead to a distance of three, then six, feet all the while staring intently at it. After his attention has been tightly fixed on the spot six feet in front of his forehead, the projector should then turn that spot ninety degrees upward so that it is parallel to the spine. He should then "reach for the vibrations at that spot" directly above his head. This purely imaginary visualization exercise and "pulling up" movement eventually has profound consequences somewhat akin to those that happened when Gopi Krishna first aroused kundalini by means of mental concentration exercises and "visualization" techniques.[59] If the aspiring projector "reaches" for the vibrations in his imagination (provided that he is in the deep state of relaxation and concentration that corresponds to Condition D), he will

---

techniques that mystics and ex-statics use to shut out distractions from the sensory world. The result in each case is similar—the individual finds that he has entered into a domain of experience and consciousness that is radically different from that of the waking state.

58. Monroe, *Journeys Out of the Body*, p. 209.
59. Gopi Krishna, *Kundalini*, pp. 12–13.

eventually get a reaction and enter a radically new domain of experience and consciousness. Referring to the reaction, Monroe states it is unmistakable when it occurs. A "surging, hissing" noise is heard as a rhythmic wave of sparks rushes into the head and then periodically up and down the body. The wave of sparks—accompanied by the hissing noise— engulfs the entire body and paralyzes it. One finds oneself in a condition of catalepsy with the body unable to respond to any desire for movement.[60] This is the stage of "vibrations" and "astral" catalepsy. At first these vibratory pulsations seem very rough and unpleasant. Monroe claimed that if dissociation were to occur it was necessary to "smooth down" these oscillations, increasing their frequency by mentally pulsing the oscillations of the ring of sparks that seems to surround the axis of the body and that go up and down periodically from the feet to the top of the head. The more rapidly these oscillations occur the "smoother" the vibrations become. Once this smooth state of vibrations has been achieved, exteriorization of the second body and consciousness becomes possible.

To summarize Monroe: If an individual focuses his mind and will one-pointedly on the task of falling into the sleep-state without losing his conscious awareness, he eventually enters into a state of profound sensory deprivation (for example, he loses his senses of touch and hearing). By maintaining conscious awareness and full concentration despite going deeper and deeper into the sleep-state, the individual's recollective efforts finally lead him into the vibrational state. By smoothing out the oscillations, he has achieved both a radically new mode of consciousness and a radically new mode of being since he is now in a condition in which his thought, his will, and his imagination have become "empowered." In other words, the data just presented suggests that this empowerment or "dynamization" of thought, will, and imagination actually precedes exteriorization rather than being its result.

Proof of the foregoing assertion is simple because the last stage of the exteriorization process assumes that this dynamization of thought and desires is already present (in tandem, of course, with a tight control over one's thoughts). Monroe affirms that once an individual has brought about the smoothed-out vibrational state, his thoughts suddenly gain the capacity to concretize themselves and completely structure the content of experience. For this reason, Monroe counsels that it is absolutely essential that one keep a very tight control over one's thoughts because "in the state

---

60. Monroe, *Journeys Out of the Body*, pp. 211–13.

of vibration, you are apparently subject to every thought, both willful and involuntary that crosses your mind. Thus you must be as close to 'no thought' or 'single thought' (concentration) as possible. If one stray thought passes through your mind you respond instantly, and sometimes in an undesirable manner."[61] It is this very same empowerment of thought that permits exteriorization to take place, for one achieves association by imagining and desiring to float upward. These thoughts and desires of floating then immediately concretize themselves in the form of an out-of-body experience, indicating that this empowerment of the thoughts and desires has already occurred. Therefore, Monroe instructs the reader that if he wishes to experiment in dissociation he must

> achieve the vibrational state and *maintain complete control* of your thought processes. . . . *Think* of getting lighter, of floating upward, of how nice it would be to float upward. Be sure to think how nice it would be as the subjective associated thought is most important. . . . *If you continue to hold only those thoughts,* you will dissociate and float up gently from your physical.[62]

This passage makes two important assertions: (1) that the empowerment of thought is a prerequisite for exteriorization and (2) that complete control over one's thoughts is not only a prerequisite for achieving those relaxation and vibrational states that precede projection but maintaining this control *continues* to be necessary even *after* the dynamization of thought, will, and imagination has taken place. Failure to maintain this recollectedness in the vibrational state will result in dreamlike experiences that will escape conscious control.

## The Two Major Functions of Recollection in the Mystical Life

In Chapter 5 I noted two things about recollection that are directly relevant to the present discussion. First, I noted that recollection serves as the means for achieving that initial breakthrough to that new realm of experience and consciousness that forms such a fundamental feature of the mystical experience. Second, I also noticed that recollection was still necessary

61. Ibid., p. 216.
62. Ibid., pp. 219–20 (last emphasis mine).

even after the mystic made his initial breakthrough into a new mode of consciousness, for if he wished to achieve more elevated spiritual states, he had to continue maintaining recollectedness in order to avoid being distracted or fascinated by the supernormal phenomena that so frequently result from successfully mastering techniques of mental and emotional concentration.

This same two-fold function of recollection also applies to ex-static experience as well. Recollection permits one to obtain an initial access to those deep states of relaxation and empowerment of thoughts and desires that serve as the preliminary condition for out-of-body experience. Recollection is still necessary even after these states are achieved because once thoughts and desires become invested with this dynamic power they need to be tightly focused and directed or else they will escape the subject's conscious control and project him into a chaotic, hallucinatory landscape of his objectified thoughts, desires, and imaginings. In both mystical experience and ex-static experience the function of recollection remains essentially the same: (1) it serves as the means for giving the subject his first contact with those domains of experience that lie beyond the reach of the five senses and (2) once this initial contact has taken place it ensures that the subject continues to shape and control the content of those experiences that follow in the wake of his first encounter with those realms beyond the five senses.

## Muldoon's Exteriorization Techniques

Muldoon's descriptions of the principal technique he used to bring about exteriorization illustrate the pivotal roles that recollection and the maintenance of conscious awareness during the dream state play in causing it. His method was similar to Monroe's insofar as he claimed that the easiest method for bringing about projection involved making the subject stay conscious while going into the hypnagogic state and then to continue that conscious awareness even as he drifted into the sleep-state. Muldoon's method emphasized the importance of constructing a dream in which the subject was rising or floating as he went into the sleep-state. For example, he suggested that constructing a dream about going up in an elevator and getting off at the top floor would be an excellent means of achieving exteriorization. If an individual could successfully control the content of such a dream *and* stay "awake" when the dream events were happening, he would discover that at that moment in the dream when he was stepping out of the elevator he would see that his incorporeal counterpart would be dissociating from the physical body. Thus Muldoon counsels the would-be projector:

> Have the dream vividly worked out in your mind, and hold it before you as your consciousness is slowly diminishing; shift yourself right into the 'elevator' just as the moment of 'unknowingness' [that moment when one actually falls into the sleep-state] comes to you and the astral body will move upward in the elevator; it will right itself above the shell [the physical body] just as you dream of standing up when the elevator reaches the top floor; it will move outward, just as you dream you are walking out of the elevator.[63]

From Muldoon's account it is clear that, just as it was for Monroe, the empowerment of thought and will precedes exteriorization and serves as its essential precondition. This is evident from the fact that there exists a simultaneity between thinking about or imagining the action of rising or moving away and what the second body actually is doing.

## Dreaming While Awake as a Technique of Exteriorization

Recollectedness forms an indispensable element in this entire procedure of "dreaming while awake" because it is hard to imagine a waking dream occurring unless the subject had previously developed a high degree of mental and volitional concentration capable of resisting both the overwhelming urge to fall asleep and the power of dream images to enchant and fascinate him, drawing away his attention from the paramount task of steering the dream in a previously determined direction. Muldoon explicitly acknowledged the importance of creating a state of one-pointed focused attention when he spoke about a technique that he claimed greatly facilitates this method of inducing projection by consciously dreaming about floating or rising. He called this technique "dynamization of projection." As one can see, dynamization of projection was a mental and volitional recollective technique involving the "saturation of the subconscious mind with the knowledge of and the desire for projection of the

63. Muldoon and Carrington, *Projection of the Astral Body*, p. 159.

astral body."[64] Muldoon emphasized that to do this one had to first "saturate the subconscious mind with the knowledge of . . . projection," that is, one had to understand the exact path the astral phantom takes as it dissociates from the physical body and then construct a dream (such as that of rising and getting out of an elevator) in which the dream-action imitates the actual behavior of the astral body. Second, this knowledge of how projection takes place must be coupled with an intense desire for a dream structured in the above manner.[65] This desire must absolutely dominate one's attention to the exclusion of everything else.

> Read about the phenomenon, think of the phenomenon, and practise the phenomenon intensely, if you would become a projector! Root an understanding of the phenomenon in your mind so deeply that it becomes a part of your life. Become so bound up in the study of astral projection that you will become almost irritable if you are interrupted when thinking and studying . . . about it. This is the big secret in making yourself "express" the phenomenon.[66]

It is clear that "dynamization of projection" is basically a method of autohypnosis.

## Fox's Techniques

Oliver Fox, in his autobiography *Astral Projection: A Record of Out-of-the-Body Experiences,* described two different methods of inducing exteriorization. The first he called the "Way of Dreams," and the second, the

---

64. Ibid., p. 222.

65. Muldoon might give one the impression that he is contradicting himself, that recollectedness is not an important prerequisite for projection since he states that "if you have formed the opinion that the mind must be calm in order to produce projection of the astral body, you will be forced to revise this idea for the passivity of the mind is a sure way to *prevent* projection" (ibid., p. 198). Oddly enough this statement occurs in the context of some parallels he is drawing between hypnosis and the procedures he outlines for self-inducing exteriorization. Muldoon is therefore not really suggesting that recollectedness is unimportant. (Indeed, how could hypnosis be anything but a species of recollective technique?) He is only observing that the mind and emotions must be concentrated on doing and desiring some particular thing—such as rising in an elevator—if projection is to take place. Autohypnotic concentration, he recognizes, must not be equated with mental blankness. Nowhere does Muldoon suggest that one should not pursue this desire for projection with a single-minded intention and devotion that entirely dominates one's consciousness, will, emotions, and imagination.

66. Ibid., p. 219.

"Way of Self-Induced Trance." The reader will see that conscious control while in the dream state and recollectedness (in the form of a tightly focused concentration of the will) serve as vital prerequisites for achieving dissociation.

Fox's Way of Dreams[67] differs from the analogous techniques of either Monroe or Muldoon insofar as the subject does not bother with trying to maintain consciousness as one drops off into the sleep-state and hypnagogic state. Instead, the individual is supposed to awaken after getting into the dream state. In order to do this, the would-be projector has to diligently practice memorizing his or her dream upon waking in the morning striving always to bring progressively more and more detail into the descriptions. Hopefully, as the aspiring projector gets greater facility and detail in memorization, he or she will also acquire an enhanced ability to scan his dreams—while they are occurring—in order to pick out bizarre or incongruous elements that will signal to the conscious mind that he is dreaming, thereby causing a gain of conscious awareness without breaking the dream. Fox observed that "the vividness or perfection of the experience was proportionate to the extent of consciousness manifesting in the dream,"[68] that is to say, the greater the degree of conscious awareness during the dream, the greater simulation of objective reality in the dream, the less one was able to differentiate dream experience from waking experience. After going into this state of the "waking dream" a few times, the would-be projector would sooner or later find himself being thrown into a condition that Fox termed the "False Awakening," a cataleptic state in which the subject imagines that he is awake but can no longer move. There is a peculiar tension pervading the atmosphere at this stage of experience; one hears surging and hissing noises (reminiscent of Monroe's description of Condition B). At this state, one's thought and will have apparently become "dynamized" for an individual is now able to bring about projection merely by willing mentally to do so. As Fox asserts, "Let him now concentrate all his will-power on the idea of jumping out of, or hurtling himself from the body, and in all probability he will succeed in making his first instantaneous projection."[69] Although there is some disagreement between Fox and Monroe as to exactly when mental and volitional empowerment takes place (Monroe places this empowerment after one has gone through Condition D and induced the vibrational state, whereas Fox suggests that it has already occurred at a stage that corresponds to Monroe's description

67. Fox, *Astral Projection*, pp. 121–25.
68. Ibid., pp. 34–35.
69. Ibid., p. 125.

of Condition B), both stress that complete concentration is necessary and that the second body responds instantaneously to the thought of projection.

Fox's second method for exteriorizing the astral body involved getting "the body to sleep while the mind is kept awake."[70] This second technique was similar to those measures that both Muldoon and Monroe employed in order to bring the conscious mind from an ordinary state of waking awareness to an awareness that was also operative during the dream-state. To induce trance and exteriorization in this manner it was necessary for the subject to lie down, begin breathing deeply and rhythmically while closing his eyes and rolling them slightly upward. Simultaneously, he should intently concentrate upon an imaginary image of a trapdoor at the top of his brain. After a while the subject begins to lose his sense of touch beginning with the feet, eventually engulfing the whole body in numbness. (Notice how Fox compresses his description of those stages that correspond to those between Condition A and Condition C in Monroe's scheme.) The subject has now become cataleptic and will then begin to see through his closed eyelids. He may also perceive flashes of light, hear noises, and see apparitions. At this point, Fox indicates that maintaining recollectedness despite these distractions remains important: "He should tell himself that such apparitions are subject to his will and powerless to harm him; and he should disregard any interrupting influence—even if it seems to proceed from his wife!" The subject then begins to sense that he has two bodies, his physical one and a "fluidic" one that, as yet, is still coincident with the physical. Empowerment of thought and will apparently supervene at this stage, for the would-be projector discovers that by imagining the fluidic body rising to the top of the head and out through the "door" he has simultaneously accomplished what he was imagining. Thus, if the would-be projector

> by a supreme effort of his will . . . force[s] this subtle vehicle [the 'fluidic' body] through the imaginary trap-door in his brain, [it will] seem to him that his incorporeal self rushes up his body and becomes condensed in that pineal point within his brain and batters against the door while the pale golden light [which suffuses what one perceives while one's eyes are closed] increases to a blaze of glory and a veritable inferno of sounds assails his ears.[71]

70. Ibid., p. 126.
71. Ibid., p. 127.

Fox's descriptions of the intensification of luminosity and the uprushing of the fluidic body toward the brain suggest processes akin to those at work in Gopi Krishna's awakening of kundalini. If the subject can successfully "force" the fluidic body through the imaginary door at the top of his head, he will immediately have the sensation of passing through the door, hear a click as he passes through, and notice that the discomfiting apparitions and noises have quieted. Although he has all the sensations of still being in the physical body, he now "can get out of bed in a leisurely fashion and walk away, *leaving his entranced body behind him on the bed*. . . . The experience is so supremely real that he may wonder if he is walking in his sleep—if he cannot see his body on the bed. His doubts will be speedily set at rest when he finds he can walk through the wall."[72] Like Monroe and Muldoon, Fox also maintained that if one's experience were to remain subject to conscious direction instead of degenerating into a series of uncontrolled dream events or terminating the projection prematurely, it was necessary that "from beginning to end the will must be master, . . . when it loses control the experiment is brought to a seemingly premature conclusion."[73] For this reason, Fox also cautioned the projector to avoid becoming too fascinated or emotionally excited by what he experiences or perceives while out of the body. He found that if one succumbs to the fascinating qualities of the objects and emotions that one perceives or feels in that condition, this absorption in the images and emotions of the dream leads to loss of control over the ex-static experience and its content.[74] The waking dream will then come to an abrupt end.

72. Ibid., p. 128.
73. Ibid., p. 131.
74. Ibid., pp. 43–44.

# 10

# Is Empowerment Unusual?

## Continuity Between Ex-static Paranormal Manifestations and Ordinary Mental and Perceptual Processes

In this study I have attempted to demonstrate that there is no radical discontinuity between the paranormal processes that occur during ex-stasis (such as traveling clairvoyance and extra-ocular vision) and those ordinary mental processes that take place while one dreams or engages in idle imaginings. The primary difference between mental (especially imaginative) processes that function as a means for acquiring various forms of supernormal knowledge and those mental processes that do not function in this way (for example, the epistemologically useless way the imagination functions in mere fantasy) appears directly related to the degree to which the subject exerts control over the fantasy-fabricating processes of the mind. Consequently, dreams that the subject consciously controls become phenomena that are qualitatively different from those dreams that the subject just passively experiences, even though the same basic psychological process of image fabrication is at work in both kinds of dreams. Similarly, imagining something while one is exteriorized is qualitatively different than ordinary imagining.

Continuing these types of observations, one starts to see evidence that various elements of the empowerment process are at work in other domains of human experience besides ex-stasis or mystical experience. For example, one of the peculiar features that the imagination possesses when it operates under conditions of ex-static empowerment is that it takes on an epistemological or noetic function that it does not ordinarily have, that is, it becomes the vehicle whereby the ex-static is able to gain supernormal knowledge. Thus an individual never gains clairvoyant knowledge about what someone he knows is doing by merely wishing he were at his home. However, this sometimes does happen during ex-stasis. In the latter circumstance, hallucinatory processes that ordinarily result in epistemologically fruitless daydreams or even delusions become transfigured into vehicles of clairvoyant perception. This epistemological or noetic dimension of the fantasy-fabricating activities of the mind does not emerge only under conditions of empowerment, however. The imagination also functions as an integral part of those procedures whereby the subject acquires objectively valid knowledge in visual perception and in hypnotic trance.

## The Hallucinatory Character of Ordinary Visual Perception

Experiments have demonstrated that to see something accurately requires that one hallucinate an optically accurate picture of an object, since one's eyeball is not an accurate camera. Just as the astral projector makes use of his imagination when he wishes to obtain supernormal knowledge about someone he knows, imagining "I wish to see so-and-so," the process of visual perception likewise involves using the imagination as a tool that helps a person obtain objectively valid knowledge about the world. Vitus Droscher writes,

> Experiments have acquainted us with a paradoxical fact: man can see "correctly" only because of his imagination. The human eye, optically speaking, is a piece of bad workmanship. . . . it is quite miraculous that our nervous systems manage in the end to synthesize the defective and distorted information received about our environment into images tallying with a reality of which the nervous system seems to have no direct grasp.[1]

One of the most dramatic exhibitions of how this noetic or knowledge-acquiring function of the imagination comes into play during visual perception comes from an experiment where a professor and some of his stu-

1. Vitus Dröscher, *The Magic of the Senses: New Discoveries in Animal Perception*, trans. Ursula Lehrburger and Oliver Coburn (London: Allen, 1969), pp. 3–4.

dents wore spectacles with prismatic lenses on them that grossly distorted everything that they saw.

> While the experiment is going on, the subject is condemned exclusively to a world reshaped by prismatic lenses, in which straight lines appear to be curved, angles are distorted, and sharp outlines seem fringed with color. Objects are not where the subject thinks he sees them, and they perform ghostly movements as soon as he moves his head; heavy objects seem to skip about when he ventures a few steps.[2]

After about six days the subject's mind begins to hallucinate a nearly "true" optical picture of what the glasses have distorted, having somehow compensated for and corrected the delusions that the spectacles caused.

The imagination performs a similar epistemological function in certain hypnotic situations in much the same way as it does during the process of visual perception. For example, under conditions of hypnosis a subject can be given suggestions that he will perceive things normally imperceptible to him. Under the influence of these hypnotically empowered suggestions he will actually extend the range of his perceptual faculties. Thus some hypnotized subjects that are shown a set of blank cards and told that a picture is on one of them can often later identify the exact card on which they mistakenly believed there was a drawing.[3] In these instances of hypnotically induced hyperesthesia, the subject's imagination, transformed in accordance with the hypnotist's suggestions, became a vehicle whereby he gained objective knowledge that he otherwise could not have obtained through his imaginatively unaided "normal" perceptual channels, since ordinary vision could not separate quickly one seemingly identical card from among the others.

Even the most unusual characteristic of the empowered mind—its capacity for objectifying what an individual is thinking, desiring, or imagining—appears in other domains of human experience besides ex-stasis. More specifically, this aspect of the empowerment process seems also to be at work in the phenomenon of hypnosis and in the process of cultural conditioning.

The concretization of thoughts sometimes operates under conditions of

2. This experiment done by Anton Hajos is cited in Dröscher, *Magic of the Senses*, p. 3.

3. Simeon Edmunds, *Hypnosis and Psychic Phenomena* (North Hollywood, Calif.: Wilshire Book Company, 1972), p. 43.

hypnotic trance. For example, the concretization of thoughts certainly seems to be at work in producing hypnotically induced stigmatization. One remarkable case was described by German investigators who hypnotized a youth and told him that a coin placed on the back of his hand was glowing hot and that a blister would form there at 5:00 P.M. He was then given the suggestion that he would forget the suggestion just given previously. "When the coin was removed a red area, the size and shape of the coin, was observed. A bandage was applied and sealed and the subject awakened. At 5:00 P.M. the patient was again hypnotized, the bandage unsealed, and a blister noted."[4] It is clear that in this case, which William Needles cites, the suggestion of the hypnotist became empowered but concretized itself somatically instead of objectifying itself mentally in the form of objects within a visionary landscape.

This parallelism between hypnotic trance and ex-stasis should not come as a surprise since the successful induction of both conditions requires that the subject first achieve one-pointed concentration of the mind. I have shown in Chapter 9 that once the mind becomes focused one-pointedly one of the results of such concentration is that it often becomes empowered. In the case of hypnotic trance, the suggestions of the hypnotist become "activated" while, during ex-stasis, it is instead the subject's own more or less consciously directed thoughts, desires, and imaginings that become empowered rather than those of someone else.

## Hallucinatory Factors in Cultural Conditioning

The capacity of the empowered mind to concretize thoughts may also become manifest during the process of cultural conditioning. Somatic objectifications of these thoughts can result from cultural suggestions just as they did from hypnotists' suggestions. Thus the Reverend Grebert, a missionary in the former French Congo, reported bizarre cases of psychological death or severe illness that were caused by the victims violating ancestral taboos that they had been told would kill them if they were ever transgressed. In one case, Grebert narrates, a small boy suddenly had a life-threatening attack of convulsions that was choking him to death. The frightened onlookers told Reverend Grebert, "He ate bananas that were cooked in a pot that had been used previously for manioc. Manioc is *eki*

4. William Needles, "Stigmata Occurring in the Course of Psychoanalysis," *Psychoanalytic Quarterly* 12, no. 1 (1943), p. 38.

for him; his grandparents told him that if he ever ate any of it—even a tiny little bit—he would die."[5] What happened in this particular case that terminated fatally was that a culturally implanted suggestion that death must follow from touching manioc "objectified" itself in the form of convulsive seizures. In other words, a cultural suggestion had become empowered somatically much the same way that the hypnotist's suggestions had become empowered when they caused the blisters to form on the young man. Cases such as this one suggest that cultural conditioning can operate on the mind in a manner that bears remarkable similarities to the ways that both hypnosis and ex-stasis affect it. Whether the contents of the mind be objectified somatically or mentally (in the form of a visual landscape perceived extra-ocularly during ex-stasis or mystical vision), the fact remains that each of the phenomena I have examined—hypnotic trance, cultural conditioning, ex-stasis, and the process of visual perception—appear to make use of specific elements of the empowerment process.

I share these observations in order to point out that we cannot completely divorce even the strangest elements of paranormal and mystical experience from domains of human experience that are familiar to us. When we notice that mystics, ex-statics, and clairvoyants tell us, or at least imply, that the imagination plays an "active" role in those processes whereby they gain knowledge about events happening at a distance from them, we realize that this seemingly bizarre active role that the imagination plays in the clairvoyant knowledge-acquisition process also appears to be taking place every time that we look at something. Similarly, when we recognize that accepting uncritically a suggestion from someone whom an individual acknowledges as an authority can actually affect the imagination in the same way that ex-stasis can affect it—that is, both situations can cause the imagination to objectify some of its contents—we begin to realize that it is not so far-fetched to entertain the idea that mystical and ex-static experiences apparently represent intensifications or exaggerations of psychological processes or processes of cultural conditioning that we experience every day without ever really pausing to appreciate some of their more wondrous aspects and implications. Taking these reflections to their logical conclusion, I suggest that mystical and ex-static experiences not only are worth studying because of their obvious importance in humanity's religious life, but they are valuable to study because they exhibit,

5. Quoted in Henri Ellenberger, *The Discovery of the Unconscious: The History and Evolution of Dynamic Psychiatry* (New York: Basic Books, 1970), pp. 22–23.

in an exaggerated and therefore clarified manner, processes that take place every time a human being becomes enculturated.

## Ex-stasis and Enculturation

Each individual has to create a meaningful and coherent picture and experience of the world in which he lives. He does this through enculturation. The resultant mental and experiential structure represents, to a significant degree, the way others have molded his imagination so that it presents to his consciousness an image and experience of the world that corresponds to their suggestions of what it ought to be. Consequently, enculturation is an attenuated form of hypnotism; both processes involve a human being in situations where others bombard his mind with suggestions that he more or less uncritically accepts. In the case of enculturation, this structure of suggestions acquires a great deal of stability and gradually becomes a worldview he shares with others.

I suggest that mystical experiences, ex-stasis, and hypnotic trance all represent situations, laboratory experiments as it were, that lay bare the psychological mechanisms that normally operate subliminally in the enculturation process. Hypnotism exhibits these mechanisms in an exaggerated way but instead of letting others implant the suggestion it substitutes a singular "other" for the plural and allows him to suggest to the subject what thoughts he will accept uncritically. Mystical and ex-static experiences allow their subjects more freedom in this latter regard. This is not to say that cultural conditioning does not play a vital role in shaping the content of their experiences and that they do not accept much of what comes from their cultural traditions uncritically just as everyone else does. Nonetheless, mystics and ex-statics seem to "play" with the cultural conditioning process in a way that no hypnotized subject or ordinary individual could imitate.[6] The hypnotized subject cannot do so because he remains largely in thrall to the hypnotist's suggestions. The ordinary person cannot do so because his existential situation does not confront him in a dramatic way with a mode of experience that seems so alien to his ordinary experience that it demands that he immediately organize it into some meaningful and coherent whole. In other words, unlike the mystic or the ex-static, the average person does not confront an existential situation where it is neces-

6. I owe this suggestion to a remark made by Kees Bolle in the course of a seminar to the effect that "mystics play with the cultural codes that everyone else takes for granted."

sary to mobilize the processes at work in cultural conditioning so that he can set them to work putting order and meaning into a novel and immeasurably rich field of experience that has more or less suddenly become present to his awareness. The average person brings order and meaning into his experience while being for the most part unconscious of those mechanisms that permit him to do so. The mystic and the ex-static, on the other hand, do much the same thing but with a much greater degree of explicit self-awareness of those mechanisms. This self-awareness is especially prominent among those mystics who mention that the modality of imaginative empowerment constitutes an important element of their experiences, for example, Ibn al-'Arabī, the author(s) of *The Tibetan Book of the Dead,* and Emanuel Swedenborg. The reader will soon see that among those mystics, as among Muldoon and Monroe, the coexistence of an empowered imagination and an experiential realm that derives its form and content from it, renders this confrontation with the mechanisms of cultural conditioning more acute.

# A Brief Recapitulation

I can summarize the principal observations I have made in Chapters 8–10 as follows: First, diverse paranormal manifestations frequently accompany out-of-body experiences. Conversely, those endowed with a wide range of supernormal gifts often report at least occasional instances when they found themselves dissociated from their physical bodies. This persistent two-way juxtaposition suggests that ex-stasis and a proclivity toward paranormal gifts bear a more than incidental relationship to each other. Second, these out-of-body experiences often occur in tandem with a remarkable dynamization or empowerment of the subject's thinking, willing, and imagining faculties so that whatever he experiences during dissociation remains embedded within a visual and emotional landscape that his "dynamized" or concretized thoughts and desires shape and vivify. Third, these ex-statically empowered thoughts and desires sometimes objectify themselves *trans*-subjectively, that is, others besides the subject can experience or perceive them or else they somehow serve as a vehicle enabling the subject to acquire supernormal knowledge about either temporally or spatially distant events. In other words, the empowered imagination can function as an organ of perception and cognition. Fourth, neither ex-stasis nor dynamization can take place unless one maintains a one-pointedly focused control and direction of one's thoughts, desires, emotions, and imaginings—neither is possible without some form of recollective technique. Fifth, recollective techniques do more than just initiate dissociation and empowerment. Failure to continue maintaining concentration and failure to continue controlling tightly the direction of one's thoughts and desires cause the ex-static experience to degenerate into nothing more than a "mere" dream or hallucination. Thus, I already noted in Chapter 9 how Monroe believed that individuals rarely obtain objectively verifiable information concerning distant physical events while exteriorized because most projectors lack that tight degree of control over their conscious and subconscious thoughts and desires that would prevent those ideas and wishes from indiscriminately objectifying themselves. Without these restraints, those uncontrolled objectifications keep projecting themselves into the ex-static's perceptual field, impacting both emotionally and perceptually with such force as to hinder him from seeing anything but his own subjectively exteriorized thoughts and desires. Monroe implies that one can obtain paranormally acquired objective knowledge about the physical world during ex-stasis provided that one quiets this perceptual and emotional interference by attempting to remain as close to "no thought" as is humanly possible. Then and only then can this state of mental and volitional quiescence give one objectively valid information about the world. Then—and only then—can this clarified and purified ex-static mode of perception begin to approximate the reliability of ordinary sense-perception. Sixth, the use of recollective techniques while dreaming radically transfigures both the ontological and affective impact of dream experience. If one maintains conscious awareness during a dream and also avoids the temptation to get emotionally absorbed in its content, then dream objects seem to become as real as the objects that we encounter while we are awake. These considerations caused Fox to conclude that controlled dreams constituted a "really new level of consciousness . . . different from the states experienced in ordinary dream and in waking life."[7] Since such controlled dreams serve as an important means for inducing out-of-body states and since tightly controlled out-of-body experiences in turn sometimes lead to instances of objective trans-subjectively verified knowledge via "traveling" clairvoyance,

7. Fox, *Astral Projection*, p. 36.

it seems safe to conclude that, on occasion, controlled dreams can represent something more than the merely private, imaginary phantasms of one's unconscious.

These findings contradict most modern theories of philosophy and psychology that rigidly separate the subjective and objective domains of experience. The findings of this study, however, imply a much broader interface between the two domains and suggest that the technique of maintaining conscious control over the subconscious and its fantasy-fabricating processes provides the most effective method for dissolving the otherwise seemingly unbridgeable gap that isolates one's own realm of private experience from the private experiences of others.

# 11

# Recollection, Empowerment, and the Genesis of Paranormal Phenomena

In Chapter 9, I stated that if scholars were to analyze carefully the structure of that peculiar mode of being that accompanies the out-of-body experience, they would discover therein the key to understanding why mystical experience so often goes hand-in-hand with a proclivity for supernormal powers of perception and action. I noted in Chapter 5 that various recollective techniques serve as prerequisites for bringing about most mystical states—except, of course, those mystical experiences that apparently come about spontaneously. Similarly, in Chapter 10, I also established that recollective techniques also serve as the principal means used to induce both exteriorization and that extraordinary dynamization and empowerment of the mind, will, and imagination so characteristic of the out-of-body state. I will now demonstrate that they play yet another vital role—recollective techniques not only serve to bring about mystical states, exteriorization, and empowerment, but they also serve as the chief means for bringing about virtually any kind of paranormal experience. In other words, the reason why supernormal manifestations of the most varied sort so often accompany mystical experiences and out-of-body experiences stems from a very simple fact—*all these seemingly disparate phenomena can have a common genesis in the recollective act.* The deliberate production of almost every type of paranormal manifestation requires that one generate a condition of recollective quiet and concentration, either with or without overt evidence of mental, volitional and imaginative empowerment.

An important Theravada scripture, the *Majjhima-Nikāya,* contains a passage that reinforces what I already said above concerning the fundamental importance of recollective concentration as an aid to obtaining supernormal powers.

> If a priest . . . should frame a wish as follows: 'Let me exercise the various powers—let me being one become multiform, let me being visible, become invisible, go without hindrance through walls, ramparts, or mountains as if through air, let me rise and sink in the ground as if in the water, let me walk on the water as if on unyielding ground, let me travel cross-legged in the air—like a winged bird, let me touch with my hand the moon and the sun . . . and let me go with my body even up to the Brahma-world'—Then he must be perfect in the precepts, *bring his thoughts to a state of quiescence,* practice diligently the trances, attain to insight, and be a frequenter of lonely places.

The text then continues to assert that if the monk desires yet other supernormal powers such as the ability to remember previous births, a "divinely clear hearing surpassing that of men," "divinely clear vision surpassing that of men" (apparently referring to clairaudience and clairvoyance), or the capacity to discern what is in men's hearts, then he must likewise acquire perfect mastery of the precepts, of techniques of mental quiescence, and of the trance-states.[1] This text clearly indicates that, at least at the level of folklore, early Buddhists believed that if one wished to obtain any kind of supernormal power, one had, among other things, to learn how to quiet the mind. Do firsthand accounts of people who claim to exercise various supernormal gifts confirm what the *Majjhima-Nikāya* says on this point? I think so. For example, Monroe continually testifies to the close connection between recollectedness and his own supernormal capabilities. He discovered that he could exercise his occasional telekinetic powers or his ability to acquire information through "traveling" clairvoyance only if he were exteriorized—a condition that requires a prior quieting of the mind. He similarly noted that his latent aptitude for precognitive insights would only come into play if he put himself into that condition of recollective stillness that immediately *precedes* the actual moment of exteriorization. Then, and only then, he wrote, "As I was lying down, *my mind stilled,* and my body relaxed" would he receive influxes of precognitive knowledge.[2]

Garrett likewise stressed that quieting the mind and imagination functioned as a prerequisite for telepathic, clairvoyant, clairaudient, and pre-

---

1. These passages from the *Majjhima-Nikāya* are taken from Warren, *Buddhism in Translations,* pp. 303–5 (emphasis mine).

2. Monroe, *Journeys Out of the Body,* p. 145 (emphasis mine).

cognitive receptivity. She maintained that in a condition of maximum telepathic receptivity, "the mind of the percipient is like a lake which, being sheltered, cannot have its smooth waters disturbed by the winds of grief or joy, of too much pain, or of too little happiness. The imagination should be alert, but not working; since too much activity on its part can change the nature of the sensory stimuli [received from incoming telepathic impressions]."[3] Not only is it important to quiet the mind but it is also important to subdue the imagination for when it is active one begins to embroider, and thereby distort, telepathic data. Therefore, objective telepathic knowledge, like any other kind of objective, scientific knowledge, requires a high degree of disciplined effort against an unrestrained subjectivity.

3. Garrett, *Telepathy*, p. 52. One may confidently assume that the prerequisites for inducing telepathic sensitivity also apply to clairvoyance and clairaudience since Garrett claims that all three forms of supernormal sensitivity "almost undoubtedly are varying manifestations of the same function" (ibid., p. 13). This confirms what one reads in other accounts written by paranormally gifted people—the ability to manifest one form of psychic ability usually implies other supernormal gifts. According to Garrett, what differentiates clairvoyance from telepathy is that telepathy, for the most part, does not "involve the use and interpretation of visual symbols; clairvoyance on the other hand does" (ibid., p. 12–13). In other words, telepathic impressions appear to one's consciousness in much the same way as one sees a television image. Consequently, there is little ambiguity regarding what the image means. However, clairvoyant impressions do not convey their meaning in such an immediate fashion. Like a dream whose manifest or apparent content may appear to be nothing more than a disconnected set of weird images with no coherent message but whose latent content contains a "true" message once one deciphers the meaning of the symbolism that forms it, clairvoyant symbols possess a similar opacity that requires an effort of translation before the true content of the message becomes clear.

It does appear that most supernormal phenomena interrelate as though they were "varying manifestations of the same function" (ibid., p. 13). For example, basing himself on self-observation, Manning suggests that even phenomena as disparate as poltergeist mediumship, automatic writing, and the ability to see auras start from a similar mental state and merely represent different ways of directing and focusing a common psychic energy. He noticed that whenever he performed automatic writing, poltergeist phenomena would temporarily cease. This caused Manning to conclude that "automatic writing appeared to be the most successful method of controlling or preventing the poltergeist phenomena, and if it looked as though disturbances were imminent, I would sit down and write. Later it became clear to me . . . that the energy I used for writing had previously been used for causing poltergeist disturbances" (Manning, *The Link*, p. 77). He accidentally discovered his ability to see auras around people in an analogous way. *While almost in the condition in which he was normally accustomed to perform automatic writing,* he suddenly found that he could see people surrounded by a "pear-shaped aura of colors" that radiated from them like colored heat waves. He learned: "*If I switched myself 'on' as though I were going to write [automatically] BUT WITHOUT ACTUALLY DOING SO, I could see auras surrounding people*" (ibid., p. 78). These latter examples clearly suggest that the varieties of paranormal manifestations ultimately stem from different ways of directing attention or psychic energy from a common mental state.

One of Garrett's pupils described her own method of preparing herself for telepathic receptivity by similarly emphasizing the crucial importance of inducing recollective quiet. She stated that when she wishes to receive telepathic impressions, "I close my eyes. I seat myself comfortably or lie down in order to be relaxed. *I let go of all thought or directed activity of the mind.* If any thought intrudes (and it usually does), I quietly push it away. This becomes a state of alert passivity—a readiness to receive." Deep-breathing techniques form an essential element of this student's preparations for bringing about this all-important state of mental quiescence. The student continues, "A preparation step to assist this receptivity is deep, slow rhythmic breathing, letting the lower abdomen expand, and expelling the air by contracting the diaphragm."[4] One should note that Garrett herself frequently refers to the role deep-breathing techniques play in bringing about mental quiescence (and a state that she calls "alertness," which I will describe in more detail later).[5] One can observe a similar— though not identical (insofar as they emphasize cessation of breathing for as long as possible rather than deep breathing)—connection between techniques of breath control (*prāṇāyāma*) and mental quiescence in certain Yoga treatises. For instance, the *Haṭhayogapradīpikā* claims that "when the breath wanders (i.e. is irregular), the mind is unsteady, but when (the breath is) still, (the mind) obtains the power of stillness."[6] Similarly, in the *Yoga-Sūtras* of Patañjali one finds the typically laconic assertion that one of the chief means for facilitating mental calmness is "by expulsion and retention of the breath."[7] In common with Monroe, Garrett, and her pupil, Patañjali and his commentators assume that one has already learned how to quiet the mind before one attempts to exercise the various supernormal powers he describes later on in his treatise. Thus the text states that "supernormal powers are accomplished by constraints (*saṃyama*). And constraint is the combination of fixed attention . . . contemplation and . . . concentration."[8] It is evident from the above description of what Patañjali and his commentators referred to as saṃyama that what I have been referring to as "mental quiescence" constitutes one of the crucial elements of those yogic practices that develop supernormal powers, since "fixed atten-

4. Garrett, *Telepathy,* pp. 59–60 (emphasis mine).
5. Garrett, *Adventures in the Supernormal,* p. 148.
6. Svātmārāma, *Haṭhayogapradīpikā,* chap. 2, v. 2, p. 22.
7. Patañjali, *Yoga-System of Patañjali* (Woods ed.), 1:34.
8. See Vācaspati Miśra's commentary on 3:1 in Pantañjali, *Yoga-System,* p. 203.

tion" is an important ingredient of saṃyama (which in turn is indispensable for achieving each of the supernormal powers the text enumerates).

A story about the great Sufi master Jalāl al-Dīn Rūmī's reputed telepathic powers provides further confirmation of my claim that the ability to
withdraw oneself from worldly distractions functions as the prerequisite
for exercising paranormal powers. The narrator relates that one day as the
great shaikh was seated among his disciples he got the feeling that one of
them had a craving for roasted sheep's head. Rūmī then ordered his companions to cook some of this delicacy for the hungry disciple. The other
disciples were surprised that Rūmī could read the other man's thoughts
and they asked him how he was able to do it. He replied:

> Because it is now thirty years that no desire has remained in me, . . .
> I have cleansed and purified myself of all desires and have become
> as clean as an unscratched mirror. When the thought of a roasted
> sheep's head entered my mind and whetted my appetite and became
> a desire, I knew that it belonged to our friend yonder for the mirror
> is without any image of itself; if an image shows in the mirror it is
> the image of another.[9]

Another Sufi miracle story associates transcendental powers with the ability to rigidly maintain concentration. A tenth-century Sufi, Abū'l-Adyān,
once got in an argument with a Zoroastrian who denied Abū'l-Adyān's
claim that he could walk through a fire without being injured. (Abū'l-
Adyān had asserted that fire only burns things if God gives it permission to
do so.) Much to the Zoroastrian's astonishment, Abū'l-Adyān then proceeded to walk through the fire without injury except for a small blister on
his foot. The Sufi later told his servant that he had received this blister at
the instant that he was emerging from the fire when he prematurely came
out of the trance-state that he had been in while crossing the hot coals. He
then added: "If I had come to myself in the midst of the fire, I would have
been burned completely."[10] Regardless of whether or not one accepts these
two accounts as true, one at least has to admit that they reflect a belief
prevalent in the folklore of Sufism that holds that he who masters the art
of concentration by that very fact also gains access to miraculous powers.

9. Jalāl al-Dīn Rūmī, *Discourses of Rūmī*, trans. A. J. Arberry (New York: Samuel
Weiser, 1972), pp. 52–53.
10. Quoted in Schimmel, *Mystical Dimensions of Islam*, p. 209.

The Selk'nam shamans of Tierra del Fuego also appear to have utilized recollective techniques as a significant part of their preparation for acquiring both the power of clairvoyant vision and the supernormal power of action-at-a-distance. The Tierra del Fuegians attributed the power of "active" vision (*yauategn*) to their shamans. Yauategn was active in the sense that the shaman who possessed it reputedly possessed the simultaneous capability to see clairvoyantly and to influence the objects that he "saw" in this supernormal manner. Martin Gusinde provides a good description of what the natives meant when they referred to a shaman's yauategn.

> [By] this term] the Indians mean the psychic vision of the witch-doctor. The *yauategn* does not consist of just the power to reproduce an object photographically; it is also able to exercise an actual influence on material objects and on the souls of other individuals. This power is depicted as an eye that leaves the witch-doctor's body and travels in a straight line to the object in view, while still remaining connected to the witch-doctor. The eye distends like a sort of "thread made from gum" (this is how the Indians expressed it): it is able to function from any side of the head like the eyes of a lobster, and may be withdrawn, like a snail's antennae.[11]

Gusinde's account shows significant resemblances to the descriptions of out-of-body experiences examined in Chapters 8 and 9. First, the Selk'nam describe the shaman's "eye" as elastic just as Muldoon and others describe the astral cord that allegedly connects the astral body to the physical body. Second, although the Fuegians do not mention that any astral "double" is attached to the other end of the witch doctor's eye, both they and Muldoon do recognize that because such a cord exists "traveling" clairvoyance is possible. And finally, like Muldoon and Monroe, the Fuegians maintain that clairvoyant vision can also be active vision. In other words, the shaman may influence the state of matter at a distance from his physical body in much the same fashion that Muldoon and Monroe both claimed to have exercised an occasional telekinetic power while clairvoyantly witnessing what they were affecting. (One will recall how Monroe claimed that he pinched a woman while he was exteriorized and actually caused her to develop a bruise at the place where his second body touched her.)[12]

11. Quoted in Ernesto de Martino, *The World of Magic,* trans. Paul Saye White (New York: Pyramid Books, 1972), p. 74.
12. Monroe, *Journeys Out of the Body,* pp. 55–57.

It should not occasion surprise when one discovers that the power of yauategn, like any other paranormal manifestation thus far analyzed, requires that the novice shaman master techniques of mental concentration. Gusinde's Selk'nam informants told him that in order to become a shaman, the candidate must try to contact the spirit of a dead shaman related to him so that he can acquire the latter's exceptional psychic powers. Without such assistance, his quest remains doomed to failure. In order for this contact and resultant acquisition of psychic powers to occur, the candidate must learn "to pass at will from waking into the hypnotic state." (One may recall at this point how both Muldoon and Monroe showed that learning how to deliberately pass successively from the waking state through the hypnagogic state into the dream-state constituted a potent means of acquiring both recollectedness and psychic power.)[13] The candidate must also try to dream of the dead shaman's image as often as possible until such a time as he believes the dead man's spirit has finally given him some of his power. When the novice finally attains a high degree of competence in this art, he should be able to summon the spirit of the dead man whenever he wishes it to appear to him. However, before he acquires this level of proficiency, the novice must, in the words of Gusinde's informants, "work very hard, dream a lot and, above all, sing without interruption, so that his waiyuwen [the soul of the dead witch doctor, together with his powers] will appear more often and remain with him longer." Gusinde elaborates by observing that

> This means that the novice [either] will concentrate even more, avoiding all distractions offered by his surroundings, or else he will enter the mysterious silence of his own ego in order to meditate upon one thought, his *waiyuwen*. (The people say) "He begins to work on his *waiyuwen* until he sees things that are far away." The novice's "strength of psychic vision" must be intensified until he is able to see the *waiyuwen* of other witch-doctors. He tries to contact these at a very early stage. When this has been achieved, he tries through his *yauategn,* to use this power at a great distance.[14]

Gusinde's description indicates that even the "primitive" Selk'nam considered that methods of mental concentration formed an essential part of any attempt to develop and manifest supernatural powers.

13. Ibid., pp. 207–11; Muldoon, *The Projection of the Astral Body,* p. 159.
14. Quoted in Martino, *World of Magic,* p. 72.

# 12

# The "Active" Approach for Inducing Paranormal Manifestations After Recollective Quiet

## What Are the "Active" and "Passive" Approaches?

The foregoing discussion clearly indicates that methods of quieting the mind form an essential part of any procedure for awakening latent paranormal sensitivities. However, mastering such methods of stilling the mind is only the beginning of any process for deliberately acquiring supernormal powers of perception and action. This being the case, what else must mystics do in order to activate these extraordinary capabilities? Generally speaking, their subsequent efforts fall into one of two broad categories that I label the "active" approach and the "passive" approach. Mystics who utilize the active approach take advantage of that peculiar condition of mental, volitional, and imaginative empowerment that, as previously observed in Chapter 9, was one possible result of stilling the mind. In other words, with the active approach the mystic directs his tightly focused and empowered mind, will, and imagination toward producing the particular supernormal phenomenon or state of consciousness that he wishes to achieve. After progressively greater efforts of such concentration he finally accomplishes his goal.

The passive approach, on the other hand, does not require this same intensity of concentration and willpower on the part of the mystic or medium. Instead, once he has recollectively abstracted himself from the sense-world, he deliberately allows phantasms, images, and emotional states that arise from the depths of his subconscious or from other sources (such as telepathic impressions) to flood into his awareness in place of the physical sense-impressions from his eyes and ears. In some cases, the first kind of passive approach, simple inspection of such images, emotional states, and phantasms suffices to determine whether or not they contain a paranormal significance or message beneath their surface appearance. What more often happens, however, is that the significance of such impressions and feeling-states is not so immediately apparent. In these cases, the second kind of passive approach, the mystic or medium then has to follow a chain of free associations that these images and emotional states suggest to him. Of course, simply following a chain of free associations does not by itself yield supernormal information. Something else is necessary: The subject must also fuse this process of free association to a peculiar kind of empathic identification with the images and emotional states that come into his awareness. Consequently, the subject is no longer just looking at what comes into his consciousness—he is also identifying with it.

Although both the active and the second kind of passive approach require some kind of effort on the subject's part, in both forms of the passive approach the primary emphasis remains centered on the subject's role as a receiver of impressions that seem to come from outside himself rather than as a generator of energies that begin from within himself and then enable him either to perceive or to influence that which lies beyond himself. In the passive method, the subject plays a role much akin to that of the medium in a seance who allows himself to be taken over by another consciousness and through that other consciousness conveys supernormal information. The role of the subject who employs the active method, on the other hand, bears an analogy to the *fakir* or yogin who, in contrast to the fundamentally passive attitude of the medium, acquires his psychic powers by heroically concentrating both his mind and will on that which he wishes to accomplish.

## The "Active" Approach in Tibetan Buddhism

My first example of the active approach comes from Tibet. Tibetans claim that magicians, monks, and other religious devotees can sometimes, through an effort of exceptionally intense mental concentration, produce materializations of their own thoughts that possess such optical vividness and quasi-tangibility that the uninitiated may take them to be real objects rather than hallucinations. Unlike ordinary hallucinations, these deliberately created illusions or materialized thought-forms (*tulpas*) possess the remarkable property of not only being subjectively perceptible to the individual who created them but they may also be perceived by others. David-Neel observed several of these mentally created apparitions during her many years in Tibet.[1] In one instance, she related how she met a Tibetan painter who fervently worshiped the terrifying wrathful deities that form an important part of the lamaist pantheon. Moreover, he not only worshiped them fervently but also spent a great deal of time drawing them. Once when he came to visit her she noticed that behind him was

> the somewhat nebulous shape of one of the fantastic beings which often appeared in his paintings. I made a startled gesture and the astonished artist took a few steps toward me, asking what was the matter. . . . I walked to the apparition with one arm stretched in front of me. My hand reached the foggy form. I felt as if touching a soft object whose substance gave way under the slight push, and the vision vanished.[2]

This illusion possessed several noteworthy qualities. First, it was not just a visual hallucination that could be perceived by another but it was also quasi-tangible. Second, even though the artist was himself not aware of the form that he had created as a result of his own concentrated mental activity, another could see the objectification of those thoughts. He confessed to David-Neel that on that very morning he had spent almost its entirety painting the particular deity she had seen and that, furthermore, in the past few weeks he had been performing a rite in which he had tried to conjure the form of that deity for magical purposes. The Tibetan's thoughts were therefore "entirely concentrated on the deity whose help he wished to secure for a rather mischievous undertaking."[3] It is evident that techniques of mental concentration remain the sine qua non for ensuring the success of any endeavor to develop one's supernormal powers.

David-Neel's acquaintance with Tibetan Buddhism was not restricted to mere observation and book-learning. She also practiced many of its rituals and meditative techniques. Consequently, it is of great interest to scholars of mysticism to analyze her own account of how she created and animated one of these tulpas. Even though she had seen a few tulpas with her own eyes, she still remained a skeptic. Before she really accepted that such phenomena were possible, she felt that she should experimentally try to create

1. David-Neel, *Magic and Mystery in Tibet*, pp. 308–12.
2. Ibid., p. 310.
3. Ibid., p. 311.

one herself. She chose to focus her attention on creating the mental illusion of a short, fat, jolly monk.

> I shut myself in *tsams* [seclusion] and proceeded to perform the prescribed concentration of thought and other rites. After a few months the phantom monk was formed. His form grew gradually fixed and life-like looking. He became a kind of guest, living in my apartment. I then broke my seclusion and started for a tour with my servants and tents. The monk included himself in the party. Though I lived in the open, riding on horseback for miles each day, the illusion persisted. I saw the fat *trapa* now and then and it was not necessary for me to think of him to make him appear. The phantom performed various actions of the kind that are natural to travelers and that I had not commanded. For instance, he walked, stopped, looked around him. The illusion was mostly visual, but sometimes I felt as if a robe was lightly touching against me and once a hand seemed to touch my shoulder. . . . Once a herdsman who brought me a present of butter saw the *tulpa* in my tent and took it for a live lama.[4]

How does David-Neel's account typify the active approach? It does so by exhibiting all three of its basic elements, namely, (1) concentration—one notices that David-Neel mentions isolation and "concentration of thought" as a preparatory phase that brought about (2) the empowerment or dynamization of thought, will, and imagination. In other words, there comes to be an exact or almost exact correspondence between what David-Neel thinks about and desires and what actually comes to be a part of her subjective and even objective experience. She is no longer merely imagining the monk or thinking about him in a purely conceptual or abstract way but she is now concretely experiencing this creature of her imagination as a visible and even quasi-tangible presence. (3) Her narrative incorporated the third element of the active approach insofar as the supernormal manifestation she produces only comes into existence after a long and vigorous effort on her part to continually direct her thoughts and desires to the task of embodying the phantom. To summarize, she must not only be capable of mastering the art of mental concentration for a short while but she must continue to focus her empowered mind in a specific direction for a long period of time.

4. Ibid., pp. 314–15.

Several other features of David-Neel's experience merit comment. For example, one notes some structural parallels between the kinds of mental and imaginative processes that took place when she was generating the tulpa and those that occur when an individual is having an out-of-body experience. First, both experiences require concentration as a preliminary. Second, the phenomenon of enthymesis plays a central role in both types of experience. Third, both types of experience raise the provocative question: To what extent can purely imaginative creations become real?[5] David-Neel's tulpa had an objective presence that even other people could occasionally detect, even though this creation was just a product of her own imagination. In this context, it occasionally happens that what an astral projector is thinking about while he is exteriorized can take on an objective presence or serve as a means for obtaining objectively verifiable information. For example, when Monroe desired to pinch a distant friend while dissociated from his physical body, his thought of pinching her apparently became "translated" into real pinch marks on her body. Similarly, there were other occasions when Monroe thought about visiting an acquaintance during an exteriorization and suddenly found himself clairvoyantly witnessing what that person was actually doing at the time. In one particular instance while he was exteriorized, Monroe desired to visit his friend Dr. Bradshaw. As soon as he thought about wanting to see Bradshaw, Monroe found himself in his astral body watching what the doctor and his wife were doing. Monroe claimed that he was later able to verify that much of what he saw his friend and his wife doing had actually happened as his astral double had witnessed it.[6]

This last observation brings us to one of the most striking peculiarities of mystical and supernormal experiences: The psychological processes at work in both employ the private imaginative and hallucinatory activities of the mind as a means of taking the individual beyond what is merely private and subjective. The mystic and the medium utilize and direct their

5. One must recognize, of course, that any Buddhist would simply declare that tangibility, solidity, and collective perceptibility are no guarantees that an object possesses an ontological status more dignified than the most evanescent dream image or hallucination. For a Tibetan Buddhist, no mode of experience, aside from the mind in a state free from thought formation is "real" in a soteriological sense. Instead of depicting nirvana as a realm that one enters into by virtue of attaining any particular transcendental state of consciousness or by having any specific kind of visionary experience, Buddhists generally depict nirvana as a knowledge state, a condition of insight together with a behavioral orientation that is consistent with that insight.

6. Monroe, *Journeys Out of the Body,* pp. 46–48.

imaginations in ways that are no longer "merely" imagining or "merely" dreaming. For them the imagination is no longer just synonymous with the domain of private subject experience. The mystic and the medium have discovered instead that when they direct and control the content of their imaginations in certain ways the subjective universe of their supposedly private dreams, thoughts, and fantasies becomes something that others can to some extent share as exemplified in the phenomena of tulpa creation and in Monroe's ability to telekinetically pinch a distant friend. They also find that various imaginative activities—for example, "thinking about" someone while one is exteriorized—can sometimes give them a means of access to clairvoyant, hence objective, modes of knowing. In all of these cases, it is clear that the imagination seems to have become transfigured into something qualitatively different from itself. The ordinarily rigid boundaries that normally separate the purely private domain of subjective fantasy and illusion from the realm of objective experience begin to dissolve and lose their usual significance. David-Neel's method for creating an objectification of her thoughts represents an extreme example of what can happen when an individual acquires exceptional proficiency in the visualization techniques that form such an important element within the ritual and meditational complex of Tibetan Tantric Buddhism.

These visualization methods have had a long history in the literature of both Hinayana and Mahayana Buddhist meditational practices. Thus, Tantric visualization procedures show some significant similarities to the *kasiṇa* meditations (meditation through fixing one's attention on colored discs) that Buddhaghosa described in the *Visuddhimagga*.[7] First, instructions for conducting both the kasiṇa meditations and the Tantric visualizations each emphasize that the practitioner must begin by secluding himself in a place where there is a minimal chance of his mental concentration being disturbed. Second, each technique emphasizes the crucial importance of completely focusing one's mental and emotional energies on the task of creating an imaginary visual image and endowing it with such vividness that the created mental image stays in the subject's field of vision even when he opens his eyes. In this way, it becomes harder and harder to differentiate the subjective images from those autonomous objects that normally occupy an individual's visual field while he is awake.[8]

7. Buddhaghosa, *Path of Purity*, 2:143–47.

8. It is worth noting that any attempt to seize control of one's imaginative processes in order to direct them seems to result in a similar vivification of the subjective imagery to the point where the individual finds it increasingly difficult to draw a hard and fast distinction

For practitioners of both the kasina meditations and the Tantric visualization techniques, when the imaginatively created image becomes as vivid and solid looking as the objective phenomena that are normally present to the subject's ordinary waking consciousness, this indicates that they have acquired that all-important one-pointedness of attention that Buddhists consider to be the sine qua non for producing any kind of extraordinary paranormal manifestation. Buddhaghosa remarks: "For abundant growth of mind-culture, he [the *kasina* meditator] should increase the afterimage."⁹ In other words, Buddhaghosa is asserting that since every aspect of mind-culture (including the production of paranormal phenomena) depends on the degree to which one has learned to concentrate one's mind, and since the vividness of the mental object is supposed to be proportional to the depth of one's concentration, it logically follows that the meditator should strive to intensify the afterimage if he wishes to develop his mental control to the fullest extent. A Tantric Buddhist such as David-Neel would have no quarrel with this line of reasoning.¹⁰

Why do Tantric Buddhists value such visualization exercises? They maintain that they serve a two-fold purpose. Most important, a successful visualization experience confirms one of the basic tenets of Mahayana Buddhism: The idea that every object that exists—whether it be objective

---

between what is imaginary and what is objective and exists autonomously. Such experiences, for example, led Oliver Fox to conclude that ordinary dreams and those "dreams of knowledge" in which the subject dreams but is simultaneously conscious that he is doing so deserved to be considered as qualitatively different from one another. The dreams of knowledge, he asserted, were "really a new level of consciousness . . . different from the states experienced in ordinary dreams and in waking life." Moreover, he discovered that when he would deliberately attempt both to prolong a dream and to maintain consciousness while in it, he would find that it became increasingly difficult to distinguish subjective from objective experience. As he put it, "My sunlit land and sea were not the physical land and sea . . . but I could not feel the *truth* of this" (Fox, *Astral Projection*, pp. 36, 38–39). David-Neel went a step further than Fox. For example, one notes that when David-Neel's tulpa subjectively grew "fixed and life-like looking" (David-Neel, *Magic and Mystery in Tibet*, p. 314) this intensification in its subjective vividness corresponded, in some measures at least, to an actual objective presence that others sometimes perceived. In other words, the subjective vividness of such mentally fabricated imagery not only indicates the degree of the meditator's mental concentration but it sometimes serves as an index of the extent to which the meditator's imaginative creation is perceptible to others. The reason why Fox's imaginative creations never seemed to have had the trans-subjective dimension that David-Neel claimed hers possessed probably relates to the lesser degree of intensity of his powers of mental concentration.

9. Buddhaghosa, *Path of Purity*, 2:175.
10. David-Neel, *Magic and Mystery in Tibet*, pp. 272, 293.

or subjective, human or divine, material or mental—is at bottom really only an illusion created by the mind, that its seeming objectivity, solidity, and tangibility are nothing more than appearances that only seem real to us because we are deluded concerning their true nature as merely subjective mental phenomena. As David-Neel puts it, the purpose of these exercises is "to lead the disciple to understand that the worlds and all phenomena which we perceive are but mirages born from our imagination. 'They emanate from the mind And into the mind they sink!' . . . This is the fundamental teaching of Tibetan mystics."[11] Consequently, when the meditator realizes that he can endow any object he chooses with apparent solidity, he not only begins to *believe* that Buddhist teachings concerning the illusory nature of even material phenomena really are true but he also begins *to know* that these teachings are true because he can empirically verify these claims. Success in vivifying and embodying mental phantasms causes the student to realize that the only real difference between tulpas and objective physical phenomena resides in the degree to which one remains conscious of the act whereby one created them. Thus, the meditator knows by immediate experience that a tulpa is an illusory fabrication because he remembers the meditative act that created it. He then will conclude that even such apparently autonomous, objective physical phenomena as rocks and trees were created by a similar mental effort and only seem to exist independently of one's own mind because one remains unconscious of the mental process that fabricated them.

Tibetan Buddhists value visualization practices for a second reason. They affirm that such experiences endow the meditator with a spiritual power or energy that he may use in a great variety of ways, either to the benefit or detriment of himself or others.[12] For example, David-Neel mentions that meditators often create tulpas as a way of providing themselves with a protector. They create the phantom of some terrifying wrathful deity, believing that when evil spirits see its frightening form they will flee headlong from it and not attempt to harm the meditator.[13] The Tibetan practice of *tumo* provides one with yet another instance of how visualization techniques and the spiritual energies that they liberate are capable of having a beneficial effect. Tumo refers to a subtle psychic fire or heat that

11. Ibid., p. 267.
12. I remind the reader that Buddhists do not equate spiritual perfection with mastery of the psychic powers.
13. David-Neel, *Magic and Mystery in Tibet*, p. 312.

certain yogins and lamas claim they are able to generate once they have mastered certain difficult hatha yoga postures, learned how to control rhythmically their breathing, focused their minds, and attained an extraordinary proficiency in effortlessly visualizing anything on which they decide to focus their imaginations. This ability to generate tumo can reputedly produce the transient supernormal ability to stay warm even when naked in the midst of the subzero winters that occur in the high altitudes of the Tibetan plateau. David-Neel attested that those stories of naked hermits wandering in the winter snows were not just legends. "Hermits really do live naked, or wearing one single thin garment during the winter in the high regions. . . . I am not the only one who had seen some of them."[14]

It is appropriate at this point to briefly examine one of the methods that tumo practitioners utilize in order to endure this bitter cold. This short investigation will also serve to illustrate how supernormal phenomena can be produced using the active approach.

A yogic text of the Kargyutpa sect of Tibetan Tantric Buddhism entitled *The Path of Knowledge: The Yoga of the Six Doctrines* incorporates as one of the six practices described in it "The Doctrine of the Psychic-Heat," a manual for generating tumo. The text proceeds on the assumption that within the human body there exists a subtle physiological system much akin to that one encountered in the previous discussions of Gopi Krishna's mystical experiences when he awakened kundalini.[15] According to this system of subtle physiology, the physical body is interpenetrated with a network of invisible psychic nerves and psychic nerve centers or chakras. (A good analogy here is that which corresponds in the physical body to the nerves and the principal nerve ganglia.) The principal invisible psychic nerve, the median nerve, is a hollow tube running from the lowest chakra situated at the base of the spine up to the highest chakra, which is situated at the very top of the head. Along this median nerve are three other chakras: one at the level of the navel, another at the level of the heart, and another at the level of the throat. Besides this median psychic nerve are two others. One on the left side of the body emerges from the left nostril

14. David-Neel, *Magic and Mystery in Tibet*, p. 229.

15. David-Neel mentions that "enlightened mystics" among the Tibetans do not consider this subtle physiological system of psychic nerves to have any physical reality. It is simply a symbolic structure whose effects, however, are nonetheless real if this physiological structure is yogically imagined as existing (*Magic and Mystery in Tibet*, p. 222). See also Gopi Krishna, *Kundalini*, pp. 175–76.

up to and over the brain, down the left side of the body, where it joins the median psychic nerve in the lowest chakra. An identical psychic nerve exists on the right side of the body. The technique described for generating tumo requires that these psychic nerves be freed from any kind of invisible blockages that may otherwise impede the flow of the subtle psychic energy (*shugs,* analogous to the Sanskrit term *prāṇa*) that the yogin supposedly extracts from the air through the use of *prāṇāyāma* (special breathing methods). The yogin then forces the *shugs* into circulation by employing hatha yoga postures that require that he sit cross-legged, "agitate his stomach with a churning motion," shake his body violently like a spirited horse shakes itself and conclude with a vigorously executed bounce made by rising a bit off his meditation cushion and then falling back down on it.[16] By repeating this series of yogic movements three times in succession, the yogin not only frees the subtle nerves from any obstructions but he also completes the preliminary step that permits him to derive full benefit from the breath-control techniques and visualizations that follow.

After he has freed the psychic nerve channels from impediments, the yogin then begins deep-breathing techniques that one-pointedly focus his mind so as to prepare it for the next task at hand. Moreover, these controlled, rhythmic breathings also introduce shugs into the subtle nerve-system.[17] The third stage then begins, that of visualization. The text instructs the meditator to visualize himself "as being the vacuous form of Vajra-Yogini [a beneficent goddess who traditionally helps yogins to achieve supernormal powers], with the three chief psychic-nerves and the four chief nerve-centers and the half-A all most vividly visualized."[18]

*The Path of Knowledge* lays special emphasis on the importance of making the image as vivid and lifelike as possible taking care, however, to keep it "vacuous," that is, semitransparent as a reminder to the yogin that even though this creation will confer very real physical benefits, it still remains ultimately illusory. The need to visualize the half of the Tibetan letter "A" stems from the author's belief that the sounds of the letters of the alphabet—and by extension their visual forms as well—possess magical efficacy that allows them to serve as vehicles for conveying psychic energy from celestial or divine sources.[19] Note that the yogin is instructed to completely

---

16. *Tibetan Yoga and Secret Doctrines,* p. 202.
17. Ibid., p. 189.
18. Ibid., p. 203.
19. Ibid., pp. 180–81, n. 2.

identify himself with this imaginatively fabricated goddess. He is to become, by a kind of mystical identification, this goddess whom he creates in his empowered imagination and he is furthermore to imagine that this goddess (who is also himself) possesses this system of subtle psychic nerves. The next step is to visualize these hollow psychic nerves as filling with a psychic fire that is ignited out of the shugs that course through them.

> While in that state of visualization, imagine at the center of each of the two palms of the hands, and at the centre of each of the two soles of the feet, a sun; and then place these suns one against the other. Then visualize in the tri-junction of the three chief psychic-nerves . . . a sun. By the rubbing together of these suns of the hands and feet, fire flareth up. This fire striketh the sun below the navel (in the tri-junction). A fire flareth up there and striketh the half-A. A fire flareth up from the half-A and permeateth the body. Then, as the expiration is going out, visualize the whole world as being permeated with fire.[20]

During these visualization exercises the meditator should perform twenty-one repetitions of the yogic bounces described above for seven days. The yogin will then acquire the ability to endure extreme cold.

One encounters here another instance where the tightly controlled imagination creates physically real effects just as it did in the examples of tulpa creation and telekinetic phenomena induced during out-of-body experiences that I referred to earlier in this chapter. As was the case with the previous examples of the active approach, supernormal efficacy first depends on the subject's being able to tightly fix his attention. The imagination of the meditator must also be in that condition that I have termed "empowerment." It is only the dynamically empowered and tightly focused thoughts and imaginings about fire and illumination that actually bring about the warming effects that the yogin desires. Thus, because David-Neel's imagination was in that condition of empowerment, others saw her tulpa in exactly the same way as she thought about it in her own imagination. If one wants to be warm, one has to think about (while the mind is empowered, of course) something warm or hot, such as fire or illumination. If one wants to have others see a phantom monk, one must likewise think about the phantom monk exactly as one wants to project

20. Ibid., p. 203.

him. Finally, if one wants to rise out of one's body then one has to think about or dream about something that rises. In each case, there is a direct and immediate correspondence between what is really experienced or generated supernormally and what one was thinking about or desiring provided that the mind and imagination were simultaneously in a condition of empowerment. Furthermore, just as David-Neel's tulpa seemed to take on the illusion of solidity in direct proportion to the vividness with which she imagined or visualized it, the objective impact of these other imaginatively created supernormal manifestations likewise seems to be directly proportional to the vividness and fixity with which they are imagined.

# The "Active" Approach Among Australian Aborigines

The descriptions that the Australian Aboriginal "clevermen" or medicinemen give in which they relate how they activate their supernormal magical powers clearly demonstrate that they, too, employ the active approach. As is typical with that method, the Australian Aborigines act as though it is necessary for the novice to learn how to focus his mind before he is able to acquire the various spiritual powers. A famous investigator of the Aborigines, A. P. Elkin, asserts that the medicineman does not acquire his exceptional powers by ingesting drugs or engaging in violent dancing but instead "through quietness and receptivity, meditation and recollection, observation and inference, concentration and decision."[21] Some medicinemen's accounts of their visionary experiences that they underwent as they were being initiated into the secrets of their vocation make it clear that the initiatory events occurred while the participant was in a trance-state akin to astral catalepsy. "While a person is experiencing the vision he cannot move, but he is conscious of what is going on around him. As one man of high degree of the Kattang tribe of New South Wales told me concerning his making: he could see and know what was happening but was as one dead, feeling nothing."[22]

A certain degree of recollective abstraction seems to be necessary either before or during the time when one is acquiring magical powers. Among the Wuradjeri tribe, when a medicineman wishes to obtain information

21. Elkin, *Aboriginal Men of High Degree*, 2d ed., p. 14.
22. Ibid., p. 62.

about what is happening at a distance clairvoyantly, he sends out his totemic familiar on a spiritual journey to gather the information he seeks. This act of sending out the totemic familiar seems to be a form of out-of-body experience in which the totemic familiar is substituted for the astral double of the projector so common in European accounts of astral projection experiences. This substitution does not always occur, however, as there are accounts of Aborigines who reportedly see the materialized double of the medicineman,[23] but generally because of the cultural assumption among them that there exists a complete identification between the mind and body of a man's totemic familiar and himself, the Aborigines usually depict out-of-body experiences as involving the exteriorization of a man's totemic familiar rather than his spiritual double. Bearing in mind that the act of sending out the totemic familiar to gather information clairvoyantly really represents another method of acquiring supernormal knowledge by means of astral projection, it should not be surprising if one discovers that some form of recollective technique is necessary in order to bring this about. Indeed, this seems to be the case for Elkin asserts that in order to gain this clairvoyant information, the medicineman has "to 'sing' or 'hum' or 'think' his spirit out. He would often do this as he was dropping off to sleep. . . . In such cases the medicineman seeks the distant information and does so through some psychic method while awake or while in a pre-controlled dream."[24]

It is evident that when the Aboriginal medicineman speaks about "singing," "humming," or "thinking" out the spirit, he is using these words in a very unusual way. The description suggests that these activities are part of a technique for inducing fixity of attention. Indeed, it is clear from this account that the medicinemen practice some form of control over their consciousness while it passes through the hypnagogic state into the dream-state in order to induce exteriorization of the consciousness-principle. This is very similar to the way contemporary practitioners of astral projection direct the flow of consciousness and thought formation as they pass from the hypnagogic state into the dream-state, so that they can bring about both mental concentration and dissociation from the physical body.

When native Australian sorcerers wish to kill someone without physically touching him, they perform a ritual known as "pointing the bone." Performance of this ritual in the proper manner supposedly results in the

23. Ibid., pp. 62–63.
24. Ibid., pp. 47–48.

victim's death. Like the other magical activities just discussed above, pointing the bone requires that the performer tightly focus his mind, will, and emotions on the task he wishes to accomplish. Performing this ritual in the proper manner involves much more than simply using the prescribed paraphernalia and uttering the prescribed words. Not only must the sorcerer possess a pointing stick or *ngathungi,* to which is attached something belonging to the intended victim such as the remnants of one of his meals, but he must also, Elkin explains, "be an expert. He must possess the power of concentration and of communicating without physical agency. . . . He must . . . throw himself into the rite, not vociferously, but through psychic concentration and direction." Without this ability of the sorcerer to concentrate his mind and without his ability to "empower" his thoughts and desires, the ritual possesses no real efficacy. One can see that this is true from the following description of the bone-pointing ritual that Elkin gives us. The sorcerer first takes a properly made pointing stick in his left hand and whispers softly,

> "Shooh ho! Let the breath leave thy body, O boy!" Then he chants a song of hate for an hour or more, after which he warms a part of the *ngathungi,* . . . concentrates his mind until he sees a picture of the victim, and then with all the emotion and energy he can summon, he whispers, "Die!" He lies down for an hour no doubt gathering fresh psychic strength, and then repeats this performance several times, each time whispering: "let the life-breath leave thy body, O boy! Die!" In fact, he keeps the mental picture of his victim before him all night. Finally, in the early morning, he performs similarly, but this time as close as possible to the victim, provided the latter is asleep.[25]

The most prominent element of the ritual is the sorcerer's complete mental and emotional focus on the task of killing his victim. Everything in the performance—the long chanting of the song of hate, the intensity and duration (lasting throughout the night) of concentration on a picture of the victim that the sorcerer creates from his imagination and memory, and the large amount of psychic energy that he projects into his utterance of the curses—clearly has the purpose of focusing the performer's mind, will, and emotions on his gruesome task. Once the sorcerer has enacted the ritual in this "proper" manner, his thoughts of hatred and murder supposedly be-

25. Ibid., p. 43.

come empowered. They have now become capable of exerting a deleterious effect on physical objects.

Although they do not assert this explicitly, the native Australians apparently believe that thoughts can materialize and then serve as a vehicle or agency of supernormal effects in much the same manner as Tibetans convert a picture of fire existing only in their imaginations into a physical source of warmth or fabricate objectifications of their own thoughts that others can sometimes physically see.[26] This assumption certainly seems to underlie aboriginal belief in the efficacy of the bone-pointing ritual. There also is some evidence that suggests that Australian medicinemen, like those Tibetans who create tulpas, are capable of materializing their spirit-familiars so that they are visible to others. For example, a white woman who lived with the Aborigines spoke of an experience that she had in which she claimed that she saw a spirit-familiar of one of the Euahlayi clevermen.

> One day I went to the camp, saw the old man in his usual airy costume, only assumed as I came in sight, a tailless shirt. . . . Presently he moved away to a quiet clear spot on the other side of the fire; he muttered something in a sing-song voice, and suddenly I saw him beating his head as if in accompaniment to his song, and then—where it came from I can't say—there beside him was a lizard. That fragment of a shirt was too transparent to have hidden that lizard; he could not have had it up his sleeve, because his sleeves were in shreds. It may have been a pet lizard that he has charmed in from the bush by his song, but I did not see it arrive.[27]

These materializations of spirit, or totemic-familiars, appear to play an important role in supernormal communications between Aborigines. For example, in Western culture it sometimes happens that at the moment when someone is either in grave danger or has just died his "double" will suddenly and unexpectedly materialize in the presence of a distant friend or loved one and then just as suddenly vanish. Such ghostly appearances are called "crisis" apparitions and take on the form of the person who is either dying or in danger. However, this is generally not the case among

---

26. Elkin noted the parallel between the techniques used by Australian clevermen to acquire supernormal powers and those of Tibetan yogins. See *Aboriginal Men of High Degree*, pp. 57–65.

27. Quoted in Ronald Rose, *Living Magic: The Realities Underlying the Psychical Practices and Beliefs of the Australian Aborigines* (New York: Rand McNally, 1956), p. 121.

native Australians, although there are exceptions—especially in the cases of those who have become acculturated to European ways. What happens instead to these Aborigines is that the crisis apparition takes on the form of the threatened individual's spirit-familiar. Consequently, when a native Australian sees one of these materialized spirit-familiars, he generally knows that one of the people he knows who has that animal as his totem is in trouble. Ronald Rose mentions an incident where an Aborigine named Earl learned that his grandmother had died.

> "He was sitting on the veranda of a hotel with three other fel-lows—white men. While they were sitting there he saw his *djurabeels*—that's his totem—that looks just like a rooster. This rooster was with the other fowls in the yard. As Earl was watching it, it came away from the other fowls, right onto the veranda. Just then a waitress came along and shooed it away. Earl knew the bird was *djurabeels,* and he said to the other men, 'You fellows won't believe this, but I'm gonna get some bad news soon!'"

Almost immediately after Earl said this he got a phone call informing him that his grandmother had indeed passed away. The native Australians are very much aware that, although other people such as the waitress may often take them to be real animals, such spirit-familiars are really only illusory. As the Aboriginal informant who told Rose the above story put it, "'That bird is not real, I know. . . . You see it with your mind.'"[28]

Materializations also function significantly in certain ritual contexts within native Australian life, especially if these rituals center around either conferring supernormal powers on someone or affecting someone or some-thing supernormally. For example, when a Wuradjeri youth decides to be-come a medicineman he must first be given a spirit-familiar or totemic assistant by the doctor or medicineman who is responsible for initiating him. Like most other Aborigines the Wuradjeri believe that one cannot possess magical powers unless one has a totem animal "sung" into one's body. The one singing the totem animal into the novice is evidently in a trance-state similar to that which is necessary if astral projection is to oc-cur. During the singing ritual, when the medicineman is transmitting his totem to the novice,

28. Rose, *Living Magic*, p. 149.

the assistant totem resident in the doctor causes itself to be doubled, so that without subtraction, it might remain with the latter and yet leave his body under the influence of the magic song. . . . Having once received the [assistant totem], the youth was instructed in the methods by which he might make use of it and was taught the song *and the ritual concentration necessary to release it from his body.*[29]

It seems that the initiating doctor's ritual concentration sets the stage for an exteriorization that then takes the form of the totem animal that the doctor wishes to project into the novice. Berndt's Wuradjeri informant told him that during one such ritual, "From the air, with a sweep of his hand, the father, who was a doctor, took a little opossum and placed it on the son's chest. While he sang, the opossum gradually sank into the flesh, until it was out of view."[30] Although there is not enough detail from this description to say with certainty that the opossum the initiating doctor supposedly materialized out of thin air was an objectification of the father's thoughts at the moment when he was transmitting his spirit-familiar to his son, one is probably safe in making this assumption. This confidence stems from my observation of the close parallels between this description of a materialization phenomenon and the kind of exteriorization phenomenon that occurs during an out-of-body experience.

I believe that the materialized opossum was probably a species of exteriorization phenomenon of the same sort as that astral phantom projected during out-of-body experiences. In other words, the opossum could be sung into the boy's body because it was a diaphanous exteriorization, a kind of astral creation, produced by the medicineman and subject to manipulation in accordance with his wishes. What parallels suggest these conclusions?

First, both kinds of exteriorization phenomena go through solid objects—in this case, the boy's body. When other native Australians described how they saw medicinemen's spirit-familiars, they likewise mentioned that these creations had the ability to pass through solid objects such as trees and rocks.[31] Second, both kinds of exteriorization phantom can serve as an extracerebral sensory organ. Monroe and other projectors sometimes gained clairvoyant information about events that were taking

29. R. M. Berndt, "Wuradjeri Magic and 'Clever Men,'" *Oceania* 17, no. 4 (June 1947), p. 334.
30. Berndt, "Wuradjeri Magic and 'Clever Men,'" p. 333.
31. Elkin, *Aboriginal Men of High Degree,* p. 54.

place at a considerable distance from their physical bodies, claiming that they acquire this information by "seeing" what was going on through the eyes of their astral double. Australian medicinemen are also supposed to be able to send out their spirit-familiars to gather information clairvoyantly while they are entranced.[32] In both cases, it is the exteriorized spirit-body that does the clairvoyant seeing, not the fleshly body. Third, both kinds of exteriorization phenomena usually require some form of mental and emotional concentration as a preparatory ritual if the event is to take place. Fourth, the empowerment of thought appears to be present in both types of exteriorization phenomena.

Although I cannot prove by direct evidence that the Wuradjeri medicineman's exteriorization is true, I argue for the existence of empowerment by indirect evidence. Why would the Wuradjeri medicineman's exteriorization take on the form of his own totem animal instead of becoming a double of his physical body? To answer this question, one needs to bear in mind Sylvan Muldoon's remarks about the role that habit and cultural conditioning play in structuring the content of out-of-body experiences. Muldoon observed that habitual or unconscious thoughts were just as important—if not more so—than conscious, deliberate thoughts in structuring the experiential content of a projection. He noted that since one always walks on the top of a floor in waking life, when an individual has an out-of-body visionary experience his astral phantom continues to walk on the tops of those floors that constitute elements of the visionary landscape, even though the astral phantom could, if it wanted to, go right through the floor. This generally does not happen because our subconscious habits keep "objectifying" themselves so that they cause the phantom to stay on the top of the floor as the physical body does in waking life. Muldoon found out that if he consciously started to think about why he was not sinking through the floor in his astral body, he would begin to go through the floor, apparently letting his conscious thoughts override unconscious habitual thoughts. Muldoon also noticed the same thing about the clothing of the astral phantom. He once asked himself, why aren't astral bodies nude? Why do they always seem to have clothes? He concluded that the astral phantoms are always seen as clothed because that is how people in our culture habitually depict themselves to their own imaginations.[33]

32. Ibid., p. 46.
33. Muldoon and Carrington, *Projection of the Astral Body*, pp. 283–91.

I argue that since the Australian spirit-familiars share all the other characteristics of the astral phantoms Muldoon and Monroe have described,
they also must occur in tandem with the empowerment of thought. Indeed,
it is precisely because empowerment is operative that the spirit-familiars
take on the particular forms that they do. After all, if one's cultural upbringing conditions them to imagine a particularly intimate relationship to
their totem animal, it is quite logical, given Muldoon's observations about
the role of habit in shaping out-of-body experience, that when a native
Australian has an out-of-body experience he will not see an astral duplicate of his physical body but rather an astral creation that takes the form
of that totem animal with which he identifies himself. When a native Australian believes "that the totem of any man is regarded . . . as the same
thing as himself,"[34] it is quite natural that, were he to produce an astral
phantom, that phantom would not clothe itself with Western clothes or
take on the form of his physical body as astral phantoms do in Western
culture. Instead, it would probably take on the form of the projector's
totem animal—especially in a ritual context where everyone's thoughts
and actions are centered on manifesting such a creature.[35]

Regardless of whether my hypothesis about the equivalence of the astral
phantom and the native Australian medicineman's totemic spirit-familiar is
correct or not, it is clear that techniques of mental concentration, coupled
with a belief in the efficacy of empowered thoughts, remain important
elements within the ritual complex of native Australian culture. Many aspects of the rituals of sorcery and the "making" of medicinemen remain
incomprehensible if one ignores the importance that the Aborigines attribute to techniques of concentration and to methods that supposedly empower thoughts. Such rituals only become comprehensible if one acknowledges that effective participation in them is not only a matter of following
certain external actions in a rigidly stereotyped order. To participate fully
and effectively participants must cultivate a distinctive psychological state.

34. Elkin, *Aboriginal Men of High Degree*, p. 67, n. 18.
35. David-Neel claimed she saw a tulpa of a demonic deity that a Tibetan painter had
unconsciously created by the force of his concentration on ritually invoking it (see David
Neel, *Magic and Mystery in Tibet*, pp. 310–11). One should recall the phenomenon of the
*djurabeels* (a materialization of an aborigine's totem animal), which shows, if it be true, that
the native Australian's intimate identification with his totem animal is capable of exteriorizing itself in the form of a phantom totem animal. I have noted in Chapter 8 that the "crisis"
apparitions of Europeans take the form of the individual in extremis while those of native
Australians take the form, not of the individual who is dying, but rather the form of his totem
animal with whom he apparently closely identified himself.

For the native Australians, as for the Tibetan yogins, the acquisition of supposed supernormal powers requires the active approach.

# The "Active" Approach in Walther's Induction of Telepathic Experiences

The next example of the active approach comes from Gerda Walther, a contemporary psychic, parapsychologist, and phenomenologist of mysticism. The two central elements of the active approach, recollection and empowerment, figure prominently in Walther's method for developing paranormal sensitivity. In "On the Psychology of Telepathy," Walther describes how she establishes a condition of telepathic rapport with another person.

> If I am looking for a person telepathically and try to get into a telepathic rapport with him or her, I usually lie down comfortably, if possible, then relax my mental hold or awareness of everything else and concentrate as much as ever I can on the person with whom I want to get in touch, i.e., I either concentrate merely on his or her aura and if I can't do that, I help myself by concentrating on the image (perhaps a real picture) of the person or the memory of a certain incident when in the company of this person; or perhaps by reading something written by him or her to get the "flavor" of his or her aura.[36]

There is, of course, nothing exceptional about Walther's emphasis on the need for relaxation, abstraction from the distractions of sense-experience, and fixity of attention. These recollective methods are common to all other partisans of the active approach. What is distinctive about Walther's method is her emphasis on the need to concentrate on the aura of the person whom she wishes to contact.

Like many other psychically gifted people, Walther claims that she sees luminous halos or auras around the bodies of other people. She furthermore claims—and she is joined by other psychics—that by the color and transparency or opacity of another's aura she can tell what mood they are

36. Walther, "On the Psychology of Telepathy," p. 442.

in and what their level of spiritual or intellectual development is.[37] The color of the person's aura

> is dependent on his mood, and may vary according to the person being glad, depressed, full of joy, or love, or anger. Yet it seems to me that the aura of one and the same person always has the same particular hue or intrinsic quality so that one can tell to whom it belongs despite these momentary differences. . . . The aura will be the brighter, luminous and transparent—so to say—the more spiritual its owner is, and it will be dull and opaque if its owner is a more or less materialistic, undeveloped person.[38]

The reason why Walther finds it necessary to focus on the aura of a person whom she wishes to contact in preference to merely focusing on a photograph or memory-image of them stems from the fact that "telepathic experiences are always penetrated by the personal atmosphere peculiar to the agent when the aura is that of a person known to the percipient. If not, then the percipient will at least know it is embedded in an 'unknown aura' of an identity obscure to the percipient."[39] In other words, every telepathic experience is embedded in the aura of the person with whom the percipient is in rapport. This sense of another person's aura is what labels the telepathic experience as coming from a specific individual. For this reason, recalling one's own previous experience of another person's aura serves as a more potent means of putting oneself in telepathic rapport with that individual than simply recalling his or her face in one's memory or looking at his or her photograph. The relative superiority Walther attributes to focusing one's recollections on another person's aura also stems from the fact that telepathic awareness and auric sensing are both phenomena that participate heavily in the affective rather than the purely intellectual or merely perceptual dimension of human experience. Thus, when Walther speaks of getting into telepathic rapport with someone she declares that it is necessary to mobilize the emotions and feelings:

37. See also Cayce, *Auras*, p. 5; Manning, *The Link;* Anonymous, *The Boy Who Saw True;* Karagulla, *Breakthrough to Creativity;* Plutarch, *On the Delay of Divine Justice (De Sera Numinis Vindicta)* quoted in G. R. S. Mead, *The Doctrine of the Subtle Body in Western Tradition* (Wheaton, Ill.: Quest Books, 1967), pp. 41–42; Garrett, *Adventures in the Supernormal.*
38. Walther, "Some Experiences Concerning the Human 'Aura,'" pp. 343–44.
39. Walther, "On the Psychology of Telepathy," p. 441.

Emotions or feelings—be they sympathetic or antipathetic, seem to help telepathy a great deal. I think it is easiest to get emotions or feelings, and in a less degree thoughts embedded in or connected with emotions. The greatest difficulty . . . is getting merely intellectual thoughts, ideas, or perceptions. I think one of the reasons why experimental telepathy doesn't get better results generally is it is mostly the mere intellectual experiences which are broadcast and emotions must needs play a very little part in them.[40]

As we saw in Chapters 3 and 9, sensing an aura involves simultaneous insights into both the emotional and spiritual interior of another human being in a way that merely perceiving their form or their photograph cannot be. The colors of an aura are more than just colors—from Walther's descriptions it is clear that not only are they colors but they are also simultaneously openings into someone else's emotional universe. Auric perception, by its very nature, possesses an intimacy that sense perceptions cannot have. Since telepathic experiences embed the percipient in a matrix of feelings rather than mere ideas, it is logical that a recollective technique for developing this sensibility would focus on recalling an experience that has the maximum capacity to evoke an emotional rather than intellectual response in the percipient.

It is evident that Walther also utilizes the empowerment of thoughts, emotions, and desires in developing her telepathic sensibilities. It is difficult to imagine how her act of concentrating on a person's aura or picture could ever actually bring her into rapport with that individual if she were not already in a state of consciousness where her thoughts, feelings, and desires were empowered. Moreover, since she claims that this exercise of concentrating the attention often works, one may deduce that empowerment is indeed present. If thinking about a person's aura actually puts one into that person's mind, there is fundamentally no structural difference between that kind of relationship between thinking and experience and what Monroe described as characteristic of that same relationship in Locale II.[41]

40. Ibid., p. 444; see also Garrett, *Telepathy,* pp. 8–9.
41. Not all of Walther's telepathic experiences, however, occurred as the result of her deliberate efforts. It often happened that telepathic impressions came to her spontaneously as though they had "invaded" her field of consciousness. See Walther, "On the Psychology of Telepathy," pp. 442–43.

# The "Active" Approach in Pantañjali's *Yoga-Sūtras*

My final example of the active approach is taken from the classic text of Raja Yoga, the *Yoga-Sūtras* of Patañjali. Patañjali devoted Book 3 of this work to a terse description of both the various supernormal powers that the perfected yogin can awaken, as well as the methods that enable him to do so. Both of the most important elements of the active approach, mental concentration and the phenomenon of empowerment, played important roles in his instructions about how to develop paranormal abilities and manifestations. Each of the supernormal capabilities or phenomena that Patañjali described required above all that the aspiring yogin learn *saṃyama*, "to practice constraint," with respect to some aspect or quality of either that supernormal power that he wishes to exercise or that supernormal phenomenon that he wishes to make manifest. What did Patañjali and his commentators mean by "to practice constraint"?

Patañjali defined samyama as an act that simultaneously incorporated three different kinds of mental focusing procedures and fused them.[42] The first component of samyama is *dhāraṇā,* that yogic practice in which one fixes the mind on one particular object to the exclusion of all else. It is basically synonymous with what I refer to as "recollection." *Dhyāna,* or "contemplation," constitutes the second component of practicing constraint and involves continuing the previously achieved dhāraṇā for a sustained period of time. In short, it is a dhāraṇā that is of more than momentary duration. The third component of samyama is *samādhi,* or "concentration." Samādhi occurs when the continuously fixed attention characteristic of dhyāna becomes so profoundly concentrated on its object that the yogin loses all sense of distinction between the act of contemplating the object and the object itself. One of the classic commentators of the *Yoga-Sūtras,* Vācaspati Miśra, asserted that in samādhi there is no longer "a distinction between the contemplation and the object-to-be-contemplated. Concentration (*samādhi*) is free from this."[43] Basically, samādhi involves the dissolution of the subject-object dualism that characterizes ordinary perception and experience. Since its achievement presumes that one has achieved dhyāna—and dhyāna in turn presupposes that one has previously mastered dhāraṇā—Patañjali saw no reason why he should not lump

42. Patañjali, *Yoga-System of Patañjali,* 3:4.
43. Ibid., 3:3. See Vācaspati Miśra's commentary.

all three processes together under the term saṃyama. "To practice constraint," then, means that one takes something as a focus of one's concentration and then puts oneself into a condition of samādhi with that particular thing as the contemplated object.

No yogin can hope to develop any supernormal powers if he does not first practice constraint. I have demonstrated above that any form of the active approach requires that the aspirant to paranormal abilities must always learn how to focus his mind, imagination, and emotions on that which he wishes to achieve or influence. I will now demonstrate that saṃyama also incorporates the second major element of the active approach, empowerment.

There is evidence that the phenomenon of mental empowerment was tacitly assumed as an element within Patañjali's system of techniques for developing supernormal powers. I suggest that the reason why the subject-object dualism disappears in samādhi stems from the fact that in samādhi the prior recollective practices of dhāraṇā and dhyāna have one-pointedly focused the mind and thereby created a condition of enthymesis, or mental empowerment. *Because of this induction of empowerment* samādhi blurs the subject-object distinction. If I am correct, samādhi is a condition where there is the same kind of simultaneity between thinking and experiencing the presence of what one is thinking about that was the prime characteristic of empowerment in other contexts. Consequently, the *Yoga-Sūtras* repeatedly assume that if a yogin wishes to acquire a particular supernormal power or knowledge he first has to focus his mind on some quality or aspect of that specific paranormal ability he wishes to develop and then put himself into a condition of samādhi with that quality or aspect as his object of meditation. Once these two things have taken place, the effect he desires will supposedly come to pass. Thus, when Patañjali counseled the yogin on how to acquire the ability to fly through the air he stated that "either as a result of constraint upon the relation between the body and the air (*ākāśa*) or (*ca*) as the result of the balanced-state of lightness, such as that of cotton-fibre, there follows the passing through air."

What was Patañjali telling the yogin to do? He was stressing that the yogin must practice constraint and thereby put his mind into a condition of samādhi with his thought focused on either one of two things: (1) "the relationship between the body and the air," that is to say, he must concentrate his mind on the way in which space allows a body to penetrate it; or (2) the attainment of a "balanced-state of lightness." What did Patañjali mean by a "balanced-state of lightness"? One of Patañjali's most important commentators, Vācaspati Miśra, explained that the balanced-state is "the state of mind which rests in the (thing) and in which it is tinged."[44] This means that the mind of the yogin is concentrated so deeply on the notion of being light like a cotton fiber that he actually experiences himself as practically weightless. The commentator Veda-Vyāsa used a helpful simile in order to clarify what the term "balanced-state" signified. Veda-Vyāsa said that when the mind of a yogin rests in the balanced-state it is like a perfectly clear gem crystal that is lying near a colored object. "Just as a crystal is tinged by the various colors of the different things next to which it lies and appears as having the form of the colored thing-next-to-which-it-lies, so the mind-stuff is influenced by referring to the object-to-be-known and . . . appears as having the form of the object-to-be-known as it is in itself."[45] In each case, the supernormal power to fly through the air came from concentrating the mind on something that pertained to flying through the air, such as the sensation of space giving way to make room for a body passing through it or the sensation of being light and puffy with air. I suggest that contemplating the notions of lightness and vacuity while the yogin's mind is simultaneously concentrated in samādhi and empowered by virtue of that concentration is what permits the yogin to actually experience a condition in which he feels weightless and airlike.

Patañjali's instructions for flying through the air merit comparison with Monroe's instructions for dissociating the astral body. Monroe, like Patañjali, emphasized the importance of tightly concentrating the mind on what one wished to do. Monroe instructed the would-be projector to first get into the vibrational state. (This was simultaneously a state of empowerment for "in the state of vibration you are apparently subject to every thought, both willful and involuntary, that crosses your mind).[46] Consequently, one must learn to control one's thoughts upon what one wishes to accomplish. "Thus you must be as close to 'no thought' or, 'single thought' (concentration) as possible."[47] In order to go from this stage to that of actual dissociation the would-be projector must "achieve the vibrational state and maintain complete control of your thought processes. . . . Think of getting lighter, of floating upward, of how nice it would be, as the subjective associated thought is most important. . . . If you continue to hold only those thoughts you will dissociate."[48]

44. Ibid., 3:42.
45. Ibid., 1:41. See Veda-Vyāsa's commentary.
46. Monroe, *Journeys Out of the Body*, p. 216.
47. Ibid.
48. Ibid., p. 219.

The parallels between Monroe's illustrations and those of Patañjali are obvious. Both descriptions presuppose the modality of empowerment because they indicate that the dynamization of thoughts will only come about if, first, the subject has previously attained proficiency in techniques of mental concentration and, second, because, in each case, a thought pertaining to some aspect of flying such as floating upward, weightlessness, or spatiality directly translates into an actual experience of flying through the air. In each case one sees that strange equivalence between thought and experience that is the hallmark of empowerment.

My suggestion that the state of samādhi that results from the practice of constraint is simultaneously a condition of mental empowerment challenges a common misconception about the nature of some of the higher states of mystical experience. More specifically, it calls into question some of the rather imprecise ways that some scholars and laymen have described the condition of mystical union. F. C. Happold exemplified this type of scholarship on the nature of mystical union.

> In mystical experience the dilemma of duality is resolved. For the
> mystic is given that unifying vision of the One in the All and the All
> in the One. There is little doubt that this sense of the Oneness of
> everything in the universe and outside it is at the heart of the most
> highly developed mystical consciousness.[49]

I am uncomfortable with this characterization of the essence of mystical experience as a "sense of the Oneness of everything in the universe." Happold's language suggests some sort of pantheistic sharing of a substance as the foundation for those feelings of mystical union referred to in the writings of some mystics. I suggest that many conditions that are described as experiences of "union" or "oneness" are really states of consciousness in which the empowerment of mind, will, and imagination is operative. In those particular conditions of enthymesis,[50] there is a simultaneity between thinking and being rather than a pantheistic sharing of a substance. For example, in the particular condition of samādhi where the yogin was instructed to focus one-pointedly on the idea of becoming light and puffy like a ball of cotton, there is not a oneness between the yogin and a ball of cotton as Happold's careless language of union might imply (had he been referring to Patañjali) but rather, as I would suggest, there is an immediate simultaneity between the thought "I am light like a puffy ball of cotton"

49. F. C. Happold, *Mysticism: A Study and an Anthology* (Baltimore: Penguin, 1973), p. 46.
50. I remind the reader that the terms "empowerment" and "enthymesis" are synonyms.

and the translation of that empowered thought into a vivid experience of actually seeming to float in the air like a puffy ball of cotton. This simultaneity of thinking and being that is characteristic of empowered thought and desire cannot really be described as an experience of union. It is something quite different; it is the "objectification" of a thought or desire. Moreover, samādhi as described in the *Yoga-Sūtras* was not a univalent "sense of Oneness with everything in the universe" because it did not bring about an identification with all objects but, instead, effected a perceptual fusion—not a fusion of substances—between the subject and a specific object or set of objects. Consequently, Patañjali took it for granted that there were as many experientially distinct forms of samādhi as there were objects on which the yogin could practice constraint. The experiential distinctiveness of each particular samādhi would follow as a direct consequence of empowerment since under such a condition each object contemplated would uniquely tinge the experience that resulted from focusing one's attention on it. For example, there is no reason to assume that the experience of samādhi that results from practicing constraint with respect to the relationship of the body with the air will be anything at all like that experience that results from practicing constraint with respect to Monroe's friend R.W.

Patañjali claimed that, in practicing constraint with respect to the body's relationship with the air, the resultant condition of samādhi allowed the yogin to fly through the air at will. However, when Monroe practiced constraint (that is, focused his attention) on the desire to visit his friend R.W., he did more than just fly through the air—he clairvoyantly experienced where she was and what she was doing. Similarly, when Monroe focused his attention on the desire to visit Dr. Bradshaw rather than R.W., the result of his empowered thought about Bradshaw was completely different from his thought about R.W.[51] Monroe's thoughts about Bradshaw took his astral body to the doctor's house, not the seaside cottage of R.W., and his clairvoyant experience of Bradshaw's actions was in no way existentially or perceptually equivalent to his out-of-body experience at R.W.'s cottage. He discovered that if he thought about visiting R.W. or Bradshaw the choice of object to focus on was no matter of indifference. In one case his destination would be wherever R.W. was and what he would perceive there would obviously differ from what he would experience at Bradshaw's residence. From these examples one may draw the following conclusion: Whenever the

51. Monroe, *Journeys Out of the Body*, pp. 46–48.

phenomenon of empowerment is operative in a mystical experience, this fact necessarily precludes the possibility of there being any experiential identity between such kinds of mystical states. Why? Because the object of contemplation and those subconscious affective and mental associations that the subject brings along with his thoughts about that particular object, directly translate themselves, as a result of the empowerment process operating on them, into an experience that is uniquely shaped by the specific object on which the subject has focused his mind.

Once he has empowered his mind by saṃyama, Patañjali's yogin obtains his supernormal power or knowledge either in a "direct" fashion from the object he contemplates or in an "indirect" fashion. I use "direct" because the paranormal ability acquired is straightforwardly related to the specific object or quality on which the yogin focuses his empowered mind. For example, the yogin gains the ability to fly through the air by focusing his mind on a quality that is immediately and obviously related to flying and floating, the quality or sensation of lightness and weightlessness. However, the connection between a particular object of saṃyama and the specific power or knowledge that supposedly results from mastering that act of constraint is not always so straightforward. The following passage from the Yoga-Sūtras illustrates how "indirect" the connection can be between a specific object of contemplation and the particular supernormal power or knowledge derived from contemplating it. Patañjali claimed that "(as a result of constraint) upon the heart (there arises) a consciousness of the mind-stuff."[52] The eleventh-century commentator Bhojarāja elaborated on this passage by explaining that the term "heart" does not really refer to the physical organ but rather to a subtle organ that lies within the corporeal heart. It is by concentrating on that subtle organ that the yogin acquires "a knowledge of his own mind as well as that of others . . . that is, he knows all fancies of his own mind as well as the passions, etc., of the minds of others."[53] Now why would focusing the mind on a space within the heart have anything to do with acquiring a telepathic power to know the passions and desires that dwell within other people's minds? This connection is anything but self-evident.

One begins to solve this puzzle once one assumes that in this particular instance the practice of constraint may have worked not because it empowered thoughts about a several-pound chunk of muscle that pumps

52. Patañjali, Yoga-System of Patañjali, 3:34.
53. Patañjali, Yoga-Sūtra of Patañjali, 3:35; commentary by Bhojarāja.

blood but for another reason. How could empowered thoughts about a chunk of muscle produce telepathic awareness? It is more likely that what was empowered were thoughts related to that more or less tacit network of conceptual and affective associations that the text called up in the yogin's mind when it referred to that subtle organ that the sacred Upanishads mention as existing within the physical heart. All the traditional commentaries on this passage of the *Yoga-Sūtra* refer either obliquely or explicitly to the Upanishadic physiology when they try to explicate the text. For this reason it will be useful to examine briefly the Upanishadic passage that seems to have had the most influence on those commentators.

The eighth book of the Chāndogya Upanishad opens with a teacher proclaiming to his students: "What is here in this city of Brahma (i.e., the body) is an abode, a small lotus-flower (i.e., the heart). Within that is a small space. What is within that should be searched out; that, assuredly, is what one should desire to understand."[54] He goes on to explain that because this small space within the heart is the dwelling place of a human being's immortal Self or soul (*ātman*), knowledge of it is the yogin's highest calling. When Veda-Vyāsa commented on Patañjali's instructions to contemplate the heart, he paraphrased those portions of the Chandogya Upanishad, except that he and the commentators that followed him made the significant substitution of *citta* (mind-stuff) where the Upanishad used the word *ātman* (Self or Soul). One can see this parallel to the Chandogya Upanishad when Veda-Vyāsa explicates 3:34 by stating that when Patañjali refers to the heart he is referring to the fact that "in this citadel of Brahma, is the house (of the mind-stuff), a tiny lotus (of the heart)—(there arises) a discernment of that."[55] Given that this system of thought underlies the *Yoga-Sūtras,* it becomes easier to understand why those who followed its system of ascesis and concentration took it for granted that practicing constraint with respect to the heart would give the yogin a knowledge about the ultimate nature of his own mind and what was in the minds of others. After all, within that system of physiology, it was just as natural for them to link the heart and the mind together as it is for us to link floating in the air with the quality or sensation of lightness.

One may recall, however, that Bhojarāja maintained that not only did performing this concentration on the heart give the yogin paranormal

---

54. Chāndogya Upanishad 8.1.1 and 8.1.4, in *The Thirteen Principal Upanishads,* pp. 262 and 263, respectively.
55. Patañjali, *Yoga-System of Patañjali,* 3:34; commentary of Veda-Vyāsa.

knowledge of the mind but also telepathic insight into the passions and desires of the human mind. The tendency to associate the heart with insight into desires and passions also seems to reflect the influence of the eighth book of the Chāndogya Upanishad. For example, immediately after the Upanishadic teacher has explained how the space within the heart is the seat of the Soul, he goes on to describe the nature of experience in the hereafter. In the afterlife, a human being experiences an objectification of his or her desires. Thus the Upanishadic teacher tells listeners, "Of whatever object he becomes desirous, whatever desire he desires, merely out of his conception it arises." The narrator goes on to explain to his pupils that although these objectified desires are real, they are covered with something that falsifies them. To remove this mysterious covering that deludes, it is necessary for the seeker to go inside his heart to his own immortal soul that dwells within that space, "for there, truly, are those real desires of his which have a covering of what is false."[56] Considering these statements, it is easier to understand how Bhojarāja could claim that meditating on the heart leads to a discernment of the desires that lie locked inside of men's minds for according to the Chāndogya Upanishad, the heart is the seat of "real desires." It is by entering into the heart, presumably by meditation, that the wise gain the ability to penetrate the veil of falsity that covers both their own desires and the desires of others. In other words, the basic theme of this Upanishadic passage seems to be that one penetrates the nature of desires when one enters into the heart. It is not difficult to imagine how this Upanishadic idea that entering into the heart is tantamount to a revelatory penetration into the nature of desire later developed into a claim that meditating on the heart provides the yogin with a telepathic knowledge about what desires lie hidden within the minds of human beings.

# The Relationship Between the Object of Concentration and the Powers Acquired by Fixing Attention Upon It

Additional material may clarify further what I mean when I assert that it is the chain of associations that an object evokes (and not the object in isolation from these associations) that often serves as the more important deter-

56. Chāndogya Upanishad 8.2.10, cited in *The Thirteen Principal Upanishads*, p. 264.

minant that structures the experience of a yogin who has empowered his mind by focusing on that particular object. For example, Muldoon spoke about the important role subconscious ideas and habits play in structuring the content of experience under conditions of mental empowerment. This discovery came about when he began to ask himself why the astral double always seems to walk on the surface of a floor during a projection even though it can just as well go through walls and through the floor. His sense-experience of suddenly falling through the floor at that very moment when he began to reflect on why his astral body was not falling through it convinced him that "the subconscious will, through habit, actually holds the body in its position. You do not think of walking in the physical, do you? Neither do you in the astral."[57] Muldoon's experience demonstrates how the tacit assumptions one brings into a condition of mental empowerment still operate significantly to shape the content of the resultant experience.

In a similar fashion, Walther reminded her readers that she generally could not establish telepathic rapport with someone whom she regarded with indifference. Her chances of success were greatest if she possessed a network of strong emotional associations, either of a positive or negative sort, with that person whom she wished to contact.[58] Once again, it is not just the physical characteristics of the object meditated on that are important. The set of affective associations that it elicits can be equally, if not more, important as a force that structures the content of experience under conditions of mental empowerment.

There is another way that the results of empowerment often transcend the specific object that serves as the subject's initial focus of concentration. The particular form of paranormal knowledge that results from centering one's empowered mind or imagination on a specific object frequently reveals information that cannot be given or implied either by that object's external features or by the set of conscious and subconscious ideational and affective associations that it evokes in the subject's mind. In other words, one's empowered thoughts or desires about an object accomplish considerably more than just the presentation of that object to one's field of consciousness. One not only senses that object's presence but one also gains additional information concerning details about the particular context of which that object is a part. It is in this sense that one can speak of a genuine element of transcendence being involved in those forms of para-

---

57. Muldoon and Carrington, *Projection of the Astral Body*, p. 290.
58. Walther, "On the Psychology of Telepathy," p. 444.

normal knowledge that result from empowered thoughts about a particular object or desire.

Monroe once put himself in a condition where he had empowered his thoughts. He then "thought heavily of the desire to 'go' to R.W." This empowered thought instantly triggered a sense of motion. Monroe then found himself in a kitchen where his friend R.W. was talking to two teen-aged girls drinking soft drinks.[59] This particular incident was one of the instances of apparently genuine traveling clairvoyance that he cited in his autobiography, since he later confirmed that at the time he visited R.W. she was indeed sitting with two girls inside a building drinking. At the time of his astral visit to R.W., Monroe had no knowledge of her specific whereabouts except that she was vacationing in New Jersey on the coast. However, this ignorance did not prevent him from actually "going" there. One may notice that Monroe's acquisition of this bit of supernormal information remained inseparably linked to his empowered thoughts of "going to see R.W." Without the thought, "I want to see R.W.," he never would have clairvoyantly seen what was happening to her. In this sense, then, one can see how this particular item of clairvoyant knowledge depended on the particular object around which he had centered his empowered imagination. Nevertheless, these empowered thoughts did much more than just present R.W.'s image to Monroe's field of consciousness. He simultaneously found out information about her surroundings that he had no way of acquiring by extrapolating from what he knew about her or her activities. How could his mere thought "I want to see R.W." actually have projected Monroe to a destination, unknown to him, where she really was? How was the information about specific details of her activities and whereabouts that day in any way hidden or implied in his thoughts about her? This example demonstrates that paranormal knowledge resulting from empowered thoughts "transcends" the subject's empowered thought-about-the-object. It indicates that there is an informational overplus somehow present in at least certain kinds of empowered thoughts. It seems as though this informational overplus glues itself to the empowered thought in an inexplicable way.[60]

59. Monroe, *Journeys Out of the Body*, pp. 55–56.
60. The observation that empowered thoughts sometimes carry veridical information about their object suggests an interesting hypothetical possibility. If thinking about R.W. actually led Monroe to objectively verifiable information concerning what she was doing, what sorts of veridical information would attach itself to empowered thoughts focused on other very different kinds of objects? For example, consider the following instruction (*Yoga-*

One other feature deserves comment. The informational overplus that attaches itself to certain kinds of empowered thoughts remains specifically connected to the particular thought that generated it. Thus, when Monroe thought about visiting R.W. he received clairvoyant information about R.W. and not about something or someone entirely unrelated to her or her immediate context at the time of the thought. Consequently, even though this information transcended what the subject could possibly have known about R.W. or extrapolated from what he knew about her, his knowledge still remained significantly related to his original object of concentration.

When one recognizes that empowered thoughts not only result in a presentation of their object to the subject's field of consciousness but also that they sometimes incorporate, in some mysterious fashion, veridical information concerning both their object and its context at the time that the subject is thinking about it, one has taken an important step toward recognizing one of the basic inadequacies of psychologism. Psychologism asserts that the phenomenon of empowerment merely creates a solipsistic landscape of objectified thoughts and feelings that engulfs the subject's field of consciousness in the manner of a dream. Furthermore, psychologism affirms that this landscape has its origin from within the conscious and subconscious mind of the percipient. Advocates of psychologism claim that any sense of exteriority or objectivity that these objectifications might have is only the illusory result of what psychoanalysts term a subconscious

---

*System of Patañjali,* 3:35) Patañjali gives the yogin who wishes to achieve *kaivalyam* (isolation), the supreme goal of Yoga. He tells the yogin that "[intuitive] Knowledge of the Self arises as the result of constraint upon that which exists for its own sake [the Self]." This passage instructs the yogin who wishes to reach kaivalyam that he must set his empowered thought (achieved by practicing constraint) on the real nature of the Self. In other words, he must center his empowered mind on the radical distinction that Sāṃkhya posits as existing between the utterly transcendent Self (*puruṣa*) and the thinking principle. In experiential terms, to what does following this instruction lead? Since the yogin focuses his empowered thought on the distinction between the Self and the thinking principle, it is clear that this empowered thought upon the distinction between the Self and the thinking principle will have to objectify itself. In one sense, then, kaivalyam will therefore become a concretization of this metaphysical assertion of Sāṃkhya. The yogin will then experience rather than merely believe the truth of this metaphysical assertion. However, my previous observation that an "informational overplus" sometimes glues itself to an empowered thought opens up the possibility that kaivalyam will be more than just a concretization of certain propositions of Sāṃkhya metaphysics and that it will also incorporate an "overplus," some kind of veridical insight, much akin to that which we saw operating in Monroe's experience. The specific form this particular veridical insight would take is anybody's guess but one should at least admit the formal possibility that it may exist as an irreducible element of that insight-state that yogins call kaivalyam.

mechanism of projection. If all that occurred as a result of empowerment was the presentation of the object-thought-about to the subject's field of consciousness, the partisans of psychologism would have a strong case. However, when empowered thoughts about an object not only present the object to consciousness but also give the subject objectively valid information about it, one realizes that regardless of superficial similarities, the phenomenon of empowerment is something fundamentally distinct from the psychoanalysts' mechanisms of projection and introjection.

# 13

# The "Passive" Approach for Inducing Paranormal Manifestations After Recollective Quiet

I began my discussion of the active approach in Chapter 12 with a brief reference to another method for acquiring supernormal sensitivities that mystics and psychically gifted people have employed. I call this method the "passive" approach. The principal feature that differentiates the passive from the active approach is that the subject acts as a passive receiver of impressions that pour into his or her field of consciousness from a source that seems to come from outside the psyche. The subject unravels the supernormal message or information that these impressions contain either by direct inspection of them or by a peculiar process of empathic identification with them.

In the active approach, the subject does not passively wait for impressions to enter his or her mind. Instead, the subject generates these information-laden impressions from within his or her own psyche by that process that I have called "empowerment." These empowered self-generated images (such as a thought about going to see someone) then serve as vehicles for supernormal knowledge once the subject focuses his or her mind intently on them. Generally speaking, aside from direct inspection, the passive approach utilizes the modality of empathic identification with a perceived object that one receives into consciousness from outside the self whereas the active approach employs the modality of empowerment in order to generate an information-laden impression or image that the subject produces from within his or her own mind.

It is important to remind the reader once again that the passive method of acquiring either supernormal knowledge or power almost invariably requires that the subject learn how to achieve one-pointedness of attention and be able to focus this attention fixedly on whatever object then presents itself to his or her field of awareness.

The phenomenon of precognition provides the clearest example of how supernormal knowledge can be obtained passively without the extraordinary mobilizations of the mind, will, and imagination (except for the initial priming step of putting the mind in a recollected state) that loom so large in descriptions of the active approach. For example, Monroe described how, from time to time, he acquired precognitive insight about coming events. He first had to put himself in a state of receptivity, that is, his body had to be completely relaxed and his mind stilled. In short, he had to be in a condition where he was ready to exteriorize but did not choose to do so. Once in this condition, it sometimes happened that he heard a hissing sound in his forebrain. Then he would experience the sensation of a small door opening exposing to his inner vision a round hole within which a dreamlike scene was taking place.[1] It took Monroe some time to learn that these particular dreamlike episodes were not just another strange kind of hallucination but were instead pictures of events that had not yet come to pass.

What is most distinctive about Monroe's precognitive visions is that he could not produce them at will. Once the subject puts himself in a receptive condition, the dreamlike images may occur but there is no guarantee that they will do so. Moreover, one does not seem to control these dream images in any way. They simply invade consciousness. In this particular instance, it was not necessary for Monroe to identify "empathically" with what presented itself to his field of awareness as is usually the case with other paranormal material acquired through the passive method. Monroe obtained the paranormal information from the visionary material simply by looking at it and recognizing that any visionary experience that took the form of a hissing followed by a small door opening probably contained precognitive material.

Garrett described the way spontaneous precognitive insights came to her in much the same way as Monroe did. She likewise mentioned that often the precognitive material quite literally invaded her field of consciousness in a way that was beyond her control. "I was troubled by the realization that coming events could register themselves beforehand in some part of my consciousness whether I wished it or not."[2] At certain times in her life, these upwellings of precognitive intuition proved so disturbing to her men-

1. Monroe, *Journeys Out of the Body*, p. 145; see also similar passages in Muldoon and Carrington, *Projection of the Astral Body*, p. 301, where he also claimed that he could not have precognitive dreams at will.

2. Garrett, *Adventures in the Supernormal*, p. 102.

tal equilibrium that she became afraid that they would drive her insane. Fortunately, she was later able to discover an autosuggestive technique that allowed her to suppress these spontaneous upwellings of unwanted material but that proved so successful that she wondered whether she had completely lost her precognitive faculty. This was not the case, however; like Monroe, Garrett found that if she allowed herself "to drop back into a relaxed and passive state," this precognitive material would once again start to invade her field of awareness.[3] In contrast to Monroe, she found that not only did precognitive insights arise spontaneously in a way that seemed completely beyond her conscious control but that there were also other occasions when she could bring about those insights intentionally. In other words, there were methods for acquiring knowledge about future events.

Nonetheless, even when Garrett recounted those instances where she intentionally tried to obtain precognitive insights, her descriptions of those procedures emphasized that she still had to preserve an essentially passive attitude with respect to that material that entered her field of consciousness as a result of those efforts. The following example comes from a description she gave of one of her precognitive experiments. In this experiment she tried to describe the subject matter contained in some paintings that were located somewhere in the same building within which she was conducting the experiment and then, after she had described them, she would attempt to sketch them. When she had concluded her part of the experiment, someone else went into other parts of the building, chose several paintings that no one in the experiment had ever seen before and then compared their content with her sketches and descriptions. During the experiment,

> One sits at a desk and from the empty canvas of the mind a "key" emerges which may be only a suggestion of a perfume, a sweet-smelling flower, a country scene. . . . One accepts the clue and presently the outside world is shut out and one is possessed by the idea. Like intuition, one idea flows from the other, actively presenting themselves out of space. Sometimes one instinctively feels that one is going to draw or describe one particular thing, but a line will arrive and change the whole contour of the scene.[4]

3. Ibid., p. 103.
4. Ibid., p. 195.

Garrett's description makes it abundantly clear that, just as in automatic writing, the subject's conscious mind plays only a very limited role in controlling the sequence of events that brings about deliberately induced precognition. Once the individual has made the initial mental effort to blank out the "canvas of the mind," the only other significant activity the conscious mind seems to perform is that of choosing which particular image it will allow to dominate his or her consciousness. Once the subject's mind chooses this image, it then dominates his or her field of consciousness to such a degree that Garrett felt compelled to say that the subject is quite literally "possessed" by it.

One can discern a two-fold sense in which the subject becomes possessed by the image he or she chooses as a clue. In the first sense, the individual is possessed because the chosen image completely dominates the field of consciousness to the extent that it prohibits any sense-impressions from having an impact on it. The subject is possessed in a second sense because, as occurs in the phenomenon of automatic writing, the clue then sets off a chain of associated images that intrude into the person's field of awareness independently of any conscious process of willing or imagining on his or her part. Garrett notes that it often happens that when she thinks that this chain of seemingly free associations is finally coalescing into a recognizable pattern, a line will suddenly pop into her field of awareness and force itself to become part of the sketch. These observations led her to conclude that in deliberately induced cases of precognition, just as in spontaneous instances of it, "At no time . . . is the conscious self concerned with the reception of the material."[5] One can detect, then, a sharp contrast between the yogin who practices saṃyama and the subject who deliberately tries to induce precognition. Although both individuals are intentionally setting out to acquire paranormal information, the latter does not do so by seeking out a particular object with the intention of purposively fixating his attention on it so as to influence it or to gain knowledge about it. Instead, the individual who uses the passive approach allows the objects he wishes to know about to come to him so that once they enter his field of awareness he can discern whatever paranormal message they may contain.

Like her methods for priming herself to receive precognitive messages, Garrett's methods for deliberately acquiring telepathic or clairvoyant knowledge also required that she must not actively seek out and focus on

5. Ibid., p. 196.

the object she wished to learn about but, instead, she had to first place herself in a state of watchful receptivity. When in that condition, she had to probe the various images that autonomously emerged into her field of awareness for whatever supernormal knowledge they may contain. Thus she categorically asserted that "when one is being telepathic or clairvoyant, impressions just happen—one is faced with them without volition."[6] Once again she stressed that the subject must adopt the passive attitude, waiting for objects and images to come rather than seeking them out. If one examines Garrett's descriptions of how she developed clairvoyant and telepathic sensitivity, one detects the same contrast between her method of acquiring supernormal knowledge and the yogic method.

> When I have an appointment with someone who is in deep need, I have been told that before my visitor's entrance into the room I have a habit of busying myself. I will move objects on my desk, or accelerate my body by attending to several things in a great hurry. . . . It is probably a means of clearing the mind of all objective material. I remember that it was required of me in the early days of my experimental work that I should spend some quiet time in concentration and meditation. This I was never able to do. Contrary to all I had been told, it was necessary for me to be in a state of nonchalance—in fact, an attitude of high carelessness.[7]

This attitude of nonchalance is poles apart from the focused intentness so characteristic of yogic saṃyama. In fact Garrett specifically rejected "concentration and meditation" as useful aids in obtaining supernormal awareness.

This last statement raises an important point. Both Garrett and the practitioners of Yoga, despite their differences, do agree that calming the mind is a vital prerequisite to any kind of supernormal activity. Even that attitude of nonchalance that seems so different from the focused intentness of yogic saṃyama is like the latter insofar as mental quiescence is a requirement for both. Consequently her rejection of "concentration and meditation" did not mean that she thought mental quiescence unimportant. Like yogic saṃyama, the "state of nonchalance" was also a condition where thinking had ceased. One should not ignore, then, Garrett's significant observation that her "tidying up" activities probably constituted a means of

6. Garrett, *Telepathy*, p. 169.
7. Garrett, *Adventures in the Supernormal*, pp. 182–83.

"clearing the mind of all objective material." This remark is not one of merely incidental significance. Elsewhere in her writing she repeatedly comes back to the importance of mental calming, a state which she always achieved by employing techniques of deep breathing.[8] In other places she related that her friends were often surprised when she told them that in a state of telepathic or clairvoyant receptivity she does not think. She explained, "It would seem then that my mind holds itself in a quiet and tranquil ease which is almost devoid of thought. The mind is either creative or completely at rest—still with the stillness of deep tranquil waters, while lights and clouds of color and imagery are at play."[9] One should notice that although thinking had ceased, the field of awareness did not remain empty for it was soon occupied by imagery of possibly clairvoyant significance that substituted for her "ordinary" thoughts or imaginings. This last sentence brings one to the major difference that separates Garrett's "state of nonchalance" from yogic saṃyama. While it is true that her method of inducing clairvoyance and telepathy was like the yogin's insofar as the mind of the would-be percipient was also devoid of thought, unlike the yogin, Garrett did not actively seek out only one particular object on which she tried to focus her attention to the complete exclusion of all other material that may have at the same time entered her field of awareness.

It is a serious misunderstanding, however, to conclude that Garrett's state of "high carelessness" was a condition where the mind was undisciplined, where, although thoughts had ceased, other kinds of mental imagery were allowed to run riot over the percipient's field of consciousness. To be sure, Garrett did not imitate the yogin trying to suppress all extraneous mental phenomena except the object of his concentration. She did allow a stream of images (possibly clairvoyant or telepathic) to enter her consciousness after she had first stopped the thinking process. Nonetheless, that stream of potentially clairvoyant and telepathic images was not just allowed to run riot but was instead subjected to a peculiar kind of information-extracting procedure that caused them to disgorge whatever supernormal content they might have possessed. Garrett extracted this paranormal information by putting herself in a peculiar emotional and perceptual state that she called "alertness." When she was in that alert state, she claimed that after she had first stopped the internal chattering of

8. Garrett, *Telepathy*, p. 52; also see Svātmārāma, *Haṭhayogapradīpikā*, chap. 2, v. 2, for reference that shows how deep breathing is a means of quieting the mind.
9. Garrett, *Telepathy*, pp. 173–74.

her thoughts, she gained a peculiar ability to "look" at those images that subsequently flooded across her field of awareness and somehow divine their content paranormally. Not only was mental calmness necessary as a priming step in every attempt to establish telepathic or clairvoyant receptivity that employed Garrett's passive methods, but it was also essential to cultivate alertness.

According to Garrett, alertness is a peculiar mood of intense anticipatory emotional exhilaration that occurs when one encounters the flux of potentially clairvoyant and telepathic images, symbols, and luminous manifestations that begin to pour into one's field of awareness after one has first stopped the thinking process by practicing deep breathing exercises. She described alertness at one point as "an eagerness to contact, apprehend, and translate the 'story'" that this flux of images and symbols may contain.[10] The affective dimension of alertness is characterized as "a sense of excitement or eagerness such as one feels on entering some unknown or forbidden territory."[11] What made alertness something different from ordinary moods of emotional exaltation and intense expectation was that it also brought about a deepening and sharpening of the subject's perceptual faculties. For example, when she spoke of the mood of alertness that accompanied her telepathic experiences, she asserted that

> anticipation becomes my mood. I clearly move out of the state in which I normally face situations into a condition which produces a better visioning, a better listening attitude. My sense of smell becomes more acute. . . . In other words, "telepathy" . . . referred to by some experimenters as a "sixth sense" certainly induces in me a marked quickening of the five more familiar senses.[12]

In Chapters 8 and 9 I noted that the phenomenon of empowerment transfigures ordinary thinking and wishing into something qualitatively different than mere thought and desire, for both, when dynamized, become transformed into tools that enable the subject either to supernormally exert action at a distance or to acquire clairvoyant knowledge about remote events. As everyone knows, thoughts and desires never have this noetic or telekinetic dimension in ordinary waking experience. From Garrett's descriptions of alertness, one can see that it brought about a somewhat anal-

10. Garrett, *Adventures in the Supernormal,* p. 172.
11. Ibid., p. 170.
12. Garrett, *Telepathy,* p. 41; and idem, *Adventures in the Supernormal,* p. 183.

ogous transformation. Alertness transfigures an emotional mood of excitement and anticipation into something qualitatively different from a mere mood, such as exaltation or eagerness. Garrett claimed that alert excitement was not only a mood—it was simultaneously an objectively real paranormal augmentation of the subject's sensory faculties. It was, in short, a noetic emotional state.

Clairvoyant or telepathic alertness is not only an emotional state that heightens one's perceptual acuity but it is also a condition of empathic identification with that which one perceives. Thus Garrett maintained that in this state of alertness, "I participate fully and intimately in events . . . and though the events that I observe are objective to me I do more than observe them—I *live* them."[13] In other words, she claimed that under conditions of clairvoyant or telepathic alertness, she did not obtain her knowledge of an object simply by looking at it or by any process of inference based on an analysis of any of its external characteristics. Instead, she had, in some peculiar way, "identified" herself with what she was perceiving. This peculiar modality of "knowledge by identification" that characterized the phenomenon of alertness appeared to have been very closely linked to her ability to see auras. She explicitly stated that the ability to see auras and other luminous phenomena was a "necessary stimulus to clairvoyance."[14] Like Gerda Walther, Edgar Cayce, and Matthew Manning,[15] Garrett also claimed that she could discern information about an individual's mood, intellectual development, moral character, and health by examining the patterns, colors, and relative degree of opacity or transparency that she could see in a person's aura.[16]

While it was true, to some extent, that Garrett gained knowledge about another's interior state by looking at that person's aura, it was also the case that this act of acquiring insight about an individual or an object through an inspection of his or its aura was something considerably more complex than the act of merely looking at it. In those cases, the act of paranormal perception went beyond merely seeing a light around an object; it also involved what I have called an "empathic identification" with it. For example, when she referred to her childhood clairvoyant experiences

13. Garrett, *Adventures in the Supernormal,* p. 183.
14. Ibid., pp. 172–73.
15. See also Karagulla, *Breakthrough to Creativity,* pp. 124–28; Muldoon, *Projection of the Astral Body,* pp. 283–87, where Muldoon quotes Caroline Larsen's observations; Anonymous, *The Boy Who Saw True,* pp. 20, 28, 93–94; Plutarch, *On the Delay of Divine Justice,* quoted in Mead, *Doctrine of the Subtle Body in Western Tradition,* pp. 41–42.
16. Garrett, *Adventures in the Supernormal,* pp. 19, 174.

Garrett noted that in that process, she did more than just look at the auras that surrounded things: "I sought to see more deeply into things and farther distances, not distances of space only but distances of being." This unusual type of vision, a kind of seeing that was simultaneously an act of perceiving the object and an intimate contact and encounter with it, depended on her sensitivity to auras.

> Each type of life had then, and still holds for me, its own particular kind of radiation. Every stone, metal, flower, or animal, substance or organism was contained within its own field of light and color, radiating both toward and away from its inner form of active, potent rays. I enter "within" the very life of this world of light, sound and color, using them as one might use a telescope to see what lies within and beyond. Thus I am able to sense the *history* of the organism or object whose nature is revealed by the quality of its radiation which I am able to contact and enter.[17]

Garrett reemphasized that clairvoyant seeing involves an intimate contact with the perceived object. "In clairvoyant vision I do not look *out* at objects in my field of observation as in ordinary seeing, but I seem to draw the perceived object toward me, so that the essence of its life and the essence of mine become, for the moment, one and the same thing."[18] Although it is difficult to comprehend fully exactly how she actually "entered into" the radiation that an object emits and thereby even penetrated into its very being, her descriptions of clairvoyant alertness leave no doubt that this intimate mode of perception derived from the informational density of auric luminosity. She explicitly stated that the nature of an object "is revealed by the quality of its radiation." As already noted in Chapter 9, the aura is much more than just a pretty pattern of lights. Like starlight that reveals a wealth of data about the size, composition, magnetic field, and temperature of a star when it is passed through a spectroscope, the light coming from a person's aura is also a source of information about the mood, health, and level of intellectual and spiritual development of the person whom it surrounds. It even appears to be an indicator of a person's thoughts as well. Thus Garrett mentioned at one point in her autobiography that she could sometimes "feel and sense the thoughts of people as

17. Ibid., p. 172.
18. Ibid., p. 183.

forms of light"[19] Likewise, Walther noted that sometimes when she experienced the auras of individuals she found "embedded in these clouds or 'rays' thoughts or thought-fragments" about persons whom those individuals were thinking about at the time she picked up their auras.[20] One might conclude, then, that for both Walther and Garrett the informational density of auric luminosity seemed to have been the essential element that permitted the clairvoyant or telepathic sensitive to gain intimate knowledge about another person's emotional state and private thoughts.

It would be a mistake, however, to imagine that clairvoyant and telepathic alertness are states where one just gathers information, although it be information of a particularly intimate character. The conditions of clairvoyant and telepathic alertness are also states where one actually shares the experience of another. One cannot simply inspect the aura the way an astronomer inspects the light of a star or galaxy in his spectroscope. How this sharing of another's experience actually takes place and why it depends on the subject's ability to see the aura, I cannot say. I can assert that Garrett—as well as Walther—claimed that this capacity to share another experience was simultaneously connected to the "vibratory nature of all things."[21] The informational density of auric light cannot explain another property of clairvoyant seeing, its capacity to compress distance and yet do so without seeming to sacrifice any vividness of detail. For example, it sometimes occurred that Garrett would clairvoyantly see a road winding a long way through the hills and disappearing into the distance beyond them. As paradoxical as it might seem, she simultaneously saw the road as ordinary eyesight would see it—perspective would diminish its dimensions as she would look into the distance and she would not see it as it went around and behind hills or mountains—and yet, at the very same time, she also saw the entire road without the hills intervening to block her view of it; nor did perspective operate to diminish its more distant reaches. Moreover, "its farther reaches are as meticulously discernible as the areas that lie close to the spot from which one is seeing. Each rut and stone is individually seen and can be described with precision."[22] In short, the conventional categories of spatiality lost their ordinary significance.

The relatively insignificant role that Garrett accorded to the imagination

19. Ibid., p. 86.
20. Walther, "Some Experiences Concerning the Human Aura," p. 345.
21. Garrett, *Adventures in the Supernormal*, p. 189.
22. Ibid., p. 179.

in the process of activating telepathic and clairvoyant sensitivity merits attention. She repeatedly stressed that telepathic sensing was not a product of the imagination. Although imagining what a person she wishes to contact will look like or be like may often help her to develop that anticipatory excitement so characteristic of supernormal alertness, once this alert state emerges,

> the world of reality produces its own knowledge, and no fancied symbol nor creation of my mind can leave so strong an impression or sense of knowing as does the field of reality itself, lying beyond the realms of imagination. In working clairvoyantly, I have tried, for my own understanding to build figures imaginatively, and to make dramas happen to them. However, they never hold together, and continually change and fall away from their type. But the clairvoyant image "happens." You come upon it. . . . You have done nothing—or, at least, so it would seem, except look within where this image is enthroned. When this happens the image or the vision is instantaneously fixed on the mind, and neither forgetfulness nor the passage of time will erase it. *It has stamped itself forever on your vision.*[23]

In contrast to those mystics and mediums who developed various procedures for acquiring supernormal abilities that utilize the active approach, such as creating tulpas, inducing out-of-body experiences and "traveling" clairvoyance, and pointing the bone, Garrett developed her telepathic and clairvoyant sensitivities without much use of methods that empowered the imagination or the dream process. What really seems to differentiate the active from the passive approach is that the latter replaces mental, imaginative, and volitional empowerment with that peculiar mood that Garrett calls "alertness." Whereas in the active approach it is the transfigured imagination that becomes the agency that transmits paranormal knowledge about an object, in the passive approach it is the transfigured emotions that function as the agents of paranormal sensitivity and a preternatural form of empathy.

23. Garrett, *Telepathy,* p. 175.

# 14

# Empowerment in the Writings of the Mystics

Since I have discussed at considerable length both the phenomenon of empowerment and some of the techniques that individuals have employed in order to obtain supernormal powers and sensibilities, it is appropriate to pause and assess how the study of such matters actually enhances one's comprehension of both mystical experience and mysticism. First, one notices that unmistakable references to the phenomenon of empowerment are not restricted solely to the autobiographies of a few nineteenth- and twentieth-century European mediums, clairvoyants, and out-of-body travelers but that references to it occur quite frequently in the writings of mystics from diverse religious traditions. Second, when writers or texts describe either the mode of being that characterizes supramundane existence or when they depict the powers that divine beings supposedly possess, they often do so in a language that distinctly alludes to the modality of empowerment. Let us now look at some examples of these references to the phenomenon of empowerment in the writings of the mystics and see how it functioned.

## The Tibetan Book of the Dead

The phenomenon of empowerment plays a prominent role in the soteriological drama that unfolds in *The Tibetan Book of the Dead,* a document that originated within the Tantric Buddhist milieu of Tibet. This text, which clearly centers around experiences of a mystical nature,[1] func-

1. See descriptions of the radiance of the Clear Light of the Void described on pp. 95–96 of *The Tibetan Book of the Dead.* Also note the descriptions of the "desire-body" and its

tions as a manual for guiding the consciousness and emotions of a person who is dying or who has just died so that he or she will achieve Buddhahood or Enlightenment instead of rebirth. It describes the various emotional states and states of consciousness that the dying or dead person experiences and teaches him or her how to distinguish those existential modalities that will ultimately lead back into the endless round of rebirths and sufferings from those that will ultimately lead to spiritual liberation.

*The Tibetan Book of the Dead* postulates that an individual who has mastered yoga can maintain full continuity of awareness throughout all six states of consciousness that human beings may experience both while they are alive and during and after death. These six different experiential modalities are known in Tibetan as *bardo* states. The first of these bardo states is normal waking consciousness (*skyes-nas bardo*). Second is the state of dream consciousness (*rmi-lam bardo*). The third state is the trance consciousness that occurs when an individual is absorbed in profound meditation or *dhyāna* (*bsam-gtan bardo*). The fourth bardo state is, soteriologically speaking, the most important of the six. *Chikhai bardo* is the mode of consciousness that occurs when one is experiencing death. In the early stages of this brief mode of consciousness, one experiences what the mind is like when it is in its natural condition, that is, free from any activity of thought formation. The fifth state of consciousness is known as "the experiencing of Reality," that is, the state of awareness that supervenes shortly after death wherein the mind begins to generate those mental states that result from the manifold kinds of karma that living beings have brought on themselves. In this stage (*chönyid bardo*), one has glimpses of Hell or Heaven and other conditions of possible existence that have come into existence because of one's karma. The sixth stage is that state of consciousness which characterizes the experience of one who is no longer just experiencing the results of karmic illusion but who has now also begun to crave rebirth in another body and is known as the *sidpa bardo*.[2] The followers of Tibetan Tantric Buddhism claim that, with the exception of the early stages of the fourth bardo, state when the mind briefly rests in its natural condition all the bardo states represent conditions of illusion and suffering because they ultimately result from the thought-forming activity

---

powers depicted in the descriptions given of the sidpa bardo state on pp. 156–60 of *Tibetan Book of the Dead*.

   2. Lama Govinda's introduction to *Tibetan Book of the Dead*, p. lxi.

of the mind or consciousness-principle and, as such, are transient and ultimately productive of birth, death, and misery.

Like all other Buddhist teachings, *The Tibetan Book of the Dead* centers its attention on answering this question: How is it possible for human beings to emerge from bondage to these various states of illusion and the horrible sufferings that attachment to them brings? Emancipation requires four conditions.

First, the individual has to realize that there exists a state that is free from suffering and illusion. This condition exists at that moment when the individual has just ceased breathing at the instant of death. "When the expiration hath ceased, the vital-force will have sunk into the nerve-center of Wisdom [this is a reference to the heart chakra described in hatha yoga] and the Knower [the mind in its cognizing function] will be experiencing the Clear Light of the Natural Condition [free from thought-formation]."[3] The text then elaborates on the nature of this soteriologically crucial experience, doing so in terms that clearly indicate that "the Clear Light of the natural condition" is an illuminated state of mystical bliss. Addressing the disembodied consciousness of the dead man, the narrator of the text explains to him that this moment when he is passing from life to death is supremely important.

> Now thou art experiencing the Radiance of the Clear Light of Pure Reality. Recognize it. O nobly-born, thy present intellect [*shes-rig,* the consciousness-principle when it is in a condition of knowing or cognizing something], in real nature void, not formed into anything as regards characteristics or color, naturally void, is the very Reality, the All-Good.
>
> Thine own intellect, which is now voidness, yet not to be regarded as the voidness of nothingness, but as being the intellect itself, unobstructed, shining, thrilling, and blissful, is the very consciousness [*rig-pa,* the consciousness-principle in its pure state when it is not cognizing something], the All-Good Buddha.
>
> Thine own consciousness, not formed into anything, in reality void, and the intellect, shining and blissful,—these two,—are inseparable. The union of them is the . . . state of Perfect Enlightenment.[4]

3. *Tibetan Book of the Dead,* p. 90.
4. Ibid., pp. 95–96.

This important passage describes the experiential state that accompanies Perfect Enlightenment in *The Tibetan Book of the Dead*. Perfect Enlightenment, according to this description, constitutes nothing other than that moment when one, first, has placed the mind in a condition of perfect, blissful, and luminous quiescence where it is not disturbed by any process of thought-formation or conceptualization; second, realizes with profound conviction that all other modes of experience are sources of suffering and delusion; and third, desires to stay in that state and is able to do so. Suffering occurs when sentient beings, as a result of craving for other states of consciousness, allow their minds to fall from this state of perfect repose and begin to yearn for those other modalities of awareness that originate from either past karma or the thought-fabricating processes of the mind. Those inferior states of consciousness take on their delusive sense of concreteness and objectivity because the subject who perceives them remains ignorant of their true nature as mere thought-formations. The principal purpose of *The Tibetan Book of the Dead* is to teach the dead person's disembodied consciousness how to recognize when it is in that condition where it is completely devoid of thought-formations, how to develop that condition if he does not already possess it, how to avoid developing any craving for thought-formations, and how to stay in that condition. When this happens, one will have achieved spiritual liberation.[5]

The second condition necessary for emancipation is that the individual must recognize that all phenomena—whether they be material or imaginary—are equally unreal and void, that is, they have no independent existence outside of the mind of the one who perceives them. How does one recognize that such concrete, solid objects like material bodies are really nothing more than mentally created illusions? Tantric Buddhists maintain that one acquires insight into illusory nature of all phenomena using two especially effective techniques. The first technique involves controlling the content of dreams and maintaining complete awareness during the transition from waking consciousness to sleep. When one realizes that one can consciously create a dream to take on any form that one wishes and that, moreover, seems as real as phenomena in the waking state, one deduces from this experience that the phenomena one encounters in the waking state are likewise unreal phantasms of the mind. They are given their semblance of autonomy and solidity in the same way that dream images acquire their appearance of substantiality, an illusion which we only recog-

5. Ibid., p. 96.

nize as such when we wake up.[6] The second of these techniques that reveals all phenomena to be illusory is the technique of visualization spoken
of in connection with David-Neel. It is especially important in *The Tibetan
Book of the Dead* for there we are told that when one is about to enter a
"womb-door" and re-enter the round of rebirths and suffering, learning
how to visualize one's tutelary deity and then dissolving the seemingly
solid hallucination that results from this mental exercise causes one to realize that all the phenomena one is encountering and that seem so real are
likewise nothing more than phantoms created by the mind.[7] This awareness of the voidness of all phenomena prevents one from craving rebirth.
After all, why would any sensible person crave a dream phantasm or
something else equally insubstantial and illusory?

The third condition necessary for spiritual emancipation is the realization that attachment to any phenomenon invariably leads one back into
the round of rebirths and suffering for all phenomena are in a state of
constant flux, arising and dissipating, being born, growing old, and dying.
Attachment to phenomena arises when one fails to recognize them as mentally created illusions. Thus when one is in the chönyid bardo or the sidpa
bardo, for example, everything one encounters is an objectification of
one's own mind, yet one thinks that they are either something to fear or
else something one should desire. When one thinks that these objectified
thoughts or desires are real, one falls into *saṃsāra*. One begins to share
that suffering-laden mode of being of all those creatures that have fallen
into it. Instead of controlling how one's thoughts objectify themselves, one
allows oneself to be controlled by one's affective responses to these objectifications. One experiences the fluctuations and vicissitudes to which all
phenomena are subject wrongfully imagining that one cannot control the
process of their appearance and disappearance as well as their affective
impact on one's mind. Because thought-formation is the source of all phenomena and, as such, one of the ultimate sources of suffering, the text
constantly repeats that while one is in the after-death state one must continually strive to keep the mind in a condition where it is without
thoughts.[8]

The fourth condition for freedom from bondage to phenomena is the

6. *Tibetan Yoga and Secret Doctrines*, ed. W. Y. Evans-Wentz, trans. Lama Kazi Dawa-
Samdup; foreword by R. R. Marett, and yogic commentary by Chen-Chi Chang, 2d ed.
(London: Oxford University Press, 1971), pp. 216–23.

7. *Tibetan Book of the Dead*, p. 176.

8. Ibid., p. 176.

cessation of craving. Craving ceases when one recognizes that all material phenomena and thought-forms are illusions and subject to the misery-producing cycle of origination and decay. This craving for phenomena receives its most effective check when the individual experiences the great peace, bliss, and illumination that result from the mind's reposing in that condition where it is free from all thought-forming activity. One then desires to stay in this condition instead of craving thought-forms and the transient, delusory pleasures that they give.

The descriptions that *The Tibetan Book of the Dead* gave concerning the nature of the afterlife states show striking parallels to the description that Monroe gave of Locale II. First, in both Locale II and in the chönyid and sidpa bardo states, the subject constructs the environment that he sees and experiences out of his own thoughts and desires that instantaneously embody themselves while he is in those states of existence. Because the chönyid bardo is an experiential modality constructed entirely out of the subject's concretized thoughts and desires and those customary ways of thinking and desiring that had become implanted in him by his past habits, that is, as a result of his karmic propensities, the narrator of the text tells the deceased not to fear what he encounters there no matter how terrifying or awesome it may seem.

> Whatever fear and terror may come to thee in the *chönyid bardo,* forget not these words; and, bearing their meaning at heart, go forward: in them lieth the vital secret of recognition:
> "Alas! when the Uncertain Experiencing of Reality is dawning upon me here,
> With every thought of fear and terror or awe for all (apparitional appearances) set aside,
> May I recognize whatever (visions) appear, as the reflections of mine own consciousness, . . .
> May I not fear the bands of Peaceful and Wrathful (Deities), mine own thought-forms."[9]

The sidpa bardo is likewise an experiential realm constructed out of one's own objectified thoughts, desires, and karmic propensities. Thus, if the karma of the deceased is bad enough that he must face judgment before the Lord of Death, he must realize that all the tortures and terrors he is being subjected to and all the loathsome demons he encounters are nothing

9. Ibid., p. 103.

more than hallucinations that he himself has created and that he mistakenly believes exist independently of his own mind.[10]

A second parallel between Locale II and the after-life existence depicted in *The Tibetan Book of the Dead* is that in both the chönyid bardo and the sidpa bardo one possesses a diaphanous counterpart to one's physical body that has both the appearance and the powers that Muldoon and Monroe attributed to the astral body.[11] The text describes the bardo-body as "a radiant body, resembling the former body . . . 'endowed with all sense-faculties, and power of unimpeded motion, possessing karmic miraculous powers, visible to pure celestial eyes [of bardo beings] of like nature.' "[12] From this description one notes several things: The bardo-body is a "double" of the physical body in regard to its appearance. It is, of course, unlike the physical body because it is diaphanous. As the lamas explained to Evans-Wentz, "As through a cloud, a sword can be plunged through the bardo-body without harming it."[13] The bardo-body also has, like the astral body, sense-perceptions, the ability to move through objects, and various supernormal powers. "Thou canst instantaneously arrive in whatever place thou wishest; thou hast the power of reaching there within the time which a man taketh to bend."[14] This remark is an unmistakable reference to the empowerment of thoughts that is operative in this state of being just as it is during astral projection. Finally, like the astral body, the bardo-body is visible only to other beings with spiritual perception. Sense perception cannot discern it. Thus one reads above that it is often the case that the deceased visits his old haunts and sees what people are doing and hears what they are saying. However, as is usually the case in astral projection, the bardo-body is likewise imperceptible to living beings and cannot influence them.[15]

The third parallel between Locale II and the posthumous bardo-states relates to the fact that habits and subconscious thoughts play a major role in shaping the content of one's respective experience in each of those realms. For example, Muldoon noticed that astral bodies always wore clothes and that, although the airlike bodies of the astral doubles could

10. Ibid., pp. 166–67.

11. Monroe, *Journeys Out of the Body*, pp. 166–78; Muldoon and Carrington, *The Projection of the Astral Body*, pp. 50–53.

12. *Tibetan Book of the Dead*, p. 156.

13. Ibid., p. 166–67, n. 3.

14. Ibid., p. 159.

15. Ibid., pp. 101–2, 160. Compare to Monroe's similar description of the properties of the astral body in *Journeys Out of the Body*, p. 47.

easily go down through a floor if they wanted to, they always walked on the surface of the floor in the same way as their physical counterparts did in the waking state. Consequently, he concluded that this astral clothing was created by the objectification of subconscious thoughts present in the projector's mind as a result of the habitual expectations he had about how he was supposed to look. He deduced that the reason the astral phantom did not walk through floors stemmed from the fact that this behavior would not have corresponded to his customary ways of walking. Muldoon therefore realized that not only could conscious thoughts influence the empowerment process in the out-of-body state but that subconscious thoughts, habits, and expectations could also exert a subliminal yet no less effective influence.[16] *The Tibetan Book of the Dead* seems to point to an analogous process of concretizing habitual and subconscious thoughts and desires that occurs within the posthumous bardo-state. For example, one finds there that the literal translation of the Tibetan word for the post-mortem bardo-body is "the thought-body of propensities."[17] This literal rendering conveys the idea that not only is the bardo-body and what it experiences an objectification of one's thoughts and desires (it is also translated as "desire-body") but it is also an embodiment of one's habits and expectations that are the products of one's conditioning by past actions and customary ways of thinking or "karmic propensities." Thus it often happens that in the first few days after death the consciousness of the one just deceased "hovereth around those places to which its activities had been limited."[18] The text implies that this particular behavior of the bardo-body is simply the result of its tendency to objectify its habitual longings for friends and family and other familiar things it enjoyed while alive. It longs to see them and, since it now has the power to concretize these desires, no sooner does it desire to see its familiar haunts than it travels to them. The text also implies that one's bardo-body takes the form of the physical body simply because the deceased has a habitual tendency to desire a body and to think of himself as always in a body. Consequently, these habitual desires and thoughts concretize themselves in the form of a human body.[19]

Having exhibited the parallels that exist between Locale II and the after-death states described in *The Tibetan Book of the Dead,* it is appropriate

16. Muldoon and Carrington, *Projection of the Astral Body*, pp. 283–85, 289–90.
17. *Tibetan Book of the Dead*, p. 104, n. 1.
18. Ibid., p. 101.
19. Ibid., p. 157.

to return to the basic problem that I set out to answer, namely, How does empowerment enter into the soteriological drama that unfolds in that text? The answer is simple. Since both the chönyid and sidpa bardo states are experiential modalities where mental, volitional, and emotional empowerment is the central characteristic of existence, the principal soteriological problem becomes that of learning how to control this empowerment process in such a way that it leads to spiritual liberation rather than to bondage and suffering.

As noted above, the author or authors of this text claimed that an individual achieves liberation from rebirth and suffering when he stops two things: first, the process of objectifying thoughts, desires, and emotions (liberation requires that the empowered mind must come to rest in a state where it is completely free of thought-formations); and second, the longing for this thought-forming activity to resume. This latter requirement can only occur if the individual has experientially comprehended how all phenomena exist merely as illusory objectifications created by his empowered mind and that both attachment and aversion for them are the root causes of all suffering.

Looking at the conditions that prevail within posthumous samsaric existence, that is, within that totality of posthumous existential modalities fettered to delusion and suffering, one notices a sharp contrast to those conditions that prevail in enlightened existence. Within saṃsāra, the endless round of rebirths, the empowered mind is not quiescent. On the contrary, it is busily engaged in objectifying the thoughts, desires, and emotional states that keep emerging within it. Nonetheless, even those individuals who are so deeply enmired in saṃsāra that they are completely unable to put their minds in the perfectly quiescent state discover that the possibility of their eventual redemption from spiritual bondage depends on their ability to discern the difference between proper and improper methods of directing the empowerment process. For example, the text mentions that even for that deceased individual who remains so deluded as a result of bad karma or ignorance that he cannot possibly escape rebirth, it is still important that he choose a good womb in which to be reborn. Otherwise, he is liable to attain rebirth in one of those realms so subject to delusion and misery that he will almost certainly not have another chance to gain liberation until eons have elapsed.

How does one choose this favorable state of rebirth for oneself? First, one has to have an "earnest" desire for rebirth in one of the happy realms of existence where it is easy to attain enlightenment and hear the *dharma* (teachings of the Buddha). Second, one has to focus one's mind one-pointedly on desiring to go there. Once these two conditions are fulfilled one instantaneously accomplishes one's wish. The problem is that one must avoid desiring what only appears to be desirable but that in reality may be a very unfavorable state of existence. To avoid this deception it is safest to desire rebirth in one of the Buddha Realms described by tradition. The text then instructs the deceased to "direct the resolution (or wish) earnestly . . . to any Realm thou mayst desire . . . direct thy wish to any realm which thou desirest most, in undistracted one-pointedness (of mind). By doing so, birth will take place in that Realm instantaneously."[20] This is a clear example of how rightly directing the empowerment process constitutes a matter of central soteriological significance. It is also insufficient for the deceased just to "think about" desiring rebirth in a Buddha Realm. He has to desire this earnestly and do so to the exclusion of all other thoughts. Monroe gave these same instructions to anyone who wished to visit someone in their astral bodies. One had to prevent stray thoughts from entering one's mind because by becoming objectified they caused one to wander from one's desired destination, and one had not only to think about going there but also imagine how pleasant it would be to do so.[21] Once an individual had satisfied all these preconditions, he had a chance of accomplishing what he wished for now that his thought-objectification processes were under his own control and direction.

References to the fundamental soteriological relevance of controlling exactly which thoughts should be allowed to become objectified abound in the descriptions of the sidpa and chönyid bardo states contained in *The Tibetan Book of the Dead.* The author or authors of the text declare that it is best to avoid any thought-formation at all while in those states but they recognize that if this is not possible one must at least not objectify thoughts or emotions whose embodiment would necessarily take the form of a degraded or hellish state of existence. Consequently, the narrator tells the deceased that since the sidpa bardo is a condition where thoughts wield enormous power, he must take great care to always be thinking good or pious thoughts.[22] For example, if it so happens that the deceased sees his relatives doing things of which he does not approve, he must at all costs avoid giving way to feelings of anger at them. If the deceased were to "feel angry with thy successors, that feeling will affect the psychological

20. Ibid., pp. 189–90.
21. Monroe, *Journeys Out of the Body,* pp. 216–20.
22. *Tibetan Book of the Dead,* p. 172.

moment in such a way that, even though thou wert destined to be born on higher and happier planes, thou wilt be obliged to be born in Hell or in the world of *pretas* [unhappy ghosts]."[23] In short, one must avoid anger because when that emotion becomes objectified under conditions of empowerment it creates an experiential landscape that is either hellish or brutish thereby greatly hindering one's possibilities of attaining enlightenment.

It is precisely because the phenomenon of empowerment figures so prominently in the afterlife states that ethical obligations become compelling. "Good" behavior or intentions under these circumstances are much more than actions or desires that tend to promote social harmony. Under conditions of empowerment, these actions or intentions derive their valuation of good or bad from the quality of the experiential states that result from them.

# Ibn al-'Arabī

To fathom the spiritual teachings of Muhyiddin Ibn al-'Arabī (1165–1240), it is also essential that one comprehend how the ex-static mode of being (empowerment) formed one of the experiential underpinnings of his thought. For example, in *The Bezels of Wisdom* Ibn al-'Arabī states that when a mystic (or "gnostic") has a vision of God, God "raises the veil between Himself and the servant and the servant sees Him in the form of his belief; indeed, He is the very content of the belief. Thus neither the Heart nor the eye (of the Heart) sees anything but the form of its belief concerning the Reality."[24] This passage refers to the modality of empowerment as active in mystical vision for whatever picture one carries around in one's imagination as to what God is like immediately objectifies itself as the content of one's experience. Ibn al-'Arabī also asserts that not only is the modality of empowerment operative in mystical experiences but it is also at work in afterlife existence. When souls come before God on the day of the Resurrection

> as men know God (in this world), so will they see Him on the day of Resurrection. . . . So, beware lest you restrict yourself to a partic-

23. Ibid., p. 170.

24. Muhyiddin Ibn al-'Arabī, *The Bezels of Wisdom* (New York: Paulist Press, 1980), p. 149.

ular tenet (concerning the Reality) and so deny any other tenet (equally reflecting Him), for you would forfeit the true knowledge of what is (the reality). Therefore, be completely and utterly receptive to all doctrinal forms, for God, Most High is too All-embracing and Great to be confined within one creed rather than another.[25]

Similarly, it is by virtue of their empowered imaginations that souls consign themselves to Hell. Ibn al-'Arabī writes that a "wind" drives such souls to Hell, "(the driver) being none other than their own desires and inclinations, and Hell the distance they imagined (to be between them and the Reality)."[26] For Ibn al-'Arabī, the drama of salvation remains crucially dependent on a proper use and understanding of that empowered imagination that comes to the soul both in the after-life and on this earth in mystical experiences.

Ibn al-'Arabī refers to this faculty of the empowered imagination by the word *himmah*. Himmah refers to that transfiguration of the mystic's imagination that allows him to do two important things: (1) it allows him to convert the imaginative faculty into an "organ" that perceives subtle realities or spiritual dimensions that otherwise lie hidden to physical sense organs and (2) it allows him to endow the creations of his own imagination with objective, extramental existence through a process involving both concentration and mental projection (similar to the way that David-Neel created her tulpa out of her own imagination). Ibn al-'Arabī is careful to distinguish between the ordinary workings of the imagination and those of the empowered imagination. Thus, in *The Book of the Spiritual Conquests of Mecca* he draws a distinction between the "conjoined" imagination (*khayāl muttaṣil*) and a "separable" or "autonomous" imagination (*khayāl munfaṣil*).[27] The former type of imaginative activity remains inseparably connected to the subject. When the subject dies, these imaginations (such as daydreams or dreams) die with him. The activities of "separable" imagination, however, lead an autonomous existence. They are capable of persisting beyond the life of the one who created them and may continue to abide as forms in that intermediate universe that exists in a dimension imperceptible to the physical senses but perceptible to those endowed with mystical vision.

25. Ibn al-'Arabī, *Bezels of Wisdom*, p. 137.
26. Ibid., p. 131. Compare this conception of Hell to Emanuel Swedenborg's views in his book, *Heaven and its Wonders and Hell* (London: Swedenborg Society, 1896), pp. 287–91, paras. 521–27.
27. Quoted in Corbin, *Creative Imagination in the Sufism of Ibn 'Arabī*, p. 359, n. 8.

Referring to the capacity of himmah to fabricate creations of the imagination that persist outside of the subject's own mind, Ibn al-'Arabī makes an oblique allusion to the distinction between khayāl muttaṣil and khayāl munfaṣil in asserting that

> every man creates by his fancy in the Imaginative faculty that which has existence nowhere else, this being a common facility. The gnostic, however, by his Concentration, creates that which has existence beyond the origin of the Concentration, indeed, the Concentration continues to maintain its existence. . . . Should the attention of the gnostic be deflected from the maintenance of what he has created, it will cease to exist, unless the gnostic commands all planes of existence.

Ibn al-'Arabī underscores the vital significance of this mystery that he has just revealed to the reader when he goes on to say that himmah is not only an imaginative modality that gnostics possess but it is also the very power with which God creates and sustains the cosmos, the power by means of which God brought all the cosmic domains, subtle, physical, and intellectual into existence. What distinguishes the mystic's himmah from the divine himmah is that God exercises this creative power with perfect attentiveness and concentration whereas the mystic always exercises it with some admixture of inattentiveness. "The Reality is never inattentive, while the servant is always inattentive to something or another. With respect to the maintenance of something he has created, the gnostic may say 'I am the Reality,' but his maintenance of that thing cannot be compared to the maintenance exercised by the Reality."[28] Because both the physical and the spiritual universes originate from the divine himmah, Ibn al-'Arabī declared that "the cosmos is but a fantasy."[29] The phenomenon of himmah is therefore something of much more than marginal significance in Ibn al-'Arabī's thought since he contended that it was only possible for human beings to come to a true understanding of the relationship that exists and should exist between creature and Creator if they were to become endowed with this power of himmah themselves.[30]

What function does developing himmah serve in the mystic's quest for spiritual perfection? Ibn al-'Arabī claimed that the mystic cultivates this

28. Ibn al-'Arabī, *Bezels of Wisdom*, p. 102.
29. Ibid., p. 124.
30. Ibid., p. 150.

transfigured power of the imagination "'only for the sake of the astonishment which occurs at the raising of the veils.' For through the knowledge which arises in contemplation, he turns to face what is beyond each appearance: the Truth beyond appearances."[31] Properly cultivated, himmah leads the mystic far beyond solipsistic reveries, bringing him qualitatively novel insights that transcend anything that he could have derived from his previous experiences. "Astonishment" results because the mystic is always discovering, as he exercises the power of his transfigured imagination, that miraculous events really are possible. He learns that there really is a spiritual universe that coexists with this world and also far transcends it, where things impossible here actually become possible there.[32] There really are conditions under which it is possible to fly through the air and clairvoyantly discern what is taking place behind walls.[33] The mystic learns that there really is a sense in which spiritual things imperceptible to the physical senses can become materialized and that material things can lose their substantiality and their capacity to hinder one's movements. These experiences and realizations constantly astonish the mystic because they unveil new dimensions of existence and experience that formerly lay hidden from him. This quickening sense of awe and wonderment helps to perfect the mystic spiritually as it causes him to thirst ever more passionately for a progressively more intimate proximity to the divine source that created this immensity that so fascinates him.

Exercising himmah permits the mystic to experience and to exhibit at the microcosmic level that same creative potency that God Himself exercised on a much larger scale and with greater perfection when He created the cosmos. Consequently, himmah opens up to the mystic the possibility of a particularly intimate understanding of God because he re-enacts the divine process of creation itself. The mystic knows God by becoming like Him even though this likeness is admittedly only a pale and fundamentally imperfect imitation of its divine archetype. The great enemy at this stage is a refusal to "face what is beyond each appearance," that is, the mystic must never allow himself to become so fascinated by the forms that his transfigured imagination presents to his spiritual vision that he starts to

31. Muhyiddin Ibn al-'Arabī, *Journey to the Lord of Power: A Sufi Manual of Retreat*, with notes from a commentary by 'Abdul-Karim Jili and an introduction by Sheikh Muzaffer Ozakh al-Jerrahi (New York: Inner Traditions International, 1981), p. 64.

32. Taken from Ibn al-'Arabī's *Meccan Revelations*, excerpted in Henry Corbin's *Spiritual Body and Celestial Earth* (Princeton: Princeton University Press, 1977), pp. 135–39.

33. Ibn al-'Arabī, *Journey to the Lord of Power*, pp. 30–35.

long for these creations of his own mind instead of for God. In other words, unwise use of himmah brings with it the very real danger of falling into solipsistic infatuation. Ibn al-'Arabī cautions, "You will not attach your *himmah*, the power of the heart's intention, to anything other than Him. And if everything in the universe should be spread out before you, receive it graciously—but do not stop there. Persist in your quest, for He is testing you. If you stay with what is offered, He will escape you."[34] For Ibn al-'Arabī, the spiritual quest is a constant struggle to accomplish two things: (1) to realize experientially, in astonished awe and with greater degrees of comprehension, that all of Creation is nothing but the handi-work of Allah and that it has no independent existence apart from Him; and (2) it is a struggle to quicken the mystic's yearning and craving for the divine presence so that this longing overwhelms and drowns out all other longings. Solipsistic infatuation numbs both the spiritual organ of under-standing and the spiritual organ of desire since it causes the deluded mystic to imagine mistakenly that just because he has attained a degree of mastery over the material world he has attained the summit of spiritual perfection and sovereignty. This spiritual smugness and hubris causes the deluded person to lose his sense of quickening amazement before the wondrous immensity and depth of God and His Creation. He becomes satisfied with experiencing the God of his own belief and he no longer truly appreciates how God utterly transcends all beliefs that human beings have about Him. For this reason, Ibn al-'Arabī considered the improper use of the trans-figured imagination (himmah) to be a deadly enemy of the mystic.

The best way to conclude this analysis of Ibn al-'Arabī's spiritual doc-trine is by quoting the following aphorism taken from *The Bezels of Wis-dom:*

> All becoming is an imagination,
> And in truth a reality.
> Who truly comprehends this,
> Has attained the mysteries of the Way.[35]

The foregoing examination of his spiritual teachings makes it clear that this succinct summary of Ibn al-'Arabī's doctrine can only be adequately interpreted if one does so from the context of the empowered imagination.

34. Ibid., p. 32.
35. Ibn al-'Arabī, *Bezels of Wisdom*, p. 197.

Only then does the paradox of something simultaneously being imaginary and real begin to resolve itself.

It is worth pausing for a moment to consider the profoundly divergent evaluations that Ibn al-'Arabī and the author(s) of *The Tibetan Book of the Dead* give to the empowerment process. For Ibn al-'Arabī, empowerment duplicates the divine creative modality. As such it plays a positive role in human salvation. Through the perfected use of himmah, one becomes increasingly aware of the utter majesty and infinite expanse of God's creation. Astonishment and awe, when confronted with this majesty and immensity that unfolds before one's newly awakened spiritual perceptions, intensify the mystic's longing for an ever more perfect knowledge of its source and in this way deepen his love of God. Because all the realms of existence are the creations of an all-good and all-powerful God, Ibn al-'Arabī does not dismiss them as realms of illusion and suffering as would a Tantric Buddhist. For this reason, the endeavor to contemplate (by exercising himmah) as many of these alternate realities as is possible in one human lifetime fulfills one of humanity's highest purposes. Considered from this perspective, the process of revelation becomes a progressive series of epistemologically and soteriologically more profound states of wonderment that disclose themselves only to the gaze of that mystic who has mastered himmah. Ibn al-'Arabī's positive evaluation of the empowerment process and of the created worlds ultimately lead him to devalue the Sufi state of *fanā'*, that condition wherein the mystic becomes completely absorbed in contemplating God's presence to the extent that he has obliterated all perception of either the physical or spiritual worlds.[36] According to Ibn al-'Arabī, the mystic must not "annihilate the worlds" in this manner but instead must infuse himself with a quickening sense of awe at the divine majesty that the spectacle of their immensity and grandeur kindles within him.

Tantric Buddhists, on the other hand, attribute no soteriological significance to contemplating the majesty of any domain of the phenomenal worlds because they contend that all phenomena whatsoever represent states of illusion and suffering brought into existence by the empowerment process of our minds. Spiritual liberation does not depend on activating the empowerment process as it does in Ibn al-'Arabī's religious metaphysic. Instead, one must stop the empowered mind from generating

---

36. See Ibn al-'Arabī's *Journey to the Lord of Power*, p. 28, and Jili's commentary on Ibn al-'Arabī's remarks on this passage, pp. 78–79.

thought-forms and cease craving or fearing all thought-forms by realizing that however real they seem to be they are nothing but illusions generated by one's own mind.

# Suhrawardī of Aleppo

One finds abundant references to empowerment, out-of-body experiences, and a mode of being that bears striking similarities to Monroe's Locale II in the writings of those Iranian Sufis who came under the influence of that mystical tradition known as Oriental theosophy. The founder of this tradition, the great spiritual master and martyr Shihābuddīn Yaḥyā Suhrawardī (1153–91), maintained—against the rationalistic Islamic Aristotelians—that one could not possibly acquire philosophical wisdom or metaphysical insight unless one were a mystic. Suhrawardī's descriptions leave no doubt that the twin phenomena of ex-stasis and empowerment were important accompaniments to this process of theosophical gnosis.

> The theosophist who has truly attained to mystical experience is one whose material body becomes like a tunic which he sometimes casts off and other times puts on. No man can be numbered among the mystical theosophists so long as he has no knowledge of the most holy leaven of mystical wisdom, and so long as he has not experienced this casting off and this putting on.[37]

In this passage Suhrawardī explicitly declares that mystical knowledge can only occur if the adept has learned how to induce out-of-body experiences. Ex-stasis and mystical knowledge are therefore inseparable. In the next sentence, moreover, Suhrawardī goes on to describe the condition of the disembodied soul once it has projected itself into the "spiritual world." His descriptions of the spiritual world closely resemble those that Monroe gave of Locale II. Like that in Locale II, Suhrawardī's spiritual world is a realm of quasi-material substance where the adept's desires and imaginings become empowered and where matter becomes infinitely plastic, taking on whatever form the subject desires it to take. Suhrawardī explains that once the mystic has obtained the ability to dissociate himself from his physical body,

37. Quoted from a selection in Corbin, *Spiritual Body and Celestial Earth*, p. 124.

from that point, he ascends toward the Light at will, and, if it
pleases him, he can manifest himself in whatever form he chooses.
This power is produced in him by the auroral Light (*nūr shāriq*)
which irradiates his person. Do you not see how it is when fire
caused iron to become red hot, and the iron takes on the appearance of fire; it irradiates and ignites? The same holds true for the
soul whose substance is that of the spiritual world. When it has
undergone the action of light and put on the robe of auroral Light,
it too is able to influence and act; it makes a sign and the sign is
obeyed; it imagines and what it imagines comes to pass accordingly.[38]

Aside from Suhrawardī's attribution of his transformative powers to the
agency of that "auroral" luminescence that penetrates his subtle body
while he is dissociated from his physical form, the parallelism with Monroe's descriptions is obvious enough. One sees the same pattern repeat
itself in both cases. The subject first puts himself into a condition of ex-
stasis, then once he has achieved this state, his will and imagination become empowered.

Suhrawardī's spiritual world of subtle bodies, of infinitely plastic quasi-
material matter, and of empowered thoughts, desires, and imaginings has a
long history in the literature of Iranian Sufism. Both Suhrawardī and the
mystics who came after him persistently mentioned this spiritual realm
(*'ālam al-mithāl*), this world of Images and archetypal Forms, and considered it to be an intermediate universe between the material world visible to
our five physical senses and that completely immaterial universe where
angelic beings dwell, the pure Intelligences devoid of any taint or residue
of corporeality. How did this intermediate universe, this Islamic analog to
Locale II, function within the theological and metaphysical framework of
the Oriental theosophy? First, it served as the locus where the "mythical"
events and places referred to in the Qur'an and the traditions of the
Prophet really took place or existed. Suhrawardī asserts that when
Muhammad spoke of the wondrous cities of Jabarsa and Jabalqa, he was
not speaking about unreal, imaginary things. These cities really exist, Suhrawardī goes on to explain, but they do not exist as places on this physical
earth or in this physical universe. They exist, but only within the 'ālam al-

38. Ibid., pp. 124–25. Compare this description of light (*nūr shāriq*) as a kind of luminosity that irradiates the body of the mystic to the description of quamaneq, in Boas, *Eskimos of Baffin Land and Hudson Bay*, pp. 133–34.

mithāl.[39] Second, the followers of the Oriental theosophy maintained that most of the miraculous events that occurred in the lives of the prophets and other great spiritual figures of Islamic history transpired within this realm rather than in the physical world. Moreover, this realm not only functions as the place where human desires and imaginings objectify themselves but it also serves as the place where the purely immaterial angelic Intelligences descend to manifest themselves to visionaries and take on a form in order to communicate with them.[40] Communication between humans and angelic beings would be impossible except for this realm of Images and archetypal Forms where the latter are able to manifest themselves in a humanly comprehensible form. Third, this intermediate universe is also where "Paradise, Hell, and the Earth of Resurrection have their existence." Paradise and Hell are not to be understood, according to the followers of the Oriental theosophy, as though they were physical places either "above" or "below" the earth. They exist on an altogether different plane of reality than the physical universe. 'Abd al-Razzāq Lāhījī states that "among the schools that admit bodily resurrection there is one that professes that the human *pneuma* (the subtle body) continues to exist in this world of autonomous Images during the interval . . . which extends from the death of the individual to the Great Resurrection."[41]

Suhrawardī also asserts that when mystics mention that they have ascended to Heaven one must not make the mistake of assuming that their material bodies went there. Quite the contrary, it is only when mystics are in their subtle bodies that they are able to visit the heavenly realms that lie within the intermediate universe beyond the confines of the material world.[42] This postulate of an intermediate universe, invisible to the five physical senses but perceptible to the mystic's awakened spiritual organ of perception, an existential modality where desires and imaginings of both human beings and angelic beings take on form, is no merely incidental feature of the theology and metaphysic of Oriental theosophy. It is instead a postulate of central importance for this school of Iranian Sufism since true knowledge and insight into the deeper mysteries of Islam can only emerge when one realizes that many of those revelatory and miraculous events of Islamic sacred history that so baffle commonsensical or literalis-

---

39. Corbin, *Spiritual Body and Celestial Earth*, p. 118.

40. See statements by Quṭbuddīn Maḥmūd Shīrāzī and Lāhījī, cited in Corbin, *Spiritual Body and Celestial Earth*, pp. 127, and 172–73, respectively.

41. Quoted in ibid., pp. 173–74.

42. Ibid., p. 126.

tic interpretations of the Qur'an actually took place or will take place in
the visionary (though no less real) geography of the 'ālam al-mithāl.


# Emanuel Swedenborg

The eighteenth-century Swedish Christian mystic Emanuel Swedenborg developed a theological system that also accorded a very prominent place to
the phenomenon of empowerment. Swedenborg frequently had visions
during which he claimed that he had visited both Heaven and Hell. His
descriptions of these after-life realms exhibit some remarkable parallels to
those that both Ibn al-'Arabī and the author(s) of *The Tibetan Book of the
Dead* gave of similar domains of posthumous existence. Swedenborg emphasized that one can only gain experiential knowledge about the nature
of these disembodied states of existence if one acquires the gift of spiritual
sight, asserting that "the things which are in heaven cannot be seen with
the bodily eyes but with the eyes of the spirit."[43] The most important parallel among Swedenborg and Ibn al-'Arabī and the author(s) of *The
Tibetan Book of the Dead*, however, was that he, too, observed that the
modality of mental and volitional empowerment constituted a central feature of afterlife existence. For example, he noted that when he was in
Heaven conversing with angels, the objects in Heaven appeared similar in
appearance to the objects one encounters in everyday waking experience.
Nonetheless, the apparent similarity between objects in Heaven and objects on earth disguised a fundamental difference: everything that exists in
Heaven derived its existence from the thoughts and desires of the spiritual
beings who dwell there.[44] Consequently, although mountains, lakes, rivers,
flowers, and animals exist in Heaven just as they do in the physical world,
"the things in the spiritual world are not fixed and static like those in the
natural world." Everything in the spiritual world seems to

> have existence about an angel and about the angelic societies, as if
> produced or created from them. They remain about them and do
> not pass away. That they are as if produced or created from them is
> seen by this that, when an angel withdraws, or when the society
> passes to another place, these things no longer appear. Also when

43. Swedenborg, *Heaven and its Wonders and Hell*, p. 81, no. 171.
44. Ibid., p. 81, no. 173.

other angels come in place of them, the appearance of all things about them is changed, the trees and fruits of the paradises are changed, in the flower garden the flowers and seeds, in the fields the herbs and grasses, also the species of animals and birds are changed. Such things have existence and are changed in this way because all these things come into existence according to the affections and consequent thoughts of the angels, for they are correspondences.[45]

Swedenborg's description of Heaven indicates that it is an existential modality quite similar to Locale II, especially insofar as both realms of experience derive their fundamental structure from a process that objectifies the thoughts and desires of the beings that dwell "within" them.

Although Locale II and Swedenborg's spiritual worlds exhibit many features in common, one must not make the mistake of hastily concluding that the two experiential conditions are identical. One notices, for example, that Swedenborg calls those objects that represent the concretization of angelic thoughts and desires "correspondences." "Correspondence" points toward a feature of Swedenborg's spiritual worlds that prevents the scholar from equating them with Locale II. In Swedenborg's system when an object in the spiritual world "corresponds" to an angel's thoughts or desires, it represents the empowerment of those thoughts and desires in an indirect manner. This differs somewhat from the way that the objectification process operates in Monroe's descriptions of Locale II. To clarify this distinction, recall that most, although by no means all, of Monroe's examples stress that what appears in Locale II represents the exact concretization of a specific thought. There is a direct one-to-one relationship between the specific thing thought about and the specific thing that actually becomes objectified. Therefore, when Monroe wanted to visit his friend Bradshaw he had to have the thought "I want to see Bradshaw" in his mind at the time he was exteriorized. The specific thought, "I want to see Bradshaw," then instantaneously concretized itself in the form of Monroe's presence at Bradshaw's residence.[46] If one follows the logic of this example a bit further, Monroe seems to suggest—with no explicit contradiction—that if one sees an apple in Locale II that apple represents the objectification of someone's thought about an apple. Consequently, Mon-

45. Emanuel Swedenborg, *Angelic Wisdom Concerning the Divine Love and Wisdom* (London: Swedenborg Society, 1969), pp. 135–36, nos. 321–22.
46. Monroe, *Journeys Out of the Body,* pp. 46–48.

roe's descriptions would imply that an apple does not appear in the landscape of Locale II without a thought—conscious or unconscious—about
an apple.

One finds references to this direct form of thought-objectification in
Swedenborg's writings as well. For example, in *Heaven and Hell* Swedenborg discusses the notion of spatiality that occurs in the spiritual world
and observes that space only appears to exist in the spiritual world for
changes of place in that realm really represent nothing more than changes
in the thoughts or desires of the beings that dwell there.[47] He then goes on
to say, in a fashion reminiscent of Monroe, that space and distance are
illusions in the spiritual world because "anyone in the spiritual world appears to be present if another intensely desires his presence, for from that
desire he sees him in thought; and vice versa, one person is removed from
another in proportion as he holds him in aversion."[48] Nonetheless,
Swedenborg's writings more often refer to a more indirect process of empowering thoughts and desires. More specifically, the thoughts and desires
of spiritual beings usually concretize themselves in accordance with a complex system of what Swedenborg called "correspondences." Thus, when
one visits the infernal spiritual realms, one notices that the souls of individuals who delighted in gluttony and other such vapid pleasures "love and
delight in dunghills and privies in the other life because mere pleasures are
spiritual filth."[49] One would have expected, according to the rules of Locale II, that their cravings for the pleasures of the table would have directly
materialized in the form of various gluttonous delights. However, since
gluttony corresponds in spiritual terms to filth, gluttonous desires objectify
themselves in accordance with this correspondence rather than directly as
would have occurred in Monroe's description of Locale II. Similarly, when
one sees crops of corn, vineyards, precious stones, windows, and crystals
in the heavenly realms, these things do not represent the objectified
thoughts of an angel who is thinking about how nice it would be to have
some corn-on-the-cob. Instead, these objects represent the objectification
of that angel's love of the divine truth declared in the Bible since those
things correspond to spiritual truth.[50] For this reason, when an angel

47. Compare Swedenborg's conception of spiritual spatiality (*Heaven and its Wonders and
Hell*, p. 89, nos. 191–92) to one by seventeenth-century Iranian Sufi Mulla Sadra, quoted in
Corbin, *Spiritual Body and Celestial Earth*, p. 166.
48. Ibid., p. 90, no. 194, and also p. 270, no. 494.
49. Ibid., p. 266, no. 488.
50. Ibid., p. 267, no. 489.

deeply desires spiritual truths, these desires concretize themselves not as a landscape of spiritual truths but rather as a landscape of the things that correspond to spiritual truth.

The omnipresence of empowerment as an experiential backdrop to Swedenborg's spirituality had important theological ramifications. First, it led him to develop a novel method for interpreting the Bible. Swedenborg claimed that since everything that exists in Heaven and Hell does so as an objectification of the thoughts and desires of the spiritual beings who dwell there and since the Bible is a document that comes from a source in the spiritual world, not the physical world, one can only understand it in a spiritual sense. In other words, one can discover a hidden message in the Bible that exists beyond its superficially apparent meaning. This hermeneutic depth derives from Swedenborg's assumption that physical objects referred to in the Bible correspond to the concretizations of specific spiritual thoughts and desires. Swedenborg's exegetical efforts centered around the attempt to go from the specific physical object mentioned in the Bible back to the specific spiritual thought or desire that it concretized. Every object mentioned in the Bible becomes pregnant with a spiritual message that can only be deciphered by one who recognizes the connection between that object and the objectified thought or desire to which it corresponds. For example, at the beginning of *Heaven and Hell,* Swedenborg interprets Matthew 24:29 where the text refers to events that will transpire when the world comes to an end: "Immediately after the tribulation of those days shall the sun be darkened, and the moon shall not give her light, and the stars shall fall from heaven." Swedenborg does not interpret this passage as referring literally to an eclipse of the sun or some other cosmic catastrophe. He asserted that spiritually ignorant men will indeed misinterpret the text in this naturalistic fashion wrongfully imagining that the text is implying "that the whole visible world will perish and that afterwards a new heaven and a new earth will be created."[51] However, the true meaning only comes to one who comprehends the science of correspondences that his experiences in the spiritual worlds had allowed him to develop. It is not the physical sun, for example, that this passage refers to but rather that to which the physical sun corresponds, humanity's love for God. When one is in the spiritual state of existence, then one's love for God objectifies itself in the form of light.[52] For that reason, the image of the sun corresponds to a spiritual love of God. Consequently, one must not interpret Matthew

51. Ibid., pp. 1–3, no. 1.
52. Ibid., p. 267, no. 489.

24:29 as saying, "Immediately after the tribulation of those days shall the sun be darkened" but rather, "Immediately after the tribulation of those days shall the love of God be darkened."

Henry Corbin has cautioned scholars against imagining that interpretations of the sort Swedenborg gives in the above example represent nothing more than allegorizations of a text.[53] One cannot abstract Swedenborg's system of correspondences from the distinctive experiential matrix that gave it birth without doing violence to his hermeneutic intention. Regarding his system of correspondences as nothing more than a catalogue of allegorical relationships runs the risk of doing exactly that.

Swedenborg's correlation of visionary images to the spiritual thoughts and desires to which they corresponded does not appear to be unique. The eleventh-century Islamic theologian Abū Ḥāmid Muḥammad al-Ghazzālī, in *Mishkat al-Anwar,* interpreted the objects that present themselves to the spiritual vision of prophets in a manner that strongly resembles Swedenborg's hermeneutic method and that seems to imply that the modality of empowerment formed an element of the prophets' visionary experiences. At one point in the text, al-Ghazzālī discussed a vision that Muhammad had in which he saw a certain Abdul-Raḥmān entering Paradise crawling. What was the meaning of this vision? al-Ghazzālī asked. He went on to explain that this vision of Abdul-Raḥmān crawling into Paradise was a waking dream. In short, Muhammad was seeing while awake what most people only see while they are dreaming. Al-Ghazzālī continued by observing that in prophetic vision the physical senses become suppressed, allowing the soul to leave its preoccupation with the objects of the sense-world and enter into the spiritual world.

> And so it sees in waking what others see in sleep. But if it has attained absolute perfection, it is not limited to apprehending the visible form merely; it passes directly from that to the inner idea, and it is disclosed to such an one that faith is drawing the soul of Abdul-Raḥmān to the World Above . . . while wealth and riches are drawing it down to this present world, the World Below.[54]

Al-Ghazzālī and Swedenborg agree that the spiritual realm is a mode of existence where ideas become embodied through the creative activity of the imagination into the forms of concrete objects familiar to us from wak-

---

53. Corbin, *Creative Imagination in the Sufism of Ibn 'Arabī,* p. 14.
54. al-Ghazzālī, *Mishkat al-Anwar,* p. 142.

ing experience. For both men spiritual wisdom consists in the art of learning how to go beyond the superficial appearance of a visionary object to the spiritual idea that it embodies or concretizes.

The omnipresence of empowerment in Swedenborg's spirituality had another important theological consequence. It served as the ultimate basis for his rejection of the Lutheran doctrine that human salvation is attained through faith alone. Against the Lutherans Swedenborg argued that good works were essential if one were to have any hope of being saved, declaring that "the life of heaven cannot be implanted in any man unless he abstains from evil."[55] His attack on the doctrine of justification stemmed from his rejection of the idea that an individual could enter Heaven by a divine act of unconditional mercy. Such viewpoints, he averred, only reveal their proponents' complete ignorance of the fundamental laws that govern a human's existence as a spiritual being. More specifically, such people fail to realize that the experiential content and quality of a human's post-mortem spiritual existence results from objectifying those desires and thoughts that predominate in the core of his personality. Thus, in a very real sense, Swedenborg maintained that it is the human being, not God, who consigns himself to Hell or to Heaven since "every spirit is from head to foot of the same quality as his love." As a result of volitional empowerment, the desire-state of a soul fabricates a spiritual environment around itself that it does not want to leave because that soul will find that any spiritual environment that does not correspond to its owner's deepest thoughts and yearnings will suffocate it. It is almost as though such a soul were a fish trying to live out of water. Such is the condition of a spiritual being that attempts to enter a spiritual environment that does not correspond to its innermost longings. The analogy of a fish out of water is not so far-fetched since Swedenborg himself reported that during one of his spiritual journeys he saw an "experiment" where angels tried to teach the souls of the damned about heavenly matters. However, they found that even among those damned souls who "were desirous that the life of the love they had contracted in the world might be taken away from them and that angelic life, or the life of heaven might be infused in its place" could not maintain their resolve because "when the love of their life was taken away they lay as if dead, and deprived of all their faculties."[56] If God were to bring such souls to Heaven by an unconditional act of mercy, this seem-

55. Swedenborg, *Heaven and its Wonders and Hell*, p. 287, no. 522.
56. Ibid., p. 291, no. 527.

ing act of kindness on His part would violate His own laws that order existence in the spiritual realms and the souls so redeemed would fall into a similar cataleptic paralysis. Such a salvation would amount to no redemption at all.

## Allusions in Saint Augustine's *City of God*

Saint Augustine finishes *The City of God* by telling his readers what the conditions of the saints will be like once they enter Heaven and receive their spiritually transfigured immortal bodies. Not surprisingly, his portrayal of heavenly existence shows it to be a mode of being where souls have become gifted with numerous paranormal powers—one of them being empowerment. As depicted by Augustine, heavenly existence exhibits several parallels to the type of existence that humans experience during extasis. However, despite the fact that Augustine refers to mystical experiences of his own in his *Confessions,* there is no certain evidence of the extent, if any, to which he derives this description of heavenly existence from his own personal experiences of illumination. He is careful to hide whatever his own experiences may have contributed to this description by taking care to construct this portrayal of heavenly blessedness only out of those suggestions that he is able to glean from Scripture. Nonetheless, the parallels between Augustine's depiction of afterlife existence and the ex-static mode of being that so often accompanies mystical illumination leave open the possibility that his personal experiences may have played some role in helping him to formulate this picture of heavenly life.

The first parallel between Augustine's picture of heavenly existence and the ex-static mode of being is that both are conditions where the will has become empowered. Augustine declares that when one is in Heaven, "Wherever the spirit wills, there, in a flash, will the body be."[57] A second parallel between the two states of being is that, in Heaven, souls will be able to discern the innermost thoughts of others. "Even our very thoughts will then be made known to one another."[58] This characteristic of heavenly existence recalls an interesting feature of Locale II that Monroe referred to earlier in Chapter 9. One will remember that Monroe mentioned that

57. Augustine, *City of God,* book 22, chap. 30, p. 541.
58. Ibid., p. 540, book 22, chap. 29.

while he was exteriorized he possessed a capacity somewhat akin to telepathy that allowed him to obtain "an undisguised awareness of [the] prime personality habits and thoughts" of the beings that he encountered there.[59] Monroe's Locale II and Augustine's description of heavenly existence share a third characteristic: they are both conditions where one possesses an extra-ocular organ of clairvoyant vision. I have observed in Chapter 9 that both Monroe and Muldoon claim that while one is exteriorized one sees without the use of his physical eyes. Augustine makes a similar claim about existence in Heaven, basing his claim on the story of Elisha and his wicked servant Gehazi narrated in 2 Kings 5. In that biblical story, the prophet Elisha clairvoyantly saw Gehazi take money from an Aramaean general whom Elisha had cured of leprosy even though Gehazi was out of the prophet's sight at that time. Referring to this story, Augustine argues that when their souls are no longer weighted down with corruptible flesh but have put on incorruptible bodies "the saints will have no more need of their bodily eyes, when they want to see, than Eliseus [Elisha] had need of his eyes to see what his servant was doing, even though the servant was a long way off."[60] Of course, Elisha's clairvoyant powers, as powerful and miraculous as they were, were still operating under the impediments of corruptible existence. However, in Heaven, these same powers will be immeasurably augmented because then visionary gifts will no longer be weighted down with carnal burdens.

One should not overlook some important differences between Monroe's and Muldoon's descriptions of the ex-static mode of being and Augustine's picture of Heaven. First, Augustine constantly emphasizes that Heaven is a condition of unutterable bliss. In contrast, Muldoon never refers to blissful experiences when he is exteriorized and Monroe only refers to occasional moments of ecstatic bliss during his out-of-body episodes.[61] Second, because Augustine defends the view that Resurrection involves an actual resuscitation of the physical body, he asserts that in Heaven one sees not only by means of the spiritual organ that he calls "the heart" but one also simultaneously sees things by means of the spiritually transfigured physical eyes. Muldoon, on the other hand, denied that such dual vision is a normal

---

59. Monroe, *Journeys Out of the Body*, p. 184.
60. Augustine, *City of God*, book 22, chap. 29, p. 535.
61. For one of the infrequent accounts of such a blissful experience in Monroe, see *Journeys Out of the Body*, pp. 122–26.

feature of the out-of-body state.[62] He emphasized, instead, that while one is exteriorized one sees by means of some nonphysical organ of vision.

# Diadochus of Photike

Another fifth-century Christian mystic, Diadochus, bishop of Photike, also refers to the phenomenon of empowerment. For Diadochus, what I have called "empowerment" was a characteristic experiential modality of both angels and disembodied souls. Like the other writers discussed in this chapter, he maintained that this capacity to objectify thoughts and desires only became manifest under conditions where the consciousness-principle had become separated from the physical body.

In "The Vision of St. Diadochus, Bishop of Photike," Diadochus referred to the phenomenon of empowerment twice. One reference appears during the course of a discussion about the exact sense in which it is proper for one to speak about angels and the soul as possessing form. He argued that both angels and the soul are entities that, properly speaking, do not possess a fixed form or figure. They are not restricted, like physical organisms, to manifesting themselves in only one specific form or shape. Instead, "it is necessary to know that they have an appearance, a beauty, and a spiritual limitation so that the splendor of their thoughts is their form and their beauty. This is why when the soul has good thoughts it is completely illuminated and visible from every part but if it has bad thoughts, without light and possessed of nothing admirable."[63] In other words, the form of an angel or a soul represents the objectification of the spiritual quality of its thoughts. Spiritually ennobling thoughts objectify themselves in a luminous and beauteous manner while spiritually degraded

62. For example, see Muldoon and Carrington, *Projection of the Astral Body*, pp. 106–8. Muldoon noticed that extra-ocular vision and ordinary ocular vision mutually excluded each other. The only exceptions to this rule were those occasional instances of dual vision that he observed when he was only a few feet from his physical body. (He called this distance "cord-activity" range because the sensation of being attached to his body by the astral cord became especially noticeable at this distance and almost completely disappeared when he went out more than a few feet from his physical body.) Beyond this distance he never had the experience of simultaneously seeing with his physical eyes and his "spiritual" eye.

63. Diadochus of Photike, "Vision de Saint Diadoque, Evêque de Photice en Epire," in *Oeuvres Spirituelles*, trans. Eduoard des Places, S.J., Sources Chrétiennes (Paris: Editions du Cerf, 1955), p. 174.

thoughts (for example, those of the apostate angels whose thoughts are directed away from God), take on the form of a physical ugliness commensurate with such spiritual baseness.

Diadochus also maintained that, in the other world of spiritual beings and disembodied souls, spiritual "substance" is so subtle and rarefied that the soul's or angel's imagination can shape it into any form it wishes in much the same way that a potter shapes clay to make a pot. Consequently, when one reads accounts about angels coming down in a particular form to communicate a message to one of the saints one must not make the mistake of imagining that that particular angel actually exists in that specific form or shape with which he manifested himself to the holy man. Instead, when angels,

> on the order of God . . . think to take on any form whatever, immediately they enter it by imagination seeing as their nature, in its great rarity, puts itself easily in the service of their will. Being given . . . that it condenses itself as by the force of their will, nothing prevents them from passing by imagination from the invisible to the visible whatever be . . . the figure in which they wish to show themselves to the pure soul.[64]

In other words, angels execute the orders of God by making use of that peculiar faculty of the empowered imagination that they possess.

# Empowered Locutions: The "Substantial Words" of Saint John of the Cross

Up to this point, I have described forms of enthymesis in which it is the individual's thoughts and desires that have undergone empowerment in one of three ways: (1) objectifying themselves in the form of a spiritual landscape that the individual "sees" with his spiritual organ of sight and in which he dwells for the duration of his vision, (2) becoming a means of locomotion in that spiritual world, or (3) transforming the imagination into an extra-ocular organ of spiritual sight. Saint John of the Cross described what appears to be another form of enthymesis in which it is not

---

64. Diadochus of Photike, "Vision de Saint Diadoque," p. 178.

the individual's thoughts and desires that have become empowered but rather it is locutions originating from beyond the individual's mind that have become empowered. These empowered locutions that John of the Cross called "substantial words" not only originate from God rather than from within the mind of the individual who hears them but they also objectify themselves differently than empowered thoughts and desires. To be more specific, whereas empowered thoughts and desires usually transform the visual environment of the individual, these empowered locutions transform the individual's actions.

According to John of the Cross, substantial words are a kind of speech or voice that the human spirit "receives, not from itself, but from some third person, sometimes when it is recollected and sometimes when it is not." Moreover, these divine words come to the individual's attention through some means other than the bodily senses.[65] In other words, John of the Cross wishes to distinguish substantial words from "interior" or "spiritual" utterances that only seem to come from outside the mystic's subconscious but that, in reality, only arise from within the mystic's own psyche. Like Garrett's and Walther's depictions of how clairvoyant, telepathic, or precognitive images "invaded" their fields of awareness from an apparently extra-mental source, John's substantial words suddenly emerge into the mystic's consciousness from a divine source that is outside of his subconscious. The peculiar quality of substantial words that intimates that they undergo the transfigurative effects of the empowerment process is that when these words are uttered to the soul they simultaneously bring about the effect which they signify. Unlike other types of locutions, substantial words possess power. This means that when such words are spoken they are not just heard and then devoid of any effects on the soul. On the contrary, when God communicates to the soul using substantial words,

> It is as if our Lord were to say . . . to the soul: "Be thou good"; and it would then be substantially good. Or as if He were to say to it: "Love thou Me"; it would then have to feel within it the substance of the love of God. Or as if it feared greatly and He said to it: "Fear thee not"; it would at once feel within itself great fortitude and tranquillity. For the saying of God and His word, as the Wise Man says, is full of power, and thus that which He says to the soul He produces substantially within it. . . . And this is the power of His

65. John of the Cross, *Ascent of Mount Carmel*, book 2, chap. 28, p. 328.

word in the Gospel, wherewith He healed the sick, raised the dead, etc. by no more than a word.[66]

Like the other writers investigated in this study, John of the Cross makes the divine mode of being a modality of empowerment. Therefore, when God speaks substantial words to the soul these utterances concretize themselves in much the same manner that an ex-static's thoughts or desires concretize themselves during the time when he is dissociated from his physical body.

It is characteristic of John of the Cross that when he did actually make a brief reference to this form of empowerment he was not concerned with its metaphysical or epistemological implications but was instead concerned with its ethical impact. Unlike Ibn al-'Arabī, who stressed the soteriological importance of the ever deepening metaphysical understanding that arose though the right use of himmah, and unlike the Tantric Buddhists for whom salvation was likewise dependent on rightly understanding the nature of the mind and its procreative role in generating our experience of existence within saṃsāra, John of the Cross stressed the soteriological primacy of ethics rather than knowledge. Because he constantly stressed that the soteriological value of spiritual phenomena must be judged solely on the basis of their ethical fruits, that is, their tendency either to foster or hinder obedience to God's will, rather than on the basis of their capacity to reveal some metaphysical truth, he had no reason to concern himself with the effects that empowerment had on the imagination.

# "Somatic" Empowerment:
# The Phenomenon of Stigmatization

How Saint Francis of Assisi received the holy stigmata provides yet another example of how empowerment can often accompany mystical experience. Although the accounts of this event come heavily embellished with hagiographical fiction, it is nonetheless significant that those who created these legends recognized that Saint Francis's stigmatization and other miraculous powers could only take place after he had developed a capacity

---

66. Ibid., book 2, chap. 31, p. 341.

272 Psychological and Parapsychological Aspects

for both recollective absorption and ex-stasis. In other words, these hagio-graphical legends confirm what I have observed about out-of-body experiences and their supernormal accompaniments. For example, the texts relate that not only was Saint Francis often rapt in ecstasy to such an extent "that he was seen by his companions raised bodily above the ground" during the period preceding his stigmatization,[67] but his angelic visitations were also preceded by a long period of recollective discipline where he spent long periods completely isolated from the world and its distractions.[68] Not surprisingly, these proclivities toward ex-static experiences and recollective quiet were often accompanied by various alleged paranormal powers such as telepathy, clairvoyance, and precognition. The text goes on to relate that "in these contemplative raptures God revealed to him not only present and future things but also the secret thoughts and desires of the friars, as his companion Brother Leo experienced during those days."[69] It has already been noted numerous times in this work how recollective quiet and ex-stasis often pave the way for the empowerment of one's thoughts, desires, and imaginings. The case of Saint Francis was no exception to this general rule. However, what was unusual about him was that the empowered contents of his mind did not objectify themselves exclusively within a spiritual landscape imperceptible to the fleshly eyes. Instead, his intense desire to imitate the life of Christ became objectified both somatically in the form of fleshly wounds and imaginatively in the form of luminous visions of Christ. Even the authors of these legends recognized that those stigmata were the result of a transfiguration operating on the saint's mind for they state that Christ, in a vision, had told Saint Francis that "he was to be utterly transformed into the direct likeness of Christ Crucified not by physical martyrdom, but by enkindling of the mind."[70] It was the activity of an ex-statically empowered mind that made Saint Francis's identification with Christ, His life, and His suffering something considerably more than just an imitation of Christ's behavior. Saint Francis's empowered desires objectified themselves in a stunningly original way demonstrating that humans could achieve, while on this earth, an unexpectedly literal transformation into the likeness of Christ not only by imitating His behavior or experiencing His presence in a vision but also somatically by bearing His wounds on one's own flesh.

67. *Little Flowers of St. Francis*, p. 180.
68. Ibid., p. 183.
69. Ibid., p. 180.
70. Ibid., p. 191.

# Allusions in Pagan Antiquity

Pagan sources from Greco-Roman Antiquity also contain allusions to the process of empowerment as the mode of divine or demiurgic activity and creativity. For example, the *Theurgia* of Iamblichos of Chalcis,[71] a text that includes references to theurgic rituals that incorporate experiences of mystical illumination during the course of their performance, mentions empowerment in much the same way as the other mystical texts discussed here. Iamblichos, like the other mystics referred to in this chapter, implies that the modality of empowerment only operates under conditions of disembodied existence when he states that "real being—that which truly is, and which is itself incorporeal—is everywhere, wherever it pleases."[72] Real being (that is, divinity), is therefore something that utterly transcends any kind of embodiment and is so constituted that, as is the case with empowered thought, willing and accomplishing are simultaneous events. Elsewhere in the *Theurgia* Iamblichos explicitly delineates the way in which demiurgic or divine creation operates, arguing that when God creates all the things of the universe He is neither rearranging matter nor bringing things together through physical motion exerted on matter. Divine creation, being utterly immaterial, operates through the empowerment or objectification of divine thoughts. When God creates "it is by thoughts put into activity, by purposes and nonmaterial ideals, through the sempiternal and supermundane soul, that he constructs the worlds."[73] "Activated" divine thoughts and intentions produce change in the "supermundane soul" and these transformations of the supermundane soul-substance in turn act as the creative agents that give rise to the phenomena of the physical world in much the same manner that activated thoughts and desires fecundate the environment of Locale II.

The *Corpus Hermeticum* similarly alludes to empowerment, especially in *libellus* XI (ii). This segment of the text is a dialogue between mind (*nous*), personified as a teacher, and Hermes, the pupil, concerning the nature of God and the universe (*kosmos*). The oblique reference to empowerment occurs at that point in the dialogue where the teacher is explaining to Hermes in exactly what sense he must comprehend the paradoxical fact that although "all things are in God" they nonetheless are not

71. Iamblichos of Chalcis, *Theurgia, or the Egyptian Mysteries,* trans. Alexander Wilder (London: William Rider & Son, 1911), pp. 116–17.
72. Iamblichos of Chalcis, *Theurgia,* p. 45.
73. Ibid., p. 161.

situated "in" God as ordinary objects are said to be situated in a place. To comprehend how God contains within Himself the entire cosmos, Hermes is told that he first has to jettison his everyday commonsensical notions of spatiality and location. Perhaps the closest analogy that does not veer too far from the truth is to imagine God containing the cosmos within Himself in the sense that the universe arises as a collection of thoughts that God thinks. "You must understand then that it is in this way that God contains within himself the Kosmos, and himself and all that is; it is as thoughts which God thinks, that all things are contained in him."[74] God's thinking activity that gives rise to the cosmos is not "thinking" in the abstract sense of mere conceptualization. Instead, the context of these assertions conveys the idea that the universe arises because God thinks activated or empowered thoughts. This impression gains confirmation from the oblique references to ex-stasis that precede and follow the above quotation. Thus one is told that if one wishes to understand the nature of God one has to become equal to him. And how can this take place? One has to "leap clear of all that is corporeal, and make (oneself) grow to a like expanse with that greatness that is beyond all measure. . . . But if you shut up your soul in your body, and abuse yourself, and say, "I know nothing, I can do nothing, I am afraid of earth and sea, I cannot mount up to heaven" . . . then, what have you to do with God?"[75] The text implies that one cannot be Godlike unless one shares God's freedom from the fetters of embodied existence. Of course, disembodied existence (ex-stasis) also implies the empowerment of thoughts and desires. Thus, Hermes is instructed that not only must he free himself from corporeality, presumably through ex-stasis, but he also must imagine spectacular things while he is disembodied because by actualizing these wild imaginings he will come to comprehend by analogy how the world came into existence as the result of a similar actualization of God's divine imaginings.

> Bid your soul travel to any land you choose, and sooner than you can bid it go, it will be there. Bid it pass from land to ocean, and it will be there no less quickly; it has not moved as one moves from place to place, but it *is* there. Bid it to fly up to heaven, and it will have no need of wings. . . . See what power and quickness is yours. And when you yourself can do all this, cannot God do it?[76]

74. *Hermetica*, 1:221.
75. Ibid., 1:221–23.
76. Ibid., 1:221. The narrator is using the word *psyche* in what appear to be three senses—it is understood here as being simultaneously (1) the life-principle that vivifies the

Playing with the soul's power to objectify thoughts in this manner and observing the wondrous extent of its powers that this playful activity reveals allows the seeker after truth to realize the true sense in which it is proper to speak of God containing the universe within Himself as "thoughts that God thinks."

The purport of these passages suggests, then, that when God creates the world and the things in it He does not think about it only in the sense of conceptualizing it. The divine world-creating thoughts are much more than mere abstract conceptualizations—they have an extra power in them that gives them their procreative energy. That "something extra" is a procreative energy that only becomes manifest when the soul (*psyche*) emancipates itself from its fleshly prison. Again, one sees that an author describing the divine mode of existence makes the assumption that the ex-static mode of being imitates the divine mode of being and therefore serves as the connecting link between the two.

---

organism, (2) that which is the faculty of rational understanding, and (3) that spirit or consciousness-principle that is capable of existing independently of the body.

# 15

# Why Paranormal Phenomena Are Not of Marginal Significance for Understanding Mysticism

## Many Scholars Have Tended to Downplay the Significance of Paranormal Phenomena in Relation to Mysticism

Many scholarly studies of mysticism leave one with the definite impression that paranormal manifestations have only a marginal significance in the mystic's life.[1] Rudolf Otto claims that "neither the mysticism of Eckhart

---

1. Some examples of this scholarly hostility to the paranormal elements in mysticism can be found in Otto, *Mysticism East and West,* and A. Godferneaux, "Sur le psychologie du mysticisme," *Revue philosophique de la France et de l'étranger* (January 1902). Positivist that he was, Godferneaux argued that all the phenomena of mysticism could be reduced to physiological or chemical causes. In other words, there was no supernatural element in mysticism. In addition, he argued that the only valid mystical experiences were those ecstasies devoid of images and forms: ecstasies with visions were the pathological by-products of brain lesions (p. 162). See also Leuba, *The Psychology of Religious Mysticism,* and Inge, *Christian Mysticism.*

Some Catholic scholars have subtly denigrated the supernormal accompaniments of mystical experience by drawing the distinction between higher intellectual visions (where the imagination is inactive) and inferior forms of visions (where forms and images produced by the imagination are present). For example, see Joseph Marechal, S.J., *Studies in the Psychology of the Mystics* (London: Burns, Oates, and Washbourne, 1927); and Zaehner, *Mysticism: Sacred and Profane.* Zaehner distinguishes between "religious" mystical experiences and the inferior "natural" mystical experiences.

Even more recent studies of mysticism continue to marginalize the paranormal dimension of mysticism by implying that the essential elements in mystical experience lie beyond any modality of consciousness where forms, figures, and images appear. For example, Forman ("Mysticism, Constructivism, and Forgetting") draws a distinction between mysticism (where experiences are "not described in terms of sensory experience or mental images") and visionary experience (where sensory experiences and mental images are present). This dichotomy subtly, though not intentionally, perpetuates the marginalization of the paranormal. See Forman, *The Problem of Pure Consciousness,* p. 6.

The works of Gerda Walther, Henry Corbin, and Mircea Eliade stand out as noteworthy

nor that of Shankara . . . has anything to do with the mysticism of the so-called 'illuminists,' with its fantastic visions, occultism, or miracle-hunting. Eckhart never saw 'visions' or experienced 'occult facts,' nor does Shankara appeal to such experiences."[2] To be sure, when contrasted to the writings of Suhrawardī of Aleppo, Emanuel Swedenborg, the Tantric Buddhists of Tibet, or Ibn al-'Arabī, the mystical spiritualities of both Meister Eckhart and Shankara attribute practically no significance to supernormal phenomena. Similarly, other great exemplars of the via negativa such as Saint John of the Cross attach no importance to the supernormal phenomena that accompany mystical experience. According to John of the Cross, desiring supernatural visions and visions actually constitutes an offense against God because it indicates that one nurtures a sinful dissatisfaction concerning the adequacy and fullness of His revelation through Scripture and Jesus Christ.[3] Why does one need supernormal revelations when one has God's fullest revelation in Christ? The exemplars of the via negativa are not the only mystics who emphasize or imply that humanity's ultimate condition of spiritual fulfillment is incompatible with a desire to exercise supernormal powers. For example, even *The Tibetan Book of the Dead* firmly counsels that one who has entered the sidpa bardo must avoid succumbing to the temptation to enjoy the miraculous powers such as the ability to change shape and to produce illusory forms that his bardo-body now possesses.[4] These precautions reflect a general tendency of Buddhist teachers to stress that the condition of detachment so fundamental to nirvana cannot coexist with any desire for exercising paranormal powers. Patañjali also maintained that the highest spiritual state, isolation (*kai-*

exceptions to this general trend of scholarly indifference or even hostility to the paranormal accompaniments of mysticism. See Walther, *Phänomenologie der Mystik;* Corbin, *Creative Imagination in the Sufism of Ibn 'Arabī.* Eliade's essays on the topic of mystical illumination ("Experiences of the Mystic Light," in *The Two and the One* [New York: Harper & Row, 1965], pp. 19–77; and "Spirit, Light, and Seed," in *Occultism, Witchcraft, and Cultural Fashions: Essays in Comparative Religions* [Chicago: University of Chicago Press, 1966], pp. 93–119), together with his essays on sense-experience and mystical experience among tribal peoples and on the symbolisms of ascension ("Sense-Experience and Mystical Experience among Primitives," and "Symbolisms of Ascension and Waking Dreams," in *Myths, Dreams and Mysteries: The Encounter between Contemporary Faiths and Archaic Realities* [New York: Harper & Row, 1960], pp. 73–98 and 99–122, respectively) are some examples of his interest in paranormal phenomena within the context of the religious life. One should also note von Hügel's remarks criticizing those who regarded all visions and ecstasies as pathological manifestations of hysteria in his *Mystical Element of Religion,* 1:336 and 2:22–42.

2. Otto, *Mysticism East and West,* p. 89.
3. John of the Cross, *Ascent of Mount Carmel,* book 2, chap. 22.
4. *Tibetan Book of the Dead,* p. 159.

*valyam*), was likewise a condition that only could come about if the yogin had renounced all desire to exercise his extraordinary powers.[5] Do all these statements imply that one must expand Otto's conclusions specific to Shankara and Eckhart so that they refer to all mystics? Do these statements force one to conclude that "authentic" mystical spirituality has no fundamental connection to supernormal modes of awareness or states of being? I disagree with this conclusion.

# Why This Study Challenges That Tendency in Scholarship

There are several reasons for my negative answer to that last question. First, when one asserts that mysticism has very little connection with supernormal phenomena, one has to carefully distinguish between the mystical experience itself and the mystic's response to that experience. While mystics may respond to supernormal phenomena by ignoring or rejecting them, this negative response does not necessarily imply that paranormal manifestations are devoid of any intrinsic or illuminating connection to the mystical experience itself. For example, even though John of the Cross warned his followers against cultivating a desire for supernatural visions, voices, and other spiritual consolations, he nevertheless realized that these extraordinary phenomena were a very frequent accompaniment of mystical states of consciousness. What decisively indicates that there is an intrinsic rather than an accidental connection between mystical states of consciousness and supernormal phenomena such as telepathy, clairvoyance, precognition, and ex-stasis is that all those manifestations share a common genesis in the recollective act.

It is necessary for scholars to be aware of this intimate linkage between recollection, mystical experience, and supernormal phenomena because this awareness enables them to place both mystical states of consciousness and their paranormal accompaniments within a larger perspective of cultural and biological activities that center around controlling the way that we focus our attention and manipulate the hallucinatory or fantasy-fabricating processes of the mind. Mystical experiences, mediumship, hypnotism, the process of enculturation, schizophrenia, dreaming, the process of visual perception, and ordinary waking experience are all different ways

5. *Yoga-System of Patañjali* (Woods trans.), 3:50.

that human beings either control (or fail to control) the way that they focus their attention and the hallucinatory, fantasy-fabricating processes within the mind. Viewed from this broader perspective, mystical states of consciousness, the phenomenon of enthymesis, and the various paranormal accompaniments of mystical experience are no longer bizarre marginalia but are, instead, exaggerations of processes that operate either subliminally or with diminished intensity in more familiar domains of human cultural, psychological, and perceptual activity. By studying the extremes, we come to a fuller understanding of the more familiar and ordinary.

There is a second reason why this study challenges the assumption that authentic mysticism has only an incidental connection to supernormal phenomena, luminous manifestations, empowerment, and other extraordinary manifestations. Such a distinction between authentic mystical states (characterized by an absence of paranormal phenomena, an absence of vivid and powerful locutions and visions, and by the absence of any desire to experience or manifest such things) and supposedly "inferior" mystical states of consciousness (where such phenomena and desires are present) incorporates an ethnocentric bias. Mystics who come from tribal societies do not seem to be concerned with differentiating between utterly transcendent, ineffable states of spiritual perfection where paranormal manifestations, visions, and locutions are either absent or ignored and mystical states of consciousness where such things are present.[6] Thus Black Elk, the Australian Aboriginal clevermen, and the Tungus and Eskimo shamans never refer to states of consciousness that are radically free of both intense visionary imagery and paranormal accompaniments and they never imply that if such a state were experienceable that it would be religiously significant.

There are five additional reasons why I think that scholars pass up a significant opportunity for deepening their understanding of mysticism when they downgrade or ignore its visionary, ex-static, and supernormal accompaniments. My analysis of mysticism and mystical experience

1. has pointed out why mystical experience is so often accompanied by supernormal powers and manifestations.

6. Examples of such transcendent and ineffable states of spiritual perfection would include the condition of kaivalyam in Patañjali's system of Sāṃkhya-Yoga, Buddhist nirvana, the concept of divine union articulated by Christian mystics who represent the via negativa (such as Meister Eckhart, Evagrius of Pontus, and Dionysius the Areopagite), and the Sufi idea that the vision of God is soteriologically superior to the vision of Paradise and all its joys.

2. provides an unusual perspective from which to challenge psychologism and positivism. While I acknowledge that many mystical experiences utilize the hallucinatory, fantasy-fabricating activities of the mind and that there are numerous, significant continuities that link mystical states of consciousness to dreaming, imagining, and even hypnotic trance, I maintain that mystical experience often operates so as to *transfigure* the dream-fabricating and imaginational activities of the mind so that they generate something very different from "ordinary" dreams or fantasies. They transform the imagination into an extra-ocular organ of perception and knowledge.

3. draws attention to why mystics consistently play such a creative role in cultural and religious life as they invigorate or re-invigorate, deepen, and expand the meaning of traditional religious symbolisms and mythologies.

4. sheds light on one of the reasons why the content of mystical experiences exhibits such persistent dependence on the mystic's cultural and historical context. It allows one to comprehend how it is that during mystical states of consciousness interpretation and experience simultaneously and reciprocally condition each other.

5. directs attention to why religious persons so persistently depict the "spiritual" domains of existence as not only ontologically superior to physical "reality" but also as realms where the thoughts and desires of the beings who inhabit them have a magical ability to instantaneously actualize themselves.

# How This Analysis of Paranormal Phenomena and Their Relationship to the Recollective Process Has Helped to Deepen Our Comprehension of Mysticism and Mystical Experience

## Why Supernormal Manifestations Accompany Mystical Experience

Why do various paranormal manifestations so often develop in tandem with both ex-stasis and mystical experience? Why are mystics and ex-statics so prone to develop various supernormal perceptual abilities such as telepathy and clairvoyance? As this study makes clear, each condition—be it mystical illumination, ex-stasis, clairvoyance, telepathy, or precognition—*when it is deliberately induced*, has its genesis in the recollectively quieted mind. Since intentionally produced ex-static states, mystical states of consciousness, and the various paranormal states each originate only when the subject has achieved this preliminary condition of mental, emotional, and imaginative quiescence, it follows that whenever the subject is psychologically primed to have a mystical experience, he is also, by virtue of those very same recollective efforts, psychologically primed to awaken whatever latent supernormal faculties he may have. This is why mystics and ex-statics often simultaneously develop supernormal sensitivities.

## A Refutation of Psychologism

Throughout Chapters 8 to 14, I have pointed to the numerous continuities that link deliberately induced mystical and ex-static experiences to such "ordinary" hallucinatory or fantasy-fabricating activities of the mind as dreaming and imagining. I have shown that in those types of mystical experiences where the empowered imagination operates, this imaginative empowerment only arises if two requirements are satisfied: The subject must first have quieted his mind and, then he must, in some form or another, gain conscious control over those often unconscious fantasy-fabricating activities of his mind. For example, I noted in Chapter 9 that consciously controlling the formation of hallucinatory images in a dream served as a very effective means of inducing both out-of-body experiences and the resulting paranormal ability to see things at a distance, a capacity that resulted from *continuing* to exercise a strong degree of control over one's thinking, imagining, and desiring processes while one was exteriorized. Tantric visualizations such as the one that David-Neel utilized in order to create her tulpa originated as a result of Herculean efforts to exercise complete control over the hallucinatory processes of the imagination. In each case, consciously controlling the fantasy-fabricating activities of the mind resulted in an extraordinary metamorphosis of the imagination. An imaginative process that normally produces only the most evanescent and insubstantial effects suddenly becomes transfigured into something else, an empowered imagination and may become an organ of supernormal perception that allows an individual to see things at a distance or establish telepathic rapport with someone merely by intensely desiring to contact that person. This empowered imagination may also create quasi-objective phenomena such as tulpas, stigmata, telekinetic manifestations of the sort to which Monroe and Muldoon referred, as well as other "miraculous" events.[7]

The point that I am trying to make is that there appears to be no sharp discontinuity between visionary mystical states where the empowered imagination is active and "ordinary" imagination, dream, or hypnotic trance.[8] All of these states appear to share a common psychological origin: They originate in the fantasy-fabricating region of the mind. What differentiates each of these states of consciousness and modes of being from the others is the degree to which the subject (or some other outside agency) does or does not exert tight conscious control over the hallucinatory activities of his mind. These states are reflected in the following possible scenarios:

1. The subject consciously manipulates the fantasy-fabricating activities of his mind. When this happens, the subject will bring about mystical or ex-static experiences in which his imagination will have also become empowered. All mystical, ex-static, and supernormal phenomena deriving from what I call the "active approach" would fall within this category. The vast bulk of my discussion has centered on phenomena of this sort.

2. A person other than the subject manipulates the fantasy-fabricating activities of his mind. This is hypnotic trance. The fact that hypnotic suggestion can sometimes bring about stigmatization implies that the imagination is also capable of being empowered in this condition just as it is during ex-stasis and mystical experience. This should not come as a surprise since one has only changed the person who is controlling the subject's mind. Its hallucinatory activities are still rather tightly constrained. Consequently, one would still expect to find that some degree of empowerment is still present.

3. An impersonal agency, rather than the subject, controls the fantasy-fabricating activities of the subject's mind. This impersonal agency is sometimes the subject's own culture. The incident of the African boy who ate manioc and who then promptly died of the psychogenically produced convulsions that resulted when he found out that he had vio-

7. See Monroe, *Journeys Out of the Body*, pp. 55–57; Muldoon, pp. 40–41, 273–75.
8. For example, in those mystical states that Swedenborg, Suhrawardī, Ibn al-'Arabī, and Mollā Sadrā described, in the mystical states that originated as a result of Tantric visualization exercises, in yogic saṃyama, and in those mystical states where stigmatization occurred.

lated an ancestral prohibition stands out as a classic example of this sort of agency (see Chapter 10). Here the culture to which the subject belonged seems to have functioned in much the same way as a hypnotist in controlling the subject's fantasy-fabricating activities since cultural suggestions took the place of the hypnotist's suggestions. In other words, that culture's system of assumptions concerning the consequences of violating the manioc taboo created a tacit but no less powerfully implanted suggestion that the boy would die from violating the taboo and, when he found out that he had inadvertently violated that prohibition, this cultural suggestion actually became objectified in the form of lethal symptoms, in much the same way that the hypnotist's suggestion that a patient would develop a blister, actually became somatically objectified in the form of a blister.

In a similar vein, the perceptual experiments described by Vitus Dröscher[9] point to the existence of some sort of mechanism that manipulates the hallucinatory activities of our mind so as to produce photographically accurate visual perception. It may very well be the case, then, that those pathological objectifications that resulted when the African culture manipulated the boy's imagination so powerfully were structurally similar to those beneficial, even vital, manipulations of the imagination that Dröscher has shown form an essential part of every human being's perceptual equipment.

4. Neither the subject nor anyone (or anything) else tightly manipulates the fantasy-fabricating activities of the subject's mind. In this situation, the fantasy-fabricating activities of the mind are allowed to operate without any attempt to control them, translating into the very ordinary conditions of dreaming and imagining. The resulting products are subjective, evanescent, and insubstantial, in a word, "imaginary" and unreal. The imaginary character of these hallucinatory creations markedly differentiates them from those subjectively vivid, sometimes even quasi-material and concrete images that result when the fantasy-fabricating activities of the mind are tightly focused and directed.

Taken as a whole, these four scenarios suggest that one of the distinctive characteristics of those mystics and ex-statics who have experiences where empowerment plays a significant role is that they self-consciously direct those mechanisms that we all unconsciously utilize whenever we participate in the process of enculturation. Those types of mystics and ex-statics

9. Dröscher, *The Magic of the Senses*, pp. 3–4.

have simply developed a variety of methods that enable them to manipulate those imaginative and hallucinatory mechanisms that we all use when we dream, fantasize, internalize the norms and worldviews of our culture, and perceive something visually.

Just as it is the case that whenever we see something we are really "hallucinating" a true picture of that object, it is likewise the case that whenever a mystic or an ex-static employs his empowered imagination so that he can clairvoyantly see what is happening at a distance, he, too, is hallucinating a correct paranormal perception. Both cases exhibit that peculiar paradox: veridical perception, whether it be clairvoyant or visual, requires the assistance of those very same hallucinatory activities of the mind that normally deform perception.

These observations also indicate that the peculiar immediate, almost infinitely plastic, responsiveness of the empowered mind to mental suggestions, thoughts, or desires is not limited exclusively to certain kinds of ex-static or mystical experiences. It can also show itself in a somewhat muted form in hypnotic trance or under circumstances of exceptionally strong cultural conditioning.

In the foregoing remarks I have repeatedly stressed the obvious continuities that connect the empowered imagination with dreams and the ordinary imagination. Do these facts therefore imply the psychologistic thesis; that is, do they necessarily force one to conclude that what a mystic or an ex-static really experiences during one of his visions or illuminations is only the psychologically projected contents of his own culturally conditioned subconscious mind that, ordinarily cut off from conscious awareness, suddenly emerge into his perceptual and experiential field and there take on the misleading appearance that it originates extramentally?[10] The adherents of psychologism point out that this delusion that the projected contents of the subject's own subconscious possess an extramental, objective origin arises because these cognitions and experiences of this projected subconscious material are novel to him and they impinge on his field of awareness with a subjective vividness that equals or even surpasses the impact that genuinely external objects make on his physical sense organs. Does this psychologistic analysis of mystical and ex-static experiences do justice to the facts? Is the mystic just experiencing his own subconscious? One must answer these questions in the negative.

Those species of visionary mysticism where empowerment operates ex-

---

10. Walther, *Phänomenologie der Mystik,* p. 24.

hibit many features that seem to support the psychologistic thesis that all visionary material has a purely intra-psychic origin. For example, one never hears of a Hindu mystic developing the stigmata of Christ's Passion or a Christian mystic having a vision of Kali or Shiva. Consequently, one thing is beyond dispute—cultural conditioning plays a crucial role in shaping the content of a mystic's experience. But do the facts allow one to go so far as to say that the entirety of a mystic's or ex-static's experience merely represents the solipsistic objectification of whatever cultural and religious expectations he or she had been conditioned to accept uncritically as the true description of reality and humankind's place in it?[11] Again, the answer appears to be no.

Several facts challenge the solipsistic implications of psychologism. The occasional appearance of telepathy, clairvoyance, and much more rarely, precognition, point beyond solipsism. Although an intra-psychic process such as the imagination in a condition of empowerment may provide the *means* for acquiring these species of paranormal knowledge, the *results* of using the imagination in this way show that the mystic or ex-static is not just objectifying the contents of his or her mind. For example, consider Monroe's clairvoyant visit to his friend R.W. who was vacationing at a location unknown to him somewhere on the New Jersey coast. This clairvoyant visit resulted from a purely imaginative act on the part of Monroe. He described this act of the imagination that led to clairvoyant perception. "I lay down . . . went into a relaxation pattern, felt the warmth (high order vibrations), then thought *heavily* of the desire to 'go' to R.W."[12] This empowered thought and desire to see R.W. objectified itself by simultaneously accomplishing three things. First, it presented R.W. to Monroe's field of awareness. He was not just daydreaming about R.W. being in his presence. He was actually there where she was, looking at her. Second, it gave Monroe veridical information about who R.W. was talking to at that very moment he was thinking about going to visit her, and so it revealed how many people were with her, the color of each person's hair, each person's age, gender, and what he or she was drinking and doing. Third, it somehow located R.W. in order to get this veridical information in spite of Monroe's own lack of specific information concerning her whereabouts and the apparent impossibility of his being able to acquire such information by any process of rational extrapolation from the data he had at

11. Solipsism is the theory that maintains that (1) the self is the only thing that really exists and (2) that the only things that this self can know are its own modifications.

12. Monroe, *Journeys Out of the Body*, p. 55 (emphasis mine).

hand. Here one has an example where an act of the imagination—the empowered imagination—took an individual beyond that solipsistic subjectivity that one ordinarily associates with the activities of the imagination. This empowered imagination can do much more than just present the object imagined to the subject's field of awareness. It can also, under certain circumstances, simultaneously function as an organ of veridical perception. When the empowered imagination objectifies itself, something extra, some overplus, attaches to that objectification that prevents one from saying that the subject is only externalizing the contents of his own mind—that Monroe only saw R.W. because he was thinking about her. The information Monroe obtained about his friend exceeded what he possibly could have known about R.W. and her activities either from his previous knowledge about her and her habits or from extrapolations based on that knowledge. My point is simply this: the empowered imagination can sometimes act as an organ of knowledge, something that the ordinary imagination can never do. For this reason, a serious error is committed if one categorically asserts that any phenomenon where the empowered imagination is active (such as in ex-static experience) possesses no more than a purely subjective significance.

The above example shows that the empowered imagination is not always merely spinning out solipsistic reveries and dream landscapes; it sometimes operates as an organ of veridical perception. One must therefore conclude that, however continuous the activities of the empowered mind might be with those of the ordinary imagination, the noetic or informational overplus that attaches to the former definitely distinguishes them from the latter and decisively refutes the solipsistic implications of psychologism. In fact, any instances of genuine clairvoyance, telepathy, or precognition that occur as the mystic or ex-static exercises his empowered imagination always exhibit this informational overplus since they always provide the subject with some kind of objectively verifiable information that exceeds what he could possibly have known or deduced about that object on which he had focused his imagination. This fact alone should seriously challenge the psychologistic thesis. After all, how could this supernormal knowledge of what others are doing or will do have come from within the subject's own mind?

The following example of telepathy further shows that telepathic material emerges into the subject's field of awareness from a source that lies outside his or her own psyche. One day a certain woman asked Garrett to establish contact with her deceased husband and deceased elder son. However, during the trance, instead of establishing mediumistic contact with the two dead men, Garrett was suddenly confronted "by the apparitional appearance of her living son, who spoke his name, and said that he had come to assure his mother that the 'ultimate tragedy of the day is not my fault' [that he had not committed suicide]." At this moment the mother got angry with Garrett for wasting her time and wanted to end what to her obviously seemed like a fruitless session. After all, she had seen her son that very morning and he was in the best of health. Garrett tried once again to establish contact with the lady's deceased husband and eldest son but then the apparition of the supposedly living son told Garrett to tell his obstinate mother to pick up the Bible and read Job 14:2, Psalms 89:45, and Jeremiah 6:2, for then she would overcome her skepticism and realize that he had indeed really been in her presence during the seance. The mother left the seance unconvinced that anything had happened that morning to her youngest son. However, Garrett later learned that the woman's son had really died that same morning in a motorcycle accident just before he was supposed to leave for India. He wanted to assure his mother that his death was not the result of suicide because he was afraid that her previous refusal to let him marry before going abroad might leave her with the erroneous impression that he had killed himself as a despondent response. The Bible verses he asked his mother to read all centered on the theme of youthful death. Thus, "He cometh forth like a flower and is cut down. . . . The days of his youth hast thou shortened. . . . Thou shalt not take thee a wife." Evidence of this sort convinced Garrett that "telepathy is not a product of the imagination."[13] Indeed, almost everything about this incident points to its extrapsychic origin: the son's death at a time when his mother had no inkling that any tragedy had occurred or would be likely to occur, the fact that he appeared in the seance unexpectedly against his mother's express wishes, and the fact that the Bible verses he cited were completely appropriate to the occasion. In any case, it seems that Garrett received information that could in no way have come from her own subconscious mind or imagination except, perhaps, the Bible verses that she might have unconsciously remembered from her childhood. Similar evidence led Walther to declare categorically that the phenomenon of telepathy forces one to acknowledge that "the concept of 'one's own' experience loses. . . its unequivocality."[14]

13. Garrett, *Telepathy*, pp. 169–71.
14. Walther, *Phänomenologie der Mystik*, p. 56.

Even those activities of the empowered imagination that do not exhibit this noetic or informational overplus still contain elements that point beyond solipsism or naive epiphenomenalism. For example, David-Neel's ability to create a tulpa showed that it was possible for the empowered imagination to create hallucinations that others could perceive.[15] She demonstrated that hallucinations, at least those that were empowered, were not always purely subjective phenomena or mere fantasies; they may actually possess an objective or at least quasi-objective presence. The proponents of psychologism or naive epiphenomenalism are mistaken in their assumption that the creations of the empowered imagination are always unreal. The evidence suggests, however, that some creations of the empowered mind possess an ontological dignity midway between that inferior status one accords those evanescent, "unreal," purely subjective phantasms that result from our ordinary dreams and imaginings and that superior ontological status one unquestioningly accords to the "real" objects that one encounters in the physical world. In fact, when one observes that, at times, the diaphanous spirit-body that the ex-static creates from his empowered imagination goes through physical matter without impediment (as when Monroe pinched R.W.) or otherwise affects matter telekinetically, one is forced to concede that the ontological inferiority we normally accord to *all* creations of the imagination may very well be unjustified.

Certain aspects of that supernormal faculty for seeing auras also contain implications that undermine the psychologistic claim that all subjective experience comes to one either out of one's subconscious or as the result of the mind's activity in processing and organizing that data which it had previously received from the five physical sense organs. For example, in *Auras*, Edgar Cayce referred to some unusual experiences a friend of his once had that indicate that the five physical senses and the subconscious are not the only sources of subjective experiences. The woman claimed that she could always tell whenever a person was lying because his aura would immediately develop a lemony-green streak when he was in the process of speaking the falsehood. Another incident in her life points to more dramatic evidence that the aura contains paranormal information that only a psychically sensitive individual can decipher. She wrote that one day while she was shopping in a department store, she approached an elevator. As she started to enter this well-lit elevator full of people, some-

15. David-Neel, *Magic and Mystery in Tibet*, pp. 314–15.

thing made her suddenly refuse to enter it. "The interior of the car, although well-lighted, seemed dark to me. Something seemed wrong." It took her a moment or two to realize what had made her so uncomfortable: "The people in the elevator had no auras." A moment after she realized what it was that had disquieted her, the elevator cable snapped and the elevator car plunged seven floors into the basement killing everyone in it.[16] Here one has a clear example of precognitive information conveyed by the absence of the auras on the people who were very shortly to die.[17] There was certainly no physical way that Cayce's friend could have known that the elevator cable was about to break. This information obviously could not have come to her from her own subconscious or from her five sense organs or by rational inference from sense data. Consequently, one can only conclude that the information had an extra-mental origin.

Cayce's friend was not the only person who claimed that she could glean extrasensory information from examining a person's aura. Garrett similarly mentioned that the luminosity that she habitually observed around both animate and inanimate objects somehow conveys information about the organism or object that it envelops. "I enter 'within' the very life of this world of light, sound, and color, using them as one might use a telescope to see what lies within and beyond. Thus I am able to sense the history of the organism or object whose nature is revealed by the quality of its radiation which I am able to contact and enter."[18] She went on to claim that this faculty of clairvoyance was impossible to develop without having a sensitivity to this extrasensory luminosity.

Walther's observations on the aura also indicate that the ability to see them constitutes an extrasensory faculty of perception radically distinct from physical sense-experience, imagination, or hallucination. She claims that the color, texture, and clarity or opacity of an aura serves as an accurate indicator of a person's health, mood, and intellectual or spiritual development. She also maintains that whenever she has compared her descriptions of some particular person's aura with those that other psychics have given her of the same person, she has invariably discovered that the two descriptions match except for small differences of detail that resulted

16. Cayce, *Auras*, p. 8.

17. Those who claim to see auras maintain that an organism only manifests one when it is alive. When it dies, the aura disappears. See Garrett, *Adventures in the Supernormal*, pp. 41–42, 86.

18. Ibid., p. 172. Garrett would not, however, maintain that the luminosity surrounding an inanimate object would be identical to that aura that surrounds one that is alive. Auras are highly individualized in structure.

from changes that had taken place in that person's mood between the time that Walther had examined him and the time that the other psychic had inspected his aura.[19] The fact that two individuals can independently arrive at almost identical descriptions of a particular person's aura demonstrates, if it be true, that the five physical senses and the rational faculty do not have any monopoly on being sources of veridical information. (Walther asserted that she asked for the other psychic's description before she told the other psychic what she saw.) In short, the faculty of sensing auras sometimes also functions as a source of objectively valid information about the world. More important, it indicates that the five physical senses, the imagination, and the subconscious are not the only sources of subjective experiences. Therefore, one may conclude that the exponents of psychologism are mistaken when they claim that all visionary and preternatural phenomena that accompany mystical experiences have a purely intrapsychic origin.

Let me reiterate the two main points I made in this subsection:

1. We must remain open to the possibility that some of the visionary and supernormal accompaniments of mystical experiences originate extramentally.

2. We must also realize that just because a visionary or ex-static phenomenon did originate from *within* the psyche of a mystic or a medium, that fact of its intra-psychic origin is not sufficient grounds for dismissing it as a mere epiphenomenon or subjective illusion. I have presented evidence that the "empowered" imagination, a phenomenon obviously generated from within the psyche of the mystic, can nevertheless function noetically as an organ of veridical extra-ocular perception and knowledge.

# Empowerment and the Essential Contextuality of Mystical Experience

In Chapter 1, I asserted that one of the fundamental characteristics of mystical experience is that it empirically verifies many elements of that description of reality, which are either explicit or implicit in the mythology that founds the mystic's particular religious and cultural tradition. Thus an

19. Walther, "Some Experiences Concerning the Human 'Aura,'" p. 344.

Eskimo shaman will have visions that seem to prove that the helping spirits posited by his community's folklore and mythology really do exist. The practitioner of hatha yoga is likely to have trance experiences that appear to prove the existence of chakras and kundalini energy. Many recent scholars of mysticism have observed phenomena of this sort and have similarly concluded that the mystic's historical situation and cultural milieu shape the content of his or her mystical experience.[20] Robert Gimello goes so far as to claim that "mystical experience is simply the psychosomatic enhancement of religious beliefs and values or of beliefs and values of other kinds held 'religiously.'"[21]

I suggest that *one of the principal reasons why mystical experiences so often empirically verify the mythology that underpins the individual mystic's religious tradition is simply that those states of consciousness frequently coincide with a condition of enthymesis.* This is actually what one ought to expect since the very same recollectedness of mind that triggers the mystical state of consciousness is also the condition that is most likely to activate the process of imaginational empowerment. Moreover, *under conditions of empowerment, it is impossible for a vision or locution to avoid being shaped by the presuppositions, desires, and anxieties that mystics bring with them into the experience from their cultural, historical, and mythological environment.*

Why is it impossible for a vision or locution originating under conditions of empowerment to avoid being contextually determined? It is impossible because the process that objectifies and concretizes the mystic's thoughts, desires, and imaginings under conditions of empowerment can never create anything in a contextual vacuum—a mystic's thoughts, desires, and imaginings have to come from some sort of context or another. Indeed, the empowerment process is incredibly sensitive to context. Let us not forget what we saw in Chapter 9: Even *unconscious* habits and prejudices often become instantaneously "objectified" under conditions of empowerment (such as astral doubles always wearing clothes because that is how the subject habitually envisions himself to his own imagination). If this is so, it stands to reason that the deeply engrained and powerfully reinforced habits, prejudices, expectations, and ideas that a mystic internalizes from his religious and cultural milieu will have an even more pow-

---

20. The most important recent works that stress the fundamental contextuality of mysticism are a series of collected essays edited by Katz, specifically, *Mysticism and Philosophical Analysis, Mysticism and Religious Traditions,* and *Mysticism and Language.*

21. Gimello, "Mysticism in Its Contexts," in Katz, *Mysticism and Religious Traditions,* p. 85.

erful influence in shaping the content of his mystical states of consciousness. Consequently, under the conditions of empowerment, it would be most unlikely that a traditional Eskimo shaman would fail to experience the presence of shore spirits in his visions because he has been brought up to believe not only that such beings exist but their assistance is essential to his people's survival. The Eskimo shaman will objectify those presuppositions about shore spirits and incorporate them into the visionary landscape of his mystical experience. His experience will therefore serve as an empirical confirmation of Eskimo religious conceptions. The same thing applies to the Hindu yogin who practices hatha yoga. If he takes it for granted that chakras, subtle nerves, and kundalini energy exist and must be experienced before spiritual liberation can occur, then it is almost certain that if he has a mystical experience that simultaneously triggers the process of imaginational empowerment, he will vividly experience the presence of those subtle energies and objects.

The foregoing analysis has an important corollary—*whenever enthymesis is operative* there can be no such thing as a "pure," unmediated mystical experience. An unmediated experience is impossible under such conditions because the empowered mind, will, and imagination are always objectifying material that the mystic has incorporated into his or her psyche from the familial and cultural environment. I suggest that the fundamental amorphousness of mystical experience to which Gershom Scholem has referred stems,[22] in part, from the fact that the mystical experiences so often mobilize the process of empowerment. For this reason, the content of such experiences cannot avoid becoming an "objectification" of and an empirical verification of the mystic's particular cultural and religious assumptions no matter what they might be. In short, whenever empowerment is an aspect of mystical experience—and I suggest that it usually is—it is impossible for any individual's mystical experience to be the same as any other person's. After all, if every person's world of private thoughts, anxieties, and desires is unique, then how can we expect that when those same thoughts and emotions are objectified through empowerment the resulting experience will be any less individualized?

Even though I agree that Katz is correct in asserting that there are no unmediated transcontextual mystical experiences (at least when empowerment is present),[23] my analysis of some of the peculiarities of the empowered imagination, mystical light, and some of the other paranormal

22. Scholem, *On the Kabbalah,* p. 8.

23. Katz, "Language, Epistemology, and Mysticism," in his *Mysticism and Philosophical Analysis,* p. 26.

enhancements of perception and emotion described in Chapters 9 through 13 suggests that we must not carry historical or contextual determinism too far. When Gimello asserts that "mystical experience is *simply* the psychosomatic enhancement of religious beliefs,"[24] he overlooks some of the subtle ways that the empowered imagination and other paranormal accompaniments of mystical experience transcend not only psychologism but also any sort of overly rigid historical or contextual determinism. I noted above that the process of enthymesis sometimes enlarges and transfigures what would otherwise be an "ordinary" thought or desire into an extraocular organ of vision. As a result, the empowered experience begins to include clairvoyantly acquired information concerning the object-thought-about or the object-desired that enters the mystic's or medium's mind from a source that is outside his or her psyche. This perceptual enlargement brings into play an element of transcendence that transforms the empowered mind, will, and imagination into something more than just exteriorizations or projections of the subject's conscious and unconscious thoughts and desires. For this reason, the partisans of psychologism are mistaken when they assume that all mystical experience is nothing more than the exteriorization of material thrown up from deep within the mystic's psyche.[25]

This same criticism of psychologism also applies to the partisans of an excessive contextual or historical determinism. Many of the mystical and ex-static experiences that are accompanied by paranormal phenomena and enthymesis are not just "psychosomatic enhancements of [the mystic's] religious beliefs and values."[26] For example, it is hard to see how Monroe's astral visit to Dr. Bradshaw and the clairvoyant information that resulted from it,[27] were psychosomatic enhancements of Monroe's religious beliefs. Similarly, Garrett cautioned her readers against assuming that telepathic and clairvoyant impressions are simply the creations of the medium's imagination or unconscious. Instead, she emphasized that the "world of reality produces its own knowledge, and no fancied symbol or creation of my mind can leave so strong an impression or sense of knowing as does

24. Gimello, "Mysticism in Its Contexts," p. 85 (emphasis mine).
25. For example, see Leuba, *The Psychology of Religious Mysticism*, p. 315; Henri Delacroix, *Études d'histoire*, p. 62. Delacroix maintained that the feelings that mystics often have of being driven by an external power come not from God but from the depths of their unconscious minds. "This God is only an interior God. This divine thing . . . is the divine in himself. . . . Those things which go beyond ordinary consciousness are the subconscious forces which are able to take a divine form."
26. Gimello, "Mysticism in Its Context," p. 85.
27. Monroe, *Journeys Out of the Body*, pp. 46–48.

the field of reality itself, lying beyond the realms of imagination. . . . The clairvoyant image 'happens.' You come upon it. . . . You have done nothing—or, so, at least, it would seem, except look within where this image is enthroned."[28] If telepathic and clairvoyant impressions do not appear to be generated from within the subject's subconscious mind, then it is also reasonable to infer that such invasive experiences are not psychosomatic enhancements of religious beliefs either.

Although I have pointed to certain extreme forms of mystical and ex-static experience that reveal the limitations of historical and contextual determinism, I still affirm that in the vast majority of cases, the mystic's historical situation and religiocultural milieu decisively shape both the existential and perceptual content of his or her visions and revelations and the specific ways that both the mystic and the community respond to them. A contextualist framework of some sort or another is still essential if one is to understand the nature of mysticism and mystical experience.

## Illuminating the Process of Enculturation

This detailed analysis of how mystics and ex-statics generate supernormal phenomena has had the additional merit of drawing attention to a third way that these individuals exhibit an extraordinary creativeness. When their imaginations are empowered, mystics explicitly and deliberately manipulate, at the level of individual experience, the same processes and mechanisms that religious traditions and cultures tacitly and unconsciously bring into play at the collective level when they create those basic orientations by which their adherents live. To put it another way, mystics and ex-statics display a remarkable degree of "playfulness" with the psychological processes that operate in enculturation.

This idea that they can sometimes consciously manipulate those mechanisms that the enculturation process subliminally imprints upon us[29] came across with particular clarity in the example of the boy who ate manioc. There one notes that the enculturation process had unobtrusively caused the boy to internalize the suggestion that if he were to violate the taboo against eating manioc he would die. This cultural suggestion actually be-

28. Garrett, *Telepathy*, p. 175.
29. Notice that I qualify this statement with the word "sometimes." One must not forget that mystics are often subject to the unconscious influences of the enculturation process just like everyone else. While their degree of sovereignty with respect to it is greater, they are by no means completely free of it.

came so strong that it had unconsciously empowered his mind, for when he violated that taboo, the culturally implanted suggestion objectified itself in fatal symptoms. This example indicates that the basic difference between enculturation as a source of empowerment and mystical recollection as a source of empowerment is that the latter process is under the subject's conscious control whereas the former is not. Except for this, the two processes preserve the same structural relationship between a suggestion and its objectification.

I have chosen what are often strange and even extreme examples of mystical experience and ex-stasis for many of the same reasons that scientists subject matter to extreme forms of stress and deformation in laboratory experiments. Sometimes one better understands the ordinary processes of nature when, to quote Francis Bacon, one "twists the lion's tail" and causes the things of nature to behave in freakish and exaggerated ways so that processes that normally operate subliminally can come to the surface. The extreme phenomena of mystical experience function in a similar way for they, too, bring to the surface some of the processes at work in enculturation that otherwise lie hidden from view. The ordinary nonviolent processes of cultural change and adaptation generally involve an unobtrusive dissolution and creation of symbolic structures and assumptions about the nature of the world that shape human experiences of reality into ordered and meaningful patterns. Mystical experiences often present people with situations that either challenge or else confirm in an unexpected way those tacitly accepted symbolic structures that give order and meaning to human existence. The Spiritualist seance of the mid-nineteenth century serves as an excellent example of the way that mystics and mediums were able to confirm in an unexpected way that religion was compatible with the prevailing materialistic conception of the world of that period. Nineteenth-century positivists and materialists had claimed that since there was no empirical evidence for the existence of either soul or spirit, religion was a delusion. The entranced mediums who "materialized" ectoplasms and generated poltergeists and spirit-rappings created experiences that both challenged and confirmed the nineteenth-century materialistic and positivistic worldview. On the one hand, they had shown that it was a mistake to consign spirit, soul, and religion to the status of illusion since they had presented empirical proof that the spiritual world had effects on matter. On the other hand, they made concessions to the materialistic worldview by creating a distinctive set of experiences that exhibited soul and spirit in such a way as to depict them as entities that possessed a peculiar sort of substantiality and corporeality akin to (but not identical to) the sort of substantiality that ordinary matter possesses.

Here we have a good example of how mediums and mystics creatively "play" with the fundamental assumptions of their respective cultures and religious traditions. At first sight, it would appear that there is no way to reconcile nineteenth-century materialism and religion. Yet this was precisely what Spiritualist mediums and mystics such as D. D. Home were able to do. They were able to create experiences that materialized spirit and soul and confirmed empirically that spirit and soul were not the unreal illusions that the opponents of religion had claimed that they were. In sum, mystics and ex-statics accomplish consciously and individually what enculturation accomplishes unconsciously and collectively. Mystics and ex-statics dissolve and create experience-ordering structures. Cultures do the same thing but they generally do it in a more subtle and unobtrusive manner over far longer stretches of time. I suggest that what I have called empowerment is not the exclusive domain of the mystic. The culture or group is also capable on occasion of unconsciously empowering the minds of its members.[30]

What do we learn from these observations? We learn that mystics are not a species set above the rest of humanity. They simply appear to exaggerate, temporally compress, and consciously control processes that are always taking place slowly and quietly, in a more attenuated form and more or less unconsciously, whenever human beings are engaged in those activities that create and sustain a cultural or religious tradition. This keenness with which mystics and ex-statics lay bare the effects of culture on human experience constitutes one of the most important aspects of their cultural and religious significance.

## Interpretation as Intrinsic to Experience

This study of how supernormal phenomena relate to mystical experiences helps to clarify John Morrison Moore's comment about the reciprocal interdependence of experience and interpretation in mysticism. "It is misleading to think of an interpretation as simply 'growing out of' an experience. . . . The relation of experience and interpretation is reciprocal and

---

30. Ellenberger's example of the boy who violated the manioc taboo comes to mind in this context. See Henri Ellenberger, *The Discovery of the Unconscious: The History and Evolution of Dynamic Psychiatry* (New York: Basic Books, 1970), pp. 22–23.

complex rather than being a simple one-way relation of dependence."[31] Moore contended that it was simplistic to imagine that somehow the experience happens first and only afterward does the one who has the experience come up with an interpretation of it. Such an erroneous view stemmed from the assumption that the interpretation of religious experience was something extrinsic to rather than constitutive of experience. Robert Gimello came to similar conclusions about the reciprocal interrelationship between experience and its interpretation. He asserted that "it seems reasonable to suggest that what has often been called interpretation, and held under that label to be extrinsic to the pure experience, is actually an essential part of the experience."[32] This reciprocity between the content of an experience and those factors by which it is interpreted comes across most clearly when one examines the phenomenon of empowerment.

It is clear that whenever enthymesis or empowerment is operative in a mystic's experience it becomes meaningless to talk about interpretation as though it were something extrinsic to experience. I demonstrated in Chapter 9 that the empowered mind instantaneously objectifies both the conscious and unconscious thoughts and desires of the mystic as well as habitual ways of thinking. For example, one never projects one's own astral double as a nude replica of oneself. It always appears clothed because one habitually imagines oneself that way. When one exteriorizes, this habitual image of oneself as clothed becomes empowered and this empowered habitual image of oneself becomes objectified almost instantaneously in the form of a clothed astral double. It therefore follows that under conditions of mental, volitional, and imaginational empowerment the content of the mystic's experience is profoundly shaped by whatever presuppositions his habits, experiences, or cultural and religious upbringing have conditioned him to accept since those are what become objectified. However, those same presuppositions and habits that objectify themselves in the visionary experience of the mystic who has recollectively empowered his imagination are also the presuppositions and habits that determine the way that he interprets his experiences. Therefore, under conditions of empowerment, it is proper to speak, as Gimello does, of interpretation as constitutive of mystical experience, since the same elements that go into generating an interpretation of that state of consciousness are also the same elements that are objectifying themselves as that experience. Interpretation is there-

---

31. Moore, *Theories of Religious Experience*, p. 187.
32. Gimello, "Mysticism and Meditation," p. 176.

fore intrinsic, not extrinsic, to experience. Moreover, interpretation and experience reciprocally condition each other. The subject's first mystical experience will, to some degree, contain novel elements that he did not expect to perceive. These new elements will then become integrated into that intellectual framework of ideas about the nature of reality that the subject carried into his first mystical experience. This framework, now modified by incorporating those novel elements of his first mystical experience, will then structure the content of subsequent experiences.

From these reflections, it is clear that under conditions of mental, volitional, and imaginational empowerment a "pure" mystical experience does not exist in sovereign isolation from any prior conditioning by one's previous experiences and one's cultural and religious assumptions. It is simplistic to imagine that the constituent elements of an interpretation are only superimposed by a process of reflection on experience *after* that experience has occurred. They are present in experience from the very beginning, shaping it even as it comes to birth.

## Empowerment and Miracle

The extensive attention I have given to the paranormal aspects of mystical and ex-static experiences has conferred an additional benefit that deserves mention. This study has shown that the modality of spiritual existence is often none other than that mode of existence where imagination has become empowered. I noted that when Swedenborg described the mode of existence that spirits possessed in Heaven and Hell their powers and existential situation there corresponded to those of an individual who had empowered his mind, will, and imagination.[33] Similarly, when Ibn al-'Arabī claimed that God created the physical universe by means of His himmah, I noted that this creative potency he ascribed to God was none other than an intensified version of that empowered desire that the mystic or ex-static can awaken when he becomes illuminated.

These investigations should also have taught one to be much more open-minded to the claims that have traditionally been made about the magical powers of "spiritual" persons—that is, shamans, medicinemen, mystics, and other specialists in the occult. This study indicated that magical practices and beliefs are not always grounded in mere superstition. For example, beliefs about the efficacy of bone-pointing among the native Australians do not ap-

33. Swedenborg, *Angelic Wisdom*, pp. 135–36, nos. 321–22.

pear to be baseless. After all, it was observed that bone-pointing rituals were not an empty assemblage of gestures and incantations but rather techniques for empowering the sorcerer's mind. As such they bore unmistakable structural resemblances to those effective visualization (and empowerment) techniques that Tantric Buddhists have utilized for noninjurious purposes. One can see other seemingly superstitious beliefs in a new light once one begins to make sense out of the paranormal dimension of mystical experience. For instance, the Colombian anthropologist Gerardo Reichel-Dolmatoff has noted that the Tukano Indians believe that a certain type of spiritual personage they call the *kumu* possesses the power to discern a person's most intimate thoughts and desires. One is tempted at first glance to dismiss these claims of power that the Tukano ascribe to the kumu as superstitious nonsense. Nevertheless, if one pays closer attention to other details of Reichel-Dolmatoff's description of the kumu, one begins to realize that there might be more to these beliefs than meets the eye. For example, when Reichel-Dolmatoff states that "the *kumu* is a luminous personage who has an interior light, a brilliant flame that shines and unveils the intimate thoughts of all people who speak to him,"[34] one immediately recognizes that being filled with an inner light invisible to ordinary human beings is always the mark of a person in a spiritually transfigured state. As I noted numerous times in Chapters 9 and 11 through 13, it is quite normal for the spiritually awakened person to possess telepathic powers.[35] One should also note parallels between the reputed ability of the kumu to discern the innermost motivations of human beings and that peculiar quasi-telepathic power Monroe previously referred to when he spoke of identifying spiritual beings and human astral forms by means of an "undisguised awareness" of their basic personality habits and thoughts. Like the kumu, Monroe claimed that he could discern the innermost thoughts and personality habits of the beings in Locale II by analyzing the light that they emitted from their auras. In other words, Monroe noticed that the radiation emitted by the auras of spiritual beings was laden with information about their most intimate thoughts and desires in much the same way that the light of a star is laden with information about its chemical composition and magnetic field.[36] Could it be that both the kumu and Monroe see auras and discern intimate secrets by reading them? One should be open to the

34. Gerardo Reichel-Dolmatoff, *Amazonian Cosmos: The Sexual and Religious Symbolism of the Tukano Indians* (Chicago: University of Chicago Press, 1971), p. 137.
35. See also Rasmussen, *Intellectual Culture of the Iglulik Eskimos*, pp. 122–24.
36. Monroe, *Journeys Out of the Body*, pp. 183–84.

possibility that those mind-reading powers that the Tukano ascribe to the kumu may have some foundation in phenomena of this sort.

The inveterate tendency of religious literature and folklore to juxtapose descriptions of miraculous events or powers with references to luminous manifestations and ex-static flight should not be surprising. I have amply demonstrated in Chapters 9 and 11 through 13 that this threefold conjunction of "miracle," illumination, and ex-stasis actually occurs in certain types of human experiences. A fuller understanding of these documents and folkloristic attitudes does not arise from "demythologizing" them, from clearing out the residuum of miracle that seems so intellectually offensive to us, but rather from making the effort to more carefully point to those human experiences that might have inspired them. It is clear from these considerations that people's conceptions of spiritual existence and spiritual beings are often something more substantial than emotionally pleasing illusions that they supposedly concoct "out of thin air." Instead, it happens (and not so infrequently) that those powers and properties that are attributed to divine beings and spiritual worlds derive from human experiences that take place under conditions of empowerment. Such extraordinary experiences of enthymesis provide human beings with concrete examples of transcendence that show individuals actually escaping from some of the common constraints that condition human existence in the material world. When one views the tireless quest for transcendence from this perspective, one begins to see that it involves something more tangible than just the wishful pursuit of an endlessly receding succession of mirages.

# PART

# II

# How Tradition Shapes Both the Mystical Experience and the Mystic's Responses to It

BOOK THREE


# MYSTICISM AMONG THE OGLALA LAKOTA: THE VISIONS OF BLACK ELK

# 16

# The Historical Setting of Black Elk's Life

## Reasons for Studying Black Elk

Black Elk is a classic example of a man whose entire life revolved around his responses to several significant mystical experiences that he had both as a child and as an adult. His account of these important visionary episodes and his attempts to order his life in accordance with their imperatives clearly exhibits the way that a mystic's social and religious environment conditions both the content of his experiences and his way of reacting to them.

Incorporating an analysis of Black Elk's spirituality into this comparative treatment of mysticism has other advantages. Such an analysis helps overcome a subtle but serious ethnocentrism that creeps into most comparative treatments of mysticism. There is a tendency among scholars to restrict comparisons to those mystics who come from the so-called world or universal religions, that is, those religions such as Christianity, Islam, and Buddhism that claim that they have a message of salvation that is relevant for *all* of humanity rather than for just one specific ethnic group. Black Elk's ancestral religious tradition, that of the Oglala Lakota (or Oglala Sioux)[1] was not universal in the sense mentioned above but tribal. Its

---

1. The word "Sioux," which used to be the term most frequently used to designate Black Elk's tribe is now falling into disfavor among both scholars and the Lakota people themselves. The reason why "Sioux" has fallen into disfavor is that it appears to have been derived from a term of insult coined by neighboring enemy tribes. For a discussion of the origins of the term, see Steltenkamp, *Black Elk,* pp. 3–5.

The people formerly designated as the Sioux were divided into three linguistic groups: (1) the western (Teton Sioux) group, who spoke the Lakota dialect (hence their name Lakota); (2) the central group (Yankton Sioux), who spoke the Nakota dialect; and (3) the eastern group (Santee Sioux), who spoke the Dakota dialect. The Lakota (or Teton Sioux) people

soteriological appeal was limited to Black Elk's own ethnic group and did not concern itself with seeking converts. I suggest that the distinction between universal and tribal religious orientations goes much deeper than the particular audience to which each type of religion appeals. The parochialism and cosmic sacrality of tribal religions also shapes the existential and imaginational horizons of mystics in different ways than the universalism and acosmism of the universal religions.[2] My analysis of Black Elk suggests three ways they differ. First, mystics from tribal religions tend to talk about the nature of spiritual power or potency in different ways than mystics in the universal religions. Second, tribal mystics seem to ignore those trance-states devoid of forms and images that often receive such a high degree of soteriological prominence in the mystical literatures of the universal religions. Third, mystics from the tribal religions tend to forge a stronger link between ritual and visionary experience than that formed in the universal religions. For these reasons alone, it is unwise to limit one's comparative analyses of mysticism solely to representatives of the universal religions.

Studying Black Elk has the second advantage of allowing the utilization of the unusually large body of ethnographic, anthropological, and autobiographical literature that has been written about the Lakota. This means that, unlike most other tribal societies, information concerning the religious life of the Lakota, especially its interior dimension, does not remain limited to one or two brief autobiographical statements or purely secondhand accounts. Instead, information on the inner spirituality of the Lakota is available through several ethnographic works such as the studies of James R. Walker and Frances Densmore.[3] It is also available through

---

were further subdivided into seven political subdivisions or *oyate* ("people" or "nation"), namely, Oglala (the "nation" from which Black Elk came), Hunkpapa, Sicangu, Mnikowoju (Minneconju), Sihasapa, Oohenunpa, and Itazipco. For a discussion of the linguistic subdivisions among the Sioux and the political subdivisions among the Lakota, see William K. Powers, *Oglala Religion* (Lincoln: University of Nebraska Press, 1977), pp. 8–15.

2. I am using the term "cosmic" in the sense that scholars of religion use it—a cosmic sacrality is a form of religion that locates the sacred in either the objects or events of nature. Acosmic sacralities, on the other hand, locate the sacred outside the realm of nature. Judaism, Christianity, and Islam are classic examples of acosmic sacralities since all three religions locate the sacred outside nature in the form of a supernatural deity. Buddhism, Vedānta, and the Yoga of Patañjali are also acosmic sacralities because they locate the sacred outside the realm of nature, outside the realms of saṃsāra and prakṛtī.

3. See James R. Walker, *Lakota Belief and Ritual* (Lincoln: University of Nebraska Press, 1980); idem, "The Sun Dance and Other Ceremonies of the Oglala Division of the Teton Dakota," *Anthropological Papers of the American Museum of Natural History* 16 (1917); and Frances Densmore, *Teton Sioux Music* (New York: Da Capo Press, 1972).

several biographical and autobiographical narratives: transcripts of Black Elk's lengthy conversations with John Neihardt in 1931 and 1944,[4] accounts of Black Elk's later life as a Catholic catechist and respected elder that Michael Steltenkamp compiled,[5] and descriptive works, including the contemporary medicineman Lame Deer's autobiography, *Lame Deer: Seeker of Visions,* Luther Standing Bear's description of life before the reservation period, *The Land of the Spotted Eagle,* and Thomas Mails's biography of the contemporary chief and medicineman Frank Fools Crow.[6] This relative abundance of biographical and autobiographical material concerning medicinemen (*pejuta wichasha*) and holy men (*wichasha wakan*) presents the scholar with a rare opportunity to acquire a substantial understanding of a mystical spirituality that, prior to the 1880s, had developed outside of the ambience of the universal religions.

4. See DeMallie, *Sixth Grandfather.* During the conversations of 1931, Black Elk, speaking through his son Benjamin as interpreter, told Neihardt the story of his life up to the Wounded Knee massacre of December 1890, and related to Neihardt the story of his principal visions and how he responded to them. This set of conversations, edited and rearranged by Neihardt—to which he added significant embellishments and made significant omissions—became the famous *Black Elk Speaks* (New York: Pocket Books, 1972), first published in 1932. The conversations of 1944 that are also included in *Sixth Grandfather* narrated the history of the Lakota from mythical times up to the coming of the white man. Material about Lakota customs was incorporated into Neihardt's fictional *When the Tree Flowered,* first published in 1951.

5. Michael Steltenkamp, *Black Elk: Holy Man of the Oglala* (Norman: University of Oklahoma Press, 1993). Steltenkamp based his account of Black Elk's life as a Catholic (after his conversion in 1904) on interviews with Black Elk's daughter Lucy Looks Twice and Black Elk's close associates. Steltenkamp's account is also enriched by extracts from descriptions of Black Elk made by priests who worked on the reservations and by other documents Steltenkamp unearthed in Marquette University's Archives of Catholic Indian Missions. Along with *Sixth Grandfather,* *Black Elk* is an indispensable source of information about Black Elk.

6. For ethnographic works on the Oglala Lakota that give insight into the inner dimension of their religious life, see Walker, *Lakota Belief and Ritual;* idem, "The Sun Dance and Other Ceremonies"; and Densmore, *Teton Sioux Music.* Important information on Lakota spirituality comes to us from Black Elk in his accounts of the seven major religious rituals of the Oglala Sioux and the mythical origin of those rites that anthropologist Joseph Epes Brown transcribed through an interpreter, Black Elk's son Benjamin Black Elk. See Joseph Epes Brown, *The Sacred Pipe: Black Elk's Account of the Seven Rites of the Oglala Sioux* (Baltimore: Penguin Books, 1971). Luther Standing Bear's book also contains an account of life during the pre-reservation period. Like Black Elk, Standing Bear was also born during the 1860s but unlike Black Elk, Standing Bear chose to leave the reservation and had a successful career in Hollywood. However, he later returned to the reservation in 1931 and became an important spokesman for the rights of the Native American. See Luther Standing Bear, *The Land of the Spotted Eagle* (Lincoln: University of Nebraska Press, 1978). For accounts of contemporary Lakota medicinemen and holy men, see John Fire Lame Deer and Richard Erdoes, *Lame Deer: Seeker of Visions* (New York: Simon & Schuster, 1972); and Thomas E. Mails, assisted by Dallas Chief Eagle, *Fools Crow* (New York: Avon Books, 1979).

# Black Elk's Life and Times

Black Elk's life spanned a period of history that saw shattering cultural changes overwhelm the Oglala Lakota. His birth in December 1863 came at a time when the traditional buffalo hunter-warrior culture of the western or Teton Lakota (of which the Oglalas were the largest of the seven groups) still remained largely intact despite the ever deepening cultural and economic contacts and sporadic conflicts that had taken place in the 1840s and 1850s between the whites and the plains Indians. To be sure, in the 1850s and 1860s the Lakota perceived that the growing white presence constituted a grievous threat to their entire way of life and existence as a nomadic group of hunters and warriors. Nonetheless, the white presence at this time was still sporadic enough and distant enough to allow the western bands of the Lakota to carry on their traditional occupations largely unmolested. As late as the 1860s their warriors still hunted the vast herds of buffalo that roamed virtually undisturbed on the plains and continued their horse-thieving raids and war parties against neighboring enemy Indian tribes, especially the Crows.

The years of Black Elk's youth and early manhood unfolded during a period that witnessed a quick succession of disasters that almost destroyed the traditional Oglala way of life. White incursions became progressively more threatening in the 1860s and 1870s despite sporadic Indian victories. A series of conflicts between 1866 and 1868 led the U.S. government to sign a treaty with the Lakota that stipulated that all of South Dakota west of the Missouri River, as well as the areas of eastern Wyoming and southern Montana near the Powder and Little Bighorn rivers, was to be forever Indian territory that whites would be forbidden to enter without permission. However, this treaty was quickly broken by 1874–75 when gold was discovered in the center of their reservation area, the Black Hills. As troops and hordes of prospectors began to move into this area it quickly became evident to the Indians that the whites intended to take this sacred land away from them. The resulting dispute led to conflict in 1876, one episode being the Indian victory over Custer's force at the Battle of the Little Bighorn.

When faced with the massive U.S. military campaign that followed in the aftermath of this brief Indian victory, the Indians split up into separate bands so as to better elude capture. This, however, made them easier to subdue when they finally did encounter units of the army. The defeated bands were moved on to further shrunken reservation lands in what is now North and South Dakota. Although Lakota led by Crazy Horse resisted throughout the winter of 1876–77, the absence of buffalo and other game eventually starved his band into submission by May 1877. This event marks a watershed in the history of the Lakota because it inaugurated the period of settled reservation life on white terms and it ended the nomadic warrior-hunter existence.

The first years of reservation life for the Lakota coincided with a series of other catastrophic events. During the years 1877–81 a few bands of Lakota fled the reservations into Canada and the northern plains where they could still live the old life undisturbed and hunt the buffalo herds that were still intact there. But the buffalo became, for all practical purposes, extinct by 1883, even in Canada. With the buffalo gone, the principal pillar of their nomadic lifestyle collapsed forcing even these rebellious remnants (including Black Elk and Sitting Bull) to return to the reservations. Because they were a society of hunters, the loss of the buffalo destroyed the fundamental basis of their entire cultural life. There could have been nothing more alien to the Lakota nomadic way of life than the sedentary agricultural existence forced on them by whites. In the days before the reservation, a man's prestige derived chiefly from his successes as a warrior, buffalo hunter, and horse thief. With confinement on the reservation (he could only leave with the U.S. agent's permission), these former avenues of social advancement were completely cut off. To the Lakota there was nothing heroic, meritorious, or challenging about agriculture or livestock herding. Consequently, their lives suddenly seemed drained of purpose. "The nation's hoop was broken," said Black Elk, meaning that the people were dispirited and at a loss for meaningful values, prisoners of a culture whose values and way of life they despised.

In 1879 the Lakota suffered the further indignity of seeing Chief Red Cloud—without the general consent of the tribe—cede large segments of their already shrunken reservation, including the Black Hills, to the whites. Furthermore, in 1881 the U.S. government outlawed the pillar of their religious life, the Sun Dance, calling it a "savage rite," a "barbarity," and "a cruel spectacle." But this was only the beginning, for "shortly thereafter, they condemned nearly all the traditional rituals and practices, and those who violated the rule were subject to instant discipline and arrest."[7] This attack on Siouan religious traditions constituted one element of a

7. Mails, *Fools Crow*, p. 31.

systematic and insensitive policy of the U.S. government to assimilate the Indians into white culture whether they wanted to be or not. This crude and brutal assimilationist attitude reflected the view that, until the Indians had learned the white way of life and adopted white religion, they were "savages," creatures who were not fully human. According to those who held these assumptions, white culture could quite justifiably be imposed on the Indians without their consent since their savage state precluded any capacity on their part for knowing what was good for themselves. One article in an Omaha newspaper from this period conveys the whites' attitude with brutal clarity as its author describes a detachment of Indians who were making their way to reservations in Oklahoma under armed escort.

> Several ladies passed through the cars, two of whom were evidently officers' wives and somewhat acquainted with the Indian language and customs. The Indians seemed delighted to see these white ladies and took pains to shake hands with them. American Horse's papoose was a chubby, sturdy little beggar, and when one of the ladies spoke to him, he set up a tremendous wail, just as natural and life-like *as if he were human.*[8]

This dehumanization of Native Americans formed an inseparable adjunct to the assimilationist policies followed on reservations during the nineteenth and early twentieth centuries.

By the early 1880s these circumstances had reduced the once proud, independent warriors and hunters of the plains into an abject dependence on an enemy whom they despised and who, in turn, despised them. Bereft of the buffalo, their guns, and most of their horses, forced into a sedentary lifestyle completely at odds with their traditional nomadic values, unskilled in the techniques of agriculture or cattle-raising, forcibly separated from their children (who were sent off to distant government schools where many of them died of tuberculosis and measles), and systematically denigrated and threatened with cultural annihilation by a policy of insensitive assimilationism, is it any wonder that many Lakota felt that these developments posed a grave threat to their continued existence as a nation and as a people? Luther Standing Bear's account of how he felt in 1879 when his father asked him if he would go away to a white school in Pennsylvania captures this mood of anxiety. Young Luther agreed to his father's request

8. Ibid., p. 27 (emphasis mine).

*not* because he was interested in learning the white way but rather because he wanted to show his father that, just like the warriors of old, he too could die bravely.

> I could think of no reason why white people wanted Indian boys and girls except to kill them, and not having the remotest idea of what a school was, I thought we were going East to die. But so well had courage and bravery been trained into us that it became a part of our unconscious thinking and acting, and personal life was nothing when it came time to do something for the tribe. . . . Accordingly, there were few cowards, most Lakota men preferring to die in the performance of some act of bravery than to die of old age. Thus, in giving myself up to go East I was proving to my father that he was honored with a brave son.[9]

If one considers the dehumanizing attitudes that many white soldiers and settlers had toward the Indians during that time as well as the fact that in recent battles with the U.S. army even women and children had been slain, Standing Bear's anxieties seem natural.

Not surprisingly, these profound fears found expression in Lakota religious life. For example, Black Elk himself repeatedly stressed the significance of his Great Vision: it had given him the power to heal and make whole *the entire tribe,* not just particular individuals.[10] Black Elk claimed that *wakan-tanka,* the Great Mystery, had sent him his Great Vision and other subsequent visions so that their revelations could be the means for him to gain "the power to make over my nation"[11] and to bring his people "back into the nation's hoop,"[12] that is, they could help him to restore his tribe's lost sense of social solidarity and rootedness in the world. Indeed, the time when Black Elk performed these visions publicly (and, by doing so, activated their otherwise dormant spiritual power) coincided with the period (1881–83) when his people were despondent about the possibility of maintaining their cultural cohesiveness and identity. The Ghost Dance movement, which swept like a wildfire through the Lakota, Cheyenne, Arapaho, and other plains tribes in 1889–90, exhibited this same existential concern for resurrecting, through ritual, that lost sense of tribal solidarity and cosmic rootedness that had formerly characterized (or sup-

9. Standing Bear, *Land of the Spotted Eagle,* pp. 230–31.
10. DeMallie, *Sixth Grandfather,* pp. 238, 293–96.
11. Ibid., p. 238.
12. Ibid., p. 294.

posedly characterized) life two decades earlier.[13] The movement's adherents claimed that the performance of its sacred ceremonies were capable of regenerating the entire cosmos and creating a new world free of whites, where the buffalo could once again roam unhindered over the plains and where the Indian could return to his old way of life free of the twin banes of war and old age. One may therefore conclude that both Black Elk's visions and the Ghost Dance rituals evolved, in part, as a religious response to the unprecedented threats that menaced the tribal solidarity of Indian peoples everywhere.

Unfortunately, even though the Ghost Dance expressly forbade its adherents to wage war against the whites,[14] its religious message was easily misconstrued as one that advocated overt hostility to the whites. The Ghost Dance movement preached, among other things, that performance of the dances would cause whites to disappear and the shirts of the participating warriors to become bulletproof. This fact, plus the extremely rapid spread of the movement among the Lakota in spite of the government agent's attempts to forbid it, caused the agent to become frightened and call in army troops to suppress what he mistakenly thought was an embryonic Indian uprising. The resulting atmosphere of tension, hostility, and mutual suspicion led to the tragic massacre at Wounded Knee in late December 1890.

What Black Elk narrated to John Neihardt during the 1931 interviews, which became the foundation for *Black Elk Speaks*, ends in January 1891 with the Wounded Knee massacre and its immediate aftermath. From reading *Black Elk Speaks*, one gains the impression that Black Elk ended his life story at this point because the Wounded Knee massacre had not only left Black Elk a defeated, broken man but that it had also irreversibly broken the spirit of the Lakota people. However, this cut-off date for the autobiography seems to have been more Neihardt's doing than Black Elk's. Neihardt originally sought the 1931 interviews with Black Elk because he was collecting material for a five-volume epic poem on the settlement of the American West. At the time he met Black Elk, he was working on volume four, which was to describe how the Ghost Dance movement and the Wounded Knee battle had affected the Lakota. For that reason, Neihardt was not interested in going beyond the Battle of Wounded Knee. Furthermore, it was Neihardt rather than Black Elk who labored under the

13. Ibid., pp. 257–59.

14. James Mooney, *The Ghost Dance Religion and the Sioux Outbreak of 1890* (Chicago: University of Chicago Press, 1965), p. 19.

illusion that the Wounded Knee massacre had finally destroyed the cultural and spiritual vitality of the Lakota.[15]

Having given this brief survey of the major events of Lakota history that occurred between 1860 and 1890, I shall now provide the reader with a summary of the major incidents in Black Elk's life.

Black Elk was born in December 1863. When he was in his ninth summer (1872), he spontaneously had what he called his Great Vision, a revelation that had a lasting impact on the way he conducted himself for the rest of his life. However, he never told anyone about this vision until he was seventeen years old (1881). During the wars of 1876, Black Elk had his first taste of battle against the army of George Armstrong Custer at the Battle of Little Bighorn. Forced onto the reservation in 1876–77 along with the rest of his band, he later fled north to Canada, where Sitting Bull had gone to escape the U.S. army. However, his longing for his relatives in South Dakota and the shortage of game soon caused him to return to reservation life. Shortly after his return (1881–83), Black Elk felt compelled to reenact publicly the events that had occurred during his Great Vision (and several subsequent ones) for the benefit of his tribesmen. He assumed that such a public reenactment might be able to restore his people to that sense of solidarity that they had lost when they had been forced onto the reservations. He also believed that this public performance of the principal events of his vision would allow him to use the spiritual power that the spirit-beings had given him at that time. One of the ways that he used that sacred power of his vision was by becoming a healer (1881–86).

In 1886 Black Elk and some of his close friends heard that Buffalo Bill's Wild West Show was looking for Indian performers to go on tours across the United States and Europe. Black Elk and his friends jumped at this opportunity for excitement and adventure. But adventure was not the only reason why Black Elk decided to join. He was also profoundly "disgusted" with the way that his people were living.[16] "Perhaps," he thought, "whites

15. Clyde Holler, "Lakota Religion and Tragedy: The Theology of *Black Elk Speaks*," *Journal of the American Academy of Religion* 52, no. 1 (March 1984), pp. 21, 36–37. It should also be noted that the research of both DeMallie and Steltenkamp has shown that Black Elk's life after 1891 was anything but a failure. Quite the contrary, Black Elk was one of the most successful of the Pine Ridge Lakota in making a spiritual, social, and economic adjustment to the new conditions that prevailed in his culture after the end of their nomadic life.

16. DeMallie, *Sixth Grandfather*, p. 245.

really can teach us a better way of life." It was at this time that Black Elk also apparently converted to Christianity (probably Episcopalianism since Buffalo Bill's contract stipulated that all Indians traveling with the show must be of the same faith and it was an Episcopal minister who traveled with the show). From letters that he wrote that were printed in the Lakota newsletter *Iapi Oaye* (Word carrier) in 1888 and 1889, Black Elk appears to have been impressed with Christianity. "Of the white man's many customs, only his faith, the white man's beliefs about God's will, and how they act according to it, I wanted to understand. . . . So Lakota people, trust in God! Now all along I trust in God. . . . I hope the people will do likewise."[17] It is clear from these remarks that, aside from the white's religion, the rest of European and American culture did not impress Black Elk. In 1889, he returned to the reservation after having toured both the eastern United States and Western Europe. In 1890, Black Elk briefly became a follower of the Ghost Dance movement, and when the whites attempted to suppress it at Wounded Knee, he fought against them and was seriously wounded during the ensuing skirmishes. It is at this point that *Black Elk Speaks* ends.

The years between Wounded Knee and Black Elk's second conversion (to Catholicism) in December 1904 saw him continue his activities as a traditional healer, using the powers that the spirits had given him in both the Great Vision and the Dog Vision. During this period, Black Elk must have also received a vision from the sacred stone spirits[18] because there are reports that he had acquired considerable renown as a practitioner of the yuwipi rites.[19] Black Elk's return to traditional Lakota religious practices did not necessarily signify that he had abandoned Christianity during the years between his conversion to the Ghost Dance in 1890 and his conversion to Catholicism in 1904. DeMallie notes that his first three sons, born

17. Ibid., pp. 9–10.
18. Black Elk does not mention any visions of sacred stone spirits in either *Sacred Pipe* (Brown) or *Sixth Grandfather* (DeMallie). I am inferring that such a vision or visions occurred from the fact that he became well known as a yuwipi practitioner.
19. John Lone Goose, a Catholic organist at Manderson who had numerous opportunities to work with Black Elk, asserted, "I first met Nick [Black Elk's name after he had converted to Catholicism] around 1900, when I was a young boy and he was not a Catholic. I don't know what they call him in English, but in Indian they call him *yuwipi* man. Sam Kills Brave, he's a Catholic, lived close to him. And before Nick converted, Kills Brave would say: 'Why don't you give up your *yuwipi* and join the Catholic Church?'" (quoted in Paul Steinmetz, S.J., *Pipe, Bible, and Peyote among the Oglala Lakota* [Knoxville: University of Tennessee Press, 1990], p. 183). Steinmetz also noted that other Lakota informants had attended some of Black Elk's yuwipi rituals in the days before he converted to Catholicism.

between 1895 and 1899, were baptized as Catholics, although it is quite possible that Black Elk's first wife, a Catholic, was the person who took the initiative rather than Black Elk himself.[20] There are also suggestions that Black Elk came into conflict with representatives of the Catholic faith during those years. For example, Black Elk related to Neihardt that during one of his traditional healing ceremonies a Catholic priest interrupted the ceremony and took all of Black Elk's ritual paraphernalia. According to Black Elk, the priest later paid dearly for disrupting the healing rite when he was fatally thrown from his horse.[21]

Black Elk's conversion to Catholicism in December 1904 marked another watershed in his spiritual life. This time his conversion to Christianity apparently became more deeply rooted. The first indication of his deep commitment to the Catholic faith was the fact that, once and for all, he gave up the practice of the traditional Lakota healing rituals.[22] Second, Black Elk became a devoted catechist and missionary to both his own people and other Native American tribes.[23] One Catholic missionary, Father Westropp, wrote of Black Elk's fervent desire to spread his new faith: "Ever since his conversion he [Black Elk] has been a fervent apostle, and he has gone around like a second St. Paul, trying to convert his tribesmen."[24] Another priest estimated that Black Elk had converted approximately four hundred Indians to Catholicism.[25]

The depth and sincerity of Black Elk's commitment to Catholicism together with his abrupt and permanent abandonment of traditional Lakota healing rituals did not signify that he had completely lost interest in the religion of his ancestors. Clyde Holler asserts that "Black Elk's position with respect to Christianity was that Christianity and traditional Lakota religion are essentially identical."[26] That may be an overstatement for, if it were true, then why would Black Elk have felt the need to abandon the yuwipi and other traditional healing rites of his people? Nevertheless, de-

20. DeMallie, *Sixth Grandfather*, p. 13.

21. Ibid., p. 239.

22. However, Black Elk did continue to perform those rituals for tourists at Duhamel's Sioux Indian Pageant though his daughter claimed that these tourist performances did not have a religious purpose—he simply regarded them as an enjoyable diversion. For example, Neihardt's daughter Hilda reports that when her father repeatedly asked Black Elk to perform a yuwipi ceremony for them, Black Elk always refused to do so. DeMallie, *Sixth Grandfather*, pp. 14–15, n. 16.

23. DeMallie, *Sixth Grandfather*, pp. 16–24; and Steltenkamp, *Black Elk*, pp. 62–65.

24. Quoted in Steltenkamp, *Black Elk*, p. 65.

25. DeMallie, *Sixth Grandfather*, p. 26.

26. Holler, "Lakota Religion and Tragedy," p. 30, n.

spite his sincere devotion to Christianity, Black Elk never lost his passionate commitment to both preserving the sacred knowledge of the old Lakota religion and transmitting it to not just the Lakota but to the world at large. Black Elk's extensive collaborations with John Neihardt in their conversations of 1931 and 1944 that led to *Black Elk Speaks* and the novel *When the Tree Flowered*,[27] respectively, and Joseph Epes Brown in 1947 in the material that later became *The Sacred Pipe* demonstrate the intensity of Black Elk's passion to preserve the pre-Christian past of his people. It is also important to note that although Black Elk gave up the performance of traditional Lakota healing rites after his conversion to Catholicism, other forms of traditional Lakota ritual were not necessarily abandoned. For example, according to his daughter's testimony, Black Elk continued to smoke the sacred pipe after his conversion to Catholicism and to practice the traditional *inipi* (sweat bath) ritual. He is also reported to have attended a Sun Dance ritual in 1928, although his role in that ceremony was not disclosed.[28] It would appear, then, that wherever Black Elk felt, to his *own* satisfaction, that the rituals of the old Lakota religion were not incompatible with his newly adopted religion he could continue practicing them.[29]

The next watershed in Black Elk's life occurred in August 1930 when he met John Neihardt. Neihardt was in the midst of writing the fourth volume of his epic poem *A Cycle of the West,* which dealt with the Lakota Ghost Dance. He met Black Elk with the hope that the old holy man might be able to give him some information that would be useful in writing that poem. Neihardt got much more than he bargained for. Black Elk saw this encounter as a precious opportunity to preserve the sacred traditions of his people and transmit them to humankind through Neihardt. Consequently, Black Elk decided to initiate Neihardt into the sacred knowledge that he possessed as a Lakota holy man. He saw himself as giving Neihardt more than just the details of his autobiography. The description of his Great Vision to Neihardt was also a ritual act that transmitted the spiritual power of that vision to Neihardt so that Neihardt could use that power to regenerate both the Lakota people and all of humankind.[30] Because Black

27. Neihardt, *Black Elk Speaks;* idem, *When the Tree Flowered: An Authentic Tale of the Old Sioux World* (New York: Macmillan, 1951).

28. Steltenkamp, *Black Elk,* pp. 60, 107, respectively.

29. It is important to stress that what Black Elk felt was compatible with Catholicism was not necessarily orthodox.

30. Holler, "Lakota Religion and Tragedy," pp. 24–25.

Elk saw himself as giving Neihardt much more than bits of information about the Ghost Dance, he requested that Neihardt return in the spring of 1931 when he would relate his life story up to Wounded Knee and initiate Neihardt into the sacred knowledge. In 1944, Neihardt had a second series of conversations with Black Elk where Black Elk related to him a history of the Lakota from mythical times up through the coming of the whites along with a miscellany about Lakota customs and mythology. Some of this material became incorporated into Neihardt's novelistic literary re-creation of the Lakota past, *When the Tree Flowered.*

A third watershed event in Black Elk's later life led to results important to scholars of Lakota religion. In the fall of 1947, Black Elk met a young anthropology student, Joseph Epes Brown, with whom he quickly struck up a friendship. Soon after their meeting, Black Elk entrusted Brown with his account (which had previously been entrusted to Black Elk by the tribe's Keeper of the Sacred Pipe) of how the seven sacred rites of the Oglala Lakota had come into existence and how they had been historically practiced. This description of most of the important rites of the Lakota was published under the title *The Sacred Pipe.*[31]

During the last two years of his life, Black Elk was restricted to a wheelchair after having broken his hip during an ice storm. According to his daughter, he passed his final months of life as a devout Catholic intensely devoted to prayer and "ready to accept his Creator's call any time."[32] Black Elk died in August 1950 at the age of eighty-six.

# Why *Black Elk Speaks* Is Not a Reliable Historical Source

My discussion of Black Elk's mysticism is not based on *Black Elk Speaks.* Instead, I have founded most of my analysis on Raymond DeMallie's published transcripts of Black Elk's 1931 conversations with John Neihardt, conversations that were the foundation for *Black Elk Speaks.*[33] *The Sixth*

---

31. One must note, however, that a description of the origin and practices of yuwipi is prominently missing from this work, a fact that becomes all the more surprising in light of Black Elk's activities as a yuwipi practitioner just before his conversion.

32. Steltenkamp, *Black Elk,* p. 122.

33. It is important to note that the transcripts are not a literal rendition of what Black Elk said to Neihardt. Black Elk spoke in Lakota; then Black Elk's son, Benjamin Black Elk,

*Grandfather,* edited and introduced by DeMallie, not only contains the complete record of the notes of the spring 1931 conversations that the two men had but also includes the transcripts of the shorter 1944 conversations that became the basis for John Neihardt's novel *When the Tree Flowered.*

*Black Elk Speaks* is a defective source of information about Black Elk's life, attitudes, and religious experiences for three reasons: (1) it omits significant data that Black Elk communicated to Neihardt during their 1931 conversations;[34] (2) it contains a significant amount of textual material that Neihardt added on his own initiative; and (3) it fails to inform the reader that not only did Black Elk convert to Catholicism in 1904 and remain passionately committed to that faith until the end of his life but that he also adapted very successfully to the revolutionary economic and social changes that confronted his people after they began living on the reservation.

One should not assume that every time Black Elk is quoted in *Black Elk Speaks* that it is Black Elk who is actually speaking. Sometimes the words placed in Black Elk's mouth are Neihardt's. Neihardt's additions often significantly change the meaning of the text. For example, chapter 25 of *Black Elk Speaks,* "The End of the Dream," concludes with three famous paragraphs where Black Elk supposedly reflects mournfully on the tragic significance of the carnage that he has just witnessed at Wounded Knee.

> And so it was all over.
>
> I did not know then how much was ended. When I look back now from this high hill of my old age, I can still see the butchered women and children lying heaped and scattered all along the crooked gulch as plain as when I saw them with eyes still young. And I can see that something else died there in the bloody mud, and was buried in the blizzard. A people's dream died there. It was a beautiful dream.
>
> And I, to whom so great a vision was given in my youth,—you see me now a pitiful old man who has done nothing, for the nation's

---

translated his father's words into English to Neihardt. John Neihardt's daughter Enid took shorthand notes of Benjamin Black Elk's English translation and then later transcribed the shorthand notes into a typed manuscript. DeMallie, *Sixth Grandfather,* pp. xxiv–xxv.

34. See DeMallie, *Sixth Grandfather,* pp. 52–55, 59, 96–99.

hoop is broken and scattered. There is no center any longer, and the sacred tree is dead.[35]

These are very eloquent and moving words but they are not, according to Holler, Black Elk's.[36] They are words that Neihardt added to the text and made to appear as though Black Elk had uttered them. Moreover, they do not appear anywhere in the original transcripts of Neihardt's conversations with Black Elk.[37]

The reader should not assume that Neihardt added these interpolations in order to deceive his audience. He was not an ethnographer but a poet. He appears to have added these interpolations for literary effect—they were Neihardt's attempt as an artist to convey the spirit rather than the strict letter of what Black Elk had conveyed to him during their 1931 conversations. Indeed, Neihardt gives an oblique warning to his readers in his 1971 preface to the Pocket Books (Simon & Schuster) edition of *Black Elk Speaks* that "it was not the facts that mattered most" in writing the book but rather the need "to re-create in English the mood and manner of the old man's narrative."[38] *Black Elk Speaks* is therefore a literary re-creation of the 1931 conversations.

Neihardt thought that he was being faithful to the spirit of Black Elk's utterances by putting these words in the holy man's mouth. Unfortunately, he did not realize that some of the words he added seriously distorted the Lakota holy man's religious message. For example, when one reads the three paragraphs from chapter 25 that I quoted above, one gains the impression that, after Wounded Knee, Black Elk was a broken man who felt that his life had been a failure and that the spiritual condition of his people was hopeless. Thus, the Black Elk of *Black Elk Speaks* seems to be saying that Lakota religion and culture are dead, the sacred hoop of the Lakota nation is broken, and the sacred tree will never bloom again; the spiritual power that the Six Grandfathers gave him in his Great Vision was squandered on a worthless man who will never put it to good use. However,

35. Neihardt, *Black Elk Speaks*, p. 230.
36. Holler, "Lakota Religion and Tragedy," pp. 36–37.
37. It should also be noted that the first three paragraphs of *Black Elk Speaks* are also not the actual words of Black Elk but rather words that Neihardt put into Black Elk's mouth for the sake of literary effect. An enumeration of this and some other significant additions that Neihardt interpolated into the text of *Black Elk Speaks* can be found in DeMallie, *Sixth Grandfather*, p. 77.
38. Neihardt, *Black Elk Speaks*, p. xiii.

when one compares what Neihardt makes Black Elk say with what Black Elk actually said in the 1931 conversations, the message is quite different.[39]

Black Elk's own words show that he did not believe that Lakota religion and culture had died—quite the contrary. In 1931 he told Neihardt: "The more I think of old times . . . it makes me feel sad, but *I hope that we can make the tree bloom for your children and mine.* . . . It was hopeless it seems before I saw you, but here you came. *Somehow the spirits have made you come to revive the tree that never bloomed.*"[40] The message in this passage is not one of despair and gloom but rather one of hope for the future. The possibility is still open that the sacred tree will bloom again. The statement reveals that from Black Elk's perspective, Neihardt's visit was pregnant with redemptive possibility. By revealing his Great Vision to Neihardt, Black Elk was not just telling a story and giving him information about the past but, much more important, he was revealing his vision to the entire world, thereby actualizing its redemptive possibilities, and transferring the spiritual power of his Great Vision to Neihardt.[41] Thus, in a letter that Neihardt wrote to publisher William Morrow in June 1931, he told Morrow that after Black Elk had described his Great Vision to him Black Elk said, "Now I have given you my vision that I have never given to anyone before and with it I have given you my power. I have no power now, but you can take it and perhaps with it you can make the tree bloom again, at least for my people and yours."[42]

Black Elk expressed similar ideas in his foreword to *The Sacred Pipe*. He declared that he was describing the seven rituals of the Lakota not out of a merely antiquarian interest in data about the past but rather because his description of these rites had redemptive possibilities—it would not only help the Lakota people respect the greatness of their own tradition but also would help to bring about peace on earth for all humankind and make it possible for all creation to live in harmony.[43] Neihardt seriously distorted Black Elk's self-image as a Lakota holy man when he depicted him in *Black Elk Speaks* as a despondent old man who had completely failed in his spiritual mission.

Examination of the original transcripts also shows that in *Black Elk*

39. See Holler, "Lakota Religion and Tragedy," pp. 36–37; and DeMallie, *Sixth Grandfather*, p. 56.
40. Quoted in DeMallie, *Sixth Grandfather*, p. 44 (emphasis mine).
41. Holler, "Lakota Religion and Tragedy," pp. 25–28.
42. Quoted in DeMallie, *Sixth Grandfather*, p. 47.
43. Brown, *Sacred Pipe*, p. xx.

*Speaks* Neihardt omitted significant events that took place during the Great Vision. For example, the stenographic record shows that Neihardt omitted entirely those episodes in the Great Vision where Black Elk and four other warriors attack a dog in the midst of flames and then kill it with lightning.[44] This omitted portion of the Great Vision bears a close resemblance to the Dog Vision that came to him nine years later. The entire episode where Black Elk receives "the soldier weed of destruction" that gives him invincible powers against his enemies in war is also completely omitted in *Black Elk Speaks*. Neihardt also considerably abbreviated that section of the Great Vision where Black Elk returns to the Six Grandfathers. The second (northern) Grandfather's gift of the butterfly cocoons and the little blue man in a cup of water (which Black Elk was instructed to swallow) are missing in *Black Elk Speaks*.[45] The result of these significant omissions is that they tend to minimize the significance that spiritual powers relating to war played in Black Elk's Great Vision. Such a picture of the young Black Elk and his spiritual world is more consistent with the universalism and yearning for peace that becomes so prominent in the teachings of the older Christian Black Elk.[46]

When one compares the description of Black Elk's Ghost Dance visions given in *Black Elk Speaks* with that given in the stenographic record of the 1931 conversations, one notices ethnographically significant omissions. For example, during one of Black Elk's Ghost Dance visions described in *Black Elk Speaks*, the reader is told that Black Elk saw a strange man whose body was painted the sacred color red. As Black Elk continued looking at him, his body began to glow with a light of many colors.[47] The original stenographic notes contain several additional features of this strange, luminous man that Neihardt omitted. First, Black Elk told Neihardt, "He did not resemble Christ." Then he added, parenthetically, that at this time he had never been exposed to white religion and did not know what Christ looked like. (This is certainly mistaken information since he had converted to Christianity when he joined Buffalo Bill's Wild West Show in 1886 some years before the Ghost Dance visions). Finally, after denying that the luminous man looked like Christ, Black Elk contradicts himself by saying that "it seemed as though there were wounds in the

44. DeMallie, *Sixth Grandfather*, pp. 131–32.

45. Ibid., pp. 135–39.

46. Black Elk confessed that although his Great Vision had given him terrible powers for war and destruction, he had deliberately refrained from using them. See ibid., pp. 136–37.

47. Neihardt, *Black Elk Speaks*, p. 208.

palms of his hands."[48] Despite Black Elk's denial that the luminous red
man of his last Ghost Dance vision was Jesus, there is nonetheless a strong
resemblance between this visionary figure as described in the original notes
and that of the crucified and transfigured Christ.

Finally, *Black Elk Speaks* fails to mention that Black Elk was a Christian
and had been a devout one for several decades. Part of the responsibility
for this serious omission lies with Neihardt for, at the time of the 1931
conversations, Neihardt was certainly aware that Black Elk was a Christian and that he no longer practiced the old Lakota healing rituals such as
yuwipi. On the other hand, Black Elk may also have been partly responsible for this omission because he seems to have been rather reticent in telling Neihardt about his life after his conversion to Catholicism and his
work as a Catholic missionary to other Native American tribes.[49]

The previous examples demonstrate that both Neihardt's additions to the
1931 conversations and his omissions of certain data from *Black Elk
Speaks* seriously distorted Black Elk's own view of his religious message
and vocation. Consequently, *Black Elk Speaks* should not be used as a
historical source for the study of Black Elk's mysticism. Instead, scholars
must utilize other sources such as the transcripts of Black Elk's 1931 conversations (through an interpreter) with Neihardt contained in DeMallie's
*The Sixth Grandfather*. Scholars who seek knowledge of the life of Black
Elk after his conversion to Catholicism in 1904 are deeply indebted to
Michael Steltenkamp's *Black Elk: Holy Man of the Oglalas,* which gives
essential information on that part of his life based on the testimony of
some of his co-workers in the church and his daughter Lucy Looks Twice.[50]
These two works, plus Brown's *The Sacred Pipe,* are essential for under-
standing Black Elk and his spirituality.

At this juncture, another question arises: Does Black Elk's intense commitment to Catholicism after 1904 make him an unreliable source of information about traditional Lakota mysticism and religion? I believe it does
not. First, the Great Vision and the Dog Vision occurred in 1872 and
1881, respectively, and would reflect his religious experience before his
first conversion to Christianity in the late 1880s. (The same cannot be said
of the content of the Ghost Dance visions as we noted earlier.) Second, the

48. DeMallie, *Sixth Grandfather,* p. 263.
49. Ibid., pp. 14–15, n. 16, 47; the transcripts refer explicitly to Black Elk's Catholicism
on p. 137.
50. Steltenkamp, *Black Elk,* p. xxi.

descriptions of his Great Vision and the Dog Vision that Black Elk gave Neihardt in the stenographic notes exhibit most of the same symbolic and mythological elements, the same concerns with acquiring healing powers and war powers, and same patterns of response that other Lakota holy men and medicinemen have described in their portrayals of their visionary encounters with the thunder-beings of the West.[51] Thus DeMallie has concluded, "There is nothing in Black Elk's great vision that is foreign to Lakota culture. The same is true of the *heyoka* vision [his Dog Vision]."[52] In the Great Vision it is significant that when the Six Grandfathers (and not the Great Spirit [in the singular]) commission him to save his people with the spiritual powers they have given him, they do not tell him he is going to save the entire human race or that the entire human race will somehow benefit from what he is going to do. The redemptive value of their gifts is limited to the tribe rather than humankind. This soteriological parochialism is what one would expect from a tribal religion that was, as yet, still relatively isolated from the religious influences of the universal religions. Instead, the Grandfathers tell him that he is going back to earth with a spiritual power that will cause hundreds, not millions, of people to be sacred.[53]

This assumption that Black Elk's mystical experiences remained congruent with the visionary experiences of non-Christianized Lakota who lived in the prereservation era finds further support when one compares his descriptions of his Great Vision and Dog Vision with the descriptions by others. For example, when Black Horse undertook his vision quest to propitiate the thunder-beings, he had an experience that showed some significant parallels to Black Elk's Great Vision. Black Horse also came to a celestial tipi in his vision where he was ushered into the presence of seven (not six) Grandfathers who assured him of their future supernatural assistance. As also happened in Black Elk's Dog Vision, Black Horse related that even though a raging storm occurred while he was in the vision pit, not a drop of rain fell within the consecrated area within which he stood while crying for his vision.[54] In the Great Vision there was an episode where horsemen, spirit messengers of the West, told Black Elk that he had

51. DeMallie, *Sixth Grandfather*, p. 84.

52. Ibid., p. 86.

53. Ibid., p. 139.

54. For evidence that Black Horse represents the pre-reservation Lakota viewpoint, see Royal B. Hassrick, *The Sioux* (Norman: University of Oklahoma Press, 1964), p. x. To see these parallels between the visions of Black Horse and Black Elk, compare Hassrick, *Sioux*, p. 235, with DeMallie, *Sixth Grandfather*, pp. 114–16, 230.

to slay a mysterious, flame-shrouded demonic man who was standing amid the confluence of several great rivers. Black Elk obeyed and as he slew him, the flame-shrouded man suddenly turned into a harmless turtle.

Lone Man's account of his wakan dream about thunder-beings incorporated a similar episode. He, too, saw horsemen coming to him from the West who told him to slay a mysterious enemy who, in this case, was painted the sacred color red. This enemy was also standing in water just as the demonic man of Black Elk's vision had done. When Lone Man obeyed these instructions from the spirits and slew the red man, he also underwent an instantaneous transformation into something harmless, a water reed.[55] These parallel visionary motifs indicate that Black Elk's Great Vision, despite its spontaneous character, was nonetheless a visionary experience quite typical of spiritual communications from the thunder-beings of the West. In other words, Black Elk's visions reveal him to have been a rather typical nineteenth-century prereservation Lakota visionary.

Although the *content* of Black Elk's Great Vision and Dog Vision does not seem to have been influenced by Christianity to any great extent, one cannot say the same thing about some of the ways that he subsequently responded to or interpreted those visions. Black Elk's universalism, that is, his desire to spread the benefits of his Great Vision to both Native Americans and whites, is alien to the ethnic parochialism that is so typical of preliterate tribal religions. This universalism and ecumenism that he exhibits in both his 1931 conversations with Neihardt and in the foreword to *The Sacred Pipe* therefore seems to reflect his subsequent exposure to and commitment to Christianity. Black Elk's rejection of the powers of destruction (the soldier-weed of destruction) that the spirits gave him in his Great Vision also suggests that the traditional Lakota obsession with prowess and glory in war has been replaced with the Christian message of universal brotherhood and peace.[56]

55. To compare Lone Man's account, see Densmore, *Teton Sioux Music,* pp. 159–60; and DeMallie, *Sixth Grandfather,* pp. 120–22, 227–32.
56. DeMallie, *Sixth Grandfather,* pp. 89–90.

# 17

# Black Elk's Great Vision

## Black Elk's Earliest Visionary Experiences

Individuals who, as adults, later demonstrate remarkable sensitivity to clairvoyant impressions or other types of extraordinary revelations such as visions or voices usually exhibit the first unmistakable glimmerings of these abilities when they are children. Eileen Garrett and Edgar Cayce are two examples of mystics who exhibited their supernormal proclivities at a very early age.[1] Black Elk also showed a similar precocious openness to supernormal experiences, hence his remarks in his autobiography that he noticed that at the age of four he began to hear strange voices calling out to him from nowhere.[2] Shortly after these first locutions occurred, he began to receive supernormal visual communications. One day when he was five years old he was riding into the woods along a creek just as a thunderstorm was starting up. Suddenly, Black Elk heard a voice and saw two men come out of the cloud holding spears. The two cloud spirits then began to sing a sacred song when a kingbird also began speaking. The bird said to Black Elk, "Look, the clouds all over are one-sided [there was something sacred about their appearance], a voice is calling you."[3] The mysterious cloud spirits came down from the north and continued to chant their sacred song. When they had finished singing this chant, they transformed themselves into geese and flew away toward the west.

Although this particular visionary episode apparently played no significant role in Black Elk's subsequent spiritual development, it does reveal that even as a young boy he experienced a peculiar kind of spiritual kin-

---

1. Garrett, *Adventures in the Supernormal*, 7–12, 15–21; Cayce, *Auras*, p. 5.
2. DeMallie, *Sixth Grandfather*, p. 108.
3. Ibid., pp. 109–10.

ship with those spiritual beings that the Oglala Lakota believe dwell within thunderstorm clouds. The Lakota highly regarded such visitations from thunder-beings because they were believed to be an especially potent source of spiritual power. These visions also carried serious obligations that one could disregard only at one's own peril.[4] According to Lakota standards, then, even this very early childhood vision had the potential to establish relationships with spirit-beings whose favor, if solicited in the proper ritual manner, could bestow great benefits on whoever pleased them or awakened their pity.

# The Great Vision

The next four years of Black Elk's childhood passed uneventfully. The strange voices did occasionally speak to him but these occurrences were infrequent. Apparently he never experienced any visual communications from spirit-beings at the same time.[5] Aside from the infrequent incidents with the voices, nothing seemed to suggest that Black Elk was any different from his other playmates. However, all this changed dramatically when he was about eight and a half years old (1872). At that time Black Elk had what he considered the most significant experience of his life, his "Great Vision." It appears that almost all of his subsequent spiritual development took form as a response to this one great visionary and auditory revelation he received while he was apparently in some condition of cataleptic ex-stasy.[6] Since various elements of this particular mystical experience played an important role in both his private religious life as well as in the larger religious life of his whole community, I shall describe the events that took place within the Great Vision in considerable detail.

The evening before his Great Vision, the nine-year-old Black Elk had been eating supper when a spirit voice began to call him saying, "It is time, they

---

4. For other descriptions of these obligations, see John Fire Lame Deer, *Lame Deer: Seeker of Visions*, pp. 241–46; Densmore, *Teton Sioux Music*, pp. 157–58, 164–66; Clark Wissler, "Societies and Ceremonial Associations in the Oglala Division of the Teton Dakota," *Anthropological Papers of the American Museum of Natural History* 11 (1916), p. 84; Walker, *Lakota Belief*, pp. 155–57, 230.

5. DeMallie, *Sixth Grandfather*, p. 110.

6. Notice that I am still maintaining the previous distinction between "ecstasy" (that sensation of great bliss that often accompanies mystical experiences) and "ex-stasy" (that sensation or experience of dissociation from the body that also commonly accompanies it).

are calling you."[7] Black Elk knew that this voice was from one of the spirits so he went outside the tipi to see who was calling him. As he did so, he noticed that his thighs were beginning to hurt. The next morning, as his band began to break camp, he suddenly found that not only could he not walk but that he also had a swollen face, arms, and legs. While he lay swollen and paralyzed, his Great Vision began.

As Black Elk lay stricken looking outside the tipi, he noticed that the two men who had appeared before him in his very first vision at the age of five were once again standing in front of him, saying, "Hurry up, your grandfather is calling you."[8] When Black Elk's spirit got up to follow them (his physical body was still paralyzed on the bed), these two messengers (*akicitas*) of the dreaded thunder-beings started to fly into the clouds. As they did so, a little cloud came down to Black Elk. Black Elk got on the small cloud. It then moved up into the sky and brought him up into the midst of the towering clouds where the two spirit messengers were.

Once Black Elk caught up with the thunder-beings' two messengers, they showed him a vision of a bay-colored horse standing amid the clouds. The bay horse began to talk to Black Elk, telling him that he was going to show him not only his own "life history" but also the life histories of the horses of the four cardinal directions. The bay horse began by pointing Black Elk toward the west, where Black Elk saw twelve black horses, each of which had a necklace of buffalo hooves. Above the heads of the black horses of the west flew birds (probably swallows, a common Lakota symbol of the thunder-beings), presenting a terrifying spectacle since lightning and thunder surrounded them. The two spirit messengers then told Black Elk to look toward the north, ninety degrees in a clockwise direction from the west, where he saw twelve white horses bedecked with necklaces of elk's teeth and with white geese flying over their heads. Black Elk's attention was then directed toward the east where he saw twelve sorrel-colored horses with horns. Eagles flew over the horses' heads. After looking at the

7. DeMallie, *Sixth Grandfather*, p. 111.

8. Here one observes an important discrepancy between *Black Elk Speaks* and the stenographic record. The transcripts show the word "grandfather" in the singular, implying that Black Elk is being summoned by the Spirit of the West, Wakinyan, the Lakota divinity associated with thunderstorms and the dreadful thunder-beings. Visions from the thunder-beings were feared because of the burdensome obligations that they imposed and the fact that failure to fulfill those obligations carried with it the risk of being struck by lightning. When Neihardt speaks of the "Grandfathers" in the plural in *Black Elk Speaks*, he is implying that all six of the Grandfathers played an equal role in bestowing their spiritual powers and concomitant obligations on Black Elk. The transcripts suggest that the Great Vision was, above all, a gift of the Spirit of the West. DeMallie, *Sixth Grandfather*, p. 114.

horses of the eastern Power, Black Elk continued to turn clockwise until he faced south. There he saw twelve buckskin-colored horses who also had horns on their heads. (There is no mention of any birds flying over the heads of these horses.)

After the bay horse presented Black Elk with the sight of these four groups of horses from each of the four cardinal directions, it told him that they were going to take him to a council that the Six Grandfathers were having. However, before Black Elk and his escort of horses began their journey to this council the bay horse turned toward each of the four cardinal directions and neighed. Great clouds of horses emerged from each direction and made thunderous sounds, neighing back to the bay horse. These innumerable swarms of horses then began to dance in a circle around Black Elk, the bay horse, and the forty-eight horses in his escort (twelve from each of the four cardinal directions). While these swarms of horses circled Black Elk, they began to turn into buffalo, elk, other animals, and birds. Thus transformed, they returned to the direction from which they had come.[9]

Once the swarms of animals and birds had disappeared in this manner, Black Elk, the bay horse, and the other forty-eight horses arrived at a tipi made of clouds that had a rainbow door.[10] On each side of the rainbow door stood one of the spirit messengers Black Elk had seen at the beginning of this vision. He was then ushered into the tipi where six old men sat: the Powers of the West, North, East, South, the Sky, and the Earth. At this point in the Great Vision, each of these Six Grandfathers presented Black Elk with the gift of a special ritual object together with a specific spiritual power, which that particular ritual object would be able to convey or make manifest provided that it were used in the proper ceremonial manner. One of the Grandfathers reassured Black Elk that there was nothing to fear. Then the Grandfather of the West told Black Elk that he was going to give Black Elk some of his great power. He then proceeded to give Black Elk a wooden cup of water as well as a bow and arrow. The bow and arrow conveyed to Black Elk the power to destroy any enemy. The wooden cup of water gave Black Elk the power to "cure all sickness."[11]

When the first Grandfather, the Power of the West, had given Black Elk

9. This description of the Great Vision is taken from *Sixth Grandfather*, pp. 111–42.

10. The cloud tipi lodge and the rainbow are symbols of Wakinyan, the Power of the West, the direction from which thunderstorms come and the dwelling place of the thunder-beings. In this vision, the various powers associated with the western direction and the thunder-beings are given precedence over the gifts that the spirits of the other directions give to Black Elk.

11. DeMallie, *Sixth Grandfather*, p. 116.

his two gifts and explained to him what power each of those gifts possessed, he suddenly ran toward the west and changed into an emaciated black horse.[12] At that moment, the second Grandfather, the Power of the North, told Black Elk to take the herb that he was handing him and hold it toward the sick black horse. This ritual gesture of pointing the herb at the black horse immediately cured the emaciated horse. When Black Elk had cured the horse in this manner, the second Grandfather told Black Elk that with that particular healing herb he would "create a nation," that is, cure many people of illness. Then the second Grandfather ran toward the north and proceeded to transform himself into a white goose. Simultaneously, all the white horses of the northern direction suddenly turned into white geese. Both the first and second Grandfathers also sang a short sacred song that was important for Black Elk to memorize in order to activate their respective gifts of power. The first Grandfather's song went like this:

> They are appearing, may you behold.
> They are appearing, may you behold.
> The thunder nation is appearing, may you behold.[13]

The third Grandfather then began to speak and bestow his sacred gifts of power. The patriarch first pointed to two men who were flying beneath the daybreak star. He told Black Elk that he who had awakened all the birds and all the four-legged creatures of the earth would now give him power. Then he handed Black Elk a peace pipe that had engraved on its stem a spotted eagle with its wings outstretched as though it were in flight. This eagle seemed to come alive as Black Elk gazed at it. With this sacred pipe, the third Grandfather continued, Black Elk would be able to heal any sick creature on earth. To emphasize this promise of curative power, the patriarch directed Black Elk to look at a strange man whose entire body was painted bright red.[14] While Black Elk looked at him, this red man lay down, rolled over, and turned into a buffalo. Then the man-turned-buffalo

12. Notice how each of the four directions is associated with a particular color. Black (or sometimes blue) is associated with the west and the terrifying powers of the thunder-beings.

13. The second Grandfather's song was the same as the first except for the last line, which read: "The white geese nation is appearing, may you behold." See DeMallie, *Sixth Grandfather*, p. 117.

14. The Sioux always associated the color red with that which quintessentially incarnates both sacredness and power. Whenever their myths or rituals involve the act of painting something or someone red or presenting something that is red, this action signifies that that object, person, or ritual deed will enjoy or bring about an exceptional intimacy with the sacred realm and the power that it brings into the world.

galloped off to join a group of sorrel horses in the east, which then turned into fat, healthy buffalo as well.[15]

The fourth Grandfather, the Power of the South, bestowed on Black Elk what he called "the power of the four quarters," symbolized by a sprouting stick, which he gave to Black Elk.[16] By bringing this sacred stick to "the nation's center of the earth," Black Elk would be able to save many people.[17] When the fourth Grandfather had given Black Elk this sacred sprouting stick, he told Black Elk to look at the earth. On it were two roads, a "good" red road going from north to south and a black "road of fearfulness" that ran from east to west.[18] This black road was the road of the thunder-beings. From the sacred red road, Black Elk was told, he would receive the power to do good and from the black road he would receive the power to destroy his people's enemies. Then the fourth Grandfather told Black Elk that we would walk the earth "with four ascents," a mysterious phrase that Black Elk interpreted to mean that the power of the vision would remain with him for four generations. Like the previous three Grandfathers, the fourth ended his speech to Black Elk by transforming himself into an animal: He began to run to the south, rolled on the ground and became a horse and then rolled on the ground yet another time and became an elk.

The fifth Grandfather, the Great Spirit or Power of the Sky, then began to speak to Black Elk. As he told Black Elk to behold his power he turned into a spotted eagle, the messenger of Wakan-Tanka (the Lakota word for

---

15. This figure of the man painted red who also changed into a buffalo exhibits many features in common with the principal figure of Siouan mythology, the White Buffalo Calf Woman, the culture heroine who first bought the sacred pipe to the Sioux. The story of her first appearance among them relates that, after she left the Siouan encampment, having given them this great gift and instructed them regarding its use, she rolled on the ground and then got up, transformed into a buffalo.

16. This sacred stick associated with the "nation's center of the earth" was an obvious reference to the freshly cut cottonwood pole that held up the tipi in which all the bands of the tribe celebrated their annual Sun Dance rite. This ritual was the most important festival of the Siouan year for not only did it bring together all the widely separated bands of the tribe for a time of reunion and happy socializing (thus it was the symbol par excellence of the nation's [or tribe's] center) but its performance also brought about a spiritual regeneration of the entire cosmos—human and nonhuman.

17. DeMallie, Sixth Grandfather, p. 118.

18. It is important to note that the black road was *not* a symbol of evil. Black was the color associated with the powerful but fearful thunder-beings. The powers of the black road, powers that enabled those who possessed them to defeat their enemies in war, were just as essential for survival as were the healing and rejuvenative powers associated with the "good" red road.

"Great Mystery"). He gave Black Elk the power to go across the earth and a mysterious power that would enable him to become a relative to all winged things as well as to the winds and the stars. He also promised Black Elk a destructive power that would allow him to defeat an enemy that even the Six Grandfathers could not defeat. After the fifth Grandfather made these promises, Black Elk noted that as the spotted eagle began to fly over his head, animals and birds came toward him "to perform a duty."[19] At that very moment the sixth Grandfather, the Power of the Earth, began to speak. He granted Black Elk the power to return to the earth, and predicted that Black Elk's "nation" would endure "great difficulties." Then, like the other Grandfathers, he began to depart and undergo a transformation. In this case, the sixth Grandfather did not turn into an animal or bird but instead changed from an ancient old man into a young man whom Black Elk realized was himself. In the Great Vision Black Elk had become the sixth Grandfather, the Spirit or Power of the Earth.[20]

What happened in this segment of the Great Vision is that each of the Six Grandfathers became, in effect, one of Black Elk's helping spirits in the form of a four-legged animal or a bird. Helping spirits were a very frequent phenomenon in the religions of hunting peoples like the Lakota. The acquisition of such a helping spirit implied that one had acquired the spiritual power that it possesses or mediates. The powers that the Six Grandfathers bestowed on Black Elk were of two basic types: (1) powers of destruction related to war magic, the powers associated with the fearful black road that allow Black Elk and his people to triumph over their enemies, and (2) powers of healing and strengthening associated with the good red road.

The next major segment of the Great Vision consisted of Black Elk (now astride the bay horse along with his escort of forty-eight horses and their riders from the four directions) walking the two sacred roads. The first road that Black Elk and his escort traversed was the fearful black road. Beginning from Pike's Peak in the west, the procession headed east. Black Elk noticed that as the journey began it seemed like all the creatures of the earth were trembling in fear. When Black Elk looked behind him, he saw that the manes of the horses and the riders on them were decorated with hail. As they rode through the sky going from west to east hail fell from his escort. Below he saw the forks of the Missouri River. In the middle of

19. The nature of this "duty" is unspecified. DeMallie, *Sixth Grandfather*, p. 119.
20. Ibid., pp. xix and 119.

the river stood the spirit of drought, a man who was surrounded by flame and dust. Around that evil spirit of drought creatures were dying. Black Elk then understood that it was his duty to slay this evil spirit of drought and thereby acquire that evil being's control over the waters.[21]

Black Elk and his escort began their attack on this evil spirit by singing sacred songs. The twelve riders on black horses attacked the man in flame from the western direction but failed to kill him. The riders from the other three directions also made sorties against him and failed.[22] After these sorties failed, the evil spirit, now painted blue, emerged from the waters. Black Elk then took the bow and arrow that the first Grandfather had given him and noticed that they had transformed into a spear that emitted lightning. The entire universe began to cheer for Black Elk, hoping that he would be able to relieve them from the oppression of this evil spirit. In one hand Black Elk held the spear and in the other he carried the other gift that the first Grandfather had given him, the wooden cup of water. Armed with these, he charged the blue man and skewered him through the heart with his lightning-emitting spear.[23] The blue man then turned into a turtle and all of the dead things that this evil spirit had killed miraculously came back to life. By killing this evil spirit, Black Elk acquired that spirit's power over the revivifying waters.[24]

Once he had vanquished the spirit of drought, Black Elk and his escort began their procession down the good red road. They came upon an encampment in the shape of a circle and halted on the south side of it. One of the spirits gave Black Elk the sacred sprouting stick and told him and his escort to begin marching north holding both the sacred stick and the sacred pipe. Then Black Elk demonstrated his healing power by reviving a

21. See DeMallie, *Sixth Grandfather*, pp. 123–24.

22. Recall the fifth Grandfather's statement that with his power Black Elk would be able to defeat an enemy that even the Six Grandfathers could not subdue.

23. According to Lakota cosmology, the thunder-beings (the powers of the sky) are locked in an eternal titanic struggle with the spirit powers that reside in the waters (symbolized by both the evil blue man of Black Elk's vision and the turtle). This element of traditional Lakota mythology has become incorporated into Black Elk's mystical experience. See DeMallie, *Sixth Grandfather*, pp. 95–96.

24. Ibid., pp. 123–24 and 139, where the second Grandfather tells Black Elk to swallow a cup of water in which a blue man was trying to escape. When Black Elk obeyed this command and swallowed the cup of water along with the blue man in it, he acquired not only the power of the water but also a strange power that he used in those conjuring ceremonies that sometimes formed a part of Lakota healing rites. This strange power was the ability to make the blue man come out and swim in the cup of water just as though he were a fish. In general, the Lakota maintain that by conquering an enemy one also acquires his spiritual powers.

tipi of dying people simply by passing in front of the tipi. Once Black Elk had cured them, he went to the center of the encampment where he handed the people both the sacred stick and the sacred pipe, telling them as he did so that with these ritual objects they would enjoy both peace and health. There was great rejoicing.

The entire encampment, along with Black Elk's escort, began to walk in a sacred manner along the good red road from south to north accompanied by the Grandfathers. The black horse rider of the west marched with a sacred herb in his possession; the white horse rider of the north carried the sacred wind with him; the sorrel rider of the east carried the Sacred Pipe; and the buckskin rider of the south carried the flowering stick as the procession headed north. Four other riders, one from each of the cardinal directions, then presented Black Elk with a sacred hoop, a symbol of tribal solidarity and prosperity. With this sacred hoop, Black Elk would have the powers and responsibilities of a chief.[25] As this solemn procession of people with the sacred ritual objects walked along the good red road, one of the old men in the procession (presumably one of the Six Grandfathers) showed Black Elk the sacred hoop and spoke these words: "Behold a good nation, a sacred nation, again they will walk toward good land, the land of plenty, and no suffering shall there be. A nation you shall create and it shall be a sacred nation (meaning that I was given the power to raise a nation)."[26] This is a very important passage in the Great Vision for it shows that the helping spirits of his vision gave Black Elk powers that would not only benefit himself but, much more important, would bring a paradisiacal prosperity, health, and social solidarity to the entire Lakota tribe.

The procession along the red road underwent what Black Elk called "four ascents" or generations. Each successive generation or "ascent" was worse than the one that had preceded it. The first ascent was a kind of tribal golden age, a time of plenty, of harmony, and freedom from suffering. The successive ascents that Black Elk witnessed became progressively more and more strife-torn and full of suffering. When the procession had reached the fourth and final ascent, Black Elk gazed upon a terrible spectacle: everywhere men, women, and children were in the worst possible extremity of suffering and want. Even the people's horses were gaunt and emaciated. Looking down from the clouds upon this scene of suffering, Black Elk suddenly noticed that on the north side of the diseased encamp-

25. Ibid., p. 123.
26. Ibid., p. 126.

ment there was a man with a lance whose whole body was painted red.[27] This sacred man walked into the center of the nation's hoop (the center of the encampment for tipis were usually arranged in a circle), rolled over, and turned into a buffalo. The buffalo then rolled over and turned into an herb, the healing herb of the north. As Black Elk looked at the herb it grew and bloomed. Black Elk was very careful to note what kind of plant it was.

This series of transformations from human to buffalo to herb in the center of the nation's hoop brought about a striking change in the condition of the sick people and horses. All of a sudden they were healthy, strong, and joyful. The horses began to neigh and dance. Then one of the spirits spoke to Black Elk and told him to look carefully at what was happening in the center of that nation's hoop (that encampment represented Black Elk's own tribe). As the spirit spoke, both the morning star and the sacred pipe with the spotted eagle flew from the east into the center of the hoop. Then the sacred flowering cottonwood stick was placed in the center of the sacred hoop.[28] Birds began singing and all of the people and animals began to rejoice. Through this sacred flowering cottonwood stick, the people and their children would prosper and multiply and humankind would be able to communicate with its four-legged and winged relatives. (Black Elk noted parenthetically that the coming of the whites had prevented this sacred tree from blooming and ushering in the scene of paradisiacal contentment that he had seen in the vision.) The paradisiacal scene was interrupted by a storm that purified the people with water. As the rain fell, one of the spirits told Black Elk that the spirits had shown him all the things that he was capable of doing on earth. Now it was Black Elk's responsibility to accomplish those things. The spirit then sang a song.

> A good nation I will make over.
> The nation above has said this to me.
> They have given me the power to make over this nation.[29]

27. The color red has many sacred associations among the Sioux. Most important, the sacred cottonwood pole that holds up the Sun Dance lodge is painted red during that most important ceremony of the Sioux. It is also the color of the buffalo calf. Red is the color associated with the Power of the East, the third Grandfather. In general, anyone painted red is assumed to be in a special state of ceremonial consecration.

28. This is a reference to the sacred cottonwood pole of the Sun Dance lodge.

29. DeMallie, *Sixth Grandfather*, p. 130.

When the storm had blown over, the encampment began marching once again down the good red road. As they left, Black Elk gave them all of his sacred paraphernalia except the sacred bow and arrow (symbols of lightning and its killing power) that he had been given by the first Grandfather.

In the next episode of the Great Vision, Black Elk exhibited some of the destructive and healing powers that the thunder-beings of the West had given him. First, Black Elk and one of his companions, One Side, armed with arrows that emitted lightning, exhibited the destructive power of the West by jointly attacking and killing a dog that dwelt amid flames.[30] Then Black Elk displayed the healing powers that the Spirit of the West had given him. The Spirit of the West told Black Elk to look at a totally emaciated black stallion that stood in front of him. The spirit said, "Behold him, for you shall make him over."[31] Then the Spirit of the West handed Black Elk an herb (the healing herb of the West). Black Elk took the herb and circumambulated the horse to the accompaniment of the peoples' cries for spirit power. Suddenly, the sickly horse neighed and rolled over and became a beautiful stallion in the full bloom of youthful vigor. This reinvigorated black stallion was clearly a symbol of the power of the thunder-beings of the west for Black Elk described it as both black (the color of the western direction) and as flashing lightning as it snorted. The black stallion then began a ritual salutation of the four directions, doing so in a clockwise fashion starting with the west.[32] The black stallion stood facing the west and neighed. Then a million happy and exuberant horses poured out of that direction. The stallion performed this same salutation for each of the other three directions with the same result. When the black stallion had concluded this ritual, the first Grandfather, the Spirit of the West, said to Black Elk, "Behold them, for these are your horses. Your horses shall come neighing to you. Your horses shall dance and you shall see. Behold them; all over the universe you have finished."[33] When the first Grandfather had finished speaking, four virgins dressed in red, the quintessential color of sacredness, stood in front of the first Grandfather. One of the

30. A similar episode occurs in Black Elk's later Dog Vision. In that vision the two spirit messengers of the thunder-beings that came to him in the Great Vision impale a dog that was surrounded by a cloud of butterflies and dragonflies. See Chapter 22.
31. DeMallie, *Sixth Grandfather*, p. 132.
32. Many Lakota rituals involve the clockwise circumambulation of an object.
33. DeMallie, *Sixth Grandfather*, p. 132.

virgins was holding the sacred pipe. The first Grandfather then sang a song:

> My horses prancing they are coming from all over the universe.
> My horses neighing they are coming, prancing they are coming.
> All over the universe my horses are coming.

When the first Grandfather had finished singing his sacred song, the black stallion began singing his own sacred song.

> They will dance, may you behold them. [four times]
> A horse nation will dance, may you behold them. [four times][34]

Black Elk pronounced the stallion's song to be indescribably beautiful. It was, as he put it, "like a radio" and could be heard everywhere in the universe by all living things, plants, animals, and birds. Everything that heard this wondrous sound began dancing. When the stallion had finished his song, Black Elk once again gazed down on a scene of paradisiacal abundance, joy, and harmony. The Spirit of the West then told Black Elk that this "day of happiness" that had spread throughout the universe was his to make. In other words, Black Elk had received so much power from all the spirits that he had the ability to bring about paradise on earth not only for the Lakota people but also for all other living things on earth.[35]

The first Grandfather then told Black Elk that the spirits were going to take him to the center of the earth, the top of a tall mountain that Black Elk later identified as Harney Peak in the Black Hills.[36] As the spirits took him to Harney Peak, Black Elk saw every color of light flashing from the mountains and radiating outward toward the four cardinal directions.[37]

---

34. Ibid., p. 133.

35. This statement is no exaggeration, for Black Elk told Neihardt that in this section of the vision, he was the sixth Grandfather, the Spirit of the Earth, and that "everything was giving me power. I was given power so that all creatures on earth would be happy." Ibid.

36. Ibid., p. 294.

37. Neihardt heavily embellished Black Elk's description of his experience on top of Harney Peak in *Black Elk Speaks*. In that book Black Elk is made to say that

> while I stood there I saw more than I can tell and I understood more than I saw; for I was seeing in a sacred manner the shapes of all things in the spirit, and the shape of all shapes as they must live together like one being. And I saw that the sacred hoop of my people was one of many hoops that made one circle, wide as daylight and starlight,

Black Elk and his retinue faced east and noticed that two winged men came out of the east. On each man's breast was a shining star. These two men from the east had an herb, the daybreak star herb, which they gave to Black Elk. They told Black Elk that with this herb he could accomplish any task. The two men then told Black Elk to drop the herb and let it fall to the earth. When the daybreak star herb hit the ground, it immediately started to grow until it flowered before Black Elk's eyes. A light that the entire universe could see radiated from its flower.[38] The first Grandfather then told Black Elk to look carefully all over the universe. In the north and the east, Black Elk saw people in a joyous mood but in the south and west a cloud covered the people and they were sick. The first Grandfather told Black Elk that this meant that in the future Black Elk would restore them to health.

The next episode of the Great Vision was completely omitted in *Black Elk Speaks*. In it, the spirits tell Black Elk that he is going to return to the Six Grandfathers. However, there is one more ordeal that he must go through before he can see them again—he must slay a terrible horned man dressed in black whose flaming body emitted lightning bolts whenever he moved.[39] Black Elk told Neihardt that this apparition was the spirit of war and everywhere around him there was pestilence and sounds of creatures in misery. The spirits told Black Elk to take a good look at this man for someday he would depend on the destructive power that this menacing creature possessed. This horned man's mighty power of destruction would allow Black Elk to annihilate all his enemies in times of war. Suddenly, the man dressed in black turned into a gopher and then into an herb.[40] This herb, which Black Elk called "the soldier-weed of destruction," was the most powerful of all the sacred herbs that he had received from the spirits in his Great Vision. Black Elk described it to Neihardt as an extremely poisonous herb of destruction so toxic that merely touching it led to instant death. Wherever it grows, it is surrounded by the skeletons of animals that had ventured too close to it.

---

and in the center grew one mighty flowering tree to shelter all the children of one mother and one father. And I saw that it was holy. (Neihardt, *Black Elk Speaks*, p. 36)

None of this material appears in the description of Black Elk's journey to the center of the earth that he gave Neihardt in the stenographic notes.

38. DeMallie, *Sixth Grandfather*, p. 134.

39. Note the close resemblance between this visionary figure and the Christian Devil.

40. The Lakota traditionally associate the gopher with powers that are useful in war.

After the spirits had shown Black Elk the soldier-weed of destruction and explained that with it he could destroy all his tribe's enemies in time of war, some of the horse riders who had escorted Black Elk participated in a titanic battle with an unseen enemy. When the battle was over, the participants from his escort turned into black-tailed deer (a symbol of invulnerability in battle). These deer then showed Black Elk how to use the herb. Then the horned man reappeared, transformed himself into a gopher again, then into the herb, and finally, into a skeleton.[41] At this point Black Elk began to notice that he had been painted the sacred color red, that his joints were painted black, and that there were white stripes symbolic of lightning on parts of his body. Moreover, every time he breathed lightning came out of his mouth. The horse he was riding was also painted with lightning designs.[42]

After Black Elk had been instructed in the ritual use of the soldier-weed of destruction, the spirits took him back to the cloud tipi and the assembly of the Six Grandfathers. As he entered the tipi, he noticed that the two spirit messengers who had appeared to him at the beginning of the vision as messengers of the Spirit of the West had now transformed themselves into white geese. Black Elk saw them and carefully listened to the sounds that they made. Later, during the Battle of Wounded Knee, Black Elk attributed his initial invulnerability to the soldiers' bullets to his imitation of these goose sounds that he had heard at this point in his Great Vision.[43]

Black Elk returned to the cloud tipi amid a scene of general rejoicing. The Six Grandfathers, the birds, the animals, the warriors, and even the lightning cheered Black Elk when he came through the door. Then each of the Six Grandfathers presented Black Elk with a wooden cup of water in which there were certain sacred objects. As each Grandfather presented Black Elk with one of these cups, he would then explain to him the power(s) that it would convey. The first Grandfather gave Black Elk a cup of water with a buffalo in it. With this cup, Black Elk would be able to feed his people and make them happy. The second Grandfather gave Black Elk a cup of water with a blue man struggling in it. He told Black Elk to swallow the blue man with the water so that he could have the power of water. Black Elk claimed that because of this gift he could make this blue man appear in a cup of water when he was healing a patient. The third

41. DeMallie, *Sixth Grandfather*, p. 137.
42. Notice once again how often the Great Vision incorporates symbols that are associated with the thunder-beings of the West.
43. DeMallie, *Sixth Grandfather*, pp. 277–78.

Grandfather presented Black Elk with a cup of water in which a star was reflected. By means of this star, Black Elk would receive the gift of wisdom. The fourth Grandfather gave Black Elk a cup of water with a red road across it. With this power, Black Elk's days on this earth would be sacred. The fourth Grandfather also presented Black Elk with a chant that he subsequently used during his healing ceremonies.[44] The fifth Grandfather gave Black Elk a cup of water with a spotted eagle in it. This gift of power gave Black Elk the penetrating sight of the eagle. Finally, the sixth Grandfather gave Black Elk a cup of water with small people swimming in it. The sixth Grandfather predicted that in the future his people would endure terrible difficulties but that through his mighty powers Black Elk would be able to sanctify and restore the nation's hoop for all six tribes of the Lakota.

When the Six Grandfathers had presented Black Elk with these gifts, the cloud tipi slowly began to disintegrate eventually vanishing altogether. Accompanied by a spotted eagle, Black Elk began to return home from the sky. As he looked down from the sky, saw his parents' tipi with himself lying in it. He then returned to his body where he still lay sick. The Great Vision was over. Black Elk's ex-static journey to the spirit-world had come to an end and, as his spirit came back to his physical body, he regained consciousness.[45]

# The Immediate Aftermath

Black Elk did not respond to his vision in the traditional Lakota manner until nine years later. Custom dictated that whenever a man had had a vision he must immediately tell a holy man (*wicasha wakan*) about all that had occurred in it so that the holy man could interpret its meaning and instruct the visionary in the performance of whatever public or private ritual and ethical obligations the spirit-beings of his vision had imposed on him as a precondition for receiving spiritual "power." The wicasha wakan

44. It is important to note that among the Lakota sacred objects usually could not manifest their spiritual power unless that power were activated by sacred songs that the helping spirit bestowed on the visionary at the same time that it presented the object.

45. Black Elk believed that he had been unconscious for twelve days during his Great Vision (DeMallie, *Sixth Grandfather*, p. 139). From the medical standpoint, this is unlikely. It is more probable that the period of unconsciousness was of much shorter duration, possibly only a few hours.

would often conclude that a public performance of parts of the vision constituted one of those ritual obligations that would allow the power to become manifest in a socially beneficial manner. For this reason, an individual's visions were never just a private affair. They were events of great social significance as well since, correctly interpreted and responded to, they could "give strength and health" to the entire tribe in much the same way that the performance of the great rituals such as the Sun Dance regenerated the entire tribe.[46]

The nine-year-old Black Elk did not tell his parents, his favorite grandfather, or other tribal elders about his Great Vision. Instead, he feared that they would somehow find out about it and think he was crazy.[47] It is also possible that the boy's reticence stemmed from the prevailing Lakota assumption that the significance of a vision or wakan dream is determined by the character of the man who has it.[48] How, then, could a child, a person of no social importance in the tribe, merit the attention of the spirits so that they would send him a "great" vision with the potential to revivify both the social order and the spiritual condition of his people and their animal relatives?

Although his Great Vision had no immediate impact on his fellow tribesmen, it did have some important consequences for his own life. First, it appears to have had an immediate effect on his physical health because no sooner had he returned from his ex-static journey than he began to recover unexpectedly from that strange paralysis, swelling, and coma that he claims had afflicted him for the previous twelve days.[49] Second, his Great Vision affected what one might call his "spiritual" nature. Black Elk related that the medicineman who had attended him during his vision illness told his father, "Your boy there is sitting in a sacred manner. I can see that there is a special duty for him to do. Just as he came in, I could see the power of lightning all through his body."[50] Not only did Black Elk's vision endow him with "the power of lightning" that a medicineman could sense but it also awakened his latent sensitivity to clairvoyant impressions. During the years between his Great Vision and his public reenactment of it at age seventeen, Black Elk received several clairvoyant premonitions about either the presence of game or enemies that he claims later proved to be

46. Brown, *Sacred Pipe*, pp. 44–45.
47. DeMallie, *Sixth Grandfather*, p. 150.
48. Densmore, *Teton Sioux Music*, p. 157; and Brown, *Sacred Pipe*, p. 44.
49. DeMallie, *Sixth Grandfather*, p. 143.
50. Ibid., p. 150.

true.[51] Third, Black Elk's Great Vision had an immediate effect insofar as it seems to have been responsible for the onset of those periodic episodes in which he acutely experienced a vivid sense of kinship with animals. While it was true that the Lakota acknowledged that men, animals, plants, and even certain inanimate objects such as rocks and thunderstorms were their "relatives," Black Elk's sense of this kinship sometimes became unusually intense even by Lakota standards. For example, a short time after his Great Vision, he went hunting with a bow and some arrows that his maternal grandfather had made for him. Because these bows and arrows reminded him of those visionary scenes where he received a bow and some arrows from the Six Grandfathers, he momentarily felt himself brought back to that peculiar feeling-state he had been in while he had been in his vision. This strange sensation of déjà vu quickly passed away and he tried to pretend that something so evanescent must only have been a dream. Perhaps, he thought to himself, even the Great Vision was just a dream. As he was thinking this, he noticed a bird that was sitting on a bush and he got ready to shoot it. However, as he prepared to do so, he "felt queer again" and remembered that he was "to be like a relative" to the birds so he did not shoot.[52] Other vignettes of this sort show that it often happened that when the "queer feeling" of his Great Vision came upon him, he felt constrained to show a special reverence to the animal that he was near at that moment. One day when both he and his father had spotted some deer while hunting, the queer feeling returned. Just as his father made ready to go off in the direction of the deer to stalk them, Black Elk suddenly blurted out that he must stay where he was for the spirits would bring the deer to them. This surprised his father but he did as Black Elk told him and the deer did actually come to them so that they killed two of them. Black Elk then went on to relate that as they were butchering the deer he became remorseful. He therefore proposed to his father that they offer one of the deer to "the wild things." This suggestion also surprised his father but, once again, he did as his son requested and ritually offered one of the slain deer to "the wild things that eat flesh" so that the Lakota people would live and the children know plenty.[53] It is significant that each incident of this sort was precipitated by something that brought back both the memories and the queer feeling that he had experienced during his Great Vision. It seems, therefore, that it was the sense of being present again in the

51. See, for example, ibid., pp. 205–8, 210–11.
52. Ibid., p. 152.
53. Ibid., pp. 155–56.

world of his vision that transformed Black Elk's behavior toward the animals. When he was not experiencing these brief rekindlings of his Great Vision, however, his conduct toward the animals did not seem to differ significantly from that of his companions.

# 18

# Three Major Characteristics of Black Elk's Great Vision

## A Source of Power

Black Elk considered his access to power the most important thing about his Great Vision. He maintained that this access not only conferred personal benefits but, even more important, it conferred them on his entire tribe. Power was therefore something that had significance for both the individual and the society at large. Most of the specific power or powers that each spirit-being gave to Black Elk belonged in one of the following two categories: powers that related to healing and powers that pertained to warfare such as the ability to destroy one's enemies in battle or powers that supposedly conferred invulnerability to enemy weapons.

There is abundant evidence indicating that the bestowal of power was the most prominent theme of the Great Vision. For example, not only did each of the four Grandfathers of the cardinal directions provide Black Elk with one or more gift objects but as each one presented his particular gift(s), he would simultaneously describe to Black Elk the specific power that was associated with it. Indeed, at the end of the Great Vision, the second Grandfather summarized its result by telling Black Elk, "All over the universe, *all* your grandfathers, the two-leggeds and on-earth walking, the day-fliers, they have had a council and appointed you and *have given you their power*."[1] The preeminent importance that obtaining power had also comes across when one recalls that although the fifth and sixth Grandfathers did not present Black Elk with any gift objects during his first visit with them, they nonetheless explicitly granted him certain spiritual powers that pertained to their specific domains of control.[2]

1. DeMallie, *Sixth Grandfather,* p. 139 (emphasis mine).
2. Ibid., p. 119.

The significance of acquiring power is reflected in the structure of the vision itself. The first third of the Great Vision centers on the theme of spirit-beings presenting Black Elk with their powers and their respective gifts. The second third of the narrative consists of a series of visionary episodes that resemble mythical events.[3] Each of these episodes exhibited in a quasi-mythical fashion how, by obeying instructions that he received from spirit-beings, Black Elk was able to utilize those gifts that they had given him so that he could liberate the spiritual power that each particular gift object mediated. By manipulating these gifts in the specific manner that the spirit-beings told him, he was then able to overcome various threats that menaced the well-being of his people and their nonhuman "relatives." The following episode was characteristic of the general tenor of the middle third of the visionary narrative.

The Spirit of the West (the first Grandfather) showed Black Elk a very sick and emaciated black horse and gave Black Elk an herb. It is worth noting that the healing power latent in this herb had nothing to do with its pharmaceutical properties since Black Elk neither touched the horse with the herb nor did he get the sick horse to ingest it. Instead, Black Elk activated the healing power of the herb by ritual means. Holding the herb, he circumambulated the horse while his retinue of horseriders called for spirit-power by uttering the chant, "A-hey, A-hey." As soon as he performed this ritual with the herb, its latent power became active. The sick horse was instantly rejuvenated and transformed into a sleek black stallion.[4]

The last third of the narrative of Black Elk's Great Vision is, in some ways, a recapitulation of the first third because it also describes gifts that each Grandfather gave Black Elk together with the powers that were associated with each specific gift. In this particular instance, the Six Grandfathers present him with cups of water in which Black Elk could see different objects. By accepting these cups of water and, in one case, swallowing the object in it, Black Elk acquired the spiritual power residing in each of them.[5] Once again, the spirits of the vision stress that the acquisition of spiritual power is the primary objective of Black Elk's journey to the other world.

3. This parallel between mythical narratives and mystics' descriptions of their experiences has been noted by Kees W. Bolle in *The Freedom of Man in Myth* (Nashville: Vanderbilt University Press, 1968), p. 166.

4. DeMallie, *Sixth Grandfather*, p. 132.

5. Ibid., pp. 137–40.

# Brings About a Harmony Between Human and Nonhuman Beings

It is significant that those climactic scenes in the Great Vision that displayed spiritually perfect conditions of existence always depicted them as situations in which humans and animals vividly experienced their kinship with each other. One particularly vivid scene in the Great Vision showed a mysterious man painted red entering a village full of pestilence with both humans and horses either dead or dying. This mysterious red man miraculously restores the people and the horses to health when he walks into the encampment, rolls over, turns into a buffalo, rolls over again, and transforms himself into an herb. Later on, in that same episode, the spirits placed a flowering cottonwood stick in the center of that same encampment, a gesture that ushered in a condition of paradisiacal harmony among all living things. Black Elk described it:

> You could hear birds singing all kinds of songs by this flowering stick and the people and animals all rejoiced and hollered. The women were sending up their tremolos. The men said . . . "Depending on the sacred stick we shall walk and it will be with us always. From this we will raise our children and under the flowering stick we will communicate with our relatives—beast and bird—as one people."[6]

This scene is a clear statement that the perfect, sacred mode of existence is one where human beings and animals shall live together "like relatives." Black Elk told Brown in *The Sacred Pipe* that "perhaps the most important reason for 'lamenting' [going out on a vision quest] is that it helps us to realize our oneness with all things, to know that all things are our relatives."[7] From these statements, one can see that, for the Lakota, truly sacred existence was essentially synonymous with a condition where man's kinship with the nonhuman order was not merely acknowledged but also experienced.

Black Elk's mystical experiences of kinship with the nonhuman realm constituted the fullest incarnation of one of the central ritual aspirations of the Lakota. Every one of their major rituals incorporated this aspiration to "live like a relative" with nonhuman "people." Each ritual included as one

6. Ibid., pp. 129–30.
7. Brown, *Sacred Pipe*, p. 46.

of its constituent elements a ceremonial smoking of the sacred pipe. The sacred pipe was much more than just a pipe—it was also a microcosm that symbolically incorporated all the classes of beings that existed within the Lakota mythological cosmos. Because it contained within itself the entire cosmos, the rite of smoking was tantamount to making an offering of all things in the universe to Wakan-Tanka, which implied, given the religious assumptions of the Sioux, that all those beings would now share in Wakan-Tanka's blessing. As White Buffalo Cow Woman told the Lakota when she first gave them this sacred rite, the fact that the pipe was a microcosm meant that "when you pray with the pipe, you pray with and for everything."[8] And since every important ritual involved the use of the sacred pipe, every ritual became a "prayer with and for everything," a means of bringing about the temporal and spiritual well-being of not only human but also animate and inanimate beings.

Whereas rituals and myths articulate an ideal of what ought to be that may sharply contrast with what actually exists,[9] mystical experiences transform these subjunctive possibilities into something that the mystic actually lives and feels. Black Elk's Great Vision was certainly no exception to this generalization for it was the experiential fulfillment of ideals attested to in every Lakota ritual. The religious preeminence that Lakota mystics accorded humans' relationships with animals—their ascription of intelligence, personality, and wisdom to them, and their supposition that animals had supernatural powers—typify the religious assumptions and preoccupations that most hunting peoples throughout the world share.[10]

One of the most common assumptions among nomadic hunters concerns the existence of a Master or Mistress of Animals, a being having the form of some animal who possesses mysterious powers that control the activities, appearances, and disappearances of all animals. In addition, this spirit-being also ensures that humans carry out their ritual obligations toward the animals under his or her care. In Chapters 2 and 4, I noted that, during times of scarcity among the Hudson Bay Eskimos, their shamans often undertook spirit journeys to the Mistress of the Animals so that, while "in the spirit," they could perform actions that would placate her anger at all the taboo violations that had made her withhold game. This

---

8. Ibid., p. 7.

9. Jonathan Z. Smith, "Bare Facts about Ritual," in his *Imagining Religion* (Chicago: University of Chicago Press, 1982), p. 63.

10. Mircea Eliade, *A History of Religious Ideas,* 3 vols. (Chicago: University of Chicago Press, 1978–84), 1:7–8.

type of divine being also made its appearance among the Lakota. Siya'ka's vision of the crow and the owl provides a classic example of a Lakota vision-seeker's encounter with a spirit-being of this genre. Siya'ka recounted that one night during his vision quest, he saw a bright light coming toward him from the east.

> It was a man. His head was tied up and he held a tomahawk in his hand. He said, "Follow me" and in an instant he changed into a crow. In my dream I followed the crow to a village. He entered the largest tent. When he entered the tent he changed into a man again. Opposite the entrance sat a young man, painted red, who welcomed me. When I was thus received, I felt highly honored, for as this was the largest tent I knew it must be the tent of the chief. The young man said he was pleased to see me there. He said, further, that all the animals and birds were his friends, and that he wished me to follow the way he had used to secure their friendship. He told me to lift my head. I did this and saw dragonflies, butterflies, and all kinds of small insects, while above them flew all kinds of birds. As soon as I cast down my eyes again and looked at the young man and at the man who had brought me thither, I saw that the young man had become transformed into an owl, and that my escort had changed again into a crow.[11]

This strange figure of the owl man in Siya'ka's vision manifested spiritual powers over animals that were typical of those possessed by Masters of Animals in other hunting cultures.

The power of the owl man of Siya'ka's vision to change into the form of an animal, to make the animals come and then disappear, and to heal them was also possessed by the Six Grandfathers of Black Elk's Great Vision. The luminous being that Black Elk encountered during one of his Ghost Dance visions also appears to have been some sort of Master of Animals figure, for he told Black Elk, "My life is such that all earthly beings that grow belong to me."[12] It is evident, then, that both the content of Black Elk's visions and the character of his responses to them reflected the existential concerns typical of not only his fellow tribe members but also of hunting peoples in general. For this reason, it is not surprising that his religious experiences, practices, and aspirations should differ pro-

11. Quoted in Densmore, *Teton Sioux Music*, p. 185.
12. DeMallie, *Sixth Grandfather*, p. 263.

foundly from those of mystics from the universal religions. After all, none of the cultures within which Christianity, Judaism, Buddhism, Islam, Hinduism, or Neoplatonism originated had any serious reason to be concerned with hunting. In these religious cultures it did not matter whether the family breadwinner brought home the game because those cultures founded their economic life on agriculture, livestock raising, or commerce. Consequently, the character of human experiential and ritual relationships to wild animals could hardly become a matter of compelling religious significance for them.

My remarks thus far have indicated some of the ways that visions displayed those sacred relationships that the Lakota had hoped to establish between humans and the nonhuman world. Their visions likewise served as sources of information about how humans could bring about those ideal conditions. The visionary scene not only presented humans and animals in situations where they co-existed in paradisiacal harmony with one another but it also often incorporated episodes where either the animals or the divine beings who protected them would give ritual instructions to the mystic that, if followed, would enable him to bring this state of affairs into existence.

# Did Not Transcend Forms or Images

In sharp contrast to the most elevated stages of yogic samādhi,[13] the more advanced affectless and imageless Hinayana Buddhist samāpattis (subtle trance-states), the various descriptions of fanā' (annihilation) that Sufis have given us, and in sharp contrast to the ineffable, imageless experiences of divine union alluded to in the writings of the classic Christian representatives of the via negativa, Black Elk never described any of his mystical experiences as being free of forms and figures or free of affect. Nothing in Black Elk's descriptions of his visions indicated that his transcendent states of consciousness involved any progression toward a dissolution of the boundaries between subject and object, or any state of awareness where forms and images disappeared from his perceptual field. Black Elk's mystical states of awareness were always full of things and objects, though they

13. Here I have in mind the "samādhi without support" that Patañjali and his commentators called asamprajñāta samādhi, a trance-state that was without support in the sense that there was no imagery of any kind upon which one could focus one's attention.

were, admittedly, spiritual things and spiritual objects rather than material ones. Thus Black Elk always experienced mystical states of consciousness where he saw a spiritual world, spiritual beings such as the Six Grandfathers who inhabited that spiritual realm, and spiritual objects that filled the landscape of that nonmaterial world. Moreover, Black Elk took it for granted that humankind's highest purpose was to seek guidance from the beings who dwelt in that wondrous world. It was an immaterial realm that presented Black Elk with vivid images and powerful emotions of joy and awe when he journeyed there in the spirit. Black Elk does not shun the concreteness and particularity of that spiritual world in his mystical visions but, rather, savors it.

Mystics in the universal religious traditions do not always savor a mystical state of consciousness full of spiritual beings, objects, images, and forms. One marked contrast to Black Elk's image-filled and affect-filled mystical experiences are the elevated and subtle trance-states known to Hinayana Buddhists as the samāpattis. In Sūtra 26 of the *Majjhima-Nikāya* there are five such states of mental abstraction, each more subtle than the one preceding it:

1. the trance of the infinity of space,
2. the trance of the infinity of consciousness,
3. the trance of nothingness,
4. the trance of neither perception nor nonperception, and
5. the trance of the cessation of perception and sensation.

The author of this Buddhist treatise describes how a monk enters the least subtle of those five trances, the trance of the infinity of space. One is told that to enter this trance the monk must first have "overpassed all perceptions of form" and then, "through the perishing of perceptions of inertia, and through ceasing to dwell [meditatively] on perceptions of diversity," finally reach a condition where he "dwells in the realm of the infinity of space."[14] It is clear that the Buddhist monk cultivating these "higher" trance-states, which bring him progressively closer to his goal of achieving nirvana, is completely indifferent to the possibility of experiencing paradisiacal realms of existence and to whatever beauty or majesty they might possess. His object is to transcend all perceptions of form and all perceptions of diversity. The Buddhist monk is therefore not concerned with encountering spirit-beings and gods or what they might tell him. No percep-

14. From the *Majjhima-Nikāya*, quoted from Warren, *Buddhism in Translations*, p. 348.

tual form or image, no matter how subtle, spiritual, or awesomely sublime it might be, interests this monk who is intent on cultivating the highest trances.

The Christian representatives of the via negativa[15] reacted to the presence of forms and images in mystical states of consciousness in ways that were quite similar to this anonymous Buddhist author. Saint John of the Cross, for example, counseled the aspirant who sought contemplative union with God to avoid all attachment to or fascination with the forms or phantasms that one receives in visions.

> These visions, inasmuch as they are of creatures . . . cannot serve the understanding as a proximate means to union with God. . . . Wherefore the soul must make no store of treasure of the forms of such visions as remain impressed upon it, neither must it lean upon them; for to do this would be to be encumbered with those forms, images, and persons which remain inwardly within it, and thus the soul would not progress toward God by denying itself all things.[16]

Diadochus of Photike gave similar advice to ascetics who strove after contemplative prayer. "We should not embark on the ascetic life in the hope of seeing visions clothed with form or shape; for if we do, Satan will find it easy to lead our soul astray. Our one purpose must be to reach the point when we perceive the love of God fully and consciously in our heart—that is, 'with all your heart, and with all your soul, and with all your mind.' "[17] The thirteenth-century Sufi, Ibn 'Ata' Illah likewise indicated that the higher states of spiritual attainment involved a progressively deepening renunciation of attachment to or fascination with visionary multiplicity. He observed that there were basically three different categories of people that one encountered on the spiritual path. The first and lowest category of seeker after wisdom is

> the one who rejoices at blessings, not in respect to their Bestower or Originator, but in respect to his pleasure in them. This man belongs to the forgetful. . . . To the second category belongs the one who

15. For example, John of the Cross, Diadochus of Photike, Dionysius the Areopagite (in his *Mystical Theology*), the anonymous author of *The Cloud of Unknowing*, and Meister Eckhart.

16. John of the Cross, *Ascent of Mount Carmel*, p. 309.

17. *Philokalia: The Complete Text*, 5 vols., trans. and ed. G. E. H. Palmer, Philip Sherrard, and Kallistos Ware (London: Faber & Faber, 1979), 1:265.

rejoices at blessings inasmuch as he sees them as blessings from Him who sent them or as grace from Him who brought it to him. . . . To the third category belongs the one who rejoices in God. Neither the exterior pleasure of the blessings nor their interior graces divert him. Instead, his vision of God, his concentration on Him, divert him from what is other-than-He, so that he contemplates only Him.[18]

These examples demonstrate that the forms and images that one encounters in visions possessed no soteriological significance for any of these three mystics. Such forms and images were regarded as hindrances to spiritual perfection because they distracted the mystic from the ultimate purposes of his quest. The spiritually perfected state was not regarded as a state of visionary illumination but rather as a state of being where one unswervingly persisted in one's steadfast love of God and one's ascetic vows despite the powerful allurements and invitations to self-indulgence that the beguiling forms and figures of his visions might throw in the way of his efforts at perfect self-control.

Similarly, when Patañjali, in his *Yoga-Sūtras,* alluded to the highest state of a yogin's meditational attainment known as *kaivalyam* (isolation), he specifically contrasted it to any notion of paradise in which the concrete multiplicity of beauteous images and forms still held their power to fascinate. He counseled the wise yogin who desired final liberation to avoid becoming fascinated by those alluring forms and visions that entice him at the penultimate stages of his meditations. At that stage, he cautioned, it often occurs that the gods and other spiritual beings try to tempt him. They will do everything to break his concentration, presenting him with strikingly beautiful maidens, elixirs that check old age and death, supernormal powers such as the ability to fly through the air, and wishing trees that, if he will but break his concentration, will grant him his every wish. The wise yogin shuns these visionary blandishments. "The lust-born gusts of sensual things are enemies. How then could it be that I . . . be led astray by these things of sense, a mere mirage, and make of myself fuel for that same fire of the round-of-rebirths as it flares up again? Fare ye well! Sen-

18. Ibn 'Ata' Illah, *The Book of Wisdom,* in Ibn 'Ata' Illah and Kwaja Abdullah Ansari, *The Book of Wisdom / Intimate Conversations;* introduction, translation, and notes of *The Book of Wisdom* by Victor Danner, and of *Intimate Conversations* by Wheeler M. Thackston, Classics of Western Spirituality Series (New York: The Paulist Press, 1978), p. 118.

sual things (deceitful) as dreams and to be craved by vile folk!"[19] Just like the highest Buddhist trance-states, kaivalyam was utterly removed from the kind of concreteness and multiplicity that one encounters in Black Elk's Great Vision. As its Sanskrit name suggests, kaivalyam was a radical "isolation" from all involvement in phenomenality whether it be material, mental, or spiritual.

For Black Elk, on the other hand, the most religiously significant spiritual states did not involve any rejection of visionary forms and images at all. One can see that this is true when one examines his description of that climactic moment of his Great Vision when he had just journeyed to the center of the world. "As I looked I could see great mountains with rocks and forests on them. I could see all colors of light flashing out of the mountains toward the four quarters. Then they [the spirits] took me on top of a high mountain where I could see all over the earth." When Black Elk and his escort of sixteen horse riders from the four cardinal directions stood facing the east, two winged men, each with a bright star on his breast, approached Black Elk and stood in front of him. At that moment, the first Grandfather told Black Elk, "Behold them, for you shall depend on them." The two winged men held an herb in their hands and gave it to Black Elk saying, "Behold this; with this on earth you shall undertake anything and accomplish it." The two winged men then instructed Black Elk to drop the herb on the earth below him. The herb fell toward the earth and "when it hit the earth it took root and grew and flowered. You could see a ray of light coming up from the flower, reaching the heavens, and all the creatures of the universe saw this light."[20]

One can see a sharp contrast between the images of spiritual fulfillment that Black Elk depicted and those of the Buddhist author of the *Majjhima-Nikāya*, John of the Cross, Diadochus, Ibn 'Ata' Illah, and Patañjali. Black Elk made no attempt to devalue the religious significance of any of those forms, figures, or spirit-beings that he had perceived. Not once did he even imply that the spiritually perfect mode of being was free from perceptual contact with concrete and particular spirits, animals, or objects. He never implied that reaching that state required one to cultivate an attitude of sublime indifference to them. Black Elk differed from the mystics quoted above insofar as the particular spirit-beings, forms, and objects of his vision later came to possess an essential, and not merely secondary, religious

19. Patañjali, *Yoga-System of Patañjali* (Woods trans.), 3:51; Veda-Vyāsa's commentary, pp. 285–87.
20. DeMallie, *Sixth Grandfather*, p. 134.

significance. In Lakota religion the specific instructions that particular spirit-beings had given to humanity in the past through visions were the source of most of their rituals. Without those visionary instructions from the spirits, most of the Lakota rituals would never have developed and the Lakota would never have learned how to behave and live on this earth in a sacred manner. Thus, if these earlier Lakota holy men had taken John of the Cross's advice and refused to pay attention to what the forms and figures in their visions had told them to do, they would never have been able to acquire those rituals necessary for their people's religious life and physical well-being. The ritual-centeredness of Lakota religion, together with the fact that these rituals generally originated in individuals' visionary experiences, prevented the Lakota from devaluing the religious significance of visionary forms and images.

What factors might account for Black Elk's contentedness with visionary multiplicity? The symbiosis between vision and ritual that one so often observes in Lakota religion appears to have been the principal factor in making Black Elk not just tolerate but welcome visionary multiplicity. Visions served as the principal means whereby power came down into the human world from its source in the spirit-world. Moreover, in Lakota religion this power that an individual received in a vision always remained inseparably linked to those specific ritual procedures that spirit-beings communicated to him during that particular vision. In other words, having a vision did not in and of itself guarantee that a holy man could utilize its power. He not only had to have the vision to acquire its power but, equally important, he had to follow those specific instructions for utilizing it that the spirit-beings gave to him. It was always crucially important for the Lakota holy man to pay close attention to what the particular beings, forms, and figures of his vision were doing and saying. Given this ritually catalyzed nature of visionary power among the Lakota, it would have been absurd for Lakota holy men or medicinemen to have followed the advice of someone like John of the Cross and suppressed or ignored the forms or images that they encountered in their visions. According to their religious assumptions, if they heeded such counsels, they would never have been able to liberate that sacralizing power that comes to man through visions. Denying or suppressing visionary multiplicity would therefore have been tantamount to denying the possibility that man could live a truly sacred life.

The compartmentalized nature of spiritual power in Lakota religion constituted another factor that contributed toward Black Elk's openness to

visionary multiplicity. Among the Lakota, spiritual power did not exist as
an amorphous potency that its possessor could direct in any way that he
wished. Instead, they maintained that there were numerous distinct kinds
of spiritual powers that one could acquire from visions each of which was
bestowed by a specific category or categories of supernatural donor(s); for
example, sacred stones or thunder-beings. This fundamentally polytheistic
or compartmentalized character of power tended to make the medicineman or holy man place a high value on the particular forms or images that
he perceived in a vision because the specific nature of that spiritual power
to which the vision had given him access remained inextricably linked to
the particular spirit-being that manifested itself to him. Consequently, if he
paid no attention to the particular details of the vision that had come to
him, he would have had no way of knowing which particular spiritual
powers he had been granted.

I suggest that it is no accident that the tendency to devalue visionary forms
and images characterizes mystical spiritualities in what Robert Bellah has
called the "historic" religions,[21] whereas the opposite tendency, that is, to
cultivate visions with forms and images, characterizes mystical spiritualities that develop among preliterate tribal religious traditions. The historic religions exemplified by Buddhism, some forms of Hinduism, Judaism, Islam, and Christianity exhibit an acosmic sacrality: the cosmos, or
nature, is no longer a vehicle for manifesting the sacred.[22] Instead, the sa-

---

21. See his famous essay "Religious Evolution," in Robert Bellah, *Beyond Belief: Essays
on Religion in a Post-Traditionalist World* (Berkeley and Los Angeles: University of California Press, 1970), pp. 20–50.

22. It is interesting to speculate on the deeper sources of this persistent acosmism in the
historic religions and its almost total absence in preliterate tribal religions. Perhaps the need
to depict the sacred in an utterly transcendent fashion stemmed from the need to make the
sacred truly universal in a political context where smaller kingdoms and tribal groups were
either becoming amalgamated into empires through conquest or else being brought into more
intimate contact with each other through trade. If God (or the sacred in some other form)
cannot be represented by any image or natural analogy, then it also stands to reason that God
cannot be debunked as merely provincial or local in origin and it is also much more difficult
to debunk Him as a product of the human imagination.

This existential disquiet with what is local in origin comes across in the thought of the
sixth-century-B.C. Greek philosopher Xenophanes of Colophon. Xenophanes is uneasy with
divine anthropomorphism and prefers to conceive of God as utterly beyond form and figure.
He implies that it is only the latter type of God that can be truly universal and survive the
criticism that He is simply the transparent creation of a particular cultural group. Xenophanes insists that God is "in no way similar to mortals either in mind or body." Thus, like

cred is regarded as located "somewhere" completely beyond the phenomenal world of nature, and salvation involves a complete freedom from entanglement in it. Thus Buddhist descriptions of nirvana emphasize its absolute dissimilarity to anything in nature: "One cannot point to its form or shape, its duration or size."[23] Similarly, both Islam and Judaism stress that God, the sole source of all that is sacred, is not only beyond nature but that He also utterly transcends all form and figure. Such acosmic forms of religiosity tend to devalue visionary forms and images since the sacred (as such systems conceive it) cannot, by its very nature, be fully revealed through them. Preliterate tribal religions, on the other hand, tended to assume that certain objects of nature reveal the sacred. Such a religious orientation has no difficulty accepting the idea that visions containing forms, images, and figures can serve as manifestations of the sacred. Consequently, it has no need to cultivate trance-states where such forms and images are absent.

---

nirvana, Yahweh, or Allah, Xenophanes' God is utterly transcendent.

It is clear that Xenophanes's theological speculations, with their emphasis on divine transcendence, developed as a response to a trading people's growing awareness of the cultural relativity of humankind's religious conceptions.

> Mortals believe that the gods are begotten and that they wear clothing like our own, and have a voice and a body. The Ethiopians make their gods snub-nosed and black; the Thracians make theirs gray-eyed and red-haired. And if oxen and horses and lions had hands and could draw with their hands and do what men do, horses would draw the gods in the shape of horses, and oxen in the shape of oxen, each giving the gods bodies similar to their own. (Quoted in John Manley Robinson, *An Introduction to Early Greek Philosophy* [Boston: Houghton Mifflin, 1968], p. 52)

Xenophanes, as an Ionian Greek and exile, had extensive contact with foreigners and their religious conceptions. It is easy to expose, in an age of frequent cross-cultural contacts, a black, snub-nosed god as a projection of an Ethiopian's image of himself, and thereby dismiss the claim that such a theology has possession of ultimate truth. However, it is not so easy to expose as culturally conditioned a conception of God that portrays Him as radically Other than human and utterly beyond the analogies of sense-experience. Sharing the enlarged cultural horizons of a trading people and group of exiles, Xenophanes could no longer tolerate any notion of divinity that was transparently parochial and so, in the process of making God more universal and less provincial, he had to remove many of His concrete attributes. The move toward an acosmic and universal sacrality was slowly beginning.

I speculate that preliterate tribal peoples did not feel this existential need to make the divine or the sacred universal (and, therefore, utterly transcendent) because they were faced with neither the political problem of integrating diverse cultural groups within an empire nor that growing awareness of cultural relativism that comes from frequent and sustained contact through trade. What is transparently local and provincial to us is not experienced as such by peoples in preliterate tribal cultures. Consequently, their religions can still remain content with both cosmic sacrality and divine anthropomorphism.

23. Quoted from *The Questions of King Milinda*, as excerpted in Conze, *Buddhist Scriptures*, p. 156.

# 19

# Principal Characteristics of Lakota Power

## Power Was an Extrapsychic Spiritual Potency

What did Black Elk and other Lakota medicinemen and holy men mean when they spoke of acquiring power from their visions and wakan dreams? The first characteristic of power that they considered was a peculiar kind of spiritual potency that an individual could only receive from a spirit-being. Spiritual power was something that came to an individual from a source external to his own mind or psyche. For example, there is not one instance in either Black Elk's conversations with Brown and Neihardt or in the ethnographic descriptions of Walker or Densmore where any Lakota holy man or medicineman ever claimed that he had obtained any of his special powers related to healing, war, or locating game without the assistance of a spirit-being. For the Lakota an individual is merely a conduit for those peculiar life-giving and life-enhancing potencies that originate from supernatural beings and that these beings send down to humanity as they see fit.

The Lakota assumption that spiritual power originates from a source that is extrapsychic or outside the human mind or psyche differs profoundly from many of the Buddhist and Hindu practitioners of yoga who claim that whenever a yogin begins to manifest supernormal powers of action or perception, he has acquired those extraordinary powers by means of his own efforts of mental discipline. Both the Tibetan Buddhist practitioner of tumo who acquires the power of keeping warm while naked in subzero temperatures and the Hindu practitioner of kundalini who activates that preternatural "liquid" light agree that they activated their respective supernormal powers and energies by means of their own efforts of mental concentration without the assistance of any god or spirit-being. Consequently, their spiritual powers had an intrapsychic origin, an origin *inside* the mind or psyche of the yogin.

# Its Linkage to Visions, *Wakan* Dreams, and Rituals

The second characteristic of Lakota power was that the spirit-beings only bestowed it when an individual either had had a vision or performed certain rituals. Although power frequently came to an individual because he had performed certain ceremonies in the proper manner, visions rather than ceremonies served as the primary sources of power. The Lakota generally maintained that the empowering rituals and ceremonies had themselves originated in the visionary experience of some individual who had lived in the past. For example, Black Elk, following the tradition handed down to him by Elk Head, the Oglala tribe's former keeper of the sacred pipe, maintained that the ceremonial details of that ultimate power-giving ritual, the Sun Dance, had their source in the instructions that supernatural beings had given to a man named Kablaya during a vision.[1] Black Elk asserted that four of the seven sacred rituals of the Lakota originated as a result of instructions that men had received in visions.[2] Black Elk was not the only member of his tribe, however, who emphasized the primacy of vision in relation to ritual. No Flesh, Little Wound, and John Blunt Horn

1. Brown, *Sacred Pipe*, p. 68.
2. Like any other statement about Lakota religion, the generalization that all rituals and all gifts of power ultimately derive from visionary experiences has some significant exceptions. For example, none of the accounts of how the sacred pipe originated that one finds in Walker, *Lakota Belief*, pp. 109–12, Densmore, *Teton Sioux Music*, pp. 63–66, or Brown, *Sacred Pipe*, pp. 3–9, mention that White Buffalo Calf Woman came to the two hunters in a vision. The myths state that she simply appeared to them while they were out hunting. There are some occasions where power is conferred without the experience of vision being necessary. Kathleen Dugan mentions that successful participation in the Sun Dance always conferred power on the dancer even if he did not have a vision during his ordeal. See Kathleen Dugan, "The Vision Quest of the Plains Indians: Its Spiritual Significance" (Ph.D. diss., New York, Fordham University, 1977), pp. 144–46.

Considerable variation also exists between one informant's description of an important mythological event and another's. One only has to contrast Black Elk's description of how the Sun Dance originated, which he gave in *Sacred Pipe*, with the account that Walker's informants gave Walker in "Sun Dance and Other Ceremonies," pp. 212–15; or contrast Lone Man's account of how the sacred pipe came to the Sioux (Densmore, *Teton Sioux Music*, pp. 63–66) with Finger's description given in Walker, *Lakota Belief*, pp. 109–12, to see how greatly they differ from one another. See also Brown, *Sacred Pipe*, p. 44.

gave Walker their separate versions of how the Hunkapi ceremony came into existence, each of them mentioning that the ritual had originated in a vision.[3]

Not only did the Lakota maintain that most of their power-bestowing rituals originated in visions but they also maintained that almost anything that possessed any supernatural efficacy—whether it were a sacred song, a pattern of behavior, or a power-laden object—had likewise originated in a vision. For example, the Lakota medicineman almost invariably claimed that he had acquired his knowledge of the use of paraphernalia from instructions that supernatural beings had once given him in a vision. Black Elk relates that when he did his first cure, the chief power that enabled him to cure a sick little boy was in an herb that the spirit-beings of his Great Vision had shown him when they took him to the center of the world.[4] The Lakota medicineman Goose similarly related that he had originally acquired his knowledge of which medicines to use in his tuberculosis-curing rites from instructions that supernatural beings had given him in a vision.

> One morning I arose before daybreak to go on a hunting trip. As I went around a butte I saw an antelope, which came toward me and stood still a short distance away from me. The antelope looked at me and then began to graze. I took my rifle and fired several shots with no effect. . . . Then the animal stopped grazing and began to move slowly away. Then I heard a voice speaking three times, and then a fourth time, and the voice said it was going to sing something, and I must listen. The voice was above me and commanded me to look at the sun. I looked and saw that the rising sun had the face of a man and was commanding all the animals and trees and everything in nature to look up. In the air, in front of the sun, was a booth made of boughs. In front of the booth was a very bright object and between this and the booth was a man. . . . The bright object was a sacred stone, and it was heated red hot. After seeing this I heard another voice telling me to look and receive what would be given me. Something in the form of a bird came down, and where it touched the ground an herb sprang up. This occurred three times. The voice above me said I was to use those three herbs in the cure of the sick. The fourth time the descending object started in the form of a bird, but a human skeleton came to the ground.

3. Walker, *Lakota Belief,* pp. 193–94, 196, 202–4.
4. DeMallie, *Sixth Grandfather,* pp. 134, 237.

Then the voice above me told me to observe the structure of the human body. I then saw the blood run into the skeleton, and a buffalo horn appeared on the back, between the shoulders, and drew the blood out of the skeleton. The voice above me said this was a sign that I would have power more than any other to cure diseases of the blood. The voice came from the sacred stone and said I must use the buffalo horn in curing diseases of the blood, a practice which I have followed ever since. I do not consider that I dreamed this as one dreams in sleep; it appeared to me when I was early on the chase.[5]

This example shows that Black Elk's methods of gaining power-laden medicinal objects from instructions given to him in a vision typified the procedure followed by other Lakota medicinemen. It was not only medicinal objects that depended on visionary experiences for their empowerment. Anthropologist Clark Wissler has observed that the protective designs that Lakota warriors painted on their shields to confer invulnerability to enemy arrows "could originate only in dreams and visions, and were painted by the person experiencing them, who prayed and sang over his work to give the shield power."[6]

The power-bestowing episodes in both Black Elk's Great Vision and Goose's vision of the talking sacred stone suggest that almost any kind of object could serve as a receptacle of supernatural power provided that some spirit-being had designated it as such and that the act of designation had occurred during a vision or wakan dream. Moreover, no Lakota claimed that he could manifest or benefit from supernatural power unless he knew which object(s) to use, how to impart power to that object, and how to use that object once it had been empowered. These instructions could only be communicated to a human from spirit-beings, who then only spoke through visions and wakan dreams.[7]

---

5. Quoted in Densmore, *Teton Sioux Music*, p. 251.

6. Clark Wissler, "Some Protective Designs of the Sioux," *Anthropological Papers of the American Museum of Natural History* 1 (1907), p. 30; see also DeMallie, *Sixth Grandfather*, pp. 261–62, 265, 272–74. The Lakota do not distinguish between waking visions and dreams as sources of power. Therefore, if a supernatural being comes to an individual in a dream, the instructions he receives in that dream are just as binding as those received in a waking vision. Dreams that occur during a vision quest are especially likely to be sources of supernatural power. For example, see Brown, *Sacred Pipe*, p. 59, and Dugan, "Vision Quest," p. 177.

7. Dugan, "Vision Quest," p. 180. Dugan has pointed out that the Lakota word for

# Compartmentalization

The third characteristic of the Lakota phenomenon of power is its tendency to be compartmentalized. The way that a specific gift of power manifests itself tends to be restricted in accordance with the mythological characteristics that the Lakota associate with the particular supernatural being
who bestowed it. In other words, those who have visions of thunder-
beings develop different capabilities than those who have visions of the
talking sacred stones because Lakota mythology and folklore have assigned different powers to each of these two types of supernatural beings.
Therefore, the Lakota do not regard power as general potency that enables
its possessor to accomplish whatever he wishes. A gift of power can only
be used for the specific purposes for which its supernatural donor designated it.

The compartmentalization of powers occurs in Black Elk's Great Vision.
For example, the fifth Grandfather, the Power of the Sky, gave Black Elk
the capability to "go across the earth." It is not surprising that the fifth
Grandfather would have bestowed this particular gift—as the Power of the
Sky his powers mythologically pertained to the control of the winds and
the winged creatures. However, the powers that the first Grandfather, the
Power of the West (the direction from which thunderstorms come and in
which, according to Lakota mythology, the thunder-beings dwell) granted
Black Elk were very different. The first Grandfather's powers pertained to
that domain over which he exercised control. Consequently, like the thunderstorm itself, the first Grandfather gave Black Elk both healing powers
(like the rain) in the form of a wooden cup of water and a power of
destruction in the form of a bow and arrow (a destructive power analogous to the power of lightning in a thunderstorm).[8]

The compartmentalization of powers was not always so neatly preserved, however. This was especially evident with respect to the powers of
healing that each of the first four Grandfathers granted Black Elk. Even
though each of these separately bestowed powers of healing differed in
subtle ways from the others (for example, the healing power given by the

---

"supernatural communication" (*wohanble*) is the same word for both "holy dream" and
"vision." This intimate linguistic connection between visions and dreams underscores the
fluidity of the boundary between visions and dreams among the Sioux.

8. DeMallie, *Sixth Grandfather*, p. 116. The association of this destructive power with
lightning is later made explicit during that episode in the Great Vision where Black Elk slays
the blue man with the bow and arrow that the first Grandfather gave him (p. 121).

Power of the West was the kind of healing associated with the revivifying power of rain after a drought, whereas that granted by the Power of the North was explicitly stated to have been the power of purification rather than revivification), Black Elk nonetheless performed his first cure indiscriminately using all the healing powers that each of the first four Grandfathers had given him. He did not treat one disease with one type of healing power and another disease with a different medicine. Unlike Goose, whose vision of the sacred stone and the buffalo horn had only given him the power to cure a specific class of diseases, diseases of the blood, Black Elk never explicitly informed Neihardt that he had ever limited his healing practices to any narrowly specified set of disease conditions. One can therefore recognize that although this tendency toward compartmentalization of spiritual power was a general one among the Lakota, there was a wide degree of individual variation from the norm. One would certainly expect variation in a nomadic tribal society where the lack of a highly stratified and tightly organized priesthood and the undeveloped communications between bands would have made the enforcement of any doctrinal and ritual orthodoxy difficult.

Black Elk's close visionary kinship to the thunder-beings and the Power of the West gave a distinctive stamp to his spiritual powers. For example, when one compares Black Elk's spiritual powers with those reputedly possessed by those who had had visions of the sacred stones, one discovers significant differences between the two classes of visionaries. This is not surprising, for the Lakota maintain that the sacred stones impart a different set of spiritual powers to those who have visions about them than do the thunder-beings. According to Densmore's informants, such stone-dreamers who fulfilled the obligations of their wakan dreams or visions acquired supernatural powers to cure sickness, foretell the future, describe where objects were hidden at a distance beyond the range of normal vision, and sometimes even the power to make stones fly around like poltergeists occasionally striking people and objects.[9] Moreover, in the yuwipi ceremonies that stone-dreamers often conduct as part of their curative rites, the visionary, while tied hand and foot in a pitch-black room, reputedly summon various spirits, which enter the darkened room in the form of bright sparks of light.[10] Since Black Elk never spoke of having had

9. See Densmore, *Teton Sioux Music*, p. 205, and Luther Standing Bear, *Land of the Spotted Eagle*, p. 208.
10. Richard Erdoes saw such phenomena during a yuwipi ceremony that he attended. See Lame Deer and Erdoes, *Lame Deer*, p. 267.

either a dream or a vision of the sacred stones or mentioned the yuwipi ritual in his autobiography or *The Sacred Pipe,* this would suggest that none of his powers derived from this source.[11] For this reason, one never finds Black Elk manifesting the power to summon spirits in the form of lights or poltergeists or locate lost objects in the manner of a yuwipi practitioner. Black Elk thus differed from Goose, who had been vouchsafed a sacred stone vision and who, as a result, claimed that he possessed the associated power to find lost objects.[12]

No accounts of the Lakota imply that the stone-dreamers ever had the capacity to influence the weather as a result of their privileged kinship with the sacred stone people. This ability appears to have been the exclusive prerogative of those who had had a visionary encounter with the thunder-beings. When Black Elk mentioned those times when he believed that he had influenced the weather, he always claimed that this control derived from the powers that either the thunder-beings or the Six Grandfathers had given him.[13] Luther Standing Bear made this same connection between Last Horse's power to dissipate a thunderstorm that threatened to wreck a festive occasion and his close visionary kinship with the thunder-beings.[14]

# Grants Access to the Spirits' Mode of Being

The fourth characteristic of power was its manifestation as a potency that allowed its possessor to accomplish things that it was normally only possible for supernatural beings to do. For example, during his visions, Black Elk often had the same ability to fly through the air that the spirit-messengers and Grandfathers of his Great Vision possessed. The Lakota took it for granted that the possession of spiritual power brought with it the potential to actuate on earth that same fullness of being that prevails in the spirit-world. It was for this reason that the spirits of his Great Vision assured Black Elk, after they had shown him all the creatures of the spirit-

11. Although Black Elk never indicated in either book that he had ever been a stone-dreamer or involved in yuwipi rituals, he apparently got involved in such practices after the Wounded Knee massacre. Several Indian witnesses who knew him just before his conversion to Catholicism stated that he had been known as a yuwipi practitioner. See Steinmetz, *Pipe, Bible, and Peyote,* pp. 157–59.

12. Densmore, *Teton Sioux Music,* p. 210.

13. Neihardt, *Black Elk Speaks,* pp. 132–35, 137, 143, 156, 231–34.

14. Luther Standing Bear, *Land of the Spotted Eagle,* pp. 206–7.

world celebrating a "day of happiness," that this same paradisiacal condition was his to make on earth.[15] Power likewise conferred the same immunity to injury from weapons that supernatural beings enjoyed.[16] Furthermore, when a supernatural personage granted someone its power, this action endowed the recipient with the former's capacities to influence the processes of nature. In general, then, the possession of power was tantamount to possession of the spirits' mode of being.

# Ritually Catalyzed

Power had an important fifth characteristic: it was usually inseparable from those rituals that liberated it. The Sioux assumed that a medicineman or holy man generally could not utilize the power that the spirit-beings had conveyed to him through his vision or dream unless he had obeyed those instructions for manifesting it that they had also given him. This linkage between power and ritual emerges with special clarity in a remark that one of Walker's informants made while he was explaining to him how a shaman or holy man endows an object with supernatural power (*ton*). He told Walker, "A shaman must impart a ton with the right ceremony done in the right manner." In other words, not only must the shaman know which particular ceremony he must perform to endow something with spiritual power, but he must also perform it in the precise way that the spirits of his vision told him to perform it. Not only was it necessary to employ the proper rituals when one endowed an object with power but it was equally necessary to follow the correct ritual procedures when one utilized the power contained in that particular power object (*wasicun*). Hence, Walker's informant added that if one wished to utilize the power in a wasicun one did so by "repeating the correct formula or singing the right song."[17]

Rituals—the invocational formulae, songs, and ceremonies that the supernaturals give the holy man during his vision—form an essential, not merely derivative, element in that process that causes power to become

15. DeMallie, *Sixth Grandfather,* p. 133.

16. This assumption that the possession of spirit power confers immunity to enemy missiles occurs repeatedly in Black Elk's autobiography; see DeMallie, *Sixth Grandfather,* pp. 157, 170, 277–78. The mythical spirit-woman Wohpe claimed immunity to arrows because she was *wakan* (sacred). See Walker, *Lakota Belief,* p. 110.

17. Walker, *Lakota Belief,* pp. 95–96.

manifest. The Lakota assumed that the curative potency of a healer's medicine resided not in the pharmaceutical properties of those herbs or objects that he used but rather in the punctiliousness with which he carried out the power-giving curative rituals that the supernaturals had given him in his vision or dream. George Sword's statement about medicine among the Lakota exhibits this preeminence of ritual considerations over pharmaceutical ones: "When one has a medicine, he must have a song for it. If the wrong song or invocation is used, the medicine will do no good."[18] One can see that with respect to the manifestation of power, rituals play a role analogous to that which catalysts play in chemical reactions. In a chemical transformation, after one has combined all the proper chemicals and brought them to the right temperature, it may still be impossible for that reaction to take place because the catalyst is missing, that is, a substance that facilitates a reaction but that is not altered by it. In applying this chemical analogy to the Lakota phenomenon of power, one observes that even if the spirit-beings have granted the individual numerous powers in a vision, this power lies imprisoned in a latent state unless the recipient also performs the proper rituals that will activate it. Fortunately, not only does the visionary get the gift of power but he also receives instructions of varying degrees of clarity that tell him how to perform those rituals that will release it. Ambiguous instructions from the spirit-beings are interpreted by the tribal elders or a holy man. Such interpretations then become invested with the same binding authority as the less ambiguous instructions.

Black Elk's autobiography contains numerous incidents and statements that attest to the fundamental rather than merely derivative nature of ritual in the process of liberating spiritual power. He informed Neihardt that an individual could not release the power contained in one of his visions until he had performed the ritual of publicly reenacting its events. The Lakota maintain that "the power vision cannot be used until the duty we got with the part of the vision has been performed upon the earth. After that the power may be used."[19] It is clear, then, that rituals of re-enactment formed an integral and essential part of those procedures that liberated the power latent within a vision.

18. Quoted in ibid., p. 91.
19. DeMallie, *Sixth Grandfather,* p. 238. This quotation is one of Enid Neihardt's parenthetical insertions into her transcript of the conversation between Black Elk and her father, John Neihardt. The importance of publicly reenacting a vision in order to utilize its power is also expressed by one of Densmore's informants in *Teton Sioux Music,* p. 157.

When one examines those scenes in the Great Vision where Black Elk exhibited the regenerative effects of his spiritual power, one notices that a similar pattern repeats itself—the moment of revivification always coincides with a ritual act. For example, in one visionary episode Black Elk cured a sickly horse simply by pointing a sacred herb at the sick creature while he circumambulated it on his spirit horse to the accompaniment of the celestial beings' chants for power.[20] This incident incorporated three simultaneous rituals: (1) pointing the herb at the sick horse, (2) circumambulating the sick horse, and (3) chanting of the spirit-beings. It is clear that the cure of the sickly horse had no connection at all with any possible pharmaceutical qualities of the sacred herb because he never fed the herb to the horse or even touched its skin with it. This visionary episode manifested spiritual power because of the ritual acts that took place within it. In other words, the rituals appear to have catalyzed some kind of spiritual transformation that effectuated the healing power that the supernaturals had bestowed on Black Elk in the Great Vision. One can be sure from the context that without these ritual procedures the horse could never have "metabolized," so to speak, the healing power that somehow inhered in both Black Elk and the sacred herb.

During his Dog Vision, Black Elk's behavior similarly proclaimed the spiritual potency and primacy of ritual. Black Elk reenacted his Dog Vision because he wanted to use the power that the thunder-beings had given him to spiritually, physically, and socially regenerate his tribe.[21] This rite of reenacting the Dog Vision, the heyoka ceremony, consisted of two principal parts. The first part involved ritually killing a dog without shedding its blood, a ceremonial offering of the dog's head, spine, and tail to the Six Powers (Grandfathers), and a ritual boiling of its meat including the head, spine, and tail.[22] The second part of the rite duplicated that scene in Black Elk's Dog Vision where two spirit-messengers riding sorrel horses streaked with black lightning designs charged at a dog that was surrounded by a cloud of butterflies and dragonflies and impaled its head on their arrows.

20. DeMallie, *Sixth Grandfather*, p. 132.
21. The Dog Vision is described in DeMallie, *Sixth Grandfather*, pp. 227–32.
22. This ritual of boiling the dog meat was not a reenactment of any particular scene within the Dog Vision but was instead a typical cultic activity of *heyokas* (sacred clowns, men who have had a vision sent to them by the thunder-beings). Since Black Elk had dreamed of thunder-beings and received power from them in the Dog Vision, this made him a member of the cultic association of the heyokas. It was therefore quite natural that the heyoka holy man, who was overseeing Black Elk's reenactment rite, would have thought it fitting to consecrate the dog's flesh in this way.

As each of these spirit-messengers (who represented the Power of the West because of the lightning designs on their horses) impaled the dog's head, the whole western portion of the sky broke into cheering. The climax of the heyoka ceremony consisted of Black Elk and his helper, One Side, mimicking the principal actions of the spirit-messengers when they impaled the dogs' head. Thus Black Elk and One Side rode sorrel horses whose sides were streaked with black lightning designs. They also imitated the spirit-beings' actions by charging at a pot of boiling dog meat with Black Elk spearing the dog's head while One Side skewered the dog's heart.[23] This ritual of impaling the dog's head and heart imbued the dog flesh with the Power of the West. As soon as Black Elk and One Side had skewered the dog, all the people immediately tried to grab some of the ritually consecrated meat. Black Elk explained that everyone clamored for the meat because even the smallest piece of the consecrated meat was like medicine in its power to spiritually and socially regenerate the people.[24] In other words, Black Elk and One Side had endowed the dog meat with supernatural power (*ton*). Their ritual behavior had acted as the catalyst that both activated the latent power in Black Elk as a result of his Dog Vision and directed some of that power into the dog meat. Nothing in Black Elk's description of this reenactment rite implies that the empirical properties of the meat possessed any power-enhancing effect. The sacrality and curative potency of the meat resulted solely from reenacting the instructions and the actions of the spirit-messengers who had shown themselves to Black Elk in his vision. Once again one sees why it is impossible to separate the Lakota phenomenon of spiritual power from the rituals that allow it to be metabolized.

Black Elk never suggested that the rituals had any lesser significance than those affective states (the "queer feeling") that sometimes betokened the presence of power. During his first cure he stated explicitly that his doubts about his ability to cure the boy only dissipated after he had experienced that emotional quickening and the onset of the queer feeling. Nonetheless, even though he certainly thought that that affective state indicated the presence of power, he still performed the medicine rituals without in any way implying that they had been any less essential to the success of his efforts to bring healing power to the child than his own concomitant

23. This particular detail of the reenactment rite diverged from the actual events of the vision insofar as the vision episode did not contain any scene where the spirit-messengers speared the dogs' hearts.
24. DeMallie, *Sixth Grandfather*, pp. 234–35.

affective and mental states.[25] In this regard, Black Elk stood apart from someone like Patañjali, who in 2:29 of his *Yoga-Sūtras* asserted that religious observances (*niyama,* or mutterings, acts of devotion to the Lord, purification, and austerities) were "subservient" to concentration. Assertions of this sort display a spirit completely alien to Black Elk's profound reverence for ritual. They show that Patañjali obviously assigned a lesser soteriological status to rituals than to certain privileged states of consciousness and metaphysical knowledge. This is not to say that Black Elk did not also have a deep regard for visionary experiences, but he never considered, as did Patañjali, that the categories of ritual and religious experience existed in any fundamental opposition to one another. For Patañjali, visionary experiences, states of samādhi, pointed away from ritual toward an ultimate state of transcendence that made all ritual irrelevant. For Black Elk, precisely the opposite held true. Visionary experiences always pointed back to ritual. They were important, not because they transcended rituals and made them irrelevant, but because they generated new rituals. Visions were the seedbeds of those new rituals that would continue to ensure the flow of life-enhancing power into the world.

I opened this analysis of power and ritual by asserting that the Lakota believed that power was inseparable from ritual. Yet one can discover occasional instances where power spontaneously manifested itself without any accompanying ritual having immediately preceded its disclosure. For example, several times before his eighteenth summer Black Elk had premonitions about the presence of either game or enemies and believed that those episodes of clairvoyance indicated that his "power was growing."[26] However, even though he construed those premonitions as manifestations of power, one does not find any evidence that ritual activity immediately preceded them. They appear to have been completely spontaneous events.

It is significant, however, that Black Elk never regarded those adolescent instances of clairvoyance as important. This is surprising, especially when one realizes that these premonitions had saved his band from both starvation and massacre. Nonetheless, for Black Elk, power in its various manifestations only became soteriologically significant—even in those cases where it saved the tribe—when its recipient had fulfilled the obligations that its bestowal required.

What conditions are necessary to fulfill the obligations of a dream or a

25. Ibid., pp. 237–39, 259–65.
26. Ibid., pp. 204–6.

vision? First, the recipient must fulfill his obligations to the supernaturals who gave him his power by obeying their wishes in his vision. Second, he must fulfill those obligations toward his people that the power-bestowing vision also imposed upon him. This usually means publicly reenacting one's vision, consulting with the elders or a holy man about its meaning and the obligations it brings, or healing the sick when one is asked.

In the foregoing analysis I established that the phenomenon of power, as the holy men and medicinemen of the Lakota have described it, possessed five principal attributes: (1) it was a peculiar kind of potency that came to an individual not from an intrapsychic source within in his own mind but rather from various kinds of spirit-beings; (2) it was only granted to someone by spirit-beings in a vision, a wakan dream, or as a result of an individual's successful participation in certain rituals like the Sun Dance; (3) it tended to be compartmentalized, that is, the manner of its manifestation tended to be delimited in accordance with the mythological attributes of that spirit-being that bestowed it; (4) it allowed its possessor to accomplish those things that it was normally only possible for spirit-beings to do; and (5) it required specific rituals in order to become manifest. Furthermore, the presence of power was often, but by no means always, accompanied by peculiar sensations of emotional quickening which Black Elk called the "queer feeling."

This delineation of the attributes of power permits an answer to the question, What was power to the Lakota? The Lakota spoke of a human being as having power whenever he came into possession of one or more of those sundry potencies—usually made manifest only by the performance of specific rituals—that spirit-beings sometimes granted to individuals, which enabled the recipients to share some of the particular capacities of the spirits; participate, to some extent, in the spirits' particular manner of behavior and way of life; and have a privileged access to them in time of need.[27] This definition stresses both the compartmentalized nature of Lakota power as well as its close association with ritual. Thus it is somewhat erroneous to refer to power in the singular. Power did not really

27. These capacities, the specific character of which depended on the nature of the particular spirit that had granted it, included the power to heal or otherwise foster those processes that either create new life or else infuse it with greater vitality, an immunity from enemy weapons, clairvoyance, the ability to affect natural phenomena such as thunderstorms, the ability to communicate intelligently with spirits and animals as though they were human, the capacity for ex-static flight, and the supernormal ability to locate game or lost objects.

exist in the generic sense for the Lakota because, even when one of their medicinemen or holy men would say that he "had power" it was understood that he was not referring to power in general but rather to a power granted by a specific spirit-being and usable only for a comparatively restricted number of purposes or situations. As a result, power was not a universal potency that, once acquired, allowed its possessor to direct it in any way that he desired.

# Notions of Spiritual Power in Other Religious Traditions

These extensive observations about the phenomenon of power in the mystical experiences of the Lakota point to some fundamental differences that distinguish it from analogous manifestations in other mystical traditions. For example, in neither the folklore and mythology about the medicinemen and holy men nor in their autobiographies does one ever find occasions where the Lakota credited these individuals with anything analogous to that power to create quasi-tangible, collectively perceptible projections of one's thoughts (*tulpas*) or mentally directed telekinetic phenomena such as Monroe's "astral pinch."[28] I suggest that stories about such prodigies that result from acts of intense mental concentration seem alien to the Lakota religious imagination because of a basic supposition that undergirded their religious universe. Unlike the yogin, who attributes his powers to his heroic efforts of mind control, the Lakota medicineman or holy man claimed that whatever power he possessed only came to him as a gift from some spirit-being. In other words, the Lakota take it for granted that mental concentration, in and of itself, does not lead to the acquisition of power. They do practice mental concentration techniques when they embark on a vision quest but they also assume that the power bestowed in a vision originates extrapsychically, that is, from outside the human psyche, as a gift received from that particular spirit-being who responded to the

28. Monroe, *Journeys Out of the Body*, pp. 55–57. Poltergeist phenomena do sometimes appear during yuwipi rituals but it is significant that the Sioux do not attribute these manifestations to the mental operations of the medicineman. Instead, they attribute those phenomena to autonomous spirit-beings who, at their pleasure, may decide to make their presence known in such a fashion. See Lame Deer and Erdoes, *Lame Deer*, pp. 194–96.

visionary's plea.[29] According to the Lakota, the mental concentration techniques prepare the vision-seeker to receive power but they do not guarantee that he will actually get it. Whether or not the seeker actually obtains that power depends entirely upon whether or not some spirit-being wishes to give it to him.

This assumption that power does not directly originate from the act of mental concentration itself causes the Lakota to react passively to their visionary experiences while they are occurring. Thus, although it is true that they actively seek visions, they are not interested in manipulating the content of those visions while they are in the process of experiencing them. One does not find in Lakota mysticism any phenomenon that is akin to the process of empowerment *(enthymesis)*. For example, it is evident that Black Elk never attempted to manipulate the content of his Great Vision. Instead, his attitude resembled that of an awestruck student who eagerly tries to remember his teacher's every word or instruction. One can say the same thing about Goose and his vision of the sacred stone. He, too, centered his attention on listening to what the spirits told him to do. Nowhere does his narrative suggest that he tried to control the content of his vision. Instead of controlling the direction or flow of a visionary experience while it is in progress (as occurs in what I have called in Chapter 12 the "active approach"), the Lakota visionary responds to his vision in a much simpler fashion. Since the revelation is the gift of an intelligent, sentient spirit-being with feelings and desires who, like any other human being, gives gifts when he is pleased and obeyed and withholds them when he is displeased or disobeyed, the vision-seeker must obey what the spirit requested in the vision. Consequently, when a vision-seeker attains success in his

29. The Lakota do state that mental concentration plays an important role in the vision quest. Thus Black Elk told Brown that when a vision-seeker prays it is not always necessary that he do so aloud. He may, if he chooses, "remain silent *with his whole attention directed to the Great Spirit* or one of his Powers. He must always be careful lest distracting thoughts come to him, yet he must be able to recognize any messenger that the Great Spirit may send to him" (quoted from Brown, *Sacred Pipe,* p. 58 [emphasis mine]). Walker's informant, George Sword, likewise emphasized that mental concentration was an integral part of the vision quest. He states that one who desires a vision must, among other things, take a sweat bath to purify himself "and then remain alone as much as possible, thinking continually of that about which he desires a vision" (quoted from Walker, *Lakota Belief,* p. 79). See also Siya'ka's instructions in Densmore, *Teton Sioux Music,* p. 184. The importance of mental concentration as a preparatory measure must not obscure the fact that once the vision appears the seeker always remains the passive recipient who obediently follows what he has been told to do by the spirit-beings of his vision. Unlike those followers of Tantric Buddhism who practice "visualization" techniques, the Lakota holy man or medicineman does not attempt to control the content of the vision while it is in progress.

quest, his primary concern remains that of following those instructions that he received in his vision.

The compartmentalized and ritually catalyzed character of Lakota power sharply differentiates it from the more plastic and transmutable kinds of spiritual potencies one often encounters in the mystical traditions of other cultures. For example, when the practitioner of Patañjali's Yoga or individuals like Matthew Manning and Robert Monroe speak about the kinds of supernormal "energy" or "force" that they possess, they describe it as an easily transmutable type of potency capable of undergoing a theoretically limitless number of metamorphoses. Each of these metamorphoses derives its distinctive character from either the object on which they have concentrated their mental attention or the particular manner in which they have focused it. For example, when Monroe's thoughts had become "empowered" he possessed a kind of psychical energy that could manifest itself in a variety of ways depending on which object he chose to focus his mind. Thus, if he thought about visiting Dr. Bradshaw in that state of mind, the energy of his empowered mind projected him into Bradshaw's presence. If, on the other hand, he thought about pinching R.W. on the thigh, then this same psychical energy manifested itself in the form of black and blue marks on her body.[30] Each of these different phenomena, as distinct as they were from each other, represented nothing more than one of those possible changes of state that this "empowered" psychic energy could undergo.

In this context Matthew Manning's "power" to generate poltergeist disturbances exhibited a similar transformability. He observed that the same kind of supernormal psychic energy that produced poltergeists could be rechanneled, by a peculiar effort of the will, into other forms of manifestation. "Automatic writing appeared to be the most successful method of controlling or preventing the poltergeist phenomena, and if it looked as though disturbances were imminent, I would sit down and write [automatically]. . . . It appeared to me that the energy I had used for writing had previously been used for causing poltergeist disturbances."[31] He later discovered, however, that if he got into a state where he was almost ready to do automatic writing but did not do so, he would sometimes see auras.[32] Manning's account suggests, then, that the direction and intensity of his mental concentration, once he was in the poltergeist-producing condition,

30. Monroe, *Journeys Out of the Body*, pp. 55–57.
31. Manning, *The Link*, p. 77.
32. Ibid., pp. 77–78.

determined the various ways that a common underlying spiritual potency could manifest itself.

The practice of restraint (*saṃyama*) described in Patañjali's system of Yoga implied a similar kind of easily deformable psychic potency manifesting itself in accordance with the particular object on which the yogin had focused his mind. In each of these examples different forms of power or spiritual force existed as a kind of energy or potency that possessed a remarkable degree of plasticity and deformability. In each instance, the subject's mind could mold the way power manifested itself. Power was deformable in an open-ended way and easily converted from one form of manifestation into another in a manner analogous to the "energy" of modern physics.

The compartmentalized and ritually catalyzed nature of Lakota power prevented it from exhibiting that convertability noted in the examples above. One of Densmore's informants made a remark that clarifies this contrast:

> A medicineman usually treated only one special disease and treated it successfully. He did this in accordance with his dream. A medicineman would not try to dream of all herbs and treat all diseases, for then he could not expect to succeed in all nor to fulfill properly the dream of any one herb or animal. He would depend on too many and fail in all. That is one reason why our medicinemen lost their power when so many diseases came among us with the advent of the white man.[33]

This quotation reveals an intellectual universe very different from that of Monroe, Manning, Patañjali, or indeed most of the other mystics examined thus far because it is one where the theoretically infinite transmutability of spiritual power was almost inconceivable. According to Densmore's informant, power is thoroughly compartmentalized. Each particular healing power was derived from the specific dream or vision that conveyed it. Consequently, to have had the general power to treat all diseases or a great number of them would have first required a correspondingly large number of power-giving visions or dreams. Second, since each particular healing power also required that one fulfill the ritual obligations of that dream or vision that had bestowed it, if one had the power to treat numerous diseases, one's ritual obligations would have had to have been

33. Densmore, *Teton Sioux Music*, pp. 244–45.

correspondingly burdensome and time-consuming. For these reasons, Densmore's informant took it for granted that spiritual power was intrinsically particularized and therefore not transformable from one mode of manifestation into another.

For the Lakota, power was like a computer program one received from a spirit-being. Like a computer program, this gift of power could only exert its effects in a restricted number of ways provided that one abided by certain rules (the rituals) that governed how one could insert information into the computer. Power was therefore something one received prepackaged from the spirit-beings and was only usable if one followed certain rather complex rules that allowed it to become manifest. The kinds of power that Manning, Monroe, and Patañjali referred to, on the other hand, suggest an analogy with the energy of modern physics. Like the energy of physics, each of these different kinds of spiritual power was a potency capable of a variety of different transformations. Each of these different kinds of spiritual energy developed its particular transformations indifferent to the ritual dimension of human existence. It was by manipulating mental processes and not by performing rituals that one created the various transmutations of spiritual power.

# 20

# Black Elk's Criteria of Discernment

Black Elk did not attribute religious significance indiscriminately to all forms of ex-static or supernormal experience. While it was true that he regarded some of his visions with great reverence, it was also true that there were others that he regarded with considerable indifference. The following ex-static episode is an example of an insignificant visionary experience.

One day in 1889, during his stay in Europe Black Elk suddenly went into a state of ex-static catalepsy similar to that which he experienced at the beginning of his Great Vision. All of a sudden the whole house he was in seemed to rise very fast into the air, swirling as it did so. A cloud then came down, Black Elk got on the cloud, and, in the spirit, left the other people he had been eating with down below. Far below him, he could see the houses, towns, green lands, and even the Atlantic Ocean itself passing quickly as he traveled over them. He continued westward until he saw the Black Hills from the air as well as that peak that had been the "center of the world" in his Great Vision. The cloud then stopped. Below him he saw his mother inside the family tipi amid a large gathering of all the different bands of his tribe. (He could not understand why all those different bands of his people were gathered together at that time since there was apparently no ceremonial reason for them to be assembled.) Although Black Elk wanted to get off his cloud and visit her, he did not do so because he feared that if he did he would die. At this moment, the cloud started to tug him back to it. He quickly traced his journey in reverse and soon found himself whirling down into a room where he lay on his back in a bed with a coffin beside him. His catalepsy had been so deep that his companions thought he had died. Black Elk regained consciousness without further incident.[1]

1. DeMallie, *Sixth Grandfather*, pp. 252–53.

Black Elk claimed that this particular ex-static journey gave him true information about what had been going on at his home when he had been transported there. The crowds of Indians from different bands had gathered at Pine Ridge to conclude the treaty of 1889 and his parents had camped in the exact place where he had seen them from his vantage point on the cloud.[2] Yet, despite certain parallels between this particular spirit-journey and his Great Vision (the premonitory catalepsy, the condition of ex-stasis, traveling on a cloud), Black Elk never implied that this specific episode had any religious or practical significance. Unlike his Great Vision, he never felt compelled to respond to it in any way. It merely conveyed a few bits of purportedly veridical information to him (just as Monroe's visit to Bradshaw had done) but that was the full extent of its impact on his life. Black Elk summed up its essential insignificance when he declared that during his entire stay in Europe the spirits had utterly forgotten him, his power was gone, and he felt as if he had been a dead man.[3]

Why did Black Elk regard this particular experience as religiously and existentially irrelevant? To answer this question, one must juxtapose the Great Vision with the insignificant one just narrated. In sharp contrast to the Great Vision, the irrelevant experience did not contain any type of communication from spirit-beings. Nowhere in the numerous Lakota accounts of visionary experiences does one find any examples of visions that compelled a response from their recipients where there was not some sort of communication between the spirit-beings and humans. Indeed, among the Lakota, the word for holy dream or vision (*wowihanble*) stresses the communicatory aspect of such experiences rather than their supernormal aspect. George Sword explained to Walker that wowihanble meant something "told to a man by something that is not a man. . . . God tells his will to man by *wowihanble*. . . . A vision is something told by a *wakan* being. . . . The *wakan* beings are the superior beings, that is, they are superior to ordinary mankind. They know what is past and present and what will be."[4] Sword's definitions of wowihanble clearly indicate that what the Lakota considered most important about holy dreams and visions was not the supernormal, veridical, or metaphysical information that they might convey but rather the messages that the supernaturals brought to the recipient. For this reason, Lakota mysticism never became, as did yoga, a quest after some radical detachment from involvement in the multiplicities of the phe-

2. Ibid., pp. 254–55.
3. Ibid., p. 294, and also p. 256.
4. Quoted in Walker, *Lakota Belief,* p. 84.

nomenal world. Lakota mysticism did not become, as did Robert Monroe's "secularized" and somewhat "technocratic" responses to his ex-static experiences, a quest for scientifically verifiable evidence that man in fact possessed supernormal powers, a conscious existence after death, or a hitherto unsuspected psychophysical energy that he could learn to manipulate in order to change the state of matter.[5] Instead, the primary focus of Lakota mysticism centered on the task of either obeying or fulfilling those messages that the spirit-beings gave in visions where they instructed the recipients about the proper rituals that they must use to acquire spiritual power, heal the sick, ensure the success of the hunt, or else ensure the overall well-being of the tribe. It is clear, then, that dreams or visions that failed to incorporate such supernatural messages could never possess any religious or existential significance no matter what other features they might possess.

The presence of some kind of communication from a spirit-being did not necessarily guarantee that a vision was important. Among the Lakota, important visions not only incorporated messages from the supernatural beings to human beings but they also contained either explicit ritual instructions for acquiring particular types of power that the recipient was expected to obey or displayed the supernatural beings engaging in some sort of ritual behavior that it was tacitly understood the recipient would try to imitate ritually on earth. The following episode provides an example of an "unimportant" visionary communication from a spirit-being. In this particular instance, Black Elk and his band were on the verge of death from starvation and extreme cold and desperately needed to locate some buffalo. One night, as he was getting ready to sleep, Black Elk heard a coyote begin to howl nearby and then hear a voice say to him, "Two-legged man, on this ridge west of you over there are buffalo. Beforehand, you shall see two two-legged people."[6] This visionary communication actually turned out to be an accurate premonition for Black Elk; his father subsequently did find bison on the west ridge exactly as the coyote had described and encountered two other starving Indians just before he made the discovery of the bison—another confirmation of the accuracy of the coyote's words. By Lakota standards, however, this clairvoyant episode was religiously insignificant because, even though the information saved his band from probable starvation, its significance did not extend beyond

5. Monroe, *Journeys Out of the Body*, pp. 263–73.
6. DeMallie, *Sixth Grandfather*, p. 208.

this immediate situation. When one contrasts this unimportant episode with those visions that Black Elk valued highly, such as the Great Vision, the Dog Vision, and the Ghost Dance visions, one notices that the latter category of visions has neither pragmatic utility nor veridicality. Their significance instead derived from the songs or chants that the spirit-beings gave Black Elk, or else from the rituals that they told him to perform, or else from certain actions that the supernaturals performed, which Black Elk was subsequently expected to reenact.

For the Lakota, "important" visions must have three essential characteristics. First, they must contain communications from spirit-beings. Second, the spirit-beings must convey, by means of such visions, essential ritual information that allows the recipient access to spiritual power. The third characteristic that made a vision important was its validation by the community, which took place in three ways: (1) the public reenactment of the vision, (2) the preparation, interpretation, and specific character of one's response to the vision had to be supervised by a holy man or a council of elders, and (3) the insistence that only those who fulfilled the highest ethical ideals of the community could possibly become the recipients of worthwhile visions. With regard to the fundamental significance of public reenactment, Black Elk leaves us no doubt, for he told Neihardt unequivocally, that no one could use the power of his vision until he had first performed it on earth for everyone to see.[7] Without this type of communal validation via public reenactment, the holy man or medicineman cannot liberate spiritual power; without this liberation of spiritual power, no vision can be truly significant.

Black Elk was not the only individual among the Lakota who stressed how important it was for the community to validate visionary experiences. Brave Buffalo, one of the most powerful medicinemen on the Standing Rock reservation at the time Densmore did her research, agreed with Black Elk that public reenactment was essential, for he told her that "it is a very strict requirement that a medicineman shall act out his dream."[8] The assumption that sharing a vision with someone else was somehow essentially related to the process of liberating its power was also implicit in a practice that another of Densmore's informants recorded. Used-as-a-Shield told her that one time in the past when he had been sick, he had solicited the services of a medicineman. As part of the healing ceremony, the medicine-

7. Ibid., p. 238.
8. Densmore, *Teton Sioux Music,* p. 248.

man shared with Used-as-a-Shield the details of the dream through which
he had gotten his healing powers.[9]

Each of these three examples exposes an important premise of Lakota
religious thought and mysticism, namely, the presupposition that the liberation of visionary power required something more than just individual effort—it also required that the entire community or some other individual
than the subject must vicariously share that power-giving revelation that
the vision contained. The idea that spiritual power could only become
manifest if the mystic publicly reenacted the vision or dream that conveyed
it formed one more extension, at the level of religious practice, of a Lakota
ethical and religious ideal of generosity that played a prominent role in
their social behavior. The tremendous social and religious value they accorded to this virtue seems to have had its origins in the exigencies of their
nomadic hunting and warring lifestyle. First, since they were nomads, the
Lakota had no need for hoarding possessions, so there was little or no
inclination for them to encourage thrift or acquisitiveness. In fact, the one
among them who dared to hoard possessions such as horses was despised
and could not hope to rise in social prominence.[10] Second, because they
were nomadic hunters and subject to the cycles of feast and famine, there
was great pressure on the Lakota to develop an ethos that stressed the duty
of sharing one's kill equally with all of one's fellow tribe members, for one
never knew when either oneself or one's family might some day be in
desperate need of aid from someone with better luck at the hunt. Concerning the custom that had prevailed in his earlier pre-reservation years, Luther Standing Bear noted:

> When food was brought into the village, the sharing must be equal
> for old, young, sick, disabled, and those who did not or could not
> hunt as well as those who hunted. There must be no hungry indi-
> viduals. . . . All shared food as long as there was any to share. If a
> hunter disobeyed the custom of sharing and was caught making
> away with game, he was severely punished by the Fox Lodge.[11]

Third, the frequency of war and the catastrophic consequences that resulted from losing a battle or skirmish, immediate death or torture from
the enemy, or starvation from the destruction of one's shelter and food-

9. Ibid., p. 247.
10. Hassrick, *Sioux*, pp. 256–57.
11. Luther Standing Bear, *Land of the Spotted Eagle*, p. 69.

stuffs made the Lakota value another kind of generosity—generosity that the warrior exhibits when he willingly sacrifices his life to ensure the safety and well-being of his people.

This willingness to share all of one's possessions with others was far more than just an ethical ideal among the Lakota. It was also a religious ideal as well. Just as the Lakota despised those who hoarded their possessions but greatly respected one who was generous in giving them away, they similarly made it a practice when they individually supplicated the spirit-beings for power not just for themselves but also for the benefit of all their fellow tribemembers—as well as their nonhuman relatives. In fact, they seem to have taken it for granted that religious acts of generosity and self-sacrifice were much more likely to elicit a favorable response from the supernaturals. For example, Black Horse donated pieces of flesh from his own forearms and thighs to the supernaturals to help ensure that the thunder-beings would visit him during his vision quest.[12] Lame Deer's mother did the same for him when he embarked on his first vision quest.[13]

The redemptive and power-giving efficacy of generosity also comes across in some examples that Black Elk described. In Black Elk's rendition of the myth of the first Sun Dance, one of the female participants in the ceremony proclaimed, "I will offer one piece of my flesh to *Wakan-Tanka* and for all moving things of the universe that they may give their powers to the people, that they with their children may walk the red path of life."[14] He emphasizes that great visions do not only bring the individuals who experience them spiritual power but they also "give strength and health to our nation."[15] Even that essential part of every Lakota's attempts to establish communication with the spirit-world, the act of smoking the sacred pipe, is depicted as a supplication that he makes on behalf of all created things. Consequently, in the myth of how the sacred pipe came to them, the White Buffalo Cow Woman told the assembled crowd that "all the things of the universe are joined to you who smoke the pipe—all send their voices to *Wakan-Tanka*. . . . When you pray with this pipe, you pray with and for everything."[16] It is also significant that White Buffalo Cow Woman made a reference to the spiritual potency of another rite that she taught the people,

12. Hassrick, *Sioux*, p. 233.
13. Lame Deer and Erdoes, *Lame Deer*, p. 13.
14. Brown, *Sacred Pipe*, p. 86.
15. Ibid., p. 44.
16. Ibid., pp. 6–7.

the ritual of soul-keeping. "It should be a sacred day when one of your people dies," she told them. "You must then keep his soul as I shall teach you and through this you will gain much power."[17] Implicit in her statement was the assumption that a religious act of sharing liberates spiritual power because, more than any other religious ritual practiced among the Lakota, the soul-keeping ceremonial involved the acquisition of power by means of an act of exceptional generosity: the family of the deceased individual had to spend at least a year making and collecting goods that they then gave away at the time the soul was ceremonially released. In fact, the couple who undertook this commitment usually ended up giving away everything that they owned.

I suggest that Black Elk's assumption that he had to publicly reenact his vision if he wished to utilize its power seems closely related to other ritual contexts in which the acquisition of spiritual power remained similarly dependent on a ceremonial proclamation or actual demonstration of the visionary's intent to share his blessings with his fellow tribemembers and his nonhuman relatives. In other words, by publicly reenacting his vision, Black Elk had incorporated into his response to his experience one of the most important elements of that nomadic hunting ethos that his tribemembers were supposed to practice in everyday life: generosity.

The community could also validate the significance of a visionary's experience in more indirect ways. In lieu of a public reenactment before the assembled tribe or band, it was often sufficient to tell one's vision to a holy man, a group of elders, or else to an assembly of those who had had the same kind of experience. They would then interpret the vision and instruct the individual on how he should correctly respond to it. (Even the highly individualistic Lakota did not leave the interpretation and response to visions up to the whim of the recipient.) After all, since visions and the beneficial power that they brought into the human world were of great importance to both the individual and his community, it was only fitting that the community would evolve methods of ensuring that the mystic properly interpreted and responded to those communications that he received from the supernaturals. One way of ensuring this was to develop a system of procedures where the representatives of the community, such as the holy man or a group of elders, would have a decisive say in interpreting the visions.

Black Horse's manner of responding to his vision from the thunder-

17. Ibid., p. 8.

beings stands as an example of how it was not always necessary to publicly reenact one's vision in order to obtain community approbation. Instead, when he had his thunder vision (which was very similar in structure and content to Black Elk's Great Vision), he did not feel the need to reenact it publicly as Black Elk had done but rather he simply proceeded to the dwelling of the holy man who had supervised his preparations for his vision quest. Both men then went to a sweat lodge where they met with an assembly of others who had also dreamed of or had visions of thunderbeings. After Black Horse and the others had purified themselves in the lodge, he shared with his mentor and the others the details of his vision. His mentor subsequently interpreted his vision for him and told him how he must respond to it.[18]

Black Elk also underscored the vital importance of seeking the advice of a holy man. Thus he declared unequivocally, "It is very important for a person who wishes to 'lament' [seek a vision] to receive aid and advice from a *wicasa wakan* so that everything is done correctly, for if things are not done in the right way, something very bad can happen."[19] Black Elk practiced what he preached, for whenever he had a vision that he thought might be significant, he sought out the advice of a holy man or a group of his peers about how he should respond to it. George Sword confirmed Black Elk's statement for he, too, mentioned that the more important a vision was, the more important it was to seek out the advice and assistance of a holy man. Sword told Walker that "if the vision desired is concerning a matter of much importance, a shaman [*wicasa wakan*] should supervise all the ceremony relative to it . . . if it is of very great importance there should be much ceremony."[20] These remarks indicate that, for the Lakota, important visions—at least those that were deliberately sought rather than spontaneous—were highly structured experiences that involved considerable advance preparation of the candidate by a wicasa wakan. These preparations created a set of expectations that the subsequent visionary experiences tended to fulfill. Thus it is not surprising that when Black Horse went on a vision quest in which he was aided in his preparations by a holy man who had had visions of thunder-beings, he likewise had a vision in which the thunder-beings visited him.[21] Furthermore, with both the deliberately sought and the spontaneous visions, it is evident that both the mys-

18. Hassrick, *Sioux*, p. 236.
19. Brown, *Sacred Pipe*, pp. 44–45.
20. Walker, *Lakota Belief*, p. 79.
21. Hassrick, *Sioux*, pp. 232–36.

tics' interpretations of the experiences and their ways of otherwise responding to them were similarly structured in accordance with the interpretations and instructions that they had received from the holy men and
other members of the community who claimed to have been knowledgeable about visions. In any case, there is no record of any important Lakota
visionary experience being either interpreted or responded to in any other
manner where the recipient failed to consult such individuals for their advice.

This insistence that the community must exert control over religiously
significant visionary experiences reflects the practices that the Lakota followed in the most important rituals. For example, the most sacred rite, the
Sun Dance, was from its start to finish a ceremony whose details were
subject to the control of the holy man who was in charge of not only
conducting the preparations for it but also the actual conduct of the ritual
itself in much the same way that a holy man might supervise both the
preparations and the interpretations of a young man's vision quest.[22]

As already mentioned, the community insisted that religiously significant
communications from the supernaturals could only come to those individuals who embodied its highest moral virtues. Black Elk acknowledged this
when he stated, "What is received through 'lamenting' [seeking a vision] is
determined in part by the character of the person who does this, for it is
only those people who are very qualified who receive the great visions . . .
which give strength and health to our nation."[23] Black Elk's assertion indicates that great visions must possess at least two characteristics: the individuals who have them must be morally upright and they must benefit the
community as a whole. Brave Buffalo also insisted that moral virtue was
an important concomitant of a visionary's life. He told Densmore, "It is a
very strict requirement that a medicineman shall act out his dream and
that he maintain absolute integrity of character. If he fails to do this he
will be punished and will not live long."[24]

This insistence that the character of visionary communications depended
on the moral character of the person who had experienced them had its
counterpart at the level of ritual and myth. For example, in both
Densmore's and Black Elk's versions of the coming of the sacred pipe,
White Buffalo Cow Woman strongly implied that the efficacy of smoking
the pipe depended on the moral character of the individual or individuals

22. Walker, "Sun Dance," p. 121.
23. Brown, Sacred Pipe, p. 44.
24. Densmore, Teton Sioux Music, p. 248.

who smoked it and the group's willingness to punish and expel wrong-doers.[25] The Lakota assumed that the Sun Dance could not achieve its purpose of effectively sending the peoples' voices to Wakan-Tanka unless the festival grounds were first cleared of morally reprehensible or ritually unclean individuals. Consequently, when the individual in charge of establishing the final ceremonial camp was about to begin setting it up, he made it a practice to proclaim that anyone knowing himself to be unworthy to appear before the sun must leave the camp circle. Furthermore, if the day were cloudy the supervisor automatically assumed that the sun was hiding himself because of his anger at someone's unworthiness. This would then lead to a repeated demand that morally reprehensible individuals leave the ceremonial grounds.[26] Densmore recounted that the two principal individuals who directed the Sun Dance and the preparations for it, the Intercessor and the Leader of the Dancers, had to be of absolutely untarnished moral character, otherwise the ritual would be rendered ineffective. Red Bird told her that "the tribe would never appoint an unworthy man to the office of Intercessor. In his prayers and offerings he represented the people and if he were not a good man *Wakan-Tanka* might not answer his petitions . . . he might even send disaster to the tribe." Another of Densmore's informants, Chased-by-Bears, corroborated Red Bird's assertion, declaring that "no man who had committed a great wrong could act as Intercessor, no matter how fully he had repented. The record of an Intercessor must be absolutely without blemish."[27] This assumption that moral or ritual impurity angered the spirit-beings and caused them to become unwilling to communicate with human beings in a socially beneficial way formed one of the basic religious premises of the Lakota. Visions from men or women of low moral character could never possess significance.

A fourth factor that determined the significance of a vision was the recipient's fidelity to the commands, instructions, or ritual procedures that the spirit-beings had given him. As Sword put it, "When one seeks a vision and receives a communication, he must obey as he is told to do so. If he does not, all the superior beings will be against him."[28] Densmore's observations concurred with those of Sword: "No one attempted to treat the sick unless he had received a dream telling him to do so, and no one ever

25. Ibid., p. 65; Brown, *Sacred Pipe*, p. 5.
26. Walker, "Sun Dance," p. 100.
27. Densmore, *Teton Sioux Music*, p. 102.
28. Quoted in Walker, *Lakota Belief*, p. 85.

disregarded the obligations of such a dream."[29] Implicit in these statements was the Lakota assumption that in visionary communications the supernaturals had actually talked to humans. It followed logically that to disobey, ignore, or forget what such a supernatural person had said was tantamount to insulting it or showing it contempt and was certain to make it angry at the individual who had done so. For this reason, Lakota visionaries—and this was certainly true of Black Elk—always took the utmost care to remember what the spirit-beings had said to them during their visions and carry out faithfully what the supernaturals had told them to do. Even if the mystic's failure to obey the directives he received in his vision or wakan dream did not cause the spirits to get angry, his forgetfulness of songs, chants, or ritual instructions would certainly vitiate the effectiveness of that power that the spirits had transmitted to him.

The fifth factor that helped to determine the value or importance of a vision was the type of spirit-being that communicated through it or the presence in it of symbols or motifs that appeared prominently in the major Lakota rituals. In other words, certain animals, supernaturals, and symbols were more important than others. Visions or wakan dreams about thunder-beings or their animal representatives (such as black horses coming out of the west with manes of lightning, swallows) were always regarded as significant.[30] In this regard the two most important of Black Elk's visions, his Great Vision and his Dog Vision, were experiences that involved the thunder-beings or their representatives. Visions of sacred stones constituted another category of religiously and socially significant experiences since the Lakota maintained that the curative powers of stone-dreamers possessed exceptional potency. Certain categories of animal visions also seemed to be regarded as especially significant since some animals like the bear and the wolf were supposed to convey useful powers. For example, the Lakota associated bears with those particular forms of healing powers most useful in curing wounded warriors, that is, the power to heal wounds and fractures, and they particularly valued visions and wakan dreams where bears spoke to humans.[31] Visions and dreams about wolves were valued because wolves were often associated with exceptional powers to locate game and deceive enemies.[32]

Visions of animals also possessed a secondary significance insofar as

29. Densmore, *Teton Sioux Music,* p. 244.
30. Ibid., p. 157.
31. See Hassrick, *Sioux,* p. 251; and DeMallie, *Sixth Grandfather,* pp. 178–79.
32. Walker, *Lakota Belief,* p. 160; and Densmore, *Teton Sioux Music,* pp. 179–83.

they determined which dream society one could join. It was the custom among the Lakota that dreamers or visionaries of a certain animal formed a cultic association composed only of those who had had the same kind of vision or wakan dream. These dream societies appear to have been cultic associations whose chief function was to instruct the dreamer or visionary on how to practice the rituals associated with the liberation of that specific spiritual power they had each been given by the particular animal that formed the object of their cult. Thunder Bear told Walker that "if the vision pertains to a particular kind or class of medicine, as, for instance, Bear medicine, he must become the pupil of some Bear medicineman and learn what the medicines are, how to prepare them, how to administer them, and the songs and ceremonies that pertain to them."[33] Thunder Bear's statement shows that it was not an invariable rule that the instructions a holy man or medicineman received concerning the specific medicines he should use, the details of their preparation, and so forth came only from the supernaturals he "saw" or "heard" in his vision or wakan dream. Apparently, each dream society could, and often did, supplement the instructions received in a vision with a repertoire of procedures that had become traditional among their members. Thunder Bear's statement also demonstrates that these dream associations functioned as one more agency that enabled Lakota society to exert some sort of control over the mystic's response to his vision. At least with respect to Bear dreamers and visionaries, the mystic did not respond to his dream or vision in a purely individualistic way—by doing only those things that the bears in his particular vision or dream had told him to do. Instead, the traditions handed down through the dream association to each of its members operated so as to stereotype their responses to their visions and wakan dreams.[34] It would be wrong, therefore, to exaggerate the individualistic element in Lakota mysticism.

The presence of certain "traditional" ritual and mythological motifs and symbols in a visionary experience also helped to invest it with greater significance. This seemed to be especially true of that vision that Black Elk

33. Walker, *Lakota Belief,* p. 132.

34. One must not confuse the dream societies or associations with the more socially prominent military societies. Membership in the latter did not depend on having a vision of a certain kind or having a vision at all but was usually the result of invitation based on one's social status or acts of exceptional bravery. It is significant, though, that every military society originated from the instructions some individual had received from a supernatural being that had appeared to him in a vision or wakan dream. See Wissler, "Societies and Ceremonial Associations," p. 62.

himself called his Great Vision. For example, one recurrent motif in the Great Vision had its counterpart in that most important myth of the Lakota, the story of how they first received the sacred pipe from White Buffalo Cow Woman. In this myth, White Buffalo Cow Woman not only became the bearer of a great spiritual gift but she also underwent a metamorphosis in which she changed from a human being into a buffalo. Several episodes in the Great Vision incorporated similar metamorphoses in which a spirit-being, either immediately prior to or subsequent to the presentation of a gift, changed from a human form into an animal form. Four of the Six Grandfathers changed from human to animal form just after they had given Black Elk their respective gifts of spiritual power. Twice in the Great Vision a mysterious masculine figure is present, the sacred man painted red, who even more strongly suggests a parallel with the White Buffalo Cow Woman.[35] This sacred red man also rolled on the ground and transformed himself into a buffalo. In another episode of the Great Vision, this metamorphosis was immediately followed by the growth of that sacred four-rayed herb that was later to play such an important role in Black Elk's first cure.

Not only were there parallels between vision and myth but there were also parallels between the Great Vision and the Sun Dance ritual. For example, one of the symbols so prominent in the Sun Dance also appeared in the Great Vision, namely, the sacred cottonwood pole that holds up the Sun Dance lodge. In the Great Vision, the sacred flowering stick that Black Elk received from the fourth Grandfather and with which he revived a village in the throes of pestilence was a cottonwood stick that functioned similarly to the cottonwood pole of the Sun Dance lodge. When the spirits who accompanied Black Elk in his Great Vision planted this stick in the center of the nation's hoop (the Sun Dance lodge was also considered to be the center of the nation's hoop while that ceremony was in progress), it came to life and sheltered all of humankind and all of the animal kingdom under its branches.[36] The symbolic connection between this sacred cottonwood stick of Black Elk's vision and the cottonwood Sun Dance pole becomes even more obvious when one remembers that Black Elk explicitly identified the stick he was carrying in his vision as a *waga chun* (cottonwood). In both situations the sacred cottonwood stick or pole functioned as a symbol that stood in the center of the nation's hoop and likewise

---

35. Brown, *Sacred Pipe*, p. 9.
36. DeMallie, *Sixth Grandfather*, p. 139, and also p. 122.

functioned as a symbol of cosmic renewal.[37] It is difficult to imagine how a vision incorporating symbols of such great religious significance to the Lakota could have been regarded indifferently.

The relevance of a vision to the public welfare constituted a sixth, and very important, criterion that helped to determine its religious and existential value. Black Elk explicitly stated that one of the things that made a vision great was its capacity to "give strength and health to our nation."[38] When he spoke about his own Great Vision, he repeatedly stressed that one of the most important things about it was that it served as a source of supernatural power that would enable him to heal individuals but, even more important, would also enable him to lead his people down the good red road of his vision as their intercessor with the spirits and thereby bring them the blessings of prosperity and social harmony.[39]

37. Brown, *Sacred Pipe*, p. 74; and DeMallie, *Sixth Grandfather*, p. 139.
38. Brown, *Sacred Pipe*, p. 44.
39. DeMallie, *Sixth Grandfather*, pp. 293–94.

# 21

# Black Elk's Response to His Great Vision

Black Elk's spiritual life centered around four events: his Great Vision of 1872, his Dog Vision of 1882, his Ghost Dance visions and brief commitment to that movement in 1890, and his conversion to Christianity in December 1904. This list suggests that, apart from his conversion to Christianity,[1] his preeminent religious concerns centered around three important mystical experiences and his responses to them. Consequently, if one wishes to fully comprehend his spirituality, one must not only analyze the content of these visions but also the nature of his responses to them.

There were two traditional ways that the Lakota could obtain visionary communications from the supernaturals. The most common way required that the would-be visionary undertake the ceremony of supplication and meditation known as the vision quest (*hanblecheyapi*). Black Elk received one of his principal visions, the Dog Vision, in this manner. However, the Lakota also acknowledged that visions could sometimes occur spontaneously without the individual's undergoing any prior ceremonial or meditative preparation.[2] Black Elk's Great Vision was this type of experience. Black Elk did not always receive his visions in such a traditional manner: his Ghost Dance visions, for example, resulted from his participation in a group dance. The method of inducing visionary ecstasy through collective dancing did not appear to have been a normal procedure among the Sioux during the pre-reservation period.[3] This break with tradition is not surprising since many of the Ghost Dance practices originated from non-Lakota sources.

---

1. Details of Black Elk's conversion are discussed in Chapter 24.
2. Walker, *Lakota Belief,* p. 85.
3. See Holler, "Lakota Religion and Tragedy," p. 41.

# The Traditional Lakota
# Response to a Vision

The traditional response of a Lakota holy man or medicineman to what he perceived as an important vision involved two procedures. First, the individual so favored generally did not attempt to interpret such a vision by himself.[4] Instead, he normally sought the advice of a holy man or a group of elders and experienced visionaries who helped him to interpret his vision. Second, the visionary usually made it a practice to follow their interpretations of what the vision meant and what the spirit-beings had told him to do in it. In those cases where the messages from the spirit-beings were transparently clear and completely unambiguous, the interpretations of the visionary and those of his advisers generally coincided because the instructions were, in such instances, self-evident. However, if the visionary events or communications were ambiguous, then the interpretations of the advisers would take on a commanding importance. Without their assistance, it would otherwise be impossible to comprehend its meaning or follow the instructions that it contained in a masked form. Moreover, ambiguous visionary communications were not considered to be properly interpreted until the advisers had come to a unanimous agreement about what it meant. Only after they had achieved this unanimity was the candidate expected to be bound by their interpretation of what it meant and what the spirit-beings in it had required him to do.[5] The adviser(s) often would decide that parts of the vision had to be reenacted publicly. The visionary was then expected to do so or he would otherwise suffer some great misfortune from the angry supernaturals. Even if he were not required to publicly perform parts of his vision, the vision served as a source of other obligations that the Lakota thought essential for the visionary to perform if he were to avoid offending the spirit-beings. These other obligations generally took the form of chants, songs, or magical ceremonies that the visionary was subsequently obligated to perform whenever he wished to liberate the power contained in the vision.

---

4. Goose's vision of the sacred stones may have been an exception to this rule. Densmore, *Teton Sioux Music,* pp. 251–52.

5. Walker, *Lakota Belief,* pp. 131–32.

# Black Elk's Initial Response

Black Elk did not initially respond to his Great Vision in accordance with the traditional procedure for it took nine years to elapse before he finally decided to consult a holy man about it. Why did he wait so long? Black Elk's age at the time he had this vision appears to have been the principal reason why he failed to tell anyone about it. The Lakota considered the importance of a vision to be dependent to a significant degree on the social status and moral character of the individual who had received it. Therefore, they accepted the view, reflected by one of Densmore's informants, that since "a young man would not be great in mind so his dream [or vision] would not be like that of a chief; it would be ordinary in kind."[6] Charles Eastman, a Santee Sioux who had ended his nomadic hunting life for a career in the white world at the age of fifteen, related an incident in his autobiography that sheds further light on this apparently widespread notion that it was somehow unseemly for children to receive significant communications from the supernaturals. Eastman recalled that when he first went to the white schools, he was dismayed to find out that his Christian teachers prayed to the Great Mystery both publicly *and* in front of children. "I had been taught that when one wishes to commune with Him . . . he must . . . retire from human sound or influence, alone in the wilderness. Here for the first time I heard Him addressed openly in the presence of a house full of young men and young girls!"[7] When one recognizes that attitudes of this sort prevailed, it is not difficult to see why a mystically precocious child might well have been reticent about divulging his vision to anyone.

During the nine years that passed before Black Elk revealed its details to anyone, the Great Vision was not without its impact on his life. First, it sometimes effected a change in the character of his relationship to animals. Thus, from time to time he would sense himself entering that feeling-state he had experienced during his vision and he would treat animals with a peculiar kind of reverence that he did not display in ordinary situations.[8] Second, Black Elk seems to have been aware from an early age that his vision had laid some kind of special obligation on him to look after the welfare of his people. When he was only twelve years old (1875) and it

---

6. Densmore, *Teton Sioux Music,* p. 157.
7. Eastman, *From the Deep Woods to Civilization,* p. 41.
8. DeMallie, *Sixth Grandfather,* pp. 152, 155–56.

became evident to the Indians that the whites were intent on taking the Black Hills away from them, Black Elk entertained the thought that perhaps if he meditated and tried to enter the world of his vision then maybe it would come back to him and somehow tell him how he could save that sacred land for his people.[9] Third, the vision seems to have served as a catalyst that activated his latent clairvoyant sensitivities for, even before he had ever revealed his vision to anyone, he had experienced several premonitions.[10]

## Revealing the Great Vision

At the age of sixteen and a half, Black Elk decided to reveal his vision to the medicineman Black Road. Black Elk had suddenly become consumed with anxiety. Despite its rapid onset, this profound emotional and spiritual unrest seems to have had its roots in a crisis that had been gestating for at least two years (since the winter of 1877–78).

Black Elk's spiritual disquiet seems principally to have been related to an intensified awareness that his Great Vision had laid some compelling obligations on him that he now had to fulfill to both his people and to the spirit-beings. He relates that during the winter of 1877–78 he began to think a great deal about his vision and started to wonder "when my duty was to come."[11] He frequently recalled that scene in the Great Vision where the Grandfathers had shown the spirits saving his people from sickness and poverty by restoring the flowering cottonwood stick to the center of the nation's hoop. Did not the spirits of his vision also tell Black Elk that he possessed the power to bring about paradisiacal conditions on earth and the power to annihilate his tribe's enemies (that episode in the Great Vision where Black Elk killed the dog amid the flames)?[12] It certainly seemed that the disastrous events and defeats of 1876–78 had confirmed the vision's prediction that his people would have to walk for a time on the terrible black road. Now, Black Elk thought to himself, it was surely time for the good part of the vision to come true. With the power his vision had given him, he would surely be able to lead his people away

9. Ibid., p. 164.
10. Ibid., pp. 207–11.
11. Ibid., p. 204.
12. Ibid., pp. 128–33.

from the black road and on to the red road.[13] It is clear that Black Elk had begun to interpret recent events as the fulfillment of a prophecy that the Grandfathers had symbolically depicted in his Great Vision when they showed him his people in despair and plague-stricken on the black road. Black Elk saw his people's recent and final defeat by the whites (spring 1877), the death of Crazy Horse (September 1877), the attempt by the whites to force them onto reservations (1877), and his band's desperate flight from the imprisoning life in the reservations to a short-lived freedom in Canada (late fall 1877 to the spring of 1879) as events that corresponded to and represented the fulfillment of that scene in the Great Vision where he had seen his tribe at death's door and then, by planting the sacred cottonwood stick in the ground, restored them to a paradisiacal vitality. If this vision were true, as Black Elk had no doubt it was, then he had to see himself as a man invested with a sacred responsibility to save his people from the catastrophes that now overwhelmed them. Although appearances might seem to suggest that his people were now in a hopeless situation, this gloomy assessment was false. In reality, they were actually ready to begin, under Black Elk's spiritual guidance, that arduous but ultimately successful journey down the red road that he saw them doing in his vision. What young man would not feel a sense of duty in such circumstances? Given these assumptions, the only questions that remained for him now were those of when his power would begin to grow so that he could indeed lead his people to victory over their enemies and what particular things he now had to do in order to ensure that this power would be utilized effectively.

One must not assume, however, that the symbolic predictions the Grandfathers gave Black Elk in his vision were the only sources of his growing sense of obligation. During the period 1877–79 Black Elk was also an adolescent at an age when Lakota boys would normally begin to enter into the serious responsibilities of manhood. Generally by the ages of fourteen or fifteen a young man would have gone out on his first war party and possibly been asked to join one of the warrior (*akicita*) societies.[14] Thus, Black Elk's heightened sense of obligation coincided with that time in a Lakota boy's life when society normally began to apply those social pressures that operated to encourage their young men to willingly make the great sacrifices that were necessary if the tribe were to survive in a warlike environment.

13. Ibid., p. 122.
14. Hassrick, *Sioux*, p. 281.

Several premonitions that subsequently saved his people from starvation and enemy attack occurred during late fall of 1877 through the early spring of 1879, when Black Elk and his band wandered with Spotted Tail's renegade bands in Canada. Black Elk interpreted those forewarnings as signs that he was amassing that spiritual power that he was going to need to save his people from their troubles. One particular clairvoyant episode especially convinced him that the supernaturals were now helping him. One day in the early spring of 1879 (on their way back to the reservation for the last time) as he was out hunting, a mysterious voice suddenly spoke out of nowhere and cautioned him to stay especially alert. He obeyed this mysterious command and saw two enemy scouts spying on his band's encampment. Before he ran back into camp to get everyone to flee, he first prayed to the Grandfathers and asked them to send him their power so that his band could escape their enemies. He believed that the Grandfathers had actually answered this prayer for, as he and his band fled through the night, thunderstorm clouds containing little rain but lots of thunder and lightning hovered over them all night long. Black Elk claimed that he heard the voices of the thunder-beings speaking. He interpreted these thunder clouds as a sign that the Grandfathers had given him power and sent the thunder-beings to protect his band from the enemy.[15] These gifts of power from the thunder nation were an ambivalent legacy, however, because the great power that they bestowed was indissolubly connected with correspondingly onerous and anxiety-provoking responsibilities.

These first pleasing indications of Black Elk's growing spiritual power quickly gave way to a state of overwhelming anxiety that seems to have begun rather abruptly in the spring of 1880. That spring his band finally returned once and for all to reservation life and when they did so, the government officials confiscated most of their horses and all of their firearms. They were no longer free and the nomadic buffalo hunting and warring days would never return. If there were ever a time when his band needed Black Elk to actualize his saving mission to his people, this was definitely the time to accomplish it. To a man who had been given such a mission to fulfill as Black Elk had, this period immediately following the entry into reservation life must have seemed like a supreme test of his spiritual vocation. The stark contrast between the visionary promise and the brutal reality must have placed him under exceptional stress.

After Black Elk's band returned to the United States from their sojourn

---

15. DeMallie, *Sixth Grandfather*, p. 211.

in Canada in the spring of 1880, Black Elk's sense of obligation and inadequacy became intolerably acute. During the next nine months, he became
afraid every time that a thundercloud appeared for it seemed that every
time it did so it would call out to him, "Behold your Grandfathers! Make
haste!" Whenever the birds sang it seemed that they were always saying to
him, "It is time! It is time!"[16] The persistence and urgency of these voices
of reproach eventually disturbed him so much that his parents sent for the
medicineman Black Road to see if he could possibly help their son.

The depressing political events of the spring of 1880 were not the only
reasons for Black Elk's feelings of depression and anxiety. By Lakota standards, Black Elk had every reason to be anxious because he had received a
gift of power from the supernaturals but had done nothing to fulfill the
obligations of that gift. Such an omission was certain to bring devastating
consequences. As George Sword told Walker, "When one . . . receives a
communication he must obey as he is told to do. If he does not, all the
superior beings will be against him."[17] Indeed, Black Elk admitted that, up
to this point, he had failed to obey his vision since he had not comprehended what the spirit-beings had wanted him to do. The fact that much
of Black Elk's power had come from the thunder-beings of the West made
his anxiety even more acute than it would have been otherwise because the
Lakota maintained that if one had dreamed or had a vision from the
thunder-beings and failed to meet its obligations, one was certain to
be struck dead by lightning.[18] One of Walker's informants, the mixed-
blood Thomas Tyon, portrayed thunder-dreamers as smitten with an anxiety similar to that which Black Elk experienced in 1880. Tyon related that
"the *heyoka* [one who has a vision or dream about the thunder-beings]
dreamer is very frightened whenever there is thunder and lightning. He
thinks he hears voices from the clouds; therefore he escapes by running
into a tipi."[19]

During the months that followed his band's return from Canada, Black
Elk had done almost exactly the same things that Tyon referred to in his
descriptions of heyoka behavior. For example, Black Elk confessed that
when autumn began that year he was glad because that signaled the end of
thunderstorm season and a respite from the reproachful voices in the

16. Ibid., p. 213.
17. Walker, *Lakota Belief*, p. 85.
18. Lame Deer and Erdoes, *Lame Deer*, p. 242; Hassrick, *Sioux*, p. 232; Densmore, *Teton
Sioux Music*, p. 159.
19. Walker, *Lakota Belief*, p. 155.

clouds who cried out to him, "It is time! It is time!" However, during the spring of 1881 this anxiety became so acute that he began to act crazy. Black Elk related, "I got so scared that I would run out of my bed and run into another tipi and . . . keep doing this all night long just as though I were crazy."[20] From this description it is clear that Black Elk was exhibiting the type of behavior common to those who had had visions or wakan dreams about thunder-beings. In the Great Vision thunder-beings (symbolized by the black horses of the West) had played a major role in his experience and given him the gift of their power. He was therefore worried that he had not fulfilled his obligations to this dreadful class of superior beings.

Black Elk's behavior during the summer of 1879 and the spring of 1880 was not all that unusual especially for a man who had had a vision of the thunder-beings and received a gift of power from them. One should not be surprised if Black Elk's method of resolving this crisis was likewise in agreement with the traditional way that thunder dreamers fulfilled their obligations to the supernaturals. Lame Deer stated that all the heyoka dreamer had to do to rid himself of his feelings of dread was to confide his vision to someone and then reenact it publicly.[21] This was exactly the course of action that Black Elk chose in order to rid himself of his "great fear."[22]

## Black Road's Advice

Distressed by their son's increasingly bizarre behavior, Black Elk's parents finally decided to consult a medicineman by the name of Black Road about his strange actions. Suspecting that his unusual behavior might be the result of some vision that he had had, Black Elk's father asked Black Road to inquire of their son whether he had experienced such a vision from the spirits. When Black Elk told Black Road about his vision, Black Road reacted to this revelation much the same as any other Lakota holy man or medicineman would have. First, he immediately made the traditional assumption that the source of Black Elk's malaise lay in his failure to fulfill a visionary obligation. For this reason, as soon as he learned that Black Elk had experienced a vision that he had not previously reported to any-

20. DeMallie, *Sixth Grandfather*, p. 214.
21. Lame Deer and Erdoes, *Lame Deer*, pp. 241–43; Densmore, *Teton Sioux Music*, pp. 159–66; Hassrick, *Sioux*, p. 232.
22. DeMallie, *Sixth Grandfather*, p. 214.

one, he concluded that he knew what the trouble was. Black Elk must do what the bay horse in his vision had wished him to do.[23] Implicit in Black Road's conclusion was that traditional Lakota assumption that dire consequences must necessarily follow if an individual disobeys or ignores what a spirit-being tells him to do in a vision. Second, Black Road told Black Elk that he had to reenact publicly the most important parts of his vision. Black Road based this bit of advice on the premise that the act of publicly performing a wakan dream or vision not only fulfills one of its most significant obligations but also functions as a prerequisite for liberating the spiritual power that it bestowed.[24] Third, Black Road consulted with another spiritually knowledgeable man, Bear Sings, about how to interpret and respond to Black Elk's vision. Fourth, when Black Road and Bear Sings queried Black Elk about the details of his experience, the particular items that interested them were the specific ritual acts that the spirit-beings performed in the vision—especially the songs that they sang in his presence—and the ritual paraphernalia that the supernaturals used in the vision.[25] Once again, these foci of concern typified the preeminent concerns that any Lakota medicineman or holy man would have had regarding a visionary experience that it was his responsibility to interpret and otherwise respond to.[26] Fifth, Black Road and Bear Sings treated Black Elk's revelation, despite its spontaneous character, just as though he had received it as the result of the deliberate effort of a vision quest. They made him fast and undergo the sweat lodge purification rite (inipi) before they asked him about the songs that the spirit-beings had sung in his presence. These acts of fasting and purification were essential formalities of both the preliminaries of the vision quest rite and its aftermath where the vision-seeker formally announced what had happened during his visions and answered his elders' questions about it. Black Road and Bear Sings treated Black Elk in much the same manner that any other Lakota medicineman or holy man would have treated an individual who had successfully returned from a

23. Ibid.
24. Ibid., p. 238. Black Elk told Neihardt that "the power vision cannot be used until the duty we got with the part of the vision has been performed upon the earth. After that, the power may be used."
25. Ibid., p. 137.
26. At this juncture it is worth making the parenthetical remark that neither Black Elk's counselors nor Black Elk himself displayed the least interest in deriving metaphysical insights from the experience, nor were they at all concerned with proving the objective reality of certain objects perceived in the vision. These metaphysical or "scientific" preoccupations, while they may have deeply interested someone like Swedenborg or Monroe, were completely alien to the religious concerns of the Lakota.

vision quest. By doing so, they ensured that Black Elk's mystical experiences received both an interpretation and a response that conformed to tradition.

# Reenacting the Great Vision: The Horse Dance Ceremony

Black Elk's advisers had decided that the ritual reenactment of an element of the Great Vision was important to the welfare of the community. Preparations for the horse dance commenced when Black Road and Bear Sings instructed the entire village to pitch their tents in a circle around a sacred tipi decorated like the cloud tipi that Black Elk saw in his Great Vision. In the middle of this encampment, Black Road and Bear Sings set up a ceremonial sacred tipi that was supposed to represent the one in which the Six Grandfathers had dwelt when Black Elk had seen them in his vision. Like the tipi in his vision, this ceremonial tipi was also painted with a rainbow over its entrance. It also had other designs painted on it that Black Elk had not seen drawn on the visionary tipi but that were meant to represent the principal gifts and helping spirits that the Powers of each of the four directions had given him in the vision. After they had done this, Black Road and Bear Sings made Black Elk fast until the horse dance was over, purify himself in the sweat lodge, and then retire with them into the sacred tipi where, in total privacy, Black Elk taught his two counselors all the songs that he had heard in his vision.

Meanwhile, Black Elk's parents busied themselves with the task of gathering the other ritual paraphernalia that their son would need for the ceremony, namely, six old men to represent the Six Grandfathers, four virgins dressed in scarlet dresses just like those whom he had seen in his vision, a bay horse like the one he had ridden in his vision, and four sets of four horses (black, white, sorrel, and buckskin) to represent those horse riders from each of the four cardinal directions that had figured so prominently in his vision. When all these were assembled, all the participants as well as their horses were ceremonially painted. Black Elk, the six old men, and the four virgins then retired to the sacred tipi where the six old men proceeded to make a circle in its center, crumble finely powdered earth over the circle, and then paint two intersecting lines that came together in the center of the circular area—a red one running north and south to represent the good red road of his vision and another running west to east to represent the black road of troubles. Representing the west and placed in that direction was a cup of water with a bow and arrow beside it; on the east side of the circular area of mellow earth they placed a buffalo hide in the shape of the morning star, a symbol of the eastern direction in his Great Vision. To each of the four virgins the six old men gave one of the sacred gifts that Black Elk had received from the Powers while he was visiting them in the other world. The virgin representing the Power of the North, the second Grandfather, carried the sacred herb that that Grandfather had given Black Elk in the Great Vision. The virgin of the East carried the sacred pipe, one of the gifts that the third Grandfather had given Black Elk in the vision. The virgin representing the southern Grandfather carried the flowering stick, one of the gifts that the southern Grandfather had given Black Elk.[27] The virgin representing the Power of the West carried the sacred hoop, another one of the several gifts that the first Grandfather had bestowed on Black Elk during his Great Vision.[28] Black Elk himself carried a red stick to represent the power of the thunder-beings (instead of carrying the bow and cup of water as he had done in his vision when he had slain the blue man).

The actual dance began when the six old men representing the Six Grandfathers of the Great Vision began to chant songs to each of the four directions, songs that were based on those that Black Elk had heard the spirits sing in his great vision.[29] As the old men chanted the song of the West, four riders on black horses drew up in formation facing the West in a manner similar to the way the riders and their horses had done in the

27. De Mallie, *Sixth Grandfather,* pp. 117–18.
28. Ibid., p. 123.
29. Compare the songs chanted by the first and second Grandfathers in the Great Vision to those that the men representing them in the horse dance sang. See Chapter 17 for the words that the first and second Grandfathers spoke to Black Elk in the Great Vision. In the horse dance (see DeMallie, *Sixth Grandfather,* p. 217) the six old men recited the first Grandfather's song:

> They will appear, may you behold them. [repeat]
> A horse nation will appear, may you behold them.
> A Thunder-nation will appear, may you behold them.
> They will appear, may you behold them. [repeat]

The song announcing the entrance of the white horsemen representing the second Grandfather went as follows (ibid., p. 218):

> They will appear, may you behold them.
> A horse nation will appear, may you behold them.
> A geese nation will appear, may you behold them.

vision. Then, as the old men chanted the song of the North, four riders on white horses symbolic of that direction drew up in formation facing north. This process continued for each of the other two directions. After this had been done, the four virgins emerged from the sacred tipi while Black Elk, mounted on a bay horse, followed them and faced west. The six old men then emerged from the tipi and stood behind Black Elk and began singing songs to each of the four directions. As they did so, each horse troop wheeled around and stood abreast behind the virgins, Black Elk, and the six old men, facing west. Then the whole group circumambulated the tipi in the traditional clockwise direction followed by the whole encampment on horseback. When the procession returned to the West again after circling the tipi, a thunderstorm began to develop. Soon it threatened to lash the encampment with violent wind, rain, and hail. However, even though it was very close to the encampment and poised to disrupt the horse dance, it did not touch the encampment. Black Elk interpreted this as a sign that the thunder-beings had come to watch the ceremony.[30]

As the storm drew close, the people began to make scarlet offerings to the virgin of the West. Then the other three virgins offered their sacred relics to the virgin representing the Spirit of the West as well. When these offerings to the West had taken place and Black Elk and the rest of the people stood solemnly facing the thunder-beings of the West, Black Elk suddenly noted that up in the thunderclouds nearby the Six Grandfathers of his Great Vision were visible to him having indeed come to watch the ritual that he was performing in order to carry out his obligations to them. In the sky he also saw the sacred tipi of his vision as well as the rainbow that he had seen then. In short, he was seeing a momentary flashback of his Great Vision. He noted that his actions as he performed the horse dance were an exact replica of what was going on above him in the cloud. A short while later, the Six Grandfathers that he saw watching him from the nearby thundercloud made a ritual salutation to Black Elk. Black Elk appears to have interpreted this as a sign that the Six Grandfathers approved of his horse dance as an authentic reenactment of what had taken place during the Great Vision. At the same time that the Six Grandfathers in the thundercloud were watching Black Elk reenact parts of his Great Vision, all the horses in the encampment suddenly became invigorated, snorting and neighing. It seemed that the horses in the encampment were beginning to imitate the behavior of the horses during that climactic scene

30. DeMallie, *Sixth Grandfather*, p. 219.

of the Great Vision where Black Elk had used an herb from the Power of the West to revitalize an emaciated black horse and transform it into a sleek black stallion whose wondrously beautiful singing had charmed the entire universe and set all the horses and other creatures into a joyous dance.[31]

During these later circumambulations of the sacred tipi, the virgin of the West who carried the sacred hoop continued to receive scarlet offerings from the sick people of the encampment. Black Elk informed Neihardt that these offerings cured them and that this restoration to health fulfilled the most important promise that the spirits had made to him in the Great Vision, namely, the promise that Black Elk was receiving powers that would enable him to "make over his nation" (or people).[32] Amid these ritual clockwise circumambulations of the tipi, Black Elk addressed the spirits telling them that he had presented both the sacred hoop and the flowering (sprouting) stick to his people. He asked for their blessing. He then looked south and experienced another flashback into a part of his Great Vision. In this particular flashback, he saw the sacred hoop and a stick in the middle of that hoop. As he looked at the stick, he noticed that it began to pop out into buds and, just as he had seen in his Great Vision, that there were little birds on top of the budding stick. For a moment it seemed as though the sacred tree of his Great Vision was about to bloom again in the middle of the nation's hoop, but it never went further than the budding stage.[33]

The next part of the horse dance had no counterpart in the Great Vision. When the four circumambulations of the sacred tipi had concluded, all the people made ready to rush the tipi and try to be the first to count coup on it,[34] conferring great honor on the one who did so. One of the old men representing a Grandfather gave the signal, the horsemen charged the tipi and couped it. Then the horses were led away and the participants in the rite went inside the sacred tipi to see if the spirits had come into it during the ceremony. Before Black Elk and the officiating medicinemen had left the sacred tipi to begin the horse dance, they had sprinkled loose dirt on the floor of the sacred tipi. This was a traditional gesture in many Lakota rituals to confirm that the spirits were pleased with its performance and that they had transferred their power to the one who had performed it

31. Ibid., pp. 132–33.
32. Ibid., p. 221.
33. Ibid., p. 223.
34. Counting coup is the custom of touching an enemy as a sign of bravery.

in their honor. If the spirits were pleased, they would leave their footprints in the loose earth. When Black Elk, Black Road, and Bear Sings looked at the freshly sprinkled earth inside the center of the tipi, they saw tiny horse tracks. This was a sure sign that the spirit horses had been dancing inside the tipi during the horse dance.[35] After Black Elk and his advisers went into the sacred tipi to see if the spirit horses had come, they concluded the horse dance ceremony in the traditional Lakota manner by offering the sacred pipe to the spirits of the four cardinal directions. The participants and their horses were then rubbed down with sage to purify them and the entire encampment joined in smoking the sacred pipe.

What immediate effect did the horse dance ceremony have? Black Elk told Neihardt that when he had finished performing it, it seemed as though he were floating on air. Both he and his people were filled with joy and revitalized by the great power that this reenactment rite had brought into the world. Many people came up to him and told him that their formerly ill kinsmen had been made well by the ceremony. Black Elk also felt, for the first time in his life, that the little blue man that he had swallowed during the Great Vision was now stirring inside of him transferring some of his power to him. The general euphoria both in himself and in his people seemed to tell Black Elk that he had truly become a medicineman with real spirit power.[36]

How does a quick inspection of this reenactment ritual augment one's knowledge about the nature of Lakota mysticism? It clarifies the relative extent to which elements intrinsic and extrinsic to Black Elk's visionary experience determined the character of his response to it.

An examination of the horse dance ritual shows how events or objects that Black Elk saw in his Great Vision, or objects presented to him within it functioned. Either they determined the character of specific sacred actions in the horse dance that he took in response to his Great Vision or they became incorporated into those sacred actions (of the horse dance) as the particular ritual objects that he used during its performance. Just as

---

35. Densmore cited a similar instance where Brave Buffalo, after having reenacted a wakan dream about elk, wanted to show the people that he really did have the powers of the elk. To do this he made the wish that, when he walked over a spot of damp ground, instead of making human footprints, he would leave behind the footprints of an elk. He claimed that this had actually happened. "A crowd of people followed him, and after he had passed over this spot they saw the footprints of an elk instead of those of a man." Densmore, *Teton Sioux Music*, p. 178.

36. DeMallie, *Sixth Grandfather*, pp. 225–26.

important as these elements "intrinsic" to the visionary experience had been in determining the structure of its reenactment, scrutiny of that ceremony also shows that elements "extrinsic" to the visionary experience itself played a significant role in determining how Black Elk responded to his vision. This means that Black Elk's reenactment of his Great Vision was not a literal reproduction of the events that had taken place within it. Black Elk and his advisers had not only omitted from the horse dance several important events that had taken place within his Great Vision but they had also added extra parts to the reenactment ritual that had no correspondence with any visionary event or object. The horse dance ceremony demonstrates some of the ways that Black Elk's community, its traditions, and its representatives, Black Road and Bear Sings, exercised a decisive influence over how he responded to his mystical experience.

Before one can begin to determine the extent to which the community and its representatives influenced the particular way that Black Elk carried out his reenactment rite, one needs to show how factors intrinsic to the visionary experience actually contributed to what took place within the ceremony. Most of the principal ritual paraphernalia, songs, and symbolic personages of the horse dance had their counterparts in the Great Vision and therefore appear to have been directly derived from it. Such a one-to-one correspondence between visionary event (or object) and ritual event (or object) would be exactly what one would expect to see in a ritual the primary purpose of which was to reenact publicly the events that had taken place within a particular vision. For example, in the Great Vision four virgins appeared dressed in scarlet, their appearance coinciding with the climactic scene of cosmic renewal that occurred toward its end.[37] These four virgins reappear in the horse dance not only dressed in scarlet as they had been in the Great Vision but also functioning in their roles as symbols and agents of physical and spiritual regeneration. Similarly, Black Elk mounted on his bay horse, the four troops of black, white, sorrel, and buckskin horses and their riders symbolic of each of the four directions, the six old men who symbolically represented the Six Grandfathers, and the sacred tipi with the rainbow over the door were all objects or personages that had appeared in the Great Vision and also later reappeared in his ceremonial reenactment of it.

Certain important rituals that took place within the horse dance clearly represented imitations of rituals that had taken place within the Great Vi-

37. Ibid., pp. 132–33.

sion. For example, in both the vision and its reenactment, Black Elk made it a practice to salute the sacred beings of the West first and then successively proceeded to do the same thing to the Powers of the other directions in a clockwise fashion until he had saluted the Powers of the South last.[38] Similarly, when Black Elk and his retinue of horses and their riders had circumambulated the encampment in the horse dance, this action was associated with a healing effect. While it was in progress, people came to the four virgins to give them little offerings wrapped in red willow bark so that they could be cured of their ailments. This ritual action had its parallel in the Great Vision when Black Elk healed the emaciated black horse and transformed him into a powerful stallion. The moment of the horse's cure coincided with Black Elk presenting an herb to the horse and making a circle over the horse.[39] These parallels between visionary event and ritual event indicate that elements intrinsic to the visionary experience played a significant role in determining the content of the latter.

While factors intrinsic to the visionary experience had a profound effect in shaping the way that Black Elk had acted in response to the events and commands that had been received in it, their significance must not cause one to overlook the equally important, if not more important, contributions that factors extrinsic to his visionary experience made toward shaping the character of his responses to it. Numerous important elements of the horse dance appeared to have lacked any correspondence with a visionary event. For example, nowhere in the Great Vision was there any reference to that act of couping the sacred tipi that Black Elk's band had performed during its ritual reenactment. One does not notice any reference in the Great Vision to the act of preparing a circle of crumbled earth in the middle of the sacred tipi as the six old men had done in the horse dance, nor was there any allusion in the Great Vision to that curative ritual of bringing offerings to the four virgins.

What factors prompted Black Road and Bear Sings to diverge from a literal reenactment of the events in Black Elk's vision? They appear to have inserted several additions into the horse dance that did not correspond to any events that had occurred in the Great Vision simply because those additions were traditional procedures that Siouan medicinemen and holy men customarily utilized whenever they wished to (1) ensure that the spiritual power latent in a vision would become manifest in a socially beneficial

38. Ibid., pp. 114–15, 116–18, 138–40.
39. Ibid., p. 132.

manner, (2) demonstrate concretely that spiritual power had actually become present in their midst, and (3) emphasize in an especially vivid way that the vision had conferred benefits on the entire community rather than on just the recipient.

Looking at the first category of additions, one notices, that when Black Road and Bear Sings had insisted that Black Elk fast during the time of the horse dance performance and the few days immediately preceding it, that he purify himself by rubbing his body with sage, and that he undergo the ceremony of purification in the sweat lodge (*inipi*), they appear to have added these ceremonial interpolations into the reenactment of his vision because they wanted its ritual format to conform to that which the Lakota had always followed whenever anyone undertook a vision quest and reported its results to the elders and one's spiritual adviser. In fact, these actions that Black Elk performed to please his counselors were none other than those traditional rites that every individual who had successfully returned from a vision quest was expected to perform before he solemnly revealed the contents of his vision(s) to them.[40] By insisting on these rites of purification, Black Road and Bear Sings intended that they fulfill the same purposes that they had in the vision quest rite, namely, that of guaranteeing that the power bestowed in the vision would manifest itself in a manner that would cause harm neither to the visionary nor to the community.

Ritual additions belonging to the second category also constituted a common feature of Lakota vision reenactment ceremonies. The visionary was not only expected to publicly reenact the principal events of his vision but also frequently expected to add to his reenactment ritual subsidiary rites that gave the observers concrete and tangible evidence that he really had privileged access to the spirits and their powers. Thus when Black Elk, his assistants, and his counselors went into the sacred tipi and claimed that the spirit horses had been dancing while he had been outside reenacting his vision, this ceremony of observing the hoofprints in the center of the sacred tipi confirmed that the spirits had been well pleased with his performance and that they had actually granted him some of their power. Other similar incidents in Lakota literature corroborate this interpretation. For example, when Brave Buffalo wanted elk prints to appear in the soft earth after he had reenacted a vision where elk had given him some of their power, he told Densmore that he wanted this manifestation to take place in order "to show these people that I have the power of the elk."[41]

40. Walker, *Lakota Belief*, pp. 129–32.
41. Densmore, *Teton Sioux Music*, p. 178.

Thunder dreamers or heyokas verified their actual possession of spiritual power by similar tangible demonstrations of its presence. They would traditionally plunge their arms into boiling water to remove pieces of dog meat that they then gave to the audience. Their ability to survive this ordeal without getting scalded served the same function as those subsidiary ceremonies that Black Elk and Brave Buffalo had performed for it showed the community that the heyokas actually had power from the thunder-beings and did not just claim they had it.[42] The actual presence of spirit-lights and poltergeist activity at yuwipi healing ceremonies was yet another example where tangible manifestations of supernormal power functioned as direct testimony to the community that an individual actually had the spirits' power rather than just claimed to have had it.[43]

Some additions that Black Road and Bear Sings made to the horse dance belong in the third category since they proclaimed that the horse dance, like Siouan rituals such as the Sun Dance and the soul-keeping rite, released a spiritual power that benefitted the community as a whole and not just the recipient of the vision. For example, nowhere in the Great Vision did Black Elk ever mention that a ceremony had taken place where everyone had smoked a sacred pipe together. Nevertheless, Black Road and Bear Sings added this ceremony to the horse dance, perhaps in order to ensure that Black Elk's visionary power would be shared by everyone in the community. This intention would certainly have remained true to that of the spirits in the Great Vision since they had persistently told him that they had given him "the center of the nation's hoop to make it live," that is, they had intended that the power they had given him would regenerate the entire nation.[44] The insertion of the couping act into the horse dance probably served as a symbolic reminder to the audience that the blessings of Black Elk's power were meant to benefit the whole community in the same way that the performance of the Sun Dance benefitted the entire community.[45]

Black Road and Bear Sings appear to have borrowed the subsidiary rite of making offerings to the four virgins from the soul-keeping ritual. This subordinate rite mimicked a part of the soul-keeping ceremony that immediately followed its climax when the hallowed soul of the deceased had

42. Lame Deer and Erdoes, *Lame Deer*, pp. 245–46.
43. Ibid., p. 196; Densmore, *Teton Sioux Music*, p. 246.
44. Neihardt, *Black Elk Speaks*, pp. 28, 32–33.
45. The act of couping the sacred tipi seems to have been borrowed from the Sun Dance for in that ritual there was also a subordinate rite where all the warriors rushed toward the sacred Sun Dance pole in order to count coup on it.

just been released in order to begin its journey to the sky where it would hopefully take along with it to Wakan-Tanka the voices and prayers of the whole encampment. After this culminating moment, the entire community rushes to touch four consecrated virgins in the hope that some of the virgins' spiritual power will transfer to them.[46] There is an obvious structural and intentional parallel between this ritual of collective healing and that collective healing ceremony involving four virgins that Black Road and Bear Sings had incorporated into the horse dance.

It is quite probable, though not provable, that Black Road and Bear Sings were members of one or more Lakota dream societies, associations of members who had experienced either a vision or a wakan dream from the same kind of spirit. If so, their membership in such a dream society would have determined the character of some of the particular extrinsic additions they made to the horse dance. For example, one of Walker's informants, Thunder Bear, stated that if a man has a vision that "pertains to a particular class or kind of medicine, as, for instance, Bear medicine, he must become the pupil of some Bear medicineman and learn what the medicines are, how to prepare them, how to administer them, and *the songs and ceremonies that pertain to them.*"[47] This passage declares that when a man has a bear vision he not only learns the ceremonies and songs that activate his spiritual power from events that took place *within* the vision but he also learns some of these empowering ceremonies and songs from sources *outside* the visionary experience, namely, from those traditions handed down to him by his fellow bear dreamers and visionaries. This being the case with bear dreamers, one would not expect to see the reenactments of visions or wakan dreams follow the exact text of the dream or vision. Instead, the traditions that had developed around a specific type of vision the individual had experienced would dictate that certain stereotyped interpolations were necessary to ensure that the reenactment would actually liberate the spiritual power within the vision. Unfortunately, since there is a dearth of specific information about what, if any, dream societies Black Road and Bear Sings belonged to, one cannot point to specific divergences in the horse dance that might have resulted from their membership in such dream cults.

So far, this analysis has focused on those elements that Black Road and Bear Sings added to the reenactment ritual that had not appeared in the

46. Brown, *Sacred Pipe*, p. 30.
47. Walker, *Lakota Belief*, p. 132 (emphasis mine).

visionary experience that it was supposedly duplicating. Yet the two medicinemen also omitted some significant episodes of the Great Vision from
its ritual reenactment. For example, those pivotal scenes where Black Elk
vanquished the strange blue man and where a sacred man painted in red
changed into a buffalo had no counterparts in the horse dance.[48] Although
one cannot say with certainty why Black Elk's advisers did not incorporate
these episodes into that ritual, it is quite possible that they failed to do so
because Black Elk never revealed that part of the vision to them. This
possible reticence on Black Elk's part seems to contradict the general rule
among the Sioux that obligated the visionary to divulge the entirety of his
dream or vision to his counselors.[49] Nevertheless, Black Elk stated that
until he met Neihardt and told him the story of his Great Vision, he had
never fully revealed to anyone what had happened in it even to Black Road
and Bear Sings. Black Elk's reticence about divulging the entirety of his
vision seems to have stemmed from his assumption that full disclosure
would drain away his spiritual power. He told Neihardt, "Now I have
given you my vision that I have never given to anyone before and with it I
have given you my power. I have no power now."[50] There is reason to
surmise that Black Elk never told them about the sacred red man turning
into a buffalo because Black Elk later felt compelled to perform what appears to have been a separate reenactment of that specific part of his vision, the buffalo ceremony.[51]

The foregoing observations clearly show that Black Elk based many of the
specific actions he took in response to the events of his vision on what
others told him to do rather than on his own purely subjective desires. His
decision not to reveal everything about the vision to his counselors indicates that his personal idiosyncrasies sometimes did play a role in determining how he reacted to it. For the most part, however, this investigation
has established that the particular character of these responsive acts depended on the confluence of a wide variety of influences that originated

48. DeMallie, *Sixth Grandfather*, pp. 120–22, 128–29.
49. Brown, *Sacred Pipe*, pp. 61–62; Walker, *Lakota Belief*, p. 131.
50. Quoted in DeMallie, *Sixth Grandfather*, p. 47.
51. Ibid., pp. 240–41. It is also possible that Black Elk told Black Road and Bear Sings
about the transformation of the red man into the buffalo but that those two may have
thought that someone from a Buffalo dream society would be more competent to advise him
on how to reenact that part of his vision. This is speculation. However, it is worth noting that
when Black Elk finally does appear to reenact this episode of the Great Vision, he consulted
Fox Belly, a Buffalo dreamer, for guidance on how to conduct that rite.

both within the visionary experience itself as well as outside it. These intrinsic and extrinsic factors limited his behavior in ways that he was not free to change in just any way that he wished.

# The Functions of Visionary Experience in Lakota Religion and Culture

What does an inspection of the horse dance and its immediate aftereffects say about how the Great Vision functioned within Black Elk's culture? First, the Great Vision served as a potent source of healing power. However, unlike that healing power or energy so often depicted in the literature about psychic healers,[52] Black Elk's healing power did not manifest itself as a psychic force or energy that he could manipulate polymorphously the way one controls the flow of electricity in different ways in order to get it to perform many dissimilar tasks. Instead, the healing power that inhered in his Great Vision only became effective either in the catalytic presence of certain sacred objects that had been revealed to him in his vision or after he had performed those specific rites that the spirit-beings or his spiritual advisers had taught him would liberate it. Both the vision and the horse dance ceremony had numerous episodes in which instances of spiritual healing had supposedly taken place. The prominence that Black Elk accorded these episodes in his autobiography as well as the apparently large number of people who made offerings to the virgins in the hope of being cured suggests that the Lakota took it for granted that one of the major functions of both the Great Vision and its reenactment was that of bringing sacred healing power into the human world. Another episode that occurred when Black Elk later reenacted that part of his Great Vision where a sacred man painted in red had rolled on the ground and then become transformed into a buffalo further reinforces what I said about the healing function of visions and their ritual reenactments. He assumed, just as he had done in the horse dance, that his public performance of this part of his vision would not only bring spiritual power into the world but, more specifically, it would also bring down healing power. For this reason, as he began to bring that rite to its conclusion, the sick started to come up to

52. See, for example, the descriptions of psychic healing energy given in the Worralls' autobiographical account of their experiences as healers. Ambrose A. and Olga N. Worrall, with Will Oursler, *Explore Your Psychic World* (New York: Harper & Row, 1976), pp. 93–97.

him and his ritual assistant with scarlet offerings, hoping, by this gesture, to get some of its curative benefits.[53]

Second, visions pointed the way to a more perfect condition of social and cosmic harmony. Black Elk believed that his Great Vision, once reenacted, would bring down into the human realm a spiritual potency that would make it possible for him to restore his nation's broken hoop and make the flowering stick that the Power of the South had given him in his vision once again flourish and bloom in the center of the nation's hoop.

What did Black Elk mean when he used the expression "to make the flowering stick flourish once again and bloom"? It referred to that event in the Great Vision where, after he had stuck a flowering stick into the center of the nation's hoop (the circular encampment of the village), a giant cottonwood tree suddenly sprang up in its place and under its protective branches a scene of paradisiacal contentment unfolded in which humans and animals mingled like relatives.[54] Those symbols of the red road, the sacred hoop, and the flowering tree were meant to convey the notion that Black Elk's reenactments of his vision were going to help bring about a radical transformation of both the cosmic and social orders that would be similar to the one that the spirits had shown him in the other world. Black Elk seriously expected that these ceremonies would bring about on earth that fullness and perfection of being that he saw in the spirit-world.

Not only did Black Elk think that his Great Vision together with his several public reenactments of different episodes within it would somehow bring about a closer contact between the human and spirit worlds but he also believed that they might play an important role in helping the Lakota to surmount the recent social, economic, and political catastrophes that had recently overwhelmed them. Black Elk expressed this socially regenerative intention through that ever-present symbol of the nation's hoop. He repeatedly expressed the hope that through the power given him in his vision, he might be able to restore the nation's hoop and bring his people back into it.[55] This symbol referred to that tradition the Lakota had followed during their nomadic heyday of setting up their tents in a circle every time they made an encampment. The idea of restoring it nostalgically recalled that old way of life that had just ended. Black Elk wished to recapture the social cohesiveness and altruism that he had experienced during those bygone times.

53. DeMallie, *Sixth Grandfather*, pp. 240–41.
54. Ibid., pp. 128–30.
55. Ibid., pp. 125–27, 129, 140, for references to the sacred hoop in the Great Vision.

One can see signs in the horse dance that indicated that Black Elk intended this ritual not only to deepen the intimacy between spirits and humans but that he also intended that it intensify his peoples' awareness of those social bonds that had formerly held them together. For example, during the horse dance the people had to move their entire encampment to a new location and set up their tipis in a circle around a sacred tipi just as though they were gathering together to celebrate a Sun Dance. Just as the Sun Dance brought the people together to share the blessings of spiritual power that its celebration brought down into their midst, the horse dance was intended to do the same. The traditional Lakota emphasis on sharing expressed itself in several other structural elements of the horse dance ritual. At one point in the ceremony each of the members of the band was individually invited to smoke the same sacred pipe the dancers had used. Similarly, everyone joined in the dancing after Black Elk and his retinue had circumambulated the encampment the first time, all participated in the ceremony of rushing to coup the sacred tipi (just as all would do in the Sun Dance preparations), and all of the sick and unhappy people within the band felt free to bring offerings to the four virgins. The general sense of euphoria that Black Elk observed pervading the encampment immediately after he and his advisers had concluded the ritual further attested to its socially regenerative effects and function. One may conclude, then, that Black Elk and his counselors had intended that the reenactment of his vision restore that social solidarity that the Lakota had lost after their military defeat.

Third, visionary experiences were a source of powers related to success in war. The American anthropologist Clark Wissler observed that most of the Oglala warrior societies originated from the visions of individuals in accordance with the following pattern: The spirits in the vision suggest that the individual found an organization or modify an existing warrior society in certain ways such as changing their rituals, their customs while out on the warpath, their ritual paraphernalia, or the societal regalia. The recipient of the vision or his companions then assemble a war party in order to test the vision's power. If they are successful, then the vision finds embodiment in a new warrior society with its distinctive vision-given rituals and regalia or else it results in the modification of an existing organization.[56] Visions not only led to the formation of new warrior associations with their distinctive practices and ritual paraphernalia but they also gave

56. Wissler, "Societies and Ceremonial Associations," pp. 23–28, 62–64.

individuals specific power objects that supposedly conferred upon them immunity from injury by enemy weapons. For example, Black Elk related that during the worst of the fighting at Wounded Knee he relied on the power of the goose's voice that the second Grandfather, the Spirit of the North, had given him during the Great Vision.[57] He claimed that he remained immune from the soldiers' bullets as long as he continued to imitate the goose by stretching out his arms and mimicking the sounds of the goose in flight.[58] He got wounded only when he momentarily stopped imitating their protective sounds and flight behavior. There were many other scenes in the Great Vision such as the episode where Black Elk received the soldier-weed of destruction in which visionary power supposedly conferred both invulnerability and invincibility in battle.[59]

Fourth, once Black Elk had publicly reenacted it, the Great Vision functioned to enhance his social prestige. One gets the impression that before the horse dance ceremony Black Elk had not been a person of any religious or social standing. This rapidly changed once he had reenacted his vision.[60] Black Elk also became the recipient of numerous gifts from those whom he had cured of their illnesses, another sign that he was beginning to acquire some degree of social prestige.

57. DeMallie, *Sixth Grandfather*, pp. 137–38.
58. Ibid., p. 277.
59. Ibid., pp. 135–37.
60. He stated that before that time none of the medicinemen had ever bothered to talk to him but that afterward they often came to speak to him about his vision. Ibid., p. 225.

# 22

# Black Elk's Dog Vision

In Chapter 21, I mentioned that Black Elk's Great Vision was not the only significant mystical experience of his life. He also considered what he called his Dog Vision, a vision that took place during the spring of 1882, to have been another. Unlike the Great Vision, however, the Dog Vision did not occur spontaneously but instead resulted from Black Elk's successful completion of a vision quest ritual (*hanblechayapi*).

Why did Black Elk decide to deliberately seek another vision even after he had apparently been so successful in both placating the superior beings and bringing spiritual benefits to his people as a result of the horse dance? First, the spirits continued to give Black Elk indications that they thought he had still not fully carried out his obligations to them. One day in September 1881, when he had gone up to a hill to call on the spirits, he was chanting the song that the two spirit-messengers (*akicitas*) of the thunder-beings had sung to him during his very first vision at the age of five. As he looked toward the west, he saw those same two spirit-messengers looking at him.[1] Even though they said nothing to him but only gestured, Black Elk divined that they wanted him to perform further unspecified ritual obligations toward them. Consequently, Black Elk would need to go out on a vision quest to learn what ritual procedures were necessary to fulfill these new obligations.

Second, Black Elk felt the need to go out on a vision quest despite his prior performance of the horse dance because he wanted to show the Oglalas at Pine Ridge that he had power from the spirits.[2] When he performed the horse dance, he had convinced the Lakota witnesses that he was a medicineman who possessed mighty powers from the spirits. How-

---

1. DeMallie, *Sixth Grandfather*, pp. 226–27.
2. Ibid.

ever, only a small number of his own Oglala people had seen him perform that ceremony and experienced its power because he had been in Montana among other bands of the Western or Teton Lakota. The only Oglalas who had benefitted from his performance of the horse dance were the small number from his particular band who had fled to Canada. The rest of the Oglalas needed to be shown that he was a man of great spiritual power. These feelings of obligation toward the Oglalas of Pine Ridge gained even more urgency when Black Elk arrived there and saw with his own eyes how they were deeply mired in a leaden depression and despair. Clearly, the revitalizing influence of his horse dance performance had not reached them and they were in desperate need of its healing powers. Somehow, as the man whom the Six Grandfathers of his Great Vision had designated as intercessor for his people, Black Elk must do something to bring the blessings of his spiritual power down to them. Consequently, when the first thunderstorms of spring came, Black Elk decided to go out on a vision quest and entreat his friends, the thunder-beings, to send their power down on the Oglalas.

Whereas today we would consider the crisis that the Lakota faced in 1880–82 as social, economic, political, and military in origin and try to resolve it by implementing specific social, political, and ecological measures such as scientific game and livestock management, the acquisition of better military hardware, and pressuring the governing powers for economic and political equality, Black Elk assumed that this crisis could be resolved by religious means. This meant that, for him, the most important and logical way to solve the crisis was to go out and seek a vision and then bring its regenerative power down into the world by reenacting it or otherwise fulfilling its obligations. His decision to respond to his peoples' distress in this manner stemmed from his conviction that social harmony and that abundance of game on which his tribe had formerly sustained itself depended chiefly on continuing efforts to set humanity in right relationship to the spirit-beings.

Black Elk's decision to embark on a vision quest followed a traditional pattern of behavior that the Lakota expected anyone to take when he found himself or his people confronted with illness, war, famine, or other personal or collective crises.[3] Moreover, custom demanded that when he sought a vision concerning a matter of especially great importance to the well-being of his social group he must also seek and follow the advice of a

3. Walker, *Lakota Belief,* pp. 105, 129.

holy man or medicineman experienced in conducting vision quests. So he sought the advice of a wise old medicineman named Few Tails, who helped him conduct the vision quest. Few Tails began the ritual in the customary manner by offering a sacred pipe to the Six Powers, the wingeds, and the four-leggeds. Then he purified Black Elk with sage and a sweat bath ceremony (*inipi*). Few Tails then took him up to a lonely butte far from all human traffic and instructed him on how he should go about entreating the spirits. In the middle of that consecrated area, Few Tails set up a flowering stick, then placed scarlet offerings of tobacco wrapped in red willow bark at each of the four cardinal points. Black Elk had to stand in the middle of the vision pit crying to the spirits for understanding. He had to advance to the western quarter from the center of the consecrated area and lament there for a time. Then he had to go back to the center and proceed in a similar fashion in a clockwise direction to the other cardinal directions all night long until a vision came to him.

When Few Tails departed, Black Elk began his ritual lamentation to the spirits. Black Elk followed his mentor's instructions crying first as he faced west, "O Great Spirit accept my offerings! O make me understand that I may know!"[4] While he beseeched the spirits in this manner, he noticed that a spotted eagle had come out of the west and sat on a pine tree directly east of him. Facing north and beseeching the spirits toward that direction, he noticed that a chicken hawk began to hover over him and stopped on a bush south of him. He then faced east and entreated the spirits. A black swallow then appeared and also alighted on a bush. As he began to lament facing south, he saw what looked like a cloud of dust come toward him, but on closer inspection he realized that it was really a swarm of butterflies, one of the common symbols of the thunder-beings.

With the cloud of butterflies swarming around him, Black Elk walked slowly backward toward the flowering stick that Few Tails had planted in the center of the vision pit. As he did so, the eagle spoke to him: "Behold these! These are your people. They are in great difficulty and you shall go there." It then seemed to Black Elk that the butterflies began emitting weeping and whimpering sounds. Then they flew south and vanished. Next the chicken hawk began to talk: "Behold! Your Grandfathers shall come forth and you shall hear them!"[5] Almost at once Black Elk found himself in the middle of a terrible thunderstorm. He could tell that the

4. DeMallie, *Sixth Grandfather*, p. 228.
5. Ibid., p. 229.

thunder-beings were present in the clouds because he could hear their voices along with the neighing of horses. As he stood looking at the storm, a vision suddenly came to him out of the blackness. The two spirit-messengers whom he had seen at the beginning of his Great Vision came into view in much the same way that they had done the first time. As they came close to the ground, Black Elk saw a cloud of butterflies beneath them and in the middle of that butterfly cloud he saw a dog's head peeping out. Mounted on sorrel horses that had lightning designs painted on them, the two men of his Great Vision charged the dog with bows and arrows to the accompaniment of cheering from the thunder-beings.[6] At this moment the butterflies changed into a swarm of swallows careening wildly in the stormy sky behind the horsemen. The first rider then lanced the dog's head and carried it away on the point of his arrow as the whole west cheered. The second rider did the same thing to a similar accompaniment of cheering from the west. Then another metamorphosis took place. The dog's head turned into a man's head. At that moment the vision disappeared and Black Elk found himself in the middle of the terrible thunderstorm again.[7] The storm passed over him as he prayed in the vision pit. Despite the pouring rain and the hail that fell, Black Elk claimed that the vision pit nevertheless remained dry and free of hail.[8]

As Black Elk dropped off to sleep, he had a wakan dream in which he saw his people sitting despondent and sick around a tipi. Looking tearfully on them, he suddenly noticed a strange light of many colors come out of the ground nearby. Then the light went out and from the place where it had issued forth, Black Elk saw an herb. As he looked at the herb and its leaves so that he might not forget what it had looked like, he heard a voice cry out to him, "Make haste! Your people need you!" He then awoke from the dream to a picture of paradisiacal contentment. As the east began to glow from the approach of the sun, he heard horses nickering and saw throngs of joyful baby faces. He then fell asleep again until Few Tails woke him up.[9]

With the Dog Vision over, Black Elk followed his mentor back to the sweat lodge, offered the sacred pipe to the Six Powers, and then, in accor-

---

6. Ibid.

7. Ibid., p. 230.

8. This same immunity from the normal effects of the thunderstorm also took place during that moment of the horse dance when Black Elk saw the thunder-beings looking down on him. In both cases, Black Elk interpreted it to mean that the thunder-beings were pleased with the proceedings.

9. DeMallie, *Sixth Grandfather*, p. 231.

dance with tradition, described what he had seen to a group of elderly men who had gathered there to help him interpret his vision.

# Black Elk's Response

Black Elk's response to the Dog Vision followed a pattern similar to the one he had pursued after he had revealed his Great Vision to Black Road. In both cases, Black Elk first consulted with a group of elders about how he should interpret its meaning and then heeded their advice on how he should respond to it. In both instances Black Elk's spiritual counselors advised him to publicly reenact portions of these visions. Furthermore, in both visions extrinsic influences played a decisive role in shaping the specific content of the respective reenactment rituals. Finally, both reenactment ceremonies (and, by extension, the visions that spawned them) functioned primarily as sources of a spiritual power that promoted healing of the sick and feelings of social solidarity.

As soon as Black Elk had described his Dog Vision to the elders, they immediately concluded that he had the duty to perform it in front of the people. They also required that he reenact his vision with the assistance of heyokas, those sacred clowns, made so by the fact that they all had had visions or wakan dreams of thunder-beings or their representative animals. Like the other dream societies, the heyokas (thunder dreamers/sacred clowns) did not publicly perform their rituals unless there was a sacred occasion for doing so. The reenactment of someone's thunder vision or dream would be the most common occasion for them to get together.[10] One therefore suspects that Black Elk had to reenact this vision with the heyokas for the simple reason that the particular character of the Dog Vision required that it be classified as a communication from the thunder-beings. Consequently, the specific character of this vision allied him with other thunder dreamers, which meant that when he publicly performed his thunder vision he would be expected to have the assistance of his fellow thunder dreamers and structure, to some extent, the content of his reenactment ritual in accordance with the traditions of that particular dream society.

When one compares the content of the Dog Vision with the content of

10. For example, see Lame Deer and Erdoes, *Lame Deer*, pp. 243–45; and Densmore, *Teton Sioux Music*, pp. 166–68.

its reenactment ritual, one finds that societal commitments influenced the content of the ritual and account for some of the ways that it diverged from the visionary experience that gave it birth.

## The Heyoka Ceremony

The first feature of the reenactment ritual that comes to one's attention is that a heyoka was put in charge of it and the ritual was conducted in accordance with the traditions of that cultic association, the thunder dreamers. Thus, instead of following the exact text of the vision and having two horseback riders spear the dog's head, the heyoka leader, Wachpanne, added two extra features traditional in all heyoka ceremonies. First, all public heyoka rituals required that the thunder dreamers act like clowns in front of the people. Black Elk related several amusing skits that he and his fellow thunder dreamers performed in order to amuse the crowd before the climax of the ceremony got under way. Second, he set a pot of boiling water near a sacred tipi in the center of the ceremonial circle. He killed a dog in the traditional manner of the heyokas, that is, without drawing blood—just as lightning kills its victims. Wachpanne then threw the dog's head, spine, tail, and heart into the pot of boiling water. This ritual boiling of dog meat and the sacrificial killing of the dog were nowhere alluded to in the Dog Vision itself but since they were essential elements of that "around-the-bucket" dance associated with all heyoka public celebrations, Wachpanne apparently chose to incorporate them into the reenactment ceremony.[11] Once again, one can see that reenacting a vision did not mean a literal reproduction before the people of every principal episode within it. Numerous extraneous factors as well as the actual content of the vision itself determined what took place in those ceremonies.

The climax of the ceremony reproduced the central event of the Dog Vision, the episode where the two horsemen speared the dogs' heads. Mounted on sorrel horses streaked with black lightning designs just like those he had seen in his vision, Black Elk and his assistant charged the pot of boiling dog meat.[12] Black Elk skewered the dog's head as the first horse-

11. Lame Deer and Erdoes, *Lame Deer*, pp. 243–45; Densmore, *Teton Sioux Music*, pp. 166–68; Walker, *Lakota Belief*, p. 156.
12. DeMallie, *Sixth Grandfather*, p. 233–34.

man had done while his assistant skewered the heart. After both men had done this, the rest of the heyokas chased after them trying to get some of the dog flesh that had now been endowed with sacred power by the ceremony. The meat was then divided up among all of the people. The rite ended in what appears to have been a general mood of euphoria similar to that which had transpired after the conclusion of the horse dance.

The above description shows that, just as occurred in the horse dance, factors extrinsic to the actual content of the Dog Vision played a large role in determining the specific character of Black Elk's response to it. Personal idiosyncrasy and whim, however, played an insignificant role in determining how he responded to this particular vision. The actual content of the vision (what he saw the spirits doing in it) certainly dictated to a significant extent some of the actions that he had to perform, but the fact remains that most of the response was dictated by what other people had told him to do. In turn, most of what they had told him to do was conditioned by the traditions of the dream societies to which they had belonged.

These observations also allow one to see that the heyoka ceremony and the Dog Vision functioned in much the same way that the horse dance and the Great Vision had functioned. Both of these visions and their respective reenactments had brought spiritual power down into the human world for the purposes of healing the sick, revivifying the cosmos, and restoring the tribe's lost sense of social solidarity. In both the Dog Vision and the Great Vision, Black Elk saw a sacred herb that, after they first appeared in the vision, suddenly brought about visionary scenes of healing and joy. Black Elk also indicated that the sacred dog meat had some sort of healing power. He stated that all the people clamored to get pieces of it because "it was like giving them medicine."[13] Other statements Black Elk made in reference to the Dog Vision and its reenactment focused on its spiritually and socially regenerative effects. He once compared the effect of the heyoka ceremony to the regenerative power of rain. Just as the rain makes the world "green and fresh,"[14] visions and their ritual reenactments also have a rejuvenating effect. In other words, against a backdrop of catastrophic cultural upheaval, Black Elk saw his Great Vision and his Dog Vision and the rituals they engendered as sources of spiritual influences that might ultimately bring about conditions of paradisiacal existence on earth.

13. Ibid., p. 234.
14. Ibid., p. 236.

These last remarks should not be construed so as to imply that Black Elk's motives for reenacting his visions were simply escapist. The evidence suggests that since he had experienced something overwhelmingly real during his visions, he saw no reason to assume that the reality of that visionary world could not also become incarnate among humanity. It was one of his cardinal assumptions that if something exists in the world of the spirits—if one sees the sacred tree blooming there—it is possible for humans to bring it into existence down here as well, provided that they imitate what the spirits do in the vision, that is, if they obey the instructions that the superior beings give them or imitate the activities that those superior beings were performing in the vision.[15] According to the Lakota, the tragic aspect of human existence stems from the fact that the presence of power in this world can never be more than sporadic and yet that very presence of it is the only thing that gives human life its meaningfulness, dignity, and full plenitude of being. These eruptions of power into the human world point beyond themselves to a spiritual reality where these comparatively weak and intermittent presences of power have become continual and strong. Given these assumptions, it is quite natural that the Lakota would conceive of religious projects that would bring this sacred power into a more constant proximity to the human world. Moreover, these religious projects did not emerge just at the moment of crisis in the late nineteenth century but appear to have been an element of Lakota religious life for a long time before the period of sustained contact with white culture. In any case, Black Elk certainly did not see himself as escaping from reality but rather saw himself as bringing it down to earth.

# The Recollective Dimension of Lakota Vision Quest Rituals

Even though Black Elk and other Lakota holy men give descriptions of the vision quest ceremony that make it clear that it consisted first and foremost of a collection of purely ritual procedures having no apparent recollective utility or intent (for example, procedures such as circumambulation of the vision pit in a clockwise direction, the ceremony of smoking a sacred pipe at the beginning and the end of the *hanblecheyapi*, the purificatory ceremony of beseeching the spirits for aid in the sweat lodge), their

15. Ibid., p. 262.

accounts also indicate that the mere performance of those sacred acts in the proper manner did not suffice to ensure success.[16] While no Lakota informant would ever have denied that the punctilious performance of the aforementioned component rituals was essential to guarantee a successful outcome, success required two other ingredients: the good will of the spirit or spirits from whom the vision-seeker desired power and the cultivation of recollectedness.[17] When Black Elk describes the various acts that take place when the vision-seeker is actually in the process of circumambulating the vision pit and beseeching the spirits for their help, he acknowledges that it is important for the lamenter to cultivate recollectedness as he does so. It is not always necessary for the vision-seeker to make his entreaties to the spirits out loud. If he wishes, "he may remain silent *with his whole attention directed to the Great Spirit or one of His Powers.*" He then went on to add in a less conditional tone that the vision-seeker "must always be careful lest distracting thoughts come to him, yet he must be alert to recognize any message which the Great Spirit may send to him."[18] George Sword's account of the vision quest ceremony provides an independent confirmation of Black Elk's statement that the seeker's ability to focus his attention was one of the prerequisites for success. Consequently, when he listed the seven things necessary for ensuring success in a vision quest, he included as the sixth item on that list the requirement that the lamenter "think continually concerning that which he wishes."[19] Thunder Bear's descriptions of the hanblecheyapi rite also referred to the cultivation of recollectedness as an integral part of the ceremony, for he declared that once the lamenter has entered into the vision pit, "he must at no time go from the place he has prepared for himself . . . but must try to keep his mind on his quest."[20]

That the Sioux would employ a ritual procedure to induce visionary experiences yet still acknowledge the importance of cultivating recollectedness should not surprise us. After all, it was observed in Chapter 5 that every effective method for inducing mystical states of consciousness incorporates some kind of explicit or implicit recollective technique as the es-

16. Black Elk's description of the vision quest ceremony that he performed to induce the Dog Vision does not mention any recollective procedure being incorporated into it. The references that link the vision quest ritual procedures to recollective techniques occur elsewhere in his writings. See Brown, *Sacred Pipe*, p. 58.

17. Ibid.

18. Ibid.

19. Walker, *Lakota Belief*, p. 81.

20. Ibid., p. 131.

sential precondition for its effectiveness. A collection of ritual acts that, when performed, failed to produce a state of focused attention in the performer would, by that very failure, never lead him into an actual mystical state of consciousness. Ritual acts of that sort might very well have great religious significance for the performer but they would never actually generate a mystical experience. The case would, of course, be quite different for an assemblage of ritual acts that did succeed in one-pointedly focusing the performer's attention. Those rituals would certainly be capable of generating visions, locutions, and other types of supernormal experiences even if the performer were not aware that his actions were actually a series of recollective procedures. Such a series of symbolic acts would simultaneously function as both a ritual and as an implicit recollective technique that the subject would have carried out unconsciously.

# 23

# Black Elk and the Ghost Dance

Once Black Elk had publicly reenacted portions of his Great Vision and had other respected medicinemen acknowledge that his Great Vision possessed exceptional power and significance, he grew more and more convinced that he was a man with a special destiny. He told Neihardt that the morning after he had performed the horse dance he felt that he was "very different from other men."[1] With the exception of the three years that he spent traveling with Buffalo Bill's Wild West Show (1886–89), the decade following his performance of the horse dance saw his sense of vocation grow progressively stronger and more sharply defined. By the time that the Ghost Dance movement had begun to affect the Lakota in 1890, Black Elk had concluded that his special vocation was that of "intercessor for my people." This vocation carried with it weighty obligations because the spiritual, material and social well-being of his people depended on how well he lived up to his obligations as intercessor and how well he had utilized the power that the spirits had given him. He told Neihardt, "I was chosen to be intercessor for my people so it was up to me to do my utmost for my people and everything that I did not do for my people—it would be my fault—if my people should perish it seemed that it would be my fault. If I were in poverty my people would also be in poverty."[2] This is an extraordinary claim for anyone to make and yet it seems that Black Elk took this claim and its concomitant responsibilities very seriously. After all, the spirits during his Great Vision had told him that the scenes of paradisiacal joy and contentment where all living things lived together in harmony and abundance were his to make.[3]

1. DeMallie, *Sixth Grandfather*, p. 225.
2. Ibid., p. 294.
3. Ibid., p. 133.

Black Elk's sense of spiritual election seems to have endured even during the years of his travel with Buffalo Bill's Wild West Show. He told Neihardt that even though his spiritual power had entirely left him at that time, he still felt that someday it would be within his power to bring his people back into the sacred hoop.[4] Even as late as 1931, many years after he had converted to Catholicism, Black Elk's belief that the spirits of his Great Vision had given him powers to bestow great blessings on his people was still very much alive. Indeed, it is precisely because the power of his Great Vision is still alive that Black Elk tells Neihardt the story of his Great Vision. By telling Neihardt the story of his Great Vision in a highly ritualized context, Black Elk was not merely conveying information to Neihardt about an interesting mystical experience. He was doing something far more profound: conveying the spiritual power of that vision to Neihardt and giving him a share of the intercessor's responsibility for actualizing its redemptive potential.[5] Neihardt told his publisher that Black Elk had once said to him, "Now I have given you my vision that I have never given to anyone before *and with it I have given you my power.* I have no power now, but you can take it and perhaps with it you can make the tree bloom again, at least for my people and yours."[6] As an old man, Black Elk realized that he was not going to live up to his full potential as an intercessor for his people. He appears to have concluded that by transferring his power to Neihardt the full potential of his Great Vision might continue to live on.[7]

In Chapter 16, I asserted that Black Elk had entertained hopes that somehow the powers he had received from both his Great Vision and Dog Vision would ultimately bring about the spiritual and social renewal of his tribe. At the peak of his youthful vigor and sensitivity to influences from the other world, he felt that he possessed the power to accomplish such mighty tasks. These utopian expectations of those years when he had reenacted his Dog Vision and portions of his Great Vision (1881–83) slowly evaporated when the Lakota were confronted with the final destruction of the bison herds (1883), the U.S. government's prohibition against the celebration of the Sun Dance (1883), the social divisions and disruptions that

4. Ibid., p. 294.

5. Holler, "Lakota Religion and Tragedy," pp. 26–28.

6. DeMallie, *Sixth Grandfather,* p. 47 (emphasis mine).

7. These remarks are not meant to convey the idea that he considered his life a complete failure. As a Catholic catechist, family man, and tribal elder, he was certainly a success and lived what others of his tribe would regard as a happy and rewarding life. See ibid., p. 26.

their attempts to adapt to the novel sedentary agricultural mode of life forced on them, and the hunger caused by inadequate government rations, a hunger that became especially acute in 1889–90. Black Elk gradually began to realize that, despite his visions and his reenactments of them, the nation's hoop was still broken. Even his great gifts of visionary power seemed to have no impact on the condition of his people as a whole. Nevertheless, his growing disillusionment about the possibility of using his powers to cure his nation of its sickness did not prevent him from keeping up his activities as a medicineman—he could at least heal individuals. During the years between the horse dance (1881) and his journey to Europe with Buffalo Bill's Wild West Show (1886), Black Elk appears to have gained considerable prominence as a traditional Lakota healer. He told Neihardt jokingly that it was too bad that he was paid in horses for his cures back then rather than in money. If he had been paid in money, he implied, he would have been a wealthy man.[8]

When Black Elk was touring Europe, he felt that his spiritual power had abandoned him.[9] However, when he came back to Pine Ridge in 1889, he felt it return to him. Once again he became deeply involved in his traditional healing activities. Nevertheless, even though he realized that he could cure individuals with the spiritual powers of his visions, he sensed that he was further than ever from his goal of healing the social and spiritual malaise of his tribe. The situation of the Lakota in the year of his return (1889) was truly desperate. They were at the edge of starvation.

Several factors contributed to this food shortage of 1889–90. First, many Lakota cattle had succumbed to disease the year before. Second, the fact that the Lakota had been summoned to the treaty council at the height of the farming season in 1889 meant that they were forced to neglect their crops when they needed attention the most. Consequently, when they returned home after the council, they came back to ruined fields. Severe drought during those two years further aggravated an already grievous harvest failure. Third, and most important, the U.S. Congress decided at the most inopportune moment, on the basis of new census figures that showed a decline in the Lakota population, to cut down the ration of food it gave to them to about one-half to two-thirds of what it had been in 1877.[10] This action, coming as it did when the Lakota had virtually no livestock or stores of grain to fall back on, brought them to the verge of

8. Ibid., p. 240.
9. Ibid., p. 256.
10. Mooney, *Ghost Dance Religion*, pp. 71–72.

starvation. As if the food situation were not demoralizing enough, they also had to contend with the loss of more than one-half of their reservation land through the treaty made in 1889. This sale seemed to give them no immediate benefits in the way of either increased rations or income. On top of starvation and the loss of their lands with little apparent compensation, the Lakota also fell prey to highly fatal epidemics of whooping cough and measles, illnesses that became even more virulent because of malnutrition. During one of those epidemics in the winter of 1889–90, Black Elk's father, sister, and several brothers died. Under these straitened circumstances so different from the strength and abundance they had known a scant fifteen years earlier, it was not surprising that Black Elk and the rest of his tribe despaired of the future.

In the middle of this pervasive mood of cultural despair, the Lakota first began to hear about a great vision that had come to a Paiute holy man who claimed to be the son of the Great Spirit. According to those stories that the Lakota obtained from the neighboring Shoshones and Arapahoes, this Paiute holy man, named Wovoka or the Wanekia (He-who-makes-live), had spoken with the Great Spirit. In a vision, the Great Spirit had shown Wovoka a ritual later known as the Ghost Dance. This ritual, along with the sacred relics that had been revealed to Wovoka in his vision, had the power to take the Indians out of this world and bring them into a new world of abundance. For this blessed event to happen, two acts had to be performed: the dance must be performed in the manner that the Great Spirit had shown Wovoka in his vision and the performers must use the special sacred relics that Wovoka gave to his followers. This new world would have no whites, all the dead Indians would be reunited with their living relatives, the buffalo would return, and humans and animals would once more live amid conditions of primeval abundance.[11] The Lakota immediately sent a delegation of three men (one of whom, Good Thunder, later married Black Elk's recently widowed mother) to visit Wovoka to see if these rumors were true. They returned full of enthusiasm for the new religion.

Numerous parallels between the Ghost Dance ritual and events that took place in his Great Vision quickly kindled Black Elk's interest in the movement. When Black Elk learned that the Ghost dancers performed their dances in a circle around a sacred pole that was an exact replica of the sacred tree in his Great Vision, that they offered scarlet relics to the

---

11. DeMallie, *Sixth Grandfather*, p. 257.

spirits and painted their faces red, and that they used both the sacred pipe and eagle feathers in the ceremony, it seemed to him that his Great Vision was coming alive again. Black Elk began to think that perhaps Wovoka had been inspired by the same forces that had inspired him during his own Great Vision. Many of the symbols and sacred paraphernalia of the Great Vision were present in the Ghost Dance as well. If the Indians as far away as Nevada seemed to be sharing and experiencing the events of his Great Vision, then maybe the time really was at hand when it would be possible to fulfill its promises of restoring the nation's hoop and making the sacred tree bloom again. Black Elk thought that perhaps the spirits had sent the Ghost Dance to remind him that it was his duty "to get to work again to bring my people into the hoop and the old religion."[12] He could not forget that the spirits had designated him as intercessor for his people and that he had been given the power to make the sacred tree bloom again and to restore the nation's hoop. Black Elk interpreted the appearance of the Ghost Dance and the parallels between it and his Great Vision as a call to action, as one more summons from the spirits that he must use his power to fulfill the promises of his Great Vision.

It is clear that Black Elk based his commitment to the Ghost Dance principally on the striking parallels that he saw between it and his own Great Vision. His own Great Vision, validated by both the Oglala religious community and its elders, was his ultimate standard of value. However, recent bereavements also played a role in Black Elk's allegiance to the Ghost Dance. There can be no doubt that the death of his father, sister, and several brothers during the epidemic and food shortages of the winter of 1889–90 made him especially receptive to the spiritual message of the Ghost Dance and its promise to reunite the living with their deceased loved ones.[13]

## Fulfilling the Promises of the Great Vision

Four things about the Ghost Dance made it plausible for Black Elk to imagine that his Great Vision was finally about to become fulfilled on earth. First, the parallels between the content of his Great Vision and the content of certain externals of the Ghost Dance rite suggested an intimate

12. Ibid., p. 258.
13. Ibid., p. 259.

connection between the two. Moreover, these parallels made it credible that the world of his vision was in the process of becoming incarnate here below. Was it not the case that people, many of whom had not even heard of his vision, were now behaving as the superior beings had done in it?

Second, the imminent expectation of seeing the dead, the intense excitement of the dance itself, and the fact that numerous participants would simultaneously be experiencing visions of the other world could not help but imply that the spirit-world was indeed moving closer to the human world and that, as a result, some apocalyptic metamorphosis was about to take place. In such an atmosphere electric with excitement, where possibly dozens of participants at the same time were falling into catalepsy and having visions from the spirit-world, it was easy to believe, especially if one were a mystic like Black Elk, that the time of redemption was indeed at hand.[14]

Third, the visions that Black Elk autohypnotically induced through energetic participation in the dance seemed to further confirm for him the imminent fulfillment of his earlier visionary expectations since they recapitulated some of those great promises of his vision that pertained to the establishment of paradisiacal conditions on earth. For example, in the first two of the Ghost Dance visions he described, he witnessed scenes of paradisiacal contentment similar to those climactic moments of his Great Vision. Thus in both the paradisiacal scenes of his Great Vision and his Ghost Dance visions he saw his people camped in a sacred hoop within the center of which grew a beautiful tree green and full of flowers.[15] In both the Ghost Dance visions and the Great Vision the supernaturals promised Black Elk that it was within his power to bring about these paradisiacal conditions on earth—the paradisiacal scenes he saw in his vision were not just displays in the spiritual world that could only be seen and experienced by mystics.[16] In both instances, both prior to and subsequent to these visionary promises, the supernaturals bestowed on Black Elk certain gift objects that they had endowed with sacred power that, if employed in the proper ritual manner, would help him fulfill those promises.

14. For a description of the frenzied excitement and expectations of a typical Ghost Dance ceremony, see Mrs. Z. A. Parker's account of a Siouan Ghost Dance in Mooney, *Ghost Dance Religion,* pp. 179–81, and also Black Elk's description of the same in *Sixth Grandfather,* pp. 259–66.

15. Cf. *Sixth Grandfather,* pp. 129–30 (scene from the Great Vision), with ibid., p. 261 (scene from the first Ghost Dance vision).

16. Cf. ibid., pp. 132–33 (from the Great Vision), with pp. 263–64 (from a Ghost Dance vision).

Fourth, there were moments during his participation in the Ghost Dance when Black Elk saw tangible evidence that he really had spiritual power. He told Neihardt that the people always let him lead the dances because he seemed to be the one among them with the most power. His power became so great that, while a Ghost Dance was in progress, all he had to do to throw the dancers into cataleptic swoons and make them see visions was to go to the center of the dancing circle and wave a red stick.[17] Such states of intense religious enthusiasm would make it easy for almost anyone caught up in its emotional excitement to imagine that a new world was indeed in the process of coming to birth.

Black Elk's enthusiasm for the Ghost Dance appears to have been rather short-lived. The transcripts show that at the time of the Wounded Knee massacre (December 29, 1890), Black Elk had doubts about "this Messiah business" and he concluded that it was not worth fighting for. When he finally decided to fight the whites at Wounded Knee, he was fighting not to preserve the Ghost Dance but rather "for my people's rights" and to avoid ridicule as a coward.[18] After the massacre had taken place, Black Elk regretted that he had placed such high hopes on the powers that the spirits conveyed to him during his Ghost Dance visions. He concluded that the outcome of that battle might have been different had he chosen to use the war powers that the spirits had given him during the Great Vision (the soldier-weed of destruction and the power of the goose voices). He told Neihardt that when he was fighting at Wounded Knee, "I did not recall the vision that I should have recalled at this time."[19]

While it is certainly true that Black Elk concluded that he had made a mistake in favoring the Ghost Dance over his Great Vision,[20] it is a serious error to conclude, as Neihardt does in *Black Elk Speaks,* that after Wounded Knee and the Ghost Dance, Black Elk had become a broken man who realized that the old Lakota religion was both powerless and dead.[21]

17. Ibid., p. 266.
18. Ibid., p. 272.
19. Ibid., p. 275.
20. As he told Neihardt, "All through this [the Ghost Dance movement and the Battle of Wounded Knee] I depended on my Messiah vision whereas perhaps I should have depended on my first great vision which had more power and this might have been where I made my great mistake." Ibid., p. 266.
21. Neihardt conveys this impression in the last three paragraphs of *Black Elk Speaks,* where he has Black Elk say that after Wounded Knee his people's dream had died, the nation's hoop had broken, and the sacred tree had died. See Neihardt, *Black Elk Speaks,* p. 230. However, it is essential to remember that these last three paragraphs are Neihardt's invention, not Black Elk's words. They do not occur anywhere in the stenographic notes.

In Black Elk's postmortem analysis of Wounded Knee and the Ghost Dance he does *not* repudiate the Great Vision and its powers, rather he concludes that the Ghost Dance vision was inferior to the Great Vision. As Holler has convincingly argued, the failure of the Ghost Dance movement and the military defeat at Wounded Knee did not destroy Black Elk's faith in either the power of the old religion or the power that had been conveyed to him in his Great Vision. Long after his conversion to Catholicism, to the end of his life, Black Elk continued to hope that it was possible for the sacred tree to bloom again with the power that the spirits gave him in his Great Vision. This unshaken confidence that the power of his Great Vision was still alive and full of redemptive promise was the reason why Black Elk described the full details of his Great Vision to Neihardt.[22] By doing so, he was not just telling a story but was also transferring the power of his Great Vision to Neihardt so that the sacred tree might bloom and the full redemptive potential of his vision might be realized.

# Lakota Elements in the Ghost Dance

The Ghost Dance came to the Lakota from the Paiute Indians of western Nevada. Consequently, it was an alien intrusion into their religious life. Its preoccupation with messiahship, an imminent apocalyptic end of the world, the return of the dead, as well as its practice of inducing ecstatic visions by frenzied dancing had no counterparts in traditional Lakota religion.[23] These elements derived from several sources: Wovoka's superficial exposure to Christianity, the traditional Paiute concern with a dance that would bring about the return of the dead, and the religious enthusiasm of the Arapaho through whom the Ghost Dance first came to the Lakota.[24] The Lakota instituted numerous changes in the ritual format of the Ghost Dance when they adopted it. First, the original version of it among the Paiutes apparently preached harmony between whites and Indians and some whites even participated in the first dances at Walker Lake, Nevada.[25] However, by the time the Ghost Dance reached the Lakota what seems to have especially appealed to them was its antiwhite message—its idea that

22. Holler, "Lakota Religion and Tragedy," pp. 19–45.

23. Many of his followers considered Wovoka to have been the son of the Great Spirit who, like his Christian counterpart Jesus Christ, had come back into the world to renew it.

24. Mooney, *Ghost Dance Religion*, pp. 62, viii, 42, respectively.

25. Ibid., p. 38.

the son of the Great Spirit was coming to destroy the whites and save only Indians.[26]

A second difference between the original Ghost Dance and the Lakota version of it was the Lakota practice of dancing around a sacred tree planted in the center of the dance circle.[27] This particular symbol of the sacred tree was obviously a reference to that holiest of Lakota religious symbols, the Sun Dance pole. If one bears in mind that the Ghost Dance sought to bring about a renewal of that paradisiacal cosmic harmony that the recently abolished Sun Dance and Black Elk's Great Vision had also tried to incarnate here on earth, it should hardly be surprising that this archetypal Lakota symbol of concord between the human, spiritual, and animal kingdoms should once again make its appearance.

A third innovation that the Lakota interpolated into the Paiute Ghost Dance was the practice of wearing "ghost shirts," shirts on which they had painted designs of certain objects the dancers had seen in their visions of the spirit-world or that they had been instructed to draw by the superior beings of their visions. In one of his own Ghost Dance visions, Black Elk had been shown some holy shirts that he then designed for the other dancers based on the patterns that he had seen.[28] It is evident that Black Elk's beliefs and practices regarding these ghost shirts were consistent with traditional Lakota war magic where one assumed that the objects, actions, or designs received in a vision could sometimes give their possessor or imitator invulnerability to weapons.[29]

These additions to the Ghost Dance ritual permitted the Lakota to assimilate it in a manner that stressed its congruence with their old religious traditions. One can see that an analogous process had taken place in Black Elk's experiential universe. Despite the nontraditional way that the Ghost Dance visions had come to him and the novel theological emphases that were present in its doctrines, Black Elk's ex-static forays into the spirit-world continued to center on the traditional Lakota concerns that had formed the cornerstone of his childhood revelations.[30] His visionary experi-

---

26. Ibid., p. 41.

27. Black Elk does not appear to have realized that the Ghost Dance, as the Paiute originally practiced it, did not include a dance around a sacred pole. He assumed that Lakota Ghost Dance practices were universal.

28. DeMallie, *Sixth Grandfather*, pp. 262, 265.

29. See Mooney, *Ghost Dance Religion*, pp. 42, 118; Wissler, "Some Protective Designs," p. 30.

30. One of the spiritual beings that Black Elk encountered in his second Ghost Dance vision appears to have had some of the features of Jesus Christ. Like Jesus, this man with

ences in the Ghost Dance continued to function the same way that they had done in the past insofar as they still served as sources of power objects and had as their ultimate purpose the regeneration of both the nonhuman cosmos and Lakota society. In short, Black Elk did not join the Ghost Dance out of a hunger for religious novelty. He only joined it when it became clear to him that it was consistent with, and indeed showed promise of being the fulfillment of, traditional Lakota religious expectations.

---

outstretched arms whose body was painted red, underwent a transfiguration in which "his body changed into all colors." Black Elk also mentioned that "it seemed as though there were wounds in the palms of his hands." On the other hand, in that very same paragraph Black Elk said that this figure "did not resemble Christ." See DeMallie, *Sixth Grandfather,* p. 263.

# 24

# Black Elk's Conversion to Christianity

I mentioned in Chapter 16 that around the time he joined Buffalo Bill's Wild West Show (in 1886) Black Elk appears to have converted to Episcopalianism. Two letters that he wrote to his people from Europe in 1888 and 1889 indicate that he was deeply impressed with the Christian religion. Indeed, Black Elk stated that of all white practices and customs it was only Christianity that seemed to be worthwhile.[1]

Black Elk's initial conversion to Christianity did not entail any abandonment of his traditional healing activities. For example, Black Elk told Neihardt that as soon as he returned to the reservation from Europe in 1889, he felt his spiritual power returning to him and he began curing people again.[2] Other Lakota informants who knew Black Elk testified that between 1889 and his conversion to Roman Catholicism in 1904, Black Elk acquired a reputation as a yuwipi practitioner and healer.[3] At times, Black Elk's healing activities got him into conflict with the Catholic Church. He told Neihardt that a "black robe" (a Catholic priest) once disrupted one of his healing rites and destroyed his ritual paraphernalia.[4]

It is difficult to determine how deeply, if at all, Black Elk was committed to Christianity during the years between Wounded Knee and his conversion to Catholicism (1891–1904). Black Elk's adherence to the old Lakota healing rites did not necessarily mean that his conversion to Episcopalianism had been insincere. Black Elk would not have been alone among his people in thinking that Christianity could coexist harmoniously with tradi-

---

1. DeMallie, *Sixth Grandfather*, pp. 9–10.
2. Ibid., p. 256.
3. Ibid., p. 239; and Paul R. Steinmetz, S.J., *Pipe, Bible and Peyote Among the Oglala Lakota,* rev. ed. (Knoxville: University of Tennessee Press, 1990), pp. 183–84.
4. DeMallie, *Sixth Grandfather*, p. 239.

tional Lakota religion.[5] On the other hand, the mere fact that Black Elk's sons were baptized as Catholics during the 1890s does not necessarily mean that he took the initiative in having them baptized. It is quite possible that his Catholic first wife was the principal force behind their baptism rather than Black Elk.

What one might call Black Elk's "second conversion" to Christianity, his conversion to Catholicism, took place in December 1904. This brought about a much more radical restructuring of his religious life than his conversion to Episcopalianism had done. First, Black Elk stopped practicing the traditional Lakota healing rituals that had previously been so important to him. His daughter Lucy Looks Twice said that after her father converted to Catholicism, "he put all his medicine practice away. He never took it up again."[6] In this regard, it is also significant that when Neihardt repeatedly asked Black Elk to perform a yuwipi ceremony for him, Black Elk always refused to do so.[7] It is true, however, that during the last two decades of his life, Black Elk frequently performed traditional Lakota dances and healing rites for tourists—for the benefit of white audiences rather than Lakota audiences. They seem to have been designed not only to bring in some pocket money but also to show the white audiences that traditional Lakota religion was worthy of their respect.[8] Despite Black Elk's continuing signs of respect for traditional Lakota religion, it does not appear that these reenactments of the old rites were intended as a challenge to the Catholic Church or its hierarchy.

5. See Steinmetz's description of what he calls the "Ecumenist I group" among present-day Lakota Christians in *Pipe, Bible and Peyote*, rev. ed., pp. 191–92.

6. Steinmetz, *Pipe, Bible and Peyote*, rev. ed., p. 184.

7. DeMallie, *Sixth Grandfather*, pp. 14–15, n. 16.

8. Steltenkamp, *Black Elk*, pp. 112–13; DeMallie, *Sixth Grandfather*, pp. 65–66. Lucy Looks Twice mentioned that her father continued to perform traditional dances and healing ceremonies for the entertainment of tourists at Duhamel's Sioux Indian Pageant. In *Sixth Grandfather*, DeMallie suggested that Black Elk's reason for performing these rites for tourists was to "teach white audiences that the old-time Lakota religion was a true religion, not devil worship as the missionaries claimed" (p. 66). Black Elk's daughter indicated that such apologetic intentions were absent. Her father performed those rites simply to entertain the audience and acquire a little money by posing for pictures. As she put it, "It was just a show . . . he never really meant it" (Steltenkamp, *Black Elk*, pp. 112–13). I am inclined to think that Black Elk's daughter overstates the discontinuity between the Catholic Black Elk and the traditionalist Black Elk. Black Elk's statement to the Laubins that, by using the sacred pipe, it would be possible to bring about a better understanding among peoples (DeMallie, *Sixth Grandfather*, p. 66) is consistent with statements he made late in his life in *Sacred Pipe*, which show that he still held parts of the old religion in high regard. I therefore find it hard to believe that he performed these dances simply for money without any element of reverence for the old ways.

Second, Black Elk's conversion to Catholicism was accompanied by a great zeal to propagate that faith to members of his own tribe and other tribes. After Black Elk converted to Catholicism he became a catechist who, as a paid assistant to the local priests, conducted the Sunday services, led the hymns and prayers, did the Bible readings, and gave religious instruction to the congregation during those frequent occasions when the priest was unable to be present.[9] Black Elk also served the Catholic Church as a successful missionary to other Indian tribes such as the Winnebago, the Arapahoes, and the Shoshones. Black Elk was so successful and zealous during his stint as a missionary (1908–16) that one of his fellow missionaries had estimated that Black Elk had been responsible for the conversion of at least four hundred Indians to Catholicism.[10]

It is not clear why this same Black Elk who had earlier gotten into conflicts with the local Catholic priests over his performance of traditional Lakota healing rites suddenly converted to Catholicism in 1904. Neihardt's daughter, Hilda, reports that when her father asked Black Elk why he had given up his healing rituals and old religion, Black Elk said to him, "My children had to live in this world."[11] What Black Elk seems to be implying by this laconic answer is that his conversion was a concession to the brutal reality of the white domination of his world. Since whites were here to stay, the Lakota had to make some adjustments to this new but unpleasant state of affairs. Black Elk's answer to Neihardt does not ring true because it fails to explain why Black Elk became so zealously committed to his new faith. His adoption of Catholicism was clearly much more than a rather reluctant concession to the needs of his children in a white world.

Lucy Looks Twice, Black Elk's daughter from his second marriage, suggests that perhaps her father converted to Catholicism because he sensed that the Catholic priests' spiritual power was greater than his own. She relates that one day in November 1904, her father was asked to heal a sick boy according to traditional Lakota rituals. As Black Elk was pounding on his drum and calling on the spirits to heal the little boy, one of the Catholic priests, Father Lindebner, arrived at the house to administer last rites to the child who had been baptized as a Catholic. Father Lindebner was furious that Black Elk was profaning the child's last moments with his pagan

9. Generally, priests conducted services in person only about once a month at a given reservation church. DeMallie, *Sixth Grandfather*, p. 16.
10. Ibid., pp. 18–26.
11. Ibid., p. 47.

rituals and jeopardizing his soul. Lindebner then hurled the drum, the rattles, and other paraphernalia out of the tent, grabbed Black Elk by the neck and threw him out, saying, as he did so, "Satan, get out!" Black Elk, the brave warrior who had fought so valiantly at Wounded Knee, remained surprisingly passive in face of this abuse. He simply sat outside "downhearted and lonely, as though he had lost all his powers."[12] When Father Lindebner finished administering last rites, he found Black Elk sitting outside in a dejected mood. When he offered Black Elk a ride in his buggy, Black Elk accepted and rode back to the local mission. Two weeks later he was baptized as a Catholic on December 6, 1904, Saint Nicholas's Day. (This is the reason why Black Elk was subsequently called Nick Black Elk.) Lucy went on to mention that after his conversion, Black Elk never again took up the practice of shamanic healing.[13] Her belief that her father converted because he felt that his spiritual powers had left him does not square with Black Elk's later expressions of faith in the redemptive possibilities of his Great Vision, however. If Black Elk truly believed that his spiritual powers had vanished, then why would he have expressed the hope that by telling Neihardt the full story of his Great Vision he was making it possible for the sacred tree to bloom once again and his people to live the joyful existence that had been shown to him in his spirit journey to the center of the world? As Holler has argued so persuasively, Black Elk collaborated with Neihardt because he still assumed, even after his conversion to Catholicism, that the Great Vision had real redemptive power for both Indians and whites.[14]

Black Elk's own view of the proper relationship between Christianity and traditional Lakota religion is not easy to discern. Some of Black Elk's statements imply that the two religions are fundamentally incompatible. For example, when he was at the peak of his activity as a missionary, Black Elk wrote a letter to the *Catholic Herald* (dated November 2, 1911) in which he stated that Lakota converts to Catholicism must put the ways of the past behind them and not look back. "Let us not talk of our ways of the past but think about the new ways our Savior has given us."[15] About two years after *Black Elk Speaks* first appeared, Black Elk signed a letter that was witnessed by his daughter Lucy Looks Twice and Father Joseph

12. Paul B. Steinmetz, S.J., *Pipe, Bible and Peyote among the Oglala Lakota* (Stockholm: Almqvist and Wiksell International, 1980), p. 158.

13. Steltenkamp, *Black Elk,* pp. 33–34.

14. Holler, "Lakota Religion and Tragedy," p. 39.

15. DeMallie, *Sixth Grandfather,* p. 21.

Zimmerman, S.J. The book had produced quite a shock to the Catholic priests on the Pine Ridge reservation since it implied that one of the Church's most prominent members was still deeply wedded to the old ways. *Black Elk Speaks* ends with a scene where Black Elk invokes the Six Grandfathers for their blessing in order to make the sacred tree bloom again. Nothing is said about Christ and His saving power in the life of this supposedly loyal Catholic. In a letter dated January 26, 1934, Black Elk tried to correct the impression that his collaboration with Neihardt on that book indicated that he had abandoned the Catholic faith. In this letter, Black Elk stated that Neihardt had talked about the old ways of the Lakota but that he had not told his audience about their current ways.[16] Black Elk went on, "In the last thirty years I am different from what the white man wrote about me. I am a Christian." For many years, he had served the Catholic Church as a missionary and catechist and all of his family were baptized in the Catholic Church. He also noted that the Bible takes a dim view of backsliders. Referring to 2 Peter 2:20–22, which states that those who, once having been shown the way of Christ, return to their own ways are worse off than if they had never known Christ, Black Elk affirmed, "I will never fall back from the true faith in Christ. . . . The old Indian prayers did not make people better. The medicine men looked for their own glory and for presents. . . . Indian medicine men did not stop sin. I want to be straight as the black-gown church teaches us to be straight to save my soul for heaven. This I want to do." This statement, at first glance, seems to be unequivocal in its condemnation of the old religion. However, even though the conclusion of *Black Elk Speaks* with its invocation to the Six Grandfathers must have acutely embarrassed Black Elk, the Catholic catechist, he never repudiated that part of the book.[17]

Although the letter implies that Black Elk had abandoned any allegiance he once had to the old religion, his actions and statements on many other occasions suggest otherwise. The stenographic notes of Black Elk's 1931 conversations with Neihardt show that the Lakota holy man was convinced that the traditional Lakota religion still had power. As I mentioned in Chapter 16, Black Elk described his Great Vision to Neihardt in the traditional manner because he believed that in doing so he was making it possible for the power conveyed in that vision to bring about the spiritual regeneration of both the white man and the Indian. He was not just giving

16. This letter is quoted in full in Steltenkamp, *Black Elk,* pp. 82–84; and in DeMallie, *Sixth Grandfather,* pp. 59–61.
17. DeMallie, *Sixth Grandfather,* p. 58.

Neihardt information of an autobiographical nature. The conveyance of this sacred information required that Black Elk perform the following ritual procedures that were typical of the old Lakota religion: (1) smoking the sacred pipe, (2) sponsoring a feast before the sacred instruction could be given just as J. R. Walker before him had been required to give a feast before the tribal elders had initiated him into the secrets of becoming a medicineman,[18] and (3) being ritually adopted into the tribe with his daughters, who were either witnesses or notetakers, and given Lakota names before this sacred information could be given to them for it was forbidden to give this information to outsiders.[19] This procedure shows that even twenty-six years after his conversion, Black Elk continued to show great respect for the ritual formalities of the old religion.

Even after the 1934 letter, Black Elk continued his relationship with Neihardt and gave him the 1944 interviews about the mythology and sacred history of the Lakotas. One must also mention Black Elk's collaboration with Joseph Epes Brown in 1947–48 that ultimately led to the publication of *The Sacred Pipe*. In that work, Black Elk expresses his passion to preserve for posterity and for all of humankind a record of Lakota religious beliefs and practices without, however, repudiating his allegiance to Christianity. Indeed, Black Elk's position in *The Sacred Pipe* seems to be that the old religion and Christianity complement, rather than oppose, each other. For example, in his foreword to that book, Black Elk acknowledged that whites were correct when they taught that Christ was crucified to redeem mankind and that He will return to earth at the Last Judgment. "This I understand and know that it is true," he writes. However, he goes on to say that the red race has its spiritual wisdom and their redeemer figure as well: the sacred pipe and the White Buffalo Calf Woman who brought it to them. The coming of the sacred pipe is a redemptive event that whites must learn to respect. They must also realize that, just as Jesus promised that He would return at the end of the world, the same thing was also true of White Buffalo Calf Woman.[20] The Catholic Black Elk is not advocating that Christ replace the Sacred Pipe and White Buffalo Calf Woman as an agent of redemption but rather he is stressing that, for the Sioux, both Christ and the pipe are co-equal partners in the drama of the red race's salvation.[21] "I have wished to make this book through no other

18. See Walker, *Lakota Belief*, p. 68.
19. Holler, "Lakota Religion and Tragedy," pp. 25–26.
20. Brown, *Sacred Pipe*, pp. xix–xx.
21. Commenting on Black Elk's position regarding the proper relationship between Chris-

desire than *to help my people in understanding the greatness and truth of our own tradition,* and also to help in bringing peace upon the earth, not only among men, but within men and the whole of creation."[22] There is no question of substituting one faith for the other. The Lakota religion is great and true just as the Christian religion is. Here Black Elk hopes to blend the two religions together harmoniously without disrespect to the spiritual greatness of either one.

It is not just the foreword to *The Sacred Pipe* that expresses Black Elk's goal of harmoniously fusing Christianity and Lakota religion. Elsewhere in that same book, Black Elk reinterpreted the rituals of the old religion from a Christian perspective. For example, when he explained to his readers the meaning of the tearing of the flesh that occurs during the Sun Dance, he stated that "the flesh represents ignorance, and, thus, as we dance and break the thong loose, it is as if we were being freed from the bonds of the flesh."[23] It is clear that Black Elk is interpreting the piercing of the dancers from the perspective of Paul's antithesis between spirit and flesh (Rom. 7:22–8:17). Black Elk's description of the *hunkapi* ceremony (the ritual of making someone an adopted relative) that he gives in *The Sacred Pipe* also shows Christian influence. When one compares Black Elk's account of that rite with the account that Walker's informant, Afraid of Bears, gave him around 1914, one notices a sharp contrast between the two versions of how this ceremony originated. Black Elk's narrative stressed that its purpose had been that of bringing about peace between two former enemies, the Sioux and the Ree.[24] However, the earlier account that Afraid of Bears gave to Walker indicated that the rite had no such purpose. Afraid of Bears's narrative, which purports to explain the origin of the ceremony in a historical event that took place in 1805 (prior to the influx of whites into the northern Plains and prior to the appearance of the pan-Indian religious movements such as the Ghost Dance and the peyote cult), says nothing at all about the rite functioning as a means of bringing about peace between warring tribes. Instead, Afraid of Bears's version empha-

---

tianity and Lakota religion in *Sacred Pipe,* Holler has written, "Christ does not replace the pipe; both have co-equal validity. . . . Black Elk is saying to the Sioux, in what was to be his last written statement, that Indians should 'pray with the pipe,' that is, not abandon traditional religious practices for Christianity." Quoted from Holler, "Black Elk's Relationship to Christianity," *American Indian Quarterly* 8 (winter 1984): 42.

22. Brown, *Sacred Pipe,* p. xx (emphasis mine).
23. Ibid., p. 85.
24. Ibid., pp. 102–3, 114–15.

sized that the ritual functioned to cement social bonds between individuals within the tribe.[25] Black Elk's ecumenical emphasis on peace between the tribes seems to belong to a religious orientation that had been colored by contact with either the Christian emphasis on the brotherhood of man or the various pan-Indian religious movements of the late nineteenth century and does not seem appropriate to the more parochial religious orientation one would expect to see in a group of nomadic warriors and hunters. War, not peace, was the central preoccupation of the Lakota during the pre-reservation period. The religious quest for harmony between Indians of different tribes was characteristic of the post-reservation period. The lack of ecumenicism, the more parochial tone, in Afraid of Bear's account would be precisely what one would expect to find in a tribal society that had yet to feel the impact of deeper contact with people from widely dissimilar cultures.

Black Elk's conversion to Christianity shaped the way that he spoke about traditional Lakota religion in another significant way: it caused him to ignore the glorification of war and the powers of destruction related to war that played such an important role in traditional Lakota religion.[26] His teachings in *The Sacred Pipe* minimize the element of warfare in Lakota religion in keeping with Christ's message of peace and love.[27] Black Elk also refused to emphasize those important parts of his Great Vision in which the spirits granted him powers of destruction that he could use to overcome his enemies in warfare. He explicitly told Neihardt that he was glad he never had the opportunity to use the soldier-weed of destruction given him in his Great Vision because it would have brought terrible injury to women and children. He was glad that he had turned his back on the temptation to exercise physical and political power that use of the weed would have given him and, instead, converted to Catholicism.[28]

What was Black Elk's final position with respect to the compatibility of Christianity and traditional Lakota religion? Did he really believe, as he stated in his January 26, 1934, letter that "the Indian religion of long ago did not benefit mankind?"[29] Or was he really a crypto-traditionalist who simply put on a show of accepting Christianity merely because his children

25. Walker, *Lakota Belief*, pp. 200–202.
26. DeMallie, *Sixth Grandfather*, p. 90.
27. For example, see Brown, *Sacred Pipe*, pp. xx, 101–2.
28. DeMallie, *Sixth Grandfather*, pp. 136–37.
29. Ibid., p. 60.

"had to live in this world" of Christians?[30] I have presented enough evidence in the foregoing pages to show that neither of these alternatives is correct. Black Elk's commitment to Christianity was deep and sincere. His activities as a Catholic catechist and missionary, his willingness to give up traditional Lakota healing rites, his ecumenical spirit that embraced all of humanity and not just the Lakota, and his willingness to downplay the traditional Lakota glorification of warfare in *The Sacred Pipe* all testify to the genuineness and depth of his Christian commitment. Nevertheless, Black Elk's devotion to Christianity did not entail a wholesale rejection of Lakota religion. While Black Elk certainly rejected those elements of the old religion that were fundamentally incompatible with Christ's message of peace, love, and brotherhood (such as the traditional glorification of war), he rejected the common Christian view that the old Indian religion was a deception of the devil.[31] Black Elk's view in his old age seems to have been that the old Lakota religion was basically good though it must now give way to something that is even better, the Catholic religion. Ben Marrowbone, a Catholic catechist who knew Black Elk very well, said that at one gathering of catechists Black Elk told the assembly, "The old way is good. God prepared us before the missionary came. Our ancestors used the pipe to know God."[32] Black Elk's daughter Lucy gives similar testimony that her father thought of the traditional Lakota religion as a preparation for Christianity in much the same way that the rituals and religion of the Israelites in the Old Testament had been a preparation for the coming of Christ and the New Testament. Seen from this perspective, the Sun Dance was not a demonic pagan rite but rather a foreshadowing of Christ's Passion and the Christian spirit of self-sacrifice. The dancers must be pure and sinless before they undergo their bloody sacrifice on the Sun Dance pole to benefit and cleanse the entire community. This parallels Christ's sinlessness before His bloody sacrifice that redeemed the entirety of humankind.[33] The crown of sage that the dancers wear at the beginning of the ceremony bears a more than coincidental resemblance to Christ's wearing of the crown of thorns that preceded His Crucifixion.

This perspective of Lakota religion as a dignified and valuable moral and religious preparation for Christianity enabled Black Elk to view the Lakota soul-keeping ritual and its practice of having the sponsoring family

30. Ibid., p. 47.
31. Ibid., p. 289.
32. Steltenkamp, *Black Elk,* p. 105.
33. Ibid., pp. 102–3.

give away all its possessions as a rite that increases "love of your neigh-bor."[34] This Christian phraseology seems designed to point to a continuity between the purpose of this ritual and the Christian obligation to love one's neighbor and show concern for the poor. Black Elk's interpretation of the ritual of the sacred pipe also stressed its continuity with Christian practice. He tells his Christian readers of *The Sacred Pipe* that when he explains to them "what our sacred pipe really is," he is confident that "they will recognize that we Indians know the One true God and that we pray to Him continually."[35]

It is evident that Black Elk's conception of Lakota religion as a morally and religiously valuable preparation for the coming of Christianity enabled him to convert to Catholicism without denigrating his ancestral religion.

What has this analysis of Black Elk's visionary experiences and his re-sponses to them shown about the nature of mysticism?

First, it has demonstrated beyond all doubt that mysticism is fundamen-tally contextual in nature. I have shown that Black Elk's religious tradition decisively shaped both the character of his responses to his visions as well as their specific content. Even though Black Elk's Great Vision was a spon-taneous event of his childhood, the imagery and symbolism within it did not emerge autonomously from his subconscious mind in complete isola-tion from his environment but, instead, derived largely from models that, even as a small child, Black Elk had already unconsciously internalized from his culture. For example, I previously demonstrated that the symbol of the sacred tree, the color red, the Grandfathers in their celestial tipi, the sacred human figure who rolls and transforms into a buffalo, the threefold association of thunder, the color black, and horsemen from the West, the four virgins, and the ritual slaying and metamorphosis of an enemy stand-ing in water were all symbolic motifs and associations that Black Elk must have consciously and unconsciously picked up from his religious environ-ment and integrated into his vision since these same motifs also appeared in other Siouan ritual, mythological, and visionary contexts.[36] These sym-bolic motifs and associations insinuated themselves into the very structure of the experience from its inception.

Black Elk's encounter with the Six Grandfathers was not just an "inter-pretation" he subsequently added to an experience which was otherwise

34. Brown, *Sacred Pipe*, p. 8.
35. Ibid., p. xx.
36. For example, in the visions of Black Horse and Lone Man referred to in Chapter 16.

identical in content to Gopi Krishna's experience of awakening kundalini or Moses' experience of Yahweh talking to him from the burning bush. The content of Gopi Krishna's experience was fundamentally dissimilar to the content of any of Black Elk's visions because, as I noted in Chapter 4, he had been exposed to the teachings of hatha yoga and the system of subtle physiology that it presupposed. Gopi Krishna could not have had a vision of the Six Grandfathers in a celestial tipi because he had never been exposed to the mythology and religion of the Lakota and vice versa. My point is simply this: Black Elk's visionary experiences and perceptions were from their very beginning thoroughly conditioned by the Lakota religious context.

Second, this analysis of Black Elk has also demonstrated that not only was the content of Black Elk's experiences contextually determined but also his responses to them were contextually conditioned. Black Elk rarely reacted to his visions autonomously. Instead, he usually made it a point to consult a holy man or medicineman about how he should respond to them and when he had done so he always obeyed their instructions. In a real sense, then, his visions were a species of community property that he was not free to dispose of in just any way that he wished.

Third, this analysis of Black Elk's visionary life has exhibited some of the ways that the mystical experiences of tribal peoples differ significantly from those that originate among mystics who belong to the various universal religions which have all been born within the cultural milieu of the oecumene, that wider world of cultures and peoples that are linked together by ties of trade or imperial domination. I suggest that mystics in tribal societies that have not yet made any deep degree of contact with the oecumene and its religious mythologies tend to develop conceptions of spiritual power that are both compartmentalized and ritually catalyzed. In sharp contrast to notions of spiritual power prevalent in tribal societies, the conceptions of spiritual power that tend to develop in the universal religions of the oecumene formulate conceptions of spiritual potency that bear a close analogy to the physicists' concept of energy, insofar as they are freely deformable spiritual potencies virtually limitless in their modes of possible manifestation. This study of Black Elk has also pointed tentatively to another major difference between the mystical experiences generated within a tribal religious milieu and those generated within the context of the universal religions—their different valuations of those mystical states of consciousness in which forms and images appear. There is a persistent strain of acosmism in the universal religions and the mysticisms that they spawn. This acosmism is persistently associated with forms of mysticism that depict the most soteriologically significant mystical experiences as states of consciousness that are devoid of forms and images. I suggest that tribal mystics—because they come from religions with a cosmic rather than acosmic sacrality—have no need to devalue visions with forms and images. The hallmark of that cosmic sacrality so characteristic of tribal spirituality is that it locates the sacred in the objects or events of nature rather than beyond nature. Consequently, there is no need to depict the sacred as beyond form or image. Black Elk never had mystical experiences devoid of forms and images and I know of no examples of such visionary experiences from a tribal religious milieu. In any case, the soteriological relevance of such imageless visions, if they are present at all, appears to be ignored in those religions.

Fourth, the constant reciprocal symbiosis between ritual and experience in Black Elk's mysticism powerfully demonstrates the fallacy of any attitude that assumes that mysticism "elevates itself in sovereign freedom above all dogmatic and ritual tradition."[37] Ritual and mysticism are not opposing religious modalities. Indeed, the prominence of ritual motifs in Black Elk's visions and the relevance of his visions to the creation of new rituals show that ritual and mystical experience reinforce each other.

37. Friedrich Heiler, *Die Bedeutung der Mystik für die Weltreligionen* (Munich: Ernst Reinhardt, 1919), p. 6; also James, *Varieties of Religious Experience,* pp. 24–25.

# Book Four

# The Mysticism of
# Saint Teresa of Avila

# 25

# Why Study Saint Teresa?

The Spanish Carmelite nun Saint Teresa of Avila (1515–82) ranks as a classic exemplar of Christian mysticism. The richness and depth of her mystical experiences, the careful and detailed way that she described them, the prominence that numerous scholars of mysticism have accorded her in their works, and the extraordinary official recognition that the Catholic Church has given her—proclaiming her a saint in 1622 and, more recently (1970), bestowing on her the singular honor of being called a Doctor of the Church—all prove that she occupied a paramount position within the tradition of Catholic spirituality and mysticism.[1] For this reason alone she would merit inclusion in this comparative study of mysticism.

However, one can easily find deeper reasons that justify devoting lengthy attention to her. First, Teresa merits such an extended study because of the capacity of her spiritual life to illuminate with exceptional clarity that relationship that links the intensification and diminution of mystical experiences to the correlative degree to which they either receive or do not receive cultural and religious legitimation. This investigation will show that, like Black Elk's, Teresa's mystical experiences underwent a major change in both their character and intensity (as did the nature of her responses to those experiences) once acknowledged religious authorities legitimized them. One therefore has every reason to expect that a comparison of these two will teach one a great deal about how the manner in which a society legitimates and controls religious behavior and religious experience determines both the content of a mystic's states of consciousness and the specific nature of his or her responses to them.

---

1. See Auguste Poulain, S.J., *The Graces of Interior Prayer: A Treatise on Mystical Theology* (London: Kegan Paul, Trench, Trubner & Company, 1921); Delacroix, *Études d'histoire*; Underhill, *Mysticism*.

Second, careful study of her life and writings quickly disabuses one of the commonly held notion that mysticism always involves, in some form or another, a quest after power. Many forms of shamanism use mystical experiences in order to acquire power over forces within the spirit-world (for example, Black Elk employed his ex-static experiences primarily for the purposes of obtaining secret ritual knowledge and power that he could then utilize to heal his tribesmen or bring about a reconciliation between man and the spiritual order). Robert Monroe's supernormal experiences gave him empirical evidence that led him to maintain that the control of ex-static states would eventually enable humans to develop telekinetic powers that they could manipulate for good or ill.[2] Such manipulative concerns remained completely alien to Teresa. Teresa neither concerned herself with acquiring occult power nor considered manipulating such a spiritual potency. Instead, she conceived of mystical experiences primarily as divinely given stimuli that inspire a soul to pursue the traditional Christian monastic virtues of charity, humility, detachment, and obedience with the fullest degree of rigor humanly possible.[3] To those who too readily identify mysticism with that quest after supernormal forms of knowledge or power, Teresa's complete indifference to these supposedly typical preoccupations of mystics serves as a much needed corrective.

Third, her detailed descriptions of her interior life put into especially sharp relief both how and why mysticism and mystical experience constitute phenomena that are fundamentally, rather than derivatively, historical or contextual in nature. When one studies Teresa's descriptions of her prayer experiences and how she responded to them, one confronts the essential contextuality or historicity of mysticism so vividly that one easily begins to see why purely psychological or phenomenological analyses that abstract the experiences from their religious and cultural contexts prevent an adequate comprehension of their nature. For example, if one examines Teresa's descriptions of those phenomena that she labeled as "union" and

---

2. Monroe, *Journeys Out of the Body*, pp. 265–66.

3. For passages in her works that express this view that mystical experiences are useful only because they foster the practice of those monastic virtues, see Teresa of Avila, *Interior Castle*, trans. and ed. E. Allison Peers (Garden City, N.Y.: Image Books, 1961), pp. 227–31; idem, *Book of the Foundations*, pp. 23–24; idem, *The Letters of St. Teresa of Avila*, trans. and ed. E. Allison Peers (London: Burns, Oates & Washbourne, 1951). See, for example, her letter of October 23, 1576, to Father Gerónimo Gracián and her letter of February 10, 1577, to her brother, Don Lorenzo de Cepeda.

"spiritual marriage,"[4] one quickly discerns that not only were those phenomena more or less distinctive states of consciousness but also that they were thoroughly Christian states of consciousness and responses to experience. They were thoroughly imbued with Christian imagery and emotions and they functioned to promote Christian religious and moral objectives. Regarded from a historical rather than purely psychological perspective, the most important things about Teresa's descriptions of "union" and "spiritual marriage" in her own eyes were not the distinctive psychological or phenomenological traits that each of these experience-states possessed but rather the fact that each was simultaneously a state of being as well as a mode of activity wherein, respectively, the central realities of Christian myth took on flesh as objects of direct experience and the Christian monastic virtues of charity, obedience, humility, and detachment from creatures became fulfilled to the fullest extent humanly possible.[5]

When one compares spiritual marriage and union to analogous phenomena in other traditions that likewise signify states of spiritual perfection accessible only to the spiritually advanced or perfect individual (for example, the *kaivalyam* [isolation] of Patañjali's system of Yoga or the nirvana of the Buddhists), one obtains an incomplete comprehension of what these terms mean if one pays attention to the psychological and phenomenological peculiarities of the experiences they refer to and ignores their intrinsic contextuality. It is important to recognize, for example, that spiritual marriage, kaivalyam, and nirvana seem to be conditions that share certain psychological and phenomenological peculiarities. Each presumes that the subject who experiences them has already largely gone beyond any fascination with or attachment to what Teresa called "imaginative visions,"[6] that is, images and phantasms of both an intrapsychic and supernormal origin that often enter into the mystic's field of consciousness after he has acquired a high degree of spiritual mastery. However, to stop at this level of description leaves out an essential aspect of each of these three states. It ignores how each of them derives its unique identity from the way in which it projects into the subject's field of experience the contents of that

4. On "union," see Teresa of Avila, *Spiritual Testimonies,* in Kiernan Kavanaugh, O.C.D., and Otilio Rodriguez, O.C.D., trans., *The Collected Works of St. Teresa of Avila* (Washington, D.C.: Institute of Carmelite Studies, 1976), 1:356; on "spiritual marriage," see Teresa of Avila, *Interior Castle,* trans. and ed. E. Allison Peers (Garden City, N.Y.: Image Books, 1961), p. 207.

5. Teresa of Avila, *Interior Castle,* pp. 209–10.

6. Teresa of Avila, *Spiritual Testimonies,* p. 354.

theology, mythology, or system of metaphysics that his religious tradition accepts as normative and effects a profound enlargement of the subject's capacity to fulfill the precepts of that ethos or system of ascetic discipline that his religious commitments require. A careful analysis of spiritual marriage and how it differs from cognate conditions of spiritual perfection in other universal religions demonstrates how and why they all constitute phenomena that are fundamentally—not merely secondarily—contextual in nature, how and why they are most emphatically not identical to one another, and why no purely psychological or phenomenological analysis can hope to do justice to them. One sees, then, that showing the fundamental historicity of Teresa's more advanced prayer states carries ramifications that point beyond the study of her mysticism alone for its implications refute those authors who would argue that the higher mystical states somehow transcend the historical environment of those who experience them.[7]

7. Heiler, *Die Bedeutung der Mystik,* p. 6; Stace, *Mysticism and Philosophy* (Philadelphia: J. B. Lippincott, 1960), esp. pp. 94–95, 341–43; Forman, *Problem of Pure Consciousness,* pp. 21–42.

# 26

# A Biographical Sketch of Saint Teresa of Avila

## Early Events and Major Influences

Teresa of Avila was born in 1515 into a family of the minor nobility. Her father, Don Alonso Sanchez y Cepeda, was one of the wealthiest men of Avila, a successful wool merchant of *converso* origins who possessed several estates, large herds of cattle, many servants, and a large residence complex that incorporated two blocks of buildings, patios, and gardens.[1] Her mother came from a distinguished lineage of considerable means. Her wedding to Don Alonso was a spectacle of such magnificence that people for years afterward remembered its splendor.[2] Although Saint Teresa's par-

---

1. It is interesting that Teresan scholars as well as her early biographers suppressed information about the *converso* origins of Teresa's paternal ancestors. (*Conversos* were Spanish Christians whose descendants had converted from Judaism to Christianity.) By the sixteenth century, being of converso origins was considered a contaminating taint so that most families such as Teresa's tried to disguise such ancestry with fictitious genealogies. This information about her tainted ancestry only became public in the 1940s. Two important Teresan scholars, Efren de la Madre de Dios and Otgar Steggink, later admitted that in their 1951 edition of *Santa Teresa y su tiempo* they had deliberately suppressed this information "in order to mitigate the moral effect of this news on our surprised readers" (quoted in Jodi Bilinkoff, *The Avila of St. Teresa: Religious Reform in a Sixteenth-Century City* [Ithaca: Cornell University Press, 1989], p. 102, n. 2). As the sixteenth century progressed, economically successful *hidalgos* (aristocrats) of converso origins, such as Teresa's father, were increasingly regarded with both distrust and contempt by the old aristocracy of Spain. After 1500 more and more legal disabilities began to be imposed on people of converso origins as Spaniards came to be obsessed with *limpieza de sangre* ("purity of blood," freedom from ancestral taint from Jewish ancestors). For example, Spanish monasteries and convents began to refuse admission to postulants who could not prove that their ancestry was free of Jewish taint. In 1566 the Spanish branch of the Mitigated Carmelites to which Teresa originally belonged required that all new candidates must prove that they had no Jewish ancestors. See Rowan Williams, *Teresa of Avila* (Harrisburg, Pa.: Morehouse Publishing, 1991), p. 18.
2. Marcelle Auclair, *Saint Teresa of Avila* (New York: Pantheon Books, 1953), pp. 4–5.

ents were wealthy and her father, in particular, liberally exercised his penchant for indulging himself in costly fineries that only the rich could afford, they never allowed such worldly vanities to dampen their religious devotion. Indeed, Teresa always spoke of her parents with the deepest respect, stating, "I never saw my parents inclined to anything but virtue." She noted that her father always took great care to show compassion to the poor, maintained his chastity, and took great care never to speak ill or falsely of anyone. Her mother likewise exemplified Christian virtue by scrupulously preserving her chastity, by avoiding that vanity that was ordinarily to be expected in someone of her great beauty, and by maintaining tranquillity in the midst of those terrible trials that her persistent poor health caused her to have to bear. Not only did Teresa portray her parents as models of Christian rectitude but she also stated that all of her brothers and sisters resembled their parents in virtue and never hindered her from serving God in any way.[3]

In view of the devoutness of her parents and the virtuousness of her siblings, it should not be surprising to learn that from an early age Teresa exhibited behavior that foreshadowed her later passionate commitment to the religious life. For example, she relates that even as a child she used to show compassion to the poor by giving them alms whenever she had the means to do so.[4] At the tender age of seven, she and her brother Rodrigo used to read the lives of the saints together and dreamed of offering themselves as martyrs in a foreign land. According to her biographer, Ribera, Teresa and her brother became so enamored with this scheme that they actually tried to run away from home in the hopes of dying for Christ in the land of the Moors.[5] When their plans collapsed in a scolding rather than martyrdom, the young Teresa still kept alive her childish religious longings by building hermitages in the orchard, by dressing up as a nun, and—if one may believe her early biographers—even making her playmates observe a rule that she had drawn up herself.[6] However, one significant thing was missing in these accounts of her childhood spirituality: there was no evidence that Teresa was a natural-born mystic. Unlike either Black Elk or Eileen Garrett, Teresa never mentioned that she had had spontaneous visions or supernormal experiences when she was a child.

3. Teresa of Avila, *Life of Teresa of Jesus*, pp. 65–66.
4. Ibid., p. 67.
5. See Stephen Clissold, *St. Teresa of Avila* (New York: Seabury Press, 1982), p. 14; Teresa of Avila, *Life of Teresa of Jesus*, p. 66, n. 5.
6. Teresa of Avila, *Life of Teresa of Jesus*, p. 67.

Instead, she had to wait until she was about twenty-three years old before she had her first mystical experience. Again unlike those of Garrett and Black Elk, these first mystical experiences do not seem to have arisen spontaneously but rather appear to have resulted from the fact that she had only recently acquainted herself with Francisco de Osuña's *Third Spiritual Alphabet* and then successfully put into practice the recollective techniques he outlined in that book.[7]

One makes a serious mistake if one imagines that Teresa's later commitment to a heroic, activist conception of the mystical life arose solely from the beneficial influence of her devout home environment or from her and her brother's reading of the lives of the saints. The religious climate that predominated among the members of her social class, the Spanish aristocracy, fostered a type of spirituality that tended to see religious commitments in the most heroic terms. Teresa and her brother were not the only members of their social class who, at that time, dreamed of offering themselves as martyrs to the Moors. Their childhood scheme found its adult counterpart in the equally quixotic dream of another contemporary Spanish aristocrat, Ignatius Loyola, who imagined that he was somehow destined to convert the Muslim world.[8] Religious sentiments of this sort emerged quite naturally among the sixteenth-century Spanish aristocracy whose members were deeply preoccupied with wars against non-Christian peoples in the New World and North Africa as well as with wars against the Protestants in northern Europe. Several of Teresa's brothers later went off to seek their fortunes and fight the heathen with the New World *conquistadores*.[9] They were therefore hardly what one would call men of peace and quiet scholarly contemplation. They were warriors and men of action. Their religiosity and that of their sister became thoroughly imbued with that activist, warrior spirit that received reinforcement from the fact that the Spanish aristocracy had only recently (in 1492) completed a five-hundred-year-long crusade against the Muslims. Spain was left with a Crusader mentality long after such ideals had become obsolete elsewhere in Western Europe.

In the sixteenth century, then, the Crusader ideals of the Spanish Reconquista were transferred to the often Crusade-like conquest of the heathen peoples of the New World. It is easy to see how these two enterprises

7. Ibid., p. 80. See also Francisco de Osuña, *The Third Spiritual Alphabet*, trans. and introd. Mary E. Gils (New York: Paulist Press, 1980).

8. In A. G. Dickens, *The Counter Reformation* (London: Thames & Hudson, 1969), p. 75.

9. Auclair, *Saint Teresa of Avila*, pp. 30, 109, 279; Clissold, *St. Teresa of Avila*, pp. 13–15.

succeeded in spawning an especially heroic conception of the religious life in which the chivalric and Crusader ideals of loyalty, courage, honor, and an unflinching willingness to suffer and die for Christ against His enemies still remained vigorously alive, especially among the members of those upper classes who fought in these conflicts. In such a martial atmosphere, the contemplative life of monks and nuns became a summons to combat against the spiritual enemies of Christ and His Church in which the cultivation of mental prayer and the monastic virtues of poverty, chastity, and obedience substituted for the physical weapons of the soldiers.[10] One must therefore see Teresa and her brother's childish yearnings for martyrdom against this larger cultural background that glorified war, suffering, and self-sacrifice.

These values central to the ethos of Christian warriors expressed themselves in a sublimated form in the mystical and ascetic writings of numerous sixteenth-century Spanish mystics such as Teresa, John of the Cross, and Ignatius Loyola. In comparison to many of their medieval predecessors, the Spaniards give a much greater prominence to the redemptive value of suffering and heroic conquest of the selfish will. For example, the French Victorine Richard of St. Victor or the German Dominican Meister Eckhart concern themselves little with the transfigurative effects of suffering or asceticism in contrast to the large part that suffering and asceticism play in the writings of John of the Cross and Teresa. It was only natural that in a nation still deeply engrossed in wars with non-Christian peoples and Protestants the images of battle and warfare would find their way into mystics' descriptions of the contemplative life. For example, when Teresa spoke about the contemplative life in *The Way of Perfection* she compared the contemplative nun to a standard-bearer in battle.

> The standard-bearer is not a combatant, yet nonetheless he is exposed to great danger, and inwardly must suffer more than anyone, for he cannot defend himself, as he is carrying the standard, which he must not allow to leave his hands, even if he is cut to pieces. Just so, contemplatives must bear aloft the standard of humility and must suffer all the blows which are aimed at them without striking any themselves.[11]

10. Clissold, *St. Teresa of Avila*, p. 13.
11. Teresa of Avila, *The Way of Perfection*, trans. and ed. E. Allison Peers (Garden City, N.Y.: Image Books, 1964), pp. 130–31.

Here is exemplified that "sublimation" of the warrior ethos referred to above. It depicts monastic asceticism as a process of combat with spiritual rather than physical enemies. Despite the spiritual rather than physical nature of the enemies, it is significant that ascetic combat still requires the same degree of fortitude, courage, and willingness to suffer and face death that a good soldier or Crusader must possess. It is clear, then, that the rhetoric of the sixteenth-century Spanish cloister borrowed much from the rhetoric of the Crusaders' camp. While I do not claim that the sixteenth-century Spaniards were the only Christian mystics who saw the ascetic and mystical life in terms of mortal combat with the enemy, the near simultaneity of the Reconquista, the conquest of the New World, and the inception of the Spanish Inquisition assured that this martial imagery achieved a much greater prominence in their writings than it did in the writings of mystics from other times and parts of Europe that were more distant from such conflicts.

Despite her early indications of religious zeal young Teresa did not continually occupy herself with religious matters. To be sure, her subsequent transition to life in a convent occurred so quickly and so joyfully that its effortlessness suggests that the seeds for such rapid and total commitment had been sown and the ground prepared for them from very early in her childhood.[12] Nonetheless, during her adolescent years, Teresa confessed that her religious impulses lay dormant and that she instead busied herself with frivolous vanities, tales of chivalry, and romantic games.[13]

When she was sixteen her father decided to send her to the local Augustinian convent as a boarder since, as a result of her mother's recent death and the marriage of her elder sister, Teresa was now a young woman living at home unchaperoned by any older female relative. In such circumstances, tradition mandated that well-to-do families send such unmarried women away to board in convents. Although Teresa was still worldly enough to resent this uprooting from her vanities and friends, she quickly began to enjoy her stay there. The good example of the nuns in this convent began to reawaken her hitherto dormant religious longings for she now began to realize that her adolescent vanities were empty and useless. However, she still had an aversion to becoming a nun.[14]

12. Teresa of Avila, *Life of Teresa of Jesus*, p. 77.
13. Ibid., pp. 68–71.
14. Ibid., p. 72.

# Her First Conversion: Teresa Becomes a Nun

Teresa eventually overcame her reservations about joining a convent through the edifying influence of two devout people: a nun at the Augustinian convent, María de Briceño, and one of her paternal uncles, Don Pedro, both of whose conversations on religious matters and holy and discreet ways of life excited her about the religious vocation. Teresa related that her first meeting with Don Pedro proved decisive in convincing her that, despite the many unpleasant renunciations that necessarily go along with it, the life of a nun was the safest course of action a woman would take if she wished to ensure her salvation. Teresa's anxieties about marriage seem also to have powerfully influenced her decision for she admitted that when she first came to live as a boarder at the Augustinian convent, she feared becoming married almost as much as she feared becoming a nun.[15] These reservations about the married state take on greater significance when one takes into account that both her mother and her father's first wife had died in childbirth. The importance of these fears about marriage receive further confirmation from a remark she made to her nuns when she later became a prioress. She explicitly told them how great a favor it was that they had chosen marriage to God rather than marriage to a man for now they no longer had to worry about dying in childbirth.[16]

Despite the edifying examples of her uncle and the devout nun at the Augustinian convent, Teresa did not decide to take on the veil with any great degree of enthusiasm. Her final decision to become a nun was not the result of any sudden experience of the overwhelming devotion or tenderness to God that she later displayed in such great abundance. It was, instead, the final result of a long, coldly rational process of analysis in which a spiritually lukewarm woman figured that since she would eventually have to suffer in Purgatory for her sins, she might just as well get the purgatorial suffering over with here in this life by joining a convent and becoming subject to its discipline.[17]

Things changed radically and rapidly once she entered the Carmelite convent of the Incarnation at Avila as a novice in 1536. Her spiritual lukewarmness suddenly left her once she made her irrevocable decision. She became filled with intense religious fervor. It was as though the seeds

15. Ibid., pp. 73–75.
16. Teresa of Avila, *Book of Foundations*, p. 203; Auclair, *Saint Teresa of Avila*, p. 29.
17. Teresa of Avila, *Life of Teresa of Jesus*, p. 75.

of religious devotion that had lain dormant since the beginning of her adolescence had finally burst into flower with great vigor. Suddenly, everything connected with the religious life—even its penances and disciplines—brought her a great joy that dissipated all her previous doubts about the religious vocation. However, up to this point nothing in her autobiography suggests that her delight in the religious life had anything mystical about it. Even though she was then twenty-three and belonged to a supposedly contemplative order, Teresa still remained a stranger to the mystical graces.

Indeed, Teresa confessed that she was ignorant about how to practice those prerequisites of mystical contemplation, recollection, and mental prayer.[18] This admission stands as a testimony to how far some of the sixteenth-century Carmelites had departed from the rigorous contemplative ideals that had inspired the founders of the order. At least in the Carmelite convent of the Mitigated observance in Avila the nuns did not give their novices any kinds of instructions about how to practice mental prayer or recollect their minds. This omission is really quite remarkable when one realizes that Carmel was originally founded as an order of contemplative religious who, like the Carthusians, centered their whole monastic routine around the quest for mystical communion with God in prayerful solitude.[19]

About a year after she started her novitiate, the sharp change in her lifestyle and diet (and perhaps her excessive penances) caused Teresa to develop a serious illness whose symptoms included cataleptic seizures, paralysis, and what she called "heart trouble."[20] To cure her of this strange malady that plagued her for several years, her superiors sent her home where she could avail herself of good medical care. It is ironic that it was there, in the secular world of pious laymen rather than in a convent of an order supposedly devoted to the life of contemplation and prayer, that Teresa first came into contact with the mystical dimension of Christianity. She asserts that it was her pious uncle, Don Pedro, whom she met once again, who introduced her to the mystical life by giving her a copy of Francisco de Osuña's *Third Spiritual Alphabet*. In that work, Osuña extolled the spiritual virtues of recollection and taught an effective method for practicing it. According to Teresa's own testimony, it was this particular book that showed her how to recollect herself and practice mental

18. Ibid., p. 80.
19. *Dictionnaire de spiritualité*, s.v. "Carmes," by Titus Brandsma, O. Carm., p. 160.
20. For a description of these symptoms, based on accounts given by her early biographers, see Auclair, *Saint Teresa of Avila*, pp. 48–50.

prayer. Furthermore, she relates that soon after she started practicing the recollective techniques that Osuña described, she began, for the first time in her life, to experience those mystical states of prayer that she called the "Prayer of Quiet" and "union."[21]

# The Stagnant Years

When one considers that Teresa's reputation largely rests on the extraordinary quality of her mysticism, it may come as a surprise to discover that her first mystical experiences contributed little to her spiritual advancement. She continued to live much as she always had. Instead, in the *Life of St. Teresa of Jesus,* she characterized the eighteen years (1538–56 or 1557) that followed her first mystical experiences as, for the most part, a time of spiritual stagnation (pp. 78, 108–9).

Does this coincidence between the onset of mystical prayer states and that long period of spiritual depression, malaise, and stagnation imply that those experiences hindered her spiritual development? Nothing could be further from the truth. The spiritually mature Teresa of the 1560s made it very clear that she thought mental prayer and those mystical states that often result from it function as superb helpmates to the religious who is striving after spiritual perfection. In the *Life of St. Teresa of Jesus,* Teresa asserts that "no one who has begun this practice [of mental prayer], however many sins he should commit, should ever forsake it. For it is the means by which we may amend our lives again, and without it amendment will be much harder" (p. 110). Here Teresa is telling us something that seemed obvious to her from the vantage point of her spiritual adulthood but that did not appear so obvious to her when she was a spiritual adolescent, namely, that the cultivation of mystical prayer experiences greatly enhances the efforts of the religious to live his or her life in rigorous accord with the most heroic precepts of Christian virtue. The joyful intimacy with God that monks or nuns are lucky enough to have fortifies their desire to do nothing to displease Him. As a result, the spiritually mature Teresa saw no conflict between the monk's or nun's desire to progress in both ascetic and moral virtue and his or her desire to enjoy mystical experiences. Far from seeing any fundamental antagonism between the mystical aspects of monastic spirituality and its moral and ascetic aspects, the mature saint

21. Teresa of Avila, *Life of St. Teresa of Jesus,* p. 80.

saw that progress in one domain naturally tended to facilitate progress in the other. During her spiritually adolescent, or stagnant, years, Teresa mistakenly assumed that such mystical graces were only given to the spiritually perfect souls. Consequently, if she seemed to be experiencing them she was simply deluding herself into thinking that a demonically counterfeited sense of the divine presence was the same thing. Whereas the spiritually mature saint saw that the mystical quest and the quest for moral and ascetic perfection reciprocally reinforced each other, the immature saint made the mistake of divorcing moral and ascetic progress from progress in acquiring mystical intimacy with God.

I contend that Teresa's capacity to give herself without any reservations to the performance of God's will rather than her own will and to integrate smoothly the cultivation of mystical prayer states and the traditional quest of monks and nuns to embody the perfect practice of the ascetic and moral virtues constitute the best indices of her progress toward spiritual maturity. Measured against these criteria, her behavior during the years 1538–57 exhibits what one would call spiritual immaturity, whereas her behavior after her so-called second conversion of 1556–57 shows that she had reached a more stable state of spiritual equilibrium that it is quite proper to designate as her "mature" phase.

There is abundant autobiographical evidence that indicates that Teresa considered the events of 1556–57 a decisive turning point in her religious development. For the first time since her first two years in the convent she described her condition as one in which she was making progress. She characterized the events of those two years as the great turning point in her spiritual life because, as she put it, "I had quite lost trust in myself and was placing all my trust in God" (p. 115). She spoke of this period of her "second conversion" as a completely new life.

> Until now the life I was describing was my own; but the life I have been living since I began to expound these matters concerning prayer is the life which God has been living in me—or so it has seemed to me. For I believe it to be impossible in so short a time to escape from such wicked deeds and sins. (pp. 219–20)

This new spiritual equilibrium that I have chosen to call her mature phase had its inception when Teresa finally acquired the courage to give up all traces of self-will, dedicate herself completely to obeying the will of God, and take the greatest care to avoid all actions, however trivial, that she or

her superiors thought would offend Him. The evidence from her autobiography suggests that Teresa experienced a sense of stagnation and malaise between 1538 and 1556 because, at that time, she was only half-
heartedly committing herself to her monastic vocation of perfect submission to the will of God. Once she actually summoned up enough courage
to make this commitment in its most rigorous form, the resulting inner
sense of certainty that she was now fully honoring her vows to God
brought her a new sense of peace and calm of conscience that she had not
known before. When this happened, her eighteen-year period of spiritual
stagnation came to an end. Henceforth, she found it easy to abandon her
penchant for engaging in idle conversations, enjoyment of petty amusements, and, most important of all, those secular friendships to which she
had become so attached. She now considered these things sinful and dangerous to her spiritual well-being since they did nothing to advance her
along the road to perfect obedience or detachment from creaturely things.

This new mature phase of Teresa's spiritual life did not just entail moral
and ascetic reformation. It also involved a far-reaching transformation in
the character of her prayer experiences. When she started to give herself
utterly to the task of obeying God's will rather than indulging her own
desires, when she no longer committed even the most venial of sins, and
when she began to spend more time praying to God instead of spending
her prayer time distracted by the petty vanities that her secular friends and
their conversations had stirred up in her mind and affections, she simultaneously began to enjoy a much deeper mystical intimacy with God.

> When I began to avoid occasions of sin and devote myself more to
> prayer, the Lord began to bestow favors upon me and it looked as
> though He were desirous that I should wish to receive them. His
> Majesty began to grant me quite frequently the Prayer of Quiet, and
> often, too, the prayer of Union, which lasted a long time (p. 220).

From these remarks one can see that experiences of the Prayer of Quiet
and the Prayer of Union that she had only known briefly and intermittently during the previous eighteen years now came to her with greater
frequency and also lasted longer. She even began to go into peculiar vehement states of ecstasy or "raptures" that she had never previously experienced. It is significant that this intensification of her mystical life acted as a
powerful stimulus to her moral reformation. For example, she mentioned
that when she had her first experience of rapturous transport, even though

she had by that time succeeded in conquering most of her sinful inclinations, she had not completely overcome her attachment to having idle conversations with her secular friends. Only when she went into this ecstatic transport and therein received locutions from God that she interpreted to mean that He wished her to give them up did she finally summon up enough courage to abandon this creaturely attachment once and for all (pp. 231–32).

These examples clearly demonstrate that, for the spiritually mature Teresa, progress in moral and ascetic virtue and progress in contemplation reciprocally reinforced each other. Only after she abandoned sinful distractions and dedicated herself totally to God did she experience an intensification of her prayer life and, in turn, as her mystical intimacy with God began to deepen she simultaneously began to tap deeper reserves of fortitude and courage that allowed her to conquer sinful proclivities she had formerly found it difficult to control.

An inspection of her autobiography shows that Teresa's behavior during the years 1538 to about 1556 or 1557 stood in sharp contrast to behavior that she displayed after her second conversion. It also shows that those earlier modes of behavior caused that spiritual malaise from which she suffered prior to her second conversion. For example, the spiritually immature Teresa of those earlier years found herself continuously attracted to petty worldly pleasures such as idle conversations with secular friends (pp. 96–97). As a result, she had difficulty devoting herself single-handedly to the service of God. But why would indulgence in these seemingly minor vices become a major cause of her spiritual discontent? First, whenever she would give in to these vain amusements, she could never do so without awakening her conscience even though some of her more lenient confessors encouraged her to ignore these distractions as sins too trivial to worry about. She would always get the feeling deep in her heart that by succumbing to these vanities she was seriously falling away from that ideal of total devotion to God's will that she had solemnly sworn to uphold when she had made her profession as a nun (pp. 113–14). The triviality of the sin could not disguise the fact that the mere fact of its commission was symptomatic of a spiritually dangerous degree of self-will. This constantly experienced contrast between the actual and the ideal continually gnawed at her conscience causing her to experience a persistent sense of spiritual distress and shame.

These venial pastimes also contributed to her spiritual malaise by preventing her from recollecting herself in prayer. Teresa found that because of her seemingly harmless habit of engaging in idle conversations, whenever she sat down to recollect herself during that time set aside for prayer, she fell prey to innumerable distractions that prevented her from attaining that single-mindedness so necessary if prayer is to enkindle devotion or intimate contact with God. "I could not shut myself within myself without at the same time shutting in a thousand vanities. I spent many years in this way, and I am now amazed that a person could have gone on for so long without giving up" (p. 105). Since she could not recollect herself without the greatest effort, she lost both the sense of intimacy with God and the emotional ardor that arises in the soul when the mind becomes recollected and sensitive to God's presence. This inability to recollect herself caused her to suffer from long spells of aridity when she would no longer feel that God was present. These long periods of divine absence slowly but surely dried up devotion.

Even when Teresa intermittently experienced mystical prayer states during this stagnant period, it is significant that, in sharp contrast to her attitude toward them that she had after her second conversion, she had difficulty comprehending how these experiences could actually help her to progress toward moral perfection. For example, she related that despite the considerable benefits that she derived from her first mystical experiences (they intensified her contempt for worldly things), sometime in 1541 or 1542 she began to have scruples about her moral fitness to have them (p. 96). Without consulting anyone, she decided that since she had been leading such a sinful life, she really had no right to be enjoying the blissful consolations that her practice of mental prayer had been giving her. For this reason, she gave up practicing mental prayer for more than a year. This decision, based on a false concept of humility, had disastrous consequences. Indeed, Teresa stated that she considered that particular decision to have been one of the gravest mistakes of her life for it almost led to her spiritual ruin (p. 101).

Why did the mature Teresa eventually conclude that giving up mental prayer was so spiritually ruinous? Abandoning mental prayer debilitates the spiritual life because it deprives the soul of the sensation that God is speaking to it and loving it. It follows that when the soul lacks this sensation of divine immediacy that mystical prayer states give it, it loses the ardor to serve God that it once had when those moments of emotionally quickening contact came to it more frequently. In turn, this loss of religious ardor leads to a morally destructive state of aridity because, by losing its yearning for the divine presence, the soul simultaneously begins to lose the major source of that fortitude that would otherwise have enabled it to have endured anything for God's sake and to have bent its own will completely and joyfully to the will of that friend whose presence formerly gave it so much joy (pp. 110–13).

To summarize, Teresa discovered that the more perfectly she embodied the Christian ascetic and moral virtues the more deeply she began to enjoy mystical intimacy with God. The reverse was also true: the more deeply she enjoyed prayerful intimacy with God, the more zealous became her practice of the Christian virtues and the mortification of her self-will. In short, Teresa—like so many other Christian mystics and monastic writers—noted that the experiential-mystical and the moral-ascetic domains of the religious life stood in reciprocal interdependence. This acute sense of the interdependence of the two domains is one of the hallmarks of Teresan spirituality.

## Teresa's Education: The Slow Escape from Stagnation

The foregoing analyses have established that Saint Teresa emerged from her lengthy period of stagnation at the same time that she began to renounce completely all vestiges of self-will so that she could give herself utterly to serving God and harmonize her contemplative experiences with her pursuit of ascetic and moral perfection. However, this study has still not shed any light on that educational process that allowed her to escape from the doldrums. It has thus far overlooked the vital role that her confessors and other spiritual guides played in the process that emancipated her from spiritual stagnation. Teresa did not "become" a mystic in the same manner that a baby naturally grows up to be an adult. Since she did not have spontaneous childhood mystical experiences as did the young Black Elk, she evidently had to learn how to develop a sensitivity to them. Who taught her how to awaken her latent capacity for experiencing mystical states? What did these people teach about mysticism? How did they affect the course of her spiritual development?

During her first two years as a nun (1536–38), Teresa obtained most of her religious inspiration and instruction from the other nuns who lived in her convent. While her convent had considerably softened the Primitive Carmelite Rule—that is, the nuns no longer rigidly observed enclosure or practiced poverty (the sisters from well-to-do families received better hous-ing than the nuns who had come from more humble backgrounds)—one must not exaggerate the laxity of her convent either.[22] Teresa herself ad-mitted that her convent included "many servants of God" from whom she could have learned a great deal had she not been so badly afflicted with spiritual blindness and pride.[23] Moreover, several other nuns at the convent were known to have practiced rigorous penances. Aside from preventing some of the more severe penances that Teresa inflicted on herself as a result of a novice's excess of ardor, neither her superiors nor the other members of her community did anything that would have dampened that religious zeal that suddenly burst into flame when she decided to join the convent.[24] One can therefore assert that the Mitigated Carmelites' relax-ation of the rigors of the Primitive Carmelite Rule did not lead to such a serious degree of moral or ascetic laxity that it would have prevented se-rious religious in the convent of the Incarnation from practicing an exem-plary monastic life there.

Like any other Catholic monk or nun, Teresa's training as a novice would have thoroughly imbued her with the idea that her ultimate reli-gious goal was to give up utterly her own will so that she could more perfectly live in accordance with the will of God. I have already mentioned above that even in the early years of her life in the convent, she suffered profoundly from pangs of conscience every time she indulged herself in petty vanities for she realized that these twinges of moral discomfort were reminders that she was neglecting her most important religious obliga-tion—to serve God unreservedly with all her heart, soul, and body.[25] For this reason, one can quite confidently state that Teresa learned about the importance of that first prerequisite to Christian spiritual progress, the need to give up all self-will, from the education she received as a novice.

However, when it came to acquiring the second of the two prerequisites to progress along the spiritual path, namely, the capacity to integrate mys-tical experience with the pursuit of moral and ascetic virtue, her education at the Carmelite convent of the Incarnation appears to have been seriously deficient. Even though many of her sisters at the convent possessed an

22. Regarding enclosure, see *Dictionnaire de spiritualité*, s.v. "Carmes," p. 168; Teresa of Avila, *Life of St. Teresa of Jesus*, p. 79. Regarding class distinctions, see Auclair, *Saint Teresa of Avila*, p. 48.

23. Teresa of Avila, *Life of St. Teresa of Jesus*, p. 78.

24. Auclair, *Saint Teresa of Avila*, p. 48.

25. Teresa of Avila, *Life of St. Teresa of Jesus*, pp. 96–97.

admirable devotion to God and furnished her with exemplary models of ascetic self-denial and moral virtue, they did not seem to have cultivated the mystical side of the religious life—at least they never taught Teresa anything about how to practice mental prayer or how to recollect herself.[26] Teresa had to learn these prerequisites of the contemplative life from reading Francisco de Osuña.

There appear to be several reasons why the Carmelite nuns of the Incarnation seem to have forgotten that even their Mitigated Rule still proclaimed that contemplation ought to be an important element in their spiritual lives.[27] First, like many other people in sixteenth-century Spain, they took it for granted that only the truly exceptional religious individual could merit genuine mystical experiences. Consequently, the ordinary religious could entertain little hope that he or she would ever experience such contemplative graces from God. Second, there was a tradition many late fifteenth-century and early sixteenth-century Spanish monasteries and convents emphasized: the performance of vocal intercessory prayers for the benefit of the deceased lay patrons of the religious establishment, a focus of spiritual concerns that tended to come at the expense of a monk's or nun's practice of interior, mental prayer.[28] The powerful lay patrons of many late fifteenth- and early sixteenth-century religious houses usually made it a precondition of their endowment that its residents pray "vocally and continuously" for the souls of their departed benefactors, kinfolk, and clients so that the prayers of the religious could shorten their patrons' stay in Purgatory.[29] Failure to perform these sometimes onerous public vocal prayers could cause the patron's descendants to pull their financial support from the delinquent religious house and force the return of the endowment to the patron's heirs.[30] In short, prior to the monastic reforms of the mid-sixteenth century that the Jesuits, the Discalced Franciscans, and the Discalced Carmelites inaugurated and that gave a renewed emphasis to the cultivation of recollection and mental prayer, there were powerful economic and social forces at work in Spain that tended to favor the performance of vocal prayer at the expense of private and silent mental prayer.

With respect to the first reason listed above, Teresa's own testimony confirms that most Spaniards of her day assumed that mystical graces were

---

26. Ibid., p. 80.
27. *Dictionnaire de spiritualité*, s.v. "Carmes," p. 166.
28. See Bilinkof, *The Avila of St. Teresa*, pp. 50–52.
29. Ibid., p. 78.
30. This almost happened to Teresa's convent in 1533; see ibid., p. 51.

only for the spiritual and moral elite and were, therefore, inaccessible to the ordinary layman and religious. For example, shortly after she read Osuña's book and started to practice his method of recollection, she began to experience the mystical Prayer of Quiet and Prayer of Union.[31] One would think that after having read Osuña and so deeply taken his teachings on prayer to heart she would have easily liberated herself from that common prejudice of her day that asserted that only the spiritually perfect souls could or should enjoy mystical experiences. After all, Osuña repeatedly emphasized that it was his intention in writing the book to make mystical prayer states accessible to all good Catholics, religious and laymen alike, and thereby combat the pernicious notion that they were only for a select few.[32] The ease with which Teresa acquired her first mystical graces after following his advice would have further operated so as to disabuse her of this prejudice. However, this did not occur. Instead, she let her uncritical acceptance of this idea that mysticism was intrinsically inaccessible slowly destroy that mood of spiritual exhilaration that initially accompanied her first experiences. Within a few years (1541 or 1542), she started to suffer from scruples concerning her moral fitness to deserve them. She reasoned that since she had behaved so sinfully by constantly indulging herself in petty amusements when she knew that she should have been serving God rather than herself, it would be very wicked of her to present an outward appearance of goodness by withdrawing to pray. Since her devotion to mental prayer and recollection only deceived others into thinking that she was good, humility demanded that she abandon this practice and live at the same shallow level of spiritual development as everyone else. Instead of praying mentally, she would henceforth pray only vocally as the ordinary person does since that pallid substitute for true converse with God was all that her sins merited.[33] As one can see, this chain of reasoning incorporates the assumption that only the spiritually perfect soul can enjoy or deserve mystical graces.

It is significant that Teresa appears to have arrived at this decision to abandon mental prayer without consulting anyone. This departure from her normal practice suggests that ideas of the sort mentioned above probably constituted part of the conventional wisdom of the period. Only the more highly educated or sophisticated religious writers such as Francisco de Osuña or Peter of Alcántara would have challenged these seemingly

31. Teresa of Avila, *Life of St. Teresa of Jesus*, p. 80.
32. Osuña, *Third Spiritual Alphabet*, 45–48, 207–8, 211.
33. Teresa of Avila, *Life of St. Teresa of Jesus*, pp. 96–97.

obvious truisms. At the time that these two men wrote, we may presume their critical opinions represented a minority viewpoint. Even though Teresa was exposed to the writings of Osuña that challenged the conventional assumption that mystical states must remain inaccessible to the average Christian, the fact that his ideas received little or no reinforcement from the other people with whom she associated at that time made it highly improbable that she would challenge the conventional point of view.

There is evidence that other people besides Teresa held the opinion that only the perfect could enjoy genuine mystical prayer states. Around 1556, as her spiritually stagnant period drew to its close, she once again started to enjoy mystical experiences frequently. Although this renewal of intimacy with God brought her great comfort, she found several things disturbing about it. First, she discovered that these experiences suppressed the functioning of her understanding so that she found herself unable to describe what she had experienced to anyone else. Second, she noted that they came to her without her being able to control either the time of their appearance or disappearance. Third, she could not help recalling that in 1546 a famous *beata* (pious laywoman) had fooled many influential people, including Queen Isabella, into thinking that she really enjoyed ecstasies from God when, in actual fact, she had made a pact with the Devil. Bearing these three facts in mind, how could Teresa be sure that her own experiences were not similarly tainted by a demonic origin, especially since these prayer states arrived and departed beyond her control and also involved a suppression of her understanding so that she could no longer think about or concentrate on scenes of Christ's Passion when she prayed to Him?[34] For these reasons, she sought the advice of an educated pious layman, Don Francisco de Salcedo, to whom she confided her mystical experiences as well as the rest of her thoughts and activities. Don Salcedo shared Teresa's anxiety about the possibility that her visions might have a demonic origin because he could not comprehend how a woman as sinful as Teresa had confessed herself to be could at the same time experience such mystical converse with God.[35] It is clear that Don Salcedo's line of reasoning displayed the same underlying assumption that formed the basis for Teresa's earlier decision to give up mental prayer for a time. Both individuals took it for granted that only the spiritually perfect could enjoy genuine mystical communion with God.

34. Ibid., pp. 220–25; Clissold, *St. Teresa of Avila*, pp. 46–47.
35. Teresa of Avila, *Life of St. Teresa of Jesus*, p. 224.

The coincidence of this prejudice in both Teresa and Don Salcedo supports my contention that this item of belief formed a part of that tacitly accepted conventional wisdom about mysticism and contemplation current in mid-sixteenth-century Spain. I suggest, moreover, that the prevalence of such notions helps to explain why some monasteries and convents such as the Incarnation no longer bothered to educate their monks and nuns about recollection and mental prayer.

Since Teresa's religious education at the Incarnation did not include any instruction about either contemplation or mental prayer and since she did not possess any natural capacity to experience supernormal states of consciousness spontaneously, one may reasonably infer that if she had she relied exclusively on what her instructresses at the convent had taught her, she never would have become a mystic. Instead, it was influences from outside her order—her confessors, the books that she read, and other spiritual people whom she met—that provided her with that knowledge and guidance that allowed her to manifest her latent mystical sensitivities.

I have shown earlier in this chapter that Osuña's book taught her the most important thing necessary for becoming a mystic insofar as it instructed her on how to recollect herself. However, I also noted that Osuña's influence did not succeed in uprooting Teresa's damaging notion that mystical experiences were only the prerogative of the perfect. Her uncritical acceptance of this idea prevented her from integrating her newly arisen experiences into the total framework of her conventual life. Because she assumed that these contemplative experiences were only for the perfect, she developed scruples that quickly caused her to turn away from mental prayer altogether.[36] The resultant suppression of her mystical states prevented them from having any beneficial effect on her quest for moral and ascetic perfection. Since she could no longer experience God's presence in prayer, she started to fall prey to frequent spells of listlessness and aridity.

Once again one finds that someone outside her Order provided Teresa with the guidance she needed just when (1543–44) she very well might have aborted her career as a mystic. When she told her father's confessor, the Dominican Vicente Barrón, about the aridity she had been experiencing and her past decision to abandon mental prayer, he impressed on her that she must under no circumstances ever give up such an exceedingly beneficial practice no matter how sinful she considered herself to be.

36. Ibid., pp. 96–97.

Thanks to this advice, Teresa suppressed her scruples and once again took up the practice of mental prayer never to abandon it. Father Barrón's advice played a crucial role in her subsequent spiritual development because her decision to follow it ensured that she would continue to practice those recollective techniques so necessary to inducing mystical states. It is quite possible that without Barrón's advice Teresa would have continued to allow her scruples concerning her fitness for mystical graces to have shut off her access to visions and locutions.

I must emphasize, however, that Father Barrón's advice did not cure her of that spiritual malaise she had been suffering from for so long. First, she discovered that her renewed practice of mental prayer actually intensified it because when she recollected herself, the closer proximity to God it produced made her realize more acutely than before how serious her faults were in God's eyes.[37] Second, Father Barrón's counsel to pray did not instill in her the courage that she still needed if she were to completely renounce all vestiges of sinful behavior. She did not acquire this degree of courage until she underwent her second conversion.

The foregoing evidence shows that by 1544 Teresa had already learned two important things. From Osuña she had learned how to bring about mystical experiences by practicing recollection. From Father Barrón she had learned that she must under no circumstances abandon those techniques of mental prayer and recollection that she had acquired from her perusal of Osuña. Despite their importance, these items of knowledge did not, in and of themselves, bring about any significant deepening of her mystical life beyond what I have already mentioned for one notices that the next twelve years of her life did not exhibit any spiritual developments of consequence. Certain things were still lacking during the years 1544–56 that prevented Teresa's contemplative and visionary experiences from coming into full bloom. What were these missing nutrients? First, Teresa needed acknowledgment from religious authorities that her experiences really came from God. Evidence will be presented later in this chapter that demonstrates that had she not received this legitimation it is almost certain that she would have suppressed and eventually obliterated her sensitivities to mystical phenomena. Second, Teresa had to take the radical step of thoroughly eradicating all traces of self-will from all her thoughts and actions. Like most of her sisters at the Incarnation, she, too, had become content with a half-hearted though sincere degree of self-renunciation and

37. Ibid., pp. 105–6.

had deluded herself into thinking that this was all that God demanded from one who had taken vows to place love of Him before love of self. I will show that her decision to actually take this extreme step in its full rigor culminated her second conversion crisis with the twofold consequence that not only did she henceforth practice the Christian virtues with the utmost scrupulosity but, by taking this step, she also profoundly enhanced the quality of her mystical relationship with God. It is significant that while her superiors at the Incarnation did not seem to have demanded or encouraged this rigorous degree of self-renunciation from her, her Jesuit confessors and spiritual guides began to pressure her to do this. Their influence prevailed and from that moment (which also happened to coincide very closely with that moment when they convinced her that her visions and locutions really did come from God rather than the Devil), one can say that Teresa had finally surmounted that spiritual maturation crisis she referred to as her "second conversion." In other words, to become a full-fledged contemplative, Teresa had to do more than just master techniques of recollection. Mastery of these techniques could do no more than awaken her latent sensitivity to mystical experiences if it were not reinforced by a deepened moral commitment and legitimation from religious authority. Only then could these sensitivities spring into full activity.

I shall now examine how the advice of her Jesuit advisers actually facilitated this metamorphosis and rescued her from developments that could have stifled the full expression of her mystical relationship with God.

# Her Second Conversion: Spiritual Maturity

For reasons that remain obscure, Teresa rather suddenly experienced an intensification of her devotion to Christ sometime in either 1555 or 1556. One day she happened to see a particularly moving image of Christ's Passion displayed in the oratory. The sight of it immediately overwhelmed her.

> So great was my distress when I thought how ill I had repaid Him for those wounds that I felt as if my heart were breaking, and I threw myself down beside Him, shedding floods of tears and beg-

ging Him to give me strength once for all so that I might not offend Him. . . . When I saw that image of which I am speaking *I think I must have made greater progress because I had quite lost trust in myself and was placing all my confidence in God.*[38]

This passage describes the beginning of that crisis known as her second conversion. Notice particularly how this watershed in her spiritual career originally had nothing to do with any kind of transformation in the character of her extraordinary visionary or auditory experiences or in the quality of her sensitivity to them. In other words, it is imperative that one understand that, at its inception, her second conversion was a crisis that pertained to the quality of her moral and ascetic commitments rather than to the quality of her mystical awareness of God. Inspection of the italicized portions above demonstrates the validity of this assertion. In them, Teresa clearly connected this turning point in her religious career to her growing awareness that, despite her solemn vows, she had failed to follow the path of self-renunciation and faith with sufficient rigor and integrity.

The above passage also contains an implicit confession that that sense of spiritual stagnation that had plagued Teresa during the previous eighteen years stemmed from the half-heartedness of her earlier commitments to God. She implies that one's degree of progress toward religious perfection is directly proportional to the degree to which one gives oneself utterly to Him. In short, by 1556 Teresa had come to the realization that ascetic and moral half-measures could no longer suffice for her. As a solemnly professed religious, how could she claim to be imitating the life of Christ if she did not strive to live the rest of her life with that same degree of poverty, humility, faith, and detachment that He had exemplified while he had dwelt among humans?

Bearing these considerations in mind, it is not surprising that Teresa looked back at this particular incident as that moment in her spiritual development when she finally began to make definite progress toward perfection. She noticed that from then on she found it easier and easier to deny herself for the sake of obeying God. Nevertheless, I must point out that these improvements did not occur overnight. She still experienced several moments of hesitancy before she actually took the final plunge. For example, she acknowledged that even after this incident she long put off consulting the Jesuit fathers who had recently (in 1554) moved into Avila about her spiritual condition because she feared that they would ask her to

38. Ibid., p. 115.

make changes in her lifestyle that would be too rigorous for her to obey. As she put it, "I did not consider myself worthy to speak to them or strong enough to obey them, and this made me still more afraid, for I felt that it would be unthinkable for me to discuss these matters with them and yet remain as I was."[39]

While I have asserted that Teresa's second conversion crisis originally had nothing to do with her mystical experiences, it did not take long for its ramifications to carry over into that domain of her religious life. She observed that soon after she began to spend more time devoted to solitary prayer instead of spending it engaging in idle conversations with friends and visitors, she started to experience a renewal of those mystical prayer states that she had enjoyed during those months that had immediately succeeded her first encounter with Osuña's writings. However, these prayer states were not only returning but they were also apparently lasting longer and occurring more frequently.[40] It is evident, then, that while Teresa did not connect the origin of her second conversion crisis to any aspect of her mystical or visionary experience, she did recognize that the deepening of her moral and ascetic commitments that this second conversion brought about had created a spiritual environment highly conducive to an intensification of her mystical state of consciousness.

One would think that with this simultaneous revivification of both Teresa's mystical life and her moral-ascetic life no further serious obstacles could have prevented her from developing her contemplative relationship with God to its fullest extent. This was not the case, however, because she soon faced another crisis briefly alluded to earlier in this chapter: she fell prey to the fear that perhaps these mystical prayer experiences and moments of blissful delight had come from the Devil rather than from God. Furthermore, Teresa was baffled by those moments when she found that her capacity to form thoughts seemed to disappear. From reading Bernadino de Laredo's *Ascent of Mt. Sion,* she suspected that her inability to think discursively for periods of time was probably not a symptom of mental pathology or demonic possession but more likely a result of the soul's union with God.[41] Nevertheless, she was still bothered by the possibility that these involuntary suspensions of thought were demonic in origin. To allay these anxieties, she turned to an educated pious layman, Don Francisco de Salcedo, for guidance. Unfortunately, Don Salcedo and Gaspar

39. Ibid., pp. 220–21.
40. Ibid., p. 220.
41. Ibid., p. 225.

Daza, a priest whom Salcedo had consulted, grimly confirmed Teresa's worst fears for they concluded that these prayer experiences had probably originated from the Devil.[42] Their judgment implied that Teresa had no other course of action open to her except to abandon mental prayer and recollection. In the *Life of St. Teresa of Jesus,* Teresa reasons that "after almost twenty years' experience of prayer I had gained nothing, but had been deluded by the devil, surely it was better for me not to pray at all" (p. 225). Had she fully accepted their conclusions and quit mental prayer, Teresa's career as a mystic would have come to a dead stop since abandoning recollection would have caused her to lose access to those extraordinary visionary and auditory states wherein she experienced intimate converse with God. Once again, she had arrived at one of those critical junctures in her spiritual development where a false step would have suffocated her sensitivity to mystical experiences. In some respects, this situation (of 1556 or 1557) was a rerun of the situation she had faced in 1541–42 when, solely on her own initiative, she made the decision to abandon the practice of mental prayer. In that earlier incident, a man to whom she owed obedience had managed to persuade her that her course of action had been founded on a faulty premise. However, now the situation was more serious. In one crucial respect the situation had been reversed for it was now the case that men to whom she owed obedience were advocating, rather than opposing, a course of action that would have deadened her sensitivity to visions and locutions.

42. It is interesting to note that even though Teresa had shown Don Salcedo and Gaspar Daza those passages in Bernardino de Laredo's *Ascent of Mt. Sion* where he described the union of the soul with God and the concomitant suspension of discursive thought that union brings about, Daza and Salcedo still believed that these states of consciousness were the work of the Devil. Recent events had made the Spanish Inquisition of Teresa's middle and later years increasingly suspicious of women mystics and practitioners of recollective prayer. As Rowan Williams has pointed out, by the middle of the sixteenth century, "to recommend the practice of *recogimiento* [recollection], particularly to women and lay people, soon became another mark of profound unreliability in Inquisitorial eyes" (quoted from Williams, *Teresa of Avila,* p. 30). The case of the Franciscan nun Magdalena de la Cruz of Córdoba in 1546 had stunned all of Spain and given women mystics a very bad reputation—a memory that still haunted Salcedo and Daza and even Teresa herself. (It is possible that she was alluding to this particular incident in chapter 23 of her *Life of St. Teresa of Jesus,* p. 220.) Like Teresa, Magdalena de la Cruz had been known widely for her virtuous life and her numerous mystical communications from God. Her reputation for piety and sanctity had caused Queen Isabella and the Inquisitor-General of Spain to seek her out. Imagine everyone's horror when, without any coercion, Magdalena freely confessed that all her mystical graces had been given to her by the Devil with whom she had made a pact at the age of five! See Clissold, *St. Teresa of Avila,* pp. 46–47.

Fortunately, at this critical juncture Don Salcedo and Gaspar Daza had both the good sense and the decency to refer Teresa to someone more experienced in these matters so that she could benefit from an informed second opinion. For this reason, they arranged for her to meet one of the Jesuit fathers and told her to give him a complete description of her life and her prayer experiences taking care to obey to the letter all the instructions that he might see fit to give her after he had heard her confession. This young Jesuit, Father Juan de Prádanos, immensely relieved Teresa when he concluded that she had nothing to fear. Quite the contrary, everything about her prayer experiences and her responses to them suggested that they came from the Holy Spirit and not from the Devil. Moreover, like Father Barrón before him, Prádanos also stressed that she must never give up the practice of mental prayer. He argued that since God was showing her His great favor by sending her blissful consolations in prayer, He might very well be using these experiences to strengthen her for some task that He had planned for her to accomplish on His behalf. Accordingly, she must cultivate the practice of prayer all the more diligently so that she could better conform herself to His will taking care, however, not to pray with the expectation that she would receive consolations and favors as a reward for doing so. Prádanos emphasized that she must always think only of God's pleasure rather than her own in such matters. He concluded his advice by urging her to practice both the virtues and her penitential mortifications more rigorously so that her prayer experiences could develop on more solid foundations and her actions could become more completely pleasing to God (pp. 226–29).

Prádanos's reassuring conclusions and counsels did far more than just give Teresa a momentary relief from anxieties—they made an immediate and permanent impact on both her prayer experiences and religious behavior. For example, she noted that immediately after he had given her the good news, her mystical experiences underwent some significant changes. She discovered that when she made a conscious effort to follow his advice to pray mentally without desiring favors and consolations, the very endeavor to resist them caused them to come to her more abundantly and more intensely than they had ever done before. She also discovered that she no longer needed to withdraw herself from all distractions and remain motionless in order to receive God's favors for He now sent them to her without such recollective efforts. It seemed to her as though human effort began to play a less and less significant role in the genesis of her prayer states while, at the same time, the role of divine grace began to play a progressively larger role. As to the impact that Prádanos's counsels and conclusions had on her religious behavior, one notices that she deepened the intensity of her commitment to moral and ascetic perfection immediately after she had her first meeting with him. For example, she relates that in the weeks that immediately followed their first meeting, she noticed that as her consolations and favors in prayer intensified she experienced a correlative intensification in her love of Christ. In turn, as her love of Christ deepened, she became more and more willing to do anything that would please Him. Consequently, she grew fonder of penances. This newly intensified concern with ascetic perfection soon became so obsessive that she could not recollect herself in prayer until she had first satisfied herself that she had thrown away all superfluities and small luxuries that a rigorous interpretation of her religious calling might require her to reject as a token of how sincerely she had committed herself to the task of renouncing the world and its vanities (p. 229).

Her compulsion to do nothing even remotely offensive to God eventually intensified to such a degree in those months that followed her talk with Prádanos that she finally accomplished something that she had been struggling for twenty years to achieve—she at long last acquired enough courage to abandon once and for all those secular friendships and conversations that had persistently nagged at her conscience. I shall now give a brief description of how she arrived at this important decision to forsake them.

One will recall that after Prádanos had reassured Teresa about the genuineness of her prayer states, she at once responded to this heartening news by immediately developing a great yearning to practice penances. She related that almost immediately after she made her confession to him and received his reply, Christ began to encourage her "to suffer things which persons who knew me, and even those nuns or my own house, considered and described as extreme" (pp. 228–29). One can see from this statement that Teresa was experiencing a resurgence of that longing for asceticism that had lain dormant since the self-sacrificing fervor of her earliest years in the convent had cooled. Nevertheless, she realized that however radical these new efforts at self-abnegation might appear when one compared them to the half-hearted endeavors of her stagnant period, they still fell short of that degree of renunciation that her religious vocation demanded from her. It particularly vexed her that she could not muster up enough courage to give up those secular friendships and visitations that continued to link her to the profane world. Even two months after her first meeting with Prádanos (shortly after he had been transferred to a new city), Teresa was still pondering whether or not to take this final step. Prádanos's successor, the Jesuit Balthazar Alvarez, continued to encourage her to sever this last connection to the outside world but she still balked at this proposal despite the otherwise admirable progress in self-abnegation she had made in the previous two months. However, Alvarez did eventually succeed in getting her to follow his suggestion that she commend the matter of her secular friendships to God and listen to His answer. She did so and spent almost an entire day in prayer beseeching God to give her the courage to conform herself completely to His will. While she prayed in this manner, there suddenly came upon her "a transport so sudden that it almost carried me away: I could make no mistake about this, so clear was it. This was the first time that the Lord had granted me the favor of any kind of rapture. I heard these words: 'I will have thee converse now, not with men but with angels.'" Teresa interpreted this locution (which she assumed had come from God) to mean that He wished her to abandon secular friendships and conversations once and for all.

This experience succeeded in accomplishing in one instant what the suggestions of several of her most respected confessors could not do—it immediately caused her to sever her secular friendships once and for all.

> Never since then have I ever been able to maintain firm friendship except with people who I believe love God and try to serve Him nor have I derived comfort from any others or cherished any private affection for them. It has not been in my power to do so. . . . Since that day I have been courageous enough to give up everything for the sake of God, who in that moment . . .was pleased to make His servant another person (pp. 231–32).

As even the most cursory inspection shows, this particular mystical experience carried with it a remarkable authoritativeness and efficacy that her previous mystical experiences had never possessed. For this reason, Teresa ranked it as an especially important milestone in her spiritual development. In one moment she had become an entirely new person in much the same way that a caterpillar turns into a butterfly.

This rapture effected her spiritual metamorphosis in two principal ways. First, it substituted God's will for her own will, that is to say, Teresa found that she possessed a natural inclination to act in accordance with God's will just as though His commandments had emerged spontaneously from the innermost depths of her soul or subconscious. Consequently, those combats between the demands of the flesh and the demands of the spirit, between her persistent desires to give in to vanities and luxuries and her other longings to reject them utterly lost most of their sharpness and no longer debilitated her as they had done during her stagnant period. Teresa henceforth found it much easier to avoid sinful temptations since the desire for them no longer seemed to arise spontaneously. Instead, her desires spontaneously gravitated, not toward sinful or worldly things, but rather toward things that she knew or thought would please God. Second, this experience marked her transformation into a new person insofar as she exhibited a much more solid confidence that it was indeed God speaking to her when she prayed. No longer does one find her zeal to serve Him or her sense of close proximity to Him crippled by scruples as had happened in the past. No longer does one find her fearing that her mystical prayer experiences derived only from her imagination (p. 100). Because of this new confidence, Teresa's mystical experiences underwent a subtle intensification after 1557. No longer were they solely restricted to those states she called the Prayer of Quiet and the Prayer of Union but they now incorporated other types of mystical states such as raptures and the intellectual vision of the Holy Trinity. Teresa began to enjoy a progressively more continuous sense of intimacy with God than she had known before. All of these considerations justify treating this particular mystical experience as both the culminating episode of her second conversion as well as that moment when one can definitely sense that she finally left behind the storms and stresses of her spiritual adolescence. She had entered into the mature phase of her mystical life, a condition wherein she started to experience a more or less continual, rather than sporadic, sense of being in immediate contact with God and also developed a much enhanced capability to conform herself radically to His will.

Why did God speak to Teresa so powerfully and so compellingly during this particular rapture and yet fail to do so in earlier visions and locutions? For example, fifteen years earlier she had an exceptionally vivid visionary encounter with God in which He similarly commanded her to shun secular friendships.

> Christ revealed Himself to me, in an attitude of great sternness, and showed me what there was in this [particular friendship] that displeased Him. I saw Him with the eyes of the soul more clearly than I ever could have seen Him with those of the body; and it made

such an impression on me that, although it is now more than twenty-six years ago, I seem to have Him present with me still.

Despite its extraordinary vividness, this particular vision did not bring about any long-lasting change in Teresa's behavior as did her rapture experience. To be sure, for a little while she did take God's admonition very seriously because she became "greatly astonished and upset about it . . . and never wanted to see that person again" but the impact of this warning soon lost its force as she quickly resumed the forbidden friendship (pp. 99–100). Did this disobedience indicate that Teresa had lost respect for God or for her vow of obedience to Him and those who stood in His place? Not at all, because she did admit that her first reaction had been one of never wishing to see that person again. At this point she clearly still held the opinion that her experience had actually come from God so she felt compelled to obey it. One can trace the beginnings of her disobedience to those moments when this certainty began to weaken.

This assurance vanished when Teresa determined that her vision had merely originated in her imagination. From that point on, she no longer felt compelled to obey it. Two factors led her to this doleful conclusion. First, her ignorance of the possibility that a human being could "see" without using the physical organ of sight led her to ascribe the quasi-ocular phenomena of visions to that only other source of such manifestations with which our everyday life acquaints us, namely, the imagination. Second, she mentioned the highly significant fact that she never discussed this particular visionary episode with anyone—not even her confessor or her friends. Consequently, she never had a chance to hear anyone in a position of religious authority contradict her conclusions (p. 100).

The conditions that prevailed in 1557 presented a striking contrast to those of fifteen years earlier insofar as Teresa no longer doubted that her visions came from God. For this reason, she had no choice but to obey them as long as they did not contradict Scripture, the teachings of the Church, or her religious superiors' orders. This radical change in the way she responded to her mystical experiences came about because men invested with great religious authority and prestige had, for the first time, started to vouch for their divine origin. During the three months that had preceded her first rapture two Jesuits—Father Prádanos and the illustrious nobleman, future saint, and future General of the Jesuit order, Francis Borgia—had unequivocally told her that they believed that her prayer experiences had come from the Holy Spirit and not from the Devil as Don

Salcedo and Gaspar Daza had led her to believe a few months before (pp. 226–30). Moreover, this judgment of these religiously prestigious men coincided with her own growing conviction that her visions and prayer states had a divine rather than a demonic or purely imaginary origin (p. 220). This coincidence guaranteed that, as long as this harmony of viewpoints lasted, whenever God would in the future speak to her in a vision she would have to obey Him most scrupulously since any failure to do so would necessarily indicate that she was committing the worst crime any religious could perpetrate—deliberately rebelling against the express commandments of God or those whom she had sworn to obey in His place. No longer could she disobey such visionary directives or admonitions on the grounds that they had originated from her imagination for she now had the most respected religious authorities reassuring her that this was not the case.

The foregoing analysis has established one simple but exceedingly important fact about the nature of those communications that Teresa received during her mystical prayer states: their power to motivate her to substitute God's will for her own will and, to a lesser extent, their subjective intensity and frequency increased in direct proportion to the extent that religiously authoritative men around her began to confirm that those messages had indeed come from God. The contrasting responses that she gave to similar visionary directives concerning the matter of secular friendships in 1542 and in 1557 substantiate this assertion. One will recall that the absence of this religious legitimation in 1542 debilitated both the vigor of her responses to her mystical experiences and, in the long run, their subjective intensity and frequency whereas the presence of such legitimation in 1557 had the opposite effect.

# Discontent with the Mitigated Rule and the Founding of the Discalced Carmelite Order

Two major events punctuated the years that immediately followed Saint Teresa's second conversion (1558–60). She developed a deep friendship with that austere Franciscan reformer and founder of the Discalced (barefoot) branch of the Franciscan order, Peter of Alcántara, and she decided in 1560 to found a convent of Discalced Carmelites in Avila.

Teresa's close friendship with Peter of Alcántara began shortly after the crisis of her second conversion had passed. One of her most loyal and vigorous supporters, the local noblewoman Doña Guiomar de Ulloa, arranged for Teresa to meet with a man whose extraordinary reputation for holiness had caused Doña Guiomar to consider him a living saint. Peter of Alcántara's spiritual credentials certainly were impressive. First, he had achieved fame as the founder of the Order of Discalced Franciscans. These monks rejected all the modifications and mitigations that the passage of time had added to the original monastic rule that Francis of Assisi had laid down for his friars. Specifically, the Discalceds made a solemn vow to live in accordance with the full rigor of Francis's Primitive Rule, especially with respect to its demands for unconditional poverty and self-abnegation. Second, Peter had also attained great renown as an ascetic by practicing radical self-mortification and poverty, which he fervently exhorted others to perform. According to Teresa's *Life*, Peter made it a habit to sleep only an hour and a half each night, never lay down (even to sleep) but instead always stood, knelt, or sat, always wore only the harshest sackcloth in both the summer and the rainy months of winter, and made it a habit to eat only once every three days (and often even less than that for he sometimes went for as long as a week without eating). In addition, Teresa testified that he was a man whose knowledge of things mystical derived from personal experience rather than from hearsay because she had, with her own eyes, observed him go into "great raptures and violent impulses for the love of God" (pp. 256–57). By introducing Peter to Teresa, Doña Guiomar evidently hoped that if this holy man arrived at the conclusion that Teresa's visions and locutions originated from God, his prestige and experience in such matters would silence once and for all those more recalcitrant critics of Teresa who still persisted in their refusal to believe that they came from Him even though her Jesuit confessors, Prádanos and Balthazar Alvarez as well as the famous Francis Borgia, had staked their reputations on such a favorable verdict.

Although Peter of Alcántara did not succeed in converting her more stubborn critics (even after this holy man had talked to him, Don Salcedo still appears to have continued to believe that her locutions and visions had come from the Devil), he did powerfully reinforce the favorable opinion of her Jesuit confessors so as to further solidify her confidence that they actually came from God. He enthusiastically reassured her that, aside from the Faith itself, nothing could be more certain than the fact that her prayer experiences had come from God. He also helped Teresa to allay her anxieties about the nature of certain ineffable, imageless, intellectual visions that she had recently begun to experience with greater frequency by drawing on his own personal experiences of the same in order to show her that their lack of imagery and their essential indescribability did not preclude them from having a divine origin or prevent them from producing spiritual benefits of the highest order (pp. 277–79). Peter of Alcántara's guidance and inspiration became especially important, even indispensable, during those two years (1560–62) when Teresa was struggling to found a new convent in Avila. First, he may have provided her with much of the inspiration that led her to found a Discalced Carmelite convent there a few years after they had first met each other. Even though she did not explicitly link her efforts to establish this convent to any inspiration that she may have received from Peter's Discalced Franciscan reform, when one considers the deep nature of the bond that existed between the two saints, the fact that each called his or her respective new order "Discalced," and the fact that each Discalced order derived its primary impulse from a common desire to restore the Primitive Rule of its respective ancestral order to its original vigor and purity, these parallels suggest a more than merely fortuitous connection between the two movements. Second, Peter of Alcántara used the full force of his considerable reputation to convince the initially balky bishop of Avila that he should allow Teresa to establish the new convent there despite considerable local opposition. And one must not forget that both Peter and María de Jesús shared joint responsibility for one of Teresa's most radical measures, her insistence that each Discalced Carmelite religious house must be founded in poverty, without any endowment. Peter of Alcántara recognized in Teresa a kindred spirit and, for this reason, continued while he was alive to do everything in his power to encourage her and assist her in her various endeavors. This bond between the two grew so strong that even after he died in October 1562, Teresa continued to have visions of him in his glorified body during which he would speak to her concerning a great variety of subjects. Teresa went so far as to assert that "since his death it has been the Lord's good pleasure that I should have more intercourse with him than I had during his life" (p. 257).

Late in 1560 Teresa decided to found another Carmelite convent in Avila whose nuns would differ from the sisters at the Incarnation by taking a vow to live in accordance with the Primitive rather than the Mitigated Rule of the Carmelite order. This decision definitely ranks as the most important religious event of her later years since it inaugurated her activities as both a foundress and a reformer of Carmelite convents and monasteries, exertions that soon became the dominant focus of her attention during the last twenty years of her life. These projects take on great importance when one views them from Teresa's own perspective because they constituted what was, for her, the highest form of service she could possibly render to God short of martyrdom. She never tired of proclaiming to others her conviction that religious perfection did not consist in the undisturbed cultivation and enjoyment of mystical experiences but was instead a mode of life wherein the joys of contemplation bring about a radical transfiguration of the mystic's will so that he or she joyfully abandons all thought of selfish gain or satisfaction and replaces these self-seeking inclinations with a burning desire to be of service to his or her neighbor and to submit to trials that will test the degree of his or her humility, loyalty, and love for God.[43] The extreme poverty that her new vows entailed as well as the persecution and abuse that she frequently had to endure from those opposed to her establishment of these new religious houses afforded her ample opportunities for testing herself.

Teresa linked this decision to found a new convent to one particularly gruesome vision that she experienced sometime during either 1559 or 1560. She related in her *Life of St. Teresa of Jesus* that one day during prayer she suddenly found herself transported into the midst of Hell. Once there she not only saw the hideous place that the devils had prepared for her but she also experienced more vividly, as though she were actually undergoing them herself, those spiritual afflictions and physical agonies that torment the souls of the damned (pp. 300–301). This shattering revelation immediately made her realize the enormity of that debt that she owed to God for she now understood from experience that Hell was something concrete and real rather than just something she had heard about and that it was only by an act of divine mercy that she had been saved from those unendurable tortures that she had just seen and experienced. This vision also greatly strengthened her courage for whenever she would compare any possible form of earthly suffering or tribulations with those that she witnessed in Hell, the earthly trials shrank into utter insignificance.

> This vision was one of the most signal favors which the Lord has bestowed upon me . . . both in taking from me all fear of the tribulations and disappointments of this life and also in strengthening me to suffer them and to give thanks to the Lord. . . . Since that

43. Teresa of Avila, *Book of Foundations*, pp. 25–26; idem, *Interior Castle*, pp. 90–91; Teresa of Avila, *Conceptions of the Love of God*, in vol. 2 of *Complete Works*, pp. 396–99.

time . . . everything has seemed light in comparison with a single moment of such suffering as I had to bear during that vision. (p. 302)

For this reason, fear of such earthly woes as hunger, ridicule, or physical punishment could no longer daunt her if she incurred them as a proof of her love for God. With this newfound strength, courage, and acute sense of indebtedness to God obtained from this vision, Teresa's thoughts soon gravitated toward the problem of how she could utilize these gifts in order to both repay God for His great favors and do adequate penance for her past heedlessness. She quickly concluded that she could best accomplish these goals if she solemnly committed herself to live the religious life with the utmost rigor and perfection.

> After I had seen this vision . . . I desired to find some way and means of doing penance for all my evil deeds and of becoming in some degree worthy to gain so great a blessing. I desired, therefore, to flee from others and to end by withdrawing myself completely from the world. . . . I would wonder what I could do for God, and it occurred to me that the first thing was to follow the vocation for a religious life which His Majesty had given me by keeping my Rule with the greatest possible perfection. (p. 304)

One can see in this statement the seeds of her coming discontent with the Mitigated Carmelite Rule.

At this point in her life Teresa had still not made up her mind to leave the convent of the Incarnation. To be sure, the vision of Hell had sown within her mind the seeds of dissatisfaction with that comparatively lax religious life she had been leading there (she complained that the nuns lived too comfortably and that the rules of enclosure were too easily relaxed) but, though sown, these seeds had still not germinated. This fact should not occasion surprise, for no one vision, in and of itself, ever caused Teresa to alter her lifestyle in accordance with its dictates—either express or implied—unless it had first received some form of legitimation from someone whose spiritual authority she respected. The story of how she established Saint Joseph's of Avila demonstrates the truth of this assertion.

For example, the first tentative thoughts about founding a new convent that this vision of Hell elicited developed no further until these suggestions had received encouragement and reinforcement from some of her colleagues. Teresa only began to proceed further in this matter after one of her associates had proposed during a discussion that they become Discalced nuns. Since this suggestion accorded so well with her own private feelings, Teresa felt confident enough to discuss the proposal with her friend Doña Guiomar de Ulloa, who enthusiastically endorsed it and agreed to help finance it. Only after receiving this reinforcement from her colleagues did Teresa again decide to seek another vision in which she hoped that God would tell her whether she should continue with the project. Predictably, she soon experienced the vision she had been seeking as well as the answer from Him that she had expected to hear. God explicitly commanded her to work on this project with all of her might. God assured her that her new convent could not fail to be established, that its nuns would set a shining example to the rest of Christendom by the perfection and austerity of their lives, that she should name it Saint Joseph's (which she did), and that He (or Saint Joseph) and the Virgin Mary would be its guardians. Furthermore, God told her to explain to her confessor Alvarez that as He Himself had sanctioned the foundation of this convent, he (Alvarez) must do nothing to oppose it (pp. 305–6). It is significant that, although this vision most vigorously encouraged—even commanded—her to carry out her project or else incur God's wrath for disobeying Him, she still refused to act in accordance with it until men of spiritual authority had first affirmed its authenticity. Thus Teresa and her ally, Doña Guiomar de Ulloa, immediately set about soliciting the opinions of Balthazar Alvarez, Peter of Alcántara, the Provincial of the Carmelite order, and the learned Dominican, Pedro Ibáñez, concerning how and if they should proceed with this project of founding a new convent of stricter observance. Teresa expressly stated that if Father Ibáñez had concluded that her proposal would have offended God or gone against obedience, she would have unhesitatingly given it up, vision or no vision, for not even a visitation from God could override her vow of obedience to a religious superior or confessor (p. 308).

With the exception of Alvarez, who initially remained noncommittal, her consultants encouraged her to continue with the foundation, Ibáñez and Peter of Alcántara being especially supportive. However, as soon as these plans became public, Teresa faced strong opposition from most of the nuns at the Incarnation (p. 310). Many of them criticized her for seeking money to found yet another convent in Avila when it was already the case that the nuns of the Incarnation often lacked enough financial support from the community to meet their needs (p. 304). Others condemned her for what they saw as pride and disloyalty: Teresa's actions could be construed as implying that she was too pure for their house. Still others resented her plans for a more strictly enclosed Carmelite convent because they did not wish to be pressured by her example into giving up the rather comfortable lifestyle the Mitigated Rule permitted. And finally, others felt insulted because they interpreted her actions to mean that Teresa thought that God was ill-served at the Incarnation (p. 310). This outcry forced the Provincial to rescind his support for her project the day before she had planned to sign the deed for the new house her friends had purchased for this purpose. Lacking the support of the Provincial, her confessor did not dare to allow her to proceed. Rather than sin against her solemn vow of unconditional obedience to her confessors, Teresa temporarily gave up the project.

During those six months when her confessor refused to condone her enterprise, Teresa obediently remained silent about establishing a new convent. Once her confessor had withdrawn his sanction, she no longer received any visionary instructions relevant to the project (p. 313). Visionary communications concerning the foundation only resumed after her confessor and another figure of religious authority, the rector of the local Jesuit college, Father Gaspar de Salazar, had once again sanctioned her project and indicated that they now had reason to believe that the Holy Spirit had inspired her to attempt it. Salazar's appointment as the new rector of the Jesuit college soon ended this period of dormancy for he quickly established an extraordinary rapport with Teresa. This rapport apparently acted as a stimulus for new visionary experiences pertaining to the foundation project. Shortly after she started this warm relationship with Salazar, she began to receive visions and locutions in which God told her to take up the matter of the new convent with Salazar and Alvarez. Salazar's position of high authority within the Jesuit order may also have played a role in activating this reemergence of "foundation visions." Since Salazar was in such a position of high authority in the same order to which Teresa's confessor Alvarez belonged, it is quite possible that she entertained hopes, perhaps subconsciously, that if she could persuade Salazar of the authenticity of her foundation visions then Salazar could use his position to pressure Alvarez to allow her to continue with that project. This was precisely what happened for once she had described these new visions and her hopes for a new foundation to Salazar and Alvarez, Salazar enthusiastically encouraged her and expressed his learned opinion that her visions were genuine.

This apparently emboldened Alvarez to finally shed his doubts about her project so that he once again allowed her to resume it (p. 315).

No longer prohibited by her confessor from founding the new convent, Teresa and her allies immediately started to work again, only this time they took great care to do everything with the utmost secrecy so that her superiors would know nothing of their plans. This ploy for keeping her superiors ignorant allowed Teresa both to keep her vow of obedience as well as to set up the new convent in what was almost certain to be opposition to their wishes. She reasoned that if they never knew of her plans until it was too late to prevent the foundation from becoming a reality, they could not order her to stop and, as long as they never issued such an order, she would be doing no wrong by continuing with the project since her confessor had sanctioned it. I must point out that this subterfuge to keep her superiors ignorant did not stem solely from Teresa's own initiative. She explicitly states that she made this important resolution to keep secrecy in the same manner that she had made others of a similar significance in her life, that is, she only made this resolution after she had first consulted learned men and had them reassure her that this tactic did not sin against obedience (p. 341).

I have observed earlier in this chapter that Teresa's periodic phases of intensified mystical activity correlated with those times in her life when one or more religiously authoritative individuals legitimated a course of action that she had considered privately for many months or years. This particular period exemplified this pattern for soon after Salazar and Alvarez gave their approval to her enterprise, she started to experience a series of visions and locutions that pertained to her project. In the most dramatic of these, both the Virgin Mary and Joseph came down in the midst of one of her "vehement" raptures, reassured her that Christ and the saints looked with the greatest favor upon her new convent, guaranteed its eventual success, and clothed her with a preternaturally luminous white garment that, as they placed it upon her, somehow cleansed her of her sins (pp. 317–18).

I emphasize that these particular visions and locutions did not just spring into Teresa's consciousness out of nowhere and then cause her to drop abruptly everything she had been doing so that she could now channel her activities into those novel directions that these extraordinary experiences had suggested to her. Nothing about her mystical experiences suggests that these visionary and auditory encounters ever put any ideas into her head that she had not already previously considered. Whereas Moses had supposedly never considered rescuing his people from their slavery in Egypt until that moment when God commanded him to do so from the burning bush and whereas Paul had supposedly never contemplated the idea of converting to Christianity until Christ spoke to him in a vision,[44] Teresa's mystical experiences never displayed this characteristic of serving as a goad to completely unanticipated courses of action. Instead, one finds that, similar to the ways that the phantasmagoria of a dream derive from either events or desires that a subject has experienced a day or two before, the content of most of Teresa's visions and locutions clearly derived from issues that had preoccupied her during the previous days or weeks. For example, in one of her deep raptures, Jesus commanded Teresa to make an endeavor to found the new convent in poverty instead of seeking an endowment for it as she had originally planned. During the preceding weeks and months, Teresa's thoughts had started to focus ever more intently on precisely that issue Jesus had raised in the vision—should she or should she not make the new convent subsist entirely on alms? She related that some time before this locution occurred she had had the good fortune to meet another Carmelite, María de Jesús, who also wanted to found a convent whose nuns would live in accordance with the Primitive Rule of their order. María de Jesús made Teresa aware for the first time that the Primitive Carmelite Rule actually forbade endowments and required that the religious live only on alms. When Teresa learned this fact, she immediately agreed that it was an excellent idea. She became so enamored of it, in fact, from then on that she vigorously defended it against the numerous learned men who brought powerful arguments to bear against such a practice.[45] Peter of Alcántara also lent his enthusiastic support to this idea of founding the new convent in poverty. With this strong reinforcement, no one could have dissuaded her from pursuing this course of action. It is clear, then, that Teresa had already made up her mind to favor poverty over endowment before she had experienced the locution in which Jesus had ordered her to do so. Her mystical experience did not formulate a novel course of action for her to follow—it merely confirmed a course of action upon which she had already resolved.

Teresa's efforts to set up a new convent in poverty finally bore fruit during the summer of 1562. Thanks to the financial support she received from a wealthy relative, she purchased a small house for this purpose and, due to the personal intervention of Peter of Alcántara, she obtained the

44. See Exodus 3:2–10; Acts 9:3–18.
45. Teresa of Avila, *Life of St. Teresa of Jesus*, pp. 331–34.

initially reluctant approval of the local bishop to establish it in Avila. The wisdom of keeping her plans secret (for example, she had her friend Doña Guiomar send off the papal authorizations as though she, rather than Teresa, hoped to found the new convent) soon became apparent. The local townspeople and clerical representatives from the other religious orders in Avila did not take kindly to the idea that their town should have to support yet another religious house on their limited economic base, especially when it had no endowment on which to rely for most of its support.[46] These opponents unsuccessfully pressured the bishop to rescind his approval of her project even to the extent of making an abortive appeal to the Royal Council when the bishop refused to yield to their demands.

Teresa characterized the four years (1563–67) when she dwelt at Saint Joseph's as the most restful period of her life. Not only did the quiet daily routine of enclosure free her from the worldly distractions that so often disturbed her prayerfulness at the Incarnation but, even more important, she discovered that the exceptional virtuousness of each of her companions powerfully reinforced her own zeal to follow the evangelical counsels with the utmost perfection.[47] Those halcyon days dedicated to solitary prayer and contemplation, the praise of God in the rituals of the canonical hours and the Mass, and the performance of humble day-to-day chores such as spinning eventually came to an end. Inspired by the example of her "angelic" companions and their great charity for one another, Teresa soon became filled with a restless desire to serve God through some form of apostolic service to others. "As time went on, my desires to do something for the good of some soul grew greater and greater, and I often felt like one who has a large amount of treasure in her charge and would like everyone to enjoy it but whose hands are tied so that she cannot distribute it."[48] Sometime around 1567 the Franciscan friar Fray Alonso Maldonado came to Avila from a missionary tour of the West Indies telling his listeners about the millions of heathen souls there who desperately needed to be brought to the true religion if they were to be saved. This speech filled Teresa with a wish to become a missionary.[49] Unfortunately, since Paul had forbidden women to preach or teach and she had already made a

---

46. Ibid., pp. 336–49.

47. These strictly enclosed nuns did not go out and beg for alms. They subsisted entirely on the unsolicited donations that they received from devout townspeople, dowries brought to them from novices, and from the small income they received from selling the products of their hand labor. See Teresa of Avila, *Book of Foundations*, pp. 1–3.

48. Ibid., p. 3.

49. Ibid., pp. 3–4.

lifelong vow to observe the strictest degree of enclosure, she could not fulfill these yearnings to imitate Francis Xavier or Fray Maldonado. Nevertheless, she continued to feel this keen urge to supplement her life of solitude and prayer with some form of apostolic service to her neighbor.

By a stroke of good fortune in the spring of 1567 the General of the Carmelite order, Fray Juan Batista Rubeo, came to visit all the Carmelite convents and monasteries as part of an inspection tour that Philip II had requested from the pope so that he could begin a general reform of the religious houses within his kingdom. The efforts of Teresa and her nuns to live in accordance with the Primitive Rule so deeply impressed Rubeo that he took it upon himself to utilize his great ecclesiastical power in support of their experiment. He therefore granted Teresa patents (Teresa claimed that she did not ask him to do this) to found new Discalced Carmelite religious houses in both Old and New Castile together with censures that forbade local provincials of the order from hindering her plans. Rubeo's action suddenly provided Teresa with a perfect outlet for her repressed longings to do missionary work of some kind. Now she could reconcile her prior religious commitments, the limitations Scripture had placed on her gender with regard to teaching and preaching, and her longing to convert souls by devoting herself to this activity that the highest authority in her order had sanctioned. As I have noted many times previously, once a religious authority figure had suggested to her a course of action that she had already incubated in her own mind for several months, she would seize upon these suggestions as though they had come from God Himself. She remarked that once "I saw how desirous our most reverend General was that more religious houses should be founded, I thought I saw them already built."[50] In no time at all Teresa had launched on a full-time career as a foundress.

It is important to mention that Teresa's new commitment to a life of more or less continuous apostolic action did not entail any serious diminution in the intensity or frequency of her mystical experiences. She did acknowledge (in 1572) that such commitments to the performance of good works do interrupt the soul's enjoyment of those contemplative favors and consolations that God sends it in its quieter hours.[51] Nonetheless, in other later works she makes it abundantly clear that, despite her busy labor as a foundress of convents and monasteries and the consequently briefer periods she had left in which she could spend time devoted to solitary prayer

50. Ibid., pp. 5–6.
51. Teresa of Avila, *Conceptions of the Love of God*, p. 398.

and recollection, she still experienced mystical states of prayer. She wrote to Rodrigo Alvarez in 1581, fourteen years after she had started busying herself with founding monasteries and convents in quick succession, telling him that while her "imaginative visions" had indeed ceased, the "intellectual vision" of the Holy Trinity and of the Sacred Humanity of Christ had become a continuous presence—a presence, she added, that was "much more sublime" than her earlier imaginative visions.[52]

Teresa immediately set to work struggling to find funds and furnishings that would enable her to set up the new religious houses. On August 15, 1567, she crowned these efforts with the opening of her second Discalced convent at Medina del Campo. That year she also met John of the Cross, the great Spanish mystical theologian, who was at that time a student at the University in Salamanca and she soon persuaded him to join her in setting up the first Discalced Carmelite monastery for friars in the tiny village of Duruelo that she inaugurated the next year. Numerous other foundations followed in rapid succession during the next nine years (1567–76) with the exception of a three-year hiatus between 1571 and 1574 when the Apostolic Delegate appointed her, against her will and, initially at least, against the wishes of its residents, prioress of her old convent, the Incarnation.

# Conflicts Between Mitigated and Discalced Carmelites

By 1575 the number of Discalced religious houses in Spain had grown large enough to require someone whom Teresa could invest with the overall responsibility for governing and administering them. She chose Father Jerónimo de la Madre de Dios (Gracián) for this task. Father Gracián became Teresa's superior within the Discalced Carmelite order since Francisco Vargas, the Apostolic Commissary for the reform of the Calced (Mitigated) Carmelites in Andalusia, had given him authority to rule over both the nuns and friars of the Discalced order.[53] At the same time, Vargas also made the mistake of appointing Father Gracián Visitor of the Mitigated

---

52. Teresa of Avila, *Spiritual Testimonies*, vol. 1 in *The Collected Works of St. Teresa of Avila*, trans. Kieran Kavanaugh, O.C.D., and Otilio Rodriguez, O.C.D., 3 vols. (Washington, D.C.: Institute of Carmelite Studies, 1976), p. 364.

53. Teresa of Avila, *Book of Foundations*, p. 121 n.

Carmelites. This appointment soon developed into a source of bitter hostility between the two groups that raged for four years (1576–80) and prevented the foundation of any more Discalced religious houses during that period.

This bitter conflict between the two Carmelite orders seems to have arisen principally from the desire of the Mitigateds to preserve the autonomy of their order from the reformist intrusions into their internal affairs that the Spanish monarch and those papal officials (such as the nuncio Ormaneto) sympathetic to his efforts to introduce greater austerity into all the religious orders within his realm sought to impose on them. When Vargas chose Father Gracián to rule over not only the Discalceds but also the Mitigateds, the Mitigated quite naturally took this as an unwarranted infringement on their ecclesiastical autonomy. Not surprisingly, they deeply resented this intrusion into their affairs by a group of religious whom they imagined had a contempt for their less rigorous manner of life. In addition, when Philip II asked the pope to send two Apostolic Visitors to Spain—Vargas for Andalusia and Pedro Fernandez for Castile—these Visitors carried with them commissions that set them directly under the jurisdiction of both the pope and the king. Consequently, those officials whom they appointed such as Father Gracián could find themselves in potential conflict with the jurisdictional authority of the General of the Carmelite order. For example, it was quite possible for the papal Visitors to give those whom they appointed commands that could directly contradict commands that these subordinates might receive from their superiors within the Carmelite order. This was what happened to Father Gracián. On the one hand, the papal Visitor Vargas gave him orders to found monasteries of Discalceds in Andalusia. On the other hand, his superior within the order, General Rubeo, had not authorized such foundations outside of Castile.[54] When Rubeo found out about Gracián setting up these foundations without his authorization, he understandably took this as an affront to his authority. As a result, when the fathers of the Mitigateds came to Rubeo with their resentments against this upstart Discalced who presumed to assert his authority over them, they found this former supporter of Teresa ready to give them a sympathetic ear.

The death of the Discalceds' principal defender, the papal nuncio Ormaneto, in June 1577, gave the Mitigateds their chance to unleash the full fury of their resentments against their more austere brethren. The new

54. Auclair, *Saint Teresa of Avila*, pp. 281–82.

papal nuncio, Felipe Sega, had been prejudiced from the very beginning against the Discalced Carmelites by one of the pope's nephews, Cardinal Buoncampagni, who also happened to be Protector of the Carmelite order. Cardinal Buoncampagni strongly supported the Mitigated Carmelite cause and opposed the Discalceds. Consequently, when the cardinal briefed Sega on the Spanish Carmelite conflict, he did everything he could to turn Sega against the Discalced.[55] As a result, Sega became an enemy of both the Discalced Carmelites and Teresa and did everything he could to assist the Mitigateds in their struggles against them.[56] Although he did not at first go so far as to invalidate Father Gracián's commission as Apostolic Visitor, as Gracián's superior he forbade him to visit any convents, thereby rendering his position a meaningless formality. Emboldened by Sega's support and the puzzling silence (which lasted almost two years) of Philip II who, at first, did nothing to make known his support of the Discalceds, the Mitigateds had many of Teresa's supporters such as John of the Cross (whom Teresa had appointed as confessor to the nuns at the Incarnation when she had governed them as their prioress a few years earlier) thrown into prison and even went so far as to attempt to place the Discalceds under the jurisdiction of the Mitigateds' provincials thereby depriving them of their organizational independence. This effort to dismantle the Discalced order climaxed in December 1578 when Sega decreed that the Discalceds must merge with their enemies and submit to their rule and that Teresa cease all correspondence with Father Gracián.[57]

This campaign of vilification and persecution eventually alienated powerful figures at the king's court who also happened to be good friends of either Teresa or her reforms. These allies finally managed to get Philip II to express once again his unequivocal support for the Discalced cause. He wrote to Sega:

> I have heard about the war which the Calced are waging against the Discalced friars and nuns. I cannot do otherwise than regard such attacks against people who have always practiced the greatest austerity and perfection with the utmost misgiving. I have been in-

55. Clissold, *St. Teresa of Avila*, p. 207.

56. Sega once described Teresa as a "restless, disobedient, and contumacious gadabout, who, under the guise of devoutness, invented false doctrines, leaving the enclosure against the orders of the Council of Trent and her own superiors, and teaching as though she were a Master, contrary to the instructions of St. Paul, who had ordered that women were not to preach" (quoted in Teresa of Avila, *Letters*, vol. 2, p. 611, n. 2).

57. Auclair, *Saint Teresa of Avila*, p. 349.

formed that you have not been helping the Discalced in any way. In future range yourself on the side of virtue.[58]

This imperial reprimand effected a quick change in Sega's behavior. On April 1, 1579, he rescinded his decree that would have placed the Discalceds under the jurisdiction of the hostile Mitigated provincials and instead placed them under the jurisdiction of a personal friend of Teresa. In 1581 Philip II authorized a final separation of the Calced and Discalced Carmelites into entirely separate provinces, which soon received papal confirmation as well. This measure guaranteed once and for all the independence of the Discalced Carmelites.

After these harrowing interruptions, Teresa resumed her work as a foundress in 1580, continuing this activity uneventfully until a few months before her death at Alba de Tormes on October 4, 1582.

# Teresa and the Carmelite Tradition

Teresa intended that her Discalced nuns reestablish that way of life that the founding fathers of Carmel had practiced. Her emphasis on enclosure, solitude, recollection, and contemplation remained true to the eremitic contemplative spirituality of those hermits. She tells her readers in the *Interior Castle* that

> all of us who wear this sacred habit of Carmel are called to prayer and contemplation—because that was the first principle of our Order and because we are descendent upon the line of those holy Fathers of ours from Mount Carmel who sought this treasure . . . in such great solitude and with such contempt for the world.[59]

Such attempts to return monastic institutions to the pristine purity and perfection that supposedly characterized them at the time of their origins were nothing new in Christian religious history. Peter of Alcántara tried to do the same thing when he founded his Order of Discalced Franciscans for he also endeavored to re-create in the present that spirituality that had existed in the earliest days of the Franciscan order. Similarly, one must not

58. Quoted in ibid., p. 353.
59. Teresa of Avila, *Interior Castle*, pp. 96–97.

forget that the great monastic reforms of the eleventh and twelfth centuries typified by the Cistercian and Carthusian orders owed much of their driving impulse to a desire to reinstate that life of solitary prayer and contemplation that the first Christian monks and hermits had practiced in the deserts of Egypt. Certainly, Teresa's desire to return to the original purity and rigor of the Primitive Rule and the life of mystical intimacy with God that was the result of such a life was one of the principal objectives of her Discalced reform. Nevertheless, she also wanted to achieve several other objectives.

Besides contemplative intimacy with God, Teresa hoped that her emphasis on the practice of obedience, solitude, recollection, and contemplation would create an environment where monks and nuns would be able to lead lives of exemplary Christian virtue in which they no longer sought their own will but only the will of God. This objective was the most important of all. As important as the life of mystical contemplation was for Teresa and her nuns, it paled in significance to this objective of achieving a perfect congruence of divine and human wills. "The highest spiritual perfection consists not in interior favors or in great raptures or in visions or in the spirit of prophecy, but in the bringing of our wills so closely into conformity with the will of God that, as soon as we realize He wills something we desire it ourselves with all our might."[60] Elsewhere, she wrote to her confessor, Father Gracián, that when it came to the mystical experiences and blissful consolations that come during prayer,

> the most potent and acceptable prayer is the prayer that leaves the best effects. . . . I should describe the best effects as those that are followed by actions—when the soul not only desires the honor of God but really strives for it. . . . Oh, that is real prayer—which cannot be said of a handful of consolations that do nothing but console ourselves. When the soul experiences these, they leave it weak and fearful and sensitive to what others think. I should not want any prayer that would not make the virtues grow in me.[61]

As these quotations demonstrate, Teresa had an "activist" notion of spiritual perfection for she conceived of the consummation of the religious vocation not in terms of some experience wherein the soul lost itself in an ecstatic absorption in God but rather in terms of acting and desiring in

60. Teresa of Avila, *Book of Foundations*, p. 23.
61. Teresa of Avila, *Letters*, letter no. 122, to Father Gracián, October 23, 1576, 1:316.

such a way that one's deeds and longings always coincided with the things that God would have done or willed. Clearly Teresa exhibited a great deal of spiritual kinship with the action-oriented religious ideals of the Jesuits, Dominicans, and Franciscans. Just as they did, she saw the active life as crowning, rather than being crowned by, the contemplative life.

Another objective of Teresa's Discalced Carmelite reform was to bolster the Catholic Church against both the heathen and the heretics. In spite of the vows of strictest enclosure she imposed on her nuns, Teresa envisioned her nuns' vocation as an apostolate of prayer. Even though her nuns had to remain strictly enclosed and thereby isolated from the world, their vocation was still one of crucial significance for the fight of the Catholic Church against her enemies. She once wrote to Father Gracián: "I do believe the aim these houses were founded for is gradually being fulfilled—I mean we should ask God to help those who are defending His honor and laboring in His service, we women who are of no use for anything else."[62] Teresa's niece, Teresita, who later became a Carmelite nun, also referred to the sublimated missionary dimension in her aunt's view of her vocation when she asserted that Teresa "determined to undertake this work [of reform] in order to make war on the heretics with her prayers and her life and with the prayers and lives of her nuns and to help the Catholics by means of spiritual exercises and continued prayer."[63] Although men had the privilege of serving God in an active missionary apostolate of teaching and preaching to the heathen, the Muslims, and the Protestants, women were forbidden by Scripture from these activities of teaching and preaching. Nevertheless, devout women did not have to despair—their prayerful life and self-abnegations for Christ and His Church were, in their own way, just as heroic and significant for the Church as the active apostolate of the men.

The religious climate of sixteenth-century Catholicism definitely left its distinctive impress on Teresa's spirituality. How else can one explain why Teresa, who otherwise so faithfully adhered to the original Carmelite rule, nonetheless chose to diverge from it by preferring a mode of life that placed the active life on a higher footing than contemplation? Her high regard for the active life despite the restraints placed on it by the practice of strict enclosure typified the pastoral orientation that animated the spirituality of most of the new religious orders that emerged during the six-

62. Teresa of Avila, *Letters*, letter no. 147, to Father Gracián, December 1576, 1:370. Similar sentiments are also expressed vividly in Teresa of Avila, *Way of Perfection*, pp. 36–37.

63. Quoted in Bilinkoff, *The Avila of St. Teresa*, p. 136.

teenth century such as the Jesuits, Ursulines, and Theatines. Teresa's preference is not surprising when one realizes that during those years that immediately preceded the foundation of Saint Joseph's and her period of spiritual activism, the men who wielded the most influence on her, namely, her confessors and advisers, came from the Jesuit, Franciscan, and Dominican orders rather than from her own. Since they had been trained in religious orders that placed a great deal of emphasis upon the pastoral aspect of the religious life—emphasizing teaching, preaching, and missionary work—one would naturally expect that their pastorally directed outlook would exert a considerable influence on her, especially in the absence of any personal contact (except for María de Jesús) with Carmelites who followed the Primitive Rule or knew much about it.[64]

The new emphasis on missionary activity that began to activate Catholicism after the discovery of the New World and the Far East must also have contributed to this preference. Indeed, Teresa confessed at the beginning of her *Book of the Foundations* that the image of the missionary saint converting the heathen souls to Christ appealed to her religious imagination even more than the ideal of martyrdom.[65] As already pointed out earlier in this chapter, in the late 1560s she had to sublimate this yearning to become a missionary because her sex and her vows of enclosure prevented her from fulfilling it. Consequently, she had to settle for a partial fulfillment of this longing through an apostolate of prayer, the feminine substitute for that active apostolate of teaching and preaching that was open to men. It is evident, then, that someone so passionately devoted to this ideal of saving souls would quite naturally gravitate toward an activist spirituality.

Before concluding this segment, it is important to appreciate more fully the radical break that Teresa's Carmelite monasticism made with the spirituality of the Mitigated Carmelites. For one thing, Teresa's Discalced Carmelite houses completely did away with all class distinctions. The Mitigated nuns at the Incarnation perpetuated the distinctions of class and caste that existed in the outside world. Many professed nuns from wealthy families continued to receive a lavish income from their properties with

64. It was María de Jesús, a Carmelite *beata* (a devout woman who either lives in a religious community without being fully professed or who lives under a rule in her own house) who first made Teresa aware that the Primitive Rule of the Carmelites forbade endowments and required that religious houses be founded in poverty. See Teresa of Avila, *Life of St. Teresa of Jesus,* pp. 331–32.
65. Teresa of Avila, *Book of Foundations,* pp. 3–4.

some of the wealthier ones even having slaves and servants live with them in the convent. Many of the aristocratic nuns insisted on being addressed with the honorific title "doña" that was reserved for members of their class. Furthermore, whereas the poorer nuns slept in common dormitories, the wealthier nuns (such as Teresa) had private rooms.[66] In marked contrast to the Mitigated Carmelites of the Incarnation, Teresa demanded that all her nuns give up all forms of wealth. "In no way should the sisters have any particular possessions, nor should such permission be granted."[67] Not only were distinctions based on wealth ignored among the Discalced but the same also held true for distinctions based on birth. Her "Constitutions" explicitly order that "never should the prioress or any other of the Sisters use the title Doña."[68]

Teresa's desire to create a form of religious community completely free of the distinctions of class, caste, and wealth also found expression in her rejection of *limpieza de sangre* (purity of blood) as a prerequisite for entrance into her order.[69] By the 1560s almost every Spanish religious institution required that novices be able to prove that their family tree was free of Jewish ancestors—a situation that made it increasingly difficult for conversos to join either the regular or the secular clergy. Teresa, whose family, one will recall, had converso ancestors on her father's side, could hardly have been expected to sympathize with this Spanish obsession with limpieza. As long as she lived, her order continued to accept postulants without any concern for their ancestral purity.[70]

Teresa also broke radically with most monastic institutions in sixteenth-century Spain by her willingness to admit otherwise qualified postulants who were too poor to bring dowries and her insistence that, whenever

66. Bilinkoff, *The Avila of St. Teresa,* pp. 113–15.

67. Teresa of Avila, *The Constitutions,* vol. 3 of *The Collected Works of St. Teresa of Avila,* trans. Kieran Kavanaugh, O.C.D., and Otilio Rodriguez, O.C.D. (Washington, D.C.: Institute of Carmelite Studies, 1985), p. 321, para. 10.

68. Teresa of Avila, *The Constitutions,* p. 329, para. 30. Teresa continually attacks the sixteenth-century Spanish obsession with titles and pedigrees. For example, in letter no. 350, to Father Gracián (February 1581), she tells him, "Oh, how it distresses me to be addressed in letters as 'Reverend.' I wish your Paternity would forbid all your subjects to do such a thing. . . . It seems to me there is no point in our using titles of honor among ourselves."

69. Teresa's disgust with the obsession of her contemporaries for purity of blood comes across in that portion of her *Book of Foundations* (15.15–16) where she described the Toledo foundation. There many people counseled her against accepting the monastic house from the donor because the donor's family was not of the noble class but apparently was of converso origins. She rejected those counsels because "glory to God, I have always esteemed virtue more than lineage."

70. Williams, *Teresa of Avila,* p. 18.

possible, new religious houses should be founded in poverty rather than with an endowment.[71]

If one compares Teresa's religious order with the typical Spanish monastic institution that existed fifty years earlier, one notices that Teresa's spiritual ideal—like that of the Jesuits to whom she was so often indebted for guidance—involved a wholesale rejection of the "aristocratic" spirituality of the earlier period.[72] Whereas convents and monasteries like the Incarnation sought endowments from wealthy aristocratic benefactors, preserved the social distinctions of the secular world behind the closed doors of the cloister, and required that their monks and nuns spend a great deal of their prayer time in the vocal recitation of choral and intercessory prayers for the benefit of the souls of their wealthy patrons (instead of spending time devoted to private, mental prayer), Teresa's convents created a spiritual community that was free of these religious influences from the Spanish aristocracy. It was an effort to create a truly egalitarian religious community in the midst of an intensely hierarchical, authoritarian, and purity-conscious society.

## Teresa's Principal Works

Teresa composed all of her extant writings after her second conversion. The first of those sixty-five accounts of her various spiritual experiences collected under the title *Spiritual Testimonies* appears to be the earliest work that we possess. Evidence suggests that she wrote it sometime around 1560, a full two years before she produced the first draft of her autobiography.[73] The second and third accounts in this collection likewise constitute her earliest works for they date from 1562 and 1563, respectively. The six longest of these accounts included in that collection, namely, numbers 1, 2, 3, 58, 59, and 65, are often referred to under the title *Relations*. They were written at the behest of her confessors who desired her to give them a

71. Thus in her letter of May 1574 (no. 54) to Father Domingo Báñez, she told him, "Believe me, my Father, it is a real delight to me whenever I accept anyone who brings nothing with her and has to be taken solely for the love of God" (*Letters*, no. 54, to Domingo Báñez, May 1574, 1:138). It should be noted that Jesuit houses were also founded without fixed incomes and that the Jesuits, like the Discalced Carmelites of Teresa's day, showed a similar indifference to lineage. See Bilinkoff, *The Avila of St. Teresa*, p. 89.

72. Bilinkoff, *The Avila of St. Teresa*, p. 52.

73. Teresa of Avila, *Spiritual Testimonies*, pp. 309, 311; Teresa of Avila, *Life of St.Teresa of Jesus*, pp. 312–13.

thorough description of those interior graces that came to her in prayer so that they could help her arrive at some understanding of them as well as have some basis for forming an intelligent judgment as to their veracity. These long accounts constitute one of the best sources for information concerning the nature of her mystical experiences since they incorporate detailed descriptions of her states of soul and the various stages of prayer that span a period of more than twenty years. One notices that whereas account number 1 dates from 1560, so that it affords the only firsthand glimpse of the saint's spiritual state before she actually wrote her auto-biography, account number 65 written in 1581 provides a glimpse of her interior state as it was during the last year of her life. Whereas the *Relations* provides a more generalized description of her locutions, visions, and other transcendent experiences, the *Spiritual Testimonies* include numerous brief accounts of various individual experiences of that sort that she received over the years. The *Spiritual Testimonies* have, at times, been published separately as *Favors of God*. It is worth observing that, in contrast to the *Relations*, which she wrote at the request of her various confessors, she apparently wrote down the latter in obedience to a divine command.[74]

Her autobiography or *Life* constitutes her most famous work. Like her other writings, she composed this one in obedience to the orders of one of her religious superiors. She completed a first draft of the text in June 1562. However, during the late summer of that year, shortly after she had founded Saint Joseph's, another one of her confessors ordered her to write a second draft that included her narrative of those events that took place in the course of its establishment. She did not complete this draft until sometime during either late 1565 or early 1566.[75]

Since her superiors refused to make public her autobiography because it contained confidential details about the spiritual state of people still living, Teresa's nuns could not benefit from the valuable information that it held concerning both the ascetic life and the contemplative life. Knowing that their mother superior had written an autobiography but had been forbidden to publish it, they besought her to write a treatise on those topics as a substitute. Consequently, sometime around either 1565 or 1566, she began her classic discussion of prayer and asceticism, *The Way of Perfection*. Although there is no means of dating its completion with any precision, it

---

74. Teresa of Avila, *Spiritual Testimonies*, p. 332.
75. Teresa of Avila, *Life of St. Teresa of Jesus*, pp. 56–59; Auclair, *Saint Teresa of Avila*, p. 441.

is known that in 1573 she had signed and attested that a particular manuscript was indeed a correct copy of it.[76] This fact allows scholars to set
1573 as the latest possible date of its completion.

*The Book of the Foundations,* her account of how she established those
convents and monasteries that succeeded Saint Joseph's, began to take
shape in 1570 when, one day after Communion, she received a communication from God telling her that she must write an account of all her
foundations and how they came to be.[77] Only after she had consulted her
confessor to confirm its genuineness did she finally start on this project
beginning it in the summer of 1573. Since she took care to add another
chapter to the narrative after she had founded each new convent and monastery, this book contains the latest material from her pen for her description of how she founded the convent at Burgos cannot have been written
any earlier than the spring of 1582.[78]

She wrote her classic treatise on the stages of the soul's mystical ascent
to spiritual perfection, *Interior Castle,* in the remarkably short period of
five months (June through November 1577) during the time of those hos-
tilities that rent asunder the Spanish Carmelites in the last half of the
1570s. This work, along with numbers 58, 59, and 65 of her *Spiritual
Testimonies,* gives the quintessence of her most mature teachings concerning both the mystical life and the pursuit of ascetic perfection. She composed *Interior Castle* at the request of Father Gracián, who had asked her
to give interested religious a description of spiritual perfection from the
vantage point of her ripest years. If she could not publish her autobiography, he reasoned, she could at least give them the results of her most
mature reflections on the stages of the interior life and her most mature
experiences of union with God.[79]

76. Auclair, *Saint Teresa of Avila,* p. 442.
77. Teresa of Avila, *Book of Foundations,* p. xvi.
78. Ibid., pp. 183–204.
79. Teresa of Avila, *Interior Castle,* pp. 8–9.

# 27

# Saint Teresa's
# Recollective Technique

So far I have restricted this examination of the intrinsic contextuality (or historicity) of Saint Teresa's mysticism almost exclusively to sketching the main events in the process of her spiritual development and describing the setting that nurtured them. I have shown that both the appearance and disappearance of her mystical states as well as their frequency and degree of intensity fluctuated in accordance with influences that she received from her social environment rather than in accordance with variations that derived from some contextually independent process within her own psyche. I repeatedly have pointed out how, once she had learned how to recollect herself, her mystical experiences tended to increase both in frequency and intensity during those periods when she received assurance from persons of religious authority that her visions and locutions had actually come from God. Whenever these prestigious individuals either withheld their approval or actually condemned them, the visions' frequency and intensity tended to decrease. This element of contextuality in her mysticism tells only a small part of the story. To appreciate the full extent to which her mysticism was historically conditioned, one still has to face the task of explaining to the reader how the peculiarities of her historical milieu determined (1) the specific character of her recollective techniques, (2) the specific content of her mystical experiences, and (3) the particular way that she responded to these experiences. I have structured the rest of this analysis of Teresa's mysticism so as to elucidate each of these three issues.

While it is true that Black Elk's Great Vision apparently came to him spontaneously without any effort of mental concentration being necessary to induce it, Teresa's initial mystical experiences did not come to her so easily. Like most mystics, she only began to experience locutions and visions after she had first learned how to control the normally helter-skelter wanderings of her mind, imagination, desires, and emotions. She discovered that the practice of recollection opened the door to mystical experiences. The set of practices that Teresa called "recollection" (*recogimiento*) functioned in much the same way as the Islamic *dhikr,* the Orthodox Christians' interiorized repetitions of the Prayer of Jesus, the breath-control procedures (*prāṇāyāma*) of Yoga, the dream-control methods of certain Tibetan Buddhists, and the kasiṇa meditations of the Hinayana Buddhists. They suppress the disruptive static that an undisciplined mind emits so that in the ensuing quiet the delicate "spiritual" sense receptors could begin to receive the subtle impressions and messages that stream into them from the spiritual realm once that interference has ceased.

Although I demonstrated in Chapter 5 that all recollective procedures function to suppress the normally random, uncontrolled activities of what we loosely term the heart and the mind, one must not imagine that it is possible to ignore the fundamental differences that distinguish the recollective techniques prevailing in one religious tradition from those in another. It is also important to realize that the ultimate concerns of the mystic's religious tradition largely determine the structural peculiarities of his or her particular recollective technique. Consequently, one must expect that mystics from a religious tradition that stresses obedience to God and love of Him as matters of primary soteriological importance will evolve recollective methods that differ substantially from those that originate in religious traditions that consider divine beings irrelevant to salvation. It necessarily follows that recollective techniques display a fundamental contextuality much like that of the mystical experiences that they induce. One can best clarify these important points when one contrasts Teresa's method of recollection with analogous techniques in a few other religious traditions, taking care to explain how these observed differences stem from specific differences present in their respective historical contexts.

# True Prayer Requires Recollectedness

Most people naively imagine that prayer consists of nothing more than a simple vocal petition that one addresses to a divine being in which one begs for some favor. This prevalent notion completely overlooks the close association that frequently exists between the phenomena of prayer and recollection. Most mystics assume that prayer loses much of its religious significance unless one learns to petition in a recollected manner. For example, in *The Way of Perfection,* Teresa leaves one no doubt that she considered recollection to be an essential element in all genuine prayer.

> It is impossible to speak to God and to the world at the same time; yet this is just what we are trying to do when we are saying our prayers and at the same time listening to the conversation of others or letting our thoughts wander on any matter that occurs to us without making an effort to control them.[1]

She reemphasized the importance of focusing the attention during prayer when she asserted that those nuns "who have formed the habit of looking at nothing and staying in no place which will distract these outward senses may be sure that they are walking an excellent road."[2] These quotations clearly show that Teresa regarded the practice of some form of recollection as an essential concomitant of true prayer. Without it, the religious who longed to speak with God could hardly hope to receive the reward that consummates perfection in the practice of prayer—the joyful sensation of standing face-to-face in the presence of God.

In spite of the above passages, which indicate that Teresa believed that recollection played a crucial role in advancing a soul toward union with God, there are other passages in her works that seem to say the opposite and appear to denigrate the use of techniques for stilling the mind. For example, in her autobiography she cautions her readers against thinking that, by their own efforts, they can stop the mental operations of the understanding—"What I say we must not do is to presume or think that we can suspend it [the understanding] ourselves, nor must we allow it to cease working."[3] Passages similar to this led one recent Teresan scholar to assert that the saint exhibits a sustained hostility to all forms of technique in prayer that aim at suspending mental activity.[4] Is it possible to reconcile these contradictory utterances from her writings? Did Teresa advocate the practice of recollection or did she not?

I contend that achieving recollectedness in prayer always remained a matter of great importance for Teresa in spite of the passages that Williams cited that seem to say otherwise. Not only are there numerous explicit passages in *The Way of Perfection* that commend the practice to her

1. Teresa of Avila, *Way of Perfection,* p. 168.
2. Ibid., p. 185.
3. Teresa of Avila, *Life of St. Teresa of Jesus,* p. 136.
4. Williams, *Teresa of Avila,* p. 71, 89.

nuns but her other writings also attest to its importance. Looking at "The Constitutions," which she wrote for her new monastic order, one notices that fostering recollectedness was obviously a matter of great concern to her. For example, Teresa was very much concerned that the way her nuns earned a living should not disrupt their ability to keep their attention focused on God. "Their earnings must not come from work requiring careful attention to fine details but from spinning and sewing or other unrefined labor *that does not so occupy the mind as to keep it from the Lord.*"[5] Teresa was obviously fearful that if their work required too much effort to do, their attention would be diverted from God and focused on their labor to the detriment of prayerfulness. Similarly, when she discusses how nuns are to spend their hour of prayer after Vespers, she shows a clear intention that they should spend that time doing whatever "helps them most toward recollection."[6]

The importance Teresa accords to recollection also comes across in her advice to her monastic superiors when she counseled them as to what they should do when they visit Discalced Carmelite convents during their periodic inspection tours. At one point she told them, "It is always important that he [the inspector] always inspect the whole house to see how recollection is preserved."[7] Teresa expressed similar sentiments about the central importance of recollection in her *Foundations*. She told her readers that after she arrived to found a new religious house, "I never would, or did, leave any monastery until it was in a fit condition, had a spirit of recollection, and was adapted according to my wishes."[8]

Given this diverse body of evidence from Teresa's own pen, why does Williams insist that she exhibited a persistent hostility to the use of techniques for stilling the mind?

I think it is safe to say that Teresa never denigrated recollection and the enormous benefits that it brought to the soul. However, toward the end of her life, especially in *The Interior Castle,* she did give more and more weight to God's initiative in inducing the condition of recollectedness and gave correspondingly less and less weight to human effort and mental techniques as means for bringing about that condition. In her earlier work, *The Way of Perfection,* she still gives considerable weight to human initia-

5. Teresa of Avila, "The Constitutions," p. 321, para. 9 (emphasis mine).
6. Ibid., p. 320, para. 7.
7. Teresa of Avila, "On Making the Visitation," in vol. 3 of *The Collected Works of St. Teresa of Avila,* p. 341, para. 15.
8. Teresa of Avila, *Book of Foundations,* p. 194.

tive in bringing about mental tranquillity and a tightly focused attention declaring that "when the soul desires to enter within herself" and shut up the faculties within herself, "this is not a supernatural state but depends upon our own volition."[9] While the Teresa of *The Way of Perfection* (1573) does not deny God a role in bringing about deeper levels of recollective prayerfulness and contemplation, she still allows human initiative a significant role in inducing the earlier stages of the recollective process.

However, by the time she wrote *The Interior Castle* (1577), she had markedly restricted the role of human initiative and effort in the recollective process and significantly expanded the role of divine grace in bringing about even the more superficial stages of recollective prayer. For example, in that work she declared that recollective withdrawal from the distractions of the senses is "not a question of our will—it happens only when God is pleased to grant us this favor."[10] This does not mean that Teresa had completely repudiated the role of human effort in the recollective process because she did continue to assert that the soul aspiring to perfection should "try, without forcing itself or causing any turmoil, to put a stop to all discursive reasoning."[11] Nevertheless, compared to *The Way of Perfection*, in *The Interior Castle* she has greatly reduced the scope of human initiative in that process.

It is clear that as Teresa grew older she felt the need to assert ever more strongly humanity's absolute dependence on divine grace even in the more superficial stages of prayer. As I said a moment ago, her growing skepticism about the efficacy of purely human actions in inducing the deeper levels of prayer did not signify any contempt for recollection. It merely indicated a shift in the relative weight she gave to human effort and divine grace in generating that blessed condition.

# Moral and Ascetic Perfection: Essential Concomitants of True Prayer

In addition to recollectedness of heart and mind, Teresa taught that genuine prayer also required a radical commitment in both intention and deed to moral and ascetic perfection. For example, she told her nuns in *The*

---

9. Teresa of Avila, *Way of Perfection*, p. 192.
10. Teresa of Avila, *Interior Castle*, p. 87.
11. Ibid., p. 89.

*Way of Perfection* that no one could hope to become a great contemplative unless that person had, first, replaced his ardent love of himself with an equally ardent and sincere love of God and his neighbor; second, acquired a thorough detachment from all created things; and third, become truly humble.[12] This effort to imitate the perfect charity, detachment, and humility of Jesus Christ always had an essential component of ascetic self-mortification in it. In other words, Teresa taught that moral perfection involved more than just the performance of virtuous deeds, it involved something that she called "subduing the body to the spirit." She went on to explain to her nuns that "subduing the body to the spirit . . . consists mainly or entirely in our ceasing to care about ourselves and our own pleasures."[13] Teresa insisted on this linkage of moral virtue to ascetic self-mortification because she and almost every other significant Catholic religious before her realized that no one could ever declare with any assurance that he possessed true humility or loved God (or his neighbor) more than himself unless he had actually verified this declaration by testing it in some concrete situation. Jesus Christ did not just claim that He loved humanity more than Himself. His humiliation before the centurions and His accusers and His mortification on the Cross proved that He actually did love humanity more than He loved Himself since He had undergone all these afflictions in order to redeem humans from their sins. The duty of Catholic religious to imitate the radical virtuousness of Jesus and the Desert Fathers mandated that they, too, carry the pursuit of virtue to similar self-denying extremes.

Teresa's conception of the integral role that both asceticism and the pursuit of moral virtue played within the total framework of the recollective process differed substantially from the way that mystics from other religious traditions have conceived of their roles. For example, Robert Monroe implied that both the quest for moral virtue as well as the quest for ascetic self-mortification had no relevance to the recollective procedure that he used to bring about his out-of-body experiences. When he describes his technique for inducing out-of-body experiences, he makes no mention of asceticism or moral virtue but insists that the following five requirements are most helpful: (1) the subject must realize that the common fears about out-of-body experiences are groundless, (2) he must learn to relax completely and avoid all distractions and worries (such as the telephone, business appointments, and problems) during that time he has

12. Teresa of Avila, *Way of Perfection,* p. 53.
13. Ibid., p. 98.

set aside for the dissociation exercises, (3) he must learn how to descend into the sleep-state while he still maintains a full consciousness that he is doing so, (4) he must learn to generate and then refine what he called the "vibrational state," and (5) he must try to control the influx of stray thoughts as much as he possibly can.[14]

This particular difference between Monroe and Teresa is not surprising. Monroe is a somewhat secularized contemporary American radio executive who induces his out-of-body experiences chiefly because he thinks that they possess significant theoretical and practical implications that bear upon the future progress of science. When he generates his out-of-body experiences, he hopes that his description of what occurs during them will extend the boundaries of scientific knowledge. Monroe considers himself a scientific investigator and, as such, has no more intrinsic need to cultivate the moral or ascetic virtues in order to ensure the success of his experiments than any other contemporary scientist has. Teresa, on the other hand, could not afford to dissociate the pursuit of the ascetic and moral virtues from the recollective process because she explicitly affirmed that our "highest perfection consists . . . in the bringing of our wills so closely into conformity with the will of God that, as soon as we realize He wills anything, we desire it ourselves with all our might."[15] Teresa taught that the mystical experiences that recollection generates derive their principal religious significance from their capacity to instill in humans a spiritual fortitude that enables them to imitate much more easily the exemplary moral and ascetic perfection of Christ.[16] These facts explain why Teresa took it for granted that the pursuit of ascetic and moral perfection had to be present as an integral element within the recollective process. Since humanity's highest spiritual purpose lay in acquiring the ascetic and moral virtues that Christ possessed and since the recollective process would hopefully bear fruit in the form of mystical experiences whose principal function would be that of making it easier for humans to acquire these moral and ascetic virtues, it was only natural that Teresa would insist that her nuns cultivate them as an integral part of their recollective endeavors. On one hand, the supreme soteriological significance that Teresa attributed to these virtues made it almost inevitable that she would incorporate them into her recollective method. On the other hand, their complete

14. Monroe, *Journeys Out of the Body*, pp. 205–16.
15. Teresa of Avila, *Book of Foundations*, p. 23.
16. Teresa of Avila, *Life of St. Teresa of Jesus*, pp. 122, 181, 208, 363, 388–89; Teresa of Avila, *Interior Castle*, pp. 227, 229.

soteriological and scientific irrelevance for Monroe made it a virtual certainty that they would not form any part of his recollective praxis.

Other mystics who differed from Monroe by acknowledging that asceticism and the cultivation of the moral virtues could facilitate recollectedness nevertheless differed from Teresa insofar as they relegated self-mortification and the pursuit of the ethical virtues to a merely accessory role within the recollective process. For example, when Patañjali listed some of the means whereby the yogin could combat those distractions that prevent concentration, he mentioned that by practicing friendliness (or benevolence) free of jealousy toward all who are experiencing happiness, by practicing compassion toward all who are experiencing pain, by feeling joy toward those who are behaving in a morally exemplary manner, and by cultivating indifference toward those who are behaving immorally, the yogin can achieve concentration. However, even though these moral virtues do function as powerful aids to concentration, it is clear that they play an accessory role within the entire recollective process that Patañjali delineates. One of Patañjali's commentators, Bhojarāja, declared that the cultivation of the moral virtues possessed only a secondary significance within the total framework of the yogin's quest for spiritual liberation. As he put it, the effect of practicing these virtues is

> external (and not an intimate portion of the yoga itself). As, in arithmetic, . . . the operations of addition, etc. are valuable (not so much in themselves but) as aids in effecting the important matter, so by exercising benevolence, etc. which are (moods of mind) opposed to aversion and covetousness, the mind . . . becomes fitted for meditation. . . . Covetousness and aversion are the very chief creators of distractions, if therefore they be radically extirpated, then . . . the mind (the more readily) becomes concentrated on one point.[17]

Bhojarāja's relegation of the moral virtues to this purely accessory role within the recollective process reflected the subordinate position that the moral virtues occupied within that general scheme of salvation that the followers of Patañjali's Yoga took for granted. According to this soteriological scheme, a human can choose two principal ways to effect his liberation from the round of rebirths. The first way, the way of virtuous deeds and scrupulous ritual observances, is a slow method that takes more

17. See Bhojarāja's commentary to *Yoga-Sūtra* 1.33, in Patañjali, *Yoga-Sūtra of Patañjali*, pp. 27–28.

than one lifetime to complete. The followers of this method count on these meritorious actions and ritual observances to bear fruit in the form of good karma, which will then cause them to achieve rebirth in a time and place that will give them favorable conditions to attain spiritual liberation. The second way, the way of Yoga, accomplishes this spiritual liberation in one lifetime. For this reason, it is much more preferable than the first way. The follower of this second way counts on the fact that his former virtuous actions have created his present favorable karma that causes him to want to study and practice Yoga. Nonetheless, these meritorious deeds and dispositions cannot function as the immediate causes of his spiritual liberation (one is assuming here that he practices his Yoga successfully). Unless the aspiring yogin also masters the art of concentration and gains a penetrating insight into the fact that his immortal soul (*puruṣa*) is a different entity from either mind-stuff (*citta*) or the various kinds of subtle and gross materiality (*prakṛti*) that make up the world, even the virtuous actions of his past lives will not release him from *saṃsāra* (the endless round of rebirths).

Christian mystics have independently arrived at Bhojarāja's insight that the cultivation of the moral and ascetic virtues can serve as a useful accessory to their recollective efforts. Even as early as the fifth century, Cassian taught that no hermit could ever hope to achieve that recollected "single-mindedness" so necessary for contemplative communion with God unless he had first spurned his parents, family, comforts, and every other earthly pleasure.[18] Teresa likewise assumed that attachment to sensual pleasures hindered recollection. For example, in her autobiography she recounted that during her early years at the Incarnation when she had still not completely weaned herself from attachment to certain sensual pleasures, she often experienced difficulty recollecting herself in prayer because of them. "I was not able to shut myself within myself (which was my whole manner of procedure in prayer); instead, I shut within myself a thousand vanities."[19]

However, one makes a serious mistake if one concludes on the basis of these citations that Christian mystics simply regarded the moral and ascetic virtues as religiously significant only because they facilitated recollection. Christian mystics did agree with Bhojarāja insofar as they too assumed that when a person possessed these virtues he concomitantly found he could recollect himself much more easily but they diverged from Bho-

18. Cassian, "Conferences," pp. 197–98.
19. Teresa of Avila, *The Book of Her Life,* vol. 1 in *Collected Works of St. Teresa of Avila,* pp. 62–63, 158–59.

jarāja when they insisted that the cultivation of the moral and ascetic virtues played an essential, not just a helpful, role in bringing about salvation regardless of whether or not they also served as a useful accessory to recollection. Teresa considered the pursuit of the moral and ascetic virtues essential to salvation because—as already noted in this chapter and Chapter 26—she subsumed the totality of spiritual struggles around efforts to conform human will to God's will.[20] Every Catholic religious had this same obligation whether or not he or she chose to follow the path of contemplation. Teresa took it for granted that both the practice of recollection and the experience of contemplating God only possessed whatever religious significance that they had because they created a disposition in men and women that made it easier for them to want to acquire the moral virtues and ascetic self-abnegation that Jesus Christ had exemplified. "His Majesty can do nothing greater for us than grant us a life which is an imitation of that lived by His Beloved Son. I feel certain, therefore, that these favors are given us to strengthen our weakness . . . so that we may be able to imitate Him in His great sufferings."[21] Anyone holding such convictions could never relegate the moral and ascetic virtues to a merely secondary instrumental role within the recollective process. If men and women only practice recollection so that this exercise may eventually better endow them with the fortitude that they will need to imitate the virtuous deeds and sufferings of Jesus Christ, how could they not consider the cultivation of those virtues an essential rather than merely useful part of that procedure?

For Patañjali and his followers, the condition of spiritual perfection that they called kaivalyam or "isolation" did not incorporate any ethical impulse with the transcendent state of consciousness that constituted its essence. Whereas Teresa's culminating condition of spiritual perfection— "the spiritual marriage of the soul to God"—symbiotically fused a mystical intimacy with God and all-consuming urge to fulfill all the ethical obligations He laid upon humankind, yogic isolation was simply a condition of naked, penetrating insight devoid of any concomitant urge to fulfill a moral obligation either to God or to one's fellow human beings. Because the moral virtues had no intrinsic connection to this condition of isolation, Patañjali was content to accord them an accessory role in that assemblage of recollective practices that eventuated in liberation from samsāra.

20. Teresa of Avila, *Book of Foundations*, p. 23.
21. Teresa of Avila, *Interior Castle*, p. 227.

# Teresa's Method of Recollection

Although its successful application assumed both a prior and concurrent rigorous cultivation of the moral and ascetic virtues, Teresa's actual "method for recollecting the thoughts" (*el modo para recoger el pensamiento*) was otherwise exceedingly simple.[22] Her procedure consisted of nothing more than having the nun try to imagine as vividly as possible that her most Beloved Spouse and dearest Friend, Jesus Christ Himself, is actually present by her side while she vocally prays to Him. As she is praying in this manner, she must also imagine that Jesus is not only beside her but that He is also humbly and lovingly instructing her how to say this prayer just as He had taught it to His beloved apostles. (Teresa assumed here that the nun was reciting the Paternoster, that very prayer that Jesus had actually taught His twelve disciples.) Thus she told her nuns, "you must look for a companion" as each of you withdraws to your cell to pray in solitude

> and who could be a better Companion than the very Master Who taught you the prayer you are about to say? Imagine that this Lord Himself is at your side and see how lovingly and humbly He is teaching you—and, believe me, you should stay with so good a friend for as long as you can before you leave Him.[23]

These recollective instructions clearly emphasize that the nuns must attempt to bring the full powers of their imaginations to bear upon the task of intensifying the feelings of devotion that they have (or ought to have) to the person of Jesus Christ. For this reason, Teresa continued to suggest other recollective stratagems that her nuns could use if her first suggestion failed to elicit feelings of tenderness toward their divine Spouse and Friend. She suggested the following meditation: Imagine that you are gazing into the eyes of someone you love far more than anyone else and that, moreover, this divine Beloved not only permits you to gaze upon His splendid countenance in this way but that He actually longs for you to do this. If that evocation of the emotions of love did not quicken the nun's feelings of devotion, perhaps this second meditation would succeed: Imagine that you are actually present at the Passion and Crucifixion of your Beloved Savior,

22. Teresa of Avila, *Obras de Santa Teresa de Jesús,* edited and annotated by Father Silverio de Santa Teresa, C.D., 9 vols., vol. 3: *Camino de Perfección,* Carmelite Mystical Library (Burgos: Tipografía de El Monte Carmelo, 1916), p. 119.
23. Teresa of Avila, *Way of Perfection,* p. 173.

Spouse, and Friend just as Peter had been. Having done this, you must now try to imagine that you are witnessing Him enduring those abject humiliations and excruciating torments that His persecutors inflicted upon Him. Even more, you must imagine that He is suffering these agonies before your very eyes all because He, loving you as He does, had offered Himself as a ransom to suffer in your place so that His blood could redeem you from your sins. Knowing this to be true, how could you not look on such a suffering Beloved without experiencing the most poignant feelings of tenderness, compassion, and remorse? How could you witness your Beloved Spouse enduring the agonies of crucifixion for your sake and not be moved to give up everything—even life itself—for His sake? And if this suffering Beloved were to look upon you (whom He loves more deeply than any earthly husband loves His wife) with his beautiful, compassionate eyes, tear-filled from the pain of His sufferings, how could your heart not burst with love and grief at such a sight?

From this brief synopsis, one can easily see why one can best characterize Teresa's method of recollection as one that possesses a predominantly "affective" emphasis, that is, it is clear that she expressly designed it not only to stop the subject's thoughts from wandering during prayer but also to intensify feelings of devotion to Christ.[24]

The markedly affective tenor of Teresa's recollective method remained consistent with its ultimate spiritual purpose: inspiring monks and nuns with both the fortitude and the longing to conform their wills perfectly to God's will.[25] We know from experience that it is far easier to act in accordance with the will of another person if we love that person. Conversely, we know that if this love is absent it is far more difficult to effect this conformity of wills. This fact explains why Teresa accentuated the affective dimension of recollection rather than its intellectual or knowledge-giving aspect. After all, if one wishes to inculcate perfect obedience to the will of Christ as Teresa did, it makes far more sense to concentrate one's efforts on evoking the subject's feelings of love for Him than it does to concentrate on giving the subject information about the nature of the Holy Trinity or about the way that spirits in Heaven see and communicate with each other. Such information may satisfy the soul's intellectual curiosity but it does not quicken devotion or endow the soul with the fortitude it needs to endure trials and tribulations for the sake of some divine person whom one loves. Both Teresa and her Franciscan mentors on prayer and

24. Ibid., pp. 173–77.
25. Teresa of Avila, *Book of Foundations*, p. 23; Teresa of Avila, *Interior Castle*, pp. 227–29.

recollection, Francisco de Osuña and Peter of Alcántara, understood that
devotion facilitates obedience, fortitude, and love of God far more effectively than knowledge does.[26] For this reason, they accentuated the affective element in prayer and paid comparatively little attention to its intellectual or knowledge-giving aspect.

# The Affective Dimension of Recollection

As I noted in Chapter 5, recollective concentration always mobilizes the
emotions to some degree. It is safe to say that without at least some mobilization of the affections and emotions no attempt to focus the attention
will ever be successful. Nevertheless, mystics vary widely in the extent to
which they employ the emotions and affections within the recollective process. Those mystics whose religious traditions emphasize the soteriological
value of love tend to create recollective techniques that employ strong
emotions as devices to focus attention whereas those whose religious traditions downplay the soteriological value of strong emotions and, instead,
stress the soteriological primacy of knowledge tend to fashion methods of
recollection that make much less use of the emotions to concentrate the
mind.

Many mystics differ sharply from Teresa insofar as they place comparatively little emphasis on the affective factors in recollection. For example,
neither the technique of prāṇāyāma that the followers of hatha yoga utilize
in order to bring about one-pointedness of concentration nor the various
forms of visualization techniques that some schools of Buddhism often
employ for the twin purposes of both concentrating the mind and giving
the student soteriologically important knowledge about the intrinsically
illusory and impermanent nature of all physical and mental phenomena
place much emphasis upon quickening the emotions.[27] Instead, the practitioners of hatha yoga bring about mental concentration by controlling the
physiological process of respiration whereas the Buddhist meditators induce recollectedness by manipulating visual images. The following synopsis of David-Neel's description of a Tibetan Tantric Buddhist visualization exercise she termed "the contemplation of one's tutelary deity or
*Yidam*" provides a good example of a recollective procedure that makes

26. For example, see Osuña, *Third Spiritual Alphabet*, pp. 315–18.
27. For example, see Svātmārāma, *Haṭhayogapradīpikā*, p. 22.

much less use of strong emotional states as a focusing device than does Teresa's recollective method.

According to David-Neel's informants, the spiritual master who assigns this exercise to his pupil does so with the ultimate hope that, by practicing it successfully, the student will learn from his own direct experience rather than by mere hearsay or book learning that no phenomenon—be it a physical object, a dream phantasm, a god, or a demon—possesses an autonomous existence independent of the perceiving subject's own mind. When the student contemplates and materializes the form of his tutelary deity (described below), he will hopefully realize that even the most tangible and substantial physical objects as well as the most vividly present forms, sounds, and feelings simply originate from his own mind and ultimately pass away as its evanescent and insubstantial by-products. The guru intends that this exercise will provide his pupil with a powerful empirical confirmation of a central tenet of Tibetan Mahayana Buddhism, namely, the assertion that, in the final analysis, all phenomena are really nothing more than mere phantasms that exist solely in the subject's mind, originate there, and eventually vanish into it.

The exercise begins with an act of deception on the guru's part. At first, he does not reveal the true purpose of the exercise to his pupil. Instead, he leads him to believe that this meditation has as its ostensible purpose the development of his pupil's magical powers. He will begin the procedure by telling his pupil: Go into solitude where you can meditate for many months if need be, completely undisturbed. I want you to focus your thoughts and imagination upon nothing else but the form of that deity whom you have chosen as your spiritual protector (that is to say, the pupil's tutelary deity or Yidam). This Yidam can be any particular spiritual being for whom the student feels a special affinity. You must try to picture your Yidam vividly in your imagination in the manner that the religious books and art works portray him. But this is not all—you must endow this purely mental image with such a degree of subjective vividness that you will see it equally clearly whether your eyes be open or closed. Even this is not enough for I eventually want you to "materialize" this vividly imagined thought-form (or *tulpa*) of your Yidam, that is, I want you to make his thought-form so vivid and intense that you can actually feel something present when you touch his form and have him talk to you.

The guru stresses the importance of materializing the thought-form of the student's Yidam for the "wrong" reason at first. He leads the novice to believe that, by accomplishing this arduous meditative task, he will not only have displayed his proficiency in the magical arts but he will also have acquired the services of a powerful spiritual protector. Many Tibetans maintain that if an individual can actually materialize the thought-image of a particular deity or demon, that materialized thought-image or tulpa will then protect its creator. It may appear in its creator's place in a manner somewhat similar to the way a Doppelgänger or "astral double" manifests itself or it may cause the individual who fabricated it to appear to evil spirits in the (usually) hideous form of the particular tutelary deity upon whom he had focused his thoughts rather than in his ordinary human form. This protects him from evil spirits because, when they see the hideous form of his Yidam instead of seeing him whom they came to harm, they flee in terror and leave the person alone.

After many months of intensive one-pointed concentration on the form of his Yidam (along with the practice of certain magical formulae that the pupil believes help to invoke its presence), the diligent student will finally start to achieve some measure of success. He announces to his guru that he is starting to materialize his Yidam. Even when he is wide awake he can see the diaphanous, ghostlike outline of his tutelary deity's form. "Very good," his guru will say. "Nevertheless, this is still a long way from being perfect, you must continue until you can actually touch the feet of your precious protector and hear him bestow his blessing upon you." Needless to say, few students possess the extraordinary mental control needed to advance to this next step.

Assume, however, that our particular student is one of the few successful ones. After many more months or years of intensive meditation on the thought-form of his Yidam, the student finally endows it with such a degree of life that he actually feels its physical presence when he reaches out to touch it. And if he is truly lucky, he will even hear the Yidam speak to him. One would have thought that the student's trials were over at this point but such is not the case. "It is good that you have accomplished what I asked you to do," the guru will say. "However, you must now try to get your Yidam to follow you out of the place where you have been meditating. This is the most difficult task of all." Again, many students fail at this point for, while it may be possible to materialize a Yidam in the undisturbed surroundings of one's hermitage, it is virtually impossible to do so in the open air or amid the cacophony of crowds. Supposing that our student succeeds in this Herculean task of mental control, he will still not necessarily have passed the test. The final elimination now takes place. The spiritually ignorant student thinks that he has now achieved the final goal. Now that he has materialized his tutelary deity, gotten it to speak to him, and even gotten it to follow him around, he thinks that the possession of such magical powers actually constitutes the highest goal of his spiritual quest. His mentor will pretend to agree with him. "You have reached the highest goal," he will say to the failed student, "I have nothing else to teach you since you now possess such a powerful spiritual protector at your side." The foolish student will then go on his way.

The student who has truly understood his guru's teachings and the teachings of the Buddha will still have misgivings at this point. He will say to his guru, "Could it not be, blessed master, that, despite the tangibility and vividness of my Yidam, my spiritual protector has no real existence at all? Could it not be that my Yidam is nothing more than a phantasm that I have created in my own mind and simply endowed with the mere semblance of life and independence?" The guru will pretend to be offended by this confession. "How can you not believe in the reality of your spiritual protector who is doing so much to help you? How can you be so ungrateful? Return again to your meditations until you have conquered this skepticism." Not even the enormous religious prestige of his guru can quell the truly wise student's doubts. After what may be months of further meditation and intellectual struggle trying to resolve these doubts, our wise student will only succeed in deepening his initial misgivings, "Alas, blessed master," he will say to his guru, "I no longer merely doubt that my Yidam is an illusion created by my own mind, I am now absolutely certain that it is an illusion." At this point the guru will then reveal the true purpose of the exercise. "At long last," he will say, "you have finally understood what I was trying to teach you. You now know beyond any shadow of a doubt that nothing whatsoever—be it gods, devas, your own Yidam, even the physical universe itself—has an autonomous existence outside of your own mind. Your mind fabricates all of these things and endows them with the appearance of autonomy. They originate in the mind, take on their semblance of concreteness and reality in the mind, and they eventually vanish into it."[28]

Juxtaposition of Teresa's recollective procedure with the Tibetan Buddhist technique of recollection reveals a striking difference in their respective emphases. Teresa's method employed intense feelings of devotion to Jesus as a means of focusing the soul's attention. These feelings of devotion to Jesus not only made it easier for a deeply pious nun to draw her

---

28. David-Neel, *Magic and Mystery in Tibet*, pp. 283–87.

attention away from worldly things but they also created a consuming ardor to do the will of her Beloved. The Buddhist technique of vivifying a visual mental image of one's tutelary deity did not quicken the pupil's emotions very much. The Tibetan guru neither suggests to his pupil that he ought to cultivate feelings of love or affection for his tutelary deity nor does he suggest that the pupil has any obligation to obey its will. Instead, the primary activity in the Buddhist recollective exercise is simply that of focusing the attention on a mental image of the deity until that mental image becomes as vivid as an actual object seen with the eyes open. The relationship that existed between the student and his tutelary deity was a purely instrumental one devoid of passion whereas, in contrast, the relationship that linked Teresa's nun and the Jesus of her meditations was that of an ardent, selfless love between two persons. The tutelary deity never really loses its status as an object—it is always an "It" rather than a "Thou." While the Buddhist pupil's tutelary deity functions as a useful protector or as a tool that enhances the student's magical powers, it is never described as a beloved friend for whose sake the meditator is willing to suffer. It is simply a useful object or tool, nothing more.

## Reasons for Teresa's Emphasis on Affect

Several influences specific to Christianity as a whole and to Catholic monasticism in particular shaped Teresa's preference for an affective technique of recollection.

First, Teresa never would have stressed the cultivation of love and devotion in her recollective technique unless the pursuit of these virtues had had some scriptural warrant. One must not forget that Teresa considered that her religious vows laid upon her the sacred obligation to follow the "evangelical counsels" as perfectly as was humanly possible.[29] These evangelical counsels place supreme importance upon both love of God and love of one's neighbor. Jesus Christ Himself had taught that what was necessary for someone to guarantee himself the blessing of eternal life was that he must love God with all his heart, with all his soul, with all his strength, and with all his mind and that he must love his neighbor as himself.[30] Paul also preached that selfless love (which he called "charity") was the greatest

29. Teresa of Avila, *Way of Perfection*, p. 36.
30. Luke 10:27.

virtue that a Christian could possess since none of the other spiritual virtues and gifts had any value if it were absent.[31] These scriptural passages show that the Christian image of a spiritually perfect mode of existence remained indissolubly linked to the cultivation of a perfect, selfless love of both God and one's fellow human beings. Consequently, it would be meaningless for a Christian to speak of a spiritual state as embodying perfection if this love of God and humans were absent in those individuals who had supposedly attained it. The Christian scriptures accorded the supreme soteriological value to the cultivation of love. It was therefore not surprising that Teresa's method of recollection placed a great deal of emphasis on the need to develop this virtue to the fullest possible extent.

Christian conceptions of spiritual perfection (such as Christian writers' descriptions of Heaven and Teresa's descriptions of that supreme mystical state that she called the Spiritual Marriage of the soul to Christ) depict it as a condition of both spiritual intimacy with God and a state of being in which the soul is filled with a profound love of God and one's fellow human beings.[32] Such images of spiritual perfection have had a profound influence on the way that Christian mystics have designed their recollective techniques and methods of interior prayer because they ensure that feelings of love and devotion play a large role in establishing contact with God. Buddhists, on the other hand, depict their state of spiritual perfection (*nirvāṇa* in Sanskrit, *nibbāna* in Pali) in a very different way that almost guarantees that the recollective techniques of Buddhist mystics will not make much use of strong emotions in the process of stilling the mind. In contrast to the Christian Heaven, Buddhist nirvana is never described as a condition of love and devotion. Instead, the individual who has attained nirvana is depicted as having a penetrating insight into the fact that all phenomena and objects are devoid of a self and having completely uprooted craving in all its forms.[33] Buddhist nirvana differs from the Christian Heaven by its essential incompatibility with intense emotional states, which by their very

31. 1 Corinthians 13.
32. Teresa's description of Spiritual Marriage as a condition of mystical intimacy with God, which was fused with an ardent love of both God and neighbor and an ardent desire to do His will, can be found in *Interior Castle*, esp. pp. 219–33.
33. The *Aṅguttara Nikāya* characterizes nirvana as follows: "O bhikkus [monks], whatever there may be [of] things conditioned or unconditioned, among them detachment (*viraga*) is the highest. That is to say, freedom from conceit, destruction of thirst (*pipasa*), the uprooting of attachment, the cutting off of continuity [the cycle of rebirths], the extinction of thirst (*tanha*) [or craving], detachment, cessation, nibānna [nirvana]." This passage from the *Aṅguttara Nikāya* is quoted in Rahula, *What the Buddha Taught*, 2d. and enl. ed., pp. 36–37.

nature give rise to a craving for their objects (e.g., the emotion of love creates a craving for the presence of the person one adores). This being the case, it is highly unlikely that Buddhist mystics will attempt to reach nirvana by using meditational techniques that arouse strong passions and feelings. For example, the author(s) of the *Majjhima Nikāya,* one of the classic Buddhist scriptures, depict the trance-states that progressively lead up to nirvana as a series of psychospiritual conditions each of which they characterize as more perfectly abstracted than its predecessor from any kind of blissful emotion commensurate with normal human experience. Whereas the author(s) describe the second level of trance as one in which the monk ceases his processes of reasoning and reflection yet still retains the experience of joy and happiness, they go on to describe the third level of trance as a condition where the monk has superseded the previous state insofar as he no longer experiences the emotions of joy and happiness he had known before. Instead, he experiences a peculiar kind of bodily rather than emotional happiness quite different in character from the previous emotional states. The author(s) characterize the fourth trance level as a condition of being radically abstracted from either bodily or emotional happiness. As they put it, it is a condition that "has neither misery nor happiness, but is contemplation refined by indifference."[34] Notice the progressive diminution of affect in these trance experiences as they begin to approximate the conditions that prevail in nirvana. As this progression would lead one to expect, nirvana itself represents the consummation of this affect-diminishing process. The classic description given in the *Anguttara Nikāya* characterizes it as having as its essence the radical annihilation of all forms of craving.[35] Nirvana supervenes only when the subject succeeds in utterly rooting out any desire or thirst to experience any phenomenon whatsoever—be it physical, imaginary, mental, supernormal, or spiritual. As such it clearly has no place for the Christian love of God and love of neighbor. Since Buddhists always describe this soteriologically supreme condition of being as possessing attributes fundamentally incompatible with any feelings of attachment such as love or devotion, one can immediately understand why they have always avoided those forms of recollective practice that place a great deal of emphasis on cultivating intense emotions. From the Buddhists' perspective, the cultivation of such emotions— even if they are directed toward God (or gods) rather than humans—make it completely impossible for the subject to reach nirvana. After all, how

34. Quoted in Warren, *Buddhism in Translations,* pp. 347–48.
35. See Rahula, *What the Buddha Taught,* 2d. and enl. ed., pp. 36–37.

can one speak of an individual as having annihilated all forms of craving if he is still consumed with a craving to experience Christ's presence?

These considerations indicate how significantly the final spiritual goals that a religious tradition sets for its adherents can determine the characteristics of a mystic's recollective technique. Because Buddhists set for themselves a spiritual goal that is inconsistent with the production of intense emotional states, one will never find them advocating recollective procedures that make any more than a merely provisional use of powerful emotional states to achieve their aim. The Christians' ultimate spiritual goal in no way forces such an exclusion of affectivity from the recollective process. On the contrary, it invites it.

## *Lectio Divina* and Its Contribution to Interior Prayer

The distinctive manner of reading sacred texts (known as *lectio divina*) that medieval Western European monks and nuns had practiced since the time of Saint Benedict of Nursia may have contributed significantly to the affective emphasis in Teresa's recollective method. In the Middle Ages monks and nuns did not read the Scriptures or the writings of the Church Fathers in the same way that we read books. A piece of advice that the Cistercian Arnoul of Boheriss gave to monks about how they should go about reading their books succinctly expresses the vast difference that distinguishes their method of reading from our own. When a monks reads, he said,

> let him seek for savor, not for science. The Holy Scripture is a well of Jacob from which the waters are drawn which will be poured out later in prayer. Thus there will be no need to go to the oratory to begin to pray; but in reading itself the means will be found for prayer and contemplation.[36]

The divergence from our own method of reading a text ought to become immediately obvious. In sharp contrast to the medieval monks and nuns, we read books with the primary intention of gleaning information from

36. Jean Leclerq, O.S.B., *The Love of Learning and the Desire for God: A Study of Monastic Culture,* trans. Catharine Misrahi (New York: Fordham University Press, 1974), p. 90.

them. Consequently, our encounter with the text almost always tends to be an affectively neutral event, that is to say, it generally does not mobilize our wills for action, vivify our imaginations, or quicken our emotions. As Arnoul of Boheriss's counsel indicates, the medieval religious never considered his act of reading a sacred book as though it were simply an affectively neutral quest for mere information about its content. Instead, he regarded the act of reading such a text as something closely akin to what monastic writers have referred to by the term "meditation" (*meditatio*). It was for this reason that Arnoul took it for granted that the act of reading was essentially synonymous with the preliminary stages of prayer and contemplation.

This element of meditatio that the religious integrated into his act of reading gave it its affect-laden character. Meditatio not only implied that one thought about or reflected on what one was reading but it also signified that one was reflecting on the subject matter with the intention of preparing oneself to do it, desiring it, or putting it into practice.[37] As a result, the monk inseparably linked the act of reading with his simultaneous endeavor to mobilize his will so that he would more readily desire to emulate those saintly men and women he had been reading about.

Besides quickening his desire to follow in the footsteps of Christ and His saints, the monk's manner of reading had the effect of vivifying his imagination so that the events taking place in the narrative acquired an added dimension of familiarity and concreteness that they would otherwise not have possessed. For one thing, the monk usually read his text aloud rather than silently as we do today. This audible pronunciation of the words implanted the contents of the texts more deeply into memory than a silent reading would have done. One must not ignore the vivifying effect of repetition either. The continuous emphasis on the Bible and a few other books both in the course of one's own private reading as well as in the liturgy and the iconography could not but impress the personalities and events depicted in them indelibly on the minds and memories of the religious.[38] This complementarity of meditatio, audible recitation, and repetition could not do other than deepen the affective impact of the textual material.

As the quote from Arnoul of Boheriss makes clear, this method of reading a text by "seeking its savor" exhibits an integral continuity with the rest of the monk's life of prayer and contemplation. One can regard the monk's manner of reading as a kind of recollective technique in its own

37. Leclerq, *Love of Learning,* pp. 20–21.
38. Ibid., pp. 89–94.

right for, by quickening the monk's desire to emulate Christ and the saints and by impressing biblical events on his imagination with a great vividness and wealth of detail, it made it much easier for him to focus his attention and emotions on God and heavenly things while he prayed. The close relationship between this method of reading and recollection may have influenced Teresa. For example, she found the reading of religious books a great aid to recollection. For many years she observed that she simply could not recollect herself if her superiors forbade her to read while she prayed. As long as they permitted her to read, she could, as she put it, "parry the blows of my many thoughts." However, when her superiors took away this prop for her recollective endeavors, her soul would at once become agitated and her thoughts would begin to wander. But let her again return to reading and all would be well again. She noted that as soon as she resumed reading her thoughts stopped wandering as though the book had somehow acted "as a bait" for her soul.[39] That the act of reading could work as such an effective brake to the tumultuous activity of her thoughts strongly implies that she had been doing this reading in the traditional way described above.

A comparison of Teresa's instructions for recollecting the thoughts and this monastic manner for reading sacred texts suggests a close relationship between the two. Monks did their reading aloud and, while doing so, simultaneously tried to picture the events that they were reading about as vividly as possible with the intention of thereby quickening within themselves the desire to imitate the religiously meritorious deeds of the good people portrayed in it. Teresa's recollective method required the same things from those who practiced it. Like the lectio divina, Teresa's method of recollecting thoughts often took place while the subject was engaged in vocal rather than silent prayer.[40] It also required that her nuns vividly picture Christ in their imaginations while they prayed just as the lectio divina required the monk to picture the events he was reading about as vividly as he could in his imagination. Teresa's method of recollection and the traditional monastic lectio divina shared the same ultimate purpose: the practitioners of both hoped that their respective activities would quicken their desire for God so that they would carry out God's will with greater fervor and alacrity than they would carry out their own selfish wishes. These parallels suggest that Teresa's particular method of recollection derived many of its features from that manner of reading sacred texts that monks

39. Teresa of Avila, *Life of St. Teresa of Jesus*, pp. 81–82.
40. Teresa of Avila, *Way of Perfection*, p. 178.

and nuns had practiced ever since the time of Benedict of Nursia. Indeed, it almost seems as though her technique of recollection was just a transposition of the lectio divina into a context where the monk or nun did not actually have the text in hand but nonetheless continued to proceed as though he or she were still reading.

Teresa's emphasis on the primacy of the feelings and the affections in the recollective act was also strongly influenced by sixteenth-century Spanish Franciscan spirituality. For example, in his *Third Spiritual Alphabet,* Francisco de Osuña asserted that it was the affective rather than the intellectual part of the soul that led men most quickly into God's presence.

> Ultimately security and repose in the heart will not be attained perfectly through speculative meditation but through recollection, which quiets the heart . . . because by ordinary thoughts we cannot approach God as closely as if our reasoning were to cease and we would be content with that simple faith whereby we endeavor to be solicitous, not to understand a great deal but to be inflamed profoundly in divine love for that highest good.[41]

This quote shows that Osuña has associated recollection with the affective part of the soul and divorced it from the practice of discursive meditation, that preliminary kind of prayer where the soul, engaging itself in intense reflection, employs its reasoning powers, the understanding and the imagination for the purpose of arriving at some deductively acquired knowledge of those things that faith teaches people about God, His love for them, and their essential dependence on Him. Teresa displayed a similar impatience with discursive meditation. She counseled that when one is trying to recollect one's thoughts, one must not waste time trying to "think about" God a great deal, "form numerous conceptions of Him," or "make long and subtle meditations with your understanding."[42] Like Osuña she preferred that her nuns bypass the intellect and the understanding and instead concentrate their attention by quickening their desires and their affections. One should not wonder at this parallel between Teresa and Osuña since the saint first learned how to practice mental prayer and recollection from reading his *Third Spiritual Alphabet.*[43]

The other Franciscans whom Teresa either read or with whom she asso-

---

41. Osuña, *Third Spiritual Alphabet,* pp. 547–48.
42. Teresa of Avila, *Way of Perfection,* p. 174.
43. Teresa of Avila, *Life of St. Teresa of Jesus,* p. 80.

ciated expressed similar sentiments about the preeminently affective character of that prayer that actually brings humanity into contact with God.
For example, Bernardino de Laredo maintained that the "hidden wisdom"
that souls acquire during contemplation had very little to do with any
intellectual apprehension or knowledge of God. He instead asserted that,
during the soul's contemplative union with God, "the soul is raised up . . .
through pure love, by the affective way alone, to union with its most loving God, without the intervention of any thought, or operation of the intellect, or understanding or natural reasoning."[44] Similarly, in Peter of Alcántara's *Golden Treatise of Mental Prayer* that Teresa evidently thought
important enough to have placed in the library of at least one of her convents,[45] one notices that even though he has devoted most of his book to a
lengthy description of how to practice discursive meditation, he nonetheless concludes his discussion of it by observing that

> we must be wary of too many speculations in this exercise and use
> rather, efficacious affections of the will rather than curious dis-
> courses of the understanding: wherefore they go not in the right
> way that meditate of divine mysteries as though they were to preach
> them to the people in a sermon.[46]

Both Bernardino and Peter could only have reinforced rather than challenged Teresa's predilection for an affective method of recollection.

This assumption, particularly widespread in sixteenth-century Spanish
Franciscan monasticism, that loving and desiring rather than the operations of the intellect serve as the vehicles that best lead the soul to true
knowledge of God and contact with Him had a long history in Catholic
spirituality. As early as the twelfth century, Bernard of Clairvaux had articulated the main outlines of this mystical theology common to Teresa
and her Catholic monastic contemporaries and immediate predecessors.
Basing himself upon 1 John 4:8, which proclaims that "God is love," Bernard taught that since Scripture states that God is love and since it is only
by making ourselves into His likeness (as much as our limitations allow us
to do this) that we can enjoy the gift of His immediate presence, it neces-

44. Bernardino de Laredo, *The Ascent of Mount Sion: Being the Third Book of the Treatise of That Name . . .* , trans. E. Allison Peers (London: Faber and Faber, 1952), p. 100.
45. Teresa of Avila, *Book of Foundations*, p. 164.
46. Peter of Alcántara, *A Golden Treatise of Mentall Praier*, trans. G. W[illoughby], microfilm reproduction of 1632 ed., published in Brussels by the widow of Hubert Antone (Ann
Arbor: University of Michigan, Microfilms, Inc., [n.d.])., p. 125.

sarily follows that it is only by imitating God's perfect love for us and by substituting God's will for our own will that we can acquire direct knowledge of Him.[47] Several parallels to Teresa's own practice and mystical theology emerge here. First, one cannot avoid noticing an unmistakable continuity between Teresa's insistence that the mystical life attains its consummation when man completely substitutes God's will for his own will and Bernard's insistence upon the supreme desirability of the same. Second, both great saints took it for granted that, as Gilson put it, "knowledge . . . is . . . profoundly impregnated with affectivity." Bernard always insisted that loving God and understanding Him were reciprocally and indissolubly intertwined.[48] This same premise undergirded the entire edifice of Teresa's mystical theology and served as one of the main reasons why she accentuated the affective rather than the intellectual element in recollection. Since love leads us most quickly and most certainly into God's presence by causing our wills to more readily conform to His will, why should anyone waste time trying to acquire knowledge of Him by such indirect means as the speculative methods of the Scholastic theologians?

The aforementioned considerations show that there was nothing fortuitous about Teresa's preference for an affective method of recollection. Her use of intense feelings of devotion as aids to recollection was the product of several concurrent influences: (1) a Christian religious environment that stressed, both in the New Testament and in its depictions of Heaven, that humankind's highest purpose was to love God and one's neighbor with all one's heart and soul, (2) the Spanish Franciscan mystics whom she read for guidance on how to practice interior prayer and recollection, and (3) the way that she read the Bible.

# The Diversity and Historicity of Recollective Techniques

A contrast of Teresa's method of recollection with other recollective procedures should correct any impression that attention-centering techniques are all basically the same from one religious tradition to the next. First, I have demonstrated that, despite a common psychological function of fo-

---

47. Etienne Gilson, *The Mystical Theology of Saint Bernard* (London: New York: Sheed & Ward, 1955), pp. 22, 27–28.
48. Gilson, *Mystical Theology of Saint Bernard*, pp. 114–15.

cusing the attention and quieting the mind and "heart," recollective techniques exhibit a considerable structural diversity. Second, and most important, I have also shown that these observed differences of form have more than just an incidental significance. For example, if the choice between a Christian nun's recollective technique that enkindles intense feelings of devotion to God and a Buddhist monk's method of either staring intently at a monotonously colored disc (*kasiṇa*)[49] or creating an intensely vivid mental image of a tutelary deity were no more than a matter of employing two different kinds of procedures that have an equal utility in concentrating the attention, then it would be clear that a mystic's choice of one or the other would be a matter of incidental significance because either choice would lead to the same result—a quieting of the mind. However, these different recollective techniques are not just different paths leading to the same goal. They do considerably more than just concentrate the subject's attention. They also prepare the individual who employs them to fulfill the ultimate spiritual goals of his particular religious tradition. Consequently, when a Christian mystic employs a technique with an affective emphasis, he is not using it simply because he thinks it a successful method for quieting his mind. The two Buddhist recollective techniques just mentioned could have worked just as well. The Christian mystic employs a meditational technique with a strong affective component not only because it concentrates his attention but also because he knows that when he employs it, it will simultaneously strengthen his love for God and his desire to serve Him. One can see, then, that the affective mobilization that he brought about by choosing this technique accomplished several religiously important purposes simultaneously. Had he chosen the Buddhist kasiṇa meditation as his recollective procedure, it is true that he would have succeeded in concentrating his attention but it is also safe to say that staring fixedly at a colored disc would never intensify his love for God. For a Christian, this Buddhist meditation would be religiously useless.

One can see from these reflections that a mystic's choice of a recollective technique is rarely the fortuitous result of certain peculiarities of his or her psychological temperament. Instead, the preponderance of facts forces one to conclude that it is the mystic's historical context rather than his psychological constitution that plays the larger role in determining his or her choice of possible methods.

49. For a brief description of the kasiṇa meditation, see p. 100.

# 28

# Distinctive Features of
# Saint Teresa's Prayer States

Even though Teresa described many visions, raptures, locutions, and ineffable sensations of God's presence, she never used any Spanish expression that one could literally translate into English as either "mystical experience" or "mysticism." The adjective "mystical" (*mística*) did make an appearance several times in her writings, but the infrequency of its occurrence and its use within only a limited context indicate that she had no intention of employing it as a blanket term referring to the whole range of extraordinary visionary and auditory phenomena that supervene after the onset of recollectedness.[1] Whenever Teresa described her beneficial visions, raptures and ecstasies, locutions, and ineffable sensations, she categorized them as either a particular type of supernatural prayer state or as a species of divine favor or consolation that God had bestowed upon her during one of those supernatural prayer states.[2] In other words, prayer states—more specifically, supernatural prayer states—provided the matrix within which

---

1. Teresa only used "mística" when she referred to that peculiar experience that she called "mystical theology" (*mística teología*). Although this phenomenon conveyed an immediate and unmistakable sense of God's presence, she was careful to add this sense of His presence "did not occur after the manner of a vision" (Teresa of Avila, *Life of St. Teresa of Jesus*, p. 119). Because she employed it in a context that clearly excluded any reference to visionary manifestations, her usage of "mística" lacked the wide-ranging character of the English word "mystical." See also pp. 127, 136.

One must also realize that when Teresa spoke about mystical theology, she was using "theology" in a way that differs from our own. For her, the word "theology" (in this context) did not refer to a process of inquiry about God but rather to an experience of Him. As such, her usage showed a greater affinity to the meaning that the early Church Fathers and the mystics of the Eastern Church have given it, namely, an "active and conscious participation in or perception of the realities of the divine world" (*Philokalia*, 1:367).

2. Teresa assumed that it was possible for the Devil to counterfeit visions and locutions. See, for example, Teresa of Avila, *Life of St. Teresa of Jesus*, p. 260.

were embedded the great variety of mystical states of consciousness that she described in her various books.

The most important characteristic that all of Teresa's soteriologically beneficial mystical experiences possessed was their "supernatural" quality. When she characterized an experience as supernatural this simultaneously indicated that the particular experience had come solely as an unmerited gift of God's grace and no amount of human moral, ascetic, and recollective effort could produce it.[3] For this reason, when Teresa described that condition that she called "perfect contemplation," she reminded her nuns that when and if that blessing should come their way, it would only do so when God, for reasons unfathomable to human understanding, had decided to bestow it upon them for such a grace "could not be gained by the merits of all the trials suffered on earth put together."[4] Her persistent emphasis on the essential incapacity of the human being to generate beneficial mystical experiences sharply differentiates her from both the followers of Patañjali's system of Yoga and the Buddhists that not only assume that all such phenomena originate from deep within the human mind but also take it for granted that one can bring them about without any divine assistance. They maintain that all the individual has to do to induce those experiences is exercise the proper degree of control over his mental processes.

In addition to sharing a supernatural origin, all of Teresa's soteriologically beneficial mystical experiences shared a second fundamental characteristic: they were experiences of companionship with God, that is, while each of them lasted, it either conveyed to the individual who experienced it an acute sensation that God now stood beside him as a loving companion or else it deepened the individual's love of God. Teresa persistently felt compelled to use the language and imagery of intimate human relationships to convey that element of mutual divine-human intimacy that seemed to permeate the existential core of every one of her mystical experi-

3. Teresa of Avila, *Spiritual Testimonies*, p. 355; Teresa of Avila, *Way of Perfection*, p. 204. Although, Teresa had high words of praise for the practice of recollection, she did not wish her nuns to think that the practice "forced" God to grant a particular soul the gift of contemplation. As Rowan Williams noted, "Just as much as any modern Protestant critic of 'mysticism,' a Karl Barth or Anders Nygren, [Teresa] is unhappy with any language that suggests God can be lured into giving favors by the straining Godwards of human eros" (Williams, *Teresa of Avila*, p. 59). For example, in *Way of Perfection*, she told her nuns that she was almost certain that if each of them had "true detachment and humility," God would grant them the gift of contemplation. Nevertheless, she was careful to add that there were no absolute guarantees that this would happen. See Teresa of Avila, *Way of Perfection*, p. 127.
4. Teresa of Avila, *Way of Perfection*, p. 171.

ences. For example, when she described the phenomenon that she called "perfect contemplation," she spoke of it as a blissful conversation that passes between God and the soul in which God "shows that He is listening to the person who is addressing Him and that, in His greatness, He is addressing her."[5] One must not forget that when she spoke about the ultimate and penultimate stages of the soul's contemplative ascent to spiritual perfection, she employed the terms "Spiritual Marriage" and "Spiritual Betrothal," respectively, as the names by which she designated each of these elevated mystical states. In so doing, she stressed that something akin to the emotions, expectations, and reciprocal obligations we associate with love and other types of intimate companionship pervaded even the most sublime of her mystical experiences. She wrote that in the experience of Spiritual Marriage one did far more than just acquire knowledge about the deepest truths of the faith. At the same time that the soul is receiving this sacred knowledge, the three Persons of the Holy Trinity "communicate Themselves to the soul and explain to it those words which the Gospel attributes to the Lord—namely, that He and the Father and the Holy Ghost will come to dwell with the soul which loves Him and keeps His commandments."[6]

Many mystical experiences in other traditions do not convey this feeling of divine-human companionship no matter how powerfully they may transform the subject's state of consciousness and his relationship to the world around him. For example, Sylvan Muldoon's first experience of out-of-body travel seems to have been nothing more than an unusual mode of perception. He experienced some strange things that both frightened and astonished him: he felt his astral body float, he saw his physical body lying on the bed beneath him as though he were looking at someone else, he felt peculiar vibrations run rapidly up and down the length of his body, he acquired the ability to travel through walls without hindrance, and he discovered that while "projected" he could easily travel to where other people were sleeping and see them as though he were physically present even though he could not make them see him nor could he make them aware that he was trying to touch them with his astral form.[7] This experience was certainly an extraordinary one but it was not an experience of spiritual companionship because it neither initiated nor continued any sort of mutual I-Thou relationship between Muldoon and a living spiritual intel-

5. Ibid., p. 170.
6. Teresa of Avila, *Interior Castle*, pp. 210–11.
7. Muldoon and Carrington, *Projection of the Astral Body*, pp. 49–53.

ligence. Muldoon admitted that during these out-of-body episodes he could not even wake up the sleeping people to get them to respond to his panic-stricken cries for assistance much less establish a dialogue with them or with some spiritual being. Consequently, this particular experience must be classified as a mere perception, a preternatural mode of consciousness devoid of any element of dialogue, a solitary act of "looking at" mere "things" that remained completely indifferent to his existence. As such, it was an experience worlds apart from the existential milieu of warm intimacy that imbued Teresa's visions and supernatural prayer states. The absence of any dialogue or companionship with God in Muldoon's out-of-body experiences should not occasion surprise for nowhere in his description of these experiences does he give the reader the impression that he was a devout Christian.

One can discern the same absence of divine-human companionship in Gopi Krishna's accounts of his mystical experiences. His first awakening of kundalini overwhelmed him emotionally and gave him a wondrous sensation that his consciousness had suddenly transcended the limitations of his physical body. "I was no longer as I knew myself to be, a small point of awareness confined in a body, but instead was a vast circle of consciousness in which the body was but a point, bathed in light and in a state of exaltation and happiness impossible to describe."[8] Despite the powerful impact that these experiences had on him, Gopi Krishna never really went beyond being a mere spectator of these events. Because this stream of liquid light that invaded his awareness exhibited none of the attributes associated with personality,[9] it could only manifest itself to him as a fascinating but utterly alien thing that he could look at but never enjoy as a friend or companion.

The absence of any of the attributes of personality in Gopi Krishna's experiences of awakening the goddess Kundalini from her slumbers at the base of his spine faithfully reflects the mythology that underlies the practice of hatha yoga. The classic treatises of hatha yoga such as the *Hathayogapradīpikā* never depict the goddess Kuṅḍalinī in anything but very impersonal terms—she is a female energy and power but she is never depicted with a fully developed divine personality to which anyone could respond with feelings of devotion and affection. Given these assumptions, it is not surprising that the practitioners of hatha yoga fail to have experiences of warm spiritual companionship with this goddess.

8. Gopi Krishna, *Kundalini*, p. 13.
9. Ibid., p. 49.

When one juxtaposes Teresa's descriptions of her supernatural prayer states and the divine favors she received during them with the various samādhis and jhānas spoken about in the classic treatises of yoga and Buddhism, one notices in the latter a similar absence of any dialogue or relationship of mutual affection between the meditator and the object upon which he meditates.[10] In sharp contrast to Teresa, none of the Buddhists or followers of Patañjali's system of Yoga ever stated or implied that the meditator should strive after those trance-states with the ultimate intention of making some spiritual being his companion or friend. However closely a Buddhist or yogin might identify himself with his chosen object of meditation (as in Tantric visualization techniques and in the yoga technique of practicing restraint or *samyama*), he always understood that the meditation object was never anything more than an object, a mere thing that one might use but never love or obey. Consequently, the objects that they perceived during their trance-states were usually just objects rather than intelligent beings endowed with personality. This fact is not surprising since neither system of religious practice accorded the slightest soteriological significance to either loving a divine Being or obeying Him.

There are some cases where Buddhists and yogins encountered entities endowed with personality during their trances but these exceptions prove the rule. In the Tibetan Buddhist practice of meditatively visualizing one's tutelary deity or Yidam, the particular deity the disciple is meditating upon sometimes will take on the appearance of being objectively real and independent of the meditator even to the extent of speaking to him and being perceptible to his touch. However, the Buddhists do not counsel the apprentice to worship, obey, or love this materialized phantom personality. Quite the contrary, they hope that the student will eventually comprehend that this seemingly real entity was nothing more than a phantom created by his own mind and from this experience of unmasking the illusion draw the conclusion that the other physical objects he believes are so real and independent of his mind have been endowed with their semblance of objective autonomy through a similar process of materializing mental phenomena.[11] Patañjali also mentioned situations where the highly accomplished yogin sometimes experiences visions in which gods speak to him and offer him the most wonderful kinds of gifts and enjoyments. However, Patañjali warned the yogin to spurn such visionary blandishments for the

10. See book 3 of Patañjali's *Yoga-Sūtras* (Ballantyne ed.); and Warren, *Buddhism in Translations,* pp. 347–49.
11. David-Neel, *Magic and Mystery in Tibet,* pp. 283–87.

gods only offer those things to divert yogins from their true goal.[12] Like the Buddhist apprentice who meditates on his tutelary deity, the yogin accomplishes nothing toward his salvation if he tries to develop a dialogue or a loving companionship with the personalities he might encounter during his trance-states. For both the Buddhist and the yogin, liberation from the round of rebirths—the one truly important goal—does not result from obeying, loving, longing for, or worshiping some entity perceived during a state of deep meditation. It only comes about when the individual employs his meditative experiences as tools that help him overcome his habitual attachment to all mental, spiritual, and physical phenomena. Consequently, both the yogin and the Buddhist would have regarded Teresa's love of God and longing for His presence as indicators that she had still not completely overcome that craving for phenomena that binds one to the round of rebirths.

Teresa's supernatural prayer states and the divine favors that took place while they were in progress had a third essential characteristic that differentiated them from experiences and revelations that did not originate from God: they always intensified the subject's desire to adhere scrupulously to His will. As Teresa pointed out, even the most rudimentary experiences of supernatural prayer cause "the soul to be less constrained in matters relating to the service of God than it was before." She then went on to say that the individual who experiences these first glimmerings of supernatural prayer "finds himself strengthened in all the virtues" as a result "and will infallibly continue to increase in them unless he turns back and commits offenses against God."[13] When the individual progresses to the more advanced stages of supernatural prayer, those first longings to serve God and obey His commandments become increasingly vehement. For example, in the Prayer of Union the soul "finds itself so anxious to praise the Lord that it would gladly . . . die a thousand deaths for His sake. . . . It has the most vehement desires for penance, for solitude, and for all to know God."[14]

This progression toward ever more vehement longings to conform oneself completely to the will of God culminates in the absolute renunciation of all self-seeking. When God grants the mystic His supreme spiritual gift, that prayer state Teresa called "Spiritual Marriage," those earlier longings to serve and obey God that he experienced during the Prayer of Union no

12. Patañjali, *Yoga-System of Patañjali*, 3:51, and commentaries on this passage by Veda-Vyāsa and Vācaspati Miśra.
13. Teresa of Avila, *Interior Castle*, pp. 90–91.
14. Ibid., p. 106.

longer seem radical enough. The mystic who has experienced the Prayer of Union no longer appears outwardly disobedient to God. Nevertheless, his inner motives betray the incompleteness of his submission to God's will. Although he thinks that his desire "to die a thousand deaths for His sake" stems from a sincere and utterly disinterested love of God, he fails to see that this yearning for martyrdom subtly disguises a selfish desire to escape this world and its burdensome obligations so that he can then enjoy God's presence uninterruptedly in Heaven. That perfect and total substitution of God's will for the mystic's own will that takes place once God has granted him the blessed privilege of Spiritual Marriage causes the mystic to realize that perfect obedience to God requires that he give up all self-seeking desires for spiritual enjoyments, even the most sublime of them. If God's will is best served by suffering for His sake in this life as Christ had done, then he must unhesitatingly embrace such suffering with a joyful heart and not long for an end to it. He must not long for the spiritual rewards that follow from fulfilling God's will but rather he must be filled with a desire to do those things that he knows God wants him to accomplish in this earthly life. For this reason, the spiritually perfect mystic no longer hopes for a quick end to earthly life. Instead, he hopes that God will give him a long life so that he can use that extra time on earth to suffer more fully for His sake just as Christ had done before him.[15]

# Teresa's Hierarchy of Prayer States

## Crude Vocal Prayer and Mental Prayer

I have already noted in this chapter that each of Teresa's religiously significant mystical experiences took place within the context of one or more of her supernatural prayer states.[16] Thus the phenomena of mystical experience and supernatural prayer were intimately linked together. I also mentioned that she made a distinction between different types of prayer states, some of purely human origin and some of divine origin, each of which corresponded to a different degree of divine-human intimacy. Whereas some of those prayer states that she described had little or no emotional

15. Ibid., pp. 219–20, 228–29.

16. I remind the reader that Teresa also assumed that it was possible for the Devil to counterfeit most of the mystical states of consciousness that she experienced. Teresa of Avila, *Life of St. Teresa of Jesus,* p. 260.

impact and conveyed little or no sense of contact with God, others—those that she considered as the more spiritually advanced—not only produced an overwhelming affective impact but also gave the subject a compelling sense of God's presence.

Teresa accorded the lowest ranking to those prayer states that had a purely human rather than a supernatural origin. Within this category, one can discern at least two distinctive classes of prayer phenomena. What I will call "crude" vocal prayer occupied the lowest class within this hierarchy of purely intrapsychic prayer experiences. (It was necessary to coin this term "crude vocal prayer" for this phenomenon because Teresa never explicitly gave it a name even though she did describe it.) According to her description, crude vocal prayer was any sort of audible petition to God in which the individual merely uttered the words of his request without making any effort to focus either his attention or his affections on God as he did so. It was nothing more than a mechanically parroted entreaty to God performed while one's heart and mind were flying after worldly thoughts and desires. This characteristic absence of even the rudiments of recollective effort or intent was one reason why Teresa considered this prayer spiritually worthless.[17] There was also another reason why she had no use for this type of prayer. She maintained that one who engaged in it displayed not only hypocrisy but also a disrespect for God. How could an individual who was supposedly preparing himself to enter into God's presence have the audacity to claim that he loved God more than himself or the things of this world when he made no effort to turn his thoughts and desires away from worldly things?[18]

Teresa distinguished a second class of intrapsychically originated prayer, which she called mental prayer (oración mental). This differed from crude vocal prayer in two ways. First, the practice of mental prayer always required that the subject integrate some element of recollective effort into his act of petitioning God (it did not matter in the least to Teresa whether the petitioning were done aloud or in silence).[19] For example, when she spoke to her nuns about how they should practice mental prayer, she warned them not to "address God while you are thinking of other things." She then went on to add that allowing one's mind to wander in an undisciplined manner during prayer stemmed from "not knowing

17. Teresa of Avila, *Interior Castle*, pp. 31–32; idem, *Way of Perfection*, p. 156.
18. Teresa of Avila, *Interior Castle*, p. 32.
19. Teresa of Avila, *Way of Perfection*, pp. 156–58; and E. W. Trueman Dicken, *The Crucible of Love* (New York: Sheed & Ward, 1963), p. 83.

what mental prayer is. . . . If anyone of you cannot say her vocal prayers with . . . attentiveness, she should know that she is not fulfilling her obligation."[20] In these passages, Teresa not only emphasized the fundamental importance of the recollective dimension of mental prayer but she also stressed that mental prayer was the only religiously significant type of intrapsychically originated prayer. For this reason, no member of her religious order could content herself with the practice of crude vocal prayer and claim that she was fulfilling her vocation to "pray without ceasing."

Second, mental prayer differed from crude vocal prayer in that it was a meditative rumination designed to foster humility and quicken the subject's feelings of devotion to God. Not only did mental prayer demand recollective concentration on God, but it also required that the subject ponder the meaning of the words he was addressing to Him, that he try to fathom the compassion and majesty of that awesome Being whom he was presuming to address, that he try to realize just how little he had really deserved God's mercy, and that he comprehend the true extent of that enormous debt that he owed his Creator and Savior.[21] Teresa's idea that mental prayer must inspire both devotion and humility shows unmistakable affinities with the earlier medieval practice of meditation. For example, her distinction between crude vocal prayer, mental prayer, and supernatural (or contemplative) prayer brings to mind the classic Victorine distinction between *cogitatio* (a "careless glance of the soul prone to restless wandering"), *meditatio* (which Richard of St. Victor characterized as both "an industrious attention of the mind concentrated diligently upon the investigation of some object" and as "the careful look of the soul zealously occupied in the search of truth"), and *contemplatio* ("a free and clear vision of the mind fixed upon the manifestation of wisdom in suspended wonder").[22] The Victorines spoke of these three phenomena as mental states rather than prayer states. Nevertheless, their trichotomy paralleled Teresa's distinction between crude vocal prayer, mental prayer, and contemplative prayer quite closely, especially when they emphasized, as she did, that the intermediate member of the triad was a phenomenon that simultaneously incorporated recollective and devotional elements, that is,

20. Teresa of Avila, *Way of Perfection,* pp. 161, 161, n.

21. Ibid., p. 171.

22. Richard of St. Victor, *Richard of Saint-Victor: Selected Writings on Contemplation,* trans. with an introduction by Clare Kirchberger (New York: Harper and Brother, 1957), p. 138.

it required both attentiveness upon some object and zeal in the pursuit of truth.

Teresa's own terminological inconsistencies initially cause difficulties when one tries to demarcate that boundary line where she considered the domain of supernatural prayer states to have begun.[23] However, there are two reasons for concluding that mental prayer did not come within that realm of manifestations that she considered supernatural. First, when she explicitly listed those prayer states that she categorized as supernatural, she conspicuously failed to include mental prayer and its accompaniments among them.[24] Second, she often contrasted mental prayer and contemplation (a phenomenon that she always described as a species of supernatural prayer) in such a way as to imply that the former did not originate supernaturally.[25]

If Teresa did not place mental prayer within the category of supernatural phenomena, did she consider the prayer state that immediately succeeded it to be supernatural?

## The Transition to Supernaturally Originated Prayer

Teresa made it clear that the transition to supernatural prayer always coincided with those moments when the individual finally reached that condition of recollectedness toward which he had directed all those meditative exercises that he had practiced during mental prayer. It was not the effort to achieve recollectedness but rather the actual achievement of recollectedness itself that she considered supernatural. It is easy to verify this by consulting any one of her principal works. For example, in her autobiography she described the first stage of supernatural prayer, which she at that time called the "Prayer of Quiet," as a "quiet and recollectedness in the soul." This description also emphasized the intrinsically supernatural character of this phenomenon for she noted that humans can do nothing to bring about this blessed condition; it comes and goes according to God's will.[26] Teresa did not change these essential attributes of the Prayer of Quiet when she wrote *The Way of Perfection*. Even though she did not refer to it as a condition of "recollectedness," she employed equivalent words to describe

23. For an excellent discussion of Teresa's terminological inconsistencies, see Dicken, *Crucible of Love*, pp. 203–11.
24. Teresa of Avila, *Spiritual Testimonies*, pp. 355–61.
25. Teresa of Avila, *Way of Perfection*, pp. 118, 171.
26. Teresa of Avila, *Life of St. Teresa of Jesus*, pp. 154–55.

it. She maintained that it took place when "the Lord grants our faculties tranquillity and our soul quiet."[27] In both of these writings two features distinguish the most rudimentary state of supernatural prayer from the phenomenon of mental prayer: (1) human beings cannot acquire it or attain it by means of their own efforts no matter how hard they try and (2) its onset is coterminous with the onset of recollectedness. While it is true that Teresa thought that all genuine mental prayer incorporated some element of recollective effort into the act of praying, she never implied that the individual who had still not advanced beyond mental prayer had actually achieved that recollectedness toward which he had been struggling. It was precisely this transition from recollective effort to recollectedness achieved that indicated that one had, in some mysterious manner, crossed the boundary line that separated mental prayer from supernatural prayer.[28]

The wonderfully clear and concise descriptions of her supernatural prayer experiences that she gave to Rodrigo Alvarez in her most mature writings, *The Interior Castle* (1577) and *Relación V* (1576), depicted the first stage of supernatural prayer in the same way that she had done in her earlier works, that is, she stressed that it was a condition essentially coterminous with the onset of recollectedness. She told her director Alvarez in *Relación V* that "the first prayer . . . that in my opinion was supernatural . . . is an interior recollection felt in the soul."[29] Similarly, when she wrote *The Interior Castle*, she observed that when the individual experiences the onset of supernatural prayer, he "involuntarily closes his eyes and desires solitude, and without the display of any human skill, . . . the senses and all external things seem gradually to lose their hold on him."[30] This descriptive continuity between her latest works pertaining to mysticism and her earliest ones shows that even at the beginning of her career as a mystic, Teresa had no difficulty identifying which phenomena heralded the soul's transition from mental prayer to supernatural prayer.

## Was the Prayer of Quiet or the Prayer of Recollection the Transitional Prayer State?

Unfortunately, even though Teresa remained consistent in describing the various attributes of this transitional prayer state, she was not consistent in

27. Teresa of Avila, *Way of Perfection*, p. 198.
28. Ibid., p. 161.
29. Teresa of Avila, *Spiritual Testimonies*, p. 355.
30. Teresa of Avila, *Interior Castle*, p. 85.

naming it.[31] This inconsistent use of terminology creates difficulties for anyone who tries to specify the relative position that each particular prayer state occupied within her hierarchy of supernatural prayer manifestations. One runs into this difficulty as soon as one attempts to answer the following question: what name did Teresa give to that first stage of supernatural prayer just described? The answer will vary depending upon which text one cites as his authority. If one bases one's authority upon either her autobiography or *The Way of Perfection,* one would have to maintain that she identified the onset of recollectedness with the Prayer of Quiet.[32] However, one gets a contradictory answer if one cites her most mature and, for that reason, most authoritative work on prayer, *The Interior Castle.* There it was the Prayer of Recollection, not the Prayer of Quiet, that corresponded to the onset of recollectedness and the most rudimentary stage of supernatural prayer. In other words, according to *The Interior Castle,* the Prayer of Quiet was not the first but rather the second stage of supernatural prayer.

There are still other nomenclatural contradictions that pertain to Teresa's descriptions of the first stages of supernatural prayer. Even if one takes *The Interior Castle* as the final authority and henceforth decides to call her first supernatural prayer state "the Prayer of Recollection," one still needs to be aware that she did not always use this term consistently either. For example, when one juxtaposes that characterization of the Prayer of Recollection that she gave in *The Interior Castle* with the one that she gave in *The Way of Perfection,* one immediately notices a major contradiction. Whereas she made it very clear in the former that the Prayer of Recollection was a supernatural condition that humans could never, under any circumstances, bring about by means of their own efforts, she did not do so in the latter book.[33] When she wrote *The Way of Perfection,* she described the manifestations allied with the term "Prayer of Recollection" (*oración de recogimiento*) in such a way as to identify it with the recollective effort rather than with the actual onset of recollectedness itself. As such, that Prayer of Recollection still remained a mere subset of that broader category of phenomena she lumped together under the term

31. For a more detailed discussion of her terminological inconsistencies, see Dicken, *Crucible of Love,* pp. 203–11.
32. Teresa of Avila, *Life of St. Teresa of Jesus,* p. 148; Teresa of Avila, *Way of Perfection,* pp. 170–71, 200–201.
33. Teresa of Avila, *Interior Castle,* pp. 85–90.

"mental prayer" instead of becoming recognized as a qualitatively distinctive phenomenon in its own right. This is probably the reason why, in that particular work, she did not consider the Prayer of Recollection to have been supernatural but rather something that humans could bring about by means of their own will.[34]

These terminological inconsistencies make it dangerous to use any important term in her prayer vocabulary unless one has already specified which particular text or texts has served as the basis for one's definition or characterization of it. For example, if one is speaking of the Prayer of Quiet, one must be sure to inform the reader whether the Prayer of Quiet being discussed is the one she described in *The Interior Castle* or the one she described in her autobiography.

The foregoing analyses lead to the following conclusion: If one bases one's authority upon Teresa's most mature work, *The Interior Castle,* one must classify the Prayer of Recollection as the most rudimentary and least developed of her supernatural prayer states. It was at this stage of prayer that mystical experiences began to occur and that God began to control the mental activities of the soul through the workings of His grace.[35]

## The Prayer of Quiet

In *The Interior Castle* Teresa employed the term "Prayer of Quiet" to designate that supernatural prayer state that was the next to develop after the Prayer of Recollection. This prayer state had two distinctive features. First, it was fundamentally incompatible with the continued practice of discursive meditation.[36] Whereas souls experiencing only the Prayer of Recollection find that they can still mobilize the imagination and the understanding to create images (such as imagining Christ's agony and humiliation as He was being scourged and mocked) or thoughts (such as thinking about the many ways that one has sinned against God's commandments in intention and deed) to elicit feelings of either devotion or contrition, those souls who have begun to experience the Prayer of Quiet suddenly find that

34. Teresa of Avila, *Obras de Santa Teresa de Jesus,* p. 135; Teresa of Avila, *Way of Perfection,* pp. 190–92.

35. Teresa mentioned that after she read Osuña's *Third Spiritual Alphabet* and began to practice recollective prayer, God soon granted her brief episodes of the Prayer of Quiet and Union. Her first imaginary visions also seem to have become manifest after she began to practice recollection. See Teresa of Avila, *Life of St. Teresa of Jesus,* pp. 80–81, 99–100.

36. Teresa of Avila, *Interior Castle,* p. 90; Teresa of Avila, *Spiritual Testimonies,* pp. 355–56.

these meditative activities hinder their prayerful intimacy with God. Instead of facilitating recollectedness as they had done before, these activities of the imagination and the understanding now become a disruptive "noise" that, if paid attention to, can only distract the soul from that deeper recollectedness and peace that it now enjoys.[37]

The Prayer of Quiet had a second important feature: it caused the subject's will to become profoundly "absorbed" or fixated upon God. When Teresa described the will as absorbed or "united in some way with the will of God,"[38] she meant that the souls of those who enter this prayer state become so amazed and overjoyed by what they experience that "they have no wish to see and hear anything but their God . . . they can think of nothing else to wish for."[39] This condition is a joyful "captivity" of the will for God has now "imprisoned" it in bonds of love so delightful that it no longer desires any earthly thing.[40]

It must be stressed that only the will became absorbed during the Prayer of Quiet. This prayer state still left the other two rational faculties of the soul, the memory and the understanding, free to wander. As a rule, their wanderings did not disturb the will because the delight it enjoyed made it difficult for it to be distracted by anything else. Nevertheless, sometimes inexperienced souls, instead of just passively enjoying the bliss that God was giving them, would attempt to chase after those two faculties in the mistaken belief that they could bring them into subjection by means of their own recollective efforts. Such attempts to control the wanderings of the memory and understanding before God had decided to restrain them Himself carried the substantial risk that they would draw the will out of its state of absorption.[41] This potential of the Prayer of Quiet to be disrupted if the soul pays attention to the activities of the memory and the understanding was one of the chief reasons why Teresa ranked it lower than those prayer states that she called "the sleep of the faculties" and the "union of all the faculties." During those "deeper" prayer states, the memory and the understanding progressively lose any potential for interfering with the will's enjoyment of God.[42]

---

37. For this image of discursive meditation as a kind of noise, see Teresa of Avila, *Life of St. Teresa of Jesus*, p. 157.

38. Teresa of Avila, *Interior Castle*, p. 83.

39. Teresa of Avila, *Way of Perfection*, p. 202.

40. Teresa of Avila, *Life of St. Teresa of Jesus*, p. 149.

41. Teresa of Avila, *Way of Perfection*, pp. 204–5; Teresa of Avila, *Life of St. Teresa of Jesus*, pp. 154–55.

42. Teresa of Avila, *Life of St. Teresa of Jesus*, p. 164.

## The Sleep of the Faculties

The phenomenon that Teresa referred to as the "sleep of the faculties" occupied the third position in her hierarchy of supernatural prayer states. For some reason, however, she failed to mention this prayer state in *The Interior Castle* even though, the year before (1576), she had mentioned it by name and briefly described its principal features to Rodrigo Alvarez.[43] This becomes all the more puzzling because she devoted two full chapters to its description in her autobiography.[44] Despite its absence from *The Interior Castle*, I have decided to incorporate it into this list of her principal supernatural prayer states because not only did it figure prominently in both her autobiography and her letter to Rodrigo Alvarez but it also possessed exactly those features that one would have expected such a manifestation to have had if it had indeed occupied the middle position between the Prayer of Quiet and her fourth prayer state, the "union of all the faculties."

The crucial thing that differentiated the sleep of the faculties from the Prayer of Quiet was that, in the former, the memory and the understanding completely lost whatever potential they had had for interrupting the will's joyful absorption in God. During the sleep of the faculties, "the will is completely occupied in God" and cannot—even if it wishes—occupy itself with anything but Him.[45] One will recall that during the Prayer of Quiet the will's absorption in God could still be disrupted if the subject deliberately allowed himself to pay attention to the "noise" that the memory and understanding continue to generate as they wander from one holy thought or imaginational construction to the next. (Teresa took it for granted that by the time the soul had reached this level of spiritual development the memory and understanding were no longer preoccupied with worldly thoughts and imaginings. Nevertheless, even holy thoughts and imaginings created noise that could disrupt the peace that the will was then enjoying.) Because of this potential threat to the will's state of absorption in God, those souls who were enjoying the Prayer of Quiet tried to remain motionless and fixated upon both the joy that they were experiencing or the love of God that this state of prayer caused them to feel. This feeling that one has to remain motionless in order to continue enjoying

43. Teresa of Avila, *Spiritual Testimonies*, p. 356. This is the famous Testimony no. 59, also known as *Relación V* in some of the other editions of her collected works.

44. Teresa of Avila, *Life of St. Teresa of Jesus*, pp. 163–73.

45. Teresa of Avila, *Spiritual Testimonies*, p. 356.

God's presence disappears when the sleep of the faculties supervenes for then the soul discovers that the thoughts, activities, and imaginings concocted by the understanding and the memory no longer have the slightest power to distract the will from its blissful absorption in God. For the first time, it is now possible for Martha and Mary to walk together, that is, the soul finds that it can now devote itself simultaneously to both the contemplative and the active life since the will can enjoy its absorption in God even while the memory and the understanding are busy with works of charity and service to God.[46] This ability is what differentiates the sleep of the faculties from the Prayer of Quiet. In the Prayer of Quiet, the soul enjoys a blissful absorption in God, but this condition is unstable. Consequently, the soul is afraid to engage in pious meditations or in pious deeds because it is afraid that those activities will distract the soul from its absorption in God. It simply wants to stay still so as not to disturb its blissful communion with Him. The soul no longer has to worry about this happening when God grants it the sleep of the faculties for then, even if the soul performs its pious meditations and actions in service to God, their performance will not disrupt its concentration.

The sleep of the faculties had two other characteristics that differentiated it from the Prayer of Quiet and also caused Teresa to accord it a higher rank within her hierarchy of prayer states. First, it noticeably enhanced both the subject's capacity and his desire to fulfill the monastic virtues. She noted that when God admits a soul into this prayer state "the virtues are . . . stronger than they were previously, in the Prayer of Quiet."[47] Second, it exhibited a far greater affective intensity than its predecessor. For this reason, she wrote that when the soul enters into this blessed condition it discovers that "the pleasure and sweetness and delight are incomparably greater than in the previous state, for the water of grace rises to the very neck of the soul."[48]

## The Union of All Faculties

Teresa gave several different names to that supernatural prayer state that she ranked immediately above the sleep of the faculties. Sometimes she referred to it as the "union of all the faculties," at other times she referred to it as the "Prayer of Union," and at still other times, she called it simply,

46. Teresa of Avila, *Life of St. Teresa of Jesus*, p. 170; and idem, *Spiritual Testimonies*, p. 356.
47. Teresa of Avila, *Life of St. Teresa of Jesus*, p. 169.
48. Ibid., p. 163.

"union." Regardless of how she referred to it or where she referred to it (she described this prayer state in her autobiography, in *Relación V* and in *The Interior Castle*), the fact remains that the phenomenon always had one fundamental feature that distinguished it from all the earlier prayer states: its onset coincided with that moment when all of the soul's faculties completely stopped functioning.

During both the Prayer of Quiet and the sleep of the faculties, the memory and the understanding as well as the five physical senses continued to function even though, in each respective prayer state, they operated with a progressively diminished capacity to disturb the will's absorption in God. Those activities cease altogether when God brings the soul into the Prayer of Union. This crippling of all the faculties has profound consequences. For example, the failure of the understanding makes it impossible for the individual to describe or apprehend what is happening to him. He experiences intense feelings of joy and love but, because his understanding has stopped functioning, he finds that he can no longer describe what it is that causes his rejoicing or in any way intellectually comprehend it. It seems as though feelings of awe have overwhelmed his powers of ratiocination. This seems to be what Teresa meant when she wrote that, during this state, "The intellect is as though in awe; the will loves more than it understands, but it doesn't understand in a describable way whether it loves or what it does."[49] The failure of the memory has radical consequences as well. The individual finds that he no longer has the power to form thoughts nor does he possess the ability to imagine things.[50] In addition, this failure of the memory temporarily anesthetizes his powers of reminiscence. "If the soul ha(s) been meditating upon any subject, this vanishes from the memory as if it had never existed."[51]

That failure of the understanding has a profound impact upon the sensible faculties, at least those of sight and hearing. The failure of the understanding does not cause visual perception or auditory perception to cease but it does make it impossible for the subject to comprehend what it is that he is seeing or hearing. For example, he finds that if he tries to read something, "He sees that the letters are there, but, as the understanding gives him no help, he cannot read them even if he so wishes. He can hear but he

49. Teresa of Avila, *Spiritual Testimonies*, p. 356; see also *Life of St. Teresa of Jesus*, p. 174 for a similar description.
50. Teresa of Avila, *Spiritual Testimonies*, p. 356; and idem, *Interior Castle*, p. 97.
51. Teresa of Avila, *Life of St. Teresa of Jesus*, p. 179.

cannot understand what he hears."[52] The naked act of perception exists but, since those percepts no longer remain connected to the parts of the brain that interpret, analyze, or otherwise make use of such perceptual information, the act of perception can no longer pose the slightest threat to concentration. If I may employ an automotive analogy, it is as though the car is "in neutral" with the engine running. Everything indicates that the car should be moving since the fuel lines, the electrical systems, the transmission, and the suspension operate well. The only problem is that someone has pushed in the clutch making it impossible for the gears to engage.

## "True" Union and "Delectable" Union

Even though it is true that Teresa often depicted "union" as a type of ecstasy, one would make a serious error if he were to conclude from this that she considered union with God to have been nothing more than a peculiar species of trance. This mistake arises from the fact that she did not employ the word "union" in a consistent and unambiguous manner.[53] She often used the word "union" as a synonym for trance or a trancelike abstraction from the world. Nevertheless, one also finds that there were numerous, significant occasions when she used the same term without its bearing any reference to states of ecstatic absorption. For example, when she talked about that important phenomenon she called "true union" (*verdadera unión*), she explicitly declared that many souls had achieved this union who had never been mystics and had never had a mystical experience of any sort.[54] "Those from whom the Lord withholds such supernatural gifts will do well to feel that they are not without hope; for true union can quite well be achieved, with the favor of Our Lord, if we endeavor to attain it by not following our own will but submitting it to whatever is the will of God."[55] As one can easily see, true union was simply the perfect conformity of the subject's will with God's will. Because it was a proclivity of the will rather than a trance-state, it was open to all Christians, mystics and nonmystics alike.

Although the term "union," as Teresa employed it in the expression "true union," did not refer to experiences of a mystical sort, those types of

52. Ibid., pp. 177–78.

53. For a discussion of her inconsistent use of the word "union," see Dicken, *Crucible of Love*, pp. 408–17.

54. Teresa of Avila, *Obras Completas*, p. 436.

55. Teresa of Avila, *Interior Castle*, p. 112; and idem, *Book of Foundations*, pp. 24–25 (5.13).

union that she included under the rubric "delectable union" (*unión regalada*) always referred to experiences that could only take place in conditions of ecstatic absorption.[56] For example, it is clear that when Teresa speaks of the "union of all the faculties" she is using the word "union" in a mystical context: the faculties are "united" only if the soul is in a condition of blissful absorption. Similarly, when she speaks of "the union of the whole soul with God,"[57] the context clearly implies some sort of mystical experience for this type of union where God gives the soul an unmistakable sensation that He has taken up His abode in its very center can only occur when the rational faculties and the physical senses have stopped functioning.

Although true union might seem somewhat prosaic when compared to the various types of phenomena that took place during delectable union, Teresa made it clear that she considered true union to be the much more valuable type of union. First, the whole of Christian perfection consists in nothing more than perfect conformity of one's own will to God's will. Given this fact, it necessarily follows that no one has any reason for desiring to go beyond true union. After all, true union is nothing other than that perfect conformity of wills that the soul has been seeking ever since it began its spiritual quest. Second, while it is true that the various types of mystical (or delectable union) must never be despised since they are precious and joyful gifts that God often sends to those who love Him, it is also true that sinners often receive them and fail to benefit from them.[58] Consequently, they do not necessarily signify that the recipient enjoys divine favor nor do they necessarily signify that the recipient is successfully conforming his own will to God's will. While perfect obedience to God's will (true union) is the closest thing humans can have of a guarantee of salvation, the experiences that correspond to the various forms of delectable union bring with them no such assurance unless they have the effect of making it easier for the recipient to obey God's will without any reservation or hesitation. It should now be easy to see why Teresa regarded the experiences of delectable union as inferior to those of true union. The experiences of delectable union only derived whatever value they had from the fact that they usually made true union much easier to achieve than it would otherwise have been.[59]

---

56. Teresa of Avila, *Obras Completas*, p. 436.

57. Teresa of Avila, *Interior Castle*, pp. 101–3.

58. Teresa of Avila, *Book of Foundations*, pp. 24–25 (5.13–15); idem, *Interior Castle*, p. 192.

59. Teresa of Avila, *Interior Castle*, p. 192.

Teresa's distinction between true union and delectable union points to an extremely important feature of her supernatural prayer states: they were not only distinctive states of consciousness but, even more significantly from Teresa's perspective, they were distinctive stages in the orientation of the individual's will toward God. The spiritually superior prayer states did two things: they effected a more perfect congruence between the mystic's will and God's will and they gave the mystic an enhanced ability to act in accordance with God's will. It was the impact of a supernatural prayer state on the mystic's will and actions—not its effects upon his consciousness—that ultimately determined its relative rank within her hierarchy of prayer states.

## Spiritual Betrothal

When Teresa wrote *The Interior Castle,* she gave the name Spiritual Betrothal to that next supernatural prayer state or, more accurately, collection of supernatural prayer states, which chronologically and hierarchically superseded the Prayer of Union. Even though she did not give this assemblage of prayer states the collective name Spiritual Betrothal until the date when she composed *The Interior Castle* (1577), her tardiness in naming the phenomenon did not mean that it had never before appeared as an important element in her religious experience. On the contrary, it is easy to show that the principal prayer states constitutive of Spiritual Betrothal had actually been around a long time. For example, one knows that Teresa's accounts of what transpired in Spiritual Betrothal accorded special pre-eminence to two prayer phenomena: a prayer state she called "rapture"[60] and a peculiar condition of "delectable" spiritual pain.[61] Those two phenomena did not appear for the first time in *The Interior Castle* but twelve years earlier in her autobiography. In that earlier text not only did she characterize the two phenomena in almost the same way that she had described them in *The Interior Castle* but she also placed them in the same temporal position that they had occupied in the later work, that is, both phenomena only became manifest after the individual had first experienced the Prayer of Union.[62]

The nature of the soul's transition from the Prayer of Union to Spiritual Betrothal differed sharply from the character of the transition that it made

60. Ibid., pp. 149–51.
61. Ibid., pp. 134–38.
62. Compare *Interior Castle,* pp. 134–38, 149–51, with Teresa of Avila, *Life of St. Teresa of Jesus,* pp. 189–202; and idem, *Spiritual Testimonies,* pp. 356–60.

when it passed from the sleep of the faculties to the Prayer of Union. Whereas the latter transition resembled a quantum leap between two discontinuous modes of experience—a jump from a condition of consciousness where all but one of the faculties and senses continued to function normally to one where none of them functioned normally—the passage from the Prayer of Union to Spiritual Betrothal was far less abrupt. As a matter of fact, Teresa pointed out that the experiences that occurred during those two prayer states were "almost identical."[63] Two assertions seem to have led her to make this statement. First, both prayer states presupposed an identical initial condition for their manifestation. Neither the phenomena of one nor the phenomena of the other could become manifest until all of the soul's faculties or senses had stopped functioning in their usual manner. Second, the experiences that transpired during each of the two prayer states were essentially continuous with one another. The progression from the Prayer of Union to the condition of Spiritual Betrothal was something like an ant's journey along a smooth curve that has no gaps in it—it is a journey along what a mathematician would call a continuum.

Abundant evidence supports each of these two assertions. With regard to the first, no one could experience the Prayer of Union until God had first caused his physical senses and his three rational faculties to cease operating in their ordinary manner. The same thing was true of the phenomena that took place during Spiritual Betrothal. For example, Teresa observed that when God wishes the soul to experience that strange phenomenon she called rapture, "He will not allow her to be disturbed either by the faculties or by the senses."[64] A similar, if not identical, disruption of the physical senses and the operations of the memory, will, and understanding also had to take place before the soul could experience that spiritually painful but much-to-be-desired gift of being "most delectably wounded" (herida sabrosisimamente) by God.[65] Thus she noticed that when this condition of blessed suffering overwhelms the soul to whom God has betrothed Himself, He makes sure that neither "the senses, the imagination, nor the faculties dares to stir."[66]

---

63. Teresa of Avila, Interior Castle, pp. 106–7; also her remark on p. 150, to the effect that "there is no closed door to separate one from the other."

64. Ibid., p. 153.

65. Teresa of Avila, Obras Completas, p. 447.

66. Teresa of Avila, Interior Castle, p. 135; but also see idem, Life of St. Teresa of Jesus, pp. 194–95. Unfortunately, Teresa seems to contradict herself on the very next page, for there she makes a confusing remark that implies that the faculties do not cease functioning

One has no difficulty locating evidence that supports my second assertion that the experiences of Spiritual Betrothal were continuous with those
that occurred during the Prayer of Union. For example, Teresa's accounts
of rapture, the most prominent among the various phenomena that took
place during Spiritual Betrothal, indicate that it did not differ all that much
from the phenomenon of union. Only two characteristics differentiated
rapture from union: it lasted longer and it caused the vital powers of the
body, especially respiration, to diminish to a greater extent than they had
done during union. As Teresa put it, "Although this diminishing of these
bodily powers occurs in union, it takes place in this prayer [rapture] with
greater force."[67] The difference between the two phenomena boils down to
this: rapture is a more vehement manifestation of the same processes that
underlie the phenomenon of union.

One can say the same thing about another phenomenon that took place
during Spiritual Betrothal, a deep trance-state, more profound than rapture, which Teresa called "transport." Just as rapture was characterized as
a more energetic manifestation of the same processes that were at work in
union, transport is essentially a more vehement expression of the same
processes that produced and sustained both union and rapture. Whereas
rapture and union cause the activities of the faculties and the physical
senses to come to a complete halt in a gradual manner, transport brings
about this cessation abruptly.[68] Other than this, Teresa gives no other criterion that would allow one to differentiate it from the other two phenomena. For this reason, I contend that union, rapture, and transport differ
from each other only in the insignificant way that three adjacent points on
a mathematical continuum such as a line or smooth curve differ from each
other. What separates one from the other is a simple difference of magnitude, not a difference of kind (such as the topological dissimilarity between
a donut and a cube).

The experiences of "delectable pain" that often afflicted the soul during
both the Prayer of Union and Spiritual Betrothal show evidence of a continuity with each other. The strikingly similar way that she described both
of these painful conditions suggests that they did not differ all that significantly from one another. For example, when she spoke about the delecta-

---

when God "most delectably" wounds the soul. In the passage in question, she asserts that
"here all the senses and faculties are active and there is no absorption; they are on the alert to
discover what can be happening." Nevertheless, she then goes on to mention that, despite this
activity, "they cause no disturbance and can neither increase this delectable pain nor remove
it" (quoted from Teresa of Avila, *Interior Castle*, pp. 136–37).

67. Teresa of Avila, *Spiritual Testimonies*, p. 356.

68. Ibid., p. 357.

ble pain of the Prayer of Union, she described it as a type of spiritual grief so intense that it "reaches to the depths of our being," tears the soul into pieces, and "grinds it to a powder."[69] She described the delectable wounds of Spiritual Betrothal in almost the same vivid way. They were spiritual agonies that seemed to penetrate to the "very bowels" of the soul.[70] The essential similarity of the two painful phenomena gains even more solid support from another parallelism. Each could only become manifest if the same preconditions had been met. The soul's faculties and physical senses had to cease their normal functioning and God, not the subject, had to decide to bestow them.[71] In other words, no individual could produce either of those two experiences of delectable pain through any process of meditative effort whatsoever no matter how hard he tried. First, their appearance, duration, and disappearance depended exclusively upon God's will. Second, meditative effort of any sort presupposed that the faculties of understanding, memory, and imagination were still functioning so that the subject could form images of what he wished to meditate upon. This type of image-creating activity was completely impossible during either the Prayer of Union or Spiritual Betrothal because both of those conditions could not occur if the physical senses or the faculties were functioning. Third, the similar origins of the delectability and the painfulness intrinsic to each of those experiences of spiritual distress points toward their essential continuity with each other. For example, we know that the feelings of pain, loneliness, and grief that overwhelmed the individual during each of those experiences arose because his soul had become "crucified between heaven and earth."[72] He was, on the one hand, filled with a love of and a longing for God so intense and exclusive that absolutely nothing worldly could any longer interest him or console him and, on the other hand, he was confronted with the painful realization that his enjoyment of his only love could only be intermittent. It is easy to see that it is the vehemence and exclusivity of the individual's longing for God coupled with his complete indifference to, or even disgust for, the things of this world that this exclusive love of God necessarily generates that causes his spiritual pain. After all, if the subject can only derive solace from God's company and He is usually absent, how can that situation produce anything but a painful emptiness when it happens? Moreover, if the subject is filled with an in-

69. Teresa of Avila, *Interior Castle*, p. 109.
70. Ibid., p. 136.
71. Ibid., pp. 109, 136.
72. Teresa of Avila, *Life of St. Teresa of Jesus*, p. 194; also compare with her description in idem, *Interior Castle*, p. 107.

eradicable disgust for anything other than God or what serves His purposes, how can his renewed contacts with those worldly things during
those frequent periods of His absence do anything but intensify the suffering and emptiness he is already feeling? The delectable element in both the
painful experiences of Spiritual Betrothal and those of the Prayer of Union
arises, in each case, from the soul's knowledge that its inability to receive
even a modicum of consolation or comfort from worldly things signifies
that it has finally chosen to love God more than things of the world. Were
this not the case, the individual would not feel His absence so acutely.
These three parallels indicate that the distressing experiences of Spiritual
Betrothal were fundamentally continuous with their counterparts in the
Prayer of Union.

Although the *content* of the experiences, both painful and blissful,
which occurred during Spiritual Betrothal and the Prayer of Union were
"almost identical," the potency of their respective *effects* was not.[73] Not
only did the beneficial effects of the experiences of Spiritual Betrothal last
far longer than those of the Prayer of Union but they also penetrated more
deeply into the core of the soul.[74] Whereas the earlier prayer states only tran-
siently endowed the individual with the monastic virtues of humility, contempt for the world, courage, love of God, and a longing to suffer for His
sake, the Spiritual Betrothal permanently endowed him with those virtues and
desires so that they became a habitual and instinctive part of his disposition.
For the first time in his life, the betrothed individual finds that he "naturally"
conforms his actions and his desires to the will of God. He can now encounter occasions of sin without fearing that they will tempt him.[75]

One can now see the real reason why Teresa valued Spiritual Betrothal
so much more than the Prayer of Union. The experiences of Spiritual Betrothal owed their superiority to one thing alone. They endowed the recipient with a will that completely and continually conformed itself to God's
will even during those moments of spiritual pain or abandonment.


## Spiritual Marriage

The phenomenon that Teresa called the "Spiritual Marriage of God with
the soul" crowned her long itinerary through the various supernatural

73. Teresa of Avila, *Interior Castle*, pp. 106–7.
74. Teresa of Avila, *Interior Castle*, pp. 165, 170–71, 202.
75. Ibid., p. 120. Thus Teresa told her nuns: "So, Christian souls, . . .withdraw from
occasions of sin—for even in this state [the Prayer of Union] the soul is *not* strong enough to
be able to run into them safely, *as it is after the betrothal has been made*" (emphasis mine).

prayer states.[76] Teresa was not the first Christian mystic to speak of the supreme contemplative experiences as a spiritual marriage between God and the soul. It is quite possible that her disciple John of the Cross influenced her to use this connubial imagery to describe her most elevated prayer state.[77] John, too, had used this term to describe the most elevated states of divine union and his association with her had become especially close during the years 1570–71 when she was prioress at the Incarnation and he worked there as a confessor. What makes this influence even more plausible is the fact that none of Teresa's works written prior to 1570 use the term Spiritual Marriage to refer to the highest states of divine union. In any case, the fact remains that both as an experience and as a radically self-abnegating disposition of the subject's will, the phenomenon that Teresa called "Spiritual Marriage" had numerous precedents in the history of Western mysticism. Her idea that the devout soul was the Bride of Christ grew out of a long tradition of allegorical interpretation that had been applied to the Song of Solomon. This notion first appeared in Origen's commentary on that particular text. Origen's commentary then made its way into Western Christendom when Jerome and Rufinus translated it into Latin. Besides Origen, Augustine also made quite a few references in his numerous works to the soul as the Bride of Christ and Cyprian expressed the view that consecrated virgins were His brides. However, Bernard of Clairvaux was the first person who actually went one step further and asserted that the spiritual marriage of the soul to Christ took place during the most elevated experiences of contemplation.[78] This association between contemplation and the spiritual marriage of the soul to Christ appeared as a persistent theme in the literature of such prominent Western mystics as Richard of St. Victor, Bonaventure, Ruysbroeck, Walter Hilton, and John of the Cross.[79]

Considered as a volitional state (as a disposition of the subject's will), the condition of Spiritual Marriage did not differ significantly from Spiritual Betrothal. Both prayer states created an existential situation where the individ-

---

76. Teresa described Spiritual Marriage as a prayer state in *Interior Castle*, p. 219.

77. See Dicken, *Crucible of Love*, p. 477.

78. See Butler, *Western Mysticism*, p. 110.

79. Richard of St. Victor, *The Mystical Ark*, book 4, chaps. 13–16; book 5, chaps. 14–15, in *The Twelve Patriarchs, The Mystical Ark, Book Three of The Trinity*, trans. Grover A. Zinn, Classics of Western Spirituality Series (New York: Paulist Press, 1979); Bonaventure, *The Triple Way*, 1:86–88, in *Works of Bonaventure*, trans. Jose de Vinck (Paterson, N.J.: St. Anthony Guild Press, 1960); Hilton, *Stairway of Perfection*, pp. 334–41; Blessed Jan Van Ruysbroeck, *Spiritual Espousals*, trans. Eric Colledge (Westminster, Md.: Christian Classics, 1983); John of the Cross, *The Living Flame of Love*, trans. E. Allison Peers (Garden City, N.Y.: Image Books, 1962), 2d redaction, 3.24–25, pp. 220–21.

ual became so filled with a love for God and so heedless of his own welfare
that he instinctively conformed his actions and his intentions exclusively to
God's will just as though God's will had been his own. As has already been
mentioned above, Teresa considered this complete substitution of God's will
for the self-seeking human will to have been the perfection of monastic ascesis. This, rather than ecstatic absorption in God, was the "true" union that
she had hoped her nuns would achieve. Because both prayer states caused the
individual's love of God and his determination to act only in accordance with
His will to persist and intensify regardless of any sufferings or spells of aridity
that might befall him, there was no reason, provided that one considered
them solely from the standpoint of their respective effects upon the subject's
will, to regard one as superior to the other.

However, as a state of consciousness, Spiritual Marriage differed significantly from its immediate predecessor. First, Teresa noted that whereas the
experiences that took place during Spiritual Betrothal and the Prayer of
Union only gave her a transient, though often intense, sensation of God's
presence, the experiences of Spiritual Marriage gave her an almost continual and absolutely indubitable sensation that all three Persons of the Holy
Trinity were now, and always would be, dwelling in the very center of her
own soul. When God decides to bestow this supreme grace of prayer upon
the soul, "the presence of the three Persons is so impossible to doubt that
it seems one experiences what St. John says, that they will make their
abode in the soul. . . . This presence is almost continual except when a lot
of sickness weighs down on one."[80] This gift of God's uninterrupted companionship was the primary reason why Teresa valued this prayer state
more than any of the others.

One must not think that Spiritual Marriage was an almost constant state
of rapture, an uninterrupted state of ecstasy, or an extreme form of the
union of all the faculties. Even though her descriptions of it make it clear
that she enjoyed an almost uninterrupted sensation of standing in the most
intimate proximity to God, Teresa's sensation of presence usually did not
impair her awareness of the physical world or cripple her capacity to act in
it. For this reason, she cautioned her nuns against the fallacy of equating
Spiritual Marriage with those states of ecstatic absorption that had predominated during the Prayer of Union. One might think that the person
who is enjoying these experiences of Spiritual Marriage "will not remain in

80. Teresa of Avila, *Spiritual Testimonies*, p. 365; also idem, *Interior Castle*, pp. 209–10,
for a similar description of the indwelling of the Holy Trinity within the innermost core of
the soul.

possession of her senses but will be so completely absorbed that she will be able to fix her mind upon nothing. But no, in all that belongs to the service of God she is more alert than before."[81] There were still moments when God presented Himself to the soul with such vehemence that action, and even thoughts, of any kind became completely impossible, but such violent ecstasies and raptures grew rarer and rarer as time went on.[82] As always, what mattered most was not the affective intensity of an experience but rather its capacity to elicit deeds of obedience and love. Second, the phenomena of Spiritual Marriage became manifest in what I shall call a more purely "spiritual" manner, that is, not only did they give Teresa indubitable proof of their divine origin but they also seemed to come into her field of awareness without the mediation of the passions, the senses, the imagination, and the faculties.[83]

The radical dissociation of this highest prayer state from anything even remotely sensual or creaturely became evident in the way that its onset transformed the character of her visionary experiences. For example, Teresa noted that during all of her other supernatural prayer states where she experienced visions, the visionary phenomena appeared in one of two possible forms. Sometimes God sent her what she called "imaginary" visions (*visiones imaginarias*) where He appeared to her soul's eye in the form of some corporeal similitude in much the same way that a dream image or a creation fashioned out of our imaginations looks like something we would see with our physical eyes. He also sent her what she called "intellectual" visions (*visiones intelectuales*), where one perceives God's presence in an ineffable and yet absolutely indubitable manner without the mediation of any visual, auditory, tactile, olfactory, or hallucinatory similitudes.[84] For example, if the intellectual vision is one of Christ, one will have the knowledge that He is present and one will know this fact without the slightest residuum of doubt even though this information has been obtained without one's seeing anything either interiorly or exteriorly. One also has the

81. Teresa of Avila, *Interior Castle*, p. 210.
82. Ibid., pp. 210–11, 223–24.
83. In *Interior Castle*, pp. 211–12, Teresa seems to have distinguished the spirit (*espíritu*) from both the "sensible" or "animal" part of the soul (the senses together with the imagination) and the "rational" part of the soul (the faculties of memory, understanding, and will). There her word "spirit" referred to that transcendent innermost core of the soul where God Himself might be pleased to set up His dwelling place if an individual gave proof that he truly loved Him and would faithfully obey His commandments.
84. Teresa of Avila, *Life of St. Teresa of Jesus*, p. 263. It is actually misleading to use "visions" since Teresa never actually "saw" anything either with the eyes of her body or the eyes of her soul when an intellectual vision was in progress.

additional knowledge of exactly where Christ is, to one's left or to one's right, for example, even though one cannot see Him, hear Him, or sense His presence and position by means of any tactile or olfactory cues.[85] The onset of Spiritual Marriage sharply diminished the frequency with which she experienced imaginary visions. Toward the end of her life (in 1581), Teresa wrote to the bishop of Osma that "the imaginative [or imaginary] visions have ceased, but it seems this intellectual vision of these three Persons and of the humanity of Christ always continues. This intellectual vision, in my opinion, is something much more sublime."[86] Whereas the Prayer of Union and Spiritual Betrothal had each created situations within which both imaginary and intellectual visions had frequently occurred, once the condition of Spiritual Marriage supervened the imaginary visions came to an end.[87]

If one surveys the entire panorama of Teresa's spiritual itinerary, one realizes that the prayer state known as the "Spiritual Marriage of the soul to God" came closest to bringing her toward a perfect fulfillment.[88] For example, one will recall that during neither the Prayer of Quiet nor the Prayer of Union did Teresa ever acquire that unwavering obedience to God's will in both act and intention that she achieved in the condition of Spiritual Marriage. Neither of these two prayer states ever succeeded in giving her an almost complete and permanent heedlessness of her own welfare, a completely disinterested love of God and her neighbor, nor did

85. Teresa of Avila, *Spiritual Testimonies*, p. 354.

86. Ibid., p. 364.

87. Teresa distinguished between three different kinds of visions in ascending order of religious value: (1) corporeal visions—those in which one sees objects with the eyes of the body; (2) imaginary visions—these are visions in which one sees objects and forms with the "eyes of the soul" rather than with the physical eyes; (3) intellectual visions—these are "visions" devoid of forms and images in which one "sees" nothing with either the eyes of the body or the eyes of the soul (nevertheless, objects are present to consciousness in a vivid and indubitable manner that transcends both the imagination and the physical senses). Teresa's distinction between these three types of visions corresponds quite closely to Augustine's distinction between corporeal, spiritual (which corresponds to Teresa's imaginary visions), and intellectual visions that he articulated in *The Literal Meaning of Genesis* (quoted in John A. Mourant, *Introduction to the Philosophy of St. Augustine* [University Park: The Pennsylvania State University Press, 1964], pp. 173–80). Teresa's ranking of those visions also corresponds to Augustine's ranking of visions. See Teresa of Avila, *Interior Castle*, p. 150; idem, *Life of St. Teresa of Jesus*, p. 263.

88. One must understand, of course, that Teresa took it for granted that human beings were incapable of complete spiritual perfection while in this life. Thus she cautioned her readers that even in this highest contemplative state human beings still fall short of perfect union with God and perfect obedience to His will. See Teresa of Avila, *Interior Castle*, p. 217.

they cause her to become completely detached from worldly or sensual concerns.[89] Each of those ascetic and moral virtues came into her possession to the highest degree of fullness possible to human beings once God had granted her the supreme gift of His sacred marriage to her soul. From then on it was no longer Teresa who lived but Christ who lived within her and through her by means of her virtuous deeds and intentions.[90] What was true regarding the effects of Spiritual Marriage upon her behavior and intentions also held true with respect to the quality of her mystical experiences. Whereas all her earlier supernatural prayer states had given her a merely transient sensation of God's presence, the onset of Spiritual Marriage transformed this transient sensation into a permanent possession.[91] Because Spiritual Marriage was the closest approximation to perfection of each one of the Christian virtues she had sought to acquire and because it was also the most perfect and intimate form of contact with God, it is no wonder that she regarded it as the supreme fulfillment of her religious vocation.

89. Ibid., pp. 219–20.
90. Ibid., pp. 214–15.
91. Ibid., pp. 210–11, 214.

# 29

# Medieval Influences on Saint Teresa's Mysticism

## Teresa's Assumptions

### Medieval Precedents for Saint Teresa's Assumption That the State of Spiritual Perfection Was a Perfect Congruence of Divine and Human Wills

As noted in Chapter 28, the condition of perfected behavior, perfected intentions, and perfected contemplation that Teresa called the "Spiritual Marriage of the soul to God" did not originate with her. Other medieval mystics and writers portrayed the spiritually perfect state of consciousness as well as the spiritually perfect disposition of the will in much the same way that she did.

It is difficult to imagine that any medieval monk or mystic, regardless of which order he belonged to, would have taken issue with Teresa's assertion that the disposition of the will most pleasing to God was one that totally conformed to His own. For example, even though Benedict neither wrote about the phenomenon of contemplation (since his Rule was addressed only to spiritual beginners and not the perfect) nor presumed that any soul could hope in this life to enjoy that intimate companionship with the gentle human Christ that Teresa proclaimed as the supreme goal of prayer, he still insisted, as much as she did, that each monk must labor unceasingly to uproot every trace of self-will. For both Teresa and Benedict the supreme virtues were humility and an unquestioning, unhesitating obedience to the will of the religious superior who served in God's place. Benedict depicted the monk's spiritual maturation process as a series of successively more perfect degrees of humility (in contrast to Teresa for whom the contemplative progresses through a succession of ever more perfect supernatural prayer states). "The first degree of humility," he wrote, "is obedience without delay." Those monks who learn to obey their abbots without the slightest hesitation and without any murmuring whether it be whispered or hidden within the heart "fulfill that saying of the Lord: 'I came not to do mine own will, but the will of him who sent me.'"[1]

Mere outward obedience did not please God. A monk could only consider himself cleansed from vice and sin and perfect in humility when he reached that point where he denied his own will not out of fear of the consequences of disobeying God but rather because he so loved God that acting in accordance with His will became the natural and instinctive thing for him to do. "Whereby he shall begin to keep, without labor, and as it were naturally and by custom, all those customs which he had hitherto observed through fear."[2] Teresa insisted that her nuns cultivate the virtues of obedience and humility as strenuously as did Benedict. "There is no path," she asserted, "which leads more quickly to the highest perfection than that of obedience." The highest perfection did not consist in receiving visions or ecstatic states of absorption but rather "in the bringing of our wills so closely into conformity with the will of God that, as soon as we realize He wills anything, we desire it ourselves with all our might."[3] The parallel between Benedict and Teresa regarding these virtues is obvious. What principally differentiates the two is not the degree of esteem that they each accord to them but rather the fact that Benedict and his early medieval followers only seemed to envision them as ascetic virtues. Teresa also spoke of these virtues as dispositions that insinuated themselves into the very fabric of the contemplative experience itself. The soul does more than just strive after and practice obedience and humility. Once the grace of Spiritual Marriage supervenes, the soul actually experiences "a self-forgetfulness which is so complete that it really seems as though the soul no longer existed, . . . so entirely is she employed in seeking the honor of God."[4] The humility and conformity to the will of God that it once had to strive for so laboriously now came to it as though they were natural tendencies of the soul.

Bernard of Clairvaux was one of the first mystics in the West who spoke

1. Quoted from *The Rule of St. Benedict,* 5.1 and 5.3, in Emmanuel Henfelder, O.S.B., *The Way of God According to The Rule of St. Benedict,* Cistercian Studies Series, no. 49 (Kalamazoo, Mich.: Cistercian Publications, 1983), pp. 232–34.

2. Quoted in Henfelder, *Way of God,* pp. 240–41.

3. Teresa of Avila, *Book of Foundations,* p. 23.

4. Teresa of Avila, *Interior Castle,* p. 219.

of the highest contemplative experiences as a Spiritual Marriage between the Bridegroom Christ and His Bride, the devout human soul. Even though Bernard did not use the term Spiritual Marriage in exactly the same way that Teresa did, there were, nonetheless, numerous parallels between the respective phenomena that bore that name.[5] Both mystics agreed that the union that took place between Christ and the soul did not entail the contemplative's loss of his identity as a unique person or involve any pantheistic fusion of substances. Instead, both regarded this "union" as a union of wills, a perfect conformity of the divine and human wills, a volitional congruence that still left the contemplative's sense of being a separate ego intact. Bernard told his monks that they must not imagine that the divine union that the soul experiences when it becomes the Bride of Christ bears any sort of resemblance to that union of substances that characterizes the consubstantiality of the three Persons of the Holy Trinity. In contrast to this indwelling of the Persons of the Holy Trinity, which is a union of three Persons who share one substance and one will, God and humans dwell in each other during the union of contemplation "in a very different way, because their wills, and their substances are different and distinct, that is, their substances are not intermingled, yet their wills are in agreement; and this union is for them a communion of wills and agreement in charity."[6] Not only did Teresa and Bernard agree that the highest contemplative state presupposed a perfect congruence of the divine and human wills, but they also agreed that this blessed condition was a state of consciousness where the forms, figures, and the phantasms of the senses and imagination had no place. For example, Bernard asserted that there were

5. For example, when Teresa referred to Christ as the Bridegroom of the soul, she always took it for granted that the Bridegroom was Christ in His Sacred Humanity, the vulnerable, gentle Christ who suffered on the Cross and longs for each soul to be His companion and friend. Bernard's Bridegroom was not Christ in His Humanity but rather Christ the Divine Word or Logos. Thus, in his sixty-first sermon on the Canticle of Canticles, Bernard asserted that his audience must "bring chaste ears to this discourse of love; and when you think of these two lovers, remember always that not a man and a woman are to be thought of, but the Word of God and a soul" (quoted in Butler, *Western Mysticism*, p. 97). In addition, there were two different senses in which Bernard spoke of Spiritual Marriage. On the one hand, he frequently used the term to refer to the marriage between Christ, the Bridegroom, and His Bride, the Church (a usage that Teresa did not employ). On the other hand, Bernard also used it in a manner similar to Teresa (with the exception just noted above), namely, to refer to that union that takes place between Christ and the devout soul at the summit of contemplation. See Butler, *Western Mysticism*, p. 97.

6. Bernard of Clairvaux, *On the Song of Songs IV*, trans. Irene Edmonds, introduction by Jean Leclerq, Cistercian Fathers Series, no. 40 (Kalamazoo, Mich.: Cistercian Publications, 1980), p. 56, ser. 71, para. 10.

two deaths that a soul goes through when it completely dies to the world during contemplation. The first death occurs when the transports of ecstasy (*ecstasis*) cause it to lose consciousness of physical existence and the temptations it creates. The second and more sublime death, which Bernard called the "death of the angels," causes the soul to depart not only from the desire for sensual things but from even the images of things sensual and corporeal. This angelic death was the only form of transport (*excessus*) that Bernard dignified with the name "contemplation." "You have not yet gone a long way unless you are able by purity of mind to fly over the phantasmata of corporeal images that rush in from all sides. Unless you have attained to this, do not promise yourself rest."[7] Bernard made the connection between this trance-state free from corporeal and imaginational imagery and the Spiritual Marriage of the soul to Christ more explicit.

> If it should ever happen to one of you to be enraptured and hidden away in this secret place . . . safe from the call and concern of the greedy senses, from the pangs of care, the guilt of sin, and the obsessive fantasies of the imagination so much more difficult to hold at bay, such a man, when he returns to us again, may well boast. . . . "The King has brought me into His bedroom."[8]

These close parallels between Teresa and Bernard with respect to the effects that the soul's Spiritual Marriage to Christ had on both the disposition of the subject's will and the activities of his imagination suggest that Bernard's descriptions of that blessed condition probably influenced Teresa.

Dominican and Franciscan writers also agreed with Bernard and Teresa about the crucial significance of total conformity to the will of God. Even the fourteenth-century Dominican Meister Eckhart, who was, in some respects, most unlike Teresa in his emphases, repeatedly stressed that the essence of spiritual perfection lay not in experiencing great visions, raptures, and illuminations but rather in creating a complete conformity between one's own will and that of God. To illustrate this point Eckhart argued that Paul's spiritual stature had had nothing to do with the sublimity or intensity of his visions. Even though those visions enabled him to

7. Quoted in Butler, *Western Mysticism*, p. 116.

8. Bernard of Clairvaux, *On the Song of Songs II,* trans. Kilian Walsh, O.C.S.O., Cistercian Fathers Series, no. 7 (Kalamazoo, Mich.: Cistercian Publications, 1976), p. 40, ser. 23, para. 16.

enjoy the supreme grace of talking to Christ they remained barren of fruit until that moment when Paul decided to completely surrender his own will to Christ. Eckhart concluded, much as Teresa had done, that "there is no way of making a person true unless he gives up his own will. In fact, apart from the complete surrender of the will, there is no traffic with God."[9]

The sixteenth-century Franciscan contemplatives whose works Teresa had read placed a similar emphasis on the cardinal necessity of perfectly conforming one's own will to God's will. Bernardino de Laredo asserted that when a "contemplative approaches perfection, he looks but little at his own profit, or devotion . . . for all his study is to be purely, simply and entirely in conformity with the will of God."[10] Francisco de Osuña stressed that perfection in the contemplative life could not take place unless the individual tried to approximate that perfect congruence of human and divine wills that Christ had exemplified. Osuña argued that the more one harmonized his own will with the will of God, the easier it became for one to recollect oneself and enjoy the fruits of contemplation. He pointed out that whereas ordinary human beings find that they must first withdraw themselves from all worldly affairs and cares before they can achieve that recollectedness essential to contemplation and union with God, Christ had no such need to withdraw Himself from daily life in order to converse with God. Osuña went on to observe that because there was this perfect and immutable congruence between Christ's will and that of His Father, Christ always enjoyed contemplative union with God whenever He wished it for no worldly object or preoccupation could impede Him or distract Him from the preeminent task of carrying out His Father's will. The reason that ordinary humans have to isolate themselves from the world is that sin has corrupted their wills so that the world becomes a constant source of distractions and allurements that always threaten to draw their desires toward the fulfillment of some goal that is contrary to the will of God. Osuña implied that once the will had diverted itself away from doing God's work, this volitional bifurcation caused the individual to become blind to that domain of spiritual realities that God only reveals to those who follow His will and whom He thinks merit the grace of contemplation.[11] Peter of Alcántara likewise insisted that states of spiritual perfection were inconceivable if this harmony of wills between man and God were

9. Meister Eckhart, *Meister Eckhart: A Modern Translation*, trans. Robert Blakney (New York: Harper & Row, 1941), pp. 15–16.

10. Bernardino de Laredo, *Ascent of Mount Sion*, p. 194.

11. Osuña, *Third Spiritual Alphabet*, pp. 159–60, 164.

absent. He contended that the number and intensity of an individual's consolations during prayer were neither criteria of sanctity nor a reliable indication as to the spiritual significance of those prayer experiences. Instead, Peter argued that "the scope of all these exercises [of meditation and prayer] and the chief end of a spiritual life" was that of conforming all of one's actions and intentions to the will of God.[12]

These examples show that Teresa's descriptions of the volitional concomitants of the highest state of contemplation had a long pedigree in Western monasticism and mysticism.

## Precedents for Saint Teresa's Assumption That the Highest Prayer State Was Largely Devoid of Imaginary Visions

In addition to being a disposition of the will, the condition of Spiritual Marriage was also a distinctive mode of consciousness. Teresa experienced this supreme prayer state as a condition in which she had an imageless and formless "intellectual vision" of the Holy Trinity dwelling deep within the innermost core of her soul and speaking to it. She mentioned that this sensation of the divine presence was constant though it did vary in intensity.[13] As I noted in Chapter 28, this state of consciousness was apparently devoid of imaginary visions, whereas in the earlier prayer states imaginary and intellectual visions had often occurred concurrently.[14]

Teresa's experience that the highest prayer state was a mode of consciousness in which God's presence is conveyed to the soul without the use of forms, shapes, or images of any kind conformed to a long-established tradition in Western European monastic spirituality that described the most perfect state of contemplation as a perceptual modality devoid of forms and images or, to put it another way, devoid of both corporeal and imaginary visions. One can trace this tradition in Western European Christianity at least as far back as Augustine of Hippo who, in *The Literal Meaning of Genesis*, distinguished between three different kinds of visions: (1) corporeal, where one sees an object in the ordinary way with one's

12. Peter of Alcántara, *Golden Treatise*, pp. 166–67.
13. Teresa of Avila, *Interior Castle*, pp. 210–11. Thus she wrote that "this Presence is not of course always realized so fully as when it first comes. . . . But . . . the soul is always aware that it is experiencing this companionship." Ibid.
14. Teresa of Avila, *Life of St. Teresa of Jesus*, p. 263. It is worth noting that Teresa claimed that she never experienced any corporeal visions. See also p. 259.

bodily eyes, (2) spiritual, corresponding closely to what Teresa called the "imaginary" type of vision where one fashions by means of thought, memory, and imagination a likeness of some corporeal object that one then perceives without the aid of the bodily eyes as occurs in dreams or mystical visions, and (3) intellectual, where one directly comprehends the meaning and nature of realities and truths that are in no way physically representable or capable of being represented in the imagination, for example, one comprehends what is meant by the abstract notion of love in the biblical commandment "Love thy neighbor as thyself [Luke 10:27]."[15] This parallelism went further than a mere terminological similarity. The two saints also ranked each type of vision in the same way. Both asserted explicitly that imaginary (or, for Augustine, "spiritual") visions were superior to corporeal visions and intellectual visions were superior to imaginary or spiritual ones.[16] Moreover, both saints regarded the intellectual type of vision as being almost completely free from the taints of delusion or error.[17]

Why did Teresa consider intellectual visions to have been superior to imaginary visions? First, she took it for granted that they were a much more direct and spiritual form of contact with God.[18] As such they were the most intimate possible form of encounter with God that one could hope for while one was imprisoned in this earthly existence. Second, and a corollary to the first, is because intellectual visions were an unmediated and purely spiritual mode of communication from God to the soul, they did not excite or disturb the passions, the faculties, or the senses. Thus Teresa wrote that intellectual visions (and locutions) "are such spiritual things that I believe no turmoil is caused by them in the faculties, or in the senses, from which the devil can take any advantage."[19] Consequently, they were almost completely free from carnal taint. Their immediacy to God, their complete independence from any involvement with the sensual

15. John A. Mourant, *Introduction to the Philosophy of Saint Augustine* (University Park, Pa.: Pennsylvania State University Press, 1964), pp. 173–77. These pages are selections from Augustine's largely untranslated *De Genesi ad litteram* (*The Literal Meaning of Genesis*).

16. Mourant, *Introduction to Augustine*, p. 180; Teresa of Avila, *Life of St. Teresa of Jesus*, pp. 259–60.

17. For example, Augustine wrote in *The Literal Meaning of Genesis*, book 12, that "intellectual vision is not liable to error; for either: he who thinks something else than what is, does not intellectually see; or: if he does intellectually see, it follows that it is true" (quoted in Butler, *Western Mysticism*, p. 37). Passages where Teresa asserts the epistemological superiority of intellectual visions can be found in Teresa of Avila, *Life of St. Teresa of Jesus*, pp. 249–52; and in idem, *Spiritual Testimonies*, p. 364.

18. Teresa of Avila, *Interior Castle*, pp. 213–14.

19. Teresa of Avila, *Life of St. Teresa of Jesus*, p. 251.

nature of humans, and their invariable effect of quickening the individual's love for God and absolute obedience to His will, made intellectual visions the type of vision that the Devil was least likely to counterfeit.[20]

On prayer and contemplation, many other influential medieval writers agreed with Augustine (and Teresa) that the highest forms of contemplation transcended both the activities of the senses and the imagination. For example, even though Gregory the Great did not make Augustine's distinction between the three types of visionary perception, he acknowledged that no soul could hope to enjoy the bliss of contemplation until it had first "learned to shut out from its eyes all the phantasmata of earthly and heavenly images."[21] When Richard of St. Victor characterized the two highest of his six stages of contemplation in *The Mystical Ark (Benjamin Major)*, he also asserted that in them "nothing from imagination, nothing from phantasy ought to suggest itself."[22] Thomas Aquinas also stressed the superiority of contemplative states that transcended the operations of the imagination. He even brought up the distinction between imaginary and intellectual visions and proclaimed that the latter were far better than the former. "The prophecy whereby a supernatural truth is seen by intellectual vision, is more excellent than that in which a supernatural truth is manifested by means of the similitudes of corporeal things in the vision of the imagination."[23] As I have already mentioned above how Bernard's descriptions of the highest states of union with God presupposed a correlative suppression of sensual and imaginative imagery, I refer the reader to my discussion of the parallelism between his conception of Spiritual Marriage and that of Teresa earlier in this chapter. Bernardino de Laredo, a Spanish Franciscan whom Teresa read, joined the other medieval authorities in affirming that "perfect contemplation" suppresses all corporeal imagery and phantasmagoria of the imagination.[24]

The foregoing examples show that both the volitional and the perceptual accompaniments of Teresa's highest prayer state corresponded quite

20. Ibid., pp. 249–51; and idem, *Interior Castle*, pp. 180–83.

21. *Homilies on Ezechiel*, 2.5.9, quoted in Butler, *Western Mysticism*, p. 69; see also Gregory's *Morals on Job*, 23:42, which, it is known, Teresa read. In that passage, Gregory writes that when the soul is seeking Truth through contemplation, "it spurns all images that present themselves to it" (quoted in Butler, *Western Mysticism*, p. 71). See also Bernardino de Laredo, *Ascent of Mount Sion*, p. 49 n.

22. Richard of St. Victor, *The Mystical Ark*, p. 263.

23. Thomas Aquinas, *Summa Theologica*, 22 vols. (London: Burns & Oates, 1935), q. 174, art. 2, obj. 4, vol. 14, p. 49.

24. Bernardino de Laredo, *Ascent of Mount Sion*, pp. 107–9, 154–56.

closely to what other medieval mystics and theologians had said about the nature of the soul's experiences during perfect contemplation. Nevertheless, it is worth noting that Teresa seems to have been rather hesitant about accepting this traditional evaluation of intellectual visions as superior to imaginary ones. In her *Life,* she stated that Peter of Alcántara "and other learned men" had told her that intellectual visions were one of the highest kinds of vision[25] and also that they were "nearer to perfection" than either imaginary or corporeal visions.[26] However, the glowing description of imaginary visions and their beneficial impact on the soul that immediately follows these remarks seems to indicate that she did not share the learned men's conviction that imaginary visions were of less spiritual value than intellectual ones. She concedes that though it is true that intellectual visions reveal God without any image of Him and are "of a higher kind, yet if the memory of it is to last, despite our weakness, and if our thoughts are to be well-occupied, it is a great thing that so Divine a Presence should be presented to the imagination."[27] Because they show Christ so vividly and majestically, because they conform so closely to our material nature that best focuses its attention on things with form and figure, and because their overwhelming beauty causes the soul to see how wretched it is in comparison to God, imaginary visions serve as a most powerful means of quickening a soul's desire for God and intensifying its zeal to obey His will.

This hunch that Teresa was, for a long time, quite skeptical of the supposed superiority of intellectual visions to imaginary ones receives further confirmation from chapter 22 of her *Life,* where she insists on challenging the learned men's view that, at the higher stages of recollective proficiency, the individual ought to abandon meditation on the Sacred Humanity of Christ and focus instead on His formless divinity. Teresa maintained that, while the learned and spiritual men must have good reasons for this opinion, her own opinion differed. From her own experience she had learned that if she wished God to reveal His great secrets to her, it was essential that she meditate on images of His Sacred Humanity. She concluded that even if one reaches "the summit of contemplation," it was absolutely essential to continue meditating on the Sacred Humanity of Christ rather than on His formless Divinity. Teresa told Father García de Toledo, "Your Reverence must seek no other way [of meditating]: that way alone is safe.

---

25. Teresa of Avila, *Life of St. Teresa of Jesus,* pp. 249–50.
26. Ibid., pp. 259–60.
27. Ibid., p. 263.

. . . it is clear, the Creator must be sought through the creatures." She also pointed out that Saints Paul, Catherine of Siena, Francis, Anthony of Padua, and Bernard all reached perfection not because they were inspired by the formless Divinity of Christ but because of their devotion to Christ's Sacred Humanity.[28]

# The Influence of Medieval Models on the Content of Saint Teresa's Imaginary Visions and Locutions

Continuity with tradition was not an exclusive characteristic of the mystical experiences that Teresa had during her most exalted supernatural prayer state. The visions and locutions that she experienced during her other supernatural prayer states also owed their form and content to models that had been popularized in medieval mystical literature and folklore. For example, Teresa frequently had imaginary visions (and locutions) where Christ appeared to her and spoke to her as though He had become her spouse.[29] Visions and locutions of this sort certainly appeared to have been inspired by that tradition of Bride mysticism that originated in the twelfth century and became popularized by Bernard of Clairvaux. Some of her other visions owed their content to the particular tenets of Catholic sacramental theology. Once while she was entranced during the celebration of Holy Communion, she felt as though her body was splattered with Christ's Blood and that His Blood filled her mouth.[30] It is obvious that this particular kind of vision where the spilling of blood is joyfully associated with the presence of Christ could only have occurred to a Christian mystic, or to someone who had been exposed to Christianity and its sacramental system. At other times, Teresa's mystical experiences reified the particular images of the Devil and the angelic hosts that had become integral parts of the corpus of medieval folklore and sixteenth-century Spanish folklore. For example, Teresa claimed that, during one of her more unpleasant visions, she actually caught a glimpse of the Devil and had him speak to her. The pictureshe gives of of the Devil, of the words he spoke and his manner of speaking them, and his manner of responding to the presentation of Chris-

28. Ibid., p. 213.
29. For example, Teresa of Avila, *Spiritual Testimonies,* p. 336.
30. Ibid., pp. 330–31.

tian symbols and ritual paraphernalia was entirely consistent with the depiction of his physical characteristics and behavior that any sixteenth-century Catholic would have obtained from the contemporary folklore. In
keeping with this tradition of folklore, Teresa saw the Devil as hideously
deformed, burning with a strange and terrible fire that was totally opposite
in nature from mystical illumination, completely filled with evil intentions,
and terrified of both holy water and the sign of the Cross.[31] In another one
of her imaginary visions, Teresa visited Hell, and in keeping with traditional sixteenth-century Catholic assumptions, she experienced it as a
place of unspeakable foulness, oppressiveness, and unending, unendurable
torment.[32] Each of these visions, whether it was a vision of Christ as Bridegroom of the soul, a vision of the Devil, or a vision of being in Hell,
derived its visual and auditory content from medieval folklore and the
teachings of the Church. In any case, it is evident that they did not emerge
as novelties created for the first time out of the depths of Teresa's unconscious in total isolation from her cultural milieu.

## Sources of Christ-Centeredness

One of the most distinctive features of Teresa's mystical experiences was
their markedly Christocentric character, that is, most of her visions and
locutions involved some sort of interchange, often tender and intimate,
between her and Jesus Christ in His Sacred Humanity. These visions and
locutions almost always had the aim and result of intensifying her obedience to His will and fortifying her longings to imitate His life. One might
think that this observation is simply stating the obvious. After all, did not
Christian mystics always have visions that involved them in some sort of
encounter with Jesus? (For example, Paul's vision on the road to Damascus and Saint Francis's vision at the time of his stigmatization.) As a
rule, most early Christian mystics do not seem to have had the Christ-
centered experiences that became much more common after the thirteenth
century. For example, none of the experiences that Augustine related in his
*Confessions* brought him into Christ's presence or involved Christ's speaking to him. Instead, he spoke of his most famous visionary encounter with
God as an experience of Him as "the Light Unchangeable" that, although

31. Teresa of Avila, *Life of St. Teresa of Jesus*, p. 288.
32. Ibid., pp. 300–302.

it made him tremble with the emotions of awe and love, did not present him with any vision of Jesus in His Humanity.[33] Similarly, nothing in Gregory the Great's writings on contemplation, neither his description of Benedict's famous vision mentioned in his *Dialogues* nor any of his other references to contemplative illumination in other works, suggested that he or any of his contemporaries ever expected or intended that their mystical experiences would initiate any kind of intimate personal exchange between them and Jesus Christ. Instead, when Gregory referred to the God that the mystic experienced during contemplative ecstasy, he characterized Him as either an "unencompassed Light" or as an immense and unfathomable "wisdom."[34] Such descriptive terminology accentuated God's majestic isolation from what was human. Such descriptions do not appear to have been derived from the experiences of those who had encountered a loving and vulnerable human Christ who longed for human companionship.

As already indicated, one notices comparatively few of these Christocentric visionary experiences prior to the twelfth century. However, sometime after that time, there took place a significant and enduring shift toward forms of religious expression and religious experience that became decidedly more Christocentric than those that had prevailed in Western Christendom since the times of Cassian, Augustine, Benedict of Nursia, and Gregory the Great. The iconography of the thirteenth and succeeding centuries underwent a rather dramatic transformation. During the period between Charlemagne and the beginning of the twelfth century, artists had generally portrayed Christ as the almost inaccessible, stern, and overwhelmingly powerful king seated upon His celestial throne far above the tumult of human affairs. The sternness with which He was usually portrayed gave one the distinct impression that a relationship of cozy, prayerful intimacy with Him was unthinkable. However, after the twelfth century, especially after the time of Saint Francis, artists throughout Western Europe began to accentuate Christ's Humanity more than they did His Divinity. Christ was no longer portrayed so often as the stern and implacable judge but rather as the tortured and suffering man on the Cross or else as the friend and companion of ordinary men and women. Portraiture not only began to depict Him as vulnerable and human but also as someone who was involved in the thick of human affairs. Aside from His halo, Christ is usually indistinguishable from the other men in the picture. This

33. Contrast Augustine's vision of the Infinite Light of his *Confessions*, book 7, chap. 10, with Teresa's visions narrated in her *Spiritual Testimonies*, pp. 325–26, 330–31, 336, 347.
34. Quoted in Butler, *Western Mysticism*, pp. 77, 79.

iconographic transformation suggests that a profound Christological shift had taken place in the Western European religious imagination sometime during the last half of the twelfth century and the first half of the thirteenth century.

This new Christological orientation toward the accessible human aspect of Christ, toward Christ as one's companion and teacher and as the archetypally suffering human, found its most vivid expression in the newly arisen Franciscan order that emerged at the beginning of the thirteenth century. Saint Francis of Assisi exemplified this new Christocentric orientation more vividly than anyone else. Whereas the earlier Benedictine writers rarely implied that it was possible for the average religious, much less a layperson, to enjoy real friendship with Christ while one was in this life, Saint Francis continually preached that this joyful companionship with Christ was available to any person who loved Him and was willing to demonstrate the sincerity of his devotion to Him by imitating His moral purity and His willingness to suffer for the sake of God and others. From the time of Saint Francis onward, Western spirituality became profoundly Christ-centered. Christian mystics in Western Europe begin to experience visions (or at least talk about such visions), where they not only enjoy the visual apparition of Christ and often converse with Him but they also make it their constant concern to ensure that these experiences end up fortifying their wills so that they can have the heroic resolve that is necessary to imitate His heroic deeds and obedience.

The foregoing observations strongly suggest that the Christocentric content of Teresa's mystical experiences owed far more to the Franciscan tradition of mysticism than it did to those forms of spirituality that had predominated during late Antiquity and the early Middle Ages. This should come as no surprise when one recalls how deeply Teresa's practice of prayer and her conception of the nature of the contemplative life was indebted to Franciscan writers (Francisco de Osuña and Bernardino de Laredo) and advisers (Peter of Alcántara).

# Saint Teresa's Lack of Curiosity About the Spiritual World

Teresa has given us one of the most detailed and subtle descriptions of the different mystical states of consciousness that has ever been written. Te-

resa's willingness to talk in such detail about the psychological peculiarities of her own experiences shows a striking affinity to such twentieth-
century mystics as Eileen Garrett, Robert Monroe, Gerda Walther, Sylvan
Muldoon, and Matthew Manning who share her "modern" fascination
with the phenomenology of their own mystical states of consciousness.

Nevertheless, one element of the modern temperament is conspicuously
absent in her descriptive focus, the scientist's limitless curiosity. Despite
her evident fascination with both the psychological details of her experiences during prayer and their impact on her moral and spiritual development, Teresa made no effort to enlarge her knowledge about either the
geography of the spiritual world or the objects and beings that dwell
within it. When Rodrigo Alvarez asked her whether, during any of her
visions, she had ever been able to locate the terrestrial paradise, she
obliquely rebuked him for his inordinate curiosity.

> What your Reverence says about water, I don't know; nor have I
> ever known where the terrestrial paradise is. . . . I have never asked
> His Majesty to give me knowledge of anything for then it would
> seem to me I had imagined it and that the devil would deceive me.
> And never, glory to God, did I have a curious desire to know
> things, nor do I care to know anything more.[35]

This reply shows a typical medieval attitude toward curiosity insofar as
she condemns it as a spiritual vice born of pride and vanity.

Two centuries after Teresa's death, some Christian mystics had lost their
inhibitions about using their visions to satisfy their curiosity about the
properties and geography of the spiritual world. For example, in Reverend
Hartley's 1778 preface to his English translation of Emanuel Swedenborg's
*Heaven and Hell,* Hartley threw out a challenge to those skeptics of his
day who argued that visions and voices and all other forms of supernatural
manifestation were nothing more than foolish superstition. His questions
show that some eighteenth-century Christians had now begun to hold the
curiosity of the scientists, naturalists, and explorers in high regard and
looked upon the spiritual world as though it were one more domain of
new facts that human beings could discover and catalogue and from which
they could extract information. Thus Hartley asked his critics, "to what
purpose is . . . your opposition to the belief of any fresh discoveries of the
other world? Is it not a subject of the highest importance to us to know,

35. Teresa of Avila, *Spiritual Testimonies,* pp. 360–61.

what and where we shall be to all eternity after a short passage over this bridge of time?"[36] The preoccupations of the scientist start to insinuate themselves into his phraseology, "are there not infinite particulars and circumstances relating to the world or spirits, which may serve as an inexhaustible fund of fresh discoveries? How comes it, then, that you are so void of all reasonable curiosity as to prefer ignorance to information in these things?" Swedenborg, who was not only a mystic but also an anatomist and geologist of some renown in his native land, shared his translator's assumption that mystics could and ought to investigate and catalogue the objects and beings of the spiritual realm in much the same way that the scientists of his day were doing such things with respect to the phenomena of the natural world. In a manner befitting his contemporaries and near contemporaries, Wilhelm von Humboldt, Isaac Newton, and Carolus Linnaeus, Swedenborg made numerous observations about the geography, the laws of motion, and even the vegetation of the heavenly and infernal regions that he had visited during his visions and ecstasies.[37] The preoccupations of eighteenth-century science not only insinuated themselves into the types of things on which he focused his attention but they also shaped the content of his mystical experiences. For example, he mentioned that the denizens of Heaven did not just take it on faith that the souls of the damned can never enjoy the blessings of the saved. He had seen the angels act like scientists and conduct numerous "experiments" that concretely verified that the souls of the damned were irreversibly set in their ways and completely incapable of repentance. During one of those celestial experiments, some of the damned souls even went so far as to allow the angels to take away from their souls the sinful loves that had rooted them in Hell and replace those base affections with spiritual ones. However, when the angels performed this spiritual surgery, the inhabitants of Hell immediately went into a total catatonic paralysis that only went away when the angels restored the original sinful affections to their souls.[38]

These different attitudes toward curiosity that distinguish Teresa and Swedenborg reflect the profound impact that the scientific revolution had made on the symbolic universe of Europeans during the course of the seventeenth and eighteenth centuries. What differentiated Teresa from those

36. Emanuel Swedenborg, *Heaven and Hell; also, The Intermediate State, or World of Spirits: A Relation of Things Heard and Seen* (London: Swedenborg Society, 1896); see Reverend T. Hartley's preface, p. xiii.

37. For example, see Swedenborg, *Heaven and Hell,* paras. 148–52, 176, 188, 191–95.

38. Ibid., para. 527.

mystics who were more directly indebted to the scientific revolution was that the latter began to treat the spiritual world as though it were just one more domain of new facts that ought to be catalogued and studied scientifically in much the same way that one studied the ordinary phenomena of nature. As Teresa's criticism of Alvarez indicated, she had no interest in collecting mere facts about the spiritual world if they had no immediate relevance to the tasks of guiding her nuns through their prayers or causing them to become more perfectly obedient to God's will.

Swedenborg and Hartley, however, reveal the typical obsessions of the scientist insofar as both seek knowledge of the spiritual world not only because it can help people to lead a more perfect religious life but also because this information acquires value the way any other scientific fact does; it satisfies humanity's yearning to enlarge its knowledge of nature to its uttermost extent. For example, even though Hartley indicated that the investigation of the world of the spirits did have considerable religious value insofar as it gave people "fresh motives and encouragements" that "promote faith, virtue, and godliness," it is significant that he did not list these religious benefits first. Instead, he began enumerating the benefits of Swedenborg's investigations by first pointing to their scientific value. Such investigations could be "an inexhaustible fund of discoveries," discoveries which would help satisfy men's "reasonable curiosity."[39]

It is also clear that neither Swedenborg nor Hartley had much use for the imageless intellectual visions that Teresa's spiritual advisers and her medieval predecessors had prized so highly. The transformation of human symbolic horizons that followed in the wake of the scientific revolution gave a new prestige to elements of complexity and multiplicity in mystics' visionary states. After all, an imageless or formless mystical experience does not give someone with a scientific bent of mind much to observe or analyze, whereas visionary experiences rich in complexity, filled with vivid images and forms, give him a more information-laden field of objects to study. It is therefore likely that the scientific revolution contributed significantly to a growing richness of imagery and detail in mystics' visions and in their descriptions of them. Indeed, if one looks at both the experiences and the descriptions of their experiences that Swedenborg, Monroe, Garrett, Muldoon, Manning, Fox, and Walther have given to us, one can see that the scientist's hunger for gathering information and making new discoveries has deeply affected each of these modern mystics. Their descrip-

39. Ibid., see translator's preface, p. xiii.

tions, sometimes minutely detailed, of the various sorts of auras and other photic manifestations are, for the most part, novel phenomena in the history of mysticism, a veritable New World of the spirit. Similarly, their descriptions of the laws of motion and the "energy" transformations (how thought creates and moves things) that govern the astral realm, their descriptions of the various sorts of spirits and other types of entities that dwell in the spiritual world, and their descriptions of what one might call its "geography" show a type of personality that, instead of fleeing from elements of multiplicity in mystical experience, tries to explore and even exploit them. In this sense, they exhibit the behavioral and existential modalities of the scientist, explorer, and technocrat.

# 30

# Saint Teresa's Criteria
# of Discernment

## "Ethical" Criteria

Christian mystics have almost always placed more emphasis on ethical rather than phenomenological or ritual criteria[1] for distinguishing religiously valuable locutions, visions, ecstasies, and supernormal events from those that are either harmful or irrelevant. I speak of these Christian criteria of discernment as ethical because Christian mystics usually categorize voices, visions, and revelations according to whether or not they subsequently improve the subject's moral behavior. For example, when Saint Teresa told her nuns how they could rest assured that their visions and revelations had come from God rather than the Devil, she stated simply that they must distinguish the two by their fruits. "Where there is humility, no harm can possibly ensue, even though the vision come from the devil; and where there is no humility, there can be no profit, even if the vision come from God."[2] Ultimately, all that matters is whether or not it spurs the recipient to imitate Christ's obedience and humility.

Teresa was certainly not the only Christian mystic or spiritual authority who emphasized ethical criteria of discernment. As early as the second century, the author (or authors) of the *Didache* warned that "not every one that speaks in the Spirit is a prophet, but only if he have the behavior,

1. Phenomenological criteria differentiate the significant from insignificant manifestations solely on the basis of their external appearances, that is, how they look (if they are visions) or how they sound or feel (if they are locutions or tactile hallucinations). A typical phenomenological scheme of classification would be that where a mystic takes it for granted that bright and clear photisms derive from a spiritually ennobling source, whereas luminous objects exhibiting a dim, mottled, or muddied appearance originate from a spiritually debased or debasing source.

2. Teresa of Avila, *Complete Works*, vol. 3: *The Foundations*, p. 42.

or ways, of the Lord."[3] Cassian likewise counseled his readers against the temptation to pay too much attention to the miraculous elements in mystical experiences. "We ought not to admire people who possess these powers on account of these powers," he wrote, instead "we should see whether they are morally reformed."[4] One can cite many other instances where Christian mystics have proclaimed the primacy of ethical criteria of discernment in a similar manner.[5]

This persistent tendency of Christian mystics to judge the soteriological value of a mystical experience by its effects on the recipient's moral behavior had its roots in the New Testament. Jesus encapsulated the essence of His teaching in just two commandments: If man desires to attain eternal life, He said, he must first love God with all his heart, soul, and strength, and second, he must love his neighbor as he loves himself (Luke 10:27). Paul also proclaimed that the moral virtues were far superior to visions and revelations. One might be able to speak in tongues, have the gift of prophecy, and a faith that could move mountains but even the most exalted of these spiritual gifts mean nothing if the one who possesses them lacks charity (1 Cor. 13:1–3).

The soteriological primacy that Jesus and Paul both accorded to the moral virtues went hand-in-hand with their disinclination to talk about possible phenomenological criteria of discernment. For example, when Jesus referred to the tribulations that would come over the earth during the Last Days, He acknowledged that there would be no way that people could distinguish the spiritual gifts and miracles of the false prophets from His own because the genuine and the counterfeit phenomena would bear a striking resemblance to each other (Matt. 24:24). Even the elect would find it difficult to tell the two apart. Paul also alluded to the uselessness of purely phenomenological criteria of discernment when he warned the Corinthians that Satan often disguises himself as an angel of light (2 Cor. 11:14). Christian mystics frequently cite or allude to this particular scriptural passage to justify the view that the only certain way to distinguish genuine visions and revelations from their demonic counterfeits is by noting how they affect the subject's moral behavior. Their argument usually

---

3. Quoted in Rufus Jones, *Studies in Mystical Religion* (London: Macmillan, 1923), p. 24.

4. This passage from Cassian's famous *Conferences* has been excerpted in *Western Asceticism*, p. 258.

5. For example, see Catherine of Siena, *The Dialogue,* trans. Suzanne Noffke, O.P., Classics of Western Spirituality Series (New York: Paulist Press, 1980), 71:133–34; Hilton, *The Stairway of Perfection,* 2.26, pp. 255–59.

develops in this fashion: if Satan can disguise himself as an angel of light, how is it possible to be sure that the vision one is seeing or the miracle that one is witnessing really comes from God rather than the Devil since the external aspects of these phenomena appear indistinguishable from one another? The answer is usually that one cannot distinguish the demonic manifestations from the divine ones by merely looking at their external appearance. For this reason, the only things one can fall back on are the ethical criteria of discernment.[6]

One cannot disentangle the Christian mystic's criteria of discernment from the principal soteriological preoccupation of the Christian religion itself, the never-ceasing struggle to bring about a perfect congruence between the human will and God's will. It is important to bear in mind that this conformity of wills was an ethical conformity rather than a ritual conformity. In other words, the God of the New Testament placed far more emphasis on the performance of virtuous deeds, works of love, humility, and compassion, as proofs that one was acting in accordance with His will than He did on the performance of ritual actions. For this reason, Christian mystics ended up formulating criteria of discernment that focused on the moral aftereffects of their spiritual experiences. They regarded as most religiously significant those mystical experiences that subsequently produced the greatest degree of morally virtuous behavior in their recipients.

Although ethical criteria of discernment always came first, Teresa did not entirely overlook phenomenological criteria for distinguishing religiously valuable visions and locutions from those that originated from within one's own overheated imagination or from the Devil. Teresa always had a high regard for intellectual visions because the absence of sensible forms and imagery in them made it less likely that the Devil would be able to counterfeit them. The sensible nature of corporeal visions made them the least desirable type of vision since the presence of sensible forms and images made it easier for the Devil to deceive the mystic.[7] When it came to distinguishing beneficial from harmful or irrelevant locutions, Teresa once again relied primarily upon ethical criteria of discernment, that is, a divine locution produces a morally uplifting effect upon the soul as soon as it is

---

6. For example, *The Philokalia*, translated from the Greek by G. E. H. Palmer, Philip Sherrard, and Kallistos Ware (London: Faber and Faber, 1979), Diadochus of Photike, "On Spiritual Discernment," chapter 40, 1:265; Catherine of Siena, *The Dialogue*, pp. 133–34; Hilton, *The Stairway of Perfection*, pp. 255–59; Teresa of Avila, *Life*, p. 151.

7. Teresa of Avila, *Life*, trans. Peers, pp. 259–60.

heard whereas that is not the case for locutions that originated either from within our imaginations or from the Devil.[8] However, she also offered phenomenological criteria as supplementary means for distinguishing the two classes of auditions. She noted that divine locutions not only made the soul conform its will more perfectly to God's will but they also came with irresistible force and intense vividness, bringing the soul new knowledge that it had no way of acquiring by other means.[9]

# Lakota Criteria Contrasted

The Lakota are a good counterexample to Teresa because they did not rank mystical experiences according to their moral aftereffects. As I already demonstrated in Chapter 20, Lakota medicinemen and holy men developed distinctive criteria of discernment that reflected the much greater role that rituals played in Siouan religious life. This is not to say that the Lakota were indifferent to moral virtues. On the contrary, they had the highest regard for bravery, fortitude, honesty, and generosity. They took it for granted that anyone who lacked these cardinal moral virtues would, by that very fact, disqualify himself from the possibility of receiving any significant visits from the spirits.[10] However, the Lakota were concerned with the moral virtues in a manner that differed profoundly from the Christian mystics. Unlike the Christians, the Lakota did not seem to have accorded much religious value to acts of repentance since nowhere in either their mythology or the narratives of their mystics' visionary experiences does one encounter instances where the protagonists receive admo-

8. Ibid., pp. 234–35.
9. Ibid., pp. 235–36.
10. Black Elk emphasized that the quality and significance of a vision depended on the moral worth of the individual who had received it. He asserted that "what is received through the 'lamenting' [the vision quest rite] is determined in part by the character of the person who does this, for it is only those who are very qualified who receive the great visions" (quoted from Brown, *The Sacred Pipe*, p. 44); Frances Densmore's informants told her virtually the same thing, "that the dream [or vision] would correspond to the character of the man" (quoted in Densmore, *Teton Sioux Music*, p. 157). The religious importance of high moral character also found expression in other domains of Lakota religious life. For example, Densmore's informants told her that the office of Intercessor, the individual in charge of the most important religious ceremonial of the Lakota, the Sun Dance, could only be given to a man of absolutely unblemished moral character. "No man who had committed a great wrong could act as Intercessor, no matter how fully he had repented. The record of an Intercessor must be absolutely without blemish" (p. 102).

nitions to repent of their moral infractions or rewards for having done so. Instead, the Lakota took it for granted that good moral character was already present prior to the onset of any religiously significant vision. Once lost, good character was difficult, if not impossible, to regain. This was one more reason why the Lakota had little incentive to dwell on the moral after-effects of their visions.

# Monroe's Criteria Contrasted

Religious mystics (those who acknowledge their allegiance to a particular religious tradition and regard it as a matter of great importance in their lives) do not hold an exclusive monopoly on the formulation of criteria of discernment. Secular mystics, who expressly disavow a commitment to anything commonly regarded as "religious," also formulate standards that allow them to distinguish between significant and insignificant mystical phenomena. In those cases, whatever functions as the religious surrogate determines the criteria of discernment.

Robert Monroe was a typical example of this "secular" type of mystic. Even though his parents had given him a typical southern American Protestant upbringing, he remained almost completely indifferent to Christianity and things religious aside from going to church as a boy and occasional visits there as an adult when friends went.[11] Moreover, even after he began to have frequent out-of-body experiences, he stated that he found "no evidence to substantiate the biblical notions of God and afterlife in a place called heaven."[12] Science was Monroe's religious surrogate. He was convinced that the expansion of scientific knowledge and the advance of technology would eventually reveal truth, liberate human beings from the crippling effects to which their uncritical acceptance of bygone dogmas had condemned them, and better the human condition. These expectations reached an almost messianic pitch of enthusiasm once Monroe discovered that he possessed a strange ability to separate his diaphanous "spirit" body or, as he called it, his "Second Body," from his physical body. Once experimentation had shown him that he could (1) control the onset of these out-of-body episodes, (2) occasionally acquire, when thus dissociated, supernormal knowledge of events that were occurring simultaneously at a considerable

11. Monroe, *Journeys Out of the Body*, p. 33.
12. Ibid., p. 116.

distance from his physical body, (3) sometimes manipulate physical objects telekinetically with his Second Body, and (4) control the content of those states of consciousness that accompanied that dissociation of the two bodies from each other,[13] Monroe began to sense that a rigorous scientific investigation and technological exploitation[14] of those hitherto unexplored domains of consciousness and existence that his out-of-body escapades had revealed to him might usher in a new era of human history, "a quantum leap as great or greater than the Copernican revolution."[15] Such investigations would do more than just add more bits of information to the inventory of "scientific" facts. This investigative endeavor also had religious connotations for it promised to settle the following weighty questions: What is man's true relationship to God? Is death a final dissolution or is there some sort of conscious existence after death? This scientific investigation of the out-of-body state would also put an end to religious conflict because it would so expand human knowledge and experience that the differences that presently divide Hindus, Buddhists, Muslims, and Christians from each other would no longer seem important. Each religion would realize that what it does is to objectify for the believer a unique universe in Locale II shaped in accordance with that tradition's conceptions of how the world is and ought to be. Insofar as each religious tradition creates an existential universe and spiritual landscape in Locale II for its adherents to "dwell" in, each religion is, by that fact, empirically "true." When this insight becomes general, how can there be religious conflict?[16]

Monroe's scientific rationalism convinced him that the things of the spirit only became relevant when they became accessible to scientific methods of investigation (and manipulation). Given this empirical emphasis, it is not surprising that Monroe regarded as most important those mystical experiences that gave him what he called "evidential" (that is, paranormally acquired) information, the validity of which he could later verify empirically but that he could not have received from either his five senses alone or from rational inference. As he put it, the "first evidential experience was indeed a sledgehammer blow. If I accepted the data as fact, it struck hard at nearly all of my life experience to that date, my training,

13. See ibid., pp. 203–27; pp. 46–48; pp. 55–57; pp. 73–77, respectively.
14. Ibid., p. 266.
15. Ibid., p. 263.
16. Ibid., p. 267.

my concepts, and my values."[17] From these evidential experiences, Monroe began to realize for the first time that his out-of-body states, and by extension, the spiritual world itself, were more than just dreams, hallucinations, or schizophrenic delusions. Experiences that failed to convey this evidential information were less important since they were difficult, if not impossible, to distinguish from ordinary dreams and hallucinations.

Nowhere in his book did Monroe show any significant degree of concern for the ethical or ritual consequences of his mystical experiences. Scientific rationalist that he was, he assumed that an individual fulfilled his highest purpose in the activity of expanding to the maximum possible extent the horizons of knowledge along with the technical applications that might result from that expansion of knowledge. Monroe's consuming passion was therefore intellectual rather than moral or ritual. When one adds to this passionate rationalism his rejection of Christianity and its concomitant notions of Heaven and Hell, it is hardly surprising that, for him, conformity to God's will lost its soteriological urgency.

17. Ibid., p. 31.

# 31

# The Contextuality of the Most Elevated States of Spiritual Perfection and Mystical Awareness

## The Anticontextualist Viewpoint Concerning the "Highest" States of Mystical Consciousness

The foregoing lengthy analyses of Black Elk and Saint Teresa repeatedly demonstrated that almost every aspect of the mystic's experience, response to that experience, and preparation for it was historically conditioned. Not only did I show that each mystic's choice of recollective techniques, methods of preparatory ascesis (or their absence), ways of responding to and interpreting his experiences, and specific criteria of distinguishing significant from insignificant or even harmful experiences derived from his religiohistorical environment, but I also demonstrated that the most intimate details of the experiences themselves, the particular imagery and symbolism that appeared in them, the distinctive emotions and desires that they generated, and the kinds of cognitions that they gave rise to, usually originated from the same source. Nevertheless, one might still object that these claims about the ineradicable historicity of mystical experiences only hold true for what one might call the less-than-ultimate mystical states, those locutions, visions, and ecstasies that still contain a residue of multiplicity in which the subject-object distinction continues to persist, external sounds and images continue to impinge upon the mystic's field of consciousness, and powerful emotions continue to inspire him with feelings of awe, affection, or dread. Some scholars have argued that the most "perfect," the most highly developed mystical states transcend the process of historical conditioning because they are radically free of any taint of multiplicity.[1] Since these ultimate mystical experiences presumably dispense

---

1. Examples of such ultimate, supposedly pure, mystical states free of all multiplicity are Plotinian *haplosis* (annihilation), Buddhist nirvana, the Upanishadic and Vedāntic experience

with all imagery and objects of consciousness and since they also supposedly unite the mystic with a radically simple, qualityless undifferentiated Unity, they transcend the processes of historical and cultural conditioning. After all, how can one speak meaningfully about historical
conditioning when both the states of consciousness themselves and their
respective transcendent Objects are so devoid of qualities?[2]

I am not convinced that the highest and purest mystical states devoid of
sensory images and forms escape the process of historical conditioning.
One difficulty with that anticontextualist thesis is the assumption of some
of its partisans that the imageless types of soteriologically superior mystical experience bring about a union with an Object that the subject encounters as an undifferentiated Unity. Stace has claimed that "the undifferentiated unity which is the mystical experience implies that there are no
distinctions within the One, or the Universal Self, that there is no distinction between object and object, and finally that there is no distinction
between subject and object."[3] Van der Leeuw also characterized the highest forms of mystical union as fusion with an Object that was totally free
of multiplicity.

Here [at the summit of the mystic's journey] both Deity and man
alike become a waste, a qualityless unnameable Nothingness, the
ground, of which German mysticism speaks so fluently. In other
words, the abrogation of the division between subject and object,
the fusion of God and man, are possible only when practice, depri-

that corresponds to the realization of the essential identity between ātman and brahman, the
kinds of mystical union alluded to by such Christian representatives of the via negativa as
Meister Eckhart and Dionysius the Areopagite, and the asampraňājta samādhi described in
Patañjali's system of Yoga.

2. One is assuming that the particular mystical state of consciousness or condition of
soteriologically superior insight has an object of consciousness. Some mystical states of consciousness are supposedly devoid of objects of consciousness, for example, the state of asamprajñāta samādhi described in Patañjali's *Yoga-Sūtras*.

There are authors who either suggest or explicitly argue that the absence of multiplicity in
the purest and most elevated mystical states implies that they are suprahistorical in nature.
Robert K. C. Forman and most of the contributors to the collection of essays he edited
challenge the contextualist approach to mysticism in *Problem of Pure Consciousness;* Heiler,
*Prayer,* pp. 146, 149–51; Gerardus Van der Leeuw, *Religion in Essence and Manifestation,* 2
vols., trans. J. E. Turner with appendices to the Torchbook edition incorporating the additions of the 2d German ed. by Hans. H. Penner, reprint of 1938 ed. (Gloucester, Mass.: Peter
Smith, 1967), 2:497, 504–5; Underhill, *Mysticism,* p. 96; Stace, *Mysticism and Philosophy,*
pp. 94–95, 341–43.

3. Stace, *Mysticism and Philosophy,* p. 236.

vation of being, *annihilatio,* have reduced both man and God together to the same Nothingness; void meets void.[4]

However ineffable and abstract these highest mystical experiences devoid of sensory images and forms might appear to be, these states of consciousness and the trancendental Objects that the mystics encounter in
them exhibit every sign of being historically conditioned. The fourteenth-
century Belgian mystic Jan van Ruysbroeck's descriptions of an elevated
nonsensuous mystical state he calls union with God "without mean" exemplify how historical conditioning insinuates itself into even the most
abstracted states of consciousness. First, when Ruysbroeck described that
union with God "without mean" that he considered to be the crowning
experience that a contemplative could aspire to in this life, he took it for
granted that this condition of ineffable peace and "delectable love" involved the mystic in an encounter with the Christian God, not Allah,
Shiva, or one of the Six Grandfathers.[5] Second, even though this Christian
God came to the mystic free of all form and imagery, He did not do so as
an "undifferentiated Unity" but rather as that mysterious fusion of three
distinct Persons whom the Christians worship as the Holy Trinity.[6] Third,
the mystic's Christian ascetic itinerary insinuated itself into the existential
core of this putative experience. For example, the feelings of "delectable
love" that the mystic ought to experience during this theoretical mystical
encounter were not erotic passions but rather Christianized spiritual emotions, *agape* rather than *eros.* As such, these purely spiritual emotions presupposed that the mystic remained free from the taint of mortal sin and
that he had undergone a lengthy period of ascetic self-denial in which he
practiced the Christian virtues of charity, chastity, humility, and obedience
so rigorously that he now lived in total conformity to the will of this
Christian God rather than in accordance with his own natural inclinations.[7]
Fourth, Ruysbroeck's perfect contemplative state did not entail any dissolution of the subject-object distinction since union with God, even union
"without mean," was a perfect coincidence of human and divine wills and
not a pantheistic fusion of the divine and human substances, such that the
mystic lost his human identity and his responsibility for his actions. Humans still remained human and God still remained God. Even in the high-

4. Van der Leeuw, *Religion in Essence and Manifestation,* 2:497.
5. Ruysbroeck, *Spiritual Espousals,* pp. 162–66.
6. Ibid., pp. 179–80.
7. Ibid., pp. 65–66.

est mystical states, the mystic retained his individuality and his correlative obligation to perform good works. The only difference was that now, at the pinnacle of the contemplative ascent, he no longer finds that his works of love detract from his experiences of contemplation because

> in either the inward man is whole and undivided, for he is wholly in God, where in delectation he rests, and he is wholly in himself, where actively he loves. And both are admonished and demanded of him each hour by God . . . each hour his spirit in justice desires to pay that which is demanded of it by God.[8]

Ruysbroeck clearly did not envision that union with God without mean involved any loss of the mystic's individuality because the mystic still had the same obligation to perform works of charity that he had always had even before he had tasted the presence of God.

This analysis of Ruysbroeck's "union without mean" shows that even when one is dealing with mystics of the via negativa it is wrong to depict their descriptions of the quintessential mystical experience in a way that suggests that they portrayed it as a transhistorical mode of being free from all taint of multiplicity. First, the transcendent Object of Ruysbroeck's experience was definitely not some radically simple *cogitatum,* devoid of all personality, that abstract "object-perceived" of every perceptual act in which there is a "consciousness of" something, but, instead, it was the specific triune God of the Christian religion.[9] Second, the relationship between subject and object that Ruysbroeck depicted in that state of consciousness was likewise one that could only emerge in the context of the medieval Christian monastic ascesis. Third, the feelings and yearnings that this experience engendered were those which only a Christian religious environment could have fostered. It was not a "delectable love" that just anyone could experience but rather a love of the Christian God and a longing to fulfill His commandments that only a Christian could have.

The observations applied to Ruysbroeck's "union without mean" apply equally to Teresa's account of those mystical experiences and their effects that she described as having taken place during that highest prayer state that she called the Spiritual Marriage of the soul to God. There was cer-

8. Ibid., p. 165.

9. Ruysbroeck concludes his description of the highest state of mystical contemplation with this wish: "That we in delectation may possess this essential unity, and that we may contemplate unity in Trinity, grant to us that Love which denies no prayer addressed to its Divinity. Amen." Ibid., p. 190.

tainly nothing transhistorical or transcontextual about her feeling of absolute assurance that all three Persons of the Holy Trinity had come to dwell in the center of her soul as her ever-present companions. Her description of this experience makes it clear that even though it took the form of an "intellectual vision" devoid of all visual imagery it was nonetheless a historically conditioned sensation that derived its distinctive existential and cognitive content from Catholic Trinitarian dogma. Teresa wrote of this experience that "what we hold by faith the soul may be said here to grasp by sight."[10] One could hardly make more explicit the organic connection between the content of her experience and the Catholic religious environment that nurtured it. The transcendental Object of her intellectual vision was the God that the Christian religion had endowed with a will and a personality, attributes that radically set Him apart from the qualityless "undifferentiated Unity" of both Van der Leeuw and Stace and distinguished Him sharply from that kind of empty, abstract objecthood that characterizes the Husserlian and Cartesian cogitatum that accompanies each and every act of perception as its object.

Teresa's descriptions of Spiritual Marriage also expose the fallacy of Van der Leeuw's and Stace's contention that the highest or purest mystical states involve some sort of dissolution of the subject-object distinction. On the contrary, Teresa always insisted that the most perfect supernatural prayer states brought about a union of wills rather than a union of substances, that is, they brought about a perfect coincidence between what the human subject wanted to do and what the Christian God wanted him to do. These prayer states neither annihilated the mystic's personality nor diminished his capacity to exercise his free choice. Precisely because Spiritual Marriage did not bring about the annihilation of the subject-object distinction, precisely because it preserved the essential separateness of God and humans and, with it, the human capacity for free choice, Teresa cautioned her nuns against ever relaxing their vigilance since even at the summit of the contemplative ascent one still had the possibility of falling away from God.[11] Needless to say, Teresa's inability to entertain the possibility that the highest mystical states could bring about a loss of the subject-object distinction had its roots in Christian anthropology for it is one of its cardinal tenets that a human being can never lose his responsibility

10. Teresa of Avila, *Interior Castle*, pp. 209–10.
11. Ibid., pp. 212, 217.

for freely choosing between the things that lead to salvation and those that lead to damnation.

The distinctive volitional orientation that accompanied the condition of Spiritual Marriage exhibited the imprint of medieval Christian monasticism. As Teresa never tired of repeating to her nuns, the entire purpose of their life of prayer and contemplation was that of better fitting them to imitate the exemplary life of love, suffering, and obedience that Jesus Christ had displayed during the time that He had dwelt upon this earth.[12] Consequently, each nun must imitate Him by conforming her will as completely to God's will as He had done, long to suffer as He had done, and yearn to imitate His exemplary humility as well as His exemplary love of God and neighbor. This quintessentially Christian orientation of the will gave far more weight to performing heroic deeds of charity and self-abnegation than it did to the quest for knowledge and wisdom and owes its distinctively act-centered focus to the Christian anthropology: because the Fall resulted from a primordial act of disobedience to God's will, the corrective process of redemption must necessarily center around the restoration of that lost obedience.

# Yogic Isolation and Sāṃkhya Metaphysics

One can therefore expect that different religious or philosophical anthropologies will lead to different volitional orientations. For example, the religious anthropology of Patañjali's system of Yoga maintains that the human descent into suffering and spiritual degradation stemmed not from any primordial act of disobedience but from a beginningless act of ignorance that led the individual to erroneously conclude that his transcendent soul (*puruṣa*) depended upon material substance (*prakṛti*) for its sustenance.[13] Not surprisingly, the antidote to such ignorance is insight, not obedience. Consequently, the follower of Patañjali bends his will toward the task of acquiring that knowledge that will save him from the harmful consequences of this ignorance. The only significant actions and desires are those that either facilitate the onset of those peculiar states of samādhi that bring about prajñā (that special sort of wisdom that destroys karmic resi-

12. Ibid., p. 227.
13. See Surendranath Dasgupta, *A History of Indian Philosophy*, 5 vols. (Delhi: Motilal Banarsidass, 1975), 1:260–62.

dues without leaving any of its own karmic residues behind) or else help him realize that his soul is an entity completely different from the subtle materiality of mind-stuff (*citta*). Moreover, Patañjali's yogin does not concern himself with the problem of whether or not his actions and desires accord with the will of some divine being. Such concerns are soteriologically irrelevant given the premises of Patañjali's religious anthropology.

One might be tempted to imagine that the condition of perfect spiritual liberation described in Patañjali's system of Yoga, isolation (*kaivalya*), would serve as a valid counterexample to my earlier criticisms of what Stace and Van der Leeuw had to say about the nature of ultimate mystical experiences. One might, after all, point out that isolation differs in one very important respect from both Ruysbroeck's union "without mean" and Teresa's condition of Spiritual Marriage: it is a state of existence completely devoid of all forms of multiplicity. This freedom from multiplicity does not suggest, however, that isolation was one instance of that transhistorical, qualityless experience of oneness with undifferentiated Unity that both Stace and Van der Leeuw considered to be the culmination of the mystic's quest. Before I explain the reasoning behind this statement, I must first clarify what it means to say that isolation is a state of being completely free of multiplicity.

I speak of isolation as totally free of multiplicity because the characterizations of it given by Patañjali and his commentators Veda-Vyāsa and Vācaspati Miśra clearly imply that it is a condition of existence radically devoid of both any sort of perception of an object and any sort of affective state. Isolation is, in short, a state of pure intellection.[14] It is a pure intellection because it is an affect-free, percept-free insight (derived from experiencing a succession of increasingly abstract trance-states) that the Self or soul (*puruṣa*) completely transcends the domain of spiritual, mental, and material phenomena. Not only is isolation pure because it is a condition of

---

14. Patañjali and his commentators describe the phenomenon of isolation in several places. The commentator Veda-Vyāsa gives a clear definition of it when, in reference to *Yoga-Sūtra* 3.50, he writes, "the absolute absence of correlation of the Self with the aspects, . . . (is) Isolation. Then the Self is nought else than the Energy of Intellect (*citi*) grounded in itself." Later on, elaborating upon Patañjali's assertion that isolation occurs "when the purity of the *sattva* and of the Self are equal" (3.55), Veda-Vyāsa explains: "When the *sattva* of the thinking-substance is freed from the defilement of the *rajas* and *tamas*, and when it has no task other than with the presented-idea of the difference (of the *sattva*) from the Self, and when the seeds of the hindrances within itself have been burned, then the *sattva* enters into a state of purity equal to that of the Self. When-this-is-so (*tadā*), purity is the cessation of the experience which is falsely attributed to the Self. In this state (of purity) Isolation follows." From Patañjali, *Yoga-System of Patañjali*, 3.50.

insight that transcends every type of feeling-state and perceptual state whatsoever (whether it be of physical, mental, or supernormal origin) but it is also pure because it leaves no karmic residue of any kind in its wake.[15]

It is important to bear in mind that if one wishes to fully comprehend the meaning of Veda-Vyāsa's characterizations of isolation, he must first have some understanding of both the philosophical vocabulary and anthropology of Sāmkhya, the system of metaphysics that underlies Patañjali's Yoga. According to Sāmkhya-Yoga, each human being has a soul or Self (*purusa*) that exists in a manner that is completely independent of any kind of mental or material phenomenon no matter how rarefied, "spiritual," or supernormal it may be. The Sāmkhya system of metaphysics maintains that not only are physical objects endowed with materiality but it also asserts that thoughts, feelings, mental representations, supernormal spiritual phenomena, and the creations of the imagination are likewise endowed with materiality though this materiality is subtle rather than gross, as is the case with physical objects. The manifold complexity of the phenomenal world, both mental and physical, has originated out of a primordially homogeneous matter-stuff known as prakṛti. This originally homogeneous prakṛti differentiates into the heterogeneous complexity of the mental and physical phenomena we observe because the three "aspects" or *gunas* that are in equilibrium in the primordial homogeneous state fall out of balance so that one predominates over the others. *Tamas,* that aspect of prakṛti associated with mental and physical inertness, is the predominant element in inanimate matter and in the sleep-state where consciousness of any kind is absent. *Rajas,* that aspect of prakṛti associated with heat and motion, is the predominant element in fire and in the mental state of irascibility. *Sattva* is that aspect of prakṛti associated with translucency and mental phenomena. As such, it is unobstructed and endowed with infinite plasticity and it is because of the predominance of this element in mental phenomena that the mind is able to conform itself to and reproduce so well the shape and color of the objects that are presented to it.

Puruṣa (the soul or Self) has absolutely no connection whatsoever with prakṛti and its manifold evolutes. It is pure inactive intelligence utterly devoid of qualities, motion, form, and any type of impurity.[16] Puruṣa is that transcendent entity that endows the inanimate (because they are of a

15. See Veda-Vyāsa's commentary on 3.50 about isolation destroying karmic residues. Patañjali, *Yoga-System of Patañjali,* 3.50, and Veda-Vyāsa's commentary; also see Dasgupta, *A History of Indian Philosophy,* 1:270–73.

16. Dasgupta, *A History of Indian Philosophy,* 1:239–40, 259–60.

"material" nature) phenomena of mental life with a spurious semblance of consciousness and intelligence. This illusion takes place because puruṣa, though it does not participate in the material world in any way, "illuminates" mental phenomena in a manner somewhat analogous to the way that light illuminates physical objects. The translucency of sattva, the subtle matter-element predominating in mental phenomena, allows the "radiance" of purusa to shine through mental phenomena without distorting them. Just as a small child can be easily led into making the error of supposing that the image he sees on an illuminated screen has an existence independent of the slide projector, humans can also (and much more easily) lose sight of the fact that the mental phenomena they perceive in front of them have no intrinsic intelligence or consciousness apart from that which the radiance of puruṣa gives them. This mistake, this tragic error of identifying one's soul or Self with the vicissitudes of unintelligent mind-stuff (*citta*) is the source of all human suffering and bondage to karma.

The arduous ascetic practices and mental disciplines of Patañjali's Yoga have the reversal of this process as their central aim. The yogin struggles to return his mind to that state of consciousness where it is so utterly free of defilement by tamas and rajas that its purity resembles that of puruṣa itself. In the state of asamprajñāta samādhi, the mind resembles the purity, formlessness, immobility, and freedom from all qualities that puruṣa possesses.[17] This is a condition where sattva manifests itself without any admixture of rajas and tamas. Those two guṇas have dropped away never to return. Karmic residues are spent. All that is left is for the yogin to realize that this pure sattva-state is *not* identical to puruṣa. Once this realization dawns, sattva drops away never to return and puruṣa is freed forever from its bondage to matter. It is quite correct to say that, at this point in his spiritual itinerary, the yogin has altogether transcended experience as we know it.[18]

17. Asamprajñāta samādhi means samādhi without support, that is, without the support of a meditative object. It is a state where the mind has reached maximum quiescence and a maximum degree of focused attention without using any object whatsoever, mental or physical, as an image upon which it has focused itself.

18. Patañjali clearly intended that the goal of his Yoga was a radical emancipation from all experience. He writes in Sūtra 3.35 that "experience is a presented-idea that fails to distinguish between the *sattva* and the Self, which are absolutely uncommingled (in the presented-idea)." Veda-Vyāsa elaborates on the nonexperiential nature of the Self when he comments on this same passage that "the Self, of which we can only say that it is Intellect (*citi*), which is other than the aspects (*guṇa*), and which is undefiled (*śuddha*) (by objects), is absolutely contrary in quality even to the *sattva* which is mutable." Because Sāṃkhya maintains that all experience is a result of one or more of the guṇas and since the Self is altogether alien to the

It should now be clear what Veda-Vyāsa meant when he defined isolation as an "absolute absence of correlation of the Self with the aspects." He was simply saying that the Self or soul (*puruṣa*), when it is in its natural state, is an entity that has absolutely no essential connection with that domain of existence where "the aspects," the three guṇas, hold sway. In other words, each individual's soul bears no necessary connection with the subtle and gross realms of prakṛti. Moreover, the liberated state is not a condition of bliss because feelings and percepts are phenomena that derive from prakṛti and, for that reason, must be fundamentally alien to the soul in its natural state.[19] Totally free of both affect and percept, at least as we know them, the condition of liberation is, instead, a purely intellectual phenomenon. When this event takes place the Self becomes nothing else except "the Energy of Intellect (*citi*) grounded in itself," that is, disconnected from everything material.

The foregoing explanations of the Sāṃkhya-Yoga metaphysics and Veda-Vyāsa's descriptions of the state that corresponds to the soul's perfect liberation from all bondage to karma and matter should help one to understand why neither Stace's nor Van der Leeuw's characterizations of ultimate mystical experience apply to the phenomenon of isolation (*kaivalyam*). First, isolation certainly did not involve any kind of experience of union since it was neither a sensation of oneness with anything nor a perfect coincidence of two separate wills. Instead, Veda-Vyāsa made it clear that isolation was simply an insight, an intellectual comprehension of a special sort that did much more than just convey information. It emancipated the soul from its imprisonment in karma, materiality, and mind-stuff.

Second, even though isolation was a condition that purportedly transcended the world of objects, sensations, emotions, thoughts, and even experience itself as we know it, it rendered these things superfluous or irrelevant in a manner that showed that the dissolution of the subject-object duality was not the final goal of yoga practice.[20] One must recall

---

guṇas and all that derives from them, it follows that isolation must be a phenomenon that transcends experience as we know it.

19. Dasgupta, *A History of Indian Philosophy*, 1:273.

20. Patañjali was evidently alluding to the phenomenon of isolation, here referred to as that highest state of freedom from passion and craving, when he wrote that "this (passionlessness) is highest when the discernment of Self results in thirstlessness for qualities and (not merely for objects)" (*Yoga-System*, 1.16). Here the word "qualities" refers to the three guṇas. Isolation is a condition where the yogin has become absolutely free of all craving for anything derived from prakṛti and the three guṇas whether it be physical objects, desires, feeling-states, thoughts, or any other kind of mental phenomenon.

once again that isolation was an insight, a condition of acute discernment, and not a condition of ecstasy. Liberation resulted from one thing only, awareness that the Self actually is something distinct from the sattva that it so closely resembles. Nothing else can actually bring about the soul's release from materiality and the round of rebirths.

At this point, several objections could be raised: Is it not true that Patañjali's system of Yoga requires the practitioner to master a succession of samādhi states?[21] And is it not an essential characteristic of yogic samādhi that it obliterates the subject-object distinction? How, then, can anyone maintain that isolation does not involve a dissolution of the subject-object duality? While one must concede that it is certainly true that the cultivation of various states of samādhi plays a significant role in the process that *precedes* isolation, the phenomenon of samādhi is not an integral element in isolation itself. First, all states of samādhi, even the highest and most subtle, asamprajñāta samādhi, still partake of the nature of prakṛti. Asamprajñāta samādhi is that state of the mind-stuff (*citta*) where sattva exists in its purest state stripped of all contaminating admixture of tamas and rajas. Nonetheless, it is still invested with a residue of materiality, slight though it be. Even pure sattva is still a derivative of prakṛti, the primordial matter-stuff. Since puruṣa is absolutely free of any residue of prakṛti, even pure sattva, it is clear that all samādhi states are alien to it. Second, the various samādhi states are not employed in yoga as ends in themselves. They are useful in the practice of yoga because, once achieved, they augment the yogin's *prajñā* (insight), a special kind of discernment that differs from ordinary types of knowledge or wisdom because not only does it give absolutely true knowledge; it also burns away all the residues of karma, both good and bad. Consequently, it really does free one from rebirths. These insights that occur as the yogin progressively masters the successive states of samādhi are therefore a kind of dress rehearsal for that final,

21. Patañjali gave his definition of samādhi in Sutra 3.3. There he distinguished samādhi from other types of concentrated attention in two ways: (1) samādhi was a total fixity of attention upon the object-to-be contemplated and (2) it was not a succession of thoughts, each of which was totally fixed on the same object, but rather, it was a single thought without any successor that was totally fixated on that object-to-be contemplated. In other words, samādhi not only totally concentrated one thought on just one object but it also killed the successive flow of fixated thoughts while it lasted. In dhyāna there is a total fixity of thoughts upon one object only but the successive appearance of identically focused thoughts has not yet ceased. Vācaspati Miśra's commentary on 3.3 shows that samādhi does indeed obliterate the subject-object dualism: "A two-termed-relation (*kalpanā*) is a distinction between the contemplation and the object-to-be contemplated. Concentration [*samādhi*] is free of this."

perfect insight that is isolation itself, that redemptive insight which irrevocably destroys all karmic residues, even the most subtle and subliminal, and releases the soul from its illusory bondage to prakṛti.

It should now be clear why isolation is not a mental state where the subject-object distinction has disappeared. Isolation is not a mental state because it is a condition of naked insight in which the soul has utterly escaped bondage from prakṛti and saṃsāra. Even the most elevated mental states and forms of samādhi differ from isolation because they are still tainted by a faint residuum of subtle materiality and bondage to the karmic process.

The transcendent abstractness of both the state of isolation itself and those penultimate states of samādhi that pave the way for it must not mislead one into thinking that either phenomenon escaped the process of historical conditioning.[22] On the contrary, one can easily see that both derived their specific existential content as well as their immediate intellectual, behavioral, and soteriological impact from the metaphysics, anthropology, and soteriology of Sāṃkhya-Yoga. For example, the purely intellectual, affect-free nature of that insight that is coterminous with isolation itself certainly owed its specific existential tone to the yogin's prior expectations, acquired by his previous exposure to Sāṃkhya doctrines, that the soul which he was now liberating from its bondage to matter and mind would be "experienced" as something totally free of anything connected with sensations and emotional states.[23] It is almost certain that if Sāṃkhya had endowed puruṣa with an affective component the way that Vedānta had endowed ultimate reality (brahman) with a threefold nature of true being, consciousness, and bliss (sat-cit-ānanda), this characterization would have insinuated itself into the existential content of the yogic experience of spiritual perfection making it a phenomenon very different from the isolation described in the Yoga-Sūtras. One would expect that a Vedāntic insight into the true nature of brahman would be experienced as an event heavily laden with a penumbra of blissful emotions.[24]

22. I am setting aside the question of whether or not any yogin has actually experienced isolation or asamprajñāta samādhi as they are described in Patañjali's Yoga-Sūtras.

23. Strictly speaking, isolation was not an experience at all, at least if one defines experience as any perception or apprehension of something that takes place by means of the mental apparatus. Isolation had nothing in common with mind-stuff (citta).

24. There is evidence that one yogin's actual experience of what he claimed was mokṣa (total liberation) really did correspond to this Vedāntic expectation. Baba Muktananda's previous exposure to Vedānta caused him to take it for granted that brahman was intrinsically blissful in nature. Consequently, it comes as no surprise that his own firsthand experience of

# Spiritual Marriage and
## *Asamprajñāta Samādhi* Contrasted

A brief comparison of the experiential content and impact of Teresan Spiritual Marriage and asamprajñāta samādhi displays clearly some of the profound ways that a mystic's prior religious and philosophical assumptions can insinuate themselves into the existential core of even the most abstract types of mystical experience.

Even though both asamprajñāta samādhi and that intellectual vision that occurred after the onset of the Spiritual Marriage state were mystical states of consciousness free of any kind of visual or imaginational imagery, this shared characteristic masks some radical differences between the two phenomena. One significant difference was that asamprajñāta samādhi was a state of consciousness utterly devoid of any object of consciousness whatsoever, whereas Teresa's intellectual vision clearly had an object, the three Persons of the Holy Trinity dwelling in the center of her soul.[25] Teresa could not see this object with the eyes of her body or the eyes of her soul but she definitely sensed that the three Persons were actually present as her companions. That the highest state of consciousness in Yoga should have taken form as a state of one-pointed concentration devoid of any meditational object stems from the central presupposition of the Sāṃkhya-Yoga system of metaphysics and soteriology, namely, that the spiritually perfect states of consciousness are conditions progressively more and more devoid of any association with the manifold forms of prakṛti. Since the mental images perceived during states of consciousness were considered products of prakṛti by Sāṃkhya-Yoga, this necessarily implied that in kaivalyam and in the subtle trance-states immediately preceding it these residues of prakṛti in its most subtle form should be absent. Teresa's commitment to the Christian scheme of salvation prevented her from conceptualizing the spiritually perfect state of consciousness as one devoid of any

---

ultimate spiritual realization confirmed its essentially blissful nature. He wrote: "I perceived the refulgent, divinely beautiful conscious light calmly throbbing as supreme bliss on all sides, within and without, above and below" (Muktananda, *Play of Consciousness*, p. 162). No true follower of Patañjali's system of Yoga would have considered such an affect-laden experience as evidence of his immediate proximity to the spiritually liberated condition because he would have been taught that mokṣa was intrinsically alien to any state of being colored by the passions and emotions. See *Yoga-System*, 1.16, and Veda-Vyāsa's commentary on it, pp. 37–38.

25. Teresa of Avila, *Interior Castle*, pp. 209–10.

object. Both the Bible and the Christian mystics taught her that the most blessed life was one where one enjoyed the most intimate companionship with God. Given this assumption, it was most unlikely that she would conceive of the most elevated mystical experiences as devoid of her divine companion.

Another significant difference between Teresa's intellectual vision of the indwelling of the Holy Trinity and asamprajñāta samādhi was that her vision, despite its absence of visual and imaginational imagery, was not a condition where the mind was immobilized. Samādhi (and saṃyama) were states of mental immobility since they presupposed that the successive appearance of thoughts and other forms of mentation had completely ceased.[26] Teresa's intellectual visions certainly did not immobilize her thought processes, her feelings, or her will. On the contrary, her certainty of God's presence in her soul co-existed with and fortified a fervent love for Him and an equally fervent longing to suffer for His sake if that should be His will. It is obvious that those feelings of love and longing would have been completely incompatible with that type of mental stasis that takes place during samādhi.

The soteriological priority that deeds of love and self-abnegation enjoyed in medieval and sixteenth-century Christian monasticism ensured that the cultivation of prayer states akin to yogic samādhi would receive little encouragement in that environment. After all, what good were states of mental immobility or ecstatic absorption in God if they failed to bear fruit in obedience, humility, and works of love? For this reason Teresa discouraged her nuns from coveting such states. "I do not covet for you those delectable states of absorption which it is possible to experience and which are given the name of union."[27]

If those moments of contemplative ecstasy were barren of good works, they did nothing to help a Christian along the road to salvation. There was another reason why Christian mystics (at least when they are compared to their Buddhist and Hindu counterparts in India) placed relatively little emphasis on immobilizing one's mental processes in prayer. They took it for granted that success in contemplation depended far more upon divine grace than it did upon human effort. Teresa assumed that all forms of genuine contemplation, all genuine mystical experiences, originated supernaturally. Consequently, no one could bring them about by means of any

26. Patañjali, *Yoga-System of Patañjali*, 3.3.
27. Teresa of Avila, *Book of Foundations*, p. 24 (5.13).

heroic amount of human effort if this element of divine grace were absent.[28] Since heroic efforts of mental discipline could never, in and of themselves, guarantee access to states of contemplative prayer, why, then, should the Christian mystic place an inordinate emphasis on cultivating them?

The insistence of Patañjali and his commentators upon the soteriological primacy of states of complete mental immobility (*samādhi*) had its roots in their commitment to the notion that the condition of spiritual liberation and the states of being immediately antecedent to it were fundamentally incompatible with the co-presence of two guṇas—rajas and tamas (especially rajas—that energetic principle of motion and activity in prakṛti).[29] They preferred these states of mental immobility to all other types of mental experience because they took it for granted that the fluctuating mind (the mind engaged in perceiving physical or spiritual objects successively), was, by that very fact of perceiving a succession of images, still contaminated by a residue of rajas. Mystical visions like those that came to Black Elk in his Great Vision or those "imaginary" visions that Teresa often had could not serve as a proximate means to isolation because they were composed of subtle material objects, mental images that changed shape and form from one moment to the next.[30] They were, in short, contaminated by rajas since the mind, even though it was in a mystical state of consciousness, was still fluctuating, moving successively from one object to the next. Only a totally immobilized mind could manifest sattva in its purest state free of any defiling admixture of rajas. Then and only then did sattva approximate the purity and qualitylessness of puruṣa and establish the one essential precondition that enabled the true saving insight to emerge.

# The Historically Conditioned Nature of Nirvana

## Scholarly Misconceptions

A number of scholars (as well as some nonspecialists who have addressed a general audience) have written books on mysticism where they take it for

28. Teresa of Avila, *Way of Perfection*, pp. 200, 206; idem, *Spiritual Testimonies*, p. 355.

29. In this context, one must not forget that Veda-Vyāsa had characterized the state of consciousness that immediately precedes isolation as a mode of being that comes only to that individual "who has cleansed the *sattva* of his thinking-substance from the defilement of *rajas* and *tamas*" (Patañjali, *Yoga-System of Patañjali*, 3.49).

30. It is important to reiterate that Sāṃkhya-Yoga classified mental images as a subtle form of matter (*prakṛti*).

granted that Buddhist nirvana is a mystical experience.[31] Stace claims that "*nirvana* is simply the final condition of a permanent mystical consciousness."[32] Heiler regarded nirvana as one of the two possible forms that quintessential mystical experience could take. Ecstasy was the quintessential form of mystical experience at its affective boiling point while nirvana was mystical experience at its affective freezing point, that is, that form which it took when the phenomenon was generated under conditions where the mystic's emotions were powerfully restrained.[33] Not only did Heiler and Stace assume that Buddhist nirvana was a mystical experience, but they also assumed that, because it was a mystical phenomenon, it transcended the process of historical conditioning and took form as a sensation of union with an Absolute that was One.[34]

Reincourt, Capra, Heiler, and Stace each made a serious but understandable mistake by ontologizing nirvana. In other words, they referred to the state of nirvana on par with the other kinds of mental phenomena and mystical states that a monk encounters during the course of his spiritual quest. Unfortunately, to speak of Buddhist nirvana as though it were just another kind of mental experience is to make the same blunder that a scholar would make if he were to treat yogic isolation as one more of the possible types of transmutation that prakṛti undergoes instead of recognizing that the distinguishing attribute of isolation is its complete alienation from all that is connected with prakṛti. One must never ontologize nirvana

31. For example, Amaury de Riencourt and Fritjof Capra imply that Buddhist nirvana is either an experience of "cosmic consciousness" (Reincourt) or a mystical apprehension of some underlying unity (Capra), which serves as the ontological foundation of all that exists. See Amaury de Riencourt, *The Eye of Shiva: Eastern Mysticism and Western Science* (New York: William Morrow & Co., 1981), p. 172, also p. 36; and Fritjof Capra, *The Tao of Physics* (New York: Bantam Books, 1981), p. 36.

32. Stace, *Mysticism and Philosophy*, p. 61.

33. Heiler, *Prayer*, pp. 139–40.

34. Heiler's definition of mysticism emphasized that not only was mysticism an experience of being "absorbed" into the "infinite unity of the Godhead" (Heiler, *Prayer*, p. 136) but it was also a phenomenon that developed its existential coloration independently of the mystic's cultural and religious environment. See also Heiler, *Die Bedeutung der Mystik für die Weltreligionen*, p. 6. Stace also stressed that the sensation of "being one with" an undifferentiated Unity constituted the sine qua non of all mystical experience. He likewise accepted Heiler's premise that the existential core of the nirvana "experience" developed independently of the subject's cultural and religious environment. Thus Stace asserted that "*Nirvana* is the Buddhist interpretation of what Plotinus spoke of as union with the One, the Vedantist as realization of identity with the Universal Self, the Christian as union with God" (Stace, *Mysticism and Philosophy*, p. 199). He is contending that the content of that particular experience that corresponds to the Buddhist's realization of nirvana is identical to the content of a Christian mystic's experience of union with God. Only the postexperiential interpretations differ, not the experiences themselves.

for the simple reason that Buddhists have always insisted that it is *asaṃ-khata* (uncompounded), whereas all mental and material phenomena whether they be subtle or gross, mystical or supernormal, are *saṃkhata* (compounded).[35] When Buddhists refer to nirvana as uncompounded they mean to stress that it is something completely different from any mental or material phenomenon. It is not constructed (compounded) out of the transient collocations of the five aggregates: name and form (matter), sensation (knowing something as pleasant or unpleasant), perception (recognition of an object through the five senses or mind), volition, and consciousness.[36]

The distinction between compounded and uncompounded phenomena derives its soteriological importance from the fact that everything compounded bears the taint of impermanence. By their very structure all compounded things exist in a ceaseless flux of coming into birth and disintegrating since each of its constituents is a collocation of the five aggregates undergoing a continual process of emergence and dissolution. Moreover, each subsidiary constituent of the main constituents of any compounded thing consists of a similar collocation of the five aggregates undergoing a similar process of emergence and dissolution ad infinitum. This endless infinitely regressing flux of emergence and dissolution has two significant consequences. First, it means that nothing compounded has a Self or an Ego. In other words, nothing in the entire domain of physical, mental, spiritual, or mystical phenomena abides in the same state permanently. Ultimately it must disintegrate. There is no eternal substrate of any kind in the realm of physical, mental, or mystical phenomena. There is no "I" that persists throughout all these transformations, there is no God that persists throughout them, there is no irreducible continually persisting

---

35. See *The Book of the Kindred Sayings (Saṃyutta–Nikāya) or Grouped Sayings*, trans. F. L. Woodward, Pali Text Society Translation Series, no. 14 (London: Published for the Pali Text Society by the Oxford University Press, [n.d.]), vol. 4, pp. 256, 359. See also Walpola Rahula, *What the Buddha Taught*, rev. ed. (New York: Grove Press, 1974), pp. 36, 40.

The classic passage that illustrates that the Buddha regarded even the most elevated mystical experiences as compounded things ultimately subject to dissolution and productive of suffering if one made the mistake of craving them occurs in the *Dhātuvibhaṅgasutta* (no. 140) of the *Majjhima-nikāya*. See *The Collection of the Middle Length Sayings (Majjhima-Nikāya)*, trans. I. B. Horner, Pali Text Society Translation Series, no. 31 (London: Published for the Pali Text Society by Luzac and Company, 1959), 3.244, pp. 290–91.

36. One will notice that the five aggregates function in Buddhist metaphysics and soteriology in a manner that parallels the way that prakṛti functions in Sāṃkhya-Yoga. In both cases, it is a penetrating insight (*prajñā* [in Pali, *paññā*]) that brings about liberation from bondage to karma and the liberated state entails a permanent, radical separation from all mental and material phenomena.

atomic particle that undergirds all the processes of nature, and there is no soul or spirit that has an eternal existence above this flux of emergence and dissolution. The appearance of any seemingly permanent entity is just that, a mere appearance, an illusion of continuity where, in fact, there is only ceaseless flux. Second, this impermanence conjoined with craving for those impermanent objects is also the root of that existential distress and suffering (*dukkha*) intrinsic to all compounded things—physical, mental, and mystical or spiritual. Whenever someone who is deluded by ignorance from penetrating into the essentially transient nature of compounded things acquires a craving for them, he assures himself misery since their innate tendency toward dissolution guarantees that sooner or later this individual will lose the presence of that thing that he craves. Worse yet, his craving for these compounded things and his ignorance of their nature as impermanent and devoid of any permanently abiding substrate or self binds him, by the workings of karma, to their ceaseless flux of emergence and dissolution.

## Wisdom (*Prajñā*)

How does one overcome this bondage to endless cycles of emergence, dissolution, and suffering? One escapes it by uprooting its causes, ignorance and craving, and acquiring wisdom (*prajñā*). It is important to realize, however, that this wisdom is not mere assent to the Buddha's teachings about the essential impermanence of compounded things, their lack of a self, and their inevitable tendency to generate suffering. Prajñā is not mere knowledge as information. Instead, Buddhists maintain that one can only acquire wisdom by direct experience of the truth of the Buddha's teachings on impermanence, suffering, and the lack of self in compounded things.[37] This wisdom based on direct experience, the only type of wisdom that really uproots ignorance, can only come to an individual after he has undergone an arduous process of ethical, mental, and intellectual discipline.

37. This Buddhist author's attitude toward mere book-learning is typical: "If you have only a (dry, smug) intellectual understanding that it [Mind in its pure state] is a clear, resplendent, unidentifiable state of clarity and Voidness, you will be unable to make any progress. . . . But if this (realization) has dawned from within (from your own meditational practice), then you have really had penetrative insight into the (nature of) the settled mind" (Wang-Ch'ug Dor-Je, the ninth Kar-ma-pa, *The Mahāmudrā Eliminating the Darkness of Ignorance*, trans. Alexander Berzin (Dharamsala, India: Library of Tibetan Works and Archives, 1981), p. 85.

The first element in this triad of discipline that leads to the extinction of ignorance is perfection in virtuous conduct (*sīla*). One abstains from killing and injury to living things, avoids hatred, gluttony, lying, and cultivates friendliness and compassion toward all creatures. This develops harmonious conditions of existence that are conducive to both mental concentration and the perfection of insight, as well as ensuring that if one does not realize nirvana in this lifetime one will at least be reborn under conditions of happiness "in the heavenly world."[38]

The second element is the practice of concentration (*samādhi*). This practice simultaneously calms and exhilarates the mind. It is, however, absolutely essential that samādhi be joined with a third element: the practice of penetrating discernment (*vipaśyanā*) into the true nature of all compounded things as transient, productive of suffering, and devoid of any self, soul, or other form of abiding substrate.[39]

Why do Buddhists consider it essential to practice one-pointed mental concentration in order to overcome ignorance? How does mental concentration have anything to do with acquiring knowledge? One cannot acquire a sufficiently penetrating insight into the true nature of compounded things if one does not join the cultivation of insight with the practice of concentration. As the *Bhāvanākrama I* asserts: "One cannot know things as they really are with an unequipoised mind, for the Bhagavat [the Buddha] has proclaimed, 'The man whose mind is equipoised knows things as they really are.'"[40] And how does concentration contribute to the perfection of discernment? It does so by energizing and exhilarating both the body and the mind. In turn, this "cathartic," this surge of mental and somatic energy, empowers the intellect so that it is capable of comprehending with much greater vividness and force of conviction the absence of a self in all compounded things.[41]

Tson-kha-pa used the following simile to clarify how concentration viv-

38. Buddhaghosa, *The Path of Purification (Visuddhimagga)*, 2 vols., trans. Bhikkhu Nyānamoli (Berkeley: Shambala, 1976), vol. 1, p. 9.

39. Tson-kha-pa (1357–1419), the founder of the Gelugpa (Yellow Hat) sect of Tibetan Buddhism, emphasized that the practice of samādhi without the concurrent cultivation of discernment could never lead one to that all-important realization that all compounded things are devoid of a self. Failure to realize this truth vividly will inevitably cause one to fall back into the habit of craving compounded things. When this happens one once again subjects oneself to the deleterious effects of karma and the endless cycle of rebirths and dissolutions (*saṃsāra*). Tson-kha-pa, *Calming the Mind*, pp. 91–92, 174–75.

40. Ibid., p. 90.

41. Ibid., p. 91.

ifies discernment and why it is necessary that one yoke the two practices together.[42] Imagine that one wants to see some objects in a dark room as they really are. For this to happen two things are necessary. First, one must have a light source, in this case, a candle. The candle represents that intellectual faculty that operates during the analytical activity of discernment. Second, one must make sure that this candle is protected from the wind so that it does not flicker or blow out. This barrier to the disruptive effects of the wind represents the mind in a state of samādhi. It is obvious that if the wind is allowed to blow on the candle this will cause the light to flicker. When this happens it is impossible to see clearly what is in the room. For example, the flickering light might cause one to see a coiled rope in the corner as though it were a snake rather than a rope or else it may create such a play of shadows in the room that one falsely takes the moving shadows to be something moving about in the room when the room is actually empty of anything capable of moving. This situation where the wind blows on the candle giving rise to visual illusions is analogous to the situation that occurs when the intellectual faculty tries to penetrate into the nature of things without the mind's being first put into a state of concentration. If one merely assents to the doctrine of non-Self (anātman) without practicing concentration, the agitations of the unsteady mind will cause the light of the intellect to flicker wildly so that it is incapable of shedding light on the truth of this doctrine. However, when concentration of the mind is yoked to discernment, it brings about a condition analogous to that which happens when the candle is protected from the wind. Then its steady light really illuminates what is in the room so that one sees things as they really are. Concentration permits the candlelight of the intellect to illuminate with maximum intensity the absence of a self in compounded things. Just as the mere absence of wind does not, by itself, illuminate the room if no light source is present, it is likewise the case that a concentrated mind, by itself, cannot shed light on the absence of self in phenomena in the absence of an intellect.

Having explained how concentration serves as an essential adjunct to discernment, I will explain why discernment is necessary. First, discernment is necessary because the penetrating insight it generates is what actually destroys the individual's ignorance about the true nature of compounded things because it shows them as they really are, impermanent, productive of suffering, and devoid of a self. One is assuming here that this

42. Ibid., p. 89.

discernment has previously been yoked to concentration since otherwise it will not have sufficient penetrative force to really bring about liberation from ignorance. Second, the penetrating insight that discernment brings into the true nature of compounded things causes the mediator to not only lose his ignorance about their true nature but also his craving for them in the same way that waking from a dream automatically dampens the intensity of one's response to the dream-images so that they no longer captivate one's attention. In this way craving and ignorance are destroyed at their very roots and with them those defilements that produce karmic fruits.[43] With this final destruction of ignorance, craving, and bondage to karma, one realizes nirvana.

## Nirvana and the Doctrine of No-Self (*Anātman*)

I have described the three practices that, when performed together, enable an individual to reach nirvana and analyzed the rationales behind each of them. Yet one last question remains: What is nirvana? The *Saṃyutta-nikāya* contains a classic characterization: [nirvana is referred to in this passage as "the Uncompounded"] "And what, brethren, is the Uncompounded [asaṃkhata]? The destruction of lust, the destruction of hatred, the destruction of illusion,—that is called the Uncompounded."[44] It is important to realize that nirvana is not only a condition of complete freedom from every form of craving and every form of hatred and aversion, and freedom from ignorance but it is also a condition where these defilements have been utterly torn up by their roots never to rise again. Since the defilements of craving, aversion, and ignorance have been totally uprooted, it is, for this reason, also a condition of total liberation from bondage to karma and rebirth for neither of these two things can operate in the absence of those three defilements.

To say that nirvana is a condition of total and final freedom from saṃsāra, a total and final freedom from craving and aversion, and a total and final freedom from ignorance does not tell the entire story. There are two other essential characteristics of nirvana that are implied by these three freedoms. First, nirvana is a freedom from ignorance and illusion of a special sort. It is not a freedom from ignorance in the sense of omniscience but a freedom from that ignorance that causes the illusion that there is a

43. Buddhaghosa, *Path of Purification*, vol. 2, p. 819.
44. *Book of the Kindred Sayings*, vol. 4, p. 256.

self in compounded things. Nirvana is simply inconceivable apart from this insight that all things are void of a permanently abiding substrate or essence. Tson-kha-pa insisted upon this point repeatedly for he maintained that without the insight that there is no self it is impossible to realize nirvana. At one point he referred to the story of a yogin named Udraka who, though he achieved a very high state of samādhi, failed to realize nirvana because he had never freed himself from the delusion that there was a self. Tson-kha-pa then went on to remark that if one "discriminates the dharmas [those seemingly ultimate constituents of the phenomenal world] as selfless; if he, discriminating those, would cultivate, that is the cause of achieving the *nirvana*-fruit."[45] One can see, then, that nirvana was not only a total and final freedom from the three things mentioned above but it was also a total and final liberation from the notion that anything has a self.

The three freedoms also imply another essential characteristic of nirvana, its freedom from suffering.[46] Since the realization of nirvana frees one from bondage to the endless cycle of rebirths and dissolutions that serves as the root cause of suffering, it stands to reason that, being emancipation from samsāra, nirvana would bring with its realization a correlative liberation from that suffering that arises as an inevitable by-product of samsaric existence.

It is important to bear in mind that, because nirvana is uncompounded (*asaṃkhata*), one makes a serious mistake if one regards it as a condition that one has "caused" or "produced." Buddhaghosa made this clear when he argued against a critic who claimed that nirvana was an experience that was created when one followed the Buddhist path of moral conduct, meditation, and insight techniques. "That is not so," Buddhaghosa answered, for nirvana "is not arousable by the path; it is only reachable, not arousable, by the path; that is why it is uncreated. It is because it is uncreated that it is free from aging and death. It is because of the absence of its creation and its aging and death it is permanent."[47] Realizing nirvana rather than creating it bears analogy to that situation of a sailor who, by opening his eyes, suddenly notices that there is a mountain in the distance. It would certainly be absurd to say that the sailor's act of opening his eyes

45. Tson-kha-pa, *Calming the Mind*, p. 92.
46. For example, Buddhaghosa identified nirvana with the third of the Four Noble Truths. He wrote, "in the ultimate sense it is *nibbāna* that is called 'the noble truth of the cessation of suffering.'" Buddhaghosa, *Path of Purification*, vol. 2, p. 577.
47. Ibid., vol. 2, p. 580. See also Rahula, *What the Buddha Taught*, 2d ed., pp. 40–41.

created the mountain. All it did was make him realize it was there as it had been all along. In a like manner, it is absurd to claim that a Buddhist monk's mental disciplines and insight techniques create nirvana. These practices simply open up his eyes so he can see that it is there.

## Why Buddhist Nirvana Is Not Akin to Yogic Samādhi or Other Forms of Mystical Union and Ecstatic Absorption

The realization of nirvana does not terminate one's participation in the world. It is not something akin to those states of ecstatic absorption that maintain themselves only by cutting off all sensory inputs. Instead, one who has realized nirvana is so completely free of either craving or aversion toward the created things that he perceives that he no longer has to worry about being defiled by them. The following conversation between King Milinda and the sage Nagasena illustrates this point very well. The king asked Nagasena whether "one who has abandoned passion" (presumably, a reference to one who has attained nirvana) continues to have the same wish as an ordinary man that his food taste good rather than bad. Nagasena answered him that the only difference between the two was that whereas the ordinary man experiences both the taste of the food and the passion (desire or loathing) that arises from tasting it, the one who is free from passion tastes the food without conceiving a passion of either desire or dislike for it.[48] In short, one who has realized nirvana continues to participate in the world but does so without being buffeted by either craving or aversion for what he experiences.

One can now see more clearly why Stace was mistaken when he asserted that "nirvana is simply the final condition of a permanent mystical consciousness." First, it would be nonsensical for any Buddhist to equate nirvana with any sort of mystical experience because nirvana was by its very nature uncompounded and uncreated and, for that reason, beyond the flux of emergence and dissolution. Mystical experiences of every kind were, when viewed from the standpoint of Buddhist psychology and metaphysics, compounded things, that is, caused and produced and subject to birth, decay, dissolution and suffering—the very things every Buddhist tries to escape from. Second, equating nirvana with any sort of presumably

48. Warren, *Buddhism in Translations,* p. 421.

eternal mystical experience would be tantamount to committing the cardinal intellectual sin of Buddhism. One would be regarding that particular mystical experience as though it had some permanently abiding substrate or self. The *Buddhacarita* contains a story that shows that Buddhist writers have expressly repudiated this notion that anyone could hope to attain nirvana by trying to permanently abide in the most elevated state of mystical consciousness. The story relates that in one of his past lives the future Buddha once entertained the idea of studying under a sage named Udraka who was accomplished in samādhi. This wise man, "knowing the fault of both ideation and non-ideation, found beyond nothingness a state of neither ideation nor non-ideation." In other words, Udraka wanted to focus his samādhi upon the most subtle object conceivable in the hopes that the extreme subtlety of his meditation object and the samādhi that would result from concentrating upon it would gain his release from saṃsāra. The story goes on to make it clear that the future Buddha was not impressed because he realized that, despite the subtlety of Udraka's meditation object, his fixation on this particular mystical state and meditation object showed that he still adhered to the notion of a Self and that his escape from saṃsāra would therefore be of short duration.[49]

In all fairness to Stace and Heiler, it is easy to slip into this error of identifying nirvana with some sort of imageless mystical experience. Descriptions of individuals attaining nirvana are often juxtaposed to descriptions of them attaining elevated states of imageless and affect-free mystical consciousness immediately prior to their realization of nirvana. A classic example of this occurs in the *Mahāparinibbāna-Sutta* of the *Dīgha-Nīkāya* where the dying Buddha goes through a progression of trance-states, each more subtle than the one that had preceded it, just before he enters into nirvana. Given this intimate juxtaposition of the Buddha's entrance into nirvana and his immediately preceding attainment of that highest trance-state, the cessation of perception and sensation, it is easy to draw the conclusion that nirvana was coterminous with that last trance-state. One of the monks in attendance, Anuruddha, drew precisely this conclusion. When he had noticed that the Buddha had entered into the cessation of perception and sensation, he told Ananda, "The Blessed One has now entered *nirvana*." If one reads too quickly it is easy to overlook Ananda's significant reply to Anuruddha's observation. In a manner consistent with the Buddhist refusal to ontologize any trance-state or mental phenomenon,

---

49. Quoted in Tson-kha-pa, *Calming the Mind*, p. 442, n. 16.

Ananda replied to him, no, the Buddha had not yet entered nirvana. He had simply arrived at the cessation of sensation and perception, nothing more.[50] The *Laṅkāvatāra Sūtra* contains many passages that also might lead a hasty reader to the false conclusion that its author(s) regarded nirvana as though it were some sort of extremely subtle, imageless mystical experience. For example, in the following passage the Buddha tells the bodhisattva Mahāmati that

> nirvana is where it is recognized that there is nothing but what is seen of the Mind itself, where there is no attachment to external objects existent or non-existent . . . where . . . all the Samadhis beginning with the Māyopama [Māyā-like] are realized, and the Citta, Manas, and Manovijñāna are put away.[51]

One might be tempted to jump to the conclusion that nirvana is that condition that arises when *citta* (mind in its pure state), *manas* (the thinking and willing faculty), and *manovijñāna* (the faculty of distinguishing ideas) are "put away," that is, when mentation entirely ceases. However, in this very same lecture the Buddha criticized those who come to this conclusion. He stated those who "conceive Nirvana to be found where a system of mentation no more operates" were guilty of error.[52] Those who might have drawn the conclusion that nirvana was a supreme imageless samādhi state also had to reckon with the Buddha's criticism (in that same passage) of those mistaken philosophers who "alarmed by the notion of form, seek their happiness in formlessness."[53] The abundant remarks of this sort one finds in the text clearly show that, despite language that is often suggestive of an identity between nirvana and imageless mystical experience, the protagonists in the *Laṅkāvatāra Sūtra,* as in almost every other Buddhist treatise, make every effort to avoid ontologizing nirvana as a particular mental state.

The foregoing analysis also shows that it is a serious error to regard nirvana as an experience of oneness or mystical union. While one cannot deny that Buddhists frequently cultivated various types of samādhi as a means of energizing their insight into the true nature of all phenomena as devoid of a self, impermanent, and productive of suffering, those states of

50. Warren, *Buddhism in Translations,* p. 109.
51. *The Laṅkāvatāra Sūtra,* trans. Daisetz Teitaro Suzuki (London: Routledge & Kegan Paul, 1968), pp. 160, 55, 86, 190–93.
52. *Laṅkāvatāra Sūtra,* p. 158.
53. Ibid.

samādhi were mere instruments that helped them to reach their final goal. One must never assume that because the instrument to realize nirvana was a mystical experience that, for that reason, nirvana itself was necessarily a mystical state. In any case, no knowledgeable Buddhist teacher would ever encourage his students to regard any type of mystical union or samādhi experience as the final goal of his practice for, if he did, this would be tantamount to craving a particular kind of mental state that one had mistakenly endowed with an eternal self. This act of ontologizing a particular mystical state would be one more variant of Udraka's mistake.

## Why Nirvana Is Not Just a Buddhist Interpretation of a Raw Experience That Is Otherwise Identical in Content to Yogic Isolation and Spiritual Marriage

The previous discussions and descriptions of nirvana, the means to realize it, and the rationales behind those techniques for its realization also expose the fallacy of Stace's claim that nirvana is simply a Buddhist "interpretation" of a raw experience that possesses the very same content as a Christian mystic's experience of divine union or a yogin's experience of isolation (*kaivalyam*). Everything presented about nirvana shows the penetrating insight that all phenomena lack a self, they are impermanent, and productive of suffering is not just an interpretation that the Buddhist places on an experience after it has happened and he has begun to reflect on it. Instead, that penetrating insight must actually constitute the existential ground of each individual's unique "experience" of realizing nirvana before any Buddhist will recognize it as such.[54] In short, apart from the concomitant insight that all things are devoid of a self, it makes no sense to speak about any experience as a realization of nirvana. For this reason, it is absurd to imagine that the existential content of a yogin's experience of isolation could be identical to that of a Buddhist monk's experience of nirvana. After all, the nirvana experience must incorporate the rejection of any at-

---

54. I place the word "experience" in quotation marks when referring to nirvana because no Buddhist would wish to ontologize any particular type of mental state as nirvana. Moreover, since nirvana is an insight into those three truths that comes about in a unique way for each particular individual, it is a mistake to speak of this insight-state as though it were a state of consciousness that had an identical content for everyone. One must not forget that each individual's particular itinerary for arriving at this insight into selflessness, impermanence, and suffering exerts a distinctive effect upon the existential content of his own particular experience of nirvana.

tachment to or craving for a self so how could it possibly be the same type of experience as kaivalyam since the latter was a phenomenon that had as its essential characteristic the liberation of *puruṣa* (the eternally existent Self or soul) from all entanglement with prakṛti? One rejected the Self while the other embraced it. How could the two insights be cognitively or existentially equivalent? From the Buddhist's perspective, the yogin's experience of isolation was a perfect example of a cardinal blunder, imagining that there was a Self behind the flux of saṃsāra and that attachment to it could release one from bondage to the cycle of rebirths.

One makes an even graver mistake if one postulates an existential equivalence between nirvana and Teresa's experience of Spiritual Marriage. Teresa's actual experience was imbued with intense feelings of love for an eternally existing God, feelings that derived from her religious obligation to love God and His commandments more than her own self. Those feelings of love had no place in the Buddhist nirvana because: (1) the Buddha had taught that there was no such thing as an eternally existent Self or God—to affirm such a thing was the cardinal mistake that roots one in saṃsāra—and (2) craving and desiring such an illusory and impermanent Self or God was incompatible with that complete absence of craving that was an essential hallmark of nirvana.

# Conclusion

What principal facts has this study established about the nature of mysticism?

It has demonstrated that almost every aspect of the phenomenon is historically and culturally conditioned. I have shown that the processes of historical and cultural conditioning penetrate even into the very marrow of the mystical experience itself determining which particular things the mystic perceives, which particular emotions or moods he feels, and which particular things he comes to know (see Chapter 4). I have also shown that the mystic's cultural and religiohistorical milieu determines the specific character of virtually every aspect of his responses in thought, deed, and intention to that experience (see Chapter 21). I have demonstrated in Chapters 20 and 30 that context determines how the mystic interprets his experiences, how he behaves in response to them, the particular kinds of desires that those experiences produce in him, and the criteria he employs to distinguish beneficial or religiously significant experiences from those that are either irrelevant or religiously dangerous. In Chapter 26 I have shown that context determines, to a large extent, the particular times of the onset and cessation of those mystical states of consciousness as well as their cycles of intensification and diminution. Furthermore, I have demonstrated in Chapter 27 that the mystic's specific choice of recollective techniques is likewise historically and culturally conditioned.

Although I have insisted on the preeminence of cultural conditioning in shaping the very marrow of the mystical state of consciousness itself, that is, its existential and perceptual content, I do not think that the evidence warrants the claim that *all* types of mystical experience are culturally conditioned. I pointed out in Chapters 13 and 15 that there are a few types of clairvoyant, telepathic, and precognitive states of consciousness that mystics and mediums have occasionally reported that actually do appear to bypass the processes of cultural conditioning. For that reason, I have suggested that the more radical formulations of the contextualist thesis need qualification.[1]

---

1. The articles of Robert Gimello and Steven Katz incorporated in the latter's collections

I have also demonstrated in Chapter 15 that both psychologism and positivism offer inadequate models for explaining the nature of the mystical state of awareness and the manifold phenomena that often accompany it. The partisans of psychologism and positivism would argue that mystical experiences and their unusual or even supernormal accompaniments are nothing but hallucinations and illusions generated from within the psyche of the mystic. I argued that this thesis is weak because it assumes that all mystical experiences and their psychomental accompaniments are generated intra-psychically and it assumes that just because a mystical state of consciousness or one of its preternatural accompaniments originates from within the psyche of the mystic it is, by that fact, a mere subjective illusion. I have argued that pointing to the intra-psychic or hallucinatory origin of a phenomenon of consciousness is *not* sufficient grounds for dismissing it as purely subjective, "unreal," or illusory. For one thing, I have shown in Chapters 9 and 12 that the recollectively "empowered" imagination of the mystic can, at times, function noetically as an organ of extra-physical perception and knowledge. In addition, I have shown in Chapter 10 that the hallucinatory processes of the imagination even appear to play a role in guaranteeing the accuracy of visual perception. Consequently, the partisans of psychologism and positivism make a mistake when they assume that the imagination does nothing but hinder accurate perception of reality.

In Chapter 12, I showed that there are special circumstances when the imagination can actually do the opposite and either (1) foster accurate visual perception or (2) enable the mystic to adapt himself better to his or her physical environment as appears to be the case in those instances of the Tibetan practice of *tumo* that have come to the attention of scholars. Tumo employs the recollectively concentrated imagination focused on an image of interior fire to generate a peculiar type of heat that actually appears to keep naked Tibetan ascetics warm in the depths of the bitter winter months. In short, I have indicated that the boundaries between that which is "unreal," imaginary, and purely subjective and that which has an objective existence separate from the perceiving subject is more fluid and uncertain than the adherents of positivism and psychologism realize.[2]

The central importance given to the phenomenon of *enthymesis* or the

---

of essays, *Mysticism and Philosophical Analysis* and *Mysticism and Religious Traditions* exemplify the more radical formulations of the contextualist thesis.

2. David-Neel's creation of a collectively perceived hallucination or thought-form (*tulpa*) was an excellent example of this fluid boundary between objective reality and the realm of purely private fantasy and illusion.

"empowerment" of the mind, will, and imagination in this study is certainly unusual but it is an emphasis that is amply justified. As I noted in Chapters 9 and 12, detailed attention to it has provided evidence that challenges some of the commonplace notions derived from positivism and psychologism that assert or imply that mystical experiences are nothing but illusions. Focus on the phenomenon of empowerment also brought another benefit in its wake—it allowed me to establish one of the reasons *why* mystical experiences exhibit that essential contextuality to which I have repeatedly referred.[3] I suggested in Chapter 15 that the intrinsic contextuality of many mystical experiences derives from a concurrent empowerment of the mystic's mind, will, and imagination that transpires once he or she enters into that extraordinary modality of consciousness which supervenes with the onset of recollectedness. Both the empowerment of thought, will, and imagination and the mystical state of consciousness itself share a common genesis in the recollective act. This point in common would suggest the possibility that the onset of a mystical state of consciousness might simultaneously trigger those psychological processes that bring about mental, volitional, and imaginational empowerment. When this happens—and I have suggested that this is more common than people think—the resulting mystical state of consciousness cannot help but be an objectification of those conscious and unconscious thoughts, desires, and expectations that the mystic received from his religious and cultural environment. Under such conditions, how can the resulting experience be anything but a context-dependent objectification of the mystic's religious beliefs? Where empowerment and the mystical state of consciousness are simultaneously activated, is it any wonder that the resulting mystical experiences so frequently tend to verify empirically that description of reality that is either explicit or implicit in the mythology that founds the mystic's particular religious and cultural tradition?

There is a third reason why I devoted so much attention to the study of empowerment and its role in the mystical life—it is an essential element in some mystics' writings. Thus I showed in Chapter 14 that the soteriological drama in *The Tibetan Book of the Dead* simply cannot be understood without reference to it and that it is also a crucial foundation of the theological and metaphysical systems that Suhrawardī of Aleppo, Ibn al-'Arabī, and Swedenborg created.

3. In other words, not only has this study established that mystical experiences exhibit a fundamental contextuality but it has also gone one step further and proffered one reason why they display this essential dependence on context.

The fourth reason I devoted so much attention to the phenomenon of "empowerment" was that it provided an unusual perspective from which to view the creativity of mystics. One might be tempted to argue that because the existential and perceptual content of a mystic's experience is so significantly shaped by influences from his or her cultural environment and historical situation, it is therefore impossible for the mystic to discover anything really new. As Gershom Scholem wrote, "the mystic's experience tends to confirm the religious authority under which he lives; its theology and symbols are *projected* into his mystical experience." It would seem, then, that mystical experience is always an inherently conservative cultural force since it is simply a mental "projection" of material that the mystic has received from his or her religious tradition. More careful attention to the phenomenon of empowerment shows that such a conclusion is premature. Despite the aforementioned remarks, Scholem realized that mystics were not always religious conservatives. "[The mystic] transforms the content of the tradition in which he lives. He contributes not only to the conservation of the tradition, but also to its development."[4] I drew the reader's attention to the ways that mystical experiences transcended the process which psychoanalysts call "projection." First, I showed in Chapters 9 and 12 that while it is true that the empowered imagination of a mystic certainly utilizes the psychological process of projection in creating an existential and perceptual "landscape" of his or her objectified thoughts, desires, and imaginings, these projected thoughts, desires, and creations of the imagination undergo a striking metamorphosis that transforms them into something qualitatively different from their "ordinary" counterparts. Ordinary wishes, imaginings, and thoughts cannot function as an extraphysical organ of clairvoyant perception and knowledge but their empowered counterparts sometimes can function in that manner. It is therefore clear that because the empowered imagination can sometimes be the vehicle of clairvoyant perceptions, it is simultaneously, by virtue of that same characteristic, a source of novel revelations—it does more than simply exteriorize the contents of the mystic's unconscious and then endow those "projections" with a spurious appearance of novelty. The empowered imagination enkindles religious creativity because it enables the mystic to encounter something that really is new; for example, those clairvoyant perceptions mentioned above. I also demonstrated in Chapter 15 that what was true of the empowered imagination was also true of the

4. Gershom Scholem, *On the Kabbalah and Its Symbolism* (New York: Schocken Books, 1965), p. 9 (emphasis mine).

emotions and feelings during certain forms of mystical awareness. Normally, feelings of excitement and eager anticipation do nothing to enhance our knowledge of the world—they simply motivate us to act. Nevertheless, in Chapter 13 I showed that in certain types of mystical consciousness such as telepathic "alertness," feelings of eager excitement undergo a peculiar metamorphosis that transforms them into extraphysical "organs" of perception and knowledge.

This study showed that mystical experiences are not only capable of transmuting both the imagination and the feelings into supraphysical organs of knowledge and revelation but it also demonstrated that the phenomenon of light underwent a similar transmutation. I drew the reader's attention to the peculiar ways that the various forms of preternatural luminosity that appear during mystical states of consciousness transcend the ordinary properties and potentialities of light (Chapters 3, 12, and 13).

This study has also drawn attention to the vital importance of recollective processes in several domains of the mystic's life and experience. Most important, I showed in Chapter 5 that almost every mystical state of awareness originates as the result of some sort of recollective act. I showed that if an individual continues to maintain his recollectively focused attention and continues to control the form and direction of those thoughts and phantasms that keep coming into his mind after his initial breakthrough to the mystical state of awareness, this prolongation of the recollective practice frequently brings about radical changes in the quality of his mystical experiences (Chapters 5, 9, and 11). This prolongation of recollectedness can bring about mystical states of consciousness where the subject experiences the empowerment of his mind. In addition, this prolongation of recollectedness into the mystical state of consciousness itself also sets the stage for the appearance of other types of paranormal phenomena (experiences of telepathy, clairvoyance, and precognition) that lack any readily discernible connection to the empowerment of the imagination (Chapter 13).

This study showed that, under conditions of recollective concentration of attention while one is entering into the hypnagogic state between waking and sleeping, dreams undergo a dramatic metamorphosis—they become much more vivid and the dream becomes empowered (Chapter 9). Conversely, I noted in Chapter 10 that once the initial practice of recollection has triggered a mystical state of consciousness, an out-of-body experience, or an empowered dream, any failure to continue focusing the attention in that state will usually result in a state of consciousness that degenerates into something indistinguishable from an ordinary dream (Chapter 15).

There was yet another way that this study pointed to the preeminence of recollection within the mystical life—many of the things that mystics do or require—many of their ascetic disciplines, many of their methods of praying, their withdrawals into solitude—are expressly designed either to facilitate the onset of recollectedness or to preserve and deepen it once it has initially been achieved (Chapter 5). Clearly, if one wishes to comprehend how mystics interact with the world, an understanding of how recollection plays a role in their lives is absolutely essential.

Finally, I have suggested that the mystic's ability to enter into a condition of recollectedness sharply differentiates his altered states of consciousness from those that prevail in the various types of hallucinatory schizophrenia (Chapter 6). In contrast to the mystic, the schizophrenic is almost completely bereft of the power to recollect himself.

This study has also broken new ground by placing mystical experiences within a wider perspective of options that human beings have for controlling—or failing to control—the more benign hallucinatory, fantasy-fabricating mechanisms of the mind that operate during dreaming and imagining (Chapters 10 and 15). As I noted in Chapters 10–12, mystics employing what I have called the "active approach" are sometimes capable of transmuting such benign hallucinatory phenomena as dreams and the imagination into organs of veridical or clairvoyant perception. Such a transmutation of hallucinatory processes presupposes two things. It assumes that the subject (the mystic) has entered into a condition of recollectedness and the subject—not some other person or outside agency—in full awareness manipulates the recollectively empowered dream or imagination. I showed that it is also possible for some agent other than the subject to seize control of his or her recollectively empowered imagination. This is precisely what happens when a hypnotist induces a trance and then takes control of the subject's recollectively empowered mind by implanting a suggestion. What is almost never recognized is that there is a third option: it is possible for the individual's own culture to function in much the same way as the hypnotist. In those instances, the individual's culture, through the enculturation process, implants suggestions in the individual's empowered imagination with the result that those culturally implanted suggestions become objectified in the same way that a hypnotist's suggestions become objectified or a mystic's self-consciously manipulated thoughts and desires become objectified under conditions of empowerment. How the culture empowers the individual's imagination in such cases remains a mystery but the fact remains that culturally implanted suggestions appear to be just as capable of embodiment or objectification as those of the hypnotist or recollected mystic. On the basis of such data, I suggested that the ability to induce what I have called enthymesis or empowerment is not the exclusive domain of mystics and mediums—or hypnotists. The culture or group also appears to be capable, on occasion, of tacitly triggering the forces that empower the minds and the imaginations of its members.

This study has directed attention to some hitherto overlooked but significant differences that distinguish the kinds of mysticism that predominate in preliterate tribal societies from those forms of it which predominate in the so-called universal religions, that is, Islam, Christianity, and Buddhism. I noted that, in contrast to their preliterate tribal counterparts, some mystics in the universal religions tend toward an experiential acosmism that, I suggested, reflected their exposure to that panoply of existential concerns that only begins to develop after humankind starts to participate in the economic, political, and cultural life of the oecumene. I observed a persistent, though by no means invariable, tendency among mystics in the universal religions to devalue what I called "visionary multiplicity," that is, visions in which the mystic perceives forms and figures (Chapter 18). Preliterate tribal mystics, on the other hand, never intimated that visions with forms or figures in them were in any way inferior to those visions or cognitive states where such imagery was absent. So far as I know, states of consciousness akin to either Teresa's formless intellectual visions, the formless (*asamprajñāta*) states of samādhi referred to in various Yoga texts, or the Buddhist nirvana described as devoid of all form or shape, size or duration, do not seem to appear in the tribal mystics' accounts of their visions.[5] I suggested that mystics in tribal religious traditions do not seek "formless" mystical states of consciousness for at least two reasons. First, in a religious tradition such as that of the Lakota where visions are accorded religious significance only if they convey ritual instructions from spirit-beings, there is no reason to cultivate a visionary state of consciousness where forms and images are altogether absent. After all, how could such a formless vision convey the ritual information of vital religious importance in which the spirits show the Lakota mystic how to act in a

5. In his famous conversations with the Buddhist sage Nagasena, King Milinda acknowledged that with respect to nirvana "one cannot point to its form or shape, its duration or size, either by simile or explanation, by reason or by argument." Quoted from Edward Conze, trans., *Buddhist Scriptures* (London: Penguin Books, 1959), p. 156.

sacred manner by imitating what they are doing in the vision? How would the Lakota mystic know which sacred objects to use if he did not see the spirit exemplars using them in his vision? Second, preliterate tribal religions are cosmic religions, that is, they assume that the sacred can become manifest through objects, beings, events, and phenomena of the natural world. That tendency toward acosmism or world rejection, that tendency to claim that the sacred—be it Yahweh, Allah, or nirvana—utterly transcends the realm of nature and that it cannot be represented by any image or simile derived from nature, has not yet made its way into the religious imagination of preliterate tribal humanity.

I also noted that mystics in tribal religious traditions tended to compartmentalize spiritual power. They referred to power as a kind of extra-psychic, ritually catalyzed potency that was divided up among many different kinds of spiritual beings or objects, each of which had a limited, specific kind of potency that it could bestow upon the mystic, medicine-man or shaman provided the latter followed the proper ritual instructions for its release. However, those mystics in the universal religions who show any interest in cultivating or manipulating spiritual power—and many do not—tend to replace the limited, spirit-specific tribal notion of power with one that depicts it as an intrapsychic, infinitely deformable type of potency much akin to the "energy" of modern physics. Furthermore, this infinitely deformable potency described by mystics of the world religions tends to require only a minimal amount of ritual catalysis, if any, in order to become manifest (Chapter 19).

This study shows that scholars of mysticism make a serious mistake when they continue to ignore the autobiographies of nineteenth- and twentieth-century clairvoyants, mediums, and out-of-body travelers as significant sources of information about the nature of mysticism. The writings of Eileen Garrett, Robert Monroe, Gerda Walther, Sylvan Muldoon, D. D. Hume, Oliver Fox, and Matthew Manning do not deserve the exile to which they have been condemned by years of scholarly neglect. They contain some of the most detailed descriptions that link the practice of recollection to the genesis of various paranormal modes of perception and action. They provide us with some of the best examples that display the connection between recollective concentration and the onset of enthymesis and they furnish us with some of the most subtle descriptions of photisms that are available. Moreover, the writings of these individuals also contain important data that challenge the validity of psychologism as an adequate model for the study of mysticism.

This scholarly neglect of the autobiographies of clairvoyants and mediums goes hand in hand with a widespread tendency to devalue mystical states of consciousness in which powerful emotions, visions, and/or locutions play a prominent part. Many scholars assume that genuine mysticism is the mysticism of the via negativa, a mysticism that is devoid of forms and images. Thus Stace can assert that "visions and voices are not mystical phenomena."[6] Why does he expel visions and voices from the domain of the mystical? He does so because he claims that "*the most important* type of mystical experience is nonsensuous, whereas visions and voices have the character of sensuous imagery."[7] Thirty years later Robert Forman will continue to restrict the term "mysticism" to those types of experiences "not described with sensory language."[8]

This restriction of the term "mysticism" to the nonsensuous forms of transcendental consciousness seems to be motivated by a concern that if one admits that genuine mystical states might contain forms and images in them, then mystical experience becomes nothing more than an illusion and a delusion since it is a phenomenon tainted by the presence of visual hallucinations that intrude into the mystic's field of awareness. When one considers the serious misunderstandings that arose in many nineteenth- and early twentieth-century studies of mysticism because earlier scholars too glibly equated mysticism and mental pathology, the attempts of recent scholars to avoid those damaging misunderstandings are certainly comprehensible. However, I have shown that there is no need for scholars to fear the hallucinatory dimension of mystical experience. Instead of quarantining mysticism from modes of consciousness that contain an admixture of visions, locutions, and powerful emotional states, it is more fruitful for scholars to direct their attention to the fascinating ways that recollective concentration transforms and transfigures hallucinatory phantasms, dream images, emotions, and the creations of the imagination into phenomena that become qualitatively different from the mere illusions that they were before the recollective process began. I submit that if we wish to go to the heart of mysticism without sacrificing any sensitivity to its rich particularity, we will do so most easily by studying the recollective transformation of these "illusory" creations of the mind and imagination.

6. Stace, *Mysticism and Philosophy*, p. 47.

7. Ibid., p. 49 (emphasis mine).

8. See Forman's introductory essay, "Mysticism, Constructivism, and Forgetting," in his *Problem of Pure Consciousness*, p. 7.

# Selected Bibliography

Almond, Philip. *Mystical Experience and Religious Doctrine*. New York: Mouton Publishers, 1982.

Anonymous. *The Boy Who Saw True*. London: Neville Spearman, 1974.

Aquinas, Saint Thomas. *The Summa Theologica*, 22 vols. London: Burns & Oates, 1935.

Arberry, A. J. *Sufism: An Account of the Mystics of Islam*. London: George Allen & Unwin, 1950.

Arbman, Ernst. *Ecstasy or Religious Trance: In the Experiences of the Ecstatics and from the Psychological Point of View*, 3 vols. Scandinavian University Books. Stockholm: Svenska Bokforlaget, 1963–70.

Auclair, Marcelle. *Saint Teresa of Avila*. New York: Pantheon Books, 1953.

Augustine of Hippo, Saint. *The City of God*, abridged ed., trans. Gerald G. Walsh, S. J., et al. Garden City, N.Y.: Image Books, 1958.

———. *The Confessions of St. Augustine*, trans. John K. Ryan. Garden City, N.Y.: Image Books, 1960.

*Autobiography of a Schizophrenic Girl*, with analytic interpretation by Marguerite Sechehaye. New York: New American Library, 1970.

Avalon, Arthur (pseud. for Sir John Woodroffe). *The Serpent Power, being the Sat-Cakra-Nirūpaṇa and Pāḍukā-Pañcaka*. New York: Dover Publications, 1974.

Beer, Frances. *Women and Mystical Experience in the Middle Ages*. Woodbridge, U.K.: Boydell Press, 1992.

Bellah, Robert. *Beyond Belief: Essays on Religion in a Post-Traditionalist World*. Berkeley and Los Angeles: University of California Press, 1970.

*A Benedictine of Stanbrook, Medieval Mystical Tradition and St. John of the Cross*. London: Burns & Oates, 1954.

Bergson, Henri. *Two Sources of Morality and Religion*. New York: Henry Holt & Co., 1935.

Bernard of Clairvaux, Saint. *On the Song of Songs II*, trans. Kilian Walsh, O.C.S.O. Cistercian Fathers Series, no. 7. Kalamazoo, Mich.: Cistercian Publications, 1976.

———. *On the Song of Songs IV*, trans. Irene Edmonds, introduction by Jean Leclerq. Cistercian Fathers Series, no. 40. Kalamazoo, Mich.: Cistercian Publications, 1980.

Berndt, R. M. "Wuradjeri Magic and 'Clever Men.'" *Oceania* 17, no. 4 (June 1947).

*The Bhagavadgītā: A New Translation*, trans. Kees W. Bolle. Berkeley and Los Angeles: University of California Press, 1979.

Bilinkoff, Jodi. *The Avila of St. Teresa: Religious Reform in a Sixteenth-Century City.* Ithaca: Cornell University Press, 1989.

Blofield, John. *The Tantric Mysticism of Tibet.* New York: Dutton, 1970.

Boas, Franz. *The Eskimo of Baffin Land and Hudson Bay,* from the notes collected by George Comor, James S. Mutch, and E. J. Peck. *Bulletin of the American Museum of Natural History,* vol. 15, pts. 1–2. New York: Published by Order of the Trustees, 1901–7.

Boehme, Jacob. *Dialogues on the Supersensual Life.* London: Methuen, 1901.

Bolle, Kees W. *The Freedom of Man in Myth.* Nashville: Vanderbilt Unversity Press, 1968.

Bonaventure, Saint. *Works of Bonaventure,* trans. Jose de Vinck. Paterson, N.J.: St. Anthony Guild Press, 1960.

*The Book of the Kindred Sayings (Samyutta-Nikāya) or Grouped Sayings,* trans. F. L. Woodward. Pali Text Society Translation Series, no. 14. London: Published for the Pali Text Society by the Oxford University Press, n.d..

Brown, Joseph Epes. *The Sacred Pipe: Black Elk's Account of the Seven Rites of the Oglala Sioux.* Baltimore: Penguin Books, 1971.

Brown, Peter. *Augustine of Hippo.* Berkeley and Los Angeles: University of California Press, 1969.

Buber, Martin. *Ecstatic Confessions.* San Francisco: Harper & Row, 1985.

Bucke, Richard Maurice. *Cosmic Consciousness: A Study in the Evolution of the Human Mind.* New York: E. P. Dutton, 1969.

Buddhaghosa, Bhadāntacariya. *The Path of Purification (Visuddhimagga),* 2 vols., trans. Bhikkhu Nyāṇamoli. Berkeley: Shambala, 1976.

———. *The Path of Purity,* 3 vols., trans. Pe Maung Tin. Pali Text Society Translation Series, nos. 11, 17, and 23. London: Pali Text Society, 1923–31.

Butler, Dom Cuthbert. *Western Mysticism.* New York: Harper & Row, 1966.

Capra, Fritjof. *The Tao of Physics.* New York: Bantam Books, 1981.

Cassian, John. "The Conferences of Cassian." In Owen Chadwick, *Western Asceticism.* London: SCM Press, 1958.

Catherine of Siena, Saint. *The Dialogue,* trans. Suzanne Noffke, O.P. Classics of Western Spirituality Series. New York: Paulist Press, 1980.

Cayce, Edgar. *Auras.* Virginia Beach, Va.: A.R.E. Press, 1973.

Chittick, William C. *The Sufi Path of Knowledge: Ibn al-'Arabī's Metaphysics of Imagination.* Albany: SUNY Press, 1989.

Clissold, Stephen. *St. Teresa of Avila.* New York: Seabury Press, 1982.

*The Collection of the Middle Length Sayings (Majjhima-Nikāya),* trans. I. B. Horner. Pali Text Society Translation Series, no. 31. London: Published for the Pali Text Society by Luzac and Company, 1959.

Conze, Edward, trans. *Buddhist Scriptures.* Baltimore: Penguin Books, 1960.

Corbin, Henry. *Creative Imagination in the Sufism of Ibn 'Arabī.* Princeton: Princeton University Press, 1969.

———. *Spiritual Body and Celestial Earth: From Mazdean Iran to Shi'ite Iran,* trans. Nancy Pearson. Princeton: Princeton University Press, 1977.

Crookall, Robert. *The Study and Practice of Astral Projection.* Secaucus, N.J.: University Books, 1966.

Dasgupta, Surendranath. *A History of Indian Philosophy,* 5 vols. Delhi: Motilal Banarsidass, 1975.

David-Neel, Alexandra. *Magic and Mystery in Tibet.* Baltimore: Penguin Books, 1971.

Delacroix, Henri. *Études d'histoire et de psychologie du mysticisme: les grandes mystiques Chrétiens.* Paris: Felix Alcan, 1908.

DeMallie, Raymond J., ed. *The Sixth Grandfather: Black Elk's Teachings Given to John Neihardt.* Lincoln: University of Nebraska Press, 1984.

Densmore, Frances. *Teton Sioux Music.* New York: Da Capo Press, 1972.

*The Dhammapada,* trans. Irving Babbitt. New York: Oxford University Press, 1936.

Diadochus of Photike. "On Spiritual Knowledge and Discrimination." In *The Philokalia,* trans. G. E. H. Palmer et al. London: Faber & Faber, 1979.

———. "Vision de Saint Diadoque, Evêque de Photice en Epire." In *Oeuvres Spirituelles,* trans. Edouard des Places, S.J. Christian Sources. Paris: Les Editions du Cerf, 1955.

Dicken, E. W. Trueman. *The Crucible of Love.* New York: Sheed & Ward, 1963.

Dickens, A. G. *The Counter Reformation.* London: Thames & Hudson, 1969.

*Dictionnaire de spiritualité,* s.v. "Carmes," by Titus Brandsma, O. Carm.

Dionysius the Areopagite. *The Divine Names and The Mystical Theology,* trans. C. E. Rolt. London: S.P.C.K., 1975.

Dröscher, Vitus. *The Magic of the Senses: New Discoveries in Animal Perception,* trans. Ursula Lehrburger and Oliver Coburn. London: Allen, 1969.

Dugan, Kathleen. "The Vision Quest of the Plains Indians: Its Spiritual Significance." Ph.D. diss., New York, Fordham University, 1977.

Dunne, J. W. *An Experiment with Time.* London: Faber & Faber, 1973.

Eastman, Charles A. *From the Deep Woods to Civilization.* Boston: Little, Brown & Company, 1926.

Edmunds, Simeon. *Hypnosis and Psychic Phenomena.* North Hollywood, Calif.: Wilshire Book Company, 1972.

Eliade, Mircea. *From Primitives to Zen: A Thematic Sourcebook of the History of Religions.* New York: Harper & Row, 1977.

———. *A History of Religious Ideas,* 3 vols. Chicago: University of Chicago Press, 1978–84.

———. *Myths, Dreams, and Mysteries: The Encounter between Contemporary Faiths and Archaic Realities.* New York: Harper and Row, 1960.

———. *Occultism, Witchcraft and Cultural Fashions: Essays in Comparative Religions.* Chicago: University of Chicago Press, 1976.

———. *The Two and the One.* New York: Harper & Row, 1965.

———. *Yoga: Immortality and Freedom.* Princeton: Princeton University Press, 1969.

Elkin, A. P. *Aboriginal Men of High Degree.* Sydney: Australian Publishing, 1945.

———. *Aboriginal Men of High Degree,* 2d ed. New York: St. Martin's Press, 1978.

Ellenberger, Henri. *The Discovery of the Unconscious: The History and Evolution of Dynamic Psychiatry.* New York: Basic Books, 1970.

Fedotov, G. P., ed. *A Treasury of Russian Spirituality.* New York: Sheed & Ward, 1948.

Forman, Robert K. C., ed. *The Problem of Pure Consciousness.* New York: Oxford University Press, 1990.

Fox, Oliver. *Astral Projection.* Secaucus, N.J.: Citadel Press, 1979.

Freud, Sigmund. *The Interpretation of Dreams.* New York: Basic Books, 1960.

Garrett, Eileen. *Adventures in the Supernormal.* New York: Creative Age Press, 1949.

———. *Telepathy: In Search of a Lost Faculty.* New York: Creative Age Press, 1945.

al-Ghazzālī, Abū-Hāmid Muḥammad. *Mishkat al-Anwar,* trans. W. H. T. Gairdner. Lahore, Pakistan: Sh. Muhammad Ashraf, 1952.

Gilson, Etienne. *The Mystical Theology of Saint Bernard.* New York: Sheed & Ward, 1955.

Gopi Krishna. *Kundalini: The Evolutionary Energy in Man.* Berkeley: Shambala, 1971.

Green, Celia. *Out-of-the-Body Experiences.* Oxford: Institute of Psychophysical Research, 1968.

Gregory of Nyssa. *From Glory to Glory: Texts from Gregory of Nyssa's Mystical Writings,* trans. Herbert Musurillo. Crestwood, N.Y.: St. Vladimir's Seminary Press, 1979.

Gregory the Great. *Dialogues, Book II: Saint Benedict,* trans. Myra L. Uhlfelder. The Library of Liberal Arts. Indianapolis: Bobbs-Merrill Company, 1967.

Happold, F. C. *Mysticism: A Study and an Anthology.* Baltimore: Penguin, 1973.

Hassrick, Royal B. *The Sioux.* Norman: University of Oklahoma Press, 1964.

Heiler, Friedrich. *Die Bedeutung der Mystik für die Weltreligionen.* Munich: Ernst Reinhardt, 1919.

———. *Prayer: A Study in the History and Psychology of Religions.* New York: Oxford University Press, 1932.

Henfelder, Emmanuel, O.S.B. *The Way of God According to The Rule of St. Benedict.* Cistercian Studies Series, no. 49. Kalamazoo, Mich.: Cistercian Publications, 1983.

*Hermetica.* 4 vols., trans. Walter Scott. Oxford: Clarendon Press, 1924.

Hildegard of Bingen. *Hildegard of Bingen's Book of Divine Works,* ed. Matthew Fox. Santa Fe, N.M.: Bear & Co., 1987.

Hilton, Walter. *The Stairway of Perfection,* trans. M. L. del Mastro. Garden City, N.Y.: Image Books, 1979.

Holler, Clyde. "Black Elk's Relationship to Christianity." *American Indian Quarterly* 8 (winter 1984): 37–49.

———. "Lakota Religion and Tragedy: The Theology of *Black Elk Speaks.*" *Journal of the American Academy of Religion* 52, no. 1 (March 1984): 19–45.

Home, D. D. *Incidents in My Life.* Secaucus, N.J.: University Books, 1972 (1862).

Hügel, Friedrich von. *The Mystical Element of Religion as Studied in Saint Catherine of Genoa and Her Friends,* 2 vols. London: J. M. Dent & Sons, 1961.

al-Hujwīrī, 'Ali B. 'Uthmān al-Jullābī. *The Kashf al-Maḥjūb,* trans. Reynold A. Nicholson. London: Luzac & Company, 1976.

Hunt, Noreen. *Cluniac Monasticism in the Middle Ages.* Hamden, Conn.: Archon Books, 1971.

Iamblichos of Chalcis. *Theurgia, or the Egyptian Mysteries,* trans. Alexander Wilder. London: William Rider & Son, 1911.

Ibn al-'Arabī, Muhyiddin. *The Bezels of Wisdom.* New York: Paulist Press, 1980.

———. *Journey to the Lord of Power: A Sufi Manual of Retreat,* with notes from a commentary by 'Abdul-Karim Jili and an introduction by Sheikh Muzaffer Ozakh al-Jerrahi. New York: Inner Traditions International, 1981.

Ibn 'Ata' Illah and Kwaja Abdullah Ansari. *The Book of Wisdom/Intimate Conversations,* introduction, translation, and notes of *The Book of Wisdom* by Victor Danner, and of *Intimate Conversations* by Wheeler M. Thackston. Classics of Western Spirituality Series. New York: Paulist Press, 1978.

Idel, Moshe. *Kabbalah: New Perspectives.* New Haven: Yale University Press, 1988.

———, ed. *Mystical Union and Monotheistic Faith: An Ecumenical Dialogue.* New York: Macmillan, 1989.

Inge, William Ralph. *Christian Mysticism.* New York: Charles Scribner's Sons, 1899.

James, William. *The Varieties of Religious Experience: A Study in Human Nature.* New York: Collier Books, 1970.

John of the Cross, Saint. *The Ascent of Mount Carmel,* 3d rev. ed., trans. E. Allison Peers. Garden City, N.Y.: Doubleday, 1958.

———. *The Living Flame of Love,* trans. E. Allison Peers. Garden City, N.Y.: Image Books, 1962.

Jones, Rufus. *Studies in Mystical Religion.* London: Macmillan, 1909.

al-Junayd. *The Life, Personality, and Writings of al-Junayd,* trans. and ed. Ali Hassan Abdel-Kader. London: Luzac & Company, 1962.

al-Kalābadhī, Abū Bakr. *The Doctrine of the Sufis,* trans. A. J. Arberry. Lahore, Pakistan: Sh. Muhammad Ashraf, 1976.

Kant, Immanuel. *An Immanuel Kant Reader,* trans. and ed. Raymond B. Blakney. New York: Harper and Brothers, 1960.

Karagulla, Shafica. *Breakthrough to Creativity.* Santa Monica, Calif.: De Vorss, 1967.

Katz, Steven T., ed. *Mysticism and Language.* New York: Oxford University Press, 1992.

———. *Mysticism and Philosophical Analysis.* New York: Oxford University Press, 1978.

———. *Mysticism and Religious Traditions.* New York: Oxford University Press, 1983.

Kerner, Justinius. *The Seeress of Prevorst,* trans. Mrs. [Catherine] Crowe. London: J. C. Moore, 1845.

Kornfield, Jack. *Living Buddhist Masters.* Santa Cruz, Calif.: Unity Press, 1977.

Lame Deer, John Fire, and Richard Erdoes. *Lame Deer: Seeker of Visions.* New York: Simon & Schuster, 1972.

*The Laṅkāvatāra Sūtra,* trans. Daisetz Teitaro Suzuki. London: Routledge & Kegan Paul, 1968.

Laredo, Bernardino de. *The Ascent of Mount Sion: Being the Third Book of the Treatise of That Name . . . ,* trans. E. Allison Peers. London: Faber & Faber, 1952.

Leclerq, Jean, O.S.B. *The Love of Learning and the Desire for God: A Study of Monastic Culture,* trans. Catharine Misrahi. New York: Fordham University Press, 1974.

Leclerq, Jean, François Vandenbroucke, and Louis Boyer. *The Spirituality of the Middle Ages,* 2 vols. London: Burns & Oates, 1968.

Leuba, James. *The Psychology of Religious Mysticism.* New York: Harcourt, Brace & Co., 1925.

Lings, Martin. *A Sufi Saint of the Twentieth Century: Shaikh Aḥmad al-'Alawī.* Berkeley and Los Angeles: University of California Press, 1973.

*The Little Flowers of St. Francis,* trans. Raphael Brown. Garden City, N.Y.: Image Books, 1958.

*The Lost Books of the Bible and the Forgotten Books of Eden.* Cleveland: World Publishing Co., 1963.

Mager, Alois, O.S.B. *Mystik als Lehre und Leben.* Innsbruck: Tyrolia Verlag, 1934.

Mails, Thomas E., assisted by Dallas Chief Eagle. *Fools Crow.* New York: Avon Books, 1979.

Manning, Matthew. *The Link.* New York: Ballantine, 1974.

Martino, Ernesto de. *The World of Magic,* trans. Paul Saye White. New York: Pyramid Books, 1972.

Mead, G. R. S. *The Doctrine of the Subtle Body in Western Tradition.* Wheaton, Ill.: Quest Books, 1967.

Meister Eckhart. *Meister Eckhart: A Modern Translation,* trans. Raymond Bernard Blakney. New York: Harper & Row, 1941.

Monroe, Robert A. *Journeys Out of the Body.* Garden City, N.Y.: Doubleday, 1971.

Mooney, James. *The Ghost Dance Religion and the Sioux Outbreak of 1890.* Chicago: University of Chicago Press, 1965.

Moore, John Morrison. *Theories of Religious Experience.* New York: Round Table Press, 1938.

Mourant, John A. *Introduction to the Philosophy of Saint Augustine.* University Park, Pa.: Pennsylvania State University Press, 1964.

Muldoon, Sylvan, and Hereward Carrington. *The Projection of the Astral Body.* New York: Samuel Weiser, 1974 (1929).

Muktananda, Baba Paramahansa. *Play of Consciousness.* California: Shree Gurudev Siddha Yoga Ashram, 1974.

Myers, F. W. H. *Human Personality and Its Survival of Bodily Death.* New Hyde Park, N.Y.: University Books, 1961.

Needles, William. "Stigmata Occurring in the Course of Psychoanalysis." *Psychoanalytic Quarterly* 12, no. 1 (1943).

Neihardt, John G. *Black Elk Speaks.* New York: Pocket Books, 1972.

———. *When the Tree Flowered: An Authentic Tale of the Old Sioux World.* New York: Macmillan, 1951.

Osuña, Francisco de. *The Third Spiritual Alphabet,* trans. and intro. Mary E. Giles. Classics of Western Spirituality Series. New York: Paulist Press, 1980.

Otto, Rudolf. *Mysticism East and West.* New York: Macmillan, 1976 (1929).

Patañjali. *Patañjali's Yoga-Sūtras: With the Commentary of Vyāsa and the Gloss of Vācaspati Miśra*, trans. Rama Prasada. New Delhi: Oriental Books Reprint, 1978.

———. *Yoga-Sūtra of Patañjali*, trans. J. R. Ballantyne and Govind Sastri Deva. Delhi: Indological Book House, 1971.

———. *The Yoga-System of Patañjali*, trans. James Haughton Woods. Harvard Oriental Series. Delhi: Motilal Banarsidass, 1977.

Perceval, John. *Perceval's Narrative: A Patient's Account of His Psychosis, 1830–1832*, ed. Gregory Bateson. New York: William Morrow & Company, 1974.

Peter of Alcántara, Saint. *A Golden Treatise of Mentall Praier*, trans. G. W[illoughby], microfilm reproduction of 1632 ed., published in Brussels by the widow of Hubert Antone. Ann Arbor: University of Michigan, Microfilms, Inc., n.d..

*Philokalia: The Complete Text*, 5 vols., trans. and ed. G. E. H. Palmer, Philip Sherrard, and Kallistos Ware. London: Faber & Faber, 1979.

Plotinus. *The Enneads*, trans. Stephen MacKenna. London: Faber & Faber, 1969.

———. *The Essential Plotinus: Representative Treatises from the Enneads*, selected and newly translated by Elmer O'Brien, S.J. New York: New American Library, 1964.

Plutarch. "On the Fortune or the Virtue of Alexander the Great." Quoted in Nels M. Bailkey, *Readings in Ancient History: From Gilgamesh to Diocletian*. Lexington, Mass.: D. C. Heath & Company, 1976.

———. *Selected Essays of Plutarch*, 2 vols., trans. A. O. Prickard. New York: Oxford University Press, 1913–18.

Poulain, Auguste, S.J. *The Graces of Interior Prayer: A Treatise on Mystical Theology*. London: Kegan Paul, Trench, Trubner & Company, 1921.

Powers, William K. *Oglala Religion*. Lincoln: University of Nebraska Press, 1977.

Proudfoot, Wayne. *Religious Experience*. Berkeley and Los Angeles: University of California Press, 1985.

Rahula, Walpola. *What the Buddha Taught*. Bedford, England: Gordon Fraser, 1967.

———. *What the Buddha Taught*, 2d and enl. ed. New York: Grove Press, 1974.

Reichel-Dolmatoff, Gerardo. *Amazonian Cosmos: The Sexual and Religious Symbolism of the Tukano Indians*. Chicago: University of Chicago Press, 1971.

Rasmussen, Knud. *Intellectual Culture of the Caribou Eskimos*, vol. 7, nos. 2 and 3 of the Report of the Fifth Thule Expedition 1921–24: The Danish Expedition to Arctic North America in Charge of Knud Rasmussen, 10 vols. in 11. Copenhagen: Gyldendalske Boghandel, Nordisk Forlag, 1930.

———. *Intellectual Culture of the Iglulik Eskimo*, vol. 7, no. 1 of the Report of the Fifth Thule Expedition 1921–24: The Danish Expedition to Arctic North America in Charge of Knud Rasmussen, 10 vols. in 11. Copenhagen: Gyldendanske Boghandel, Nordisk Forlag, 1929.

Ribet, Jerome. *La mystique divine, distinguées des contrefaçons diaboliques et des analogies humaines*, 4 vols. Paris: C. Poussielgue, 1895–1903.

Richard of St. Victor. *Richard of Saint-Victor: Selected Writings on Contemplation*, trans. with an introduction by Clare Kirchberger. New York: Harper and Brother, 1957.

————. *The Twelve Patriarchs, The Mystical Ark, Book Three of The Trinity,* trans. Grover A. Zinn. Classics of Western Spirituality Series. New York: Paulist Press, 1979.

Riencourt, Amaury de. *The Eye of Shiva: Eastern Mysticism and Western Science.* New York: William Morrow & Company, 1981.

Robinson, John Manley. *An Introduction to Early Greek Philosophy.* Boston: Houghton Mifflin, 1968.

Rose, Ronald. *Living Magic: The Realities Underlying the Psychical Practices and Beliefs of the Australian Aborigines.* New York: Rand McNally, 1956.

*The Rule of St. Benedict,* trans. and ed. Aldoff Justin McCann. London: Burns & Oates, 1963.

Rūmī, Jalāl al-Din. *Discourses of Rūmī,* trans. A. J. Arberry. New York: Samuel Weiser, 1972.

Ruysbroeck, Blessed Jan Van. *Spiritual Espousals,* trans. Eric Colledge. Westminster, Md.: Christian Classics, 1983.

Saṅkara, *Vivekachūḍāmaṇi,* trans. Swami Mahavananda. Calcutta: Advaita Ashram, 1966.

*The Secret of the Golden Flower,* trans. Thomas Cleary. New York: Harper-Collins, 1991.

Schimmel, Anne-Marie. *The Mystical Dimensions of Islam.* Chapel Hill: University of North Carolina Press, 1975.

Scholem, Gershom. "Eine Kabbalistische Deutung der Prophetik als Selbstbegegnung." *Monatsschrift für Geschichte und Wissenschaft des Judentums* 74 (1930): 285–90.

————. *On the Kabbalah and Its Symbolism.* New York: Schocken Books, 1969.

————. *Major Trends in Jewish Mysticism.* New York: Schocken Books, 1961.

Sharafuddin Maneri. *The Hundred Letters,* trans. Paul Jackson, S.J. New York: Paulist Press, 1980.

Shirokogoroff, S. *The Psychomental Complex of the Tungus.* London: Kegan Paul, Trench & Trubner, 1935.

Smith, Jonathan Z. *Imagining Religion.* Chicago: University of Chicago Press, 1982.

Snellgrove, David, ed. and trans. *Four Lamas of Dolpo.* Cambridge, Mass.: Harvard University Press, 1967.

Staal, Frits. *Exploring Mysticism: A Methodological Essay.* Berkeley and Los Angeles: University of California Press, 1975.

Stace, Walter T. *Mysticism and Philosophy.* Philadelphia: J. B. Lippincott, 1960.

Standing Bear, Luther. *The Land of the Spotted Eagle.* Lincoln: University of Nebraska Press, 1978.

Steinmetz, Paul B., S.J. *Pipe, Bible, and Peyote Among the Oglala Lakota.* Stockholm: Almqvist & Wiksell International, 1980.

————. *Pipe, Bible, and Peyote Among the Oglala Lakota,* rev. ed. Knoxville: University of Tennessee Press, 1990.

Steltenkamp, Michael F. *Black Elk: Holy Man of the Oglala.* Norman: University of Oklahoma Press, 1993.

Suzuki, Daisetz Teitaro. *Mysticism Christian and Buddhist.* London: George Allen & Unwin, 1957.

Svātmārāma. *The Haṭhayogapradīpikā of Svātmārāma with the Commentary Jyotsnā of Brahmānanda*. Adyar, India: Adyar Library and Research Center, 1972.

Swedenborg, Emanuel. *Angelic Wisdom Concerning the Divine Love and Wisdom*. London: Swedenborg Society, 1969.

——. *Heaven and Hell; also, The Intermediate State, or World of Spirits: A Relation of Things Heard and Seen*. London: Swedenborg Society, 1896.

——. *Heaven and Its Wonders and Hell*. London: Swedenborg Society, 1896.

Teresa of Avila, Saint. *The Book of Her Life*, vol. 1. In *Collected Works of St. Teresa of Avila*, 3 vols., trans. Kieran Kavanaugh, O.C.D., and Otilio Rodriguez, O.C.D. Washington, D.C.: Institute of Carmelite Studies, 1976.

——. *Book of the Foundations*, vol. 3. In *The Complete Works of Saint Teresa of Jesus*, 3 vols., trans. and ed. E. Allison Peers. London: Sheed & Ward, 1957.

——. *The Collected Works of St. Teresa of Avila*, 3 vols., trans. Kieran Kavanaugh, O.C.D., and Otilio Rodriguez, O.C.D. Washington, D.C.: Institute of Carmelite Studies, 1976.

——. *The Complete Works of St. Teresa of Jesus*, 3 vols., trans. and ed. E. Allison Peers. London: Sheed & Ward, 1978.

——. *Conceptions of the Love of God*, vol. 2. In *The Complete Works of Saint Teresa of Jesus*, 3 vols., trans. and ed. E. Allison Peers. London: Sheed & Ward, 1957.

——. "The Constitutions." In vol. 3 of *The Collected Works of St. Teresa of Avila*, trans. Kieran Kavanaugh, O.C.D., and Otilio Rodriguez, O.C.D. Washington, D.C.: Institute of Carmelite Studies, 1985.

——. *Interior Castle*, trans. and ed. E. Allison Peers. Garden City, N.Y.: Image Books, 1961.

——. *The Letters of Saint Teresa of Avila*, 2 vols., trans. and ed. E. Allison Peers. London: Burns, Oates & Washbourne, 1951.

——. *The Life of St. Teresa of Jesus: The Autobiography of St. Teresa of Avila*, trans. and ed. and with an introduction by E. Allison Peers. Garden City, N.Y.: Image Books, 1960.

——. *Obras Completas, estudio preliminar y notas explicativas por Luis Santullano*. Madrid: Aguilar, 1957.

——. *Obras de Santa Teresa de Jesus*, ed. and ann. P. Silverio de Santa Teresa, C.D., 9 vols., vol. 3: *Camino de Perfección*. Library of Carmelite Mystics. Burgos: Tipografía de El Monte Carmelo, 1916.

——. "On Making the Visitation." In vol. 3 of *The Collected Works of St. Teresa of Avila*, trans. Kieran Kavanaugh, O.C.D., and Otilio Rodriguez, O.C.D. Washington, D.C.: Institute of Carmelite Studies, 1985.

——. *Spiritual Testimonies*, vol. 1. In *The Collected Works of St. Teresa of Avila*, trans. Kieran Kavanaugh, O.C.D., and Otilio Rodriguez, O.C.D., Washington, D.C.: Institute of Carmelite Studies, 1976.

*Thirty Minor Upanishads, Including the Yoga Upanishads*, trans. K. Narayanasvami Aiyar. El Reno, Okla.: Santarasa Publications, 1980. Reprint of 1914 ed.

———. *The Way of Perfection,* trans. and ed. E. Allison Peers. Garden City, N.Y.: Image Books, 1964.

Thomas à Kempis. *The Imitation of Christ,* trans. Leo Sherley-Price. Harmondsworth: Penguin Books, 1983.

Thurston, Herbert, S.J. *Ghosts and Poltergeists.* Chicago: Henry Regnery Company, 1953.

*The Tibetan Book of the Dead,* trans. Lama Kazi Dawa Samdup, and ed. W. Y. Evans-Wentz. New York: Oxford University Press, 1960.

*The Tibetan Book of the Great Liberation,* ed. W. Y. Evans-Wentz. New York: Oxford University Press, 1975.

*Tibetan Yoga and Secret Doctrines,* 2d ed., ed. W. Y. Evans-Wentz, trans. by Lama Kazi Dawa-Samdup; foreword by R. R. Marett; yogic commentary by Chen-Chi Chang. New York: Oxford University Press, 1971.

Tson-kha-pa. *Calming the Mind and Discerning the Real . . . from the Lam rim chen mo of Tson-kha-pa,* trans. Alex Wayman. Delhi: Motilal Banarsidass, 1979.

Tyrrell, G. N. M. *Apparitions.* New York: Collier, 1953.

Underhill, Evelyn. *Mysticism: A Study in the Nature and Development of Man's Spiritual Consciousness.* New York: E. P. Dutton, 1961 (1911).

———. *Mysticism: A Study in the Nature and Development of Man's Spiritual Consciousness,* 12th ed. New York: World Publishing, 1955.

———. *The Mystics of the Church.* London: James Clarke, n.d..

Upanishads. *The Thirteen Principal Upanishads,* 2d ed. and rev., trans. Robert E. Hume. New York: Oxford University Press, 1975.

Van der Leeuw, Gerardus. *Religion in Essence and Manifestation,* 2 vols., trans. J. E. Turner with appendices to the Torchbook edition incorporating the additions of the 2d German ed. by Hans H. Penner. Gloucester, Mass.: Peter Smith, 1967. Reprint of 1938 ed.

Vijñāna Bhikṣu. *The Yogasāra-Saṃgraha,* trans. Gangānātha Jhā. Bombay: Tatva-Vivechaka Press, 1894.

Vonnegut, Mark. *The Eden Express.* New York: Bantam Books, 1976.

Waley, Arthur, trans. *Three Ways of Thought in Ancient China.* London: George Allen & Unwin, 1974.

Walker, James R. *Lakota Belief and Ritual.* Lincoln: University of Nebraska Press, 1980.

———. "The Sun Dance and Other Ceremonies of the Oglala Division of the Teton Dakota." *Anthropological Papers of the American Museum of Natural History* 16, pt. 2 (1917): 50–221.

Walther, Gerda. "On the Psychology of Telepathy." *Journal: American Society for Psychical Research* 25, no. 10 (October 1931): 438–46.

———. *Phänomenologie der Mystik.* Olten und Freiburg im Breisgau: Walter Verlag, 1955.

———. "Some Experiences Concerning the Human Aura." *Journal: American Society for Psychical Research* 26 (September 1932): 339–46.

Wang-Ch'ug Dor-Je, the ninth Kar-ma-pa. *The Mahāmudrā Eliminating the Darkness of Ignorance,* trans. Alexander Berzin. Dharamsala, India: Library of Tibetan Works and Archives, 1981.

Warren, Henry Clarke. *Buddhism in Translations*. New York: Atheneum, 1974.

Watt, W. Montgomery. *The Faith and Practice of al-Ghazālī*. London: George Allen & Unwin, 1970.

William of St. Thierry. *The Golden Epistle*. Kalamazoo, Mich.: Cistercian Publications, 1976.

Williams, Rowan. *Teresa of Avila*. Harrisburg, Pa.: Morehouse Publishing, 1991.

Wissler, Clark. "Societies and Ceremonial Associations in the Oglala Division of the Teton Dakota." *Anthropological Papers of the American Museum of Natural History* 11, pt. 1 (1916): 1–99.

———. "Some Protective Designs of the Sioux." *Anthropological Papers of the American Museum of Natural History* 1 (1907): 21–53.

Woods, Richard, O.P., ed. *Understanding Mysticism*. Garden City, N.Y.: Image Books, 1980.

Worrall, Ambrose A., and Olga N. Worrall, with Will Oursler. *Explore Your Psychic World*. New York: Harper & Row, 1976.

Zaehner, R. C. *Mysticism Sacred and Profane*. New York: Oxford University Press, 1961.

# Index

Abū'l-Adyān, 193
acosmism, 306 n. 2, 354–55, 442–43
active approach, to inducing supernormal
   phenomena, 197–200
   among Australian Aborigines, 207–15
   in: Patañjali's Yoga-Sūtras, 218–25;
      Tibetan Buddhism, 197–207
   used by Walther, 215–17
Acts of the Apostles, 37–38, 46
Adam, 70–71
*Adventures in the Supernormal* (Garrett),
   14
Afraid of Bears, 438–39
Africa, religious taboos, 183–84, 282–83,
   294–95
afterlife
   Augustine on, 18 n. 41, 150–51, 160
   in: Christianity, 260–61, 265–66; Is-
      lam, 251–52; in Sufism, 258–59; in
      Tibetan Buddhism, 242, 246, 249,
      250–51
   Swedenborg on, 260–61, 265–66
   Teresa's visions of, 482–83
alertness, telepathic and clairvoyant, 235–
   37, 239
Almond, Philip, 12 n. 25, 13, 13 n. 27,
   15
Alvarez, Balthazar, 476, 484
Alvarez, Rodrigo, 490, 537, 541, 569
amorphousness, of mystical experiences,
   41, 75–92, 130–31, 292
anātman, 600–601
*Aṅguttara Nikāya,* 519
anesthesia, 170 n. 57
antinomian mystics, 115
Aquinas, Thomas, 563
Arbman, Ernst, 127
Arjuna, 46–47
Arnoul of Boheriss, 520, 521
asamprajñāta samādhi, 16, 110, 588, 590,
   592–94

*Ascent of Mt. Sion* (Bernardino de Laredo), 472
ascetism
   of Christian mystics, 115–16, 454–55,
      463, 509–10
   Discalced orders and, 480, 481–82,
      483–88, 489–98, 504
   mystical experiences and, 505–10
   recollection and, 115–16
   Saint Teresa's view of, 454, 463, 475–
      77, 505–6, 507, 509, 510
*Astral Projection: A Record of Out-of-
   the-Body Experiences* (Fox), 176
astral projection. *See* ex-stasis
Aua (Eskimo shaman), 46
   enlightenment, 35, 50, 51, 52–53, 55,
      57, 58
   radiance, 60
   religious influences, 76–77
   supernormal perception, 44
Augustine of Hippo
   experience of Infinite Light, 38–39, 45–
      46, 48, 53–54, 55, 57, 59, 60
   mystical experiences, 86, 142–43, 566–
      67
   on: Bride of Christ, 551; empowerment,
      150–51, 266–67; heaven, 18 n. 41,
      150–51, 160, 266–67
*Auras* (Cayce), 288–89
auras, 64–67, 68, 217, 288–90
   absence of, 289
   clairvoyance and, 237–39
   colors in, 68, 167, 215–16, 288
   induction of ability to see, 167, 167 n.
      54, 191 n. 3
   objectification of thoughts and, 160
   of: doubles, 155; inanimate objects,
      289, 289 n. 18
   telepathy and, 216, 299
Australian Aborigines
   clever men, 106–7